Before They
Were the Cubs

ALSO BY JACK BALES

Willie Morris:
An Exhaustive Annotated Bibliography
and a Biography (McFarland, 2006; softcover 2010)

Before They Were the Cubs

*The Early Years of Chicago's
First Professional Baseball Team*

JACK BALES

McFarland & Company, Inc., Publishers
Jefferson, North Carolina

LIBRARY OF CONGRESS CATALOGUING-IN-PUBLICATION DATA

Names: Bales, Jack, author.
Title: Before they were the Cubs : the early years of Chicago's first professional baseball team / Jack Bales.
Description: Jefferson, North Carolina : McFarland & Company, Inc., Publishers, 2019 | Includes bibliographical references and index.
Identifiers: LCCN 2019003390 | ISBN 9781476674674 (paperback : acid free paper) ∞
Subjects: LCSH: Chicago Cubs (Baseball team)—History—19th century. | Baseball—Illinois—Chicago—History—19th century.
Classification: LCC GV875.C6 B34 2019 | DDC 796.357/640977311—dc23
LC record available at https://lccn.loc.gov/2019003390

BRITISH LIBRARY CATALOGUING DATA ARE AVAILABLE

ISBN (print) 978-1-4766-7467-4
ISBN (ebook) 978-1-4766-3506-4

© 2019 Jack Bales. All rights reserved

No part of this book may be reproduced or transmitted in any form or by any means, electronic or mechanical, including photocopying or recording, or by any information storage and retrieval system, without permission in writing from the publisher.

Front cover: The 1870 Chicago White Stockings (author's collection)

Printed in the United States of America

McFarland & Company, Inc., Publishers
Box 611, Jefferson, North Carolina 28640
www.mcfarlandpub.com

For Laura and Patrick
Robert, David, Jane, Peggy, Kate, Beth, R. J.
and for Dick, naturally

Chicago needs a representative club; an organization as great as her enterprise and wealth,—one that will not allow the second-rate clubs of every village in the northwest to carry away all the honors in base ball contests.
—*Chicago Times*, July 22, 1868

Somewhere along about Christmas in 1869, I noticed an advertisement in a New York paper which read something as follows: "Ball players wanted to form a team to represent Chicago and to defeat the Cincinnati Red Stockings." ... I answered the ad and in due time got a reply. It happened that I was among the first to write. The Chicago people told me they ... desired me to organize a club to beat the Red Stockings in 1870 and d— the expense!
—*El Paso (Texas) Herald*, August 17, 1916.
From an interview with Jimmy Wood, the first member of the Chicago baseball team that in 1902 became known as the Cubs.

We were beaten! We know it, we feel it, but how could we help it? The umpire was against us, the weather was against us, the crowd was against us, the heavens were against us, the ground was against us, the pestilential air of the Chicago river was against us, the Chicago Nine was against us, and last, but not least, the score was against us.
—*Cincinnati Daily Gazette*, October 14, 1870

Table of Contents

Preface   1

Chronology   6

Prologue   9

1. A New Team for Chicago (1868–1870)   11
2. A Fiery Second Season (1871)   47
3. Recovery After Disaster (1872–1875)   60
4. William Hulbert and the First League Pennant (1875–1876)   86
5. Reversal of Fortune (1877–1879)   108
6. Successes and Struggles (1880–1884)   122
7. On Top of the League (1885–1886)   142
8. Fading Glory (1887–1890)   162
9. Dark Days and Grim Years (1891–1902)   176

Postscript: Return to Greatness (1902–1908)   198

Appendix: Year-End Standings of the Chicago Team, 1871–1908   203

Chapter Notes   205

Bibliography   245

Index   247

Preface

In the summer of 2004, I casually picked up the June issue of *Vine Line*, the official magazine of the Chicago Cubs, to read the letters to the editor. One fan related that he had been having a heated argument with a friend, who said that the team had not always played at Wrigley Field. The fan had "begged to differ" and asked *Vine Line*, "Will you please settle this disagreement, and set the record straight?"

The magazine's editor obliged, explaining that the Cubs had called a number of ballparks home before settling down in 1916 at what was then Weeghman Park (renamed Cubs Park in 1919 and Wrigley Field in 1926). The fan's misconception was not at all unusual, as many people believe the Cubs have always played at the iconic, ivy-decorated "green cathedral" on Clark and Addison Streets.[1]

The query in *Vine Line* gave me the idea for this book, as I knew the team boasted a rich, storied history during its nineteenth-century formative years, with names such as White Stockings, Colts, and Orphans. I own dozens of volumes on the Cubs, but few document this history. One book in my collection is George Will's labor of love, *A Nice Little Place on the North Side* (2014). Well, the Chicago club had nice little places on the South and West Sides, too, but ballparks such as the 23rd Street Grounds and the West Side Grounds are now largely forgotten footnotes in Cubs lore. These footnotes deserve to be featured more prominently in the pages of Chicago baseball chronicles.

The organization now known as the Chicago Cubs was the city's first "professional" team; that is, the ballplayers received salaries for their services. It has been a member of the National League since the governing body's inception in 1876 and is the only one of the eight charter clubs still playing in the city in which the franchise started. In *Before They Were the Cubs* I draw upon hundreds of primary and secondary works to trace the history of the team, from its early planning stages in 1868 to 1902, when a sportswriter referred to the young players as Cubs in the March 27 issue of the *Chicago Daily News*. The club did not officially adopt the name until a few years later, as I discuss in a postscript covering 1902 through the end of the 1908 season. Photographs, display ads, baseball cartoons, drawings, a chronology, and an appendix complement the text.

My sources include books, contemporary newspapers, sporting publications (such as the *New York Clipper*, *Sporting Life*, *The Sporting News*, and volumes of *Spalding's Base Ball Guide*), periodicals, memoirs, and archival records in the collection of the Chicago History Museum. Lengthy quotations, reprinted articles, game-day reports, and other direct evidence from firsthand accounts provide not only a colorful narrative of baseball in nineteenth- and early twentieth-century America, but also a documentary history of the Chicago team and its members before they were the Cubs.

Like countless other baseball researchers, I am indebted to websites such as http://www.baseball-almanac.com/, https://www.baseball-reference.com/, http://www.retrosheet.org/, and the various resources that the Society for American Baseball Research maintains (http://www.sabr.org/). The notes and bibliographies in secondary works turned up significant books and articles. Databases gave me access to full-text, online archives of newspapers and periodicals.

I also took advantage of newspapers on microfilm. I spent several years poring over numerous microfilm reels, looking for not only articles that recorded the team's past, but also vivid, descriptive passages that illuminated and enlivened that past.

I was not disappointed. When Chicago Base Ball Association president William A. Hulbert reorganized the association in 1876 under a new charter as the Chicago Ball Club, the Chicago *Inter Ocean* provided the details in a lengthy analysis. As president of both the Chicago club and the National League, Hulbert was a dedicated—but also demanding—business executive. While I was scanning the pages of the *Chicago Times*, I serendipitously came across a blistering letter he wrote in 1877 to a slumping Paul Hines, telling the ballplayer he would "not consent to pay first-class prices for third-rate play." Journalist Finley Peter Dunne was well known for his bold, lively essays, and as I read the 1887 *Chicago Daily News*, I enjoyed his account of right fielder Billy Sunday (who played baseball before he became an evangelist) dashing across the field to catch a fly ball:

> Sunday ... saw that the ball would light between the clubhouse and a row of benches about ten feet distant.... The people opened a gap, and with a tremendous leap he cleared the bench, his speed carrying him against the brick wall with great force. Ten thousand pairs of eyes saw him throw his arms above his head, and they were ready to applaud the act, but no one expected that he had caught the ball. As he turned and limped away from the wall, holding aloft the ball for judgment, the shouts of the crowd could be heard for blocks away.[2]

Nineteenth-century sportswriters were masters of florid and flowery prose, and they were skilled in the use of hyperbole, similes, metaphors, and various types of allusions. On May 17, 1877, for example, a *Chicago Daily Tribune* reporter complained that the new league baseball was "too soft," for during a game it quickly "grew flabby on the outside, so that one could be picked up by the slack like a kitten by the scruff of its neck or a small boy by the slack of his breeches." After former Chicago players John Clarkson and Mike Kelly helped the Boston Beaneaters trounce the White Stockings, 20–5, on May 15, 1888, the *Chicago Times* writer declared that pitcher Clarkson "breathed on his enemies and they were as are the snow banks of last winter. The unrivaled Kelly smote the enemy's curves and they sailed away like robins seeking the summer."

The reporter added that the Beaneaters beat the Chicago players "as no nine young men have been beaten since the Pecatonica Blues won their long tin horn." During an 1866 baseball tournament, the Pecatonica, Illinois, club lost a game by the lopsided score of 49–1. The team had the dubious distinction of winning a silver-mounted tin horn engraved with the word "Practice," for being the club that had lost by the biggest margin. As baseball historians Peter Morris and David Nemec observe in *The Rank and File of 19th Century Major League Baseball*, "The name Pecatonica remained a byword for futility for decades."[3]

Since some of my original source documents occasionally provided different accounts of the same topic or events, I had to be cautious interpreting those accounts. I particularly noticed discrepancies in early twentieth-century coverage of the Chicago club's ownership. Some journalists assumed that controlling partner Jim Hart was the majority stockholder and owner, while others maintained that he held only a minority stock interest. Even today it is difficult to assess the circumstances, for as Chicago Cubs historian Ed Hartig explains, "There are too many contradictions of what some newspapers said happened versus what others said happened." While I was reading articles, I tried to identify contradictions—and possible biases of authors—before making any conclusions.

As I delved into hundreds of historical works, I discovered intriguing details that I incorporated into my text. I knew, for example, that beginning in 1888 the baseball players wore gray and black uniforms and were informally called the "Black Stockings," but I had not realized that Virginia Anson, the wife of team captain Adrian "Cap" Anson, had designed the outfits. The men stopped wearing them prior to the 1894 season, supposedly for superstitious reasons as the players had failed to win a league championship during the years they wore black. I also wanted to determine when and why the club left the South Side Park for the West Side Grounds. It was in June 1893, as club president Jim Hart had leased the former ballpark to the promoters of a college baseball tournament.

Like all researchers, I had to make arbitrary decisions. Box scores among publications occasionally conflicted with each other. What data should I use? Should I refer to players by their given names or their nicknames? How should I treat team names, which varied among newspapers of the time? I chose the online resource Retrosheet as an authority record, but with the exception of two players' names on the website: Cap Anson and King Kelly. Adrian Anson did not acquire his nickname until he became captain of the Chicago team in 1879, so until Chapter 5 I do not refer to him as "Cap." Mike Kelly was not called "King" until after he left Chicago in 1887 and joined the Boston team. I examine Kelly's move to Boston in my last chapter, so I decided it was easier just to leave his name as "Mike" throughout the rest of the book.[4]

A ballpark was often known by more than one name. Philip J. Lowry has meticulously researched the history of ballparks, and I use the names in his *Green Cathedrals: The Ultimate Celebration of Major League and Negro League Ballparks* (2006).

Magazine and newspaper title changes always frustrate bibliographers and researchers, and I relied heavily upon Library of Congress authority records. For example, Chicago's *Tribune* was titled the *Chicago Daily Tribune* from 1860–1864, the *Chicago Tribune* from 1864–1872, the *Chicago Daily Tribune* from 1872–1963, and the *Chicago Tribune* from 1963 to the present. Chicago's *Inter Ocean* (1872–1879) was later called the *Daily Inter Ocean* (1879–1902). Over the years another Chicago newspaper alternated between the *Chicago Times* and simply the *Times*. Citations to works from magazines and newspapers include the titles in use when the items were published.

For citations to newspapers whose titles do not include the names of cities, I note the identifying localities in parentheses, such as the *(Chicago) Inter Ocean* and the *(New York) Sun*. For citations to newspapers not nationally well known, I include the state abbreviations in parentheses; for instance, the *Hot Springs (SD) Weekly Star*. These procedures conform to the guidelines outlined in *The Chicago Manual of Style*, 17th edition.

Endnotes after each section document the works I used in my text and furnish resources for persons desiring additional information. Nineteenth-century newspaper articles were often published under multiple titles; for instance, an article may have a headline, followed by a title, followed by subtitles and subheadings. To avoid confusion, I generally reference article headlines, and to assist researchers, I include the newspaper page numbers on which the articles appeared.

In my endnotes I abbreviate a few often-cited publications, such as the *Chicago Daily Tribune* (*CDT*), the *Chicago Tribune* (*CT*), and *Sporting Life* (*SL*). I include on page 205 a list of these works and their abbreviations.

All quotations appear exactly as they were originally published, and I have not corrected grammar, altered punctuation, added capitalization, or changed the spelling of words (unless by inserting bracketed material or by indicating changes with appropriate endnotes).[5]

While I, alone, am responsible for any of this book's faults, the credit for many of its virtues belongs to the people who have assisted me over the years. Society for American Baseball Research member Raymond D. Kush, whose article "The Building of Chicago's Wrigley Field" was published in SABR's *Baseball Research Journal* in 1981, read the manuscript with an experienced and critical editor's eye. His numerous suggestions and comments improved this book immeasurably. Chicago Cubs historian Ed Hartig has spent decades researching the Cubs and their ballparks, and he patiently answered all of my questions with thoughtful observations, detailed analyses, and much-appreciated interest. Art Ahrens, who has written several books on the Cubs, not only provided encouragement, but also resources that he located for me at the Chicago Public Library.

I am grateful to my colleagues, past and present, at the University of Mary Washington in Fredericksburg, Virginia, where I have been employed as the reference and humanities librarian since 1980. Carla Bailey, Virginia's virtuosa of interlibrary loan, has worked with me on all of my projects and painstakingly tracked down everything I needed, even when confronted with incomplete—and occasionally incorrect—citations. I routinely "set up shop" in the microfilm reading area when the library was closed, and staff members helped keep recalcitrant microfilm reader-printers running for me (even responding to my frantic and frustrated text messages on Sunday mornings). Thank you, Suzanne Crosnicker, Brianne Dort, Shannon Hauser, Andrea Meckley, James Pape, and Sara Parker-Gray.

University librarian Rosemary Arneson and her support allowed me to travel to conferences to give presentations about my research and helped me finish this book ahead of schedule. Pauline Jenkins provided advice as well as unmatched expertise with navigating the often rough waters of state forms and regulations. Also furnishing encouragement and assistance were my longtime colleagues and good friends Linda Carver, Tina Faulconer, Christie Glancy, Phyllis Johnson, and Roy Strohl. Suzanne Chase, Carolyn Parsons, Angie White, and Megan Lindsey expertly scanned illustrations and photographs. Katherine Perdue viewed all of my technical obstacles as personal challenges, and she readily—and cheerfully—came up with solutions. Peter Catlin, Elizabeth Heitsch, and Erin Wysong, my reference department colleagues, have contributed marvelously to a congenial, productive work environment.

Beth Perkins has helped me with assorted writing projects since the mid–1980s and has had my back from the beginning. Renee Davis, an indefatigable researcher and genealogist, provided answers to many questions. I also appreciate the dedication of Sarah Appleby, Paul Boger, Caitlin DeMarco, Summer Durrant, Tammy Hefner, Donna Hudgins, Wanda Pittman, Nicole St. John, and Olivia Vander Bleek.

University of Mary Washington president Troy Paino, a sports historian himself, provided much encouragement as I was writing this book. John Morello, UMW associate provost for academic affairs, approved travel grants that enabled me to research at various libraries around the country. Bill and Terrie Crawley have been my supporters—both professionally as well as personally—for decades, and I am grateful for their friendship and fellowship. I know of few people who are fascinated with the English language the way Bill is, and over the years he has provided countless solutions to my grammatical and writing puzzles.

Former UMW baseball coach Tom Sheridan patiently answered numerous questions about the game. A few years ago I presented a talk on my Cubs work in one of Claudine Ferrell's history classes, and she, her students, and I routinely discuss research processes and problems. Contributing support in many ways were Beverley Shelesky and Paulette Watson. Persons furnishing technical assistance include James Ashmore, Barry Buchanan, Martha Burtis, Don Edwards, Bob Grattan, Edward Gray, Jim Groom, Tim Newman, Tommy Pack, Jessica Reingold, Andy Rush, Jerry Slezak, and Ray Usler.

The Chicago History Museum owns and maintains a fine collection of early Chicago Cubs records. Ellen Keith and Lesley Martin made them readily available to me and assisted with various aspects of my research. I spent a week at the National Baseball Hall of Fame, and director of research and Cubs fan Tim Wiles pulled numerous files and showed me some of the Hall's treasured items, such as decades-old Cubs uniforms. Veteran researcher and writer Mike Hill was always available to talk over the myriad of details that accompany the completion of a book. Donald R. Eldred and Jim Davis have for more than forty years provided inspiration and sound advice. I enjoyed discussing the Cubs' early history with Larry Names, author of *Bury My Heart at Wrigley Field* (1996). I also wish to express my appreciation to Bill Anderson, Rosemary Barra, Porter Blakemore, Steve Gallik, Bill Gowen, Bill Hageman, Jim Hall, Scott Harris, Dan Hubbard, David Hunt, Rick Hurley, Rob Kasper, Steve Klein, Milton Kline, Jack Kramer, Ken Machande, Jeff McClurken, Nina Mikhalevsky, Gary Mitchem, Pat Moore, Peter Morris, Willie Morris (who, after showing me the baseball diamond used in the filming of his boyhood memoir *My Dog Skip*, urged me to write a book on the Cubs), Joe Nicholas, David Rapp, Christina A. Reynen, Tom Riley, Stuart Shea, David Smith, Trey Strecker, Cecilia Tan, John Thorn, Tom Wolf, and Grant Woodwell.

This book has truly been a "family affair." Kate Bales provided technical expertise— and true craftsmanship!—as she enhanced the quality of many of my photographs and illustrations. I would have been lost without her. Baseball statistician Mike Bales answered my questions about the sport. Tom Bales helped with database searching. David Bales designed the masthead for my Chicago Cubs website, http://WrigleyIvy.com, and worked on some of my photos. Phyllis Bales assisted me with a variety of writing details. My twin brother, Dick Bales, and I have always been a true "band of brothers," and I could always count on him to drop everything and help out (such as taking off work to go through newspapers on microfilm in Chicago libraries).

My children, Patrick and Laura Bales, have told me that some of their earliest memories are of me working on writing projects and poring over books. They also recall my reading to them, particularly at night before bedtime, and I am reminded of a sentence near the end of one of my favorite books about reading and book collecting, *84, Charing Cross Road* by Helene Hanff: "I owe [them] so much."

Chronology

1868   The Chicago Excelsior baseball club loses to the Cincinnati Buckeyes on July 21, 43–22, prompting the *Chicago Times* to declare that Chicago needs a team "that will not allow the second-rate clubs of every village in the northwest to carry away all the honors in base ball contests."

1869   Chicago men meet at a local hotel on October 1 to organize a new baseball club. The team members would include not amateurs who played for fun, but professionals who received salaries.

1870   The new Chicago team plays at Ogden Park (Ontario Street near Lake Michigan) and Dexter Park (42nd and Halsted Streets, near the Union Stock Yards). While in St. Louis to play a game on April 29, the baseball players purportedly acquire their name after a young boy in a crowd calls out, "Oh, look at the White Stockings!" On November 1 the White Stockings defeat the New York Mutuals, 7–5, in a controversial match and claim the season's championship.

1871   The Chicago team plays at White Stocking Grounds (also called Lake Front Park), bounded by Michigan Avenue, Randolph Street, Madison Street, and the Illinois Central Railroad tracks. On October 8 the Chicago Fire burns down several square miles of the city, including the White Stockings' stadium and grounds. Most of the players lose their homes and possessions and finish the season wearing borrowed uniforms. The baseball club suspends all of its activities.

1872   Chicagoans interested in bringing professional baseball back to the city form the Chicago Base Ball Association and arrange for the construction of a new ballpark. The 23rd Street Grounds is bounded by 23rd Street, Burnside Street (later Dearborn), Clark Street, and 22nd Street (later Cermak Road).

1873   Chicago's newspapers announce in August that a baseball team is organized for the 1874 season.

1874   On May 13 the White Stockings play their first regular-season game since 1871, beating the Philadelphia Athletics, 4–0, at Chicago's 23rd Street Grounds.

1875   Chicago Base Ball Association secretary William A. Hulbert signs some of baseball's best-known players, including Adrian Anson and Albert G. "Al" Spalding. Hulbert is elected president of the association later in the year.

1876	William Hulbert and other baseball executives form the National League in February, and the White Stockings join as one of eight charter members. Hulbert reorganizes the Chicago Base Ball Association as the Chicago Ball Club. The club's White Stockings, with Al Spalding as team captain, win the league's first championship. Hulbert is elected president of the National League in December.
1877	Al Spalding stops playing professional baseball at the end of the season, although he remains with the White Stockings as William Hulbert's secretary.
1878	Players inaugurate White Stocking Park (also called Lake Front Park and Lake Park), built on the same location as the ballpark that burned down in 1871.
1879	Adrian "Cap" Anson takes the field as player-captain of the White Stockings.
1880	The White Stockings, led by Cap Anson, win the National League pennant with an astonishing record of 67–17–2 (and a winning percentage of .798).
1881	The White Stockings again end the season first in the National League. The American Association baseball league is formed in November.
1882	William Hulbert dies on April 10. Al Spalding is elected president of the Chicago Ball Club. The White Stockings win their third consecutive National League pennant and play the American Association's Cincinnati Red Stockings in a two-game exhibition series. Each team wins one game.
1883–1884	The White Stockings fail to win the National League pennant, finishing the 1883 season in second place and the 1884 season in fourth place.
1885	The White Stockings move to the West Side Park (bounded by Congress, Harrison, Loomis, and Throop Streets). They nose out the New York Giants for first place in the National League. Chicago's seven-game championship series with the American Association's St. Louis Browns ends in a controversial draw.
1886	The White Stockings defeat the Detroit Wolverines in a thrilling pennant race, but Chicago loses to the American Association's St. Louis Browns in the post-season championship series.
1887–1888	Al Spalding sells some key players in late 1886 and early 1887. The White Stockings place third in the National League in 1887 and second in 1888.
1889	The White Stockings again fail to win the National League pennant. Players from around the country, frustrated with the restrictive policies of team owners, form the Players' League at the end of the year. One of the new league teams is the Chicago Pirates.
1890	Al Spalding hires young players to replace the men who leave the White Stockings for the Players' League, and sportswriters adopt the nickname "Colts" for the youthful Chicago team. The Colts finish the National League season in second place. With so many teams competing for fans, all the clubs suffer financially, and the Players' League folds after one season. Al Spalding purchases the Chicago Pirates and their Brotherhood Park (soon

known as South Side Park), located at the corner of 35th Street and Wentworth Avenue.

1891 Al Spalding retires prior to the start of the season and Jim Hart is elected club president. Monday, Wednesday, and Friday games are held at the West Side Park and games on Tuesday, Thursday, and Saturday are played at the South Side Park (National League rules prohibit Sunday games). The Colts fail to win the league pennant.

1892 The Colts play all of their games at their grounds on the city's South Side, as attendance in 1891 was larger at the South Side Park than at the West Side Park. The National League allows games on Sundays, although the Colts' ballpark lease prohibits Sunday games. The Colts end the season with a losing record, their first since 1877. Jim Hart sells the West Side Park and the club begins construction of a new park on the West Side.

1893 The Colts play Sunday games at their new West Side Grounds, bounded by Polk, Taylor, Wood, and Lincoln (later Wolcott) Streets, while the remaining games are scheduled at their park on the city's South Side. In June they leave the South Side Park and begin playing all their games at the West Side Grounds. The Colts compile another losing record.

1894–1897 A fire at the West Side Grounds on August 5, 1894, traps spectators behind a barbed wire fence. Hundreds are injured, although no one is killed. The Colts struggle during these four years and are never in contention for the championship.

1898–1900 Cap Anson is forced to retire at the end of January 1898, and since the Colts have lost their "father," they become known as the "Orphans." Tom Burns succeeds Anson as manager for the 1898 and 1899 seasons, followed by Tom Loftus, who assumes the managerial role for 1900. The team continues to struggle.

1901 American League teams take the field for the first time, among them a Chicago club that adopts the name White Stockings, which is soon shortened to White Sox. The White Sox, under owner Charles Comiskey, finish first in the American League, while the Orphans end the season with their lowest winning percentage since the team was founded (.381). Tom Loftus resigns and Frank Selee takes over as manager. Selee starts to rebuild the team.

1902–1908 The *Chicago Daily News* coins a new name for the team when it uses "Cubs" in its March 27, 1902, issue to reflect Selee's signing of promising young players. The name slowly catches on with sportswriters and fans. The club members show improvement, and they compile winning seasons in 1903 and 1904. Selee resigns in 1905 due to illness and is replaced by player Frank Chance (originally signed in 1898), and the team has another winning season. With Chance as player-manager, the Cubs win National League pennants in 1906, 1907, and 1908, as well as World Series titles in 1907 and 1908.

Prologue

For Midwestern baseball fans, much of the 1870 season was merely a preliminary to the game on October 13. "The all-absorbing topic of conversation in base ball circles in this city and elsewhere is the probable result of the grand match," the *Cincinnati Daily Gazette* declared. "This game," the newspaper added, "will probably draw the largest crowd that has ever been seen on a ball field outside of New York, and the excitement during its progress will be immense." Wrote the *Chicago Tribune*: "No contest with the ball and bat ever excited such an interest throughout the entire West.... The interest is by no means confined to Chicago and Cincinnati, but extends equally through Illinois and Ohio, while other and adjacent States have fixed their attention upon the great event."[1]

It promised to be both a grand match and a great event, as it would feature the long-anticipated duel between the Chicago White Stockings and Cincinnati Red Stockings. In the late 1860s the professional, salaried Red Stockings had vanquished baseball teams all over the country, garnering effusive headlines from sportswriters. At that time the City of Chicago boasted of only amateur clubs, and although these included a few well-known powerhouses, none of them had received the acclaim accorded the Cincinnati club.

Chicago set out to change that. Well-respected second baseman Jimmy Wood had been the first player added to the 1870 Chicago roster, and others soon followed. Decades later Wood reminisced about those early years: "Chicago wasn't such a wonderfully large city then and it was doing everything possible to boom the town. And it was jealous of Cincinnati because of the great publicity Cincinnati had gained through the medium of its 1869 ball team.... And so Chicago decided that it must have a team to beat the Reds."[2]

Chicago got its baseball team, but the "great publicity" came slowly. By the middle of the 1870 season, sportswriters argued that yes, the White Stockings were winning games, but the competition was not particularly formidable (they had defeated one team by the score of 157–1). According to the *Chicago Republican,* the White Stockings had "proven themselves only capable of beating second-rate clubs." The *Chicago Tribune* went even further when it scoffed that the ballplayers had simply been playing mediocre clubs of "infants," and had "nervously shrunk" from challenging "full grown men."

Newspapers also pointed out that the Chicagoans had yet to take on the Red Stockings, against whom all teams—particularly the Illinois upstarts—were measured. "The sporting world of the entire country," the *Tribune* went on, were pitting [Chicago] in imaginary contests against the best-organized club in the world—the Cincinnatis—even before it had played the game with a creditable competitor."[3]

The sportswriters need not have concerned themselves with the White Stockings, nor with their games, real or imaginary. The Chicago ballplayers would soon enough be facing "creditable competitors."

And after that they would take on Cincinnati.

1

A NEW TEAM FOR CHICAGO (1868–1870)

> Chicago has started a subscription which already foots up $20,000 for the purpose of organizing a base ball nine to beat Cincinnati next year.
> —*(New York) Sun*, August 13, 1869

It was perfect weather for baseball in Chicago. July 21, 1868, turned out to be "as favorable as could have been hoped for," wrote a reporter for the *Chicago Tribune*. "The sky was clouded over, the scorching sun-rays hidden, and a brisk breeze drove away the sultriness of the air." Although quite a few people thought it would rain, they proved to be mistaken and it seemed that nothing could mar the pleasant summer day. By mid-afternoon some 2,000 persons had converged on the baseball grounds on State Street to see the contest between the Excelsior Club of Chicago and the Buckeye Club of Cincinnati. And not just men and boys mingled about, for "there were ladies, too, in carriages and upon the stands, eager and interested."[1]

Perhaps part of this intense interest was that the game was no mere pick-up match between small-town local teams. Three thousand baseball fans had recently gathered on the Cincinnati home grounds to see the Buckeyes face off against the Athletic Club of Philadelphia, while a year earlier 10,000 spectators had been on hand for a game featuring the Excelsiors, the "crack" ball club of the Midwest, according to the *Tribune*. In 1867 the Chicago athletes had won 10 games and lost only one, and although their current season was not going as well, enthusiastic onlookers still packed the grounds whenever the team played.[2]

Darkness brought an end to the competition after eight innings, with the Excelsiors losing, 43–22. The *Tribune* sportswriter, disgusted at what he called "mediocre playing," suggested that the team members might want to "give up playing entirely, and disorganize." If, however, they wished to "retrieve their fortunes and again hold the first place among Western clubs," then they needed to "root out from among themselves the men who have ... clogged their progress and made them weak at the bat and in the field, and replace them by others who are willing to practice." After all, the reporter concluded, "It is better to have poor players who have the will to practice, than to rely upon those who rest upon laurels gained in the past."

These were rather blunt words, but the *Chicago Times* was even more outspoken in its coverage of the hometown team:

Many persons, including the Excelsior club, were confident in their ability to defeat the Buckeyes; the result has shown that the Excelsiors can beat nobody. Such an exhibition of "muffing" as that made by the Excelsiors is unparalleled in the annals of the game in America. Chicago needs a representative club; an organization as great as her enterprise and wealth,—one that will not allow the second-rate clubs of every village in the northwest to carry away all the honors in base ball contests. The Excelsior club evidently cannot fill the bill; its repeated defeats are inexcusable.[3]

Given the seriousness and intensity with which Chicago residents viewed their baseball teams, the candor of the two newspapers is not surprising. Following the Civil War, in the summer of 1866, a *Chicago Tribune* editorial had pronounced the arrival of "the age of base ball." Participation in the sport had declined during the war years and many teams—including the Excelsior Club, which had been active as early as 1858—discontinued their activities. With the chaotic conflict over, the *Tribune* urged Americans not to lose themselves in "the incessant toil of business" but recognize that "life must have vent" and that "play is the simple sign of exuberant life." To maintain this spirit of enthusiasm, the newspaper continued, "There is nothing better than a game of ball to train the attention and alertness at once of mind, eye and nerve."[4]

And Chicago had indeed turned its attention to baseball. Chicago's postwar economic growth would be accompanied by a corresponding rise in the city's population—more than 240,000 residents in 1868 as compared to some 112,000 in 1860. In 1866 the city boasted 32 organized teams, up from a mere handful in 1860.[5] The Excelsiors had reorganized and were "raring to go," as one modern baseball historian put it, and soon they were regularly defeating the area's other clubs. In September 1868, two months after the team's humiliating defeat at the hands of the Cincinnati Buckeyes, the "Excelsior boys" were back in the public's good graces and "redeeming themselves in a highly satisfactory manner," according to a Chicago newspaper. But money—or the lack of it—was a constant problem, and the team soon needed to raise funds for operating expenses. Although a subscription committee was formed of several men "with 'cheek' enough to go among our citizens and ask for money," contributions were few, and in November the club disbanded.[6] Nevertheless, hopes were still high that a new team could restore baseball luster to the city of Chicago.

CINCINNATI vs. CHICAGO.

GAME OF

BASE BALL.

"BUCKEYE," of Cincinnati,

vs.

"EXCELSIOR," of Chicago.

1,000 Reserved Seats for Ladies in Covered Amphitheatre.

Tuesday, July 21st, at 2 o'clock.

ADMISSION, 25 CENTS.

After the Chicago Excelsiors lost to the Cincinnati Buckeyes on July 21, 1868, baseball-minded Chicagoans met to organize the city's first team to be comprised not of amateurs, but of players who received salaries. This team, soon to be called the White Stockings, became known in the early twentieth century as the Cubs (*Chicago Tribune*, July 21, 1868).

"Sporting. Base Ball." *Chicago Tribune*, November 7, 1868, p. 4.

The Excelsior Base Ball Club is no more, it having dissolved its organization. Several reasons for the event are assigned, among them the insolvency of the club, which fell badly in arrears for its current expenses; and also the fact that several of the star players have left the city. It is probable, however, that the remaining members of the first nine will constitute the nucleus for a stronger organization to be formed next spring, although, perhaps, under a different club name. This will undoubtedly be done, since it is imperative that Chicago should boast of a base ball club which can not only beat anything in the West, but which shall be able to vindicate Chicago's importance as the first city on the continent, by bidding defiance to any and all clubs in America. We look to see such an organization perfected next year.

◆ ◆ ◆

Wanted: A Baseball Team to Beat the World (1869)

With the demise of the Excelsior Club, Chicagoans were left without a first-class baseball team, a fact not lost on the newspapers of other cities. "Perhaps the only thing in which Chicago has not put forth efforts to outstrip New-York is in a ball club," chided a writer for the *New-York Tribune* in early April 1869. The Excelsiors had finished the 1868 season with a record of seven wins, seven losses, and one tie, which undoubtedly led the reporter to contend that the team's "playing strength" was not sufficient "to make even a respectable stand against the heavy clubs outside."[7]

One of those leading clubs was the Cincinnati Red Stockings. Formed in 1866, it quickly emerged as one of early baseball's true powerhouses. In 1868 the team had finished the season with a win-loss record of 36–7, and the following year the club members won all 57 games that they played. Of course, it certainly helped that the Red Stockings was one of the first teams that did not rely on local, amateur ballplayers; instead it recruited highly skilled athletes from outside the city who were compensated for their baseball prowess. As a reporter commented in August 1869, "It is generally known that this [Cincinnati] club is made up of professionals from every part of the country. About every one of them is well known in base ball circles the country over."[8]

It was precisely this type of national recognition that rankled Chicagoans. For years Chicago had competed with Cincinnati (and also St. Louis) for bragging rights as to which was the greatest Midwestern city, and now Cincinnati was upping the ante with its first-class baseball team. "This was too much for Chicago to bear," declared the city's own *Western Monthly*. "She would not see her commercial rival on the Ohio bearing off the honors of the national game…. So Chicago went to work."

And it wasted no time in doing so. In late September, word went out around town that on October 1 there would be "a meeting of all citizens of Chicago who are interested in securing to this city a base ball club which shall beat the world." A large turnout of the city's "leading citizens" was expected.[9]

"Base Ball. The Professional Club Project." *Chicago Tribune*, October 2, 1869, p. 4.

A meeting of gentlemen interested in securing a first-class professional ball club for Chicago was held last evening at the Briggs House, the attendance numbering about fifty persons. Mr. S. W. Tanner was called to the chair, and stated the object of the meeting—the perfecting of an organization which should get together a professional base ball nine: a nine which should play ball and nothing else; a nine which should beat the world. It was proposed to organize a club and solicit subscriptions for this purpose. Fred. Erb[y] was elected Secretary. He said that a number of gentlemen had signified to him their willingness to further the proposed plan. Mr. W. H. Anderson gave assurance that the Board of Trade would contribute liberally. In reply to an inquiry, Mr. Erb[y] gave it as his option that at least $10,000 would be required to secure and maintain a club. His plan would be not to form a stock corporation, but to keep a record of subscriptions, and at the close of the season declare dividends, if any, *pro rata*. Messrs. George Treadway, Matthew Renner, W. H. Anderson, F. H. Tanner, and F. W. Budd were appointed a committee to ascertain what can be done toward raising funds, and to investigate the subject of suitable grounds for the permanent use of the club. After a rambling and informal discussion, resolutions were adopted declaring that a first class base ball club should be organized in Chicago, and calling upon the citizens to contribute toward it. The meeting then adjourned until Thursday evening next at the same place.

◆ ◆ ◆

The *Chicago Tribune* followed its report with an announcement on October 12, 1869, that "some of the most eminent citizens of Chicago" were interested in establishing a baseball club of professional, salaried players in the city. In a meeting that evening at the Briggs House, a well-known Chicago hotel, real estate tycoon Potter Palmer was elected president of the newly formed Chicago Base Ball Club. Various vice presidents included Philip H. Sheridan (Union general in the Civil War), industrialist and inventor George M. Pullman, J. M. Richards (president of the Chicago Board of Trade), *Chicago Tribune* City Editor Samuel J. Medill (brother of *Tribune* Managing Editor Joseph Medill), railroad executive J. W. Midgley, *Chicago Times* Editor Franc B. Wilkie, and businessman and politician (and later U.S. Senator from Illinois) Charles B. Farwell. David A. Gage (a former Chicago city treasurer who would soon be reelected to that office) became treasurer of the organization, and T. Z. Cowles, sports editor of the *Chicago Tribune*, assumed the corresponding secretary's position. Tom Foley, a well-known proprietor of a Chicago billiards hall and the group's general and business manager, dealt with day-to-day activities, as did an executive committee.[10]

Team general and business manager Tom Foley was the proprietor of a Chicago billiards hall. A leading player as well as an authority on the cue sport, the *Chicago Daily Tribune* of November 12, 1911, called him the "Father of American Billiards" (Al Spink, *One Thousand Sport Stories*, vol. 2, 1921).

With competition fierce among the professional teams for the best ballplayers, the Chicagoans wasted little time getting organized. That month they advertised for top players in *The Spirit of the Times* and the *New York Clipper*, two of the leading sports weeklies of the day.[11] "To Base Ball Players" appeared in the *New York Clipper* less than three weeks after the Chicago Base Ball Club's first meeting.

"To Base Ball Players." *New York Clipper*, October 30, 1869, p. 237.

Some time since, shortly after the return of the noted Cincinnati Club from their successful eastern tour, it was intimated that a number of the leading citizens of the Garden City, envious of the fame won for Porkopolis by the invincible "Red Stockings," contemplated the organization of a professional nine which would be strong enough to effectually clip the wings of the aforesaid club, and transfer the laurel wreath to Chicago.[12] This statement gave rise to vague rumors, but until now it was without tangible shape or official endorsement. A perusal of the communication which appears underneath, however, will show that the Chicago[a]ns have entered into this matter in earnest, and if the "Red Stockings" should roll on in their triumphal chariot through the season of '70, it will not be because strenuous exertions have been lacking to prevent their so doing. Read the card:—

TO THE EDITOR OF THE CLIPPER.—On the 12th of October 1869, was organized, in Chicago, the "Chicago Base Ball Club," having for its object the employment of a picked nine, composed of first class professional base ball players, to have their headquarters in Chicago during the season of 1870, or thereafter, if so agreeable to all concerned.[13] In compliance with the direction of the Executive Committee, the undersigned hereby calls the attention of base ball players to the subject. All professionals desirous of connecting themselves with the Chicago Club are requested to address, stating terms as to salary, etc., and with the full understanding that all communications will be held as strictly confidential.

T. [Z.] COWLES,
Corresponding Secretary C. B. B. C., Room 24, Tribune Building. Chicago, Ill.

As an evidence of the soundness and reliability of the movement, it is only necessary to state that Potter Palmer is President and David A. Gage Treasurer of the new club.

◆ ◆ ◆

The New Chicago Club (1870)

T. Z. Cowles and his associates knew that just a few judiciously placed ads would not attract enough talented players to "clip the wings," as the *Clipper* had phrased it, of even amateur baseball clubs, let alone the Red Stockings. Consequently, recruiting trips were arranged. On November 25, 1869, the New York *Sun* commented that Chicago team representatives had traveled to New York and Philadelphia "to secure talent for the new enterprise." Salary money for this "talent" was collected by selling stock certificates, and within a year $15,000 was raised after 48 persons had purchased 600 shares at $25.00 each. In addition, the 150 people who each contributed $10.00 were given season tickets and club honorary memberships.[14]

All these efforts boded well for both Chicago and the baseball club. On November 26, sports fans were no doubt elated to open their newspapers and read that the organization had held a "special meeting" and that "good progress has been made in the subscription of stock and in the receipt of applications from professionals throughout the country for positions in the nine." In addition, the "Executive Committee was requested to proceed without delay" to select and acquire the needed players.

Unfortunately, the committee did not heed the cautionary words "without delay." By January 1870 the *Chicago Tribune* was grousing that due to the "bungling inefficiency" on the part of team officials, a number of outstanding players had slipped through Chicago's procrastinating fingers and signed with other teams. "The thing has fizzled," the *Tribune* exclaimed. "To-day, over three months after the preliminary organization was effected, the famous Chicago Nine, which was to have beaten the 'Red Stockings' in particular and the world in general, consists of two players!" Although the project had been an ambitious undertaking, the paper continued, team organizers had had all the financial and moral support they needed. All that had to be done was the "exercise of a little prompt, energetic, discreet activity." Most of the administrators, however, were apparently incapable of handling such a task. Details that should have been kept confidential, the *Tribune* said, were made public. Furthermore, instead of quickly selecting and signing top ballplayers, "These bunglers allowed the days, and weeks, and months to slip by, doing many things which they ought not to have done, and leaving undone many things which they ought to have done."[15]

The *New York Clipper* also wondered whether Chicago would have a new baseball team. "When the club was first started," the *Clipper* wrote, "considerable of a splurge was made by those having the matter in charge.... After making overtures to nearly every first-class player in the country, the managers of the new club have come to the conclusion that getting up a ball club on paper is one thing, and getting together nine players and making them 'stick' quite another." The sporting publication continued, commenting on the various players the officials contacted:

> Thus far, [Jimmy] Wood of the [Brooklyn] Eckfords, and [Ned] Cuthbert of the [Philadelphia] Athletics, are only those who have signed papers. [John] Hatfield and [Candy] Nelson of the [New York] Mutuals, are claimed as members of the new nine, but as yet neither has signed papers. Tom Foley, the billiardist, who is the business manager of the concern, is getting discouraged, it is said. He thought at first that all he had to do was to offer the players he wanted an engagement, and they would take the next train for Chicago. George Wright, [Rynie] Wolters, Charl[ie] Mills, Joe Start, Dick McBride, [Wes] Fisler, [Count] Sensenderfer, [Bill] Craver, [Al] Spaulding [sic], of the Forest City [team] of Rockford, Ill., and others were offered positions on the nine at $1,500 a year, and in some instances the offers reached $2,000. In this connection, the following gossip from our Philadelphia correspondent may be interesting:—"Wood of the Eckfords was in our city last week, trying to drum up recruits, and I believe Cuthbert signed an agreement, but Fisler or Sensenderfer would not.... Wood says that Hatfield and Nelson have signed papers, but I doubt it very much. Wood nearly talked Dick McBride to death, wishing him to go out, but Dick, I guess, will stay; but if he goes, no matters, as Fis[l]er will play with the Athletics next season."[16]

Just two days after the *Tribune* lambasted the managers of the Chicago Base Ball Club, the newspaper reported that the organization's members had met the previous evening and elected new officers. The *Tribune* went on to say that despite the committee's setbacks, the investors appeared to still support the club's efforts in building a first-class baseball team. Although not enough stock in the organization had been sold to engage the entire squad, the paper's sportswriter hoped "the players will be secured, at some rate or other, as fast as practicable."[17]

One principal member of the team was already working to acquire those players.

James "Jimmy" Wood, who had been the stalwart second baseman for the renowned Eckford Club of Brooklyn, New York, had in November agreed to captain the Chicago team at a salary of $2,000 for the season. Wood "is a fine looking, splendidly formed fellow of 26," one sportswriter enthusiastically observed. "He stands five feet eight and a half, weighs 150 pounds, ... and has been by occupation a machinist." Wood had played a major role in helping the Eckfords claim two national championships—one in 1862 and another a year later in which the team had gone undefeated. Since he was accustomed to the success enjoyed by the winning teams of the Eckford Club, he had no intention of letting his new club fail before it even played its first game. Suitably armed with the authority to sign players, Wood "came to the rescue," as the *Tribune* exclaimed in January, "with five men who had been dropped in the formation of Eastern clubs for this year, making in all seven players who are now under engagement."[18]

More ballplayers soon came to Chicago. On March 11 the *Tribune* revealed that club official Tom Foley had returned from a recruiting trip out east "bringing confirmation" that he had signed additional men to the team. Two days later the newspaper admitted it was wrong in doubting that the club's administrators could bring a "first-class" team to Chicago:

> Not long since it was highly uncertain whether or not Chicago was to have a first-class professional base-ball club for the season—the chances being, just then, decidedly in the direction of "not." At that time we took occasion to comment upon the lack of energy and decision manifested by the parties who had the matter in hand, and to plainly point to the probability that, with such management, the attempt to secure a first-class nine would result in a total failure. As opposition naturally incited increased activity, and as our comments were then (incorrectly) construed as being prompted by opposition to the movement, the result was that renewed efforts were put forth, this time with vigor and promptness, and in the right direction, and Chicago has a first-class ball club in consequence. Can the new nine beat the Red Stockings, the invincible, invariable conquerors of last season? Everybody will want information upon this point, but everybody must wait and see. A decided opinion either way could scarcely be given at present. Last year the Red Stockings were the only nine in America which could boast of maintaining a discipline almost equal in diet, habits, and general physical *regime* to that enforced upon a crew of professional oarsmen, or a pugilist in training: this year their example will be emulated by all the other crack clubs in the country, our own included, and the Cincinnati nine will not stand alone in that peculiarity which, more than any other explanation which could be given, was the real secret of their victorious career....
>
> ... The Chicago Base Ball Club ... [has] standing as a first-class club beyond a doubt. It is, however, in the way of batting that the nine is deemed to be preeminently strong. There is not a man of the ten who is not as good as the best in other clubs at the bat, and there are those whose wielding of the willow is considered as being usually equivalent to anything from second base to the home plate for the striker, not to mention the chance occupants of the sand bags who are sent in thereby. In the in and out fields, before, behind and at the bat, there is not a man whom rival clubs deem weak; and, after its month's sojourn at the South for practice, it will be, indeed, surprising if the Chicago Club does not lay out warm work for the best which the country can bring against it.[19]

Birth of the White Stockings (1870)

The *Chicago Tribune* was not alone in its praise of the members of the city's new baseball club. "As a nine they are very strong," the *New York Clipper* declared in March 1870, "especially in the outfield. They have the best outfield of any of our clubs, while the infield is very strong, the second base and short especially." The *Tribune* profiled Chicago's players that month and contended that second baseman Jimmy Wood "probably has no equal in America." The newspaper added that as team captain, Wood carried "the responsibility of maintaining discipline, directing the movements on and off the field, and who, more than any other individual player, must assume the burden of defeat or the glory of success. That he is equal to the task, no one familiar with his reputation for morality, integrity of character, executive tact, and base ball proficiency, can doubt."[20]

Although most of the other members of Chicago's club were perhaps not as nationally well known as Wood, they also earned recognition in the pages of the *Tribune*, which just two months previously had called the city's baseball project "a total failure." The men—some of whom would play more than one position during the season—included catcher William "Bill" Craver, formerly of the Unions of Lansingburgh, New York (also known as the Troy Haymakers); right fielder Edgar "Ned" Cuthbert, who had won "high renown" in the outfield of the Athletic Club of Philadelphia, according to the *Tribune*; William "Clipper" Flynn, who had played "each and every position" while with the Unions; shortstop Charles "Charlie" Hodes, whose "intense ambition to excel" had made him a well-respected member of the Brooklyn Eckfords; center fielder Marshall King, from the Unions, whom an "eminent Eastern sporting authority" called "the best centre fielder in America"; first baseman Michael "Bub" McAtee, who had played first base and shortstop for several years with the Unions and whose "record as a baseman is up to that of the best"; third baseman Levi Meyerle, formerly with the Philadelphia Athletics, who "can pitch or catch, take the field or a base, doing either most efficiently"; pitcher Edward "Ed" Pinkham, from the Brooklyn Eckfords; and left fielder and "splendid player" Frederick "Fred" Treacey, previously with the Brooklyn Eckfords.[21]

Soon the players headed to the ball field. The *Chicago Tribune* reported on March 30 that "the boys had a bout yesterday afternoon with an amateur nine hastily made up from members of various local clubs, the game being played merely with a view to practice." More games followed, with the *Tribune* and other newspapers following the team's progress. "A new professional nine of great ability is said to have been organized under the auspices of the Chicago Club," wrote the Philadelphia *Evening Telegraph* on April 11. "It is a strong team," the *New York Times* had commented four days earlier.

Interest was rather high on April 23, therefore, when the newly formed Chicago team faced off against the city's Garden City Club, a well-known amateur squad. The competition "attracted one of the largest crowds which ever attended a ball match in Chicago," a Chicago sportswriter observed. And even though the Garden City Club lost, 48–2, the reporter was quick to point out that the amateurs performed well on the ball field, unlike the members of another club who had played the new team the day before. After all, during the Garden City contest "the professionals were restricted to forty-eight runs, instead of seventy-five, as on the other occasion."[22]

During their coverage of these games, Chicago's newspapers usually referred to the city's professional team simply as the Chicago Base Ball Club, the Chicago Club, or the Chicago nine. But that would soon change. The men were planning on leaving the city April 28 on a "southern tour" of baseball clubs.[23] The Chicago athletes—resplendent in new uniforms—would have a name bestowed on them shortly after their arrival in St. Louis to play the Unions and Empires:

> ST. LOUIS, April 29.—The Chicago Base Ball Club inaugurated the match game season of 1870, to-day, by a contest with the Unions, of St. Louis, and achieved one of the greatest victories on record.

1. A New Team for Chicago (1868–1870)

Chicago's new baseball team for 1870 included, from left to right: Ned Cuthbert, Fred Treacey, Charlie Hodes, Levi Meyerle, Ed Pinkham, Jimmy Wood, Michael "Bub" McAtee, Bill Craver, Marshall King, and William "Clipper" Flynn (author's collection).

ARRIVAL AT ST. LOUIS.

The Chicago nine reached this city at 11 o'clock this forenoon, after a safe and comfortable journey over the Illinois Central, being supplied with quarters in the sleeping car, and proceeded to the Laclede Hotel, where they were allotted spacious and nicely furnished rooms, the same suite as that occupied by the Red Stockings on the occasion of their visit here last season.

TO THE FIELD.

Dinner over, the club entered carriages supplied by the Unions, and were driven to the base ball park, about four miles northwest of the city, where both clubs were soon on hand in readiness for work.

UNIFORM OF THE CHICAGO NINE.

The Chicago nine were clad in their new uniform, which they had donned for the first time, and an elegant one it is. It consists of a blue cap adorned with a white star in the centre, white flannel shirt, trimmed with blue and bearing the letter C upon the breast worked in blue. Pants of bright blue flannel, with white cord, and supported by a belt of blue and white; stockings of pure white British thread, shoes of white goatskin, with the customary spikes, the *ensemble* constituting by far the showiest and handsomest uniform ever started by a base ball club. Already the snowy purity of the hose has suggested the name of "White Stockings" for the nine, and it is likely to become as generally accepted, not to say as famous, as that of the sanguinary extremities.[24]

The "White Stockings" beat the St. Louis Unions by a score of 47–1, and the Chicago team won again the next day against the St. Louis Empires, 36–8. Using the club's new name, the *Chicago Tribune* subtitled its coverage of the second game with "Another Victory for the Chicago 'White Stockings.'"

Many clubs during this period were simply referred to by their cities, such as the Chicagos or Bostons. The team names themselves were often coined not by their respective clubs but by the newspapers' sportswriters. The names would catch the public's fancy and eventually, through popular use, become a part of the club's history. As for the "White Stockings," in the *Tribune*'s May 19 summation of the team's successful, high-scoring road trip through the South, it recounted who may have originated the name.

The detailed article also included some disquieting reports of dissension in the club and "petty backbiting and jangling" among a few of the players. The newspaper concluded that the team needed "a firmer controlling power than has yet been exercised." The future of the White Stockings depended on it.[25]

"Sporting Matters. The Recent Southern Tour of the White Stockings—Summary of Events. What Was Accomplished, and What Remains to Be Done. The Individual Averages—Programme for the Eastern Tour of the Chicago Club." *Chicago Tribune*, May 19, 1870, p. 4.

BASE BALL.
THE SOUTHERN TOUR OF THE WHITE STOCKINGS.

The recent extended trip of the White Stockings, of Chicago, through the South was a remarkable one in all respects, attracting, both here and elsewhere, a degree of interest and attention such as has rarely been excited by the movements of any base ball club. The achievements of the new professional nine, were in some instances, unparalleled, and a brief *resume* of the events of the tour will be found of interest. On the 28th of April the Chicago Club started on its journey, the objective point being New Orleans, where the club were to be the guests of the Lone Stars, of that city. The party consisted of the ten players of the club, with Tom Foley as business manager, Johnnie Oberlander as scorer, and a reporter of THE TRIBUNE, the latter having been assigned as the chronicler of the journey.

ST. LOUIS

was selected as the site for the opening of the campaign, and it was here that the White Stockings received their christening. The name was suggested by the distinctive peculiarities of the new uniform, which was here donned for the first time, and the neatest and most notable features of which were the snow-white leg coverings. A bare-footed urchin in the crowd exclaimed: "Oh, look at the White Stockings!" The boy's choice of an appellation has since been uniformly endorsed throughout the country.[26] On the afternoon of April 29, the series of victories was inaugurated by the White Stockings, who defeated the Union Club of St. Louis by a score of 47 to 1. The following day the Empires of that city tried it on, and were dispersed of to the tune of 36 to 8. The stay of the White Stockings at St. Louis was an extremely pleasant one, and was rendered especially so by the polite attentions and courtesies of the Union and Empire Clubs. Sunday afternoon found the Chicago party embarked for

NEW ORLEANS,

where they arrived safely on Tuesday morning, May 3. They were met at the depot by Toby Hart, Esq., the genial President of the Lone Star Club, who had already provided elegant accommodations at a private boarding house, on Canal street. The Red Stockings had left New Orleans the day previous. After a respite of three days, the Chicago club met the Atlantics, on Friday, and defeated them by the remarkable score of 51 to 0. This was a magnificent game on the part of the White Stockings, and by no means a poor one by the Atlantics. Twice during the game the latter had filled each of the bases, with no man out, and the skill and strategy which was able to prevent the scoring of a single run under these critical circumstances is so manifest to those familiar with base ball as to need no comment.

One incident deserves notice. The Atlantics were in, and each base was filled, and no out as yet. The back-stop stood sixty feet behind the plate, and its face was padded, and the ground in front covered with sawdust to prevent the bounding back of passed balls. [Bill] Craver had shrewdly noticed the precise point at which every passed ball stopped, and formed a plan to bag the man on third. He contrived to give [Levi] M[e]yerle[27] a hint of his design, and as the striker stood at the bat, Craver being close behind, he gave the required sign to Meyerle, who pitched a very low ball, giving it but a moderate rate of speed. Purposely Craver allowed the ball to pass between his legs and go rolling on toward the back stop. The man on third saw the opening, and stepped into the trap. Quick as a flash Craver wheeled and ran for the ball, while Meyerle, well up to the dodge, ran forward to the home plate, and there received the ball from Craver in ample time to secure the runner from third. It was a dangerous trick, to be sure, but the striker at the bat was very liable to make a hit which would bring in the man at third, and Craver, having calculated the chances, concluded to run the risk. He succeeded, and the inning resulted in a whitewash, after all.

AN "EFFICIENT" UMPIRE.

On the Sunday following, occurred the game with the Lone Stars, the peculiar incidents of which were duly commented upon in THE TRIBUNE'S report by telegraph. The umpire was a most efficient member of the playing ten of the Lone Stars, whom he had evidently concluded beforehand were to be victorious. He certainly did more to secure that end than did all the other players put together, but at last was compelled to undergo the mortification of having demonstrated his unfitness to no purpose. It should not be inferred that the Lone Star nine were parties to the transaction; their well-known character for strict honor and integrity would not permit of such an insinuation. They openly declared themselves disgusted at the umpire's conduct, and admitted that it materially detracted from the credit they would otherwise have taken to themselves in holding the White Stockings to so close a score. The behavior of the professionals was far from creditable. That they suffered intense provocation and exasperation is true, and they must have been more than human to have fully preserved their equanimity; but that they should have been so completely demoralized was disgraceful. They are paid to play base ball, and they are not worthy to hold their positions if they are so poorly provided with tempers as to sacrifice skill and efficiency to mere personal pique, however aggravating may be the circumstances. They protested that they could not help it, but they should be made to understand that they must help it, and that they are held strictly accountable for gross inefficiency, under whatever circumstances. In the game with the Lees the umpiring was wholly against the pitcher and in favor of the striker, but the White Stockings had learned a lesson from the occurrences of the day previous, and succeeded in keeping cool and in playing a better game, although several of the positions were changed by reason of disabilities. On Wednesday they wound up matters by administering a severe drubbing to the Southerns, who have since badly worsted the Lone Stars. In the latter half of the seventh inning the score stood at 41 to 9, with [Jimmy] Wood at the bat and but two men out. The pitching of the Southerns was being punished at a fearful rate, and the fielding nine, appalled at the certain prospect that the completion of nine full innings would run up the score to nearly ten to one, refused to even play out the inning in hand, and quitted the game. Thursday morning, May 12, saw the White Stockings on board the train for the North, and a warm-hearted leave-taking ensued with the Lone Stars, at whose hands they had experienced the most assiduous attention. The stay in New Orleans was rendered by them peculiarly pleasant throughout, and the Chicago Club will be only too well pleased to reciprocate the treatment bestowed by their genial entertainers. The game in

MEMPHIS

with the Bluff City Club was the finest played by the White Stockings with regard to the batting, the character of which is indicated in the subjoined table, showing the number of first-base hits, and the number of total bases made on hits. For the enlight[en]ment of such as are not versed in the inner details of base ball, it should be stated a first base hit is one which is sent out of the reach of any fielder, and by which the striker is enabled to reach the first base. If a ground ball or high fly is muffed in the in or out field, and the striker gets to first in consequence, or, if he goes to first on called balls, he does not receive the credit of a first base hit. The total base line shows the whole number of bases made on clean, safe hits, as described above. For instance, [Fred] Treac[e]y,[28] in the course of his fifteen first base hits, made four home runs, four bases on each run, and sixteen bases in all, to which add the making of second base twice, and his total score is brought to 35. Below is the table:

Player	First base	Total bases
[Marshall] King	16	19
[Charlie] Hodes	11	12
[Jimmy] Wood	15	21
[Ned] Cuthbert	9	16
[Bub] McAtee	16	16
[Fred] Treacey	15	35
[Bill] Craver	13	21
[Levi] Meyerle	13	20
[Ed] Pinkham	11	21
Total	119	181

Leaving Memphis on Saturday evening, the White Stockings made Kankakee on Monday morning, and, in the afternoon, finished up the trip by a score of 111 to 5 against the Grove City Club.

AVERAGES.

The following table gives the individual average of each member of the White Stockings in the games played on the Southern tour, as to outs, runs, and first and total bases:

Players	No. of Games	Outs	Av.	Runs	Av.	1.B.	Av.	T.B.	Av.
[Marshall] King	7	17	2.4	44	6.3	40	5.7	56	8.0
[Charlie] Hodes	7	33	4.7	42	6.0	38	5.4	50	7.1
[Jimmy] Wood	8	22	2.7	58	7.3	46	5.8	57	7.1
[Ned] Cuthbert	8	21	2.6	58	7.3	41	5.1	63	7.9
[Fred] Treacey	8	26	3.3	50	6.3	45	5.6	75	9.4
[Bill] Craver	8	18	2.2	57	7.1	46	5.8	80	10.0
[Levi] Meyerle	8	25	3.1	48	6.0	40	5.0	62	7.8
[Ed] Pinkh[a]m	8	26	3.3	50	6.3	41	5.1	63	7.9
[Bub] McAtee	5	12	2.4	43	8.6	34	6.8	40	8.0
[Clipper] Flynn	5	10	2.0	35	7.0	29	5.8	41	8.2
Total				485		400		587	

THE GAMES PLAYED.

Chicago	Runs	Opponents	Runs
Chicago	47	Union, St. Louis	1
Chicago	36	Empire, St. Louis	8
Chicago	51	Atlantic, New Orleans	0

Chicago	Runs	Opponents	Runs
Chicago	18	Lone Star, New Orleans	10
Chicago	24	R[obert] E. Lee, New Orleans	14
Chicago	41	Southern, New Orleans	9
Chicago	157	Bluff City, Memphis	1
Chicago	111	Grove City, Kankakee	5
Total	485		48

This gives the White Stockings an average of 60.6 runs to each game, against 6 runs by their opponents, or over 10 to 1.

THE PROGRESS OF THE CLUB.

Since the return of the White Stockings to Chicago the public mind has been agitated upon two propositions: First, "To what extent, if any, has the nine improved in its collective play?" Second, "Will they beat the Red Stockings?"

As to the first inquiry, the writer can affirm, having been with the club throughout, that there are grounds for encouragement; that material improvement has taken place in this respect; that a feeling of club pride and club interest, so wholly lacking when the picked nine was first got together, has arisen and is on the increase. The practice has done an immense deal of good in establishing a confidence among the players, and in perfecting a knowledge of each other's style of play. There is yet, however, vast room for improvement in the personal feelings and relations of the various members, the general tendency being toward petty backbiting and jangling. This can only be overcome by time and a firmer controlling power than has yet been exercised. Time will do its share, and Jimmy Wood *must* do the rest. He has a difficult task—more difficult than would ever be suspected with the club at home—but we believe he is equal to it, and that when the proper time arrives he will surprise some of the troublesome, turbulent elements of his team with a check both sudden and effectual. And there are one or two terribly turbulent spirits among them—spirits which must be ruled, or they will ruin all about them. They shall be nameless now, and, we hope, forever; but a recurrence of some of the characteristic incidents of the Southern trip could not fail to involve a publicity and an individual and collective odium most undesirable to those directly concerned, and damaging to the good name of the club. "Will they beat the Red Stockings?" To this, not an opinion, but a theory. Everybody concedes that the individual efficiency of the Chicago Club throughout is greater than that of the Red Stockings, and no one denies that our nine is capable of doing as fine fielding as they. The batting of the White Stockings has been demonstrated to be superior, both upon swift and slow pitching. Then, if anything like the perfection of the Reds in collective play can be secured by the Chicago nine, the stronger batting of the latter will be a great point in their favor, and the chances for wrestling the supremacy from the hitherto invincibles may be said to be extremely good. All this, as we have said, depends upon what the Chicago Club shall accomplish in the way of mutual efficiency, and the situation, generally considered, is rather promising than otherwise.

THE EASTERN TOUR.

The programme of the White Stockings for their Eastern tour has now been definitely arranged as to date of games, and is as follows:

Leaving Chicago on the afternoon of Sunday, June 19, the club will arrive in Cleveland early on the following day, and there the series of match games will be inaugurated:

No. 1—Forest City, Cleveland, Monday, June 20.
No. 2—Niagaras, Buffalo, Tuesday, June 21.

No. 3—Flour City, Rochester, New York, Wednesday, June 22
No game on Thursday.
No. 4—Ontario, Oswego, Friday, June 24.
No. 5—Central City, Syracuse, Saturday, June 25.
No game on Sunday.
No. 6—Haymakers, Troy, Monday, June 27.
No. 7—Trimountains, Boston, June 28.
No game on Wednesday.
No. 8—Lowells, Boston, Thursday, June 30.
No. 9—Harvards, Boston, Friday, July 1.
No. 10—Yales, New Haven, Saturday, July 2.
No game on Sunday.
No. 11—Atlantics, Brooklyn, Monday, July 4.
No game Tuesday.
No. 12—Mutuals, New York, Wednesday, July 6.
No. 13—Eckfords, Brooklyn, Thursday, July 7.
No. 14—Unions, Morrisania, Friday, July 8.
No games on Saturday and Sunday.
No. 15—Athletics, Philadelphia, Monday, July 11.
No. 16—Keystone, Philadelphia, Tuesday, July 12.
No game on Wednesday.
No. 17—Marylands, Baltimore, Thursday, July 14.
No. 18—Pastimes, Baltimore, Friday, July 15.
No. 19—Olympics, Washington, Saturday, July 16.
No game on Sunday.
No. 20—Nationals, Washington, Monday, July 18.
No. 21—The leading club of Harrisburg, Penn., Tuesday, July 19.
No. 22—Allegh[e]nys, Pittsburgh, Wednesday, July 20.
No. 23—Kekiongas, Fort Wayne, Ind., Thursday, July 21.

Due allowance has been made for the intervention of bad weather, and it is quite probable that other games will be arranged for some of the vacant days.

With the White Stockings' busy 1870 schedule and a growing fan base, the team needed a suitable ballpark. Many of Chicago's clubs played at Ogden Park, located on Ontario Street near Lake Michigan on the city's North Side. Unfortunately, the park had no benches or seats for spectators, who had to stand along the baselines to watch games. A year earlier, for a match between the Cincinnati Red Stockings and the Forest Citys of Rockford, Illinois, a platform with a small number of seats was constructed, but it collapsed shortly before the game started. Conditions were probably not any better for the athletes themselves. As one local Chicago reporter bluntly declared in his game-day coverage, "It was very evident to those who have any knowledge of the game of base ball, that the Ogden Park is a place very poorly adapted to first-class players of the game." With its shallow outfield, even an average player could muster a home run or two. The two clubs therefore agreed even before they took the field that whenever a ball was hit over the fence, the batter could advance only two bases.[29]

In addition to Ogden Park, the 1870 White Stockings also played games at Dexter

Park, adjacent to the Union Stock Yards on the city's South Side. Dexter Park was actually a horse racing track, with the baseball diamond laid out inside the oval. *Baseball in Old Chicago*, a 1939 project of the Writers' Program of the Work Projects Administration (WPA) in the State of Illinois, notes that the park "was located about six miles southwest of what is now the loop, in the vicinity of 42nd and Halsted streets, where the International Amphitheatre now stands." Although some argued that getting to Dexter Park from nearly anywhere in the city was a simple matter, the WPA Chicago baseball history related that "many people considered it entirely too far out. The park was connected with the city by a steam railroad and a street car line, but the street cars of that day were horse cars, and a six-mile ride in a horse car was not a pleasant experience."

Dexter Park received some much-needed improvements in the spring of 1870.

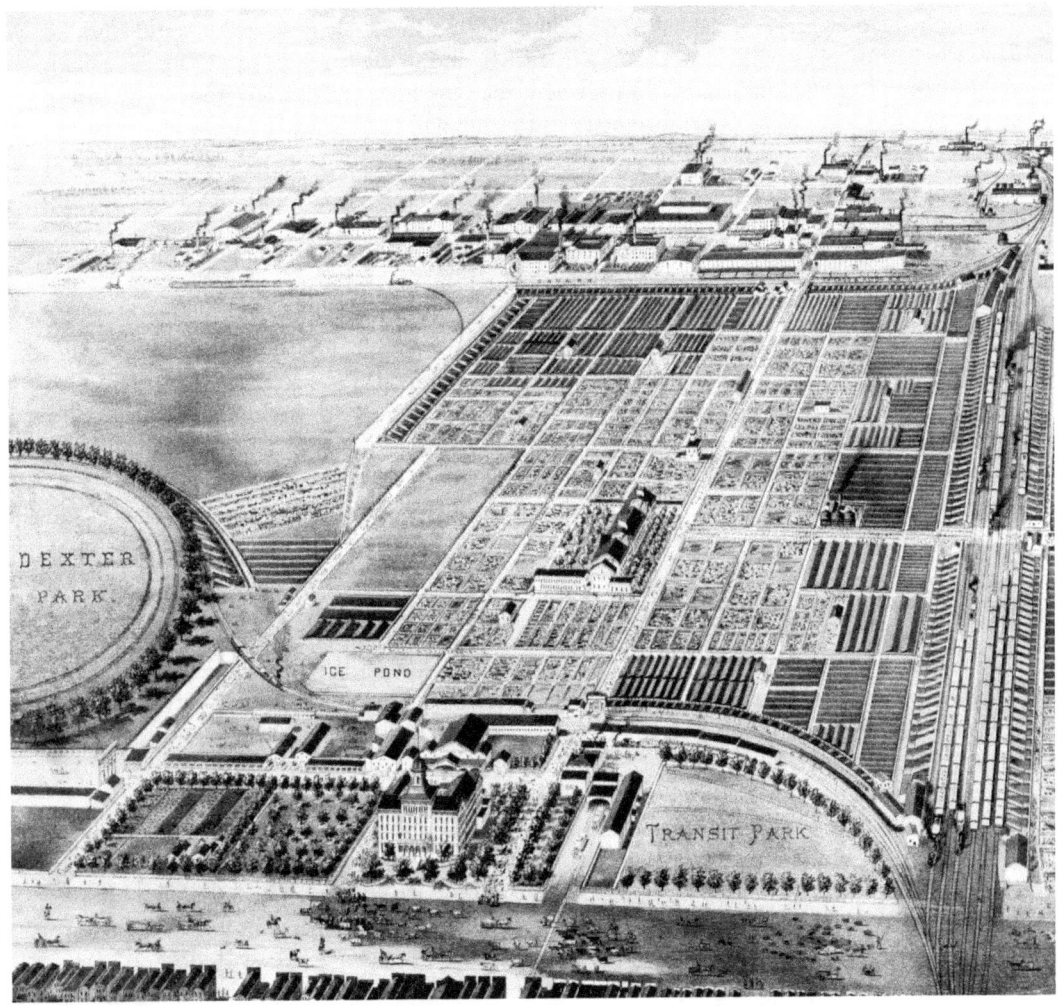

In 1870, the Chicago White Stockings played at Dexter Park, adjacent to the Union Stock Yards on the city's South Side. Dexter Park was actually a horse racing track, with the baseball diamond laid out inside the oval. This 1877 panoramic view of the Union Stock Yards from the east shows the packing houses to the far west and Dexter Park to the south (Charles Rascher, "The Great Union Stock Yards of Chicago." Chicago: Walsh & Co., 1878; Library of Congress, LC-DIG-pga-02434).

Shortly before the White Stockings played their first game at the new facility, a *Chicago Tribune* sportswriter reviewed the renovations and pronounced them "nearly perfect."[30]

"Sporting Matters. The New Base Ball Grounds of the White Stockings." *Chicago Tribune*, May 27, 1870, p. 4. [Note: This article originally appeared as one long passage, and a few paragraph breaks have been added for ease of readability.]

Base Ball.
THE NEW GROUNDS OF THE WHITE STOCKINGS.

While the White Stockings have been on their travels, gaining renown and needed practice, busy hands have been at work preparing the club grounds for the season of 1870. These are located at Dexter Park, inside the racing course, where ample space has been set apart for the purposes of base ball. The field is laid out precisely west of the grand stand, and the batting plate will be nearly on a line with, and immediately beyond, the octagonal club-house. The diamond-shaped space which the base lines enclose will front to the southwest, which is an admirable arrangement, as the sun will thereby be at the backs of the pitcher, second baseman, short stop, and fielders, and upon the side faces of both the first and third basemen, the catcher being the only player who must squarely face the sun at any time.

About sixty feet behind the home plate will be placed the back stop, and directly in the rear, and circling on either side, will be erected the tiers of seats, made somewhat after the style of circus seats, portable, so that the upper tiers may be taken down when the park is used for racing purposes. In addition to these, it is contemplated to construct a low tier of permanent benches around the right and left circumferences of a circle 650 feet in diameter, which is sufficiently large for the purposes of the entire field. Back of these seats will be ample room for carriages around the entire circle.

The plan provides for the comfortable and eligible seating of about 12,000 persons. Add to this the carriage room, the balconies of the club-house, the ladies' stand overlooking the race course, and a portion of the grand stand itself, and the total facilities for viewing the game of base ball are such as to provide for an attendance of over 30,000 people. The calculations are on a grand scale, but it is believed that nothing short of the vast provisions to be made at Dexter Park would be adequate for the accommodation of the multitude which will assemble there on the occasion of the contest between the two great stocking nines, the Whites and the Reds.

By means of filling, grading, and rolling, together with a complete system of drainage, the surface of the field has been splendidly adapted to the uses of the game. The ground is smooth, level, and compact, and is covered with a fine sward of grass. In fact, the whole arrangement is as nearly perfect as could be desired by either players or spectators. No objection can be urged upon the score of distance, as there is no spot in or about Chicago for reaching which there are so many facilities. With three separate lines of steam railway, a well-equipped street railroad, and a smooth, attractive carriage-way over the entire distance, the five miles between Dexter Park and Chicago, are rendered a very easy, short and comfortable trip. The new grounds will be formally inaugurated and thrown open to the public on the [16th] of June by a game between the White Stockings and the Forest City Club, of Rockford.[31]

◆ ◆ ◆

The White Stockings defeated the Forest City Club of Cleveland, 15–9, during a June 3 "practice game" at the new ball grounds. When the Chicago team formally opened the ballpark on June 16, it trounced the Forest Citys of Rockford, Illinois, exactly two to one, 28–14.

The White Stockings continued to compete at both ball fields for the rest of the season. Contemporary newspaper articles indicate that home games against professional teams were usually played at the spacious Dexter Park, while contests against amateur opponents were held at the smaller Ogden Park.[32]

Growing Pains (1870)

The *Chicago Tribune* sportswriter had been quite accurate when he observed in mid–May 1870 that despite the White Stockings' successful southern tour, there was "vast room for improvement" in the personal relationships developing among the team members. Even the *New York Times*, in its review of the 1870 baseball season, noted that a major "fault of the Chicago organization was in not having a harmonious nine." One of the team's "troublesome, turbulent elements" whom the *Tribune* did not name was undoubtedly catcher Bill Craver. Suspicions (as well as charges) of gambling and game-fixing dogged him throughout his career, and the White Stockings dismissed him in August 1870.[33]

Besides the internal strife, sportswriters also raised their eyebrows at the White Stockings' "lack of discipline," which occasionally led to sloppy play on the ball field. After Chicago lost, 30–20, to the Brooklyn Atlantics on July 4, the *New-York Tribune* wrote that "in the field the White Stockings showed little skill, while at the bat they hammered away, regardless of the course the ball might take. They appeared to have had no training as a nine, and played for individual show, no one member appearing to feel otherwise than that he was best, his coadjutors falling far below him." In its own game-day coverage, the New York *Star* contemptuously called the White Stockings "simply a number of base-ball hacks ... who never were anything more than third-rate players until they took the notion of going to Chicago and coming back as representatives of the West *a la* 'Red Stockings.' ... They were soundly thrashed, and were, moreover, exposed as humbugs, mountebanks, and side-show people of no ability, except in the Barnum style of base-balling."

Chicago's newspapers were no less caustic. For example, one local sportswriter soundly chastised the White Stockings for their "wretched" performance during a 13–4 loss to the New York Mutuals on July 6. He particularly contrasted the style of play between the two clubs when he derisively explained how the White Stockings scored no runs in five innings: "The Mutuals waited for balls until they got good ones, and those wanting it took their first [base] on called balls. On the contrary, Chicago batted at everything, high and low; batted like mere countrymen instead of ball players, and the consequence was that their flys were gobbled as fast as they were sent up, and their low hits to short picked up as fast as they were knocked down, and five whitewashes were the consequence."[34]

Perhaps the club schedule had lulled the Chicago men into feelings of false complacency. For the first part of the season (from April until June 3), the White Stockings had squared off against only amateur opponents who provided little competition. On

May 13, for example, they had pounded the Bluff City Club of Memphis, 157–1. The *Chicago Tribune* wrote that after seven innings, the Tennesseans wanted the White Stockings to let them score just two more runs and then call the game as darkness approached. But Chicago business manager Tom Foley and captain Jimmy Wood, however, "stubbornly refused to let up an atom, and ordered the boys to go on with their 'rat kill[in]g,' which they did most effectually."

Such obstinacy did not go unnoticed by the newspapers. On June 3 the Chicago team bested the members of Cleveland's Forest City Club by the score of 15–9. The *Tribune* tempered its write-up of this "sharp and exciting contest" by referring to Chicago's "succession of easy victories wrested from clubs of an inferior order." The reporter went on to contend that the White Stockings' games "heretofore have been with that class of clubs whom to beat was no honor, and from the scores of which no particular satisfaction could be derived in estimating their abilities."[35]

Following their uninspired performance against the New York Mutuals on July 6, the White Stockings began compiling a solid record, winning eight of nine games from July 8 to July 18. They were in "excellent health and spirits" and "first-rate condition," according to one Chicago sportswriter, and looked forward to meeting New York again on July 23. Any dreams of victory, however, were quickly shattered. With a 9–0 loss on that day, the Chicago team became the first member of the National Association of Base Ball Players (the sport's governing organization) to be held scoreless in a professional game. Furthermore, a new word—"Chicagoed"—would enter baseball's lexicon. As the *New York Herald* related:

> It may be proper here to remark that since the Mutual game at Chicago on Saturday the word "skunked" will not be used hereafter.
>
> "CHICAGOED"
>
> will be the expression to signify what has been known heretofore as "skunked," "whitewashed," "goose-egged."[36]

After the disastrous July 23 game against the Mutuals, New York journalists were not alone in singling out the White Stockings' deficiencies. The *Chicago Republican* wrote a particularly biting attack, in which the newspaper denounced the players, berated the club officials, and called for an "immediate reorganization" of the team "under some vigorous management."

"Base-Ball. The Great Whitewashed Nine—A Few Remarks Concerning the Same." *Chicago Republican*, July 25, 1870, p. 4.

THE DEFEAT OF THE CHICAGOS.

Concerning the most overwhelming defeat of the professional nine base-ball players, called the Chicago Club, on Saturday, there can be little or nothing said by way of extenuation. They were beaten in the most extraordinary manner, and most unaccountably, except on the hypothesis that they can not play base-ball—and even that has about ceased to be hypothetical. They have, thus far, proven themselves only capable of beating second-rate clubs—the few first-class organizations they have met having all come off victorious. If any are so foolish as to believe that they have "sold" any games let them be at once and forever undeceived. Not that they are too immaculate to do the little ingenious speculating that other similar organizations do, but, in fact, no one has as yet had any occasion, or evinced any determination to buy.

The club has made a miserably poor record. That it has done so is partly the fault of the players, and partly the fault of the managers—the management having been for the most part entirely inefficient, and worse than the playing. The insubordinate spirit of some members of the nine has been painfully prominent—so much so that a well-meaning but weak captain has never been able to have full control of his men, and, in looking for support from the officers, he has invariably been in the fix of the boy in the parable who wanted bread and got a stone. A degree of firmness, such as is shown by the managers of all Eastern clubs, has never been manifested, and attempts have been made to quell the little disturbances on the sugar-candy principle, when the ultimatum should have been, "Shut up or pack up—tend to your business or leave." And so each individual has been allowed to look out for No. 1 alone, and the interests of the club and the money of its backers have alike been allowed to go by default.

This great fault may have accounted for some of the reverses the club has met, but not for the defeat of Saturday. The play of the Mutuals was as near perfection as possible, but three errors being made on their side, and they not serious enough to admit of a tally for their opponents. Their fielding, out and in, could not have been improved upon. The outfielding of the Chicagos was fine, but the infield was even weaker than usual, errors being credited to those players that would have looked badly in an amateur club. The new pitcher [Mark Burns] proved a failure. [Bill] Craver, well as he caught, could not stop all of his wild balls, and every pass was taken advantage of. But the real cause of the nine whitewashes lay in the batting. The great club that went forth heralded as the "heavy batting" nine, found a pitcher they could not play against, and when a hit was made, the ball was sure to go straight up in the air, and never allowed to touch the ground. The "heavy batting" was far below that of the Amateur Club, who made eleven runs the day before against the same opponents. As willow swingers, there never were sadder failures, and in that lay the result of the game—which, however, would have been won by the superior infielding of the Mutuals had the batting been ever so good.

The defeat is extremely humiliating to Chicago people, particularly to those who took their cue from certain daily papers, and allowed their prejudice, for all that is of Chicago to get the better of their judgment. This is the organization that was gotten up for the purpose of "cleaning out," the Red Stockings, and sweeping directly into the championship. They are in a fair way of doing so now, for they have achieved an honor at the hands of the Mutuals that no other club has been thought worthy of. But one other such game is on record.[37] Now, all that remains is the immediate reorganization of the club, for the next season, under some vigorous management. The money that has already been squandered on the institution would have procured a much better team, and there is no chance of its being got back, for people have become disgusted, and won't go to see them play. If the present concern is to be continued, we protest that it be under some other name than that of "The Chicago Club," for Chicago is not accustomed to turn out such enterprising failures.

◆ ◆ ◆

Shutouts were rare in the early years of baseball, a time when pitchers tossed "lively" rubber balls underhanded and when batters requested where they wanted their pitches located. Perhaps that's why the White Stockings' failure to score even one run was so embarrassing to fans in Chicago. When the *Chicago Tribune* recapped the whitewash it wrote: "Who would have thought it? What sane individual, conversant with the general subject, would have incurred the risk of an examination before a commission of lunacy, by admitting the bare possibility, much less by uttering the prediction?"

Probably no "sane individual" would have predicted that the Chicago ballplayers would be defeated in their next two games as well, falling to the Cambridge Harvards and the Philadelphia Athletics on July 26 and August 1. Losing by scores of 11–6 and 18–11, however, at least prevented the White Stockings from being "Chicagoed," and the *Tribune* even praised their excellent batting. Moreover, the newspaper affirmed that despite the team's "repeated drubbings," the city's residents were still "fond of looking at a fine game of base ball."[38]

And uppermost in these fans' minds was beating the mighty Red Stockings. Some reorganization was clearly needed, and not just on the baseball diamond. Impatient stockholders felt that the board of trustees' mismanagement of the club contributed to the team's poor performance. "The mixture of merchant chiefs, war heroes, and sporting characters in the 'front office' was just a little too mixed up to jell properly," according to *Baseball in Old Chicago*, "and, after some heated spats and shake-ups of the officers, the shareholders began to realize that while professional baseball might be a business, it was not quite the same as keeping a store or running a hotel." To bring some much-needed leadership to the Chicago Base Ball Club, Norman T. Gassette, Clerk of the Circuit Court of Cook County, was elected president in August 1870. Other newly elected officers joined him and the dependable Tom Foley on an executive committee, which was responsible for managing the entire organization.[39]

Less than two weeks after the committee's formation, catcher and perennial malcontent Bill Craver was drummed off the team, accused of gambling, insubordination, and, as the baseball club's secretary recorded in his meeting minutes, having an "utter disregard of the rules." Marshall King took Craver's place as catcher, and business manager Tom Foley shrewdly hired infielder Ed Duffy away from the Brooklyn Eckfords. In the words of *Baseball in Old Chicago*, the pieces of the ball club finally all seemed to "jell properly." On August 30 the White Stockings beat the Brooklyn Atlantics, 12–4, no small feat considering that the Atlantics the previous June had given Cincinnati its first loss in more than a year. After the Chicago players followed this victory with a 13–6 win over the Forest City Club of Rockford, Illinois, the *Chicago Tribune* lauded not only the team's superb fielding and batting but also its "perfect harmony, good will, and discipline"—the same characteristics that sportswriters found lacking in the team earlier in the spring.[40]

The season was now about three-quarters finished, and Chicago would play half of its remaining 18 games (including two with the Red Stockings) against highly regarded professional teams. The *Tribune* was optimistic, however, reporting that in Cincinnati on September 7 the Chicago ballplayers "will take the field against the Red Stockings for the first time. They will enter the contest in good condition, and it will be strange indeed if they do not acquit themselves with credit."

The Chicago ballplayers came through and brought glory to both themselves and their city after a 10–6 win over their despised adversaries. "The mission of the White Stockings has been accomplished," the newspaper's sportswriter gloated. "The organization was effected with a direct view to beating the Red Stockings, and they have done it. The white is above the red, and Chicago can crow over Cincinnati to her heart's content.... Every man was bent on doing his best to win the game, knowing that the Cincinnati people entertained a profound contempt for the $18,000 nine, as they were fond of calling it."[41]

Chicagoans planned to welcome the team in grand style upon its return to the city.

Although the White Stockings were not scheduled to get back to Chicago until after nine o'clock on the evening of September 9, some 3,000 fans greeted them at the Union Depot. The *Tribune* related that as the train pulled into the station, "There arose a prolonged cheer so long and so hearty that the echo must have reached a certain dejected town on the Ohio River." Cheers broke out again when the ballplayers showed off their trophy: a month-old pig wearing red stockings and bearing a placard reading "Porkopolis, Sept. 7, 1870." The newspaper remarked that "it is contemplated to give his pigship a suitable bringing up, and when he shall have reached the enormous dimensions to which all things Chicagoan attain, his unctuous adipose will be forwarded to Cincinnati as a salve for her wounded pride."

In the meantime, Cincinnati's fans had to forgo the salve while nursing their many wounds. They complained (with some justification) about the umpire's bad calls, though others said that his decisions adversely affected the Chicago nine as well. The Red Stockings had played without their injured star shortstop, George Wright, and the Cincinnati sportswriters agreed that his absence was a terrible loss for the team, if not a principal reason for its defeat. Not surprisingly, the Red Stockings asked for a rematch, to be held after Wright resumed his place in the lineup.

Chicago residents naturally had no use for Cincinnati's excuses. The White Stockings, confident after their huge win and anxious to redeem themselves after their notable losses on their summer eastern tour, prepared for another trip out east. The *Chicago Tribune* was just as upbeat as the players and certainly did not expect them to be "Chicagoed" again: "The recent superb play of the White Stockings, together with the fact that the nine never was so strong or in so perfect working condition as now, warrants the prediction that the purpose of the proposed tour will not altogether fall short of accomplishment, and no one need be surprised if they return to Chicago the foremost club in America."[42]

The ballplayers left the city on September 20, traveling to New York on the Pittsburgh & Fort Wayne Railroad. Although their recent wins were still fresh in their minds, they had not forgotten their losses either, and now they desired nothing more than to play the clubs that had pummeled them during their first trip east. At the top of the list was undoubtedly the Mutual Club. After all, the New York Mutuals had badly beaten the White Stockings twice that season, including the infamous game in which the Chicago club failed to score a run and lost, 9–0. The Mutuals had also previously defeated two other strong teams, the Brooklyn Atlantics and the Philadelphia Athletics, so many Chicago fans predicted a close game, particularly with "that spectral 'nine to nothing' continually before our eyes."

And before the White Stockings' eyes was their tough schedule. On September 23 the team would face the Brooklyn Eckfords, and this match would be quickly followed by games with three more outstanding teams: the Brooklyn Atlantics, the Philadelphia Athletics, and the New York Mutuals. Interest in the game with the Mutuals was undoubtedly heightened after the Chicago nine won their first three contests of the trip. Even the *New York Times* was suitably impressed, writing that the game with the Athletics "was decidedly the best played here this season. The batting of both sides was at times heavy, and the fielding first-class."[43]

The *Times* also praised the White Stockings the following day, after they beat the Mutual Club by the resounding score of 22–11.

"Out-Door Sports. Base-Ball. The White Stockings Again Victorious—Signal Defeat of the New Champions." *New York Times*, September 28, 1870, p. 8.

The White Stockings nine of the Chicago Club may now exclaim, with the Roman General, *Veni, Vidi, Vici*, for the result of their second tour East has been a series of signal victories over the strongest nines of New-York, Brooklyn and Philadelphia. The Chicago nine arrived in town last week, and opened play with the Eckford Club, winning easily by a score of 22 to 8. Their play in this match did not warrant any great expectations in regard to their other games; but their noteworthy victory over the Atlantics by a score of 9 to 4, followed up, as it was, with their grand triumph in Philadelphia over the Athletics, their umpire and their crowd, by a score of 12 to 11, led to quite an unusual degree of interest being taken in the contest of yesterday, with the new champion nine of the Mutual Club, and consequently there was an immense assemblage of spectators gathered on the Union Grounds, Brooklyn, yesterday afternoon, fully 5,000 people paying the half dollar admission fee on the occasion, while almost as many were congregated outside the inclosure. The first game of the series between the first Chicago nine and the Mutuals resulted in a score of 13 to 4 in favor of the New-Yorkers, and on the occasion of the second game in Chicago the Mutuals won by a score of 9 to 0. The Chicago nine after this signal defeat was "reconstructed," [Bill] CRAVER being expelled from the Club for alleged dishonorable conduct, and [Ed] DUFFY, of the Eckfords, substituted. With this new nine victory began to perch upon the Chicago banner, and the climax of success was reached when they defeated the famous Red Stockings by a score of 10 to 6. Being desirous of redeeming the defeat previously sustained in this City and Philadelphia, they came on last week once more to try conclusions with our strong nines, and also with the intention of taking home the coveted whip pennant, if such a feat were possible of accomplishment. With this object in view they played the three crack clubs of the East—Atlantics, Athletics and Mutuals, and the result has been a degree of success only equaled by the career of the Red Stockings through our Eastern cities in 1869. The contest of yesterday was the culminating point, and should they be fortunate enough to defeat the Mutual Club on the occasion of the return game at Chicago—to be played in a week or so there—the whip pennant, the emblem of the championship, will then fly from the Chicago flag-staff at Dexter Park.

The game of yesterday was not what was expected, neither nine doing themselves justice, the Mutuals, especially, making a very poor display at the bat and in the field in fact; the poorest since their defeat by the Athletics. Had they supported their pitcher as they did last Thursday, the Chicagos would have sustained defeat. Of course the result will set Chicago wild. If they had a procession to greet the gents of the White Hose after their victory in Cincinnati, the city ought to turn out *en masse* to welcome them from their "Sedan triumphs" in the East.[44] Below we give the full score of the match, which gives all further particulars:

CHICAGO	R.	1B.	P.O.	A.	MUTUAL	R.	1B.	P.O.	A.
[Bub] McAtee, 1st b.	4	2	9	0	[John] Hatfield, s.s.	2	2	5	3
[Jimmy] Wood, 2d b.	2	2	1	3	[Dave] Eggler, c.f.	0	0	4	0
[Ned] Cuthbert, c.f.	2	4	0	0	[Dan] Patterson, l.f.	1	0	1	0
[Clipper] Flynn, r.f.	3	4	3	0	[John] Nelson, 3d b.	2	1	3	1
[Fred] Treac[el]y, l.f.	4	1	4	0	E[verett] Mills, 1st b.	2	2	8	0
[Marshall] King, c.	2	3	4	0	[Phonney] Martin, r.f.	1	3	0	0
[Levi] Meyerle, 3d b.	3	2	2	1	C[harlie] Mills, c.	2	1	4	1
[Ed] Pinkham, p.	2	3	2	1	[Rynie] Wolters, p.	0	1	0	1
[Ed] Duffy, s.s.	0	0	2	3	[Marty] Swandell, 2d b.	1	0	2	3
Total	22	2[1]	27	8	Total	11	10	27	9

	INNINGS									
	1	2	3	4	5	6	7	8	9	
Chicago	2	3	2	0	1	4	4	0	6	22
Mutual	1	0	2	3	0	3	1	1	0	11

Umpire—Mr. [Bob] FERGUSON, of the Atlantic Club.
Time of Game—Two hours and fifteen minutes.
Runs Earned—Chicago, 4; Mutual, 4.
First Base by Errors—Chicago, 9; Mutual, 4.
Fielding Errors—Chicago, 12; Mutual, 22.

◆ ◆ ◆

A Controversial Championship (1870)

Following the Chicago ballplayers' huge win over the Mutual Club on September 27, they set out for home, stopping in Fort Wayne, Indiana, where they defeated the amateur Kekionga club. In the following week, three more amateur teams fell to the White Stockings in quick succession, which augured well for their second contest against opponent Cincinnati on October 13.

Although the *Cincinnati Daily Gazette*'s comment that "the game will be the most bitterly contested and exciting contest of the season" could be construed as typical journalism hyperbole, even casual observers knew that this was no ordinary match. A Chicago sportswriter reported on October 12 that "people who have been meditating a visit to Chicago all summer, on business or pleasure, have arranged to be here tomorrow, and those who otherwise would have returned home will stay over." Spectators from Indiana, Wisconsin, and Iowa were already on hand, and an excursion train from Cincinnati was expected. Railway lines leading to Dexter Park were in readiness, and there was "no lack of facilities for reaching and returning from the grounds."[45]

Everything else was ready as well. To ward off complaints about the umpire, both sides agreed upon the competent, well-respected Bob Ferguson of the Brooklyn Atlantics. (Until well into the 1870s, home teams usually hired local persons to umpire games, which naturally led to charges of favoritism.) Shortstop George Wright had recovered from his injuries and would be back on the field for Cincinnati; indeed, he and his teammates all arrived in Chicago "in excellent physical condition," according to the *Chicago Tribune*, "and determined to demonstrate that the Whites can't do it again." As for the White Stockings, "It is only necessary to say that they are wholly sound in wind and limb, and will enter the contest with the will to do all that skill and pluck can accomplish toward winning the game."

And win they did, much to the frustration of a Cincinnati sportswriter who charged that the umpire, weather, crowd, heavens, ground, and even "the pestilential air of the Chicago river" were all in league against the Red Stockings.[46] The intense rivalry between the two clubs is illustrated in the game-day coverage from the *Chicago Times* and the *Cincinnati Daily Gazette*.

"Sporting. The Great Base-Ball Event of the Season of 1870. Match Between the Chicagos and the Red Stockings. The Former Victorious by a Score of 16 to 13. An Immense Crowd and an Exciting Contest." *Chicago Times*, October 14, 1870, p. 4.

ENGLEWOOD, Oct. 13, 6 P.M.—A party of about 600 men came down on our suburb from the north a few moments ago. They act strangely and look hungry. Please inform Superintendent Kennedy of their helpless situation.

LATER.—The invaders have departed eastward for Cincinnati. Several of the crowd wear white knee-breeches and red stockings.

HYDE PARK, Oct. 13, 7 P.M.—A straggling band of roughs, barefooted and coatless, passed through this place a few moments since toward Calumet. Their conversation indicated some great financial affliction. What's up?

CALUMET, Oct. 13, 9:30 P.M.—The people of this metropolis are greatly annoyed by the presence of an unusually large number of dangerous-looking characters who appear to have come from your city. However, they are quite harmless, but very reticent. Among themselves such expressions as "put-up job," "d—d umpire," "dead broke," etc., are common. One hungry chap, called "Gris," is discoursing on "Indian meal" to a thoughtful squad.

MICHIGAN CITY, Oct. 13, 12 P.M.—What in the d—il's the matter? Just now a scaly-looking crowd of about 600 persons passed through here, and asked the best road to Cincinnati; said they came from Chicago. They only stopped to bathe their feet.

The above telegrams were received at this office on last evening. As they indicated the occurrence of something of unusual importance, a reporter was dispatched to learn, if possible, what had taken place. Shortly he returned, and stated that there was a rumor current of a game of base-ball having been played during the afternoon at Dexter park, in which a number of Cincinnati men had been deeply interested in a financial way. With his characteristic enterprise, THE TIMES reporter followed up this rumor, and at length ascertained, after great difficulty (Chicago people taking but little interest in such games, especially with inferior clubs from abroad), that nine stripling base-ball players from Hamilton county, Ohio, had had the temerity to come to the city and play the champions; that a large number of their fellow-citizens had accompanied the so-called Red Stockings, and had lost a vast amount of money upon the game; that, in fact, the aforesaid Hamilton county chaps had come to realize the singular situation of that individual who was 500 miles from home, without a cent or friend. Among other things, the reporter gleaned the following facts concerning the game, which are given for the benefit of Cincinnati subscribers, Chicago people being but little interested in such one-sided affairs:

After 12 o'clock every train of cars on the Rock Island, and the Pittsburgh and Fort Wayne roads, and every avenue leading southward, were crowded with passengers for Dexter park, mostly from Cincinnati. Indeed, every regular train from that city since Monday, three special trains on Wednesday, and two on yesterday, were taken up with visitors from that town, who insanely believed that their favorite club would harvest a victory here. To humor the boys, the Chicagos consented to play with them, and yesterday afternoon was a most auspicious occasion. The day was clear and cool, and the grounds were perfection.

At 2:40 o'clock, when the game was called, there were not less than 15,000 persons on the grounds. Every seat was full, and a cordon of vehicles encircled the field. The clubhouse was especially reserved for ladies, who, when occasion offered, lent their voices and hands to swell the enthusiasm, which was, out of courtesy to the visiting nine, pretty evenly distributed.

The ever-courteous Chicagos consented to take the first turn at the bat, and [Bub] McAtee spraed himself around the home plate.[47] His effort was not very successful. In fact, the home nine, anticipating no honor in beating their opponents, encouraged them in the hope of victory until the eighth inning, when they shook off their apathy and took the game. The Chicagos were not ambitious for distinction in such a game, but with such accomplished players honor will follow them, whether or no. [Ed] Duffy unquestionably took the greatest share. Not an error can be made upon his record. At short he was greatly superior to George Wright, both in blocking and throwing balls. But in base running he achieved the greatest success. His play between the first and second bases when McAtee struck to [Charlie] Swe[as]y, in the fourth inning, was noticeably brilliant, both in design and execution. [Jimmy] Wood played with his usual energy and skill. Sly Levi [Meyerle] covered himself with glory again. [Clipper] Flynn misjudged several balls at right, and [Ned] Cuthbert did the same in centre field. McAtee was terribly unfortunate at the bat, though nearly every hit was a grounder and would have been safe ordinarily. The others played well, as a matter of course.

On the part of the Reds, no especially fine playing was developed, except in the in field, which has always been remarkably strong, while the out field has ever been remarkably weak. The pitching and catching were moderately good. In the eighth inning, Harry Wright was substituted for [Asa] Brainard, who took the right field, [Cal] McVey covering centre. The change did not appear to be especially beneficial, as the Chicago lads punished his pitching even worse than they did that of Brainard. In the middle of the ninth inning they came back to first principles again, Brainard taking his regular position.

Robert Ferguson, of the Brooklyn Atlantics, acted as umpire, and in a highly creditable manner. He struck a happy mean in calling balls and strikes which Chicago umpires would do well to imitate.

The Chicagos, losing the toss, went first to the bat.... [Paragraphs of inning-by-inning coverage are omitted.]

THE SCORE

CINCINNATIS	O.	R.	B.	TB	CHICAGOS	O.	R.	B.	TB
Geo[rge] Wright, ss.	2	2	2	3	[Bub] McAtee, 1st b.	6	0	0	0
[Charlie] Gould, 1st b.	3	2	2	2	[Jimmy] Wood, 2d b.	3	2	3	3
[Fred] Waterman, 3d b.	2	1	2	4	[Ned] Cuthbert, c.f.	2	3	2	4
[Doug] Allison, c.	2	3	3	3	[Clipper] Flynn, r.f.	3	2	2	3
H[arry] Wright, c.f.	3	2	1	1	[Fred] Treacey, l.f.	2	2	2	2
[Andy] Leonard, l.f.	3	2	0	0	[Marshall] King, c.	2	3	1	1
[Asa] Brainard, p.	3	1	4	4	[Levi] Meyerle, 3d b.	2	2	2	4
[Charlie] Sweasy, 2d b.	4	0	1	1	[Ed] Pinkham, p.	4	0	2	2
[Cal] McVey, r.f.	5	0	0	0	[Ed] Duffy, s.s.	3	2	2	3
Total	27	13	15	18	Total	27	16	16	22

INNINGS

	1	2	3	4	5	6	7	8	9	
Cincinnatis	0	0	1	0	0	4	0	3	5	13
Chicagos	1	0	0	0	0	0	1	6	8	16

RUNS EARNED

	1	2	3	4	5	6	7	8	9	
Cincinnatis	0	0	1	0	0	2	0	0	2	5
Chicagos	0	0	0	0	0	0	0	2	4	6

Umpire—Robert F[e]rguson of the Atlantics.
Scorer—[J. M.] Thatcher and [Ed] Atwater.
Time of game—Two hours and 45 minutes.
Flys caught—Treacey 2, Wood 1, Flynn 2. Total Chicagos 5. G. Wright 1, Sweasy 1, McVey 1, Leonard 2, Brainard 1, Gould 1. Total Cincinnatis 7.
Flys missed—Treacey 1, Flynn 1, Brainard 1, Waterman 1, Leonard 1.
Passed balls—King 5, Allison 4.
Foul flys caught—King 2, McAtee 1.
Foul bounds—King 2, Sweasy 1.
Bases on called balls—Meyerle 1, Wood 1, H. Wright 1.

PERSONAL.

The game was witnessed by Messrs. A. P. C. Bonte, president of the Cincinnati club; A. G. Corre, vice president; W. P. Noble, secretary; S. S. Davis, director, Alexander Henderson, Cincinnati *Chronicle*; A. M. Griswold, Cincinnati *Times*; Joseph M. Miller, Cincinnati *Commercial*; Louis O'Shaughnessy, Cincinnati *Enquirer*, and a very large number of other visitors from Cincinnati and elsewhere.

HOW THE NEWS WAS RECEIVED AT CINCINNATI.

CINCINNATI, Oct. 13.—Large crowds collected about the newspaper offices, watching with interest the bulletins of the game between the Red Stockings and the Chicago club. The streets were filled with people while awaiting the result of the last inning, but they suddenly scattered when the figures were posted.

"Base Ball. Our Champion Red Stockings. Their Sedan at the Hands of the Chicago Club. How It Occurred." *Cincinnati Daily Gazette*, October 14, 1870, p. 3.[48]

Special Dispatch to the Cincinnati Gazette.
CHICAGO, October 13.

We were beaten! We know it, we feel it, but how could we help it? The umpire was against us, the weather was against us, the crowd was against us, the heavens were against us, the ground was against us, the pestilential air of the Chicago river was against us, the Chicago Nine was against us, and last, but not least, the score was against us.

Our gallant boys entered the city where they were doomed to be sacrificed at about eleven o'clock on Wednesday evening, and at once sought their temporary abiding place, the Briggs House. The night was spent by the boys in the arms of the god of sleep, and when the blazing rays of the rising sun burst upon the city of wickedness, not a sound issued from th[ei]r chambers but the labored breathing, indicative of the deepest repose.

At about 10 o'clock the offerings to the Chicago idols came slowly down the staircase of the hotel and wended their way in melancholy procession into the breakfast room, where they were fed upon tea [an]d crackers, to make them feel light and ready for the fray. They moved around the hotel after disposing of this frugal repast, and were followed by a train of mourners, whose woe-begone and anxious looking countenances told too well that they hailed from Cincinnati, and were looking for a faint ray of hope in the lengthened and solemn looking faces of the gallant boys.

On the way to the ground, which is situated on the outskirts of the city, we were saluted by numbers of rising Chicagoans of a tender age with demoniac screeches, violent contortions of the facial muscles, requests to go to a certain place where the thermometer indicates the same high figure all the year round, and other pleasantries too numerous to mention. We heeded them not, but with resigned expressions and folded arms looked stolidly in one particular direction until we reached the place of execution, Dexter Park.

An immense crowd, among whom were a large number of the most beautiful ladies in Chicago, were awaiting the approach of the doomed knights of the bat and ball, and when the Red Stockings were discovered a long and loud cheer swelled forth and announced to the expectant persons, who occupied eligible positions for viewing the operation at a distance of two or three squares away, that the entertainment would soon be inaugurated. The executioners, under the lead of one Jimmy Wood, had been upon the field for some time previous to the arrival of their victims, and had donned their usual attire. The preliminaries were soon arranged, and a gentleman named Robert Ferguson, who is a member of the Atlantic Club, of Brooklyn, was chosen to see that the unfortunates were dispatched without any unnecessary delay. The spokesman of the Red Stockings was then asked if they had anything to say, and replied "No," whereupon, everything being in readiness at about half-past 2 o'clock, Michael McAtee, of the White Stockings, toed the scratch ready to deliver the first blow on behalf of his companions in white stockings. From a Chicago correspondent we have the following detailed account of the game: ... [Paragraphs of inning-by-inning coverage are omitted.]

REMARKS.

Of course Chicago will become a gigantic lunatic asylum, and continue so for some time to come. There will be illuminations, and bonfires, and mass meetings, and congratulations, addresses to the victors, and mock expressions of condolence with those unfortunates who bet upon the Reds, and votes of thanks tendered the victors, and, and [sic]—new suits of clothes furnished the gallant Whites.

We shall no more look with exultant eyes upon the tirades of abuse of the "Mountebank Muffins" with which the Chicago papers in days gone by were so prolific. We shall no more hear the Journal entreating the managers of the Chicago Club to adopt a new title for the organization; we shall no longer hear dreadful tales about how Mart King was "indisposed," Jimmy Wood was too easy upon his subordinates, [Ned] Cuthbert was "cranky," McAtee had a game leg, [Levi] Meyerle a smashed finger and the majority of the nine too great a fondness for diluted spirits.

But instead of this multitude of complaints with which the Chicago papers formerly regaled their readers, we shall in the future peruse long, double leaded articles with flaming head lines [sic] about the Invincible White Stockings, and the dead and buried Red Stockings.

We shall learn with astonishment unbounded, that the defunct Red Legs never did anything so noticeable after all, and that their glory has faded into insignificance when compared with the marvelous, the unapproachable, the almost incredible exploits on the ball field of the nine players who wear stockings of pure and undefiled whiteness, and do their carousing in the Garden City.

It will be trumpeted forth to the base ball world by the Chicago papers that the greatest catcher, pitcher, first baseman, second baseman, third baseman, short stop, left fielder, center fielder, right fielder and business manager dwell in the great city of the universe—Chicago—and that the greatest collection of base ball humbugs this side of Cleveland is contained in the insignificant city of Cincinnati.

The Chicago Club will now find itself in a similar predicament to that in which Alexander the Great was placed once upon a time, and will sigh for more clubs to conquer as he did for more worlds to be placed within marching distance of his legion.

When winter puts an end to field sports, we presume the victors in yesterday's contest will be elected to represent the base ball public of Chicago in the Common Council, while the unlucky Red Legs will spend their leisure hours in reflecting that all are not invincible who wear red stockings, and that a little more attention to their profession and a little less intermingling in political affairs is necessary to enable them to resume the victorious mantle they have themselves thrown from their shoulders, and once more stand forth as the *invincible* Red Stockings.

◆ ◆ ◆

Contrary to the hopes of the somewhat bitter Cincinnati sportswriter, the era of the "invincible Red Stockings" was over. Following a 12–5 loss on October 15 to the Forest City Club of Rockford, Illinois, the *Cincinnati Daily Gazette* lamented that the Reds "are in a demoralized condition, from which nothing better can be expected than defeat, unless some sharp remedy is quickly applied."

None was forthcoming, however, and with ball game attendance and gate receipts declining, the club's executive board issued a statement on November 21 that the team would not take the field in 1871. President A. P. C. Bonte and Secretary William P. Noble wrote in the board's letter that "we have arrived at the conclusion that to employ a nine for the coming season, at the enormous salaries now demanded by professional players, would plunge our club deeply in debt at the end of the year." With the Red Stockings thereby disbanded, the ballplayers sought employment with other teams.[49]

The Chicago nine still had a major game to play before it could take home the whip pennant, the symbol of the baseball championship. According to custom, winning this large flag was determined not by a team's win-loss record but by defeating the existing champion two games out of three. The Mutuals had secured the honor on September 22 when they triumphed over the Brooklyn Atlantics; a second White Stockings win over the New York club would cause the whip pennant to change hands.

In this convoluted system, the winner of a best-of-three series did not have to be the team with the season's best record, nor did pennant contenders even have to play the same number of games. Furthermore, as noted in *Baseball in Old Chicago*, at this time "games were scheduled on a go-as-you-please basis," so a championship club could retain the whip pennant by simply avoiding tough challengers.[50]

The Mutuals arrived in Chicago on the morning of October 30, eager to face the White Stockings and confident that they could defend their title. It was the last game of the season for the White Stockings, and as the *Chicago Times* remarked, they had a "double incentive to wipe out the disgrace of the 9 to nothing game, and attain the championship." A heavy rain storm postponed the match, but on November 1 both the weather and the manicured grounds at Dexter Park promised a lively game of baseball.

And lively it was! After eight innings, Chicago led, 7–5. In the top of the ninth inning, the Mutuals scored eight runs, giving them a comfortable lead of 13–7. "The Mutuals were jubilant," a *New York Times* sportswriter exclaimed. "They felt that victory could not be wrested from them at so late a juncture."

In the bottom of the ninth inning, however, Chicago narrowed the lead to 13–12. With one out and with Ed Duffy on first base, Mutual Rynie Wolters pitched ball after ball to Bub McAtee, who just stood at the plate without swinging. "After delivering more than a dozen," the New York reporter continued, "none of which suited McAtee, Wolters threw down the ball in disgust, declaring he would not pitch any longer. His complaint was that the umpire called balls on him unjustly, and neglected to call strikes." Several

Mutuals players begged Wolters to continue, but he refused. With spectators milling around the players and darkness falling, the umpire called the game, the score reverting to the last completed inning. The White Stockings walked off the field with a 7–5 win and a season record of 65–8 (22–7 against professional teams).[51]

Since Chicago defeated the Mutuals twice after the New Yorkers took the championship from the Atlantics, the White Stockings insisted they were baseball's top team. The Mutuals argued that their last two contests with Chicago were not regular match games, but unofficial exhibition games that did not count in the standings, so they refused to surrender the whip pennant. During the year, the Red Stockings had lost the fewest number of games, but they had also lost twice to both the Atlantics and the White Stockings. Other teams claimed bragging rights based on their own records. "Who are the champions for 1870?" asked the bewildered *New York Clipper*, admitting that "we find it a rather tough problem to solve." It is little wonder that a *New York Times* sportswriter, trying to make sense of the chaotic situation a few months after the season ended, declared that "it would puzzle a Philadelphia lawyer to find out which was the champion club of 1870."

The White Stockings naturally believed they were entitled to the whip pennant and were indignant upon not receiving it from the Mutuals. The city of Chicago, however, knew who the champions were and took immediate steps to recognize them.

"The Sporting World. Base Ball Championship Pennant." *Chicago Tribune*, November 16, 1870, p. 4.

Base Ball.
THE CHAMPIONSHIP PENNANT
which, as is well known, was wrested from the Mutuals by the White Stockings, about two weeks ago, was not surrendered by the former club, which still insists that it is the champion. But Chicago knows better, and has supplied the real champions with a handsome pennant, in place of the one which the recalcitrant New Yorkers refused to give up. The streamer is forty-two feet in length, with a blue field and white stars at the head, to which are attached single stripes of red and white, tapering to a point. It is on exhibition at Foley's [a billiards hall, run by White Stockings business manager Tom Foley], and is the object of much interest. It will be displayed for the first time on the field at the

COMPLIMENTARY BENEFIT
which the White Stockings are to receive at Dexter Park, this afternoon, when some of the Forest Citys, of Rockford, are expected to join with [Charlie] Hodes and [George] Keerl, of the Whites, and a sufficient number of the leading amateur players of the city, in making up a strong picked nine. The game will be the last of the season, and will doubtless be an interesting one.[52]

Epilogue

Many years after the White Stockings received their championship pennant, original club member Jimmy Wood and former officials T. Z. Cowles and Tom Foley recalled the team's early days. Reporter and sportswriter Frank G. Menke interviewed Wood for a series of six syndicated newspaper articles published in August 1916, of which the fourth is reprinted here.[53] Two years later, ex-sports editor Cowles reminisced about the White Stockings in the *Chicago Daily Tribune*. Foley's recollections were published in 1921 in the *Auburn (New York) Citizen*; by that time he had long given up baseball for billiards, his first passion.[54]

Memories and reminiscences, especially after half a century, are rarely infallible, and it is not surprising that the narratives exhibit a few errors and embellishments. For example, although Wood says that he canceled the team's games in June and July of 1870, a check of the box scores proves otherwise. His difficulties in acquiring players probably stemmed from the fact that most of them had already signed with other teams, not because they thought it was a waste of time to take on the supposedly invincible Cincinnati Red Stockings. Cowles implies that George Zettlein was a member of the 1870 White Stockings, though actually he did not come on board until 1871. Real estate magnate Potter Palmer was the club's first president, not Philip Sheridan, who was a vice president. A few of the scores in Foley's account are wrong (and have been corrected, here, within brackets).

Despite these inaccuracies, the articles offer colorful, firsthand reflections about the White Stockings by persons intimately associated with the team.

"Baseball of Bygone Days: Wood Organizes Ball Team to Beat Cincinnati Stars." Hard Hitting Chicagoans Clean Up Every Thing in South—As Related by James Wood, Captain and Manager of White Stockings in 1870–71 to Frank G. Menke. *El Paso (Texas) Herald*, August 17, 1916, home edition, p. 9.

SOMEWHERE along about Christmas in 1869, I noticed an advertisement in a New York paper which read something as follows:

"Ball players wanted to form a team to represent Chicago and to defeat the Cincinnati Red Stockings."

During the period of the late 60's and early 70's there was keen rivalry between Chicago and Cincinnati in a commercial way. Chicago wasn't such a wonderfully large city then and it was doing everything possible to boom the town. And it was jealous of Cincinnati because of the great publicity Cincinnati had gained through the medium of its 1869 ball team which had won 56 out of its 57 games, the other resulting in a 17 to 17 tie with the Union team of Lansingburg.[55]

And so Chicago decided that it must have a team to beat the Reds. Baseball wasn't played to any great extent in the Illinois metropolis prior to that time. All the crack players were in the east. That is why the advertisement appeared in New York.

Organizes the Team

I answered the ad and in due time got a reply. It happened that I was among the first to write. The Chicago people told me they, under advice from [Cincinnati player-manager] Harry Wright, desired me to organize a club to beat the Red Stockings in 1870 and d—the expense!

So I started to recruit my team. I figured the task would be easy, yet I found it the most difficult one of my life. Only a few of the many baseball stars that I approached cared to join a team that had as its ultimate purpose the beating of the Reds in a three game series.

"It can't be done," most of the players answered me. "Those Reds are unbeatable and we aren't going to waste all of next spring and summer practising for it."

Finally after much persuasion, I signed up a number of men who were real players but only after I had advanced them money out of my own pocket. The Chicago people hadn't sent me any funds. Just as soon as some of those players had squandered their first advance money in drinking or gambling, they came for more, threatening to jump their contracts if we didn't "come through." Finally, when my advance totalled beyond $1200 and the players kept demanding more, I asked my father to go to Chicago and ascertain the financial responsibility of the Chicagoans.

Father wired back:

"Go the limit; Chicagoans will make good all your advances."

Team Complete with 11 Men

When I got the message, I hurried to Troy (N. Y.) with Tom Foley, the representative of the Chicagoans, to get [Cherokee] Fisher and [Bill] Craver who had played in 1869 with the Troy Haymakers. Both were terrific hitters and I needed them but I knew they would come high, as salaries went in those days. However, we signed up both men, contracting Fisher for $800 and [C]rave[r] for $2000. Then my team—11 men—was complete.[56]

Team Went South

Early in the spring of 1870, we arranged the details of our training trip to New Orleans. It was the second southern trip ever undertaken by a ball club. Foley, who was a champion billiardist and one of the Chicago backers and is still living in Chicago, accompanied us south.

During our first week in the Louisiana town we practised among ourselves. Then we commenced to take on the teams in New Orleans. I began by scheduling the weakest first, working up gradually to the hardest. We defeated the weaker teams in New Orleans—and then we beat the strongest. In each succeeding game my club appeared stronger both in batting and in fielding. Toward the end of our season in New Orleans we played an all-star New Orleans nine and won with ease.

Played a Double New Orleans Team

Then I made the proposition that our regular nine should play a double team of New Orleans men, giving them 18 players in the field. The game itself was rather amusing because the New Orleans captain had so many players under his command and he didn't know where to play them all. However, he put one man behind the plate to assist the catcher, four extras in the outfield, giving him seven altogether, and the rest were sprinkled around the infield, making a total of eight infielders.

Pitted against such a collection, we won almost as easily as we had in playing nine men. In our final game in New Orleans I allowed the rival team six outs per innings to our three—and once again we won.

Won All Along the Line

We worked our way north gradually, as the teams do today, playing all the crack southern teams enroute and winning all of our games by overwhelming scores. We beat the Memphis team, champions of Tennessee 157 to 1—and Foley was very angry because we had permitted the southerners to score their lone tally!

At last we reached Chicago—and we got a wild ovation. The town had gone crazy over baseball. Our wonderful showing in New Orleans and our clean sweep through the south had caused the Chicagoans to feel that our chief aim—to defeat the Red Stockings—was a certainty.

Defeated Rockford, Too

Our first real game in the north was against the crack Rockford (Ills.) team—the club on which Adrian Anson and A. G. Spalding got their start. The Rockford people backed their team heavily in the betting that preceded that game—but we swamped them. We scored 14 runs in the first inning and after the fifth were so far ahead that I gave my boys orders to take it easy, and by that additional victory set Chicago further aflame with baseball enthusiasm.

Then we started east to play out the schedule which was so arranged that the Cincinnati series did not come until the end of the season. Our success continued. My boys were wonderful batters and every additional contest they engaged in seemed to increase their hitting power.

Hitting Was Chief Asset

In those days ability to hit was the main asset of a player. In his batting power lay his baseball value. Not much attention was paid to perfecting a team in fielding. It was figured that fielding would come naturally but that batting must be developed.

During the latter part of May two of my players took sick while we were on tour and I had to send them home. Shortly afterward two others joined the "hospital squad." I filled in with amateurs, sent to me from Chicago, but I found quickly that they wouldn't do.

So, along about June 4 when I found that my ailing quartet was not convalescing very rapidly, I cancelled all our remaining June and July games and stayed in Chicago.

Late in July when all the players were back in shape we resumed team playing practice. All during the time the four boys were sick I kept the others at batting practise for two hours a day and the expertness in the hitting line continued to increase. About August 4 we resumed our schedule and played out the season, winning all of our games from the resumption in August until the end.[57]

Then Came the Big Game

And then came the grand climax of the year—the task for which we had been preparing ourselves: the battle with the Cincinnati Red Stockings.

As challengers we were compelled to play the first game of the series—a best two out of three affairs—on the home diamond of the Reds: on the same field where they never had tasted defeat. Only once during the two years—1869 and 1870—had the Reds been beaten and that was suffered on foreign territory, the Atlantics of Brooklyn, turning the trick in 1[1] innings, 8 to 7.[58]

Three Games Scheduled

It being necessary for the first game to be played in Cincinnati and the second in Chicago; the place for the third—if a third game was necessary—was to be determined by a flip of a coin.

Chicago Rooters Pessimistic

When we went to Cincinnati for that first game even our most loyal rooters were pessimistic. It was not that they lacked confidence in our ability, but because they feared we would be "jobbed" by some Cincinnati umpire, or menaced so by the rowdy crowds that we wouldn't play our real game because of fear of violence if we should win.

But we did win and the story of that game, together with the second in Chicago which was witnessed by a crowd beyond 50,000 shall form the next chapter in this recital.[59]

"Ye Sporting Ed of 1868 Harks Back 50 Years. Tells of First Chicago Baseball Club Formed in 1870." By T. Z. Cowles. *Chicago Daily Tribune*, May 26, 1918, sec. 2, pp. 1, 4. [Note: A paragraph preceding Cowles's memoir mentions that "Mr. Cowles was sporting editor of 'The Tribune' from 1868 to 1875 and night editor from 1875 to 1883. For the last twenty-one years he has been editor of The American Economist."]

Fifty years ago, in 1868, I became sporting editor of THE CHICAGO TRIBUNE. Sam Medill was then city editor and THE TRIBUNE office was up one flight of stairs in a dingy brick building across from the Sherman house on Clark street.

THE TRIBUNE sporting editor of 1918 asks me to tell something of the sports of half a century back, what they were like as compared with the sports of today, and to recall some experiences and reminiscences of the earlier period.

Chicago in 1868 was an important sporting center, as it is today. It was, in many respects, the nursery of some sports that have since become national and indeed universal. This is true of at least two branches of sports—baseball and billiards. In both of these Chicago has led the country.

Chicago a Sporting Center.

More than any other city Chicago has nationalized baseball and helped to make it in fact the national game. The same is true of billiards. Practically all the big American players on the green cloth were developed in Chicago. But we shall get to that later. The baseball season is now and we will commence the story with Chicago's share in the glory of the diamond.

I was in at the birth of the first professional ball club in Chicago. It was organized in the winter of 1869–'70. Gen. Phil Sheridan, at that time in command of the department of the Missouri, with headquarters in Chicago, was the first president of the club.[60] Tom Foley was financial secretary, and THE TRIBUNE sporting editor the recording secretary. All through that winter there was a lot of letter writing to eastern players and by the first of April 1870, a team had been secured.

Jimmy Wood First Player.

Jimmy Wood of the Eckfords of Brooklyn was the first player signed. Charl[ie] Holdes [sic] of the same club came with him as shortstop. Philadelphia contributed Edgar Cuthbert for left field, and Levi M[e]yerle for third base and change pitcher.[61] [George] Zettlein, the main pitcher, hailed from Brooklyn. The rest of the bunch detached themselves from the Haymakers of Troy, and a tough bunch they were, too: Bill Craver, catcher; [Bub] McA[t]ee, first base; Mart King, center field; and "Clipper" Flynn, right field.

Jimmy Wood was a star second baseman for that period. He covered a wide field, was a good pickup and short thrower, but a rather weak batter. He was far below the class of Fred Pfeffer in later years, or of Eddie Collins, Larry Doyle, or any of the middle sackers of the big leagues of today. Patient, good tempered, and zealous Jimmy was, but not a crack ball player as we rate them nowadays. At that he was much the best of the Chicago infield of 1870.

Estimate of Zettlein.

Zettlein was a strong, fairly fast pitcher of the straight arm school of that period, and had as much control as the average.

M[e]yerle wasn't much, either at third base or in the pitcher's box. He had difficulty in finding the plate and perpetrated many a wild pitch.

Craver was one of the best catchers of that time. He was never known to wear a shield, mask, or gloves of any kind. He caught with bare hands, was a good thrower to second, and safe on foul flies. In those days the batter was out on a foul fly if caught on the bound. So the catcher always played far back when the bases were empty, and thereby got many outs on foul bounds. That rule did not remain long in force, and fouls had to be caught on the fly.

Catcher Without Protection.

"Mart" King—his front name was Marshall—served as change catcher when Craver's hands had lost so many finger nails that he could no longer hang onto the ball. "Mart" was a hero in purpose if not a star in performance. No hurt could drive him out of the game. He, too, spurned all protection contrivances. Once a foul tip landed squarely between his eyes. It didn't even knock him down. He winced a little, shook his head, and went on with the game. A finger nail tor[n] from its roots meant nothing to him. He would wrap a rag around it and go on with the game. His heavy build made him a slow runner, and he missed many a fly that the center fielders of later years would invariably gather in.

There were no sacrifice hits in those days. Times at bat were not included in the box score. Batting percentages were not kept. The best batter was the fellow who hit hardest and longest and brought in somebody ahead of him.

Wager with Cap Anson.

Speaking of sacrifice hits recalls a bet between Capt. Anson and the writer. "Anse" was just then strong on "placing" the ball. This was in 1881, when the grounds were on the lake front. Dropping in at the clubhouse as the boys were dressing after a game, I found a warm discussion going on regarding the necessity of placing the ball.

"Anse" was arguing in the affirmative, and Larry Corcoran was chief spokesman on the other side. They asked me what I thought about it.

"There's nothing in it," I said. "The thing for a batter to do is to hit the ball on the nose, and hit it hard."

"You're all wrong," said Anson. "When a man is on first base, hit to right field. That increases the chances of the runner getting to second, even though the batter is fielded out at first base."

Suit of Clothes at Stake.

After more talk, pro and con, the captain accepted this proposition: "You are now batting close to .400. There are sixteen straight games ahead on the home grounds. I'll bet you a $75 suit of clothes that if you undertake to place the ball every time you go to bat your batting average will drop below zero."

"I'll make you the same bet," said Pitcher Corcoran.

"No," said "Anse"; "one at a time will be enough."

For the next ten games his average dropped away below .300. Placing the ball was interfering sadly with his safe hitting and his driving in of runs. No man ever equaled Anson in the number of runs sent across the home plate by his bat.

Boss Hulbert Pays Bet.

"Boss" [William] Hulbert, president of the club, noticed the slump and inquired the reason. Somebody told him about the bet. He said: "If you'll call it off I'll pay the Anson end of it. It's raising hell with his batting."

And so it was. I accepted Hulbert's offer and took the suit of clothes. Anson stopped trying to place the ball, his batting average went back toward the normal .400, and the club lost less games. After that, nothing more was heard from him about sacrifice hitting.

Big Four of Hard Hitters.

Hard hitting is what wins ball games, and Anson was in his time the best hard hitter—and that means the best batter—that the game ever saw. For years together the Chicago batting order was: [George] Gore, [Abner] Dalrymple, [Mike] Kelly, [Cap] Anson. It was a cold day when one or more runs failed to come through that combination.

◆ ◆ ◆

"Memories of Old White Stockings." By Al Spink. *Auburn (New York) Citizen*, November 3, 1921, p. 9. [Note: In the paragraph that precedes the list of game scores, the original article does not include any closing quotation marks after the opening quotation marks.][62]

The veteran, Tom Foley, sat in his billiard room the other night, keeping tab on the games, as he has kept tab of them for more than half a century, and chatted merrily of the sports of today and yesterday.

Tom was the manager of the Chicago White Stockings of 1870, Chicago's first professional baseball club, and all that are left of that old team are Tom himself and Captain Jimmy Wood.

Between his work of keeping tab on the billiard players Tom found time to talk about his old team, and grayhaired fans stood around and listened to his tale and at times corroborated all he had to say.

"It seems strange to me," said Tom, "that the two leaders of the Chicago White [Stockings] and Cincinnati Reds of 1870 are still alive, while nearly all the players of those teams have passed on.

"George Wright, alive and well, like Babe Ruth today, was the leading batsman of that olden time.

"When I set out to organize a team for Chicago in 1869, a team that would beat the up to that time invincible Cincinnati Reds, I threw out a line for Wright, who was then the captain and short fielder of that team.[63]

"It was in 1869, after the Cincinnati Reds had beaten every team they met that a friend asked me why I did not organize a team for Chicago that would beat the Reds.

"Even George Wright, then the captain of the invincible Reds, asked me that question."

Duel Over Wright

"I said I would if he would come and captain the nine," continued Tom. "And that Winter I had a duel with the Cincinnati people over Wright. I would make him an offer and they would raise it. I would come back and they would see my raise. I finally offered him $2,500, only to see that covered, and then I got Jimmy Wood to captain and play second.

"The team of 1870 included W. H. Craver, catcher; yes, Bill Craver, blacklisted in after years and now dead; Ed Pinkham, pitcher and third base; Mike McAntee [sic], first; James Wood, second; Levi Meyerle, third and change pitcher; Ed Cuthbert, right field; Marshall King, center field and change catcher; Fred Treac[e]y, left field, and 'Clipper' Flynn, substitute.

"It was hard work at first and we lost $3,000 on the initial season. Salaries were high, from $1,600 to $2,500, and the game was looked upon as a sort of forbidden sport. The players were regarded by some people as loafers and there was many a young clerk who lost his job for slipping away to attend the games. The Dexter Park grounds were a loser, but we did better when we located on the lake front.

"We sold a number of shares of stock to various prominent citizens, who took the stock from a feeling of local pride more than with the thought that they could make anything on the deal, and we went into the second season in dead earnest. It cost us $8,000 to fix up the Lake Fr[o]nt Park and we were therefore $11,000 behind when the season began. Our success that year was wonderful, and we were even up and had seven big games to play when the fire wiped us out of existence.

"The game was very exciting in those days on account of the lively batting. As I have said, we paid our men good money. We had to, for the Eastern Clubs discouraged and back-capped us in every way, and scared many players out of coming to join us.[64]

"[George] Zettlein and Al Spaulding [sic] were, in my opinion, the best pitchers of that olden day, and Craver and King were as good as any of the catchers.

"As to our first Southern trip, well, we had lots of fun and won eight games, all that were played. The scores were:

Chicago, 47; Unions of St. Louis, 1.
Chicago, 36; Empires of St. Louis, 8.
Chicago, 51; Atlantics of New Orleans, 0.
Chicago, 1[8]; Lone Stars of New Orleans, [10].
Chicago, 24; Robert E. Lee of New Orleans, 14.
Chicago, 41; Southerns of New Orleans, 9.
Chicago, 157; Bluff City of Memphis, 1.
Chicago 111; [Grove City] of Kankakee, [5].

The Bluff City game will live in history as one of the most fearful and wonderful ever played.

And the umpire's troubles were just the same in 1870 as they are in 1921.

2

A FIERY SECOND SEASON (1871)

> The Chicago club, it will be remembered, lost everything but their lives in the late fire, and the appearance they made yesterday in their suits of various hues and make was ludicrous in the extreme. [Ed] Pinkham wore a Mutual shirt, a pair of Mutual pants and a pair of red stockings.... Some wore black hats, some wore caps, a few had regular ball hats, while others again played bareheaded.
> —*New York Herald*, October 31, 1871

Following the White Stockings' triumphant inaugural year, Chicago's baseball fans looked forward to the start of the 1871 season. Admittedly, the new sporting venture had not been financially successful, for the club was $3,000 in debt, including $1,565 it owed to players. Nevertheless, the *Chicago Tribune* declared in November 1870 that "the stockholders have lost neither faith nor enthusiasm, and it need surprise no one, if, after the 1st of January, they announce a nine which will challenge comparison with any in the land."

The *Chicago Republican* was a bit more restrained in its assessment, simply commenting that "the White Stocking nine, as at present made up, is thought to be, and undoubtedly is, some improvement on that of last year." Most of that nine would be returning players, though Clipper Flynn and Levi Meyerle left during the offseason and signed with other clubs (newspapers reported that Charlie Hodes was also leaving, but he later re-signed with Chicago). In their places, business manager Tom Foley recruited outfielder Joe Simmons from the Rockford Forest City Club, pitcher George Zettlein from the Brooklyn Atlantics, substitute Tom Foley from the Rockford Forest Citys (no relation to the Chicago team official), and pitcher Ed Atwater from the disbanded Cincinnati Red Stockings. Philadelphian Ned Cuthbert had intended to play again with the White Stockings, but when his wife complained about him being away from home, he returned east and signed with the Philadelphia Athletics.[1]

Baseball itself was undergoing changes as well. The sport's central administrative body was the National Association of Base Ball Players (NABBP), which had formally been organized in March 1858 to oversee and govern the game. By the end of 1870 the NABBP included more than 500 amateur teams (whose members played for recreation), and 15 professional teams (whose players competed for money). The salaried teams were growing in popularity, as members realized that winning teams, which boasted the best players, would generate high interest and consequently high ticket sales and profits.

Not everyone favored the spread of professionalism throughout the sport. Although the *New York Times* editorially admitted that baseball and other games were "a means of mental and physical health and development," it claimed that vigorous participation in these activities could lead to "dissipation or gambling" and could "exercise mischievous influences.... The moment [sports] cease to be practiced for mere recreation, they cease to be beneficial."[2]

The exaggerated circumstances outlined in the editorial notwithstanding, there was no denying that some matters needed to be corrected. Gambling, throwing games (called "hippodroming"), and the excess drinking of alcohol were problems among both amateur and professional players. Clubs often complained of "revolvers," persons who broke their contracts or agreements by jumping from team to team as they sought the best salaries and working conditions. Game scheduling was at best haphazard, which made the playing for—and the awarding of—national championships particularly difficult.

Club directors would soon address these concerns, though contrary to the opinion of the *New York Times*, many persons believed that baseball could be played for more than just recreational purposes. After all, a professional team provided a source of civic pride within a community and furnished opportunities for paying fans to see top-notch players participate in highly competitive contests. Members of amateur teams, on the other hand, devoted most of their time to their jobs and other pursuits. They could not hope to compete against those for whom baseball *was* their job, and they found it difficult to generate the revenue that a club needed to attract good ballplayers and pay expenses. As a Chicago sportswriter maintained:

> Attractive as is the idea of base ball devotees, who play the game solely for the love of it, and the splendid exercise which it affords, it has been pretty thoroughly demonstrated that it will not work. Amateur players have neither the time nor the inclination to devote themselves to such a *regime* of arduous practice as is necessary in order to attain perfection in the game. Without the perfection to which professionals have brought it, base ball becomes of no possible account as a species of amusement. The public will neither support it, morally or pecuniarily, and it will drop back into the obscure position which it occupied in Chicago a year or two ago.[3]

Baseball officials had no intention of letting that happen. On the rainy evening of March 17, 1871, representatives from the Chicago White Stockings and nine other professional clubs gathered in New York City at Collier's Rooms, a saloon on the corner of Broadway and 13th Street, and formed the National Association of Professional Base Ball Players (soon to be referred to as simply the National Association), the forebear of today's major leagues. As detailed in the published proceedings, the main purpose of the meeting was to authorize "a championship title to be contested for by the various professional clubs in the country." Rules were discussed and resolutions drawn up. Teams interested in belonging to the association were each charged a ten-dollar entry fee. They would handle their own scheduling of games, with "each club to play best three in five games with every other contesting club, at such time and place as they may agree upon." The team winning the most games "shall be declared champions of the United States."

Despite having the word "national" in its name, the new organization represented relatively few baseball clubs. In 1870 professional teams had filled their schedules by playing games against amateur clubs, and the professionals would continue the practice in 1871. The White Stockings soon began packing their bags to head south, for as the *Chicago Tribune* announced on March 7, they intended to "open the season this year, as last, with a Southern tour of some extent." The newspaper added that their first game would be against the amateur Lone Stars of New Orleans, "now probably the strongest club in the South." Chicago team members left the city on March 16 via the Illinois Central Railroad and looked forward to "at least a month of good practice" before returning to Chicago for their first home game.[4]

The White Stockings would play this game on a new ball field. The team had called Dexter Park home for less than a year, but the grounds' location, some six miles from downtown, had proved to be less than ideal for fans. They had to pay not only for the tickets but also for the time-consuming transportation to the park (30 minutes by railroad, a little more than 30 minutes by carriage, and an hour by horse car). "In view of these facts," the *Tribune* reasoned, "it is not difficult to appreciate the strong public feeling in favor of the location of the White Stocking grounds as centrally as possible." The team's managers agreed, and in March the city of Chicago leased a section of Lake Park to the club for a new ballpark. The playing field would be 375 feet in length (from home plate to the outfield fence along the foul lines). The rectangular ballpark in the city's downtown area at Michigan Avenue and Randolph Street would be known variously as White Stocking Grounds, Lake Front Park, Union Base-Ball Grounds, and Lake Shore Park. The site, which had been used as a dump before the White Stockings took it over, is now part of Chicago's Millennium Park.[5]

The *Chicago Tribune* discussed in early March how "the Chicago Club propose[d] to fit up the lake front":

> Since the passage of the resolution by which the Common Council agreed to lease the lake front to the Chicago Club, there has been a lively interest among the better class of citizens to know what difference the laying-out of the ground for ball purposes will make in its appearance and usefulness as a public park. The plans of the cub management are such as every citizen cannot but approve, and some of the improvements which they propose to make will render the barren waste at the foot of Randolph and Washington streets a much pleasanter place than it has lately been, or is likely soon to be under the present control of the grounds.
>
> The portion of ground leased, or to be leased, to the Chicago Club, will be 500 feet in length by 225 in width, and will commence at a point 225 feet south of the line of Randolph street. This will be surrounded by a low fence—six feet or thereabouts—painted white, and kept entirely free from advertising of all kinds, whether by bills, stencils, or other device. In the northwest corner will be placed the grand stand, which will be directly behind the catcher, and will, therefore, afford the best view of the games. The lower tier of this stand, with accommodations for about 400 persons, will be set aside for the Mayor, Comptroller, Common Council, Board of Public Works, Judges, and the stockholders of the club, with especial reference to the comfort of the ladies who are supposed to come with these dignitaries. Above them will be two more tiers of seats, well shaded from the sun and convenient in every regard. These seats will be numbered and reserved for the use of those who possess season tickets. Every person buying a ticket for the season, therefore, will have with him a voucher for his seat for every inning of every game, so that he can come and go as he pleases, without feeling any doubt that his seat will be empty when he chooses to occupy it. Near the grand stand will be placed a covered stand for reporters and scorers, which will be constructed with reference to its possible use as a band stand. Still another separate stand will be devoted to the use of those ladies who attend without the means of access to the grand stand. This last edifice will have accommodations for at least two hundred ladies and gentlemen. The general attendance will be accommodated in the usual sloping stair seats, which will be placed across the north end of the enclosure and behind the third base. The seating facilities already mentioned, together with some seats partially extended down the east and west sides, will give plenty of room for something over 7,000 persons, allowing each person as much or more room than would be assigned him in any theatre. Seats for the season will be sold before long at the price of $15 for the right to witness every match of the season, and the understanding that the seat shall at all times be empty except when used by the person who has

bought it. The rest of the arrangements for seating will be free, with the exception of a few of the largest games, when a small additional fee may be charged for reserving seats....

The diamond will be laid out, as has been hinted, with the home plate and second base on a line drawn from the northwest to the southeast corners of the enclosure. A careful survey of the ground shows that this arrangement will give a batting range of about one hundred and twenty yards on a line drawn from home base through third base to the fence. Taking into account that a lively ball has hardly ever been batted more than 125 yards, and that a dead one will be used, this will prove amply sufficient for batting room.[6]

With club officials in Chicago attending to details about the new park, the White Stockings relaxed on the train as they traveled across the country to launch their southern tour. After they arrived in New Orleans ("in good health and spirits," according to one observer), they began working out by holding practice games each morning at a local ballpark. Followers of the team were undoubtedly pleased to read in the *Chicago Tribune* on March 25 that new pitchers George Zettlein and Ed Atwater "are getting down to their work in a manner that is beautiful to behold; but if the former does not astonish the Lone Stars on Sunday next he will disappoint about five thousand people who are arranging to be at the park on that occasion." Team members were also pleased with their new right fielder, Joe Simmons, though the reporter noted that "it is as first baseman that he really excels."

Both Zettlein and Simmons lived up to the newspaper's expectations in the White Stockings' inaugural game of the season on March 26, which they won, 9–6. "Simmons' play at first was the admiration of every one. He was simply superb. He is not only a strong player, but a shrewd one, ever ready to take advantage of his opponent's mistakes and miscalculations."

As for Zettlein, he "was the great object of interest. Hundreds of those in attendance came with the single object of witnessing the wonderful pitching of 'Old Accuracy,' and they were not sent home disappointed. Zettlein was in the very best humor, and the way he sent the sphere into [catcher Charlie] Hodes was a matter of astonishment to the batsmen of the Star organization. As will be seen by the score, they only succeeded in hitting him for four bases, and it must be understood that these Lone Star boys are no slouches with the ash."

Other teams were also proficient at batting, but the White Stockings still managed to defeat them. One sportswriter mentioned that the New Orleans Excelsiors had been "hankering to get a whack at the White Stockings," but when the two teams met on March 31, it appeared that the Chicagoans did all the whacking. Not only did the Excelsiors lose, 29–0, but the pitching of George Zettlein left them "sorely demoralized" as well.[7]

The White Stockings departed New Orleans for Memphis on April 17, and from there they traveled to St. Louis. They finished their nine-game road trip on April 23 with the enviable record of all wins. The *Chicago Tribune* commented that the players did not score nearly as many runs as they had during their southern tour the preceding spring (266 as opposed to 485), which "may seem to show a depreciation of batting ability." The newspaper added, however, that the team's competitors this year "were all, with, perhaps, one exception, strong organizations, and this fact, coupled with the use of the new dead ball instead of the almost rubber one played with last year, will show why the scores were not so large." (A "dead" ball with little rubber in it did not bounce as high nor could it be hit as far as the so-called "lively" ball.)

Whatever the reason—if any—for the low number of runs scored, it apparently did not bother the White Stockings, for the *Chicago Times* reported that they returned home on April 24 "feeling and looking the very picture of good health and contentment.... They are not only healthful, but filled with enthusiasm and very anxious to get at some of the leading clubs in the country."[8]

They would be able to play these clubs in their new park. Shortly before the season opened, the *Chicago Republican* declared that the White Stocking officers "deserve the heartiest commendation for the manner in which the [grounds] arrangements have been made."

"Base Ball. The Lake Park Grounds—Description—The Grand Stand—Unsurpassed Accommodation for Spectators—Inaugural Game This Afternoon." *Chicago Republican*, April 29, 1871, p. 4.

The Lake Park ball grounds are nearly completed, and when fully so, will be the finest in the country. Not so large as some, yet enough to meet all ordinary requirements.

The first view reveals a high, smooth-planed board fence, that portion fronting on Michigan avenue being painted white. Passing along, we come to the ticket office, which is on the avenue, near the entrance on the northwest corner. These entrances—one on the avenue and the other fronting north—are ten feet in width and closed by sliding doors.

INTERIOR.

Entering we find ourselves under long ranges of seats, the means of reaching the interior of the grounds being through a passage with seats overhead and on the sides. A few steps further on a full view of the ground is afforded, and we cannot but express delight at the

BEAUTY OF THE SCENE.

Before us lies the smooth, green surface upon which so many hard-fought struggles are to take place during the season. None will recognize the space, as it not long ago appeared. The transformation has been complete and from side to side all is green and pleasant to the eye.

The pitcher, striker and catcher bases, have been placed on a line running from [south]east to [north]west, thus taking best advantage of the space inclosed.[9] The infield looks like a huge green cloth with a stripe of white near the border.

THE FIELD OF GREEN.

This space has been sodded in a most compact manner, the rich green extending twenty feet beyond the base lines. Back of the catcher's position the

GRAND STAND

is now in course of erection, and when that is completed everything will be in readiness for the season. The stand will accommodate about 1,000 spectators, and will be occupied solely by stockholders, holders of season tickets, and reporters. Every seat will be numbered, and none but the holders of tickets can occupy them.

THE SEATS.

Extending from each side of the grand stand are the uncovered seats, capable of accommodating fully 6,000 persons. These seats are most admirably arranged, and for comfort and convenience are far better than on any other grounds in the country. Reaching around the upper portion of the ground, from the line of the first base to that of the third, they afford every facility for witnessing the game. Two feet in width, they enable spectators to sit comfortably, and also give plenty of room for the feet of those occupying the range next above. Extending the entire front of the range of seats is a wire fence placed a sufficient distance from the lower tier to permit free passage, and at the same time preventing all encroachment upon the field devoted to the players.

DESERVING GREAT PRAISE.

President [Norman] Gassette and his able coadjutors, Tom Foley and Secretary [J. M.] Thatcher, deserve the heartiest commendation for the manner in which the arrangements have been made. Money has been most liberally expended, and every precaution taken to avoid accident or discomfort.

OPENING GAME.

The grounds will be inaugurated this afternoon by a game between the White Stockings and a picked nine, composed of the following players: [Ed] Atwater, pitcher; [Tom] Foley, catcher; Bredburg, third base; Hallinan, short stop; Grant, left field; Graves, center field. The first and second bases and right field will be filled by selection from the following list: Stevens, Whitehead, Eb Smith, and Tanner.[10]

Some 1,500 spectators braved the chilly afternoon to see the Chicago club christen its new baseball grounds with a game against some of the best amateur players in the city. Newspaper reporters, who had publicized the big event with feature articles, were on hand to not only report on the game but also to inspect the new field. Although the *Chicago Times* sportswriter complained about "the noise and smoke from the neighboring locomotives," he admitted that "the infield has been nicely sodded, while a coat of whitewash on the interior walls adds much to the general fine appearance." The *Tribune* reported that "the grounds are as yet in an unfinished state, the grand stand being scarcely begun, but the game ... may be considered as effectually setting at rest all doubts concerning their capacity. The space is entirely ample for the purposes required." The match that day also showed how the ballpark's location near the "business part of the city" was a marked improvement over that of Dexter Park, as "the attendance was augmented until after 4 o'clock by the gradual dropping in of merchants, business men, clerks, etc."

The White Stockings themselves, the newspaper continued, attracted a "vast amount of favorable comment by their neat appearance in their new uniforms." Although their clothes were similar to those worn the previous year, their pants were "of a trifle darker shade of blue," and instead of caps, each player had on "a tasty white cloth hat, trimmed with blue cord." As for the match itself, both teams played well, with the professionals winning, 12-5. The *Tribune* related that "the game was an exceedingly pretty one, and developed a degree of proficiency on the part of the White Stockings far beyond that which they had reached at the corresponding date last year. It is evident both that their practice in the South has benefited them largely, and that a state of harmony and excellent discipline prevails."[11]

The Chicagoans would need all that harmony and discipline once the National Association of Professional Base Ball Players launched its inaugural season the following week. Nine teams would compete for the championship: the Boston Red Stockings, Chicago White Stockings, Cleveland Forest Citys, Fort Wayne (Indiana) Kekiongas, New York Mutuals, Philadelphia Athletics, Rockford (Illinois) Forest Citys, Troy (New York) Haymakers, and the Washington (D.C.) Olympics.[12]

On May 8 the White Stockings kicked off their season at home in front of some

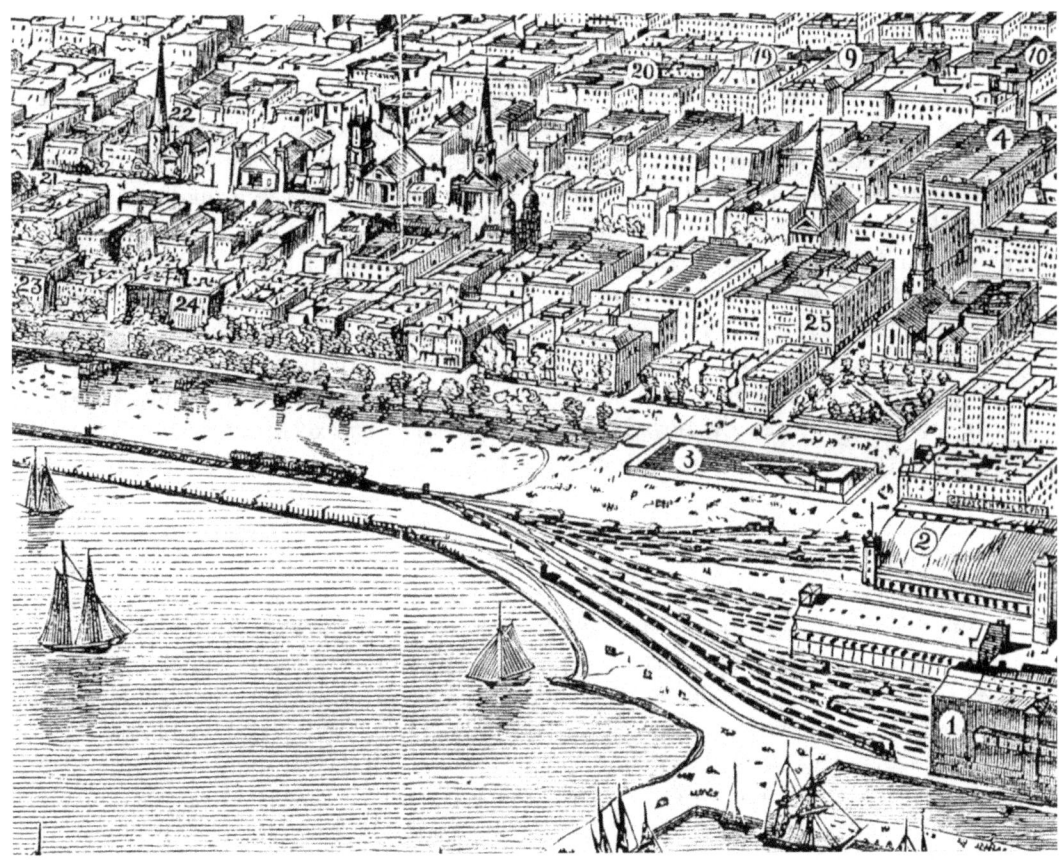

In 1871 the White Stockings played at a rectangular ballpark at Michigan Avenue and Randolph Street, just west of Lake Michigan (number 3, right center). Contrary to the illustration, the grandstand and home plate were actually in the northwest corner of the park, not the northeast. The top, first-base side was along Michigan Avenue; to the east, beyond left field, were the tracks of the Illinois Central Railroad. The Chicago Fire of October 8, 1871, incinerated not only the stadium and grounds, but also the homes of most of the players (Theodore R. Davis, "Bird's-Eye View of Chicago as It Was Before the Great Fire." *Harper's Weekly*, October 21, 1871).

5,000 boisterous spectators with a 14–12 victory over the Cleveland Forest City Club (a game marked by Cleveland's Ezra Sutton hitting the first home run in National Association history). The Chicago players won their next few contests as well, but on May 19 nearly 6,000 fans saw them come perilously close to ending their successful streak. A *Chicago Tribune* sportswriter, struggling to find something to which he could compare the ball game, explained that "perhaps the nearest approach to a correct and faithful simile would be to liken it to a man blown to atoms in a powder magazine, and then getting himself together again and coming up smiling."

The reporter was probably not too far off the mark. Chicago was facing the Washington Olympics, who had left the nation's capital with "their strongest and best team." At the end of the eighth inning it looked hopeless for the White Stockings, as they were down, 4–0. Captain Jimmy Wood seemed a bit shaken, but when his players came to bat in the ninth inning, he shouted, "We need a run from every man on the team. See that we get them!"

Wood got precisely what he demanded. When the first four men scored, tying the game in the ninth inning, 4–4, "The crowd fairly ran riot with excitement," according to the Chicago reporter. "Men threw their hats into the air, and cheered until they were hoarse, while the ladies in the pavilion waved their handkerchiefs and clapped their hands, and did all sorts of excitable things. It is related of Lotta [Crabtree], the popular little actress, who was present, that in her ardent enthusiasm she brought down her parasol upon the shoulders of a dignified old lady who sat in front of her, breaking the parasol, and astounding the old lady, who had never attended a base ball match before, and couldn't see what there was to make such a fuss about."

The "fuss" continued as the White Stockings scored five more runs in the ninth inning. The Olympics tried to stage a comeback, and although they did manage to bring three men home, they lost the game, 9–7. Chicago club president Norman Gassette "almost embraced the boys," the *Chicago Republican* exclaimed, while the team business manager, Tom Foley, and secretary J. M. Thatcher "dance[d] a high-flyer can can."[13]

By May 27 the White Stockings had played—and won—18 games, including six against professional teams that counted towards the national championship. The Chicago team members left the city that morning to play some of the eastern baseball clubs. After beating the Brooklyn Eckfords, 10–5, on May 29, the White Stockings scored a seventh professional win with a 16–14 victory against the Boston Red Stockings on June 2. Three days later, some 6,000 to 7,000 enthusiastic fans gathered at the ballpark in Brooklyn to see the Chicago team take on the New York Mutuals. The *New York Times* related that the Chicagoans had "arrived from Boston duly flushed with their triumph over the strong nine of the Boston Club." Moreover, since the Troy Haymakers had recently "badly whipped" the Mutuals, 25–10, the White Stockings felt "pretty confident" of winning the upcoming game.

Perhaps they were overconfident, as an 8–5 defeat to the Mutuals was followed by a 15–11 loss against the Philadelphia Athletics on June 8. From Philadelphia the Chicago team members traveled to Baltimore to play an amateur club, and from there they went to Washington, D.C., where on June 13 they were thrashed by the Olympics, 13–3. The poor play of the visiting team prompted the *Chicago Tribune* to jeer that many in attendance "were led to ask how it was that this club ever won its present reputation."[14]

The White Stockings, however, did not exactly have to limp home with their tails between their legs. They had won eight of the 11 games they played on their road trip (a June 15 game against the Mutuals was rained out), and their mid-June record against teams in the National Association was 7–3. The *Chicago Republican* did bring up, however, "the steadiness with which [the White Stockings] made errors and won by accidents since the opening of the season." The *Chicago Tribune* told its readers that "the players feel sore over their defeats, and, contrary to the general custom of ball-tossers, do not attribute them to 'bad luck,' but candidly confess that 'bad play' was the cause of it." The White Stockings were particularly "sore" about losing to Washington, though the newspaper was quick to say that business manager Tom Foley "feels almost morally certain" that the Olympics would be defeated "when that nine revisits Chicago on the 30th inst."

Foley was wise to hedge his bets as to the certainty of a forthcoming victory, for the White Stockings lost to the Olympics, 13–8, on June 30. The Chicago ballplayers did win six professional games in a row after that, however, and although the Cleveland Forest

City Club defeated them, 12–10, on August 10, the White Stockings squeaked out a 12–11 nail-biter of a victory on August 16 against the Olympics. With a 10–8 triumph against Boston on September 29, Chicago stood alongside Philadelphia at the top of the National Association, with each team having 18 victories and just seven losses. Since the two clubs had squared off four times and had each won two games, the Chicago players were looking forward to their final eastern tour and the deciding game with the Athletics on October 17.[15]

They never made it to the train station. Unfortunately, there was a little matter of a fire. And not just *any* fire. The summer of 1871 was particularly hot and dry in Chicago; moreover, by the first week of October, hot southwest winds had sucked all the moisture from wooden buildings, leaving behind "a desiccated husk of a city," according to a Chicago Fire historian. After a fire broke out on Sunday evening, October 8, in Patrick and Catherine O'Leary's barn on Chicago's West Side, it did not take long for it to incinerate three-and-one-third square miles in the heart of the city. Included among the property destroyed were not only the White Stockings' stadium and grounds but also the homes and possessions of most of the players.

Baseball and the plight of the local professional team, however, were far from the minds of most Chicagoans. "Up to Sunday night the dozen men who formed the White Stocking nine undoubtedly occupied a larger share of the public attention than any other body of private citizens in the city," the *Chicago Tribune* affirmed. "By way of contrast, it may be said that they occupied very much inferior positions in the attention of the people on Monday and Tuesday."

But the team members and their jobs commanded the full attention of captain Jimmy Wood. His club had already signed men from other teams for the 1872 season, and Wood soon began contacting officials from those organizations to cancel ballplayer contracts with the White Stockings. He also wrote the *New York Clipper* and asked that it publicize the Chicago team's predicament so that its players could sign new contracts, adding in his letter that "we are one and all now in the market."

The *Clipper* was one step ahead of Wood. It had suggested just a few days after the fire that baseball clubs hold benefit games "for the sufferers from the great fire" (and also rather callously mentioned that Chicago's ballplayers could now be obtained "at quite a discount"). A week later the *Clipper* quoted from Wood's letter and once again urged clubs to assist the White Stockings.[16]

"Aid for Chicago." *New York Clipper*, October 14, 1871, p. 219.

The disastrous conflagration which has visited Chicago this past week will have the effect of putting a close to the ball-playing season in that city as far as the playing of any more professional contests is concerned, and in view of the present condition of affairs the Chicago Club had better change their programme so as to play their concluding games with the Haymakers alternately at Troy and Brooklyn. In view also of the distress which has been occasioned by the dire misfortune which has afflicted the Lake City, and remembering the large sums of money which the professional clubs of the country have received at their contests in Chicago, it becomes them, one and all, to join hands in arranging a series of benefit performances, the receipts of which should be handed over to the Mayor of Chicago in response to his call for aid for the sufferers from the great fire.

◆ ◆ ◆

"The Chicago Club for 1872." *New York Clipper*, October 21, 1871, p. 226. [Note: The salary for Ed Pinkham in the original article appeared as ",500." Because the salaries in the table are arranged from highest to lowest, his undoubtedly should have been $1,500, which, when added to the others, equals the $25,100 total.]

The following are the names of the players engaged by the Chicago Club for 1872, and the salaries each was to have received:—

Players	Clubs in 1871	Positions	Salary
N[ick] E. Young	Olympic	Financial Secretary	$2,500
[Jimmy] Wood	Chicago	Captain and 2d base	2,500
[Mike] M[cGe]ary	Haymaker	Catcher	2,500
[Doug] Allison	Olympic	Catcher	2,000
[Davy] Force	Olympic	Short Stop	2,000
[Phonney] Martin	Eckford	Pitcher	2,000
[George] Zettlein	Chicago	Pitcher	2,000
[Everett] Mills	Olympic	First Base	1,800
[Fred] Treac[e]y	Chicago	Left Field	1,650
[Ned] Cuthbert	Athletic	Centre Field	1,650
[Candy] Nelson	Eckford	Third Base	1,500
[Ed] Pinkham	Chicago	Substitute	[1],500
[Charlie] Hodes	Chicago	Substitute	1,500
Total			$25,100

Mr. Young and the Olympic players who have been engaged for 1872, have received no advance salary, and they one and all express themselves as ready to release the Chicago club from their engagement. The new ground of the club was entirely destroyed by the fire, and, moreover, all the wealthy backers of the club are penniless, having lost all they had. Under such circumstances it is almost impossible that the club can take the field next year, even were there not another obstacle in the way, viz., a people having neither means nor inclination to support a professional club by patronizing their games. Chicago will want all her means to supply the necessities of life, and in re-building homes for their suffering people for a year to come at least, and therefore there is no likelihood of their dealing in such a recreative luxury as a professional base ball club. The best thing all the engaged professionals can do is to follow the example of the Olympic players and release the Chicago club from their bonds and seek new fields for the 1872 campaign.

On Monday, Oct. 16th, we received a letter from Captain [Jimmy] Wood, of the late Chicago club, in which he desires us to officially state that, in consequence of the Chicago club grounds being totally destroyed, and the club entirely bankrupt, all players now connected with the club, and those engaged for 1872, are *released from their engagements* and free to seek service in other clubs. He says he has not been able to write to each to this effect, but that he soon will do so. In the meantime he sends them word through the CLIPPER, so that they may not lose any opportunity to engage with other clubs. Mr. Wood says—in his own words:— "*So we are one and all now in the market.*" He also writes word that the White Stocking players have all, except two, been burnt out, and have lost all they had, including savings in the banks, and that they have availed themselves of the offers of free passes to come east to play the concluding games of their championship matches. The captain of the White Stocking nine also adds:—"Our only resort now is the generosity of the eastern public in this our trying ordeal."

Under such circumstances the White Stockings come to us a portion of the sufferers from the Chicago fire, and in such case should be the recipients of the sympathy and assistance of the professional fraternity as expressed through the medium of a benefit match for the burnt out ball tossers. Let such a match be arranged at once. One of the series with the Haymakers might be selected for the purpose. The Philadelphia *Age*, of Oct. 14th, states that "on Thursday and Friday games will be played between the Athletic and Mutual Clubs *for the benefit of the Chicago sufferers*. The first will be played in this city, with [Candy] Cummings as pitcher for the Athletic, and [Phonney] Martin for the Mutuals; the second game, in New York, with Cummings for the Mutual, and Martin for the Athletic. This organization of the nines should draw immense crowds." The receipts at these contests will go to the general funds. Those of the match we suggest will be for the benefit of those of the White Stocking nine who were burnt out.

As the *Clipper* article relates, the White Stockings received offers of free railroad passes to travel east to finish the baseball season. Their first stop was Troy, New York. The fire prevented them from playing a scheduled October 12 match-up at home with the Haymakers, so on October 21 the two teams squared off for the first game of the two-game series. One Chicago newspaper observed that although the large crowd gathered at the field naturally cheered for the home team, "much less feeling was manifest than might have been expected." The paper quickly opined that "the misfortunes of the visiting club had undoubtedly much to do with this." The White Stockings won the first game against the Haymakers by the score of 11–5 but lost the second contest two days later, 19–12.

Although the article had not mentioned it, the rag-tag appearance of the Chicago players provided a visible reminder of their woeful predicament. Gone were the attractive, well-tailored shirts and pants with which the men had started the season, and in their places was a motley assortment of borrowed, mismatched clothing. The *Chicago Tribune* vividly described the players after another game:

> Not two of the nine were dressed alike, all their uniforms having been consumed at the fire. They presented a most extraordinary appearance from the parti-colored nature of their dress. All who could get white stockings did so, but they were not many. One man wore a Mutual shirt and Eckford hose; another an Atlantic shirt, Mutual pants, and Flyaway hose, and so on; each man being obliged to borrow a shirt from any one who was willing to lend. Where so much depends on the freedom of limb, it is very necessary that the uniforms of the players should fit them well and easily, and therefore their play to-day with tight shirts, short pants, and hose in many cases a world too wide, was indeed as creditable as it was surprising.[17]

With their possessions in ashes and having had few opportunities for practice, the demoralized White Stockings deserved a fair amount of credit for even showing up. The Chicago players scheduled a few unofficial exhibition games to bring in some much-needed revenue, but rainy weather forced the cancellation of the games. In addition, a crucial match against Philadelphia was postponed several times before finally taking place on October 30. To make matters even worse, gate receipts were meager as fewer than 600 spectators showed up at the neutral ballpark in Brooklyn ("and a large portion of them were from Philadelphia," a sportswriter pointed out). A 4–1 loss against the top-ranked Athletics removed the White Stockings from competition for the championship.

Even though the season officially ended on October 31, Chicago played another game with the Haymakers on November 2 in a vain attempt to improve its record. The National Association ruled, however, that despite the fire, the season was over and the match did not count (the White Stockings lost anyway, 13–9). The association declared the Athletics, with their 21 game wins and seven losses and six series victories, the 1871 baseball champions. The Boston Red Stockings' 20-10-1 record and five series wins put them in second place, followed by the White Stockings with a win-loss record of 19–9 and four series victories. (A club that won a best three-out-of five games from a team throughout the season won the series.)

With arguments swirling about the league on controversial issues such as series wins vs. game wins, player eligibility, forfeited games, and incomplete schedules, it is not surprising that Chicago and other clubs grumbled about the National Association's decision to award the championship to Philadelphia. Wins and losses aside, an examination of the White Stockings' individual records shows that while pitcher George Zettlein led the league with his sparkling 2.73 earned run average, only Fred Treacey and Jimmy Wood hit above .300 (.339 and .378, respectively)—and the club as a whole batted a lackluster .270. In comparison, the pennant-winning Athletics' overall batting average was 50 points higher at .320. In terms of run production, the White Stockings' modest 302 runs garnered them only a fifth-place tie with the New York Mutuals, behind the Boston Red Stockings (401), the Philadelphia Athletics (376), the Troy Haymakers (351) and the Washington Olympics (310).[18]

Epilogue

The season was over, but even with free rail passes, the impoverished White Stockings desperately needed cash before they could go home. On the day after their deciding match with Philadelphia, the White Stockings (clad in the uniforms of the Brooklyn Eckford Club) took on the New York Mutuals in an unofficial exhibition game at the Union Grounds in Brooklyn, which would not count in the standings. "The attendance was very small," the New York *World* reported, "which was the more to be regretted, as the Chicago men have been considerably inconvenienced by the disaster which recently befell their city, and a good sum taken at the gate would have considerably benefited them." Even though they lost, 11–3, the New York newspaper graciously acknowledged that they played "an exceedingly creditable game throughout, and the wonder was that, laboring under the disadvantages they played under, they should have done so well."

The White Stockings returned home, and from time to time the Chicago press mentioned the names of those who were fortunate enough to secure roster spots on other teams. The Troy Haymakers particularly benefited from the Chicago club's devastating circumstances; they picked up the contracts of Charlie Hodes, Marshall King, Bub McAtee, George Zettlein, and also Jimmy Wood, who would captain this team just as he had the White Stockings.[19]

During a November 11 meeting of the Chicago Base Ball Club, secretary J. M. Thatcher reported that some $1,500 had been disbursed since the fire, most of it towards the ballplayers' salaries. Although the catastrophe had destroyed all of the club's records and account books, Thatcher believed that there was roughly $2,000 in the organization's treasury.

Naturally, the club's future was on everybody's mind. The *Chicago Tribune* disclosed that nothing was decided at the meeting because only about 20 stockholders were present, and they felt that everyone needed to be "advised of the present condition of affairs before taking any steps for the future."

The *Tribune* was more direct and candid as it continued, insisting that since Chicago residents were facing an overwhelming amount of work as they struggled to rebuild their city, time and money could not—nor should not—be spent on baseball:

> It would seem as though Chicago would, for next year, have enough on its hands in the care of its destitute and in the work of rebuilding, without any further dabbling in professional base ball. Even if it were possible—which it is not—to reconcile with our present position of alms-takers from the entire world the maintenance of an expensive professional nine, we have no grounds on which to play games, and to fit up grounds will cost from four to five thousand dollars. The year 1872 will be a season of work in Chicago—hard, unceasing work for everybody, and we shall have little time to devote to an amusement, the enjoyment of which takes an entire afternoon. There will be no afternoons to spare, for some time to come, in Chicago. Base ball is a luxury which we can dispense with for at least one year, and there should be no further steps toward the reorganization of the White Stocking nine.

The Chicago Base Ball Club, perhaps heeding the newspaper's words, soon canceled and surrendered its stock, and a committee was appointed to wrap up all of the details. Baseball, however, remained on the minds of many Chicagoans throughout the following months as the city's amateur clubs attracted both players and spectators. With the construction of a new ballpark in 1872, interest in the sport would continue, as professional teams traveled to Chicago to compete against each other as well as local clubs. The city's White Stockings would again take the field in 1874 and, two years later, one of the men responsible for their return would help form a new league that would replace the National Association and help bolster professional baseball in the years ahead.[20]

3

RECOVERY AFTER DISASTER
(1872–1875)

> Mr. T. S. Fauntleroy, Treasurer of the Chicago Base Ball Association, which clings to life with remarkable tenacity for such a decrepi[t] institution, has called a special meeting of the stockholders for 8 o'clock to-morrow evening, at the Uhlich House. The object of the gathering is to do whatever may be possible to revive the interest in the game this season, as well as to take active measures to secure a nine for next year.
> —*Chicago Daily Tribune*, July 17, 1873

A New Ballpark (1872)

In April 1872, New York City's *Spirit of the Times* newspaper lamented that "there can be no doubt that the breaking up of the Chicago Club, in consequence of the fire last fall, was a heavy blow to the professional section of the base-ball community." Although the impact was indeed serious, Chicago's amateur teams did their best to fill the void left by the White Stockings' unfortunate and involuntary dissolution. On January 11, for example, a large number of persons had attended a special meeting of the well-known Aetna Base Ball Club. The group was "fully determined," the *Chicago Tribune* reported, "to preserve the Aetna organization for 1872, and to put in the field a nine as good as ever." The city's newspapers were soon also covering the Phoenix Club, newly formed in May, and the Active Base Ball Club, whose members played their first game of the season in late July (with each Active player wearing "a new and neat uniform").[1]

Even though the future of the White Stockings was on hold for a while, in early April some 50 baseball-minded individuals—including former officials of the Chicago Base Ball Club—gathered together in the parlor of the Uhlich House, a local hotel. They reasoned that if a suitable park was built in Chicago, perhaps professional teams could be enticed to compete against the city's amateur clubs. Not only could the money earned by leasing the grounds go towards building a solid team for Chicago, but sports fans would also be able to see some first-class baseball. After all, ex–White Stocking Jimmy Wood, now captain of the Troy Haymakers, had already expressed a desire to bring his team to Chicago.

It seemed like an ideal situation, and the men began selling stock to raise money towards the construction of a new ballpark. During an April 24 meeting of the newly formed Chicago Base Ball Association, secretary J. M. Thatcher said that the organization had made arrangements to use land on the city's South Side at the corner of 23rd and State Streets, but that roughly $4,000 was needed to build a facility and pay the rent for the baseball season. According to one report, Thatcher "had assurances from the Troy, Baltimore, and Cleveland Clubs that they would come here to play, and bring other clubs with them. There was no doubt about the success of the undertaking, if the necessary funds were forthcoming."[2]

The association quickly addressed the financial part of the project, and two weeks later, at a meeting on May 6, Treasurer Edwin F. Dexter announced that he had collected $2,050 on subscribed stock. Furthermore, secretary Thatcher told the members that work had begun upon the new baseball grounds and was progressing quickly. He added that the fence was already up, seats were being constructed, and sod would be laid soon. A few paragraphs from a newspaper article published the previous day furnished additional information:

> The "home plate" will be situated in the centre of the short diameter of the ground, and about 125 feet from the north line of fencing. From the home plate to the west line of fencing, it is just 100 yards along the "foul line," necessitating a pretty sharp hit for a foul ball to go on to the railroad track. There will be plenty of room in the out-field for home runs, if necessary....
>
> The batter will strike in a southeasterly direction generally, or across the wind, which is generally from the southwest in this windy town. The sun will be on or toward the batter's right, and out of the fielder's eyes....
>
> Nothing remains to be noticed about the grounds but the fencing, which is stout and better adapted to the demands of the ground than that on the lake front enclosure, occupying less room. The grounds are near the State street cars, and Twenty-third street will be put in order for the accommodation of vehicles. Better grounds and better accommodations could not have been met with in this or any city.

By the following week about all that remained to be completed was the grandstand, which would be constructed behind home plate, "as in the case of the old Lake Shore grounds," according to one observer. There were few other similarities between the two facilities, however. In fact, in terms of size, the new park, with dimensions of 600 feet by 400 feet, was certainly an improvement over the older, smaller one.

A quarter-mile track, 20 feet in width, and a dressing room were added to the grounds so that the Chicago Athletic Club as well as baseball players could use the field. Although the city's new park would be formally opened on May 29 with a game between the Baltimore and Cleveland teams, the athletic club actually inaugurated the grounds on May 25 with a series of sporting events.[3]

In his coverage of the various competitions, a sportswriter pointed out that Burnside Street (later Dearborn) bordered the park on the east—not the farther east State Street, which J. M. Thatcher had mentioned during the association's April 24 meeting. An article on the refurbishing of the park relates that "a side-track will be laid from State street to the entrance of the grounds, so that spectators can ride directly to the gates." Clark Street bordered the park on the west, 23rd Street on the south, and 22nd Street (later Cermak Road) on the north. The reporter provided baseball fans with other significant details about the new ballpark:

> The public has awaited with some little curiosity the result of the efforts being made to secure a comfortable base ball ground for the coming season. The lovers of the national game who were present on the occasion of the first meeting of the Chicago Athletic Club were enthusiastic over the condition of affairs. A few weeks of honest labor have transformed the rough, uneven vacant lot into a ball ground equal to any in the United States. The new park is nearly a third larger than the lake front

grounds whereon so many matches were contested, and the preparation for the purposes for which it is designed reflects credit upon the management. An enormous roller has been kept in active operation for some days, and the ground has been well rolled. The grass has been reduced with a mower, and is still being mowed at intervals. The outfield requires a little more attention from the roller still, but one more rain storm, and a thorough rolling after it, will leave nothing to be desired. The infield is all that the most fastidious ball-player could desire, the general expression being that it was a diamond of the first water. It has all been carefully sodded, rolled, watered, mowed and re-rolled, until the turf is as compact and smooth as a lawn, and the reputation of the Chicago Base Ball Park will be fully sustained by the enclosure on the corner of Burnside and Twenty-third streets. It is as accessible to the citizens now as the old grounds were, the car and omnibus lines bringing it within a quarter of an hour's distance of State and Madison streets. The arrangement of the grand stand has been altered somewhat, the management having decided to put it on the north line of fencing, and immediately behind the back stop, as in the old grounds. Seats have been erected around the north and west sides of the grounds for the accommodation of 3,500 visitors, so that no very great danger of standing need be feared.[4]

The White Stockings Return (1873)

On May 29 and 30, 1872, the Baltimore Canaries and Cleveland Forest Citys played the first baseball games in the recently completed park, soon called the 23rd Street Grounds. The two professional clubs had barely vacated the premises before fans streamed in on June 1 to see the amateur Aetnas take on Evanston University. Although members of the Chicago Base Ball Association took pride in hosting the various games, they remembered that they had constructed their new facility—as well as founded their organization—with a higher goal in mind: to sign players for a new White Stockings team. "Shall we get up a nine for next year?" asked Treasurer T. S. Fauntleroy. "If so, how? [A]nd who shall do it?" The *Chicago Tribune* reported in a lengthy June 13 article that the association was contemplating "to take time by the forelock, and proceed at once to the engagement of players to constitute the Chicago professional nine for the season of 1873, and it has been virtually decided to hold a meeting soon and appoint a Committee, whose duty it shall be to select and secure a nine for next year."

The *Tribune*, however, believed that it was still too early in the summer to determine if outstanding (and highly paid) players would continue to perform well throughout the long baseball season. "It may transpire," the newspaper explained, "as it has often done, that those who stood the highest at the beginning of the year relapse into inefficiency before the season's play is ended, and are never again heard of as first class ball players." The *Tribune* added that some of the high-priced men who were supposed to have played for the White Stockings in 1872 had recently "made an unparalleled exhibition of successful and uninterrupted muffinism."[5]

The Chicago Base Ball Association apparently took this candid assessment to heart. At its July 1 meeting, secretary J. M. Thatcher moved that a committee be appointed to look into securing a team for the city, but the motion was not seconded and was rejected "on the ground that it was premature." By the end of November, however, association members were still not ready to commit themselves. According to one report, "The financial difficulties experienced by Eastern professional associations the past season ha[ve] deterred [Chicago association directors] from taking any hasty action…. It has been discovered that the best paid professionals are not the most successful players, and that expensive nines are not to be the rule the coming ball season."

These "financial difficulties" represented a typical problem with baseball clubs of this era. A team's heavy salary obligations often stretched its limited resources, occasionally causing its collapse. For example, the legendary Cincinnati Red Stockings had disbanded following the 1870 season due to ballplayer salary demands, and the Cleveland Forest Citys had folded in 1872 after the club rashly increased wages to hold its star athletes. Although the Chicago Base Ball Association did not yet have to contend with salary issues, it did find itself facing a different set of economic circumstances. As the city struggled to rebuild itself in the aftermath of the October 1871 fire, enterprising men could easily forego sports and choose steady jobs in the various construction trades. As pointed out in a newspaper editorial on July 28, "Any 'nine' can at any time find constant employment.... If they keep sober and work well, they can save more money than they can at baseball.... No city in the country offers so much employment at such high wages for athletic young men as Chicago."[6]

The 1872 championship baseball season closed with the Boston Red Stockings solidly in first place with a record of 39 wins, eight losses, and one tie. Unfortunately, the year itself ended with little likelihood that a Chicago professional team would soon enjoy the amenities at the city's modern baseball grounds. Although the Chicago Base Ball Association continued its attempts to both secure a team for Chicago and attract established clubs to play at the new field, many of its members lost interest in baseball by June 1873. A reorganization of the association in July, however, apparently aroused them from their indifference and lethargy. The *Chicago Times* reported that association members were "doing everything possible" to bring teams to Chicago; in fact, because the businessmen had "progressed with such rapidity," the newspaper announced on July 21 that the Boston Red Stockings and the Philadelphias (also known as the Philadelphia White Stockings or Philadelphia Whites) would soon be competing against each other in Chicago.

The August 16, 1873, match-up between Boston and Philadelphia marked the first professional game held in Chicago that season. With both teams playing exceptionally well that year (and with many former Chicago players on the Philadelphia team), some 6,000 excited fans thronged the 23rd Street Grounds on a glorious summer afternoon. "The attendance was very large," one Chicago newspaper commented, "and the interest manifested in the sport by the spectators recalled to mind the days when we boasted a base ball club of our own that could whip anything in the thirty-seven States."

Perhaps that era would soon return. With the reorganization of the Chicago Base Ball Association came a new board of directors and new officers. Norman T. Gassette, who had resigned as head of the group in June 1872, returned and was reelected president. A leader known for asserting authority and taking charge, Gassette promised he would do his best for the club, and he promptly set off for the east coast to scout for players. His journey proved successful and on the day of the Boston-Philadelphia game, Chicago's newspapers announced his big news: he had engaged a White Stocking team for 1874.[7]

"Out-Door Amusements. A New Nine Engaged for Chicago." *Chicago Times*, August 16, 1873, p. 3.

Chicago's old base-ball club went off with the smoke, together with about everything that could be called Chicago's. We had to forego the satisfaction of seeing the "Chicago's" obtain the championship of '71, and for a year thereafter relin[q]uish the game—but not the love of it. That still seems to burn in the excitable Chicago breast as deeply as ever. And now that Chicago is getting back more than her old glories, she has determined to again possess a crack "nine." The president of the base-ball association left this city for the east with full authority from its members to secure the best players that the country affords. He has just returned and reports the most complete success. Contracts with players have been signed, and the "White Stocking" nine of 1874 is in existence. This is the first club that has yet been formed for the ensuing season. The players constitute men of the most distinguished base-ball ability, and will compose a team that will be formidable to any that can hereafter be organized. The management did well in getting so early into the field, and the result has been they have had the pick of the choicest players, as there are no members of the profession who are loth to represent the favorite city of base-ball.

◆ ◆ ◆

"Sporting Matters. The New Professional Club." *Chicago Daily Tribune*, August 17, 1873, p. 3.

The number of people who went out to see the match yesterday between the "Red" and "White" Stockings fully demonstrated that the people of Chicago have not lost their love for the "National Game," and that Chicago merits the reputation she has of being the greatest base-ball city in the country. But next year Chicago will have a club which she can well be proud of. The following gentlemen intend to bring the "champion pennant" of 1874 to Chicago: The most important and difficult position to fill is the manager's. There never has been but three A 1 managers of ball clubs in the country, viz: Mr. [John] Joyce, who brought the old "Cincinnati Red Stockings" to the enviable position they occupied in 1869; Hicks Hay[h]urst, who has been the mentor for the Athletics of Philadelphia from the Year 1, and last, but not least, Nicholas Young, of Washington, who will have charge of the destinies of the "Chicagos" next year. Nick, as he is generally called, is the best man in the country to note the peculiar fitness of players for certain positions, and their unfitness for others. Taking a number of disorganized nines in Washington composed of players generally considered second rate, he has trained and brought out a nine that defeated the Philadelphia White Stockings the other day very badly. Next to the manager in importance comes the Captain. Harry Wright and James Wood are the only two good Captains among professional ball-players. The others either lack judgment, are quick-tempered, or have some other disqualifications. James Wood, or as the boys say, "Jimmy," is to be Captain of the Chicagos. He will also guard the second base, a position in which he has no superiors and but one equal, viz.: [Ross] Barnes. Jimmy is an old [Brooklyn] "Eckford" player, beginning with Dickie Pearce, [Jim] Creighton (who was the first swift pitcher), and Harry Wright. In 1870–71 he was the Captain and second baseman of the "Old Whites." The catcher's position will be filled by Fergus Malone. Fergy is an old Philadelphia player, but first got his reputation in the Olympics of Washington. He is a fine catcher, assisting the pitcher a great deal by using his brains in his playing, or, as it is termed, "head work." Last year he played catcher, short stop, and first base for the Athletics, all of which positions he filled creditably, but his position unquestionably is behind the bat, where he now plays in the Philadelphias. George Zettlein is to pitch. While in the famous Atlantics of New York, in 1867–68 and '69, the "Charmer" acquired the reputation of being one of the swiftest, most accurate, and enduring pitchers in the country; but George did not use his head enough. He has improved wonderfully in that respect since he came under Jimmy Wood's tutelage. David W. Force, or "Little George Wright," as he used to be called in Washington, one of the few good short-stops in the country, is to fill that position in the coming nine. In the Olympic nine of Washington he did most excellent service. Then he went to Troy to play in the Haymakers. On the breaking up of that nine Nick Young persuaded him to go to

Baltimore, where he now is. He plays third base in the Baltimores, but he is not tall enough to play a base, and should play short. James A. Devlin, of the present White Stockings, will play first base. He is comparatively unknown outside of Philadelphia, where he has long enjoyed a reputation as one of the best players of the Quaker City, being a member of the amateur Olympics.

We have spoken of the second baseman, "Jimmy" Wood. We now come to third base, a most difficult position to fill well, and Levi Meyerle has played it as well as it can be played. He is also a very useful man, being able to play *any* position creditably. He, too, is an old Philadelphian. He first came into notice in the Athletics, where he has caught, pitched, and played almost every other position. He is not one of your variable players, who has good and bad days. He is always good.

Left field will be attended to by Edgar E. Cuthbert, better known to Chicagoans as "Cuthy." He is the best fielder in the country. A sure catch, swift runner, and a wonderfully accurate, strong thrower. We all remember that "Cuthy" made the winning run in the memorable game in Cincinnati, when the "Whites" first conqu[e]red the then thought invincible "Red Stockings." Ned is an old "Athletic" player, who played in Chicago in 1870–71, and last year played with the Athletics, whom he left to join the "Philadelphias."

If "Cuthy" has an equal in fielding it is Frederick S. Treac[e]y, who will be the invincible in centre-field next year. Fred first became noted in the Eckford Club, which he left to come to Chicago and play in the Whites. Last year he played in the Athletics, but, with "Cuthy," he went over to the Philadelphias.

John Glenn is to play right-field next year in the Chicagos. He is a Rochester player, who gained prominence in the Excelsiors of that place, the club that beat the Athletics on their first annual tour. In the Olympics, of Washington, John played field and first base, both of which positions he plays finely. This year Nick Young has him in Washington.

◆ ◆ ◆

It probably was no coincidence that Norman Gassette's announcement came on the day of the big Boston-Philadelphia game. After all, not only had Philadelphia players Ned Cuthbert, Jim Devlin, Fergy Malone, Levi Meyerle, Fred Treacey, Jimmy Wood, and George Zettlein just signed with Chicago, but several of them had also played for the original White Stockings. Gassette undoubtedly realized that his news would help fill ballpark seats and generate much enthusiasm for next season's Chicago team. As the *Chicago Times* observed on game day:

> The members of both clubs have hosts of friends in this city from whom they received early visits. The knights of the ball and bat were accordingly the recipients of many hearty welcomes from their admirers. Noticeably true was this in the case of the "Philadelphias" or rather the "White Stockings," now of another city to be sure, but largely the old "White Stockings" of Chicago.... They were greeted by their Chicago friends with a heartiness that left not a suspicion that they were any less admired, or that time and absence had caused them to be scarce less remembered than when they upheld Chicago prowess on the ball field.

Gassette and the other members of the Chicago Base Ball Association were determined to bring that athletic prowess back to their city. They could probably count on gate receipts and the rental of their new park to provide financial assistance, as the two well-attended Boston-Philadelphia games had brought in a sizable profit. Although Boston wanted to return to Chicago, other eastern clubs faced busy schedules and could not spare the time; therefore, no additional professional games were played at the 23rd Street Grounds that year.[8]

The 1873 baseball season drew to a close in late October, with the Boston Red Stockings winning the championship title with 43 wins, 16 losses, and one tie, and the Philadelphia White Stockings taking second place with 36 wins and 17 losses. On November 10 the *Chicago Daily Tribune* looked ahead to "next year's great nines." It cautioned that talent alone could not win a championship, as a team needed "thorough discipline and good management" to lead it to first place. Fortunately, the White Stockings had already signed two strong directors. "The future nine," the *Tribune* wrote, "that we hope and expect so much from, has in MR. NICHOLAS YOUNG, of Washington, one of the most experienced and able managers of ball clubs in the country, and in James Wood a Captain second to none."

The paper emphasized, however, that each time the team members walked onto the ball field, they had to play "an earnest, intelligent, and reliable game," as "we don't want a nine that plays a brilliant game one day and a muffin the next." The *Tribune* concluded by urging the city's baseball fans simply to "hope for the best."[9]

Chicago's New White Stockings Take the Field (1874)

Even before the first pitch of Opening Day, newspapers predicted an eventful year for the new White Stockings. On March 7 the *New York Times* declared that "the Chicago Club, under the management of 'Nick' Young, propose making things lively this season." The New York *World* reminisced that Chicago had originally organized a nine so it could defeat Cincinnati's Red Stockings. The Illinois team had indeed triumphed over its rival, the paper continued, and now Chicago "sends forth a company fully as powerful, and including a number of members of her old organization."

The forthcoming season was, however, a long and demanding one, and no matter how powerful the ballplayers were, they still needed much practice time. The *Los Angeles Daily Herald* announced on March 19 that the team was expected to arrive in Chicago soon—and would be playing in a refurbished ballpark. "Its play-grounds," the newspaper informed its readers, "are to be fitted up in magnificent style—the grand stand alone seating about 12,000." This was a somewhat grandiose figure; as the *Chicago Daily Tribune* pointed out a few weeks later, the actual seating capacity for the entire park was roughly 7,000.[10]

"Local Miscellany. Base-Ball Gossip." *Chicago Daily Tribune*, April 5, 1874, p. 4.

It is just beginning to be fairly realized that Chicago is to have a first-class base-ball club this season, and that the memorable contests which took place during 1870, 1871, and 1872 are to be repeated upon the green diamond. It may be doubted whether we shall ever see again the immense crowds, the strong interest and the hearty enthusiasm which used to attend the old White Stocking games, but it is certain that the really excellent nine for 187[4] will to a great degree succeed in reviving the old-time popularity of the national game.

WITH THE SINGLE EXCEPTION OF [FERGY] MALONE,

the catcher, the nine is on hand, ready for business, though the weather has been too cold for outdoor practice. Malone is due next Wednesday, and the club will be in shape to begin operations. Jimmy Wood, the Captain, and second baseman, is still confined to his bed with a disabled knee, though he is in a fair way to recover. It will, however, be at least two months before he can hope to take his place in the nine. His base will be played by [Paul] Hines, who has filled the position with credit heretofore, though, were he a "hangel from 'eving" [angel from evening], no one in Chicago would believe that he could fill Jimmy Wood's place. Hines is a splendid ball player by reputation, and the management have no doubt of his ability to take care of base No. 2.

THE OTHER POSITIONS

will be as before announced—[George] Zettlein, pitcher; [Fergy] Malone, catcher; [Jim] Devlin, first; [Davy] Force, short; [Levi] Meyerle, third; [Ned] Cuthbert, left; [Fred] Treac[e]y, centre; and [Ed] Pinkham, right field and change pitcher. Pinkham is in perfect health once more, and will doubtless avail himself of the opportunity to show that he can play ball. His left-hand delivery will once more be brought in to bother opposing batsmen when they "get on" Zettlein's pitching too heavily,—more especially the Bostons, who never could bat Pinkham. Treac[e]y, too, has some lost ground to recover in Chicago, and, judging from his fine physical condition, he will get it back. All in all, the nine promises to be a tough lot for the Eastern clubs to tackle, and will, no doubt, be found to be the strongest Chicago has ever had.

THE FIRST GAMES.

About the 18th or 20th of this month the White Stockings will go to St. Louis, there to play the Empires and St. Louis Red Stockings three games each, and practice on alternate days. They will be under the charge of Mr. [Nick] Young, the manager, and will be absent about two weeks. The championship season begins in Chicago on the 13th of May, when the Athletics, of Philadelphia, play the White Stockings on the latter's grounds, corner of State and Twenty-third streets. On the 16th of May the Athletics and White Stockings will try it again; on the 20th and 23d the Whites play the New York Mutuals; on the 27th and 30th (probably) the Philadelphias play here; and on June 3, 6, and 8, the champion Bostons will fly the whip pennant here, and play three games to hold it, if they can, against Chicago.

This year, it should be borne in mind, the championship series consists of ten games, making seventy in all which each club must play, as there are seven contesting clubs in the field. According to the rule, one-half of these games must be played in Chicago, and it is believed that the inducements here will be so strong as to give a larger number of games in this city.... ["Visiting Nines," a section about the seven other professional teams, is omitted.]

FIRST EASTERN TRIP.

The White Stockings start on their first Eastern trip on the 9th of June. The only games thus far arranged are with the Bostons on the 24th, 26th, and 27th of June.

THE GROUNDS.

Work on the Twenty-second street grounds is rapidly pushed forward, the plans for the stands having been drawn up by Mr. Roberts, a well-known architect. The grand stand will contain 1,388 sittings, and will be furnished with comfortable settees, numbered. Three hundred season seats in this stand will be sold at $10 each, or at the rate of about 25 cents for each game. These seats will be ready for sale this week. Then there will be the complimentary stand for the stockholders and other persons on the free-list. This will be an exclusive affair, containing 300 seats. The total seating-capacity of the grounds will be not far from 7,000. A side-track will be laid from State street to the entrance of the grounds, so that spectators can ride directly to the gates. All games will commence promptly at 3:45 p.m.

◆ ◆ ◆

By the middle of April the players had convened in Chicago, ready to begin working out and practicing. "Every pleasant day has seen them engaged in limbering up after the winter's inactivity," the city's baseball fans read in their newspapers, "and the arrow-like straightness and speed with which they send the ball along from base to base and far into the field, combined with their accuracy of catch and batting vim, opens up pleasant visions of victories to come."

Not so pleasant, however, was the condition of team captain and second baseman Jimmy Wood. During the 1873–74 off-season, Wood had made the ill-considered decision of using his pocketknife to lance an abscess on his left thigh. Before he could clean the blade, he accidentally dropped the knife, cutting his right leg. Infection set in, and Wood had been forced to remain in his home, unable to play baseball. Although one report in early April suggested that Wood was "in a fair way to recover," that was really not the case. Consequently, the White Stockings had to begin their season without him. As a Chicago newspaper related, on April 17 they faced a team "composed of some of our best amateur players," with Paul Hines assuming Wood's position at second base. "The professionals played remarkably well," the paper observed, "astonishing even themselves in many instances," and they won by the score of 44–3.[11]

After a 24–3 Chicago victory the next day against many of the same athletes, the White Stockings left for St. Louis to practice and to play exhibition games against local amateur clubs. The visitors competed against some of the area's best squads but managed to continue their winning streak. In an analysis of the National Association's eight professional teams of 1874—others included the Boston Red Stockings, New York Mutuals, Philadelphia Athletics, Philadelphia White Stockings (nicknamed the Pearls after the 1873 season), Hartford Dark Blues, Brooklyn Atlantics, and the Baltimore Canaries—the *New York Herald* pointed out that "the Chicago White Stockings are a hard set to win a game from. Not only are they expert fielders, but they are very heavy hitters and always play a steady game." The *Chicago Daily Tribune* also commented on the fierce hitting of the visiting team in its coverage of the Chicago ballplayers' final match in St. Louis, a 39–13 triumph against the St. Louis Red Stockings on May 2: "The batting of the Reds was the best ever shown by a St. Louis club, but the fearful batting of the White-Legs seemed to demoralize them somewhat in the field at times."

Whatever the teams' moods and spirits were like during the games, on May 2 the White Stockings left for home on excellent terms with their various St. Louis rivals. The Red Stockings even accompanied the Chicagoans, as the two clubs were scheduled to face each other four times at the 23rd Street Grounds. A beat writer from one Chicago newspaper predicted that these games, scheduled for May 6–9, would give the Whites "all the practice necessary before the meeting with the Athletics on the 13th." The prescient sportswriter may have been on to something, as four consecutive wins kept the home team's perfect record intact. With the season's initial exhibition matches now over and Chicago's club off to an excellent start, the city's baseball fans undoubtedly awaited the match on May 13—the first White Stockings regular-season game in Chicago since 1871—with eager anticipation.[12]

"The Ball and Bat. First Championship Game in Chicago—The Athletics "Chicagoed" by the White Stockings." *New York Times*, May 14, 1874, p. 5.

Special Dispatch to the New-York Times.

CHICAGO, May 13.—The first championship game played in this city this season took place this afternoon between the White Stockings and Athletics, of Philadelphia. The result was the disastrous defeat of the Athletics. Nine times in succession were they whitewashed, but they played an up-hill game with great pluck, and kept the Chicagos down to four runs. The game was witnessed by at least 5,000 persons, and the début of our professionals was so successful that everybody went home satisfied that Chicago has one of, if not the best nine in the country. While there were several errors committed on both sides, the fielding was at times magnificent. Take, for instance, the seventh inning, when the Athletics had three men on bases, only one man out, and [Adrian] Anson, their heavy hitter, at the bat, they were whitewashed after all. It was, from first to last, a fine exhibition of the national game, for though seven of the Athletics got to first on errors, not one of them could reach the home-plate. Of the ten mistakes made by the visiting club, Anson alone made five errors. The score was as follows:

WHITE STOCKINGS.	R.	1B.	E.	ATHLETIC.	R.	1B.	E.
[Ned] Cuthbert, l. f.	1	0	0	[Mike] McGeary, c.	0	0	2
[Davy] Force, s. s.	1	1	2	[Dick] McBride, p.	0	0	0
[Fergy] Malo[ne], c.	1	1	3	[Adrian] Anson, 3d b.	0	3	5
[Levi] Meyerle, 3d b.	0	0	2	[Wes] Fis[l]er, 1st b.	0	0	1
[Fred] Treac[e]y, c. f.	0	0	2	[Ezra] Sutton, s. s.	0	2	0
[Jim] Devlin, 1st b.	1	1	0	[Joe] Battin, 2d b.	0	1	2
[Paul] Hines, 2d b.	0	0	3	[Count] Sensenderfer, r. f.	0	0	0
[John] Glenn, r. f.	0	0	0	[Count] Gedney, l. f.	0	0	0
[George] Zettlein, p.	0	1	0	[John] McMullin, c. f.	0	2	0
Total	4	4	1[2]	Total	0	8	10

INNINGS.

	1st.	2d.	3d.	4th.	5th.	6th.	7th.	8th.	9th.
White Stockings	2	0	0	0	0	0	1	0	1–4
Athletic	0	0	0	0	0	0	0	0	0–0

Umpire—Mr. Al. Reach, of the Athletics, of Philadelphia.
Time of Game—Two hours and five minutes.

◆ ◆ ◆

"It was a most extraordinary contest from beginning to end," exclaimed the *Chicago Daily Tribune* following the White Stockings' first victory of the season. The paper added that 5,000 to 6,000 spectators were on hand and that "a large number of the most prominent men in the city, accompanied by their families, were observed in the grand stand, which was gay with the bright colors and other finery of the fair sex, and the outside seats were filled with as respectable and orderly an assemblage as was ever gathered together."

One wonders if the onlookers were as "respectable and orderly" on May 23, after the Chicago ballplayers lost their third game in a row. Although the *Tribune* may have buoyed fans' spirits when it confidently declared the next day that "there is plenty of time to regain lost ground," on June 17 the club's record was a disheartening six wins and seven losses. That afternoon the White Stockings were leading the Pearls after the third inning, 6–1, but according to one sportswriter, "The miserable play of [George] Zettlein and [Ned] Cuthbert soon settled the question as to who would be the victors."

But why was Zettlein's and Cuthbert's play so "miserable"? Were they just in a slump, or was there a more sinister reason? Although the two Chicago men were not charged with gambling or game-fixing, the *Tribune* reported that manager Nick Young pulled them from the line-up of the next day's road game against the New York Mutuals, "suspicion being openly attached to their action during the matches in Philadelphia." Unfortunately, matters only got worse. The newspaper pointed out that on June 18, the anniversary of Napoleon's defeat at the hands of the Duke of Wellington, the Chicago players "m[et] their Waterloo in New York" as they ignominiously succumbed to the Mutuals by the lopsided score of 38–1.[13]

The White Stockings were then about a third of the way through a grueling road trip. The earlier resignation of Ed Pinkham and the poor play of some of the team members had spurred Young to change a few of the batting and fielding positions; in addition, the club had brought John Peters over from the St. Louis Red Stockings to play second base, with Paul Hines moving to center field. This reorganization did little to improve the club's fortunes, however, and as scattered wins were overshadowed by multiple losses, the *Tribune* grumbled in late June that players were "wander[ing] listlessly through the Eastern States, conquering an insignificant club here and there, and being conquered by every one which it would be an honor to defeat."

The newspaper's jabs held some validity. On July 2 the three top clubs in the eight-member National Association were the Boston Red Stockings—the reigning champions from 1872 and 1873—followed by the Philadelphia Athletics and the New York Mutuals. At that time the White Stockings' win-loss record against Boston was 1–5, against Philadelphia 1–2, and against New York 0–4. On the other hand, Chicago stood 2–0 against the Baltimore Canaries, the worst team in the league, and 3–0 against the Hartford Dark Blues, the second-worst.

The White Stockings' performance on the field might be explained by both the physical and mental conditions of some team members. Jimmy Wood's injured leg and his uncertain future as a ballplayer had certainly cast a pall over the club, as had the health of other team members. In May the *Chicago Daily Tribune* told its readers that "the White Stockings have been crippled from the outset by the disability of Wood, and also by [Levi] Meyerle's lame shoulder, which reduced his throwing and batting to positively nothing." Catcher Fergy Malone's sore hands made it difficult for him to field baseballs—particularly the wild throws of Dan Collins, who had been acquired in early June as a substitute pitcher. On June 19 the *New York Times* commented that "nearly all of [the White Stocking] players were ailing." Perhaps, then, it was not surprising that the team members limped home on July 3 with just eight wins in their first 22 games and only four victories during their 13-game road trip.

By that time, however, the *Tribune* had lost any sympathy it might have had for the players and vented its frustration about the team's "sorry record":

> A party of much demoralized ball-players yesterday arrived in the city, which they consent to call their temporary headquarters for and in consideration of sums ranging from $1,000 to $2,200 each for about four months of service such as it is. Whether their employers fee[l] good over the bargain, and consider that they have earned their money, is no affair of ours; but, whether these nine or ten professional base ball players have reflected credit upon the city whose name they bear, and have so conducted themselves as to sustain the standing of a deservedly popular class of out-door amusements, is a matter of some general consequence. The so-called Chicago Club has made a sorry record on its first Eastern trip. It has, in fact, accomplished the most absolute failure of the season, and has

attracted a vast amount of attention on that account. Base ball is proverbially prolific of surprises, but the White Stockings have fairly won the title of

THE CHAMPION ASTONISHERS.

When the nine was first organized, it was unanimously agreed, on the strength of the previous records of the respective players, that the team was second to none. This was admitted everywhere, and a brilliant season was predicted. But nobody then anticipated that these heavy-salaried importations were going to progress backwards—that [Levi] M[e]yerle was to prove worse than worthless; that [George] Zettlein was to change rank from the best to the poorest pitcher in America; that [Davy] Force was to fall away in his batting, and [Ned] Cuthbert in his fielding; that [Jim] Devlin would degenerate so rapidly; and that, worst of all, it would be necessary to place on the sick-list the finest Captain and second-baseman in the country, and fill his place with an amateur player. Nobody could foresee all this, which has come to pass before the season is half over.[14]

Despite the White Stockings' uninspired performance during their eastern road trip, more than 10,000 spectators packed the 23rd Street Grounds for their July 4 home game. Although a local reporter scoffed that "the large attendance was no doubt owing chiefly to the fact that it was a general holiday, and very little to the expectation of seeing a close or exciting contest," the Chicago players pulled out a narrow 10-inning victory (17–16) over the Boston Red Stockings. The White Stockings lost their next game with Boston but thrashed the Baltimore Canaries, 9–1, on July 8. Chicago and Baltimore faced off again three days later, with the Chicago *Inter Ocean* remarking that "if one might judge of the character of the game by the play of last Wednesday, it would be predicted that there will be a brilliant display on the diamond field."

The White Stockings defeated the Canaries, 17–12, but neither team presented much of a "brilliant display"; in fact, the *Chicago Daily Tribune* referred to the game as "an exceedingly commonplace and tedious affair on both sides." One can understand why the Chicago players probably did not have their hearts in it. Just one day prior, former White Stocking captain and second baseman Jimmy Wood had to have his right leg amputated due to complications resulting from his cut and infection. "This will be sad news to Wood's hosts of friends here and elsewhere," the *Tribune* related. "By his forced withdrawal from the diamond field the national game loses one of its best, most honorable, and most gentlemanly players."

The loss of Wood was even more poignant because he had been the first ballplayer signed to the White Stockings and was therefore, indirectly, the first Chicago Cub.[15]

"Base Ball. Unfortunate Jimmy Wood." *(Chicago) Inter Ocean*, July 11, 1874, p. 9.

It will be painful news to his many friends in this city and throughout the country to learn that the popular and gallant "Jimmy" Wood, as his friends are wont to call him, has been obliged to suffer the amputation of his right leg, and that his handsome service and cheery voice may never again be seen or heard on the diamond field.

Some time ago, a little abscess formed itself on his left thigh, and Jimmy, not thinking the services of a phys[i]cian requisite, opened it with a pocket-knife. Unfortunately before clasping in the blade, with the poison of the abscess on it, the knife fell from his hands and the point of the blade entered his right leg just below the knee. In a few days the poison began to work, and produced a disease of the joint to such a degree as to produce a stiffness. By careful nursing, the wound gradually closed, and although the stiffness remained, the doctors thought that by the use of a harness the leg might be brought back to its proper position. They succeeded, however, in only bringing the foot to about a couple of inches from the ground, and finding that it did not succeed, a final attempt, resulting in its amputation, was tried yesterday.

About 1:30 o'clock yesterday afternoon Doctors A. Reeves Jackson, Gunn, and Bevan repaired to the residence of Captain Wood, and after putting him under the influence of ether, proceeded to straighten the leg, and then to keep it in place by the use of splints. The attempt was not successful, for hardly had the doctors got half way through the assumed task before the bone broke, cutting an artery. The artery was immediately secured, and upon investigation it was found that the bone below the knee was decayed and diseased. There was only one way left to save the victim's life, and the leg was amputated just above the knee.

Since the operation Jimmy seems to feel better, there being no pain or sickness with the exception of what was caused by the ether. Since the leg has been amputated and investigated the disease has been found to have been worse than it was thought to be, and shows that even if this accident had not hastened the amputation, it would have been found necessary to amputate the limb in a short while.

As Jimmy is in good health and all the diseased portion of the leg has been amputated, the doctors apprehend no future danger, and predict that in a short while he will be out of bed and in his usual state of health, although with but one leg. In his sore misfortune, James Wood will have the earnest sympathy of many friends, who would be glad to be permitted to testify in some substantial manner their recognition and appreciation of his past honorable career on the ball-field. And in this connection it is suggested that a complimentary benefit be given him by the White Stockings and other professional clubs of the country. It would be only a graceful act of recognition of past merit, and it is hoped the White Stockings will take the lead in the move, as no doubt they will be happy to do.

When the Chicago Base Ball Club in October 1869 advertised for "first class professional base ball players ... desirous of connecting themselves with the Chicago Club," second baseman Jimmy Wood was the first player the organization signed. A well-known and respected player of the day, Wood captained Chicago's White Stockings in both 1870 and 1871. "No blot has ever tarnished his reputation," the *Chicago Republican* declared in its January 27, 1871, issue, "and never have his actions either upon or off the field been imputed to dishonorable motives." An accidental knife wound to his right leg during the 1873-74 off-season led to infection and the amputation of the limb. Outfitted with an artificial leg, he was able to manage the Chicago team in 1874 and 1875, but was not hired in 1876 after Al Spalding assumed the managerial duties. Wood held a variety of jobs around the country following his Chicago baseball career. He died in San Francisco on November 20, 1928, just one day before his 85th birthday (Al Spink, *One Thousand Sport Stories*, vol. 1, 1921).

◆ ◆ ◆

The *Inter Ocean*'s suggestion was an excellent one, and Jimmy Wood's benefit exhibition game between the White Stockings and the Brooklyn Atlantics took place on July

29 at the 23rd Street Grounds. The *Chicago Daily Tribune* wrote that "it was to assist him out of the pecuniary difficulties which his physical troubles entailed upon him that the benefit was gotten up, and his host of friends nobly responded." They certainly had, for even though the game did not count in the standings, more than 3,000 persons bought tickets and helped raise about $3,000 for the former second baseman of the Chicago club. Catcher Fergy Malone had assumed Wood's position as captain, and under his direction, the White Stockings won by the score of 5–4. The players on both teams "were in the best of spirits," the *Tribune* continued, "and the utmost good feeling existed among them. Each man played his position as if the possession of the championship pennant depended upon his individual efforts on that particular occasion."[16]

The White Stockings needed such strong efforts—and more—if they wanted to secure that pennant. By July 15 their record of 13–15 relegated them to fourth place in the National Association, 12 games behind the front-running Boston Red Stockings. The Philadelphia Athletics were 4½ games out of first place, while the New York Mutuals were in third and 10½ games back. Chicago still had a chance, however, for in mid-season the two leading championship contenders took a European sabbatical of sorts. On July 16 the Red Stockings and Athletics sailed for England, where they played a series of exhibition games there and in Ireland to promote the sport of baseball. The trip, regrettably, was neither financially nor promotionally successful. Despite the players engaging in some goodwill cricket matches, the locals showed only polite interest in baseball.

With the National Association's leaders out of the country for almost two months, a few of the remaining six teams had the chance to gain some ground in the standings by playing weaker opponents. Although the Chicago players did not fare particularly well—between September 2 and September 10 they lost seven games in a row—the New Yorkers took full advantage of the unusual opportunity. When the Red Stockings and Athletics returned to the United States on September 9, Boston found itself only five games in front of the second-place Mutuals, with the Philadelphia Athletics, Philadelphia Pearls, and the Chicago White Stockings trailing behind.[17]

The Mutuals and Pearls, however, had other issues to confront besides their win-loss records. In early August the *Chicago Daily Tribune* dramatically claimed that "for the first time in the history of base ball in Chicago the national game has been disgraced by palpable and unblushing fraud.... As long ago as 1868 it used to be said and believed of the Mutuals of New York that they were governed by a ring of gamblers, and games were won or lost according as the gamblers had placed their money. That reputation has clung to the Mutual Club up to the present time."

The newspaper further contended that in the fourth inning of an August 5 game with the White Stockings, Mutuals pitcher Bobby Mathews overshot second base, allowing White Stocking Levi Meyerle to advance to third. A subsequent hit brought Meyerle home. In the fifth inning, with the White Stockings down, 4–2, "It was announced that Mathews was too sick to pitch, and he left the nine. This action, together with his previous play, led the spectators to believe that a fraud was being perpetrated, and the hisses were loud and long as Mathews left the field."

The "easy" delivery of the next New York pitcher, along with a "listlessly" batting Mutuals team, secured a 5–4 Chicago victory. "It was a well-played game by the White Stockings," continued the *Tribune*, "but it seemed as though the Mutuals had no thought of winning at any stage. There is ample reason to believe that at least four of the players were hired to lose the game; the rest naturally were discouraged and disheartened by the fact."

The *Tribune* added that it did not think that any Chicago player or club official knew about the "fraud." The loud accusations from both the press and the fans forced the manager of the Mutuals to produce a letter from Mathews's doctor, who stated that the ballplayer had been ill for two days and had pitched on August 5 "against my advice." The furor died down soon afterwards.[18]

The Pearls did not get off so easily. In early September, reports surfaced that Philadelphia player John Radcliff had attempted to bribe respected umpire Billy McLean prior to the July 15 game with the White Stockings (which Chicago won, 10-3). On August 20 McLean formally charged Radcliff in a sworn affidavit, part of which stated:

> William McLean, residing at 197 Grand avenue, being sworn, doth depose and say: I was in Chicago at the time the Philadelphia Base-Ball Club arrived in that city to play the Chicago Club, and it was understood between the two clubs that I was to umpire all three games to be played in that city. Previous to the first game being played, and on the same day, I was approached by John Radcliffe [sic], one of the players of the Philadelphia Base-Ball Club. He took me to one side, in the hotel (the Clifton) where they were stopping, and told me that he had $350 which he gave to his brother to bet in Philadelphia on [t]he result of this game, stating at the same time that it was all the money he had, and that he would give me one-half if I gave my decision in favor of the White Stockings. He also stated that there were four others in with him. He named them as [Candy] Cummings, [Nat] Hicks, [Bill] Craver, and [Denny] Mack, and himself, and wanted the game to result in favor of the Whites. When he offered me one-half of the $350, I told him I would have nothing to do with it, and I said I would umpire the game the same as I had done all the other games.

The stockholders of the Philadelphia ball club met on September 8 and voted 26-15 to expel Radcliff from the team. The four other players were censured "for the loose manner in which they have been playing." Radcliff, however, appealed the decision before the National Association's Judiciary Committee, and its members reinstated him. Although he had to sit out the last few weeks of the 1874 baseball season, he resumed his career the next year with the newly formed Philadelphia Centennials.

The Pearls never did have much of a chance to overtake the mighty Red Stockings, and although the Mutuals came close towards the end of September, Boston closed the 1874 season with a healthy lead of 7½ games over the New Yorkers. The Athletics finished in third place while the White Stockings, who at no time posed much of a threat, ended up in fifth, 18½ games out of first place and 1½ games behind the Pearls. The *Chicago Daily Tribune* published the teams' standings on November 1 and a sportswriter optimistically summed up the White Stockings' performance: "The Chicagos made but a poor showing in the race, but hope to do better next time."[19]

William Hulbert Takes Charge of the White Stockings ... and Takes on Baseball (1874–1875)

Unlike the *Tribune's* reporter, an official of the Chicago Base Ball Association viewed the new season with more than just "hope" on his mind. William A. Hulbert intended not only to improve the fortunes of the White Stockings, but also to rectify some of the problems that had existed for years and which almost seemed inherent to baseball itself. Although the National Association was founded in 1871 in part to curb gambling and the throwing of ball games (commonly referred to as "hippodroming"), the largely player-run organization with no central leadership was simply not up to the task; consequently, dishonest betting and other troublesome concerns remained. During a speech at a March

1914 banquet in New York City, former baseball executive Abraham G. Mills recalled some of the circumstances surrounding the sport's early years:

> As now, each summer's campaign was planned during the preceding winter and the habit was general on the part of the clubs to take on obligations in the way of players' salaries that were not justified, as the spring games would inevitably demonstrate that the majority of such clubs could have no hope of winning even a respectable number of games. Moreover, this condition was greatly aggravated by the general practice, on the part of the richer clubs, of stripping the weaker ones of their best playing talent. Then would follow the collapse of a number of these clubs in mid-season, leaving their players unpaid, while the winning clubs, owing to the disbandment of the weaker ones, would also frequently fail from inability to arrange a paying number of games.
>
> In such a condition of things, it was manifestly impossible to establish and maintain that discipline which is indispensable to success in every form of team contest, and the lack or laxity of discipline was largely responsible for the grosser evils which were then rife, such as dissipation, gambling and even in some cases selling of games.

This game-fixing kept many outraged fans away from the ballparks, as did excess alcohol consumption and rowdiness on the part of spectators and players alike. Because the National Association was open to any organization that called itself a professional club and could pay the entry fee of $10, clubs from small cities often lacked the financial backing that teams from larger communities enjoyed. The Red Stockings' continued supremacy over the league led discouraged players to simply give up, leaving other ball clubs to fight for second or third place. Some teams joined just to make a few dollars through ticket sales of home games but then disbanded before their expensive road trips. Baseball administrators constantly worried about money, and since the mediocre teams in the association seldom drew large crowds of paying customers to their games, all clubs to some extent suffered financially.[20]

Ballplayers received fairly high salaries, but because most men signed only one-year contracts, there was little team loyalty. Players often broke their contracts to join clubs that offered better wages and/or working conditions, such as the well-heeled Boston Red Stockings, New York Mutuals, and Philadelphia Athletics. These contract-breaking athletes were called "revolvers," and an egregious example of "revolving" particularly angered William Hulbert. On September 18, 1874, Chicago infielder Davy Force had renewed his contract with the team, but on December 5 he also signed one with the Philadelphia Athletics. Although the facts seemed simple enough, the case involved several thorny issues, including whether a contracted player could sign a new agreement for the following year with another—or even his own—team. The matter was referred to the National Association's Judiciary Committee, which ruled on March 1, 1875, at the association's national convention in Philadelphia that Force was bound by the terms of his September 18 contract. Later that day, however, new members of the committee were elected and on March 2 the five-man group, which included three members of the Philadelphia club, reversed the previous decision and decided in favor of Davy Force and the Athletics.

This crafty maneuver infuriated Hulbert and the White Stockings as well as other baseball clubs and officials, though some teams sided with the Athletics. Persons aligned with Philadelphia pointed out that the Chicago club was guilty of fraud as Force's contract had actually been signed on November 2 but backdated to September 18. The original Judiciary Committee explained in its report that there were two Davy Force contracts with the White Stockings and that the first was "imperfect" as it was "not attested by witnesses." Consequently, team executives drew up a new contract that was signed on

November 2, "but dated back to Sept. 18,—that being the date of their original but imperfect contract."

The Chicago club officials saw nothing wrong with their attempt to correct the "imperfect contract," particularly as the backdated agreement was still signed prior to the December 5 Athletics contract. Although rules of the National Association stipulated that the Judiciary Committee had to be notified of all disputes before November 15, the White Stockings felt that this regulation did not apply to their case because the Athletics had signed Force after the deadline.[21]

The *New York Clipper*, which was widely read by baseball men, had no sympathy with the White Stockings, insisting that the team's contract with Force "was rendered void by antedating."

"Chicago vs. Athletic." *New York Clipper*, March 27, 1875, p. 411.

The Chicago papers are at it again, getting up sensational excitements. The latest effort is to stir up ill-will between the Chicago and Athletic Clubs. *The Chicago Inter-ocean* of March 13 says:

"The new judiciary committee of the national association of professional baseball players has reversed the unanimous decision of the old committee assigning Force to the Chicago Club, and giving him to the Athletic Club. This is remarkable when it is considered that the new committee was appointed by the President of the Athletic Club, who is himself one of its members. The fraternity generally consider this decision a defiant usurpation of authority, as under the rules of the association the new committee for 1875 have no jurisdiction over disputes arising on contracts made in 1874. Force signed with the Chicago Club Sept. 18, 1874, and with the Athletics Dec. 5, 1874. It is thought hardly probable the latter club will play with them during this season."

Why will partisan journalists persist in this business of creating strife between professional organizations? Surely they ought to know that it injures the clubs collectively and individually. Unless the Chicago and Athletic Clubs are managed by officials grossly incompetent to fill the positions assigned them, they will play their regular series of games out like men. What is this Force business that it should be the cause of the two clubs breaking up that harmony which should be the highest aim of the professional clubs to maintain in their intercourse together, if only for policy sake or to serve their pecuniary interests? The Force contract of September was rendered void by antedating, and the only legal contract was that of Dec. 5, so the facts in the case show. As for the Judiciary Committee of 1874 they unquestionably had no jurisdiction in the case, the matter of the complaint not having been presented to them before November 15. As for the action of the other committee they were the only parties who could legally adjudicate upon the question, so it appears to us. But let it be as it may, the case now is this: Force wanted to play with the Athletics, and the committee of 1875 have decided that their claim on him is the only good one. Under these circumstances there is now no case for a protest against Force's playing, and the statement that the two clubs will not play together is absurd. Please drop the subject, gentlemen. It is settled and ended. Make your arrangements to play as hitherto.

◆ ◆ ◆

William Hulbert was present at the Philadelphia convention and saw firsthand what he regarded as a blatant act of duplicity on the part of the revamped Judiciary Committee. He also could see how the wealthy teams in the East, with their powerful and influential managers, tipped the competitive balance throughout the National Association. Baseball historian Lee Allen put it rather concisely: "Not only did these [eastern] teams control most of the best players, they also controlled the operation of the league." As Hulbert discussed association policies with baseball administrators who he believed put their own interests above the well-being of the entire sport, he began to ponder on how their influence could be weakened.[22]

His background as a businessman and baseball executive made Hulbert an ideal candidate for the task at hand. Born in 1832 in Burlington Flats, New York (some fifteen miles west of Cooperstown), he was two years old when his parents moved to Chicago. After attending a college preparatory school in Beloit, Wisconsin, for one year, he returned to Chicago, where he became successful in the coal industry and in wholesale groceries and obtained a position on the Chicago Board of Trade. Energetic, self-confident, and proud of his hometown, he often remarked that "I would rather be a lamp-post in Chicago than a millionaire in any other city."

Although he was not an athlete himself, Hulbert was also proud of Chicago baseball, and in 1870 he had purchased three shares of stock in the fledgling White Stockings organization. Two years later he became a club director, and by 1874 he was secretary, handling with efficiency team correspondence and details associated with player contracts. After Chicago Base Ball Association president George W. Gage died in September 1875, he was elected as Gage's successor.[23]

Hulbert, his fellow association members, and Chicago's baseball fans saw little to complain about at the 23rd Street Grounds during the first few weeks of the 1875 season. Between May 11 and June 3 the White Stockings won nine games in a row, and by mid-June their record was 13–5—a far different start from the year before. But then, besides the record number of 13 teams in the National Association, 1875 proved to be a distinctive year for all of baseball. Thanks to pitchers' growing expertise with the curve ball, both batting averages and game scores were dropping. One news account reported, for example, that in a late-season game the Hartford Dark Blues easily defeated the St. Louis Brown Stockings, 8–2, largely because "the St. Louis men utterly failed to master [Tommy] Bond's parabolic curves, and no less than eight of them struck out on his pitching." Small wonder, then, that the baseball year had already seen the association's first 1–0 game (between Chicago and St. Louis) as well as its first no-hitter (between Chicago and Philadelphia).[24]

On June 19 the White Stockings took part in another historic pitching duel, during which a runner did not cross home plate until the eleventh inning. The *Chicago Daily Tribune* exclaimed that the White Stockings' 1–0 "whitewash" over the Hartfords proved to be "the most brilliant contest in the history of the game." The *New York Clipper* was no less effusive in its account:

> For the first time in the history of professional playing we have to record a game in which neither of the contesting nines could score a run until after nine full innings had been played. We have been waiting some years to see this feat accomplished in a regular match, but hitherto the nearest approach to such a model score has been one to nothing. In Chicago, on Saturday, June 19, the deed was done, and the Chicago White Stockings and the Dark Blues of Hartford are entitled to the credit of being the first to play such a model game, their match proving to be the finest display of baseball playing, and the most exciting contest yet recorded in the annals of the national game.

Unfortunately, though, the White Stockings followed their "model game" with more defeats than victories, and within a few short weeks they found themselves once again floundering in the middle of the National Association's standings. The Boston Red Stockings, thanks to the stellar pitching of Albert G. "Al" Spalding, were well on their way to their fourth consecutive pennant (as well as a five-year win-loss record of 225–60).[25]

William Hulbert, however, had a different scenario in mind for the following season, for in July 1875, he had quietly signed Boston's ace pitcher. Spalding would not only join the White Stockings as field manager (captain), replacing non-playing manager Jimmy Wood, but would also assume the club's secretarial responsibilities. Hulbert also received commitments from Spalding's teammates Ross Barnes, James "Deacon" White, and Cal McVey, as well as two stars of the Philadelphia Athletics, Adrian Anson and Ezra Sutton (though the latter changed his mind and remained with the Athletics).

> Minutes of July 16, 1875, meeting of directors of the Chicago Base Ball Association. Record book of the Board of Directors of the Chicago Base Ball Association. Chicago Cubs Records, box 4, volume 4. Chicago History Museum.
>
>> Meeting held at Dexters Old Store on 22nd Street Friday evening July 16th 1875
>> Present Gage Wadsworth Dexter Bartlett + Hulbert—
>> Meeting called to hear Hulberts report
>> Hulbert stated to meeting that pursuant to instructions of Directory (meeting July 3) he had visited Boston New York + Philadelphia[.][26] That he had had a long and full conference with Mr A. G. Spalding and that he had finally entered into an arrangment [sic] with Mr Spalding—and that preliminary Articles of Agreement were duly drawn and signed by Spalding + Hulbert (acting in behalf of the Association)[.] Viz—The Association guarantees Mr Spalding a salary of Two thousand dollars for the season of 1876 and in addition twenty five per cent of the <u>net</u> profits arriving from the business of the Association for the season of 1876—These provisions to be incorporated in the <u>general</u> contract with said Spalding—A special or sub contract also to be made with Spalding conveynying [sic] thirty per cent of the net profits arriving from the business of the Ass^n for 1876—(The provisions of the sub contract it was agreed should be kept a secret—i.e. no persons outside the directory, were, under any circumstances, to be made aquainted [sic] with its provisions)—
>>
>> It was further agreed that Mr Spalding should by the Directory of the Ass^n be duly elected "Manager" and that his term of Office should be from Novr. 1st 1875 to Nov 15th 1876—
>>
>> The understanding and agreement with Mr Spalding—(and Mr Hulbert as representative of the Association—promised in behalf of his fellow Directors that the same should in good faith be carried out)—was that Spalding was to have charge, of and conduct in his own person, all the detail business of the Association—The supervision of the Directory to be general—It being of course understood, that the Directory should have full control of the general policy of the club—but they are expected to act as a <u>body</u> and not in their individual capacity—
>>
>> The following named players were also engaged by Mr Hulbert—
>>
>>> Mr Roscoe C Barnes   salary $2,000
>>>   and twenty five per cent net profits business of the Ass^n season 1876—
>>> Calvin A. McVey   salary   2,000
>>>   Contract for two years from Nov 1/75—salary payable Monthly—
>>> Ja^s White   salary   2,400
>>> $100 Additional provided club proves financial success
>>> Adrian C. Anson   salary   2,000
>>> $50 paid in cash $150 to be paid when regular contract is signed
>>> Ezra B Sutton   salary   2,000
>>> $50 paid in cash $350 in installments during Winter
>>> Jno P. Peters   salary   1,500

The foregoing is a fair transcript of what Mʳ Hulbert said and his action is approved by us, and we hereby ratify + confirm the same[.]

[Signed]
Chas. S. Bartlett   Geo. W. Gage
E. F. Dexter   Philip Wadsworth

◆ ◆ ◆

Despite the attempts of White Stocking officials to keep their player acquisitions a secret, word soon leaked out, and the *Tribune* broke the story on July 20. A few days later, the newspaper revealed how officials of the Boston club first learned of Chicago's coup in securing the "Big Four," as Al Spalding, Deacon White, Ross Barnes, and Cal McVey were commonly referred to in baseball circles:

> To say that the Boston managers were surprised at the news of the split in their nine is to give but a slight idea of their feeling. They were stunned. They got their first intimation on Tuesday noon, while dining at Taunton [Massachusetts], where they were playing the Taunton nine, eight hours after THE TRIBUNE had published the fact. McVey remarked casually that he wasn't going to play ball in Boston next year. This didn't surprise [manager] Harry [Wright], for he thought it a jest; but after dinner he spoke to White, who said that he, Spalding, McVey, and Barnes had agreed to go to Chicago.[27]

The managers of the Boston Red Stockings were not the only ones stunned by the announcement. The city's fans were particularly devastated when they heard that their beloved team, whose record had given them bragging rights throughout the baseball world, was to break up.

Untitled editorial. *Worcester (Massachusetts) Daily Spy*, July 24, 1875, p. 2. [Note: This editorial originally appeared as one long passage, and a paragraph break has been added for ease of readability.]

Boston is in mourning. Like Rachel weeping for her children, she refuses to be comforted because the famous base ball nine, the perennial champions, the city's most cherished possession, has been captured by Chicago. "There is probably no paragraph of news this week," says the [Boston Daily] Advertiser, "that has caused so much real vexation out of doors as this." Boston sacrificed the Paddock elms cheerfully, and awaits with composure the loss of the Old South. She bore with wonderful fortitude the wasting of her finest business streets and the destruction of untold millions of property in the great fire, but she has never known real bereavement before. The blow is prostrating. "Take any shape but this," she cries in her anguish. She could bear to lose the great organ, Faneuil Hall, or the Ancient and Honorable Artillery company, though she sets a high value on each of them, but she can not smile through her tears in parting with the Boston nine. Of course she is grieved at the manner of their taking off, the cutting ingratitude of their desertion. They had a right to go if they chose, but since Boston's pride in them was something unique, compounded of admiration and confidence, it is thought that they should at least have given an opportunity to test the desire that they should remain.

Chicago perhaps promises them higher wages than they have received in Boston, but in their residence of several years in the latter city they should have learned that Boston has rewards, in comparison with which money is contemptible, to bestow upon her illustrious sons and faithful servants. Money, indeed, she does not spare to gratify her affections or her pride, but she would have tempted the hesitating champions with nobler gifts if they had given her the opportunity. They might have had their portraits in Faneuil Hall, or their statues in the public garden over against that pitcher, dignified and graceful, but not quite up to the champion standard of animation and energy, who now stands there in enduring bronze. Such honors as those would not be too great for [Al] Spalding, for whom as a pitcher there is no substitute in the country, or for [Deacon] White, the catcher, who has no equal behind the bat. Perhaps [Ross] Barnes and [Cal] McVey ought to be content with more moderate honors, since their places, the Advertiser admits, may be fairly supplied, adding, however, "We do not believe they are likely to be filled with men as good in the field, with the bat and at base running." Perhaps a vote of thanks from the city council would be considered an adequate testimonial to their merit. But if so much would have been conceded to these members of the nine, what reward is too great for Capt. Harry Wright, who has organized victory, and so often helped to achieve it, and who stands by his colors, "among the faithless, faithful only he!" Men far less worthy have been immortalized in bronze and marble. Boston must devise some new form of distinction for the man who she chiefly delights to honor. The Advertiser manfully exhorts to "all the cheerfulness possible under the disastrous blow." The advice is good, but it is of little avail just now, while the wound is still fresh. We understand that tears fell fast in Boston yesterday, and they had a very damp and melancholy time.

◆ ◆ ◆

After catcher Deacon White read the article in the *Boston Daily Advertiser* that the Worcester newspaper mentioned, he wrote a letter to the *Boston Daily Globe* to "correct the erroneous impression" that he was obligated to stay with the Red Stockings for another season. He said that he had met with club president Nicholas Apollonio that spring, right before the team set off on its western tour. Apollonio wanted him to stay with the Red Stockings, "but at the same time," White explained, he "gave me to understand in plain terms that their salary list was as high as they could afford to pay, and, to use his own words, 'they could not and did not propose to compete with "fancy" western prices.'" The ballplayer added that Chicago later offered him "the 'fancy' price that the Boston Club did not propose to compete with."

White's justification for leaving Boston did little to appease eastern baseball fans and journalists, who branded him and his teammates as "seceders"—hardly a term of affection in this post–Civil War era. The Chicago White Stockings were also roundly criticized, as newspapers and magazines across the country protested the barefaced audacity of the club's strategic business move. *Forest and Stream* fumed that "there are apparently two ways of getting at the base ball whip pennant—the one is by winning it squarely by superior play in the field, and the other is to break up the team which is successful in holding it year after year, and then try and wedge your new team into the vacant place edgeways." The *New York Clipper* editorially vented its own sharp opinion: "No sooner does Boston show her ability to be champion ball-tosser, than Chicago seeks to overthrow her and rob her of her well-deserved laurels by inducing several of the champions to 'go West,' for a certain consideration, the consideration being sums ranging from two thousand dollars up to four thousand per player, the manager, Spalding, being promised the latter sum, we are told."[28]

Al Spalding was probably well worth that amount; however, the July 16 minutes of the Chicago Base Ball Association stipulated that his salary for 1876 would be half the sum the *New York Clipper* printed, though he would also receive 25 percent of the year's net profit. The team's new pitcher and captain was one of the best known—and one of the most formidable—players during these early years of baseball. In his youth he had pitched for the Forest City Club of Rockford, Illinois, and in 1867, when he was just 16 years old, he had helped defeat the powerful Washington Nationals team. Three years later, with the young man as its pitcher, the Forest Citys dealt Cincinnati one of the Red Stockings' few losses that season. After the Red Stockings disbanded in November 1870, their player-manager, Harry Wright, moved to Boston to organize a new team. Wright and the Boston Red Stockings lured Spalding away from Rockford in 1871, thereby launching the National Association's only baseball dynasty. Just as the Red Stockings dominated the league in pennants, Spalding as top pitcher led the association in game victories.[29]

With Al Spalding poised to return home to Illinois, William Hulbert intended that the White Stockings collect those victories. The truth be told, at about this time the Chicago team needed some favorable publicity as well as a few wins. A 5-2 loss normally would not raise any questions, but during a 12-inning match between the White Stockings and the Philadelphia Pearls on June 24, both sides were charged with 21 errors—11 to Philadelphia and 10 to Chicago. Two days later, the *Chicago Daily Tribune* revealed what had led to such poor playing: After the White Stockings learned during the game that the Pearls had conspired with gamblers and were attempting to purposely lose, the Chicago players themselves also tried to lose in retaliation for not being included in the crooked deal. With each team doing its best to throw the game to the other, the competition was literally a "comedy of errors," though the paper and the city's fans were not laughing. "There has been just enough of this suspicious business in base ball in Chicago," the *Tribune* lashed out, "and it would be better for the game if the crowd would tear down the fence and stands rather than ever suffer another player to be bought or sold on Chicago ground."

The indignant *Tribune* was not yet through with the White Stockings, for on June 27 it angrily insisted that "there seems no good excuse for keeping up the present Chicago nine. They are not what Chicago wants, and already the public is thoroughly disgusted with them." In another article published the same day, the paper declared that "the recent revelations in base-ball matters show that that noble and healthful game is being operated in the behoof of betting men, and it is quite certain, if managements wish to preserve the respectability which it has hitherto enjoyed, they must act summarily in weeding out the purchaseable material."

William Hulbert and his club officers apparently took the paper's words to heart. Catcher and team captain Dick Higham purportedly had overthrown second base to help the Pearls, and on June 29 the *Tribune* announced that the White Stockings' directors had removed him from his baseball duties, "for today's game at least." In addition, they appointed left fielder John Glenn to replace him as captain. The club officials also offered a reward of $500 "for evidence to prove that any member of the nine has been tampered with in any way in connection with the playing of games."[30]

Higham resumed his normal position behind the plate within a week. Although no mention was made of the reward money, the *Tribune* later noted that the White Stockings had "gotten rid of her suspected players." Even so, Hulbert realized that more needed to be accomplished to return the sport to, as the newspaper had written on June 27, "that noble and healthful game." For starters, baseball officials themselves had to accept—and act on—*Forest and Stream*'s curt summation of the situation: "The existing National Association of Professional [Base Ball] Players is an organization which can be run in the interests of either the honest or the knavish class of the professional players of the country." Hulbert and a few like-minded team executives chose the former, and rumors soon began to circulate about a "Western clique" of baseball clubs that were determined to restructure the association. At the forefront of this faction was Hulbert, though he had in mind not merely a few organizational changes but rather the National Association's demise and the formation of a new national league.

Helping William Hulbert alter the course of baseball was his friend Lewis Meacham, a sports reporter for the *Chicago Daily Tribune*. On October 24, 1875, shortly before the end of the season, the *Tribune* ran a piece undoubtedly written by Meacham titled "The Professional Base Ball Association—What It Must Do to Be Saved." Because the article reflects Hulbert's thoughts on the subject, modern-day sports historians credit the journalist as the "mouthpiece" and public voice of the White Stockings president; in fact, even the *Tribune*'s 1882 obituary of Hulbert acknowledges that he and Meacham "matured the plan of the National League."[31]

The early success of the White Stockings—and of baseball itself—was due to William Ambrose Hulbert. As secretary of the Chicago Base Ball Association, he signed some of the sport's top players for the 1876 season. He saw firsthand that baseball's National Association could not adequately govern the teams and the players, and before the season had even started he spearheaded the formation of a new administrative body, the National League. His White Stockings won the league's inaugural championship, and under his watch the team also captured National League pennants in 1880 and 1881.

Hulbert had been elected president of the Chicago Base Ball Association in the fall of 1875 and president of the National League in December of 1876. He held both offices until his death on April 10, 1882. At its annual meeting in December that year, the National League adopted several resolutions, one of which recognized "that to [Hulbert] alone is due the credit of having founded this League, and to his able leadership, sound judgment and impartial management, are chiefly due the success it has thus far attained." William Hulbert was inducted into the National Baseball Hall of Fame in 1995 (Adrian C. Anson, *A Ball Player's Career*, 1900).

"Sporting. The Professional Base Ball Association—What It Must Do to Be Saved. The Coming Trouble for the Game and Its Remedy." *Chicago Daily Tribune*, October 24, 1875, p. 12.

BASE BALL.
A VITAL QUESTION FOR 1876.

A glance over the ball-field for the season now nearly closed presents a problem for 1876 of more than ordinary importance to the game as an exhibition. At the beginning of this season thirteen clubs entered for the championship; three have disbanded, and three more—the Atlantic, New Haven, and St. Louis Reds—are out of the championship race by reason of not having played any return games. Of the last-named three, the Atlantics are

A SAMPLE OF TOO MANY
PROFESSIONAL CLUBS;

they had never any organization, any association, any backing, or any elements of permanency or responsibility of any kind; they were simply a gang of amateurs and rejected professionals, who played such clubs as they could get to come to them, and shared the proceeds. They were not even a mob, for a mob must have a head. During the season so far they have played thirty-eight different men in their nine, and it has been too evident that whenever a game was to come off some one went out into the highways and byways and picked up almost the first nine he met. No one supposes that they ever intended to play any Western games; they simply entered the ring to force clubs to play as many games as possible with them, they taking two-thirds the receipts as on home ground. No large audiences have attended their games, because nobody felt any interest in the gang, and first-class visiting clubs under heavy expense have lost money every time they played with them, while the two-thirds which went to the gang was reason enough to induce them to get on as many games as they could.

A great part of this same description would apply to

THE ST. LOUIS REDS,

whose manager is said to have announced in March that he did not intend to go East at all. The club in question was formed by a man who thought he could make something out of a ball field on some ground controlled by him. In forming the club the manager calculated on nothing more than a few games on his own ground and then a country tour.

The case of the New Haven Club was somewhat different, and their fault appears to have been more that they went into the ball business without counting the cost than that they meant to deal unfairly with anybody. The town is too small to support a club, and yet the intense rivalry between it and Hartford led to the establishment of one which could not be sustained.

Now this same trick is to be attempted in 1876. Already announcements are made for the following

CLUBS FOR 1876,

eighteen in all:

Chicago [White Stockings],	Philadelphia [White Stockings],
St. Louis [Brown Stockings],	Americus [of Philadelphia],
Cincinnati [Red Stockings],	New Haven [Elm Citys],
Louisville [Grays],	Atlantic [of Brooklyn],
Mutual [of New York],	St. Louis Reds,
New York [a new club],	Buffalo [Bisons],
Hartford [Dark Blues],	Cleveland [Blues],
Boston [Red Stockings],	Burlington [Illinois]
Athletic [of Philadelphia],	Washington [Nationals of D.C.].[32]

Some of these enterprises may be still-born, but others will spring up to take their places, and the Centennial year will be opened with not less than a dozen and a half professional clubs. This may be fun for the little fellows, but it will be death to the first nine clubs named, who are really the only ones in the list who have much showing of permanency.

It may be asked why the advent of more clubs and a more general interest in the game will hurt it. The answer is

STATISTICAL:

the ball season in Chicago lasts about six months, or, in round numbers, 180 days. Deduct from this Sundays, rainy days, time used in traveling and in needed rest, and it will be seen that not more than ninety (or at the outside 100) games can be played. The total expense account of the Chicago Club for next year will approximate $28,000, and others in the ring will reach somewhat near the same figures. Thus it may be seen that every championship game played by the Chicago Club in 1876 will cost the management not far from $300. Nine clubs have been referred to above as on a solid basis; ten games all around, as this year, would give eighty games for each club and forty for each city which sustains a club, and this would give the nines some leeway, to be used in playing amateurs or exhibition games. On this plan every club of the nine first named could live respectably, pay good salaries, and perhaps a modest dividend, and put the exhibition on a sound basis.

ON THE OTHER HAND,

if the whole gang be let in, half of the games will not pay expenses. The best clubs in the country have played championship games for receipts of $10, $20, $30, when their opponents were the second class of clubs. Games of this class have been played this year with the St. Louis Reds, the Keokuks, the Washingtons, the Atlantics, and the New Havens. It doesn't require much figuring to see that this is a losing business where the game actually costs the first-class club from ten to twenty times what it takes in.

It may be noted that the Chicago Club played four games in Philadelphia on its present trip, and that their hotel bills in the city during their stay were more by $60 than their receipts from all the five games. This has a bearing on another point discussed further on.

The question which agitates the club management is,

"WHAT CAN WE DO ABOUT IT?"

They see the trouble ahead and are trying to work out their financial salvation. They know well enough that if eighteen clubs come into the ring next year, the poorest half of the list will utterly swamp the whole and destroy the prospects of the whole game. At the same time, the managers say they can hardly see how to keep the duffers out. It has been the custom to vote everybody in who applied, and unless some concerted action be at once taken the same thing will be done at the professional association this winter.

The remedy is not difficult, and it lies in the hands of a few men. When the Professional Association meets it should at once adopt the following

PRINCIPLES TO GOVERN THE CHAMPIONSHIP CONTESTS

for next year:

First—No club should be allowed to enter for the championship unless it be backed by a responsible association, financially capable of finishing a season when begun.

This, if adopted, would cut off the Atlantic Club and other co-operative frauds.

Second—No club should be admitted from a city of less size than 100,000 inhabitants,—excepting only Hartford.

This would cut off the New Havens and other clubs in places so small that, under the most favorable circumstances, a first-class club could never expect to get its expenses paid for going to them.

Third—No two clubs should be admitted from the same city.

The evil effects of having more than one club in a city have been shown in Philadelphia this year. First, the Centennials went under, and then the Philadelphias and Athletics divided the interest, so that both of them have ended the season at a loss, poorer than poverty, and owing their players. One club can live in Philadelphia, but two must starve—not only themselves, but visiting clubs. This is shown in the statement of White Stocking receipts given above. And it is well known that the Athletic Club owes $6,000 as its showing for the year, while the Philadelphias are not much better off—or would not be but for some peculiar practices.

Fourth—The faith of the management of a club should be shown by the deposit of $1,000, or perhaps $1,500, in the hands of the association before the season begins. This sum not to be played for, but returned to each club which carries out its agreements and plays its return games. If it refuses to play all the games that it agrees to, let the sum be forfeited.

The adoption of these restrictions would limit the contestants next year to Chicago, Cincinnati, St. Louis, and Louisville in the West; Athletic, New York, and Mutual in the Middle States, and Hartford and Boston in the East; and with such an association the game would be prosperous, and the people who attended championship games would have a guarantee that they were to see the best clubs and the best games possible.

It may be doubted whether the Professional Association will be willing to vote the restrictions proposed, and, if they do not, it will be

THE PLAIN DUTY

of the nine clubs named to withdraw from the Association as it now stands, and form an organization of their own,—a close corporation, too. Every club which has a backing should discuss this matter before the meeting of [the] Professional Association, and so instruct their representative that he will feel at liberty to take such action as may be for the best interests of the game.

◆ ◆ ◆

Epilogue

One week after the *Chicago Daily Tribune* published Meacham's (and Hulbert's) manifesto, the newspaper covered the end of the 1875 baseball year. Of the 13 original teams, the Philadelphia Centennials, the Keokuk Westerns, and the Washington Nationals had disbanded during the season, while the St. Louis Reds, the Brooklyn Atlantics, and the New Haven Elm Citys did not play all of their scheduled games and posted few victories in the games they did play.

Boston, with 71 wins, eight losses, and three ties, finished the season 18½ games in front of the second-place Hartford Dark Blues, who ended with a 54–28–4 record. Chicago closed the year in sixth place, a distant 35 games out of first and just ½ game ahead of the New York Mutuals. The White Stockings' record of 30–37–2 did not inspire much hope for the future, particularly when the *Tribune* reminded readers of the team's mediocre performance in 1874, when they ended up "fifth in a field of eight."

The newspaper also included in its baseball coverage the number of base hits made by every man who had played in the National Association in 1875. Heading the list was slugger Ross Barnes, and close on his heels were Deacon White and Cal McVey. Perhaps the knowledge that these three ballplayers would be wearing White Stockings uniforms the following year led the sportswriter to add a note of bravado to his article. Next to a chart listing end-of-the-season team standings was a declaration about the Chicago players that may have both heartened the city's fans and warned opposing clubs: "We shall see what 'the boys of '76' will do, when the table is made up a year hence."[33]

New faces were on the horizon for the Chicago White Stockings. And "the boys of '76" would be working hard to ensure that that year's table would be dramatically different from the one in 1875.

4

WILLIAM HULBERT AND THE FIRST LEAGUE PENNANT (1875–1876)

> The *New York Sportsman*, one of the higher grade of sporting papers, has the following paragraph: "The Chicagos are now considered to have the championship within their grasp, and many people will be glad of it. [Al] Spalding's fine management, and the able co-operation of such men as [Ross] Barnes, [Deacon] White, and [Cal] McVey, certainly deserve the reward in reserve for all honest and capable nines, and it is gratifying to the friends of Mr. [William] Hulbert, the President of the Chicago Club, that his endeavors and indefatigability will be recognized and appreciated."
> —*Chicago Daily Tribune*, August 6, 1876

Baseball pitcher Albert G. "Al" Spalding was impressed with White Stockings president William A. Hulbert and his no-nonsense manner as soon as he met him in early 1875. "He seemed strong, forceful, self-reliant," Spalding recalled years later. "I admired his business-like way of considering things…. He was a master of [the] business system."

After dealing with a variety of complicated issues in the National Association of Professional Base Ball Players, Hulbert knew that he had to master the business of baseball. As for Spalding, he was looking forward to some changes in his life. The succession of Red Stockings championships "was becoming monotonous," he admitted. With Boston victorious in most of its games, fans were losing interest in baseball as there were few close contests and even fewer tight pennant races. Furthermore, Spalding saw firsthand the many deficiencies of the National Association and wanted to assist Hulbert in improving the situation. "I was sick and sore of existing conditions; ready to get away from them—the sooner the better," Spalding wrote in his baseball memoir. Hulbert was gratified by the attitude of the young pitcher, whom the *New York Clipper* praised not only for his skill as a baseball player, but also for his "education and gentlemanly qualities [that] place him above the generality of baseball pitchers."

Spalding, like Hulbert, viewed professional baseball in a "business-like way," and they both believed that the sport should be run on sound business principles. They felt that if the owners, not the players, were in charge and if strict rules and guidelines were followed, the team executives could then turn substantial profits on their investments. Of course, the two men also realized that the success of their plans depended upon the support of these baseball officials, who may or may not agree with their ideas.[1]

Fortunately, Hulbert possessed some financial leverage that could help sway a few votes. His Chicago White Stockings, thanks to their enthusiastic fan base, routinely drew large crowds. Hefty ticket sales consequently resulted in substantial revenue for both the home team (which received two-thirds of the gate receipts) and visiting clubs (which were given the other third). In 1869 the price of a ticket had been 25 cents, but by the early 1870s, a person paid 50 cents to attend a professional game.

One thousand spectators at a game was considered a respectable turn-out, but most of the time Chicago at least doubled that figure for its home competitions; when prominent clubs were in town, attendance soared even higher. Sportswriters in the 1870s often overestimated baseball attendance figures, but according to one Chicago newspaper, "between 7,000 and 8,000" fans swarmed to the 23rd Street Grounds for a June 8, 1875, White Stockings game against Boston.[2]

To show how the White Stockings supported eastern teams, in November the *Chicago Daily Tribune* published "some financial figures." The newspaper listed the income of eastern clubs for the games they had played in Chicago during 1874 and 1875 and contrasted the dollar amounts with the money that the White Stockings had earned during their away games in those same cities. For example, the five games that Boston played in Chicago that season enabled the visitors to earn $2,983, an average of about $596 a game. On the other hand, when the White Stockings that year played in Boston, the Chicago players took home just $1,038 for the five games, or about $207 per game. Ballplayers were certainly well aware of this pay differential, for as *The Spirit of the Times* sporting newspaper commented about Chicago games, "It pays out there, the boys say." In fact, those eastern boys occasionally earned more money, even with travel expenses, playing in Chicago than they did in cities and towns closer to home.

The *Tribune* was quick to point out that although the Philadelphia White Stockings had received, on average, almost exactly the same amount each year it played Chicago at the 23rd Street Grounds ($219 in 1874 and $214 in 1875), the Chicago White Stockings' share of the proceeds for their games in Philadelphia had decreased by more than 50 percent (from $143 in 1874 to $58 in 1875). The newspaper also explained that the "suicidal policy" of one city maintaining two ball clubs (in this case Philadelphia with both its White Stockings and Athletics) naturally diluted fan attendance.

In a summary of its examination, the *Tribune* contended:

> In order to make these figures general in their application it may be said that in 1874 Eastern clubs played twenty-eight games in Chicago and received an average of $399 a game, while in the same year the Chicagos played thirty-one games East and received an average of $132. In 1875 the Eastern clubs played twenty-four games in Chicago, and received an average of $296, while during the same year the Chicagos played twenty-eight games East, and received an average of $88 each game.[3]

The *Tribune* concluded that the "moral of this preachment" was that the western teams "must be treated as an equal" by the teams in the East. Hulbert had not forgotten the Davy Force incident in Philadelphia, and in December 1875, he and Spalding took their first step towards demanding that equality. That month the two men, along with *Chicago Daily Tribune* journalist Lewis Meacham, secretly met in Louisville, Kentucky, with representatives of three western clubs: Charles A. Fowle and Nathaniel Hazard (St. Louis Brown Stockings); Walter N. Haldeman, Charles E. Chase, and Thomas Shirley (Louisville Grays); and John A. Joyce (Cincinnati Red Stockings). The Chicagoans had already drafted a constitution for a new baseball league, and the group pored over the document and talked about their plans to revamp the sport. It was a "thorough and animated discussion," according to Spalding, and during the two-day organizational meeting "the revolution was then and there decided upon." The men selected Hulbert and Fowle to contact the eastern clubs of Boston, New York, Philadelphia (the Athletics), and Hartford. On January 23, 1876, the two baseball executives wrote the team presidents the following letter:

> The undersigned have been appointed by the Chicago, Cincinnati, Louisville, and St. Louis Clubs a committee to confer with you on matters of interest to the game at large, with special reference to the reformation of existing abuses, and the formation of a new association, and we are clothed with full authority in writing from the above named clubs to bind them to any arrangement we may make with you. We therefore invite your club to send a representative clothed with like authority to meet us at the Grand Central Hotel, in the City of New York, on Wednesday, the 2d day of February next, at 12 m[eridiem]. After careful consideration of the needs of the professional clubs, the organizations we represent are of the firm belief that existing circumstances demand prompt and vigorous action by those who are the natural sponsors of the game. It is the earnest recommendation of our constituents that all past troubles and differences be ignored and forgotten, and that the conference we propose shall be a calm, friendly, and deliberate discussion, looking solely to the general good of the clubs who are calculated to give character and permanency to the game. We are confident that the propositions we have to submit will meet with your approval and support, and we shall be pleased to meet you at the time and place above mentioned.
>
> Yours respectfully,
> W. A. HULBERT,
> CHAS. A. FOWLE.[4]

Baseball in Old Chicago (1939) mentions that people who knew Hulbert described him as having "a forceful, magnetic personality." Perhaps he used that to good advantage in early 1876, for delegates from all four eastern clubs attended his and Fowle's New York City meeting. Hulbert and Fowle represented the western clubs of Chicago, Louisville, Cincinnati, and St. Louis; other emissaries included Nicholas Apollonio and Harry Wright (Boston), Morgan Bulkeley (Hartford), George W. Thompson and Al Reach (Philadelphia Athletics), William H. Cammeyer (New York), and Nicholas E. Young, secretary of the National Association and former White Stockings manager, who would become the league's secretary and treasurer. Al Spalding wrote years later that when details of the new plan and formation of a new league were explained to the eastern representatives, "They entered into it with enthusiasm; and the result was, then and there, the organization of the present National League of professional base-ball clubs."

The men ratified a new constitution, which effectively changed baseball's governing organization from an association of players to a league of clubs. Each team's league entry fee was $100 (as compared to the National Association's meager assessment of $10, which often led to irresponsible and mediocre teams applying for membership). To ensure steady and sizable gate receipts, the constitution stipulated that no club could be admitted to the National League from a city of fewer than 75,000 residents, "except by unanimous vote of the League." Furthermore, no club from the same city as a member club—or from a locality within five miles of the city—could be admitted to the league. The constitution also included sections on clubs forfeiting league membership, the handling of disputes and complaints, player contracts, gambling, and playing and field rules. A five-man board of directors would govern the eight-team league and help enforce regulations.

The season's schedule called for 70 games, with each team playing its seven opponents five games at home and five games away; these games could not be played on Sundays. The club that won the most games would be entitled to fly the league pennant during the subsequent baseball season. According to the constitution, "The emblem of the championship shall be a pennant (of the national colors).... It shall be inscribed with the motto, 'Champion Base Ball Club of the United States,' with the name of the club and the year in which the title was won."[5]

On February 13, the *Chicago Daily Tribune* summarized the "effect of the formation" of the National League of Professional Base Ball Clubs: "It will make first-class games more frequent, and will tend to more evenly match the clubs, because within a year almost every superior and honest player in the country will be in one of the League organizations.... There is no reason why the game should not be as honorably managed as a bank, and perhaps it will be,—anyway the League has done its part in the matter; and the prophecy is herewith ventured that it will be successful." Hulbert's work to ensure that success helped speed the inevitable demise of the old National Association. Morgan Bulkeley of the Hartford club became the National League's first president, but Hulbert still remained at the forefront of league activities.

The hands-on Chicago executive also remained committed to the success of the White Stockings. With new men such as pitcher Al Spalding and catcher James "Deacon" White on board, he undoubtedly felt that the team could make a strong run for the 1876 championship pennant. Newspapers and magazines—including some that had roundly chastised the club for "breaking up" the famed Boston Red Stockings—admitted that the talented Chicago players would be a formidable presence on the ball diamond. The *New York World* profiled the various teams scheduled to play in the National League's inaugural season, and of the White Stockings it wrote: "The nine will contain the most effective pitcher and the best catcher in the professional fraternity, and the other players are up to the highest standard, while all are thoroughly reliable men." The *New York Times* praised team captain Spalding and concluded that "the Chicago Club is, individually, stronger than any of the strong nines they have yet put forth." The well-known sporting publication, the *New York Clipper*, had predicted in August 1875 that some teams would certainly "do their best to polish off Chicago!" Furthermore, the *Clipper* continued, with assorted rival clubs competing with one another, "Things will be hot and lively next year."[6]

That "hot and lively" season of 1876 opened with the eight charter members of the National League of Professional Base Ball Clubs in contention for the championship pennant: Boston, Chicago, Cincinnati, Hartford, Louisville, New York, Philadelphia, and St. Louis. With games scheduled to begin in April, the White Stockings started assembling in Chicago in early March to begin their training sessions. The Chicago newspapers reported that due to the inclement spring weather, they had begun practicing in the gymnasium at the Chicago Athenaeum on Washington Street for about four hours a day. "A padded partition has been erected at one end of the room for the benefit of the pitcher and catcher," wrote the *Chicago Post and Mail*, "and a swinging sand-bag furnishes facilities for the development of muscle in the way of batting." Concluded the *Chicago Daily Tribune*: The players "have now worked off the first soreness, and are as nimble as cats,—all except [John] Peters, whose way of getting up a ball is fitly compared to that of a sparrow picking up a worm."[7]

Both newspapers also told their readers that the White Stockings would soon take the field in new uniforms. During the preceding season the team had worn heavy white flannel uniforms with the collars and cuffs trimmed in blue. As described in an April 1875 newspaper article, each shirt had the word "Chicago" sewn across the front in black letters, "handsomely embroidered with a dark background of blue. The knee-breeches are white and of the same material, with a blue cord down the sides.... A jaunty white-flannel cap, 'white stockings,' and shoes made to order" completed the outfit.

The uniforms of 1876 would be fairly similar to the older ones, though they would not have the word "Chicago" embroidered on the shirt fronts. Also, instead of the "jaunty" white caps, team captain Spalding furnished each of his men with a different colored cap so that spectators would be able to tell the players apart. Game score cards listed each man's name next to the color of his cap. Although a *Tribune* reporter initially felt that "a collection of heads under the proposed plan would look like a Dutch bed of tulips," he later conceded that "it is fair to say that [the caps] do not look by any means as badly as might have been expected. They are square-topped, and have the colors in bands on the side and in solid color on top."[8]

The sportswriter may have had misgivings about the colorful new caps, but he enthusiastically approved of the club's lease of a "fine mansion" for the ballplayers' clubhouse. Located at the southeast corner of Wabash Avenue and 23rd Street, the two-story Gothic frame house was just slightly more than a block from the White Stockings' grounds and contained a reception room, parlor, reading room, and billiard room. The reporter exclaimed that "the new move is a most excellent one and will work to the good of the men in many ways. It will relieve them of the necessity of or excuse for standing around street corners, as some of last year's nine were in the habit of doing; and will give them an excellent place for billiards and other games to pass away what time the manager does not require them to put in practice. Other first-class clubs have always had club-houses, but it has remained for the present management of the Chicagos to fit up one of the finest establishments of the kind in the country."

After the long winter, the ballpark, too, needed a bit of "fitting up," including some fresh paint here and there, a new fence along the east side of the enclosure, and a few other improvements. By the first part of April the players had all reported for spring training, and, with opening day fast approaching, baseball fans avidly devoured news stories about the men and their activities. A few months earlier, a *Tribune* sportswriter had interviewed team captain Al Spalding. Judging from the leading questions, the anonymous reporter was likely Lewis Meacham, who shared Spalding's and Hulbert's thoughts on reorganizing baseball. During a discussion of the "prominent clubs for 1876," for example, the writer asked Spalding if it was true that the better teams were in the West. "'You are perfectly right,' promptly answered our informant, 'the four best clubs are located in Louisville, Cincinnati, St. Louis and Chicago.'" Following are Spalding's remarks about the White Stockings:

"The Chicago nine consist of [Deacon] White, c.; [Al] Spalding, p.; [Cal] McVey, 1st b.; [Ross] Barnes, 2d b.; [Adrian] Anson, 3d b.; [John] Peters, s. s.; [John] Glenn, l. f.; [Paul] Hines, c. f.; [Bob] Addy or [Oscar] Bielaski, r. f. Also, [Fred] Cone as assistant business manager, and to be in condition to play should occasion demand. This gives Chicago eleven good men."

WHO THEY ARE.

"White is recognized as the best catcher in the country. He first made his appearance with the Forest City Club, at Cleaveland [*sic*]. He was with the Boston nine at the time of their departure for England, but did not go. Mr. White is a very exemplary young man, and is a good Christian as well as a good ball-player."

"A combination of elements," timidly suggested the reporter, "rarely met with."

Mr. Spalding affected not to observe this remark, and hurried on at a much faster rate.

"Of myself, it will suffice to say that I made my *debut* with the Forest City Club, in 1866, and remained with them until 1871, when I joined the Bostons. I was sent over to England to negotiate for the European games, and afterwards went with the club to that country.

"McVey is a native of Iowa (the Chicago nine is composed of nearly all Western men). He is one of the strongest and best winning players, and is considered the best batter in the profession. Barnes is from Rockford. He joined the Forest City Club [in] 1867, and went to England with the Bostons. He is rightly called the best general base-ball player in the country. It is an indisputable fact that

HE LED THE BATTING AVERAGE

of the Boston Club all the time he remained in it. It would be no vain boast to say that he has led the batting average of the world—in fact, McVey and Barnes are acknowledged the best batters in the world. Anson is also a Western man, being a native of Iowa, and is a thorough representative of the sturdy Western breed. He stands 6 feet 3 inches, and his pluck and endurance is only equal to his strength and size. He is a strong batter, and is one of those fellows who never know when they are whipped. We expect that Anson will show us some fine play at third base next season. The three years that he played in Rockford bears me out in this opinion.

AN INFANT PHENOMENA.

"Peters may not inappropriately be termed the infant phenomena. He made his first appearance as a professional player last year, and exhibited some excellent qualification[s]. He is a good base-runner, first-rate batter, and withal a good general player. He is very popular in Chicago, and has always been connected with a Chicago club, and is a great favorite in the city. Glenn is from Rochester, N. Y. He is an old ball-player, always having been considered very strong, and is thoroughly reliable. His play at left field has not been surpassed this season. He first made his appearance as a professional in Washington. Hines is also from the East. He is a very good batter, and is considered by many as the best out-fielder the game has ever produced. His reputation stands high in Chicago.

ANOTHER ROCKFORD MAN.

"Addy is also a native of Rockford, making his first professional bow in the Rockford Club, and remaining a member until its last breath had been given, and the famous old club ceased to exist. After being with the Bostons a short time, he returned in 1872, and commenced the business of tinsmith at Rockford. In 1873 he joined the Philadelphias, and played with them during the time of their success. He afterwards left them and joined the Bostons again. It was 'Addy's play,' says H.[arry] Wright, 'that won for the Bostons the championship in 1873.' In 1874, Addy played with the Hartfords, and this year he again identified himself with the Philadelphias. Since his engagement with the Chicagos he has had the tempting offer of $2,500 to go East this year; but, though that is more than he will get in Chicago, his regard for principle overbalanced pecuniary benefit, and Addy will lend his cheering presence to the Chicago nine. He is a great base-runner, but added to this his buoyant manner puts life into the game, and the fact that he never gives up frequently stimulates other players at a critical time when the reinstatement of confidence is the most needed. Bielaski is from Washington, and first became eminent as a professional base-ball player four years ago. He has always played right field, where he has no superior. His picking up of sharp hits and throwing men out at first base is his particular hobby, and he frequently carries this hobby to such an extent that it makes it quite distressing for his adversaries. Cone is another Rockford man, and first distinguished himself by playing first base and field in 1871. He has not played much since then. He is engaged by the Chicagos rather more in reference to business ability, though he will be in good condition to keep up his end if called upon."[9]

The Season Starts (1876)

The White Stockings did their best to get in the "good condition" that Spalding had mentioned, despite the cold and rainy spring of 1876. Impatient fans, waiting for the season to begin, read in their newspapers on April 2 that the "unkind weather" was keeping the White Stockings from practicing outside, but that the men were "making up for it by solid work in the gymnasium. No Chicago nine ever went into the field with as much training as the present club has already had in the two or three weeks which they have spent at work."[10]

Not all publications, however, glowingly extolled the virtues of the White Stockings and their training regimen. The *New York Clipper* reviewed and analyzed all of the National League's clubs as to their "respective chances for success in the coming campaign." As the *Clipper* summarized the Chicago ballplayers' strengths and weaknesses, it maintained a cautionary wait-and-see attitude concerning the team's prospects:

Next on the list come the "coming champions," as the sanguine journalists of the Lake City term

THE CHICAGO CLUB,

which is to be run under a new regime this season, and with the following noted players: Albert G. Spalding, p.; James White, c.; Calvin A. McVey, 1st b.; Roscoe C. Barnes, 2d b.; Adrian C. Anson, 3d b.; John P. Peters, s. s.; Paul A. Hines, c. f., Oscar Bielaski, sub.; John W. Glenn; l. f.; J. Fred Cone, sub.; Robert Addy, r. f.; and [Fred] Andrus, the latter of whom has been engaged only on three months' trial. It is not quite certain about Anson, as the latter is making arrangements to open a racket court in Philadelphia, and may not play ball at all this season.

It is a team very strong in home-players for each position; but it is weak in one respect, and that is in not having a regular change pitcher. McVey is ambitious of pitching honors, and he is a fine catcher, but he cannot play both positions at once very well. No nine is complete without two regular pitchers and catchers. Both of these players will get used up at times. Besides which, it is a point in strategic play to change your pitcher at once, if he is at all being punished; and when such change is made it is necessary that the pitcher who replaces the regular player of the nine should have his *own catcher* to catch for him. Each of these positions should be filled by men familiar with each other's play in their respective positions. A catcher should know all the peculiarities of his pitcher's delivery before he can catch from him with the best effect. Many a fine catcher has been misjudged in the estimate made upon his play when facing a pitcher he was not accustomed to; and pitchers who are accustomed to strategic work require a catcher who knows all their signals, and is familiar with their delivery.

White and Spalding work beautifully together; so do [Tom] Miller and [George] Bradley, and [Nat] Hicks and [Bobby] Mathews; so did [Dick] McBride and [John] Clapp.[11] It is this familiarity with each other's playing points—weak and strong together—which will make the Chicago infield so strong. White, Spalding, McVey and Barnes being all at home in their positions. Peters is an earnest worker and a very active short-fielder; but the third base has no special guardian as yet, and the outfield is not so strong as it might be.

Still the team as a whole is the best the club have ever presented, and they *ought* to win the Western championship at least. It will depend a great deal, however, on how the Chicago baseball writers treat the new team. Some players are indifferent to the comments of the press, especially those of the "crooked" class, who, so long as they get chances to play their "own little games," don't "scare worth a cent" at anything the papers say. But your right-dealing, square men, as a class, are sensitive on the subject of press comment; and just such partial criticism as emanates from partisan writers, and the betting class of reporters, plays the mischief with some of the best players. They weaken under it terribly at times. This has been one of the chief obstacles to the success of Chicago club teams. One day it has been fulsome praise after victory, and another day unjust censure and gross abuse following defeat. This kind of thing the new Chicago nine will weaken under, and, therefore, much depends upon how the local press treat them.[12]

The *New York Clipper* failed to consider the integrity of Adrian Anson when it mentioned that he "may not play ball at all this season." The highly respected and popular Athletic had signed a contract to join the White Stockings, but his future wife did not want to leave her family and friends in Philadelphia and begged him to try and get released from his agreement. William Hulbert refused to let him go, and Anson, rather than break his contract like many "revolvers" had, donned a Chicago uniform.

The White Stockings were scheduled to play their first game on April 20. Although spring rains had flooded the 23rd Street Grounds earlier that month, forcing the ballplayers to seek out drier parks for practice, conditions had improved by the time both teams took the field. "The grounds were found in fair shape," commented a reporter, "considering their natural moist failings, and did very well to play on." The White Stockings certainly had no complaints; they easily defeated, 37–6, a team comprised of their own Fred Andrus and Fred Cone plus seven local amateur players.

Two days later, the White Stockings beat the Franklins of Chicago, a baseball club that the *Chicago Daily Tribune* believed to be the strongest team of amateurs in the state. The sportswriter singled out not only the "hard hitting of the professionals" and their "fine, close, active fielding" in his coverage of the 28–3 victory, but also their handsome apparel. The Chicago ballplayers "appeared to rather better advantage" than they had during their previous game, he contended. "The addition of a dark-blue tie to each man's uniform relieved the monotony of clear white, and gave a very pretty effect." With the men's brightly colored caps enhancing that effect, "The Club dress is now the tastiest and neatest in the whole list."[13]

Almost lost in the *Tribune*'s commentary on the grounds and the players' clothing were the brief notations that these games were umpired by Jimmy Wood, the White Stockings' former manager and captain. After Wood had his infected right leg amputated in 1874, he was outfitted with an artificial limb in the spring of 1875. He stayed on as the White Stockings' manager that year, but he lost his position when Al Spalding took over in 1876. On April 9, a small notice in the

Chicago's White Stockings wore ties, as well as their well-known white stockings, as this photograph of Adrian Anson shows (*Literary Digest*, May 6, 1922).

newspaper informed baseball fans that "it is predicted that Jimmy Wood will umpire most of the games out West. It will be the means of saving Eastern clubs a large amount of cash. The cost to bring an umpire from the East is from $50 to $100. 'Woodsey' would make an excellent umpire, as he is honest in his convictions, and by this means he would be enabled to put up a dollar or two for a 'rainy day.'"

The conscientious "Woodsey" apparently enjoyed being back on the ball field. Although he was widely respected, players occasionally took advantage of his good nature, and at least one Franklin team member crassly disparaged his umpiring skills during the game on April 22. A new baseball rule that year stipulated that before a batter received a called third strike, the umpire first had to warn him if, after the second strike, he did not swing at a well-pitched ball (which in essence gave the batter four strikes). A newspaper wrote in its game coverage that "the veteran Jimmy Wood filled the position of umpire satisfactorily, and interpreted the new rules concerning strikes and balls excellently well. The only fault found with him was by a captious Franklin [player], who declared that on one occasion [Wood] got so mixed up that he scratched his wooden leg in despair. This, however, is an unwarranted and unproved assertion."[14]

Another new rule for the National League's inaugural season required the home team to provide the game balls (previously the visiting club furnished them). The *Chicago Daily Tribune* voiced its approval of this change as spectators would then "be able to properly compare the home nine's play with different clubs which was impossible under the old rule when a different kind of ball was used every game."

The *Tribune* had an excellent point, as the composition of the baseball had indeed varied over the years. Throughout the 1860s, the "lively" ball with its large amount of rubber led to long flies, blistering grounders, erratic bounces, and high-scoring games. "Hitting was an easy matter due to lively baseballs and underhand pitching," baseball historian Peter Morris observes in his *A Game of Inches*, "while fielders faced the multiple handicaps of uneven fields, no gloves, and the sun in their eyes."

The amount and type of rubber in the ball fluctuated in the 1870s, but with the formation of the National League came specifications for bats, bases, and a less lively type of baseball. This league-sanctioned "dead" ball—which could still be hit well into the outfield and beyond—was made of woolen yarn and covered with leather; in accordance with 1876 official rules, each ball could "not contain more than one ounce of vulcanized rubber in mould [sic] form" (manufacturers of livelier balls often used as much as four ounces of rubber strips). Despite this mandate, which was well known throughout the sport, for a few years some teams continued to choose baseballs that did not conform to league standards.

Batters during the 1870s and into the 1880s could request "high" (waist to shoulder) and "low" (knee to waist) balls from the pitcher, who threw from just 45 feet from home plate, as opposed to 60½ feet today. This relatively short distance enabled a strong pitcher to complete—and win—40 or more games each season.[15]

In baseball's very early years, umpires issued strikes only when a batter swung and missed. By the 1870s they could call strikes, but they had wide discretion in doing so, for an umpire did not want "to make a batter suffer the ignominy of being called out on strikes." Until the early 1900s, officials did not call foul balls as strikes, though a batter was out if his foul ball was caught on the first bounce. Few batters struck out, as the balls thrown underhanded—at slow speeds compared to overhand pitches—were relatively easy to hit.

Umpires originally did not call balls, but by the 1870s a batter took a walk to first base after nine called balls. "It took nine balls to walk somebody," Bill James explains in his well-known *Baseball Abstract*, "so nobody got too many. Not many walks, not many homers, but lots of singles and lots of errors.... It wasn't at all unusual for a team to make three, four, maybe more errors in an inning—and that made the innings long enough to get out of hand" (that is, additional runs would score).

Batters often got on base not only through errors but also due to "fair-foul" hitting, which played a significant role in early baseball. Prior to 1877, any ball hit into fair territory was deemed a fair ball, even if it rolled foul before passing first or third base. Famed second baseman Ross Barnes was well known for his ability to reach first base by bunting balls that rolled foul; during his years in the National Association, from 1871 through 1875, this expertise helped him compile a staggering batting average of .391.[16]

The White Stockings were counting on that batting prowess when they left Chicago on April 24 for their initial games of the new National League championship season. The *Chicago Daily Tribune* billed the Tuesday, April 25, match with the Louisville Grays as "the first of the Centennial season in the West, and, as such, will interest the entire country." With the United States caught up in 100th anniversary celebrations, such embellishment is understandable. The Centennial Exposition would open in just a few weeks in Philadelphia—where Alexander Graham Bell would demonstrate his recently patented "speaking telegraph"—and Americans were in a celebratory mood.

As it turned out, the game clearly did warrant some attention, as Chicago's Al Spalding pitched the National League's first shutout.[17]

"Sporting News. First Game of Chicago's Great Champion Base-Ball Club. A Handsome Victory Over the Louisville Nine—Score 4 to 0." *Chicago Daily Tribune*, April 26, 1876, pp. 1–2.

BASE-BALL.
VICTORY NUMBER ONE—CHICAGO VS. LOUISVILLE.

Special Dispatch to The Chicago Tribune.

LOUISVILLE, Ky., April 25.—When this city entered the professional base-ball business it was done with rather more judgment than is usual in first adventures, and the nine was picked out with rather more good sense than is usual in like cases. When Chicago, warned by many failures, undertook her present team, it was proper that it be a strong one. The two clubs met to-day with the result to have been expected.

Louisville has one of the finest parks in the country for the national game, and its stands are well arranged but small. Chicago people had been led to believe that the excitement here was great enough to draw out many people, and the papers thought 10,000 would be a small figure. The result was about 2,000 or a little less. But the saving character of the Louisville people was well shown in the crowd on a hill adjoining the grounds. This elevation commands a clear view of the game over a short fence, and it was crowded and packed with masses of citizens, who chose to husband their cash and steal half-a-dollar each from the clubs. The audience which did not pay was fully as large as that which did.

THE GROUND

was not in good shape, and was fully as moist as the Chicago park, being sticky and soft in the outfield, and very dead all over. The character of the game depended largely on this fact.

Just before the game a jeweler of the city presented to each of the Louisville team a gold badge as a testimonial, etc. The sporting reporter of the [Louisville] *Courier-Journal* was included in the distribution, and flowery speeches were made on all sides.

THE GAME.

Promptly at 3:30 [Al] Spalding spun his copper, won the toss, and sent his opponents to bat. [Joe] Gerhardt led off with a high safe hit to centre field, and received much applause therefor. He got to second on [Scott] Hastings' out by [John] Peters to [Cal] McVey, and there stuck fast, [Jack] Chapman suffering by the hands of [Adrian] Anson to first base, and [Jim] Devlin striking out after Anson had missed his foul fly. The Chicagos followed suit in the whitewash way.

The second inning of the Louisvilles was opened by [George] Bechtel, who got to first on [Deacon] White's fumble and bad throw of his third strike. [Chick] Fulmer followed with a high fly, which never touched the ground because of one Peters. When [John] Carbine came up to retrieve matters, Spalding sent him in a beauty, and he drove it high out into centre field, while the crowd set up a howl of joy, and chorused "There's nobody there!" Bechtel, who was on first, thought so too, and lit out for second just in time to see [Paul] Hines paddle placidly up and make a beautiful running catch, and then a clean double play by a fast long throw to McVey. The crowd adjourned the shouting, and Hines came in and went to bat. He hit hard at the first one, and sent it to Carbine so briskly that he couldn't hold it, giving Hines a life. Spalding put a corker to centre-field, Hines going to third. After Spalding had been run out and [Bob] Addy had retired at first, White drove a fierce one to Gerhardt, who gathered it well but threw it wildly to Carbine, letting in Hines with the first tally.

THE THIRD INNING

for the Louisvilles brought them nothing, though [Pop] Snyder made a clean hit. [John] Glenn opened the White Stocking half with a safe hit to centre, but was run out while trying to steal second. [Ross] Barnes waited for a good one so long that he was sent to the base on called balls. After Anson had scored an out, McVey tried Gerhardt with a hard hit, and the third baseman repeated his previous performance, making a throw wild enough to let in Barnes, making the second run of the game.

IN THE FOURTH INNING

Spalding, Addy, and White made clean hits before an out was scored, and the bases were full. While Peters was at the bat Devlin made a perceptible balk, letting in Spalding, but his was the only run of the inning.

The other White Stocking run was made in the seventh inning. After Peters and Glenn had gone out, Barnes came to the bat, and, despairing of safe hits, got on the first fair ball, and, as the phrase goes, "hit it hard and wished it well." It went into Chapman's territory, and that gentleman promptly muffed it while Barnes went to second. Anson followed with a clear long hit which sent Barnes home and scored the fourth and last run of the game.

The other error beside those noted to Anson and White was committed by Hines in the seventh inning, when he muffed a high fly from Fulmer. The full score of the game is as follows:

CHICAGO.	T	R	B	P	A	E	LOUISVILLE.	T	R	B	P	A	E
[Ross] Barnes, 2b	4	2	0	2	2	0	[Joe] Gerhardt, 3b	4	0	1	3	1	2
[Adrian] Anson, 3b	4	0	1	1	4	1	[Scott] Hastings, cf	4	0	2	2	0	0
[Cal] McVey, 1b	4	0	0	14	1	0	[Jack] Chapman, lf	4	0	2	0	0	1
[Paul] Hines, cf	4	1	1	4	0	1	[Jim] Devlin, p	4	0	1	1	0	1
[Al] Spalding, p	5	1	3	1	3	0	[George] Bechtel, rf	4	0	0	0	0	0

CHICAGO.	T	R	B	P	A	E	LOUISVILLE.	T	R	B	P	A	E
[Bob] Addy, rf	4	0	1	1	0	0	[Chick] Fulmer, ss	4	0	0	0	3	0
[Deacon] White, c	4	0	1	2	1	1	[John] Carbine, 1b	4	0	0	12	0	1
[John] Peters, ss	4	0	0	2	4	0	[Pop] Snyder, c	3	0	1	5	3	1
[John] Glenn, lf	4	0	1	0	0	0	[Ed] Som[ervil]le, 2b	3	0	0	4	4	0
Total	37	4	8	27	15	3	Total	34	0	7	27	11	6

Innings	1	2	3	4	5	6	7	8	9
Chicago	0	1	1	1	0	0	1	0	0 — 4
Louisville	0	0	0	0	0	0	0	0	0 — 0

Runs earned—None.
First base on errors—Barnes, 1; McVey, 1; Hines, 1; White, 1. Bechtel, 1; Fulmer, 1.
Bases on called balls—Barnes, 1.
Left on bases—Anson, 1; McVey, 1; Addy, 1; White, 1. Gerhardt, 1; Hastings, 1; Chapman, 1; Devlin, 1; Snyder, 1; Fulmer, 1.
Time of game—One hour and fifty minutes.
Umpire—L. B. Warren, St. Louis.

THE BATTING.

People in Chicago who believe that they have the strongest batting team in the League will look at the above score with doubt on that point when they see the best men without credit for even a single hit. It should be explained that the ball was the deadest possible to be found, and with it long hits were impossible. Then, again, the ground was soggy, and the ball could not be hit hard enough to bound. Another reason that cannot hereafter be alleged was that none of the nine have for several months faced a swift pitcher, and were consequently out of shape for that delivery. But what the White Stockings missed in batting they amply made up in fielding, for prettier work was never seen on a field than their share of to-day's game.

THE CREDIT OF THE VICTORY

belongs to Spalding more than to any one else, and it is safe to say that better pitching was hardly ever seen. Anson and Peters faced some stiff hits and fielded them in beautiful style, the throwing of both men being as accurate as rifle-shooting. Barnes, as usual, skirmished all around, and made a particularly fine pick-up and throw of what looked like a clean hit. McVey played his position without an error, and, indeed, without much excuse for one. Hines rather astonished the audience by his fast running and generally sure fielding.

TAKEN AS A WHOLE,

the first game of the Chicagos of 1876 was a creditable one, and promises well for the score at the end of the season.

The Louisville team were beaten to-day by their fielding errors, as well as by their utter inability to hit Spalding's delivery. They have not yet worked together long enough to play as a unit, and yet they show the power to trouble any team in the country to take away a ball from them. The crowd, especially the backers of the club, are deeply chagrined this evening at the score, but not so much at the loss of the game. Very little money was wagered, the Chicagoans generally refusing to give the odds of five to one which were demanded before the game. The general expression is, "Wait till Thursday, when the next game comes off!" For my part, I promise you for the Chicagos a far better batting game.

NINE MEN AND AN UMPIRE.

There was, during the game, considerable open dissatisfaction with Mr. Warren's umpiring, but it seemed no better based than the usual cry in cases where the home club is getting beaten. As nearly as an unprejudiced observer could judge, Mr. Warren made four errors of judgment—two in which the Chicagos took the worst, and two in which they gained. The most important were: Glenn ran in and took a low fly near the ground, making a beautiful catch, which the umpire would not recognize, and again, when White was touched off third and was declared not out. Inasmuch as White took no run by the error, it would seem that the criticism was unimportant. Still, the talk was so loud this evening that Welch, of this city, was agreed upon as umpire for Thursday's game. He did very good work for the games in Chicago last year.

LOUISVILLE IS DISPLEASED,

but unrepentant, this evening, and finds its consolation only in rejoicing at the defeat of the St. Louis Club by the Cincinnati pony team. Louisville proposes to wreak its revenge on Cincinnati for anything that Chicago has done or can do.

The *Courier-Journal* of to-morrow morning looks at the results of yesterday's game philosophically, and says that not much more could have been expected of its new nine. It in effect consoles itself with the idea that a trifle closer fielding would have made a tie game, and that Devlin must prove a hard pitcher for any club to hit.

[FRED] CONE

has severed his connection with the Chicago Club, and has taken a situation in the Matteson House. The act was wholly voluntary on his part, and resulted from his seeing that the White Stocking team of twelve men was too large, and must in some way be reduced.

The Chicago victory—the first shutout in National League history—included Paul Hines's "first tally," to quote the *Tribune*'s coverage, in the second inning that gave the White Stockings their first major league run. The sportswriter observed that after the victory the "deeply chagrined" Louisville supporters consoled themselves by calling out, "Wait till Thursday, when the next game comes off!" The Grays and their fans would have to wait a while longer than Thursday, however, for that afternoon's game ended in a second Al Spalding shutout, 10–0.

The White Stockings next set out for Cincinnati. Their two matches with the Red Stockings resulted in not just another two wins, but also another milestone: the National League's first home run. With two outs in the fifth inning on May 2, second baseman Ross Barnes came through and "made the finest hit of the game," the *Tribune* exclaimed, "straight down the left field to the carriages, for a clean home run." Although the *Chicago Evening Journal* did not mention Barnes's accomplishment (and even carped that the White Stockings' performance on the field "was less worthy of admiration than in previous games"), the team's 4–0 record did inspire a front-page notice in the newspaper: "The White Stockings—Chicago's champion base ball club—have started out admirably in the campaign of 1876. Thus far they have played four match games—two with the 'crack club' of Louisville, and two with the pride of Cincinnati's base ball people—coming out with flying colors in every contest."[18]

It would not last, of course. Cal McVey went home after the first Cincinnati game to help his wife tend to their sick child. With McVey out of the lineup, May 5 saw not only the first Chicago loss of the season, but also a somewhat embarrassing one: a 1–0 shutout at the hands of the St. Louis Brown Stockings.

The *St. Louis Globe-Democrat* gloated that after pitcher George Bradley and the other Browns "goose-egged Chicago" with their victory, "About 2,000 spectators evinc[ed] their appreciation of the act by loud and continuous applause." The *St. Louis Republican* underscored the shutout by belittling the visitors as "the boasted Chicagooses," exulting that "men forgot their wives, mothers, sweethearts, bets; yea, they forgot their corns in the anxiety of the moment." The paper reported, perhaps apocryphally, that as the last few fans left the ballpark and the gates closed behind them, "A little boy went up the avenue, and this was the song the little boy sang":

> There's a town in the North called She-cag-o,
> Which is known far and wide for her brag-o;
> She sent her Whites down
> To sink the brave Browns,
> But only ran afoul of a snag-o.[19]

Even without McVey on board, the Whites encountered nary a "snag-o" when they played the "brave Browns" a few days later, defeating them 3–2. The *Tribune* bragged that the Chicago ballplayers returned home on May 9 "bringing with them five creditable victories and leaving one scalp in St. Louis—a record which is, so far, the best in the country." The White Stockings would next take the field on May 10 for their first National League home contest, and the newspaper anticipated that "there will undoubtedly be an immense crowd—the more so that it will be a reception game to the best club Chicago ever had."

The *Tribune* was correct; an "immense crowd" of fans did indeed help the White Stockings inaugurate the professional baseball season in Chicago. Better yet, that crowd cheered Al Spalding and his men—including the returned Cal McVey—to a 6–0 shutout against the Cincinnati Red Stockings. The sportswriter explained that the players' use of a regulation baseball provided opportunities for outfielders to demonstrate their athletic expertise, and he recounted the team's difficulties on the road with less-than-adequate baseballs. In fact, the *Tribune*'s reporter had suggested just a few days earlier that factors contributing to the Chicago players' loss in St. Louis were the rain-soaked grounds and the sodden "putty ball" that, when hit, "simply gave a dull thud like a chunk of mud." The livelier ball that the White Stockings provided during each of their own home games was manufactured according to National League specifications by Louis H. Mahn of Jamaica Plain, Massachusetts. Mahn's league-approved "double cover" baseball, with its ounce of rubber and two stitched leather covers, was a favorite among the sluggers on the Chicago team.

From the *Tribune*'s account of the White Stockings' victory:

It looks as if the Chicago Club management had done it at last—had selected a club to fitly represent this city, and therefore to excel all other clubs in the West, if not in the country. This club of ours went away down into the rural districts, and won pretty much all the games it played, which circumstance was so strange to Chicago that its people who take an interest in the game inquired when the nine was coming back, and when it could be seen here; and, finding out, arranged to attend the first game and give the boys a reception.

That was what made 5,000 or 6,000 people stand in line yesterday and go through all sorts of trouble to get tickets and seats for Chicago's opening game of the Centennial year. Then, too, the weather encouraged the attendance, for a finer day for a game was hardly ever seen....

There was some little curiosity among the audience to know how Capt. Spalding proposed to play his Chicago games in the vital point of the kind of ball used. During his trip he had been almost constantly supplied with the deadest kind of dumpy balls, it being the privilege of the home club in every case to furnish the ball, and it was with no little satisfaction that the knowing ones among the

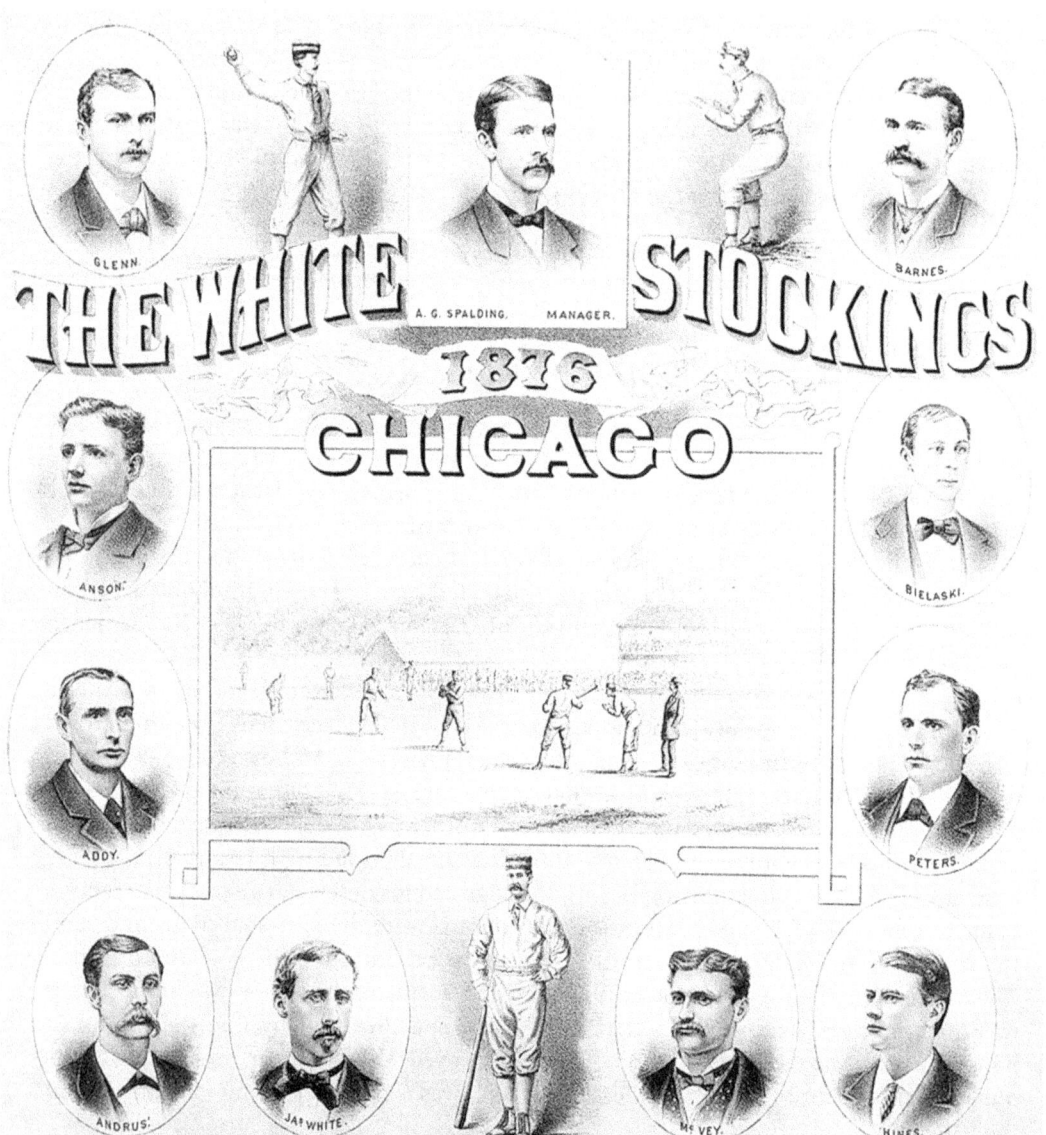

The 1876 White Stockings, clockwise from upper left: John Glenn, Al Spalding, Ross Barnes, Oscar Bielaski, John Peters, Paul Hines, Cal McVey, James "Deacon" White, Fred Andrus, Bob Addy, and Adrian Anson (author's collection).

audience noted that a Mahn, or double-cover, ball was in use. With this kind there is some chance for the beauties of out-fielding as well as batting to be displayed, and the audience are not forced to sit for a couple of hours and see successive hits passed about among the in-fielders, while the out-fielders have no chance to show whether they are ball-players or not. It is clear that the base-ball audience of Chicago will be pleased to see the game played on all its merits, and will therefore thank the Whites to play with a ball, and not a lump of duff....

The meed of praise at yesterday's game is due to neither nine, nor to the umpire, so much as to the attendance. THE TRIBUNE believes that so well-behaved, good-humored, and impartial an audience can be found nowhere else in the country. Yesterday, for instance, they applauded good plays by both sides with a judgment and fairness that deserves much credit. [Charley] Jones and [Paul] Hines,

[Ross] Barnes and [Charlie] Sweasy, [Adrian] Anson and [Amos] Booth, were treated equally well, while during the whole game there was not an abusive expression used. To those who have heard the howling mob of St. Louis, the change is a pleasure.[20]

Newspapers praised the stellar pitching of Al Spalding during the game, and the White Stockings' fielding also received its share of accolades. "Anson at third base played as fine if not finer than was ever seen on third base in this city before," asserted the *Chicago Evening Journal*. The *New York Clipper* wrote that "Spalding's pitching was too puzzling for the good batters of the visiting team, who made but three base-hits during the game. The Chicagos fielded magnificently, the only error being a miss by [Cal] McVey of a low whizzer."

This was not the first time the sporting paper had pointed out Chicago's strong defense. After the White Stockings' match against a strong amateur team at the beginning of the season, the *Clipper* had declared that "the notable feature of the game, as far as the professionals were concerned, was the generally fine throwing to second and third bases, which positions had a good deal of work.... [This] quality will win plenty of games."

It certainly helped. The Chicago men took another game from Cincinnati as well as two from Louisville, and they were ready for St. Louis—the same team that had "goose-egged Chicago" earlier in the month. Eight thousand exuberant spectators were on hand for the May 19 contest, which George Bradley and his Brown Stockings won, 4–1. That loss proved a bit costly for the White Stockings. They had played 11 regular season games and had lost only two. The Hartford Dark Blues, however, had a 9–1 record and were leading by one-half game in the standings (with St. Louis and Boston in third and fourth place, respectively). But the home team had another chance at the Browns and through "nerve, work, running, play, courage, and hang-on," as a reporter summarized, the Whites came back the next day to win, 6–3.

On the evening of May 21, the Chicago club members boarded the Michigan Central Railroad to begin their eastern road trip. The first stop would be Hartford, followed by Boston, Philadelphia, and then New York. For a month the White Stockings had distinguished themselves on the playing field, and the *Tribune* exulted that they were leaving "with an excellent record and many good wishes."

But the season did not end until late September, and the players would need more than their 10–2 record to claim the championship. Tempering the *Tribune*'s hearty bon voyage was the more pragmatic observation that "this week will tell a story for either the Hartford or Chicago Club."[21]

A White Stockings Pennant (1876)

The White Stockings were not the only western team traveling to the East. All four of them—Chicago, Cincinnati, Louisville, and St. Louis—would be on the road in May and June to play Hartford, Boston, New York, and Philadelphia. In mid–May the *New York Clipper* published a review of the season's "professional campaign." It contended that the West seemed to be "getting the better of the East," for the various win-loss records showed "superior fielding and pitching on the part of the Western-club nines." The three-game series between Chicago and Hartford on May 23, 25, and 27 was of particular interest to the *Clipper*, as both teams had the best records in their respective sections of the country.

After the White Stockings won the first game from the Dark Blues, lost the second, and took the third, Chicago held a one-game lead in the National League standings. The *Chicago Daily Tribune* celebrated the victories with an editorial:

> The four Western base-ball League clubs which last Tuesday went Down East to test the mettle of the Eastern League clubs have made a creditable showing thus far, the score standing two out of three in favor of the Chicago, St. Louis, and Louisville Clubs, though the Cincinnati's record is that of three consecutive defeats. The heavy work has fallen to the lot of the Chicago Club, which has met the crack Eastern nine, the Hartfords, who were relied upon to save the championship for the East; and the result is that the Chicagos won two out of the three games, which unmistakably indicates that, unless some extraordinary mishap befall them, they will win the championship.[22]

It was still rather early in the season for the *Tribune* to conclude brashly that the White Stockings would "unmistakably" take home the championship pennant. They had to face Hartford again later in the summer; moreover, of immediate concern as they traveled throughout the East was the Boston club—from which William Hulbert had snatched Al Spalding, Deacon White, Ross Barnes, and Cal McVey the previous year. In his memoir, *A Ball Player's Career* (1900), Adrian Anson recalled that even though the Hartfords were the White Stockings' toughest opponents, "All through the season of 1876 the most intense rivalry existed between the Chicago and Boston Clubs." He wrote that Boston officials, "smarting under the fact that the 'big four' had been hired away from them by the Western Metropolis," had managed to put together a strong team and were looking forward to playing the White Stockings. The two teams had not competed against each other since Spalding, White, Barnes, and McVey had left, and it seemed to Anson "as if all Boston had determined to be present" at the game, with the main attraction being "the advent of the 'Big Four' in a new uniform." The former Boston players "were given a great ovation when they put in an appearance, and of course the whole team shared in the honors that were showered upon them."

Sportswriters naturally covered this momentous occasion. In 1961, Preston D. Orem published *Baseball (1845–1881): From the Newspaper Accounts*. In it he wrote a vivid passage about the White Stockings' first game in Boston, which took place before an overflow crowd on May 30:

> Boston had prepared for Chicago on Memorial Day [then called Decoration Day]. Seats for 500 more had been prepared and all stands checked by the building inspectors. Long before 2 p. m. every reserved seat was taken. The horse cars were full, gateways choked, and the people could not get into the grounds fast enough. The only thing that kept the enclosure from being packed completely full, playing field and all, was the cessation of ticket sales. There were no tickets sold for one hour before the game started at 3:20. Yet so great was the rush that hundreds were pushed by the receivers before they could give up their tickets. As many more climbed the fence and readily paid for so doing, glad to get in at any price.
>
> Inside the grounds the sight was indeed a remarkable one. On each side [was] a densely packed sea of heads way down to the end of the long circle. The low seats in front were filled and in front of these there were spectators seated three and four rows deep. Further down each telegraph pole was a perch for two or three admirers of the national game, every foot of room on the lower fence was covered, and a thousand were seated on the grass below the centre field. The canvas was spread so thoroughly to shutout [sic] the view of the game that the number of outside spectators is comparatively small. People kept coming in and yet for half an hour before the game, before the ground was at last cleared and the game begun, the number of spectators did not seem perceptibly to increase.
>
> While the players were practicing the crowd toed the baselines and throwing was soon stopped as it was seen the game could not proceed until the crowd was pushed back. 69 policemen, players of both sides, and officers of the club, worked for 20 minutes to get the crowd back, a long tedious

process. To get them "outside" was impossible as there was not room enough but they were finally placed in bounds enough for play to start. The people were remarkably impartial and goodnatured [*sic*]. The crowd estimate was 12,000, including those who made their way in without paying. Receipts were $5,050.

The *Chicago Daily Tribune* figured that "not less than 14,000 persons went through the gates and over the fences, while another thousand had free seats on neighboring house-tops." The newspaper emphasized that the Chicago ballplayers' 5–1 victory was due in part because "the Whites took every chance, and made their runs in that way, while the Bostons were at times too timorous, and again foolishly risky.... [The] whole game was an almost perfect exhibition of the principle of taking all the chances yourself, and nipping your opponent when he tries to do the same thing; rattle the other club, but never get rattled yourself."

The White Stockings not only rattled Boston for two more games, but they also swept the Philadelphia Athletics in a three-game series and won two out of three against the New York Mutuals. The Chicago ballplayers returned home on Tuesday morning, June 20, with a 20–4 record and a one-game lead over the Hartford Dark Blues.[23]

After the White Stockings' last game of their road trip, a 10–3 victory over the New York Mutuals, the *New York Clipper* published its report of the Chicago team:

> Judging of the new Chicago team from what we know of the players, and what we have seen them do in the field and at the bat against one of the strongest of the League nines in these three games, we have to state that the present White Stocking nine is the equal of the strongest as a whole, and in some respects excels all others of the League-club teams. The Whites have in the person of [Ross] Barnes a model second-base player and a most scientific batsman, and an expert and skillful base-runner. They have an unsurpassed centre-fielder in [Paul] Hines, and one of the best of left-fielders in [John] Glenn. Their catcher [Deacon White] has no superior, and in [Cal] McVey they have not only an excellent first-baseman, but a good change-pitcher and a very good change-catcher. Their short-stop, too, is a first-class player in his position, [John] Peters being very active and a quick and accurate thrower. Their right-fielder, [Oscar] Bielaski, is an excellent player in his position, and [Adrian] Anson fills third base very acceptably; but if any position could be improved upon to any extent, that is the place where there is some room. They have a good substitute, too, in [Bob] Addy. In regard to their pitcher, captain and manager [Al Spalding], it is only necessary to state that his ability to act in all three positions has been plainly shown by the success attending his team.

The nation's political parties focused their attention on their own road trips in June 1876. While the White Stockings were finishing up their journey out East, Republicans were busy at their national convention in Cincinnati nominating Ohio Governor Rutherford B. Hayes for president. Soon after this—at around the time Americans were learning details about the death of General George Custer near Montana's Little Bighorn River—Democrats assembled in St. Louis and nominated New York Governor Samuel J. Tilden as their candidate for the position. With the eastern baseball tour and convention oratory concluded by the end of the month, players, politicians, and the rest of America looked forward to the country's centennial celebrations on July 4.

Of course, it would not be Independence Day without fireworks, and Chicago was no exception. Later on a Chicago newspaper recalled that July 4 "was ushered in with the usual pyrotechnic pandemonium. Firecrackers, pistols, and gunpowder did their level best to let the sleeping city know that the Fourth had arrived."[24]

The White Stockings had arrived, too, and were prepared to set off their own type of fireworks that afternoon at the ballpark. The Hartford Dark Blues were in town, and the Chicago players were determined to put some distance in the standings between the two teams.

The Hartfords and pitcher Tommy Bond, however, had other ideas. A year earlier, the *New York Clipper* had noted that Bond "pitched with a degree of speed and mastery of the ball." He evidently had not lost any of his skills over the intervening months, for the Hartfords managed to shut out the White Stockings, 3–0, and beat them again two days later, 6–2. "It is rather curious," the *Chicago Daily Tribune* observed on July 7, "how the Hartford and Chicago Clubs kept side by side all the season in the race for the flag, and still more curious how the two games of this week have changed the positions of the organizations, making the Whites second instead of first."

The White Stockings set out to change that order. Not only did they defeat the Dark Blues in the third game, 9–3—relying on back-up pitcher Cal McVey rather than Al Spalding—but they also began an 11-game winning streak that put them solidly back in first place. During this period, McVey achieved distinction with his bat as well as his arm, collecting six hits in each of two consecutive games (July 22 and July 25). On July 22 Chicago trounced Louisville, 30–7, as the Whites scored 10 runs in the first inning and 8 in the fourth, and three days later they crushed Cincinnati, 23–3. On July 27, it was Ross Barnes's turn as he went six for six during another White Stocking romp over Cincinnati, 17–3.[25]

Unlike a number of their rival clubs, the White Stockings' directors were making no efforts to acquire ballplayers for the next season. On July 30, the *Tribune* printed a list of men signed to various clubs and added that "this may be a good place to drop a paragraph in answer to several letters addressed to THE TRIBUNE asking why the Chicago Club management don't engage their team for next year. The answer is that Mr. Hulbert is doing just what is wisest under the circumstances; and, as he should be given the credit for assembling the only first-class team Chicago ever had, so he should be let alone in his movements for 1877. He will do just what is best, no doubt."

There is little doubt that what occurred was certainly best for William Hulbert. An article in the *Inter Ocean* newspaper points out that the Chicago Base Ball Association's three-year charter had expired in the spring of 1876, and "it therefore follows that [club officers] were not in a position to make any contracts for 1877." Hulbert and two trusted associates, Edwin F. Dexter and William M. Murray, soon thereafter formed a new group, the Chicago Ball Club. They applied for a new charter of incorporation with $20,000 of capital stock divided into 200 shares of $100 each. Hulbert, not surprisingly, acquired a majority interest of stock and was elected president of the organization. Other board members of the fledgling Chicago Ball Club included Al Spalding (secretary), Dexter, Murray, and John B. Lyon. As a reporter summarized, "The affairs of the old Association were closed out, and its property sold, mainly to the new club, the proceeds divided, and it passed away to give room to the new dispensation."[26]

"Bats Are Trumps. A Thorough Reorganization of the Chicago Base Ball Association Under a New Charter." *(Chicago) Inter Ocean*, July 31, 1876, p. 8.

BASE BALL.
A CHANGE IN THE CHICAGO CLUB.

Lovers of the national game, and their name is legion, have naturally enough manifested considerable interest of late as to the constitution of the League nines for the coming year. Particularly has this been the case in Chicago, the home of the champion nine, for the possession of the pennant may be treated by this time as an assured fact. From different quarters rumors, more or less authentic, have come in regard to engagements made with the different clubs, and through it all the Chicagos have made no sign. Certain outside newspapers have busied themselves with speculations and surmises as to the future, several asserting that three or four of the best men were to leave the Whites at the end of the season.

That this is not the fact may be at once stated, and an explanation as to the seeming delay may here be fitly made. The present Chicago Base Ball Association first took shape in 1872, after the fire, when a piece of ground was obtained and invitations issued to Eastern clubs to visit the city. Among the original stockholders were such men as Norman T. Gassette, W. A. Hulbert, George W. Gage, Charles Bartlett, Charles and Walter Hough, and a number of others. The capital stock was originally $5,000, but in 1873 it was increased to $10,000, in shares of $100 each, a charter was obtained, and work begun in earnest. An assessment was levied on the original stockholders, but the holders of thirty-eight shares failed to step up to the captain's desk and settle, the consequence being that their shares were forfeited to the association. The year 1875 was a moderately successful one, the club clearing over $4,000, thus enabling them to pay the rent of their present grounds for a year in advance.

In November last a meeting of the stockholders was held, at which W. A. Hulbert was elected president. Charles Bartlett, Treasurer, and a Board of Directors was also chosen, and a power given to them to engage a nine for the coming year. How well they performed that duty the record of the diamond field for this year shows, and there are very few persons indeed likely to question their judgment. By hard work and at great expense a selection was made from among the finest players of the country, and the result was that Chicago has to-day the champion base-ball team of the world. The public, satisfied with the efforts made, showed their appreciation of them by a liberal attendance of the games, and a constantly-increasing interest in the fortunes of the boys was developed. The formation of the National League helped greatly to raise the tone of base ball generally, and acted very favorably in this city, where it was well known that the home nine were not only first-class players but gentlemen all through.

Some months ago it was discovered that the charter granted in 1873 only ran three years, and consequently expired last spring. Under the State law the management were therefore unable to open up any new business, though fully empowered to wind up the affairs of the old company, having two years in which to do so. It therefore follows that they were not in a position to make any contracts for 1877, and the cause for the supposed dilatoriness is thus at once shown. Of course it became necessary to take immediate steps to procure a new charter, and some ten days ago the announcement was made that this had been obtained. The corporators were W. A. Hulbert, E. F. Dexter, and W. M. Murray, and the capital was fixed at $20,000, in shares of $100 each. The success of this year's work so far has been unexampled in the history of the game, and there was naturally little difficulty in placing the shares. Mr. Hulbert retained a large interest, Mr. Murray and Mr. J. DeKoven subscribed liberally, Messrs. Gassette, Dexter, and Bartlett also took shares, while A. G. Spalding, the pitcher of the nine, and [Ross] Barnes, the second baseman, also became stockholders to a considerable amount. Two or three more of the boys showed their faith in the nine and their intention of sticking to Chicago by subscribing, and the few shares remaining were eagerly snapped up by one of the largest capitalists of Chicago.

Pending these negotiations it was felt wisest to say as little as possible about them, although the course of events has been an open secret in the more well-informed sporting circles for some little time. Now, however, that everything has been arranged, THE INTER-OCEAN is happy to be the first to announce the fact that the White Stockings, almost as a body, will play again next year. There will not, in any case, be more than two changes in the composition of the team. It is even hoped that these changes may be further diminished, and efforts are now being made in this direction.

In this connection it may be stated that one or two of the minor stockholders in the old company hold themselves somewhat aggrieved by being left out of the new one, and accuse Mr. Hulbert of sharp practice. They will hold a meeting on Tuesday evening, at which time they will place their complaints in formal shape.

◆ ◆ ◆

The *Inter Ocean* underestimated the number of persons who felt "somewhat aggrieved" at being excluded from the new baseball organization. The *Chicago Times* reported that about a dozen of the 20 or 30 disenfranchised stockholders met on Tuesday, August 1, and they agreed to hire an attorney "to ascertain what their rights are and fight for them." Researcher Preston D. Orem, who pored over many nineteenth-century newspapers while compiling his baseball history, concluded that "matters were apparently fixed up" and that Hulbert "was obviously just scuttling some individuals he considered undesirables." One cannot help but wonder if Hulbert, the shrewd businessman that he was, deliberately let the association's charter quietly lapse so he could rid himself of meddlesome stockholders who did not share his vision for the White Stockings. A Chicago reporter approvingly commented in his summary of the reorganization that the new club "contains within its small number of stockholders all the best elements of the support of the game in this city."

With the baseball organization now restructured to his liking, Hulbert wasted little time in engaging players for 1877. The *Tribune* reported on September 17 that "the club has made several contracts for next year," including the re-signing of Al Spalding, Ross Barnes, John Peters, and Cal McVey ("though, as a matter of fact, [McVey] signed for two years when he came here"). That day the newspaper also covered the "close of the second eastern tour of the western clubs." It had been a successful trip for the White Stockings, for they had won seven out of their eight final road games. Only a few home matches now remained on the team's schedule, so the elated *Tribune* sportswriter could probably be excused for exclaiming that "it may be said that it is impossible to lose the pennant, and Mr. Hulbert may as well think about a pole to hang it on."[27]

William Hulbert was able to make that decision on September 26 after his White Stockings defeated the Hartford Dark Blues, 7–6, to clinch the first National League pennant. After beating them again the next day in the season finale, the Whites finished with a 52–14 record for a win-loss percentage of .788. Hartford followed six games back, with the St. Louis Brown Stockings and the Bostons in third and fourth place, respectively.

In looking at the White Stockings' team and individual batting records and solid pitching performances, it is small wonder that they won almost four out of every five games. In 1876, the White Stockings dominated the league with their batting average of .337, trailed far behind by Hartford at .267 and Boston at .266. Individually, second baseman Ross Barnes's average of .429 was baseball's best (helped by his mastery of the fair-foul single). Behind him were George Hall of the Philadelphia Athletics (.366), Adrian Anson (.356), John Peters (.351), and Cal McVey (.347). David Nemec observes in his *The Great Encyclopedia of Nineteenth Century Major League Baseball* that first baseman McVey, third baseman Anson, and shortstop Peters teamed with second baseman Barnes "to give Chicago the finest hitting infield quartet in major league history. Barnes and Peters paced all fielders at their respective positions as well, and centerfielder Paul Hines led all gardeners in fielding average."

The Chicago ballplayers topped the league both collectively in hits (926), as well as individually, with contributions from Ross Barnes (138), John Peters (111), Adrian Anson (110), and Cal McVey (107). Runner-up Boston had some 200 fewer hits. The White Stockings also scored the most runs with 624, far outpacing Boston, which hit a second-best 471. Ross Barnes once again took first-place honors with his own 126 runs, followed by Boston's George Wright (72), John Peters (70), and Deacon White (66). Backed by the White Stockings' commanding offense and stellar defense, pitcher Al Spalding led the National League in wins with 47, finishing the season with a 1.75 earned run average.

An editorial published in the *Chicago Evening Journal* at the end of the season proclaimed that "at last Chicago has won the championship. Cincinnati was the first city to bring the game to its best. Boston then took it up, and now Chicago has fairly eclipsed them all." The sportswriter for the *Evening Journal* added to the paper's celebration with additional congratulations:

> For a number of years the management of the Chicago Base Ball Association have been working hard to secure the whip pennant, and to that effect they have from year to year engaged players whom they thought would be able to wrest the championship from the Bostons. Before the closing of the base-ball season of 1875 it was formally announced that the four players, [Ross] Barnes, [Al] Spalding, [Cal] McVey, and [Deacon] White, were engaged with [Adrian] Anson, of the Athletics, to play in Chicago for 1876. How well they have done, the admirers of base ball are aware. They have won the coveted flag, and Chicago is happy. Every man in the club has shown himself to be a gentleman as well as a ball-player, and there has never been a breath of suspicion against them. Each and every man has done his duty, both on the field and off. They have made friends in and out of the profession, and are a credit to the city of their adoption.[28]

Epilogue

On September 28 the Chicago team left town on a three-week road trip to play exhibition games with clubs in Janesville, Wisconsin; Clinton and Marshalltown, Iowa; Freeport, Illinois; St. Louis, Missouri; St. Paul and Minneapolis, Minnesota; and Milwaukee, Wisconsin. The White Stockings were already thinking ahead to 1877, for as the *Chicago Evening Journal* commented, "They take with them, for trial, an amateur catcher who has promise of blooming out into anybody's equal." (They would need a good catcher to replace the dependable Deacon White, who next year would be playing for Boston.)

The White Stockings returned to Chicago on the evening of October 21. The *Chicago Daily Tribune* wrote that that day's exhibition game between the White Stockings and Milwaukee's West End club marked "the close of the season, and the champion White Stockings of 1876 will probably not play together again." The same article also listed the names of the men who had agreed to play for Chicago the following year. The sportswriter declared that the team comprised "the strongest nine ever made up," and he compared their superb batting records to those of other players in the National League. He was quick to add that "THE TRIBUNE does not, however, propose to assert now that the championship for 1877 is won, or anything like it."

But the *Tribune* most likely *was* thinking along those lines, as were undoubtedly thousands of the city's baseball fans. They would have done well simply to bask in the afterglow of their team's hard-won victory rather than anticipate future success. Come spring, it would soon be apparent to the loyal supporters of the White Stockings that the new season would not end so triumphantly.[29]

5

REVERSAL OF FORTUNE (1877–1879)

> This season the Chicago team lacked nearly every essential of success which they possessed in 1876.... [Al] Spalding ran the Chicago machine in 1876—he did not run it, except nominally, in 1877. The result of the bad management of the club for 1877 is that they occupy almost the last position.
> —*New York Clipper*, October 13, 1877

Defeats and Disappointments (1877–1878)

After the White Stockings finished playing their exhibition games in October 1876, they returned to Chicago, attended to some business and personal matters, and then set out for their homes. Many of the players lived in the city and planned to enjoy a few months of rest, though as a local sportswriter had reported in February that year, team captain Al Spalding had moved to Chicago not only to play baseball but also "to open a large emporium." There he planned to sell sporting supplies and "turn his place into the headquarters for the Western Base Ball Clubs." Spalding and his brother, Walter, launched their Western Base Ball Emporium a few weeks later at 118 Randolph Street.[1]

The two Spalding brothers quickly recognized that a new business needed publicity to succeed. By April the *New York Clipper* was publishing advertisements for their sporting goods, particularly for "Spalding's New League Ball" (which bore the Spalding name but was actually produced by Louis H. Mahn's company in Massachusetts). The *Clipper* itself even promoted the new partnership; an April editorial note directed readers to an eye-catching A. G. Spalding & Bro. baseball advertisement, adding that the two businessmen "announce to the baseball fraternity that special attention is paid by this house to the getting-up of club uniforms, and that they are prepared to supply all the necessary outfit[s] for baseball and sporting associations."

Al Spalding was lucky that he could rely on his second job as a baseball store proprietor, as his days as a baseball pitcher were numbered. In mid–September 1876, the *Chicago Daily Tribune* reported "with great pleasure" that the White Stockings had reengaged the Chicago hurler, "the most successful pitcher in the country." Just a month later, however, Chicagoans were startled to read in the newspaper that the team had also signed George Bradley, St. Louis's star pitcher, who that year had posted a 1.23 earned run average—the lowest in the National League.

The *Tribune* was quick to discredit the rumor that Bradley "superseded" Spalding. Nevertheless, the *New York Clipper* pointed out that Spalding could not throw a curve ball, while Bradley was both a proficient and a prominent member of this "new school of pitchers." Spalding probably recognized his shortcoming, for according to biographer Arthur Bartlett, "The fact seems to be that Spalding had now decided to bring his own pitching career to an end. He was only twenty-six years old, but perhaps he was already beginning to detect signs of decreasing effectiveness and was determined to leave the box while his reputation was still at its peak." Spalding would still occasionally pitch during the next season, but in most games he would take the field as the White Stockings' first baseman. He would also continue his role as team manager, club secretary, and trusted colleague of White Stockings president William A. Hulbert.[2]

BASE BALL.

Western Base Ball Emporium.

A. G. SPALDING & BRO.,

Wholesale and Retail Dealers in

BASE BALL AND CRICKET GOODS,

Croquet, Archery, Fishing Tackle, Fine Cutlery, etc., etc.,

No. 118 East Randolph-st., Chicago, Ill.

On February 19, 1876, the *Chicago Post and Mail* reported that Chicago baseball team "manager Spalding and his brother will soon open a base ball and sporting goods emporium at 118 Randolph street near Clark. It will be headquarters for base ball people." This classified advertisement appeared in the *Chicago Daily Tribune* on April 30, 1876.

As team officials, Hulbert and Spalding (along with their friend Lewis Meacham of the *Chicago Daily Tribune*) attended the National League's first convention, held in Cleveland from December 7–8, 1876. One of the first items on the agenda was a candid discussion of the New York Mutuals and Philadelphia Athletics. Although league regulations required teams to play all of their scheduled games, in September both clubs had canceled their final road trips out West due to financial difficulties. Spalding recalled years later that this rule violation "so incensed Hulbert and his Western associates" that at the Cleveland meeting, New York and Philadelphia were summarily expelled from the National League. The two clubs "pleaded for mercy," Spalding said, "but in vain." The failure of teams to finish out their seasons was characteristic of the earlier National Association, and baseball's executives were determined that the sport—and its fans—would not relive those scandal-ridden times. As Spalding declared, "This showed something of the character of Hulbert and his associates."

With this rather unpleasant task out of the way, Hulbert and the other directors turned their attention to more routine matters. During a discussion of the league ball, they selected a Louis H. Mahn baseball that contained the customary ounce of molded rubber. To prevent teams from using their own baseballs of widely varying quality, the officers stipulated that the National League secretary would furnish the balls to each team. This regulation would ensure that a home team could not, for example, use a rubber-less baseball with little bounce when they faced a hard-hitting opponent.

After they addressed these and other baseball matters, the meeting delegates unanimously elected William Hulbert president of the National League for 1877. With the convention over, Hulbert, Spalding, and Meacham left Cleveland and returned home, comfortable with the knowledge that the National League would field teams representing Boston, Cincinnati, Hartford, Louisville, St. Louis—and, of course, Chicago.[3]

"Turf and Field. Base-Ball. The White Stockings." *Chicago Daily Tribune*, March 11, 1877, p. 7.

The Chicago team for 1877, who have before them the arduous but not entirely unpleasant duty of playing under the shadow of the championship flag, have manifested a pleasant alacrity in getting to the work laid out for them, and seven of the ten are now in the city. Besides the four who have spent the winter here—Messrs. [Al] Spalding, [Ross] Barnes, [Cal] McVey, and [John] Glenn—the new comers are, curiously, the three new members of the nine—[George] Bradley, [Charlie] Waitt, and [Harry] Smith. The first named has been ailing a little, but is now much better, and will no doubt take the field in the best of trim. Waitt is also well fitted for business, and rather anxious to have it commence. The other new man, Harry W. Smith, of Indianapolis, happened in Friday, looking with favor upon all that he saw, except the snow. It is a good part of the country to come from,—that Hoosier State. They have plucky ball-players thereabouts. McVey will do for a sample, and if Smith gets on as well as Mac has, he will do quite well enough for any team.

The Club management have laid aside so much of the ideas of former years as related to a gymnasium to work in, and have arranged to have the team exercise in a large loft over No. 76 Randolph street. Here is a room about 40 by 150 feet, admirably adapted for all all [sic] kinds of practice. The windows have been protected by wire netting, and the whole fitted up for use.

The three members of the nine who have not yet arrived are [Adrian] Anson, [John] Peters, and [Paul] Hines, but they will "fetch up" before Thursday, when the whole party will get to work. They expect to put in four hours per day,—10 to 12 a. m. and 2 to 4 p. m.,—and it should not take many days of that kind of work to get the knots out of the cords. Nothing is known as yet about the first games, but it is quite likely that they will not take place here.

The indefatigable and earnest McVey, who had been pining away all winter for lack of somebody to bruise up his hands, fell on Bradley as soon as he arrived in the city, and, getting him in a hall, proceeded to examine his delivery to see if it had improved any during the winter. When the examination was concluded, Mac stepped out and informed a friend that if anybody hit Bradley clean for a base this year it would be a scratch.

It has been for some time a favorite subject for speculation with outsiders as to what the Chicago Club proposed to do for a catcher to replace [Deacon] White. It was not enough to assure the doubters that McVey was competent to do the work; they wagged their wise heads and declared that there was some "dark horse," some "incipient African in the hedge." It looks now as if they were right, for the Chicago Club has during the past week sent to Mr. [Nick] Young the notice of contract made with M. L. Finley. Exactly how good a man Finley may be can only be told after he has seen service. He is understood to be from Pekin, in this State, and is said to be one of the best men in the country in his place; quick to detect a point, sharp in making returns, and generally excellent in change.

◆ ◆ ◆

Finley was indeed contracted to take Deacon White's place as catcher, although Cal McVey was behind the plate for the White Stockings' first pre-season game on April 21. With George Bradley as pitcher and Al Spalding at first base, the Chicago team defeated the amateur Fairbanks Club ("the most prominent local organization," according to the

Chicago Daily Tribune), by the score of 11–1. Keeping with the previous year's custom, each White Stocking wore a different colored cap, though with the new season "it was necessary to make some changes to meet the difference in the team." Continued the *Tribune*:

> The attendance was fair, and the interest mainly cent[e]red, of course, in the play of the team which Chicago sends out this season to try for another flag to take the place of the one which floated for the first time yesterday. This pennant is some forty feet long, with the national colors, and an inscription to the effect that the Chicago Club is entitled to fly the champion flag of the year 1876....
>
> The game, like all opening and one-sided contests, was a source of great amusement to the audience, who seemed to be especially pleased with the fact that the amateurs could not make any sort of show against Bradley's curves, and struck out with freedom. Ten out of twenty-seven outs were made in this way, giving the curly-haired man a big record to start with. The audience greeted the old friends in their old places with the proper degree of enthusiasm, and then turned their critical attention on the work of Spalding, Bradley, and McVey. They were abundantly satisfied, and expressed that fact repeatedly. Bradley was in perfect trim, and apparently as effective as ever in his life. He will find that, so far from there being a prejudice against him here, the public are prepared to look on him favorably for his ability last year. McVey surprised the audience who had not seen his catching, by his accuracy and pluck, and above all, by the accuracy of his throwing.... Spalding and Bradley seemed to be equally at home on first, and neither of them made an error in that position.[4]

Despite Bradley's expertise with the curve ball, McVey's prowess behind the plate, and Spalding's ease at adapting to his new position, the White Stockings did not live up to pre-season expectations. They won their regular season opener but then lost four in a row, spurring one Chicago sportswriter to offer his brusque analysis of the situation: "It is getting to be about time that some of the Chicago team reformed their batting and infused some such life into it as used to please audiences and win games."

As it turned out, "life" was also found lacking in the new ball. The *Chicago Daily Tribune* observed that the ball was simply "too soft," for after only a brief period of use it "grew flabby on the outside, so that one could be picked up by the slack like a kitten by the scruff of its neck or a small boy by the slack of his breeches." During a meeting in Cincinnati on April 26, William Hulbert and the other National League directors first discussed the 1877 baseball schedule and then turned their attention to the new league baseball. From the *Tribune*:

> The only other matter of interest beside the schedule considered at the League meeting was a change in the character of the ball to be used in championship games. Mr. [Louis H.] Mahn, official maker to the League, had carried out his contract to the letter, and furnished the balls strictly according to the specifications; but when tried in practice they were found not to "act" up to what the clubs expected, and such a change was ordered as would make them more lively, to the end that the audience might see some ball-playing. It is proper to add that this move is an eminently wise one, and accords perfectly with the temper of Western audiences, especially those in Chicago. There has never been any special admiration for "kedunk" hits and 1–0 games in this city. People who pay an admittance fee want to see something going on, and nothing disgusts them more than to see a strong, active man hit a ball a furious blow and then have it hop along toward the short-stop. It isn't manly, and it isn't baseball. It's some sort of a child's game.

A new, livelier ball made its appearance in Chicago on May 10 during the White Stockings' game against the Hartfords of Brooklyn. It was bad enough that the home team lost, 14–10, but as the *Tribune* pointed out, Louis Mahn "had overdone the matter" while redesigning the baseball. Because he had used cotton yarn rather than the softer, league-prescribed woolen yarn, the ball had "the same degree of pliability that would exist in a billiard-ball covered with thin and tightly-stretched horse-hide." The White

Stockings, the *Tribune* went on, "while anxious to play with a hard, manly, lively sphere, were not prepared for, and not agreeable to, the wooden ball, as the new one was called, because they were getting laid up and disabled on all sides."

Something needed to be done—and quickly—so the league directors conferred with Mahn during a hastily called meeting in Indianapolis. They decided that each baseball would contain three-quarters of an ounce of rubber rather than one ounce and that the rubber would be wrapped in woolen yarn, not cotton. "This will at the same time furnish a live ball," the *Tribune* explained, "and one that can be handled without the danger and errors attending the use of cotton-finished [baseballs]."[5]

The White Stockings faced another dilemma of a more personal nature. The day of the league meeting, May 17, would mark Ross Barnes's last game until late August. The star hitter had been feeling run down and quite debilitated ever since the beginning of spring practice. "I tell you," he exclaimed in frustration, "this is terrible; to be anxious to do a thing which you know you can do, and yet find that you are bodily unable to do it. I know what I can do, and what I have done, and yet I haven't the strength to do the same again."

Barnes may have been suffering from ague, a malaria-like sickness characterized by alternating periods of chills and fever. While he recuperated at his home in Rockford, Illinois, newcomer Harry Smith filled in for him at second base. As for the other White Stockings, they also seemed unable to play baseball with the same precision and dexterity the team had demonstrated during the previous season. "The great hitters of last year became hitters at wind, or poor, feeble bunters to pitcher or second base," the *Tribune* complained on June 1 after a 3–1 loss. Two days later the paper attributed an embarrassing 9–2 defeat to "loose fielding and scandalously weak batting," though the latter, it dryly added, had been so noticeable during the season that "it excited no special comment."

Not so reserved was team captain Al Spalding, for after a 13–1 thrashing on June 19, he was heard to blurt out, "Tell THE TRIBUNE we are no good." This was the third loss in a row, and the newspaper certainly saw no reason to argue with him. "The White Stockings were thoroughly beaten this afternoon by the Hartfords," it reported. The *Tribune* went a step further by making an ironic allusion to past glory, the derision obvious by the use of quotation marks: "For the Chicago 'Champions' it was a bad day all around."[6]

It was also more than a little humiliating, for the lopsided defeat handed the White Stockings their 12th loss of the year in just their first 19 games. The *Chicago Times* attributed at least part of the team's dismal showing to "the ill-luck which has rested on the Chicagos during the present season like an incubus." After all, there was probably little that could have prevented Ross Barnes's illness and the other players' injuries, including utility player Harry Smith's broken thumb, outfielder Dave Rowe's strained arm, and catcher Cal McVey's battered hands and dislocated thumb. Still, as the *Times* pointed out after the June 19 loss, pitcher George Bradley "had no such fine support behind the bat as he had last year in St. Louis," nor did he have much in the outfield. It was also true that Bradley had not exhibited as much command with the lively baseball as he had shown the previous year with the softer ball.

There was, however, plenty of blame to go around, as various White Stockings throughout the season had committed numerous fielding errors and other careless mistakes. For instance, "a great deal of muffing," to quote the *New York Clipper*, had been on display during the 18–9 loss against Boston on May 12, in which the Chicago men made 22 errors. Following a June road trip in which the White Stockings lost all four games, the *Clipper* evaluated the team and explained the players' lack of success on the ball field:

> When the Chicago Club won the championship in 1876 they did it with a united, harmonized team, one in which every player was in his home position, and the most important positions were occupied by men made familiar with one another's play by years of practice together under able management. Not content with letting well enough alone, and endeavoring to retain the honors so creditably won by availing themselves of the services of the nine which had won the pennant, they proceeded to organize a new and what they regarded as a stronger team. In doing this they took from their leading rivals their pitcher, erroneously calculating that this was all they wanted to secure certain victory in 1877. Now, it happens that half the strength of a pitcher's play lies in his having not only a catcher fully competent to support him, but especially a catcher who is familiar with the pitcher's peculiar style of delivery. In taking [George] Bradley from the St. Louis Club they only withdrew one half the strength of that club's battery. They should also have engaged [John] Clapp, or should have made sure of being able to supply his place. They did neither, and the result is their present weakness in having no man behind the bat able to give Bradley the same efficient support he had in 1876. Here lies one of the causes of the existing demoralization of the present Chicago nine. Another cause is the result of misfortune rather than faulty management, and that is the loss of [Ross] Barnes' valuable services to the team. Barnes was the king-pin of the nine, as it were. With him in position, the team felt a confidence they failed to possess without him. To let [Deacon] White leave the quartet which went from the East to the West in 1876 was bad enough; but to lose Barnes, the model second-baseman of the fraternity, was a loss the club could ill afford to sustain at any time, and least of all in 1877.
>
> In March we said that the success of the Chicago experiment in engaging Bradley depended upon the ability [Cal] McVey would display in supporting him behind the bat. Now, McVey is simply a change-catcher. Compared with White, Clapp, [Pop] Snyder, and other leading catchers, he stands fourth or fifth on the list. Certainly he is not capable of filling the position of Bradley's assistant, as the experience of the past month's play has shown. His hands get puffed up too soon, for one thing. [Adrian] Anson is not even so good as McVey, and no substitute for either has yet been found. With used-up catchers, without Barnes at second, and with the majority of their nine in new positions, the Chicago Club came East in June to sustain the high reputation of the fine team which in 1876 bore down all opposition in the Eastern States, and won for the West the honors of the championship. Is it at all surprising, under such circumstances, that the Chicagos leave the East in June, 1877, a beaten club?[7]

According to the *Chicago Daily Tribune*, the White Stockings left the East not only beaten, but also "particularly unfortunate." On the afternoon of June 21, they were preparing to take the field for the final game of their road trip when outfielder Jimmy Hallinan, just acquired from Cincinnati, began warming up with Cal McVey. The newspaper revealed that before Hallinan "had been in the White Stocking uniform ten minutes," he severely ruptured his left index finger on one of McVey's fastballs, and, as a result, had to postpone his debut with the White Stockings.

Hallinan finally got to wear his new uniform five days later in a game with St. Louis, as did his former teammate, newly signed Chicago outfielder Charley Jones. Both men were widely regarded as experienced, skilled players, and baseball fans had been looking forward to a spirited afternoon of baseball. The White Stockings had also been eagerly awaiting the arrival of the two men, and after an 11–0 victory the *Chicago Times* declared that Hallinan and Jones "seemed to put new life into the rest of the nine. The old members seemed inspired with fresh confidence, and the result was that they played such a game, both at the bat and in the field, as has not been played by them this season."[8]

This newfound confidence did not last long. William Hulbert had signed Hallinan and Jones after the Cincinnati Red Stockings, staggering under financial woes, disbanded on June 18. Jones was able to play in just one more Chicago game—another win over St.

Louis—before Hulbert released him from his contract so he could return to a reorganized Cincinnati club. Hallinan stayed in Chicago, but as the weeks went by, neither he nor his teammates particularly distinguished themselves against their opponents, and the club's sporadic wins were outnumbered by troubling losses. After the Chicagoans lost two games in mid-July (on their way to four successive defeats), the *Chicago Times* sarcastically observed that "the White Stockings introduced a style of fielding which entirely does away with base-hits on the part of their opponents. With a liberal number of well-placed errors on the one side, the men of the other side are enabled to make runs without the necessity of safe batting. It is something of an innovation in base-ball, to be sure, but the Whites are struggling resolutely to introduce it."

William Hulbert wanted nothing to do with such a dubious team innovation. One player's lackluster performance and apparent apathy particularly infuriated the club president, and on July 29 he wrote a scathing letter to the slumping Paul Hines:

> Mr. P. A. HINES: This club will not consent to pay first-class prices for third-rate play. We have the right to expect of you that you will fully maintain your reputation for skill at bat, in the field, and in base-running. You have fallen off amazingly in all respects, and you show an indifference to the interest of your club which would warrant us in dismissing you. If you desire to retain your position with us you must wake up, and attend to your business in first-class shape. I hereby warn you that unless you do improve in respect to the matters to which I have, in this letter, called your attention, you will be dismissed and your pay stopped.
>
> The official record of your play this season is as follows—all league games:
>
> Games, 30; runs, 19; base-hits, 29. Last year, 64 games, 62 runs, 101 base-hits.
>
> You see, therefore, that you are not playing much more than half as well as last year. Yet you draw full pay, and, at the same time, rate as last year. You must not expect that this will continue. I tell you frankly, the club will not stand it. In the first 15 games this year you made 15 runs and 17 base-hits. In the last 15 games, 5 runs and 12 base-hits. You are not trying to play. Your father would not like to have you home with half your salary lost.
>
> Yours,
> W. A. HULB[E]RT.
> P[residen]t. Chicago Ball Club.
>
> In the last 10 games, 4 runs—3 [on] July 4; 1 [on] June 28—and 6 base-hits.[9]

The *Chicago Times* contended that Hulbert's fault-finding throughout the year led to the team's discouragement and lack of initiative. Perhaps his letter was a wake-up call of sorts; box scores for August show that Hines improved—on August 2 he had three hits and the *Tribune* awarded him "fielding honors"—and the club itself that month compiled a 7–4 record. Ross Barnes rejoined his teammates at the end of August and took his old position at second base against a newly formed Buffalo, New York, squad. His long illness, however, appeared to have sapped his strength, as he failed to get a hit and contributed little on the playing field. His physical weakness was also evident in a game against the Hartfords a few days later, prompting the *New York Clipper* to observe with some regret that "the Barnes of 1876 is not the Barnes of 1877."

The same could have been said about the White Stockings as a whole. They limped through September and October winning just six games out of 17 (6–10–1), and their .278 batting average for the year was not nearly as impressive as their .337 average in 1876. Infielder Adrian Anson dubbed 1877 "a year of disaster as far as Chicago was concerned," for the team finished the season buried fifth among the National League's six clubs, 15½ games behind first-place Boston. A *Chicago Daily Tribune* editorial insisted that "it is useless to speculate on the causes which led to this melancholy result," but that did not prevent sportswriters from arriving at their own conclusions. Some of the reasons mirrored the *New York Clipper*'s lengthy mid-season commentary: the unfortunate absence of Ross Barnes, George Bradley's failure to control the season's lively ball, and the team's lack of a top-notch catcher. The *Tribune*, for its part, believed that the various new players on the team were mere amateurs and that the year had been "a dismal and damaging series of experiments with kids." The *Clipper* chimed in once again, this time bluntly pointing a finger at Al Spalding's management:

> For integrity of character and general ability and intelligence in the business of running a baseball team, Mr. Spalding is the equal of the best. By his fine play in his position, his judgment in selecting his team, and his general efficiency in managing his nine, in 1876 he took his new team to the platform of the season's championship, and there duly received his reward. But this season he had too many irons in the fire, and in his attempt to Captain the nine, to run the general business of the club, and at the same time manage his own baseball business and store, he undertook more than any one man could properly attend to, and the result was a measureable failure.[10]

Spalding already knew that he had "too many irons in the fire." His and his brother's thriving sporting goods store was keeping even their mother busy: on one occasion she herself had to sew the name "INDIANAPOLIS" on the front of 11 team shirts to ensure that an order would be delivered on schedule. The ball player also realized that with his fading athletic skills, it was indeed time to step off the field, for in August he had announced his intention to retire from active play at the end of the season. He would, though, still retain administrative club duties under president William Hulbert.

Spalding was not the only Chicago player leaving the 23rd Street Grounds. After the 1877 season, fellow "Big Four" member Ross Barnes joined the Tecumseh Club of London, Ontario. Barnes had appeared in only 22 games that year and hit .272 (as compared to 1876, when he appeared in 66 games and hit a league-leading .429). A rule change for 1877 had limited his specialty, the fair-foul single, to a simple foul, though the decline in his batting average probably stemmed from his long illness rather than the new regulation.[11]

George Bradley pitched only one season for the White Stockings, electing instead to play for Massachusetts' New Bedford Club in 1878. Cal McVey signed with Cincinnati, as did his former "Big Four" comrade, Boston player Deacon White. Heading east to the Providence Grays was Paul Hines, whose alleged indifference during the summer had aroused William Hulbert's ire. The ballplayer probably never got back in the team president's good graces; in a summation of the White Stockings' "year of disaster," to quote Adrian Anson, the *Chicago Daily Tribune* stated that Hines's fielding average at second base had "dropped down to .774," which was "not near as good as Jimmy Wood would be with his cork leg."

That the *Tribune* should bring up the celebrated former captain was hardly surprising. Wood had been a fixture of Chicago baseball since helping to establish the first White Stockings team, and he was still active in the sport despite his artificial leg. He occasionally umpired games, and during the 1877 season he had organized at least one tournament at the 23rd Street Grounds. He later ran minor-league baseball clubs.[12]

By the fall, Chicagoans wondered whether the White Stockings would be returning to the 23rd Street Grounds or, for that matter, even be hosting a team for the 1878 season. Chicago's newspapers certainly expressed their doubts on both subjects. Reporters pointed out that the organization's directors apparently had not signed the lease on the South Side ballpark, nor had they signed any players. Furthermore, although the White

Stockings were probably the only professional club that had turned a profit in 1876, it was unlikely that any team ended the 1877 season financially stable.[13]

Fans were reassured when the Chicago Ball Club announced in November that not only would a team take the field the following year, but the players also would represent the city in a new ballpark. William Hulbert and the other directors had secured a lease on the same property that the White Stockings had played on in 1871—until the entire area's untimely destruction during the Great Chicago Fire. Club officials recognized that the site's central location between Michigan Avenue and the Illinois Central Railroad tracks (south of Randolph Street) would make the new grounds easily accessible to the city's many baseball fans. The *New York Clipper* heartily approved of the change, noting that the "very desirable ball-field" would attract "a paying audience at every match." White Stocking Park (also called Lake Front Park and Lake Park) would open in 1878.[14]

"Sporting. Base-Ball. The New Park." *Chicago Daily Tribune*, March 24, 1878, p. 7.

Work on the new ground is being pushed as fast as possible, a large force of men being employed. The grading is being done with loam and a mixture of street-dirt, the latter giving enough manure to the composition to insure the rapid growth of the grass which will be sown in the outfield. The diamond and a little space outside it will be covered with sod brought from outside the city. This is the same plan adopted with the Lake-Front ground in 1871, and it was eminently successful in procuring a handsome and even field. The diamond has been laid out in the southwest corner of the inclosure, so that a line from home to second base runs in a northeasterly by north direction. It will take a very long hit to get a ball over [the] left-field fence in fair ground, but it will not be impossible to hit over [the] right-field fence.[15] These cases can be easily covered by a ground rule that will be equally just to both sides,—say two bases for a hit over the fence. The fence around the ground will be of planed and matched boards and painted. It will no doubt have to be hued to prevent the small boy from cutting a peep-hole, as he would be sure to do if left to his own wicked devices. The grand stand will be in the southwest corner, just behind the catcher, and it will run part way down toward the east. There will not be room for so many seats back of third base as before, and the bulk of the seating capacity will be from the grand stand along the south line to the southeast corner, and thence along the east line to the foul line.[16]

◆ ◆ ◆

The *Chicago Times*, in a comparison of the old and new baseball fields, wrote that "the old grounds at Twenty-third street are about 390 by 600 feet; the lake front about 330 by 600, making a difference of about 60 feet in width. This can be overcome to a good extent, by laying out the field diagonally." The newspaper reported that six hundred persons would be able to view the games comfortably in the grandstand, with other seats accommodating two thousand more. Plans called for the rear of the grandstand to contain two large dressing rooms and the park's ticket office.

Because the city had dumped charred rubble all along the lakefront after the Chicago Fire, much preparatory work was required before grass could be planted and sod put down. "The field has been harrowed over and over until all the stones and foreign substances were removed," the *Tribune* told its readers shortly before the grounds were completed. "Then a heavy roller was put on and has been kept in motion a good part of the time until the field has assumed a respectable appearance."[17]

The grounds may have been respectable, but the size of the field certainly wasn't.

5. Reversal of Fortune (1877–1879)

As the sketch in the lower left indicates, fans at the White Stockings' ballpark enjoyed views of Lake Michigan as well as baseball games. The park opened in 1878 (*Harper's Weekly*, May 12, 1883).

Contrary to what the *Tribune* wrote in its article of March 24, the foul lines proved to be quite short (just 196 feet, for example, from home plate to the right-field fence), and the wall in straightaway center was a mere 300 feet from the plate. Sluggers found it so easy to clout balls over the outfield fences that such hits were declared ground-rule doubles, not home runs.[18]

Two Discouraging Seasons (1878–1879)

The White Stockings' gleaming new ballpark was about the only bright spot for the Chicago players during the 1878 baseball season. For that matter, even the entire National League faced quite a few setbacks. Financial costs had taken a toll on the six clubs of 1877—Boston, Chicago, Cincinnati, Louisville, Hartford, and St. Louis—and the latter two lacked the funds to field professional teams that year.

Louisville did not host a club in 1878, as well, though for a different reason. Marking professional baseball's first major scandal, in October 1877 two members of the Grays had confessed that gamblers had paid them and two other teammates to lose games deliberately. The club quickly expelled all four, and the National League permanently banned them from league play. Their exile in effect also banished the rest of the Grays, as the sudden loss of the foursome compelled the club to resign from the league.

Taking the three teams' places in 1878 were clubs from Indianapolis, Milwaukee, and Providence. When the *New York Clipper* announced the National League's six contenders, it added that "if the Boston nine do not retain possession of the pennant at the close of the season we shall be greatly surprised." The prescient *Clipper*'s faith in Boston was well deserved, for the club finished four games in front of second-place Cincinnati. The White Stockings' 30–30–1 record relegated them to fourth place in the league's standings, 11 games behind Boston.[19]

The White Stockings surely thought the season would go much differently. They lifted their fans' spirits early on, beginning during the pre-season. The White Stockings inaugurated their new ballpark on April 20 with a 14–1 victory against a strong team captained by none other than Al Spalding, who played second base. "The Fun Has Begun," the *Chicago Times* gloated, exclaiming that "on the part of the professionals the play was almost faultless." The newspaper concluded that the day's competition "was one that augurs well for the efficiency of the nine in its championship games."

The exhibition match, umpired by former White Stocking Jimmy Wood, certainly did bode well for the team, for the club opened the season with three victories against the recently formed Indianapolis Blues. The "fun" the *Times* mentioned, though, stopped after that, for Chicago lost nine of its next 10 games. A boost in the standings after a nine-game winning streak in July was wiped out by eight consecutive losses in August and September, which put the team well out of pennant contention. What led to the apparent collapse of the White Stockings? The *Chicago Daily Tribune* had a couple of ideas on the subject. "It will easily be remembered," the newspaper tersely wrote at the end of September, "that it has been their habit to lose games by being outbatted and outfielded."[20]

Sagging team morale might also have played a role. With Al Spalding no longer on the active roster, Hulbert had needed a new player-manager, so he hired Bob Ferguson of the Hartfords of Brooklyn. Chicago's newspapers had approved of the choice. "Ferguson is a good, steady, reliable player," said the *Times*. The *Tribune* recounted his long baseball career and wrote that "of course Ferguson is a veteran,—in play, experience, and cleverness.... It is not too much to say that he is the best judge of a young player in the game, a model disciplinarian, and can get as much work out of his men as any one can."

Ferguson was indeed a "reliable player," as the *Tribune* observed—he batted .351 in 1878—but he was not a particularly "steady" one. His hot temper was well known around the baseball world, as was his penchant for loudly berating his players in public. Al Spalding thought he was "one of the best ball players of his time" but also admitted that he was "no master of the arts of finesse. He had no tact. He knew nothing of the subtle science of handling men by strategy rather than by force." On top of his poor managerial skills, Ferguson occasionally butted heads with William Hulbert, and probably few were surprised when the club failed to renew his contract at the end of the season.[21]

Taking over Ferguson's supervisory duties was Adrian Anson, whose role as team captain would be acknowledged by the nickname "Cap." When the *Chicago Daily Tribune* headlined "The Chicagos of 1879," the paper remarked that "it would be superfluous to say anything to Chicago people about Anson; he plays to win, and is one of the few men in the country who don't care for a personal record, or, rather, who thinks more of his Club's record than he does of his own."

As the new manager, Anson had some changes in mind to improve his club's record. He had played third base in 1876 and 1877, and patrolled the outfield in 1878 while Ferguson was manager. When Anson's White Stockings played a solid amateur team on a raw and chilly April afternoon, the new captain positioned himself on first base. Not only did his club win the game, 35–5, but Anson also helped turn a triple play in the fourth inning, hurling the ball "like a shot" from first to home plate, according to a local sportswriter.

Of course, Anson had some timely assistance during the game, too. The Milwaukee and Indianapolis clubs had disbanded following the 1878 season due to financial difficulties, and the Chicago team immediately saw the opportunity to add some new faces to its lineup. These players included outfielders Abner Dalrymple and George "Orator" Shafer, infielders Joe Quest and Edward "Ned" Williamson, and catcher Frank Sylvester "Silver" Flint. George Gore, formerly of the New Bedford Club in Massachusetts, also joined the White Stockings in his first appearance as a professional ballplayer. The *Chicago Times* reported in its game-day coverage that the men all "worked well and smoothly together, showing an unexpected degree of fielding skill at this season."[22]

The National League's eight teams (Boston, Buffalo, Chicago, Cincinnati, Cleveland, Providence, Syracuse, and Troy) officially opened the 1879 season on May 1. In their first two series, the White Stockings swept the league's newly added Syracuse Stars and Troy Trojans from New York and then took two out of three from Rhode Island's Providence Grays. The Chicagoans continued to demonstrate the "fielding skill" that the *Times* had referred to, and at the end of the month won all six games with Boston. By August 1, the White Stockings' league-leading record of 34–12–2 put them 5½ games in front of second-place Providence.

Chicago did not stay in first place for long. It was bad enough that catcher Silver Flint injured his hand during an exhibition game in Dubuque, Iowa, but in the summer Cap Anson struggled with, as one paper put it, a "billious [sic] fever." His condition grew worse, with reporters describing his ailment as a liver affliction. In a mid–August article aptly titled "Anson's Liver," the *Chicago Daily Tribune* colorfully summed up the situation:

> The Whites not only lost the little one-horse game in Dubuque, but they also lost their grip. One of Flint's thumbs suffered the loss of a nail (neatly peeled off by a foul ball) and Anson's liver was affected. The thumb recovered, but the liver is still out of condition. In a general way and in ordinary times Mr. Anson's liver is not, perhaps, a more important affair than any of the internal organs of the ordinary citizen, but these are not ordinary times, and just now that liver and its workings are the source of intense anxiety to thousands of young men with standing collars who are mildly insane on the subject of base-ball, and who worship Anson as the only man who can save Chicago from ruin. It is a tight place for the town and no mistake.[23]

Anson tried to ignore his illness and continue to play, but all too frequently he had to scratch his name out of the lineup. Center fielder Jack Remsen moved over to first base, but his skills clearly did not equal those of the team's leader. A loss on August 19, the third in a row, dropped Chicago to 1½ games behind the Grays, and the *Tribune* bemoaned that "it looks now as if the White Stockings had bidden good-by to the championship, which, but a few weeks ago they were supposed to have practically in their hands."

Meanwhile, Anson bid farewell to his teammates as he went home to Marshalltown, Iowa, to recuperate. The White Stockings with Silver Flint as captain battled on without him, but they again ended the season in fourth place, 10½ games behind the Providence Grays.

Chicago's disappointing finish, however, could hardly be blamed on Cap Anson. Pitcher Terry Larkin compiled a 31–23 record for the year, but he had thrown poorly throughout August and September, and during one particularly bad stretch lost eight games and tied one. Interestingly, in its account of the "accidents and misfortunes" that had overwhelmed the team after July 1, the *Chicago Daily Tribune* pointed out that Larkin was "simply an addition to the long list of ball-players who have ruined themselves by dissipation." The *Tribune* also noted that players George Gore and Abner Dalrymple had gone on the sick list at about the same time as Anson.

The *Chicago Times* likewise reflected on the disheartening season, though it added a tribute to the White Stockings' captain:

Though the Chicago team held the lead from the latter part of May till the latter part of August almost uninterruptedly, it at no time was so far in advance but that a little bad luck or a little letdown in play would suffice to spoil its lead. Then Providence went to the front, and, by steady, nervy play, held the lead to the close, but only by such a slight advantage that nothing but strict attention to business could maintain it.

There was yet another exceptional feature in the season:

THE INFLUENCE OF LUCK

on the result.... The hardest luck was reserved for Chicago; that, too, at a time when it could not repair the damage, and make up by subsequent steady play for past unavoidable losses. But the sickness of [Cap] Anson was not the only piece of ill-fortune against which the team had to contend. [Silver] Flint disjointed a finger in an 'off' game; [Ned] Williamson and [Jack] Remsen went lame on the home-stretch, and there was general demoralization. Further than that, Chicago practically met a different set of clubs from those contended against by her chief rivals, Boston and Providence. When the eastern clubs played the first round in the west, and the western clubs returned the visit, Cincinnati, Buffalo, and Cleveland were at their weakest, and it was no trouble to get away with them. When Chicago came to do battle with them they were playing as they had not played before during the season, as the eastern clubs found to their cost when they made their second trip west.

During all this time of weakness in the west, Boston and Providence were piling up victories which stood them in good stead at the finish. Had Buffalo and Cincinnati played games of equal strength to those with Chicago in their first half of the series with the eastern clubs, Chicago would have secured such a lead that it could not have been overcome in the last four weeks of the season.

In view of all these peculiarly adverse circumstances, no one will scarcely question the assertion that Chicago had the strongest team of the year, and that, but for these unforeseeable and unavoidable haps, the whip-pennant of 1879 would have floated from the flag-staff of White Stocking park.

In this connection,

A WORD IN REGARD TO CAPT. ANSON

will not be out of place. In trying the double experiment of making him captain of the team and putting him on first base, President Hulbert showed a thorough knowledge of the capabilities of the man. His playing of the position was a revelation, and it is safe to say that, in the general efficiency of his work there he had no equal in the country, as long as he was well. But it was as captain of the nine that he showed himself most completely master of the situation, and of the game. Quick to see and take advantage of every point, whether of strength on his own side, or weakness in the other side, he inspired confidence in the team he commanded, and his steady, unshakable coolness in the tightest pinch, begot in his men a like feeling. As a certain batsman in time of need, he was without an equal; but it was in the coaching of his men, when running the bases, that his ability appeared to the most striking advantage. In taking judicious chances for gaining a base he was *facile princeps*. He seemed to have a sort of intuition as to when he could count upon a baseman making a muff, or a fielder, or a wild throw, and he rarely erred. A man was seldom put out when following his directions about running. The value of his work in this department was abundantly shown as soon as he became too sick to play, and game after game was lost by poor base running. His aggregate value to the team, in all the departments, came out boldly when it went out without him, and rapidly dropped from first to [fourth] place, failing to go down any further only because the lead secured while he was at its head rendered it impossible in the allotted time.[24]

Epilogue

The White Stockings' season, however, was not a complete disaster. Chicago was one of the few clubs to turn a profit in 1879, just as it had in 1878. The team also led the National League in attendance both years. Secretary Al Spalding's business continued to flourish; his "Spalding League Ball" had been used by the professional teams in 1879, and the league adopted it again for 1880.[25]

Cap Anson fared well, too. After recuperating at his family home in Iowa, he returned to Chicago at the end of September "looking as hearty as ever," according to the *Chicago Daily Tribune*. He and other team members soon left for California to play a series of exhibition games. While they were gone, the *Tribune* told its readers that Anson was in fine physical condition, and it confidently declared that he would resume his place "on the field next May with all his abilities unimpaired."

White Stocking fans were counting on Anson's good health. So, too, were the club's directors, who were determined to do their part to assure his—and the team's—success. "So far as the home management is concerned," the *Chicago Times* reported in October, "earnest endeavor will be made to snatch victory from defeat, and that no pains will be spared to have Chicago fitly represented in the championship arena during the season of 1880."

As for the White Stockings themselves, a sportswriter announced that the players were "supremely happy" and "absolutely rolling in good things" in California. The team would be back home by the end of the year, and Chicagoans were hoping all those "good things" would still be at hand—especially when the new season started up in the spring.[26]

The name "Spalding" usually brings to mind the sporting goods store by that name, though founder Albert G. "Al" Spalding's reputation also rests on his career as a baseball player and White Stocking executive. By mid-1875, the 24-year-old pitcher had already led the Boston Red Stockings to three National Association championships when William A. Hulbert of the White Stockings convinced him to sign with the Chicago team. Spalding soon moved to Chicago and opened his baseball "emporium." A year later, the White Stockings—with Spalding as team captain as well as club secretary—won the National League's championship in the league's inaugural season.

Spalding found it difficult, however, to juggle both baseball and a business, and he decided to end his playing career after the 1877 season. He still retained his administrative duties with the club, and when Hulbert died in 1882, he assumed the presidency. Under his sharp managerial eye, the White Stockings took home National League pennants in 1882, 1885, and 1886. He also published an annual baseball guide of statistics, analyses, and season summaries.

Spalding retired in 1891, though for years he retained his ties to both the Chicago club and the National League. In 1911 he published his history of baseball—and his own role in the sport—titled *America's National Game*. He died four years later. Al Spalding was elected to the National Baseball Hall of Fame in 1939. This photograph was taken in November 1879, when he was 29 years old (Albert Meader Chesley, *Indoor and Outdoor Gymnastic Games*, 1913).

6

SUCCESSES AND STRUGGLES (1880–1884)

> To those interested in base-ball, and who have from year to year followed the varying fortunes of the several clubs, the mere mention of the Chicago nine ... brings to memory scenes of many a well-contested game and hard-earned victory.
> —*Harper's Weekly*, October 14, 1882

Chicago Flies a Pennant (1880)

Despite the heavy rain that had fallen on Friday, April 2, 1880, more than a dozen White Stockings were practicing on the field Saturday morning. Exhibition games were scheduled for the middle of the month, and the players—as well as the park itself—were ready for the new season. "The Chicago team kept up gymnasium practice all Winter," the *Chicago Evening Journal* observed, "and have had out-door work ever since it was warm enough to handle the ball. The grounds have been put in good condition, and the seats have received a fresh coat of paint."

Fresh new faces also dotted the ball field. On April 22 the *Evening Journal* published a "review of the composition of the eight league clubs which are to contest for the 1880 championship," and the sportswriter inserted his glowing appraisal of the White Stockings:

> In the Chicago team is to be found, in the opinion of most experts, the coming nine of 1880. The Chicago pitchers and catchers are this season the strongest they have placed in the field since 1876. They consist of [Silver] Flint and [Fred] Goldsmith and [Mike] Kelly and [Larry] Corcoran. The two pitchers are among the most effective in the country, and are trustworthy both as regards integrity and habits. In this respect the team has been greatly strengthened since 1879. Then, too, their in-field support is very strong, having [Cap] Anson, [Joe] Quest, [Ned] Williamson and [Tom] Burns, with [Tommy] Beals to assist if necessary, and [Abner] Dalrymple, [George] Gore and Kelly in the out-field."[1]

Right fielder Mike Kelly also played catcher. During his lengthy career he gained prominence for his strong arm, aggressive base running, daring base stealing, and especially his flamboyant slides, which inspired crowds to scream "slide, Kelly, slide" during games. He was also a genial, charismatic raconteur with a fondness for liquor. White Stockings manager Cap Anson recalled years later that Kelly "was a good fielder when not bowled up, but when he was he sometimes failed to judge a fly ball correctly, though he would generally manage to get pretty close in under it. In such cases he would remark with a comical leer: 'By Gad, I made it hit me gloves, anyhow.'"[2]

But Kelly (who in later years was often called "King" Kelly) was proficient at the plate, as were his teammates. In the spring of 1880, the White Stockings boasted a solid core of returning players in Dalrymple, Flint, Gore, Quest, and Williamson, thanks to baseball's new "five-men rule," which allowed a club to reserve and hold up to five of its ballplayers for each season. Anson, healthy and fully recovered from his illness the previous year, was counting on these veterans, as well as on newcomers Kelly, shortstop Burns, and pitchers Goldsmith and Corcoran.

With the latter two men, Anson could alternate his pitchers and not run the risk of overworking either one of them. In an article reviewing the 1879 baseball year, the *New York Clipper* had praised Goldsmith as "one of the most effective of the season's pitchers" and one who would likely "prove more effective next season than ever before." The *Clipper* had also profiled Corcoran, observing that "he has wonderful speed for his strength, and with it a troublesome curve. He also has more than ordinary command of the ball in delivery for so swift a pitcher.... He is reticent in his work, a plucky fielder, has plenty of endurance, and is to be relied upon for faithfulness in his position."

That dependability came through in the White Stockings' first game, played on May 1 against the Stars, the reorganized Cincinnati team. Corcoran not only pitched a 4–3 victory, but he also opened the ninth inning "with a corking hit to left field," as one newspaper reported, eventually scoring a run.[3]

Chicago lost the next game, but it then began steamrolling the seven teams of the National League, which besides Cincinnati included clubs from Boston, Buffalo, Cleveland, Providence, Troy, and Worcester. "It has proved itself so far," a sportswriter gloated on May 23, "to be the strongest League nine in every essential particular,—batting, baserunning, fielding, and earnest, united, harmonious play." The White Stockings compiled a 21-0-1 record from June 2 to July 8, which put them in firm command of first place. The string of wins, however, ended on July 10. Early in the season they had beaten Cleveland three games in a row, and they were probably expecting a similar outcome when they met up with the Ohio players again. But as the *New York Clipper* pointed out, there is "nothing sure" about the outcome of a baseball game:

> The one special attraction of baseball to sporting men is its glorious uncertainty. Even when a perfectly managed and strong team is opposed to inferior players, there is nothing sure about the result of the contest. This is regarded as a special merit of the game by those who use it for betting purposes. Nines may go into a contest eager to win, playing a perfectly fair game and striving their best for victory, and yet a nine which they could ordinarily defeat without difficulty will master them when least expected. This was the case on Saturday last, when the Chicago team entered the field at Cleveland. It was dollars to cents against the home-nine's escaping defeat. From June 4 to July 9 the Chicago team had not lost a single game, while within that period the Clevelands had lost ten out of the twenty games they had played. The Chicagos entered upon the contest flushed with twenty successive victories over the strong Eastern nines, and they had previously defeated the Clevelands in three straight games by the totals of 21 to 12. Here was material for an overconfident feeling; and, moreover, just here was a position for the Clevelands which has time and again yielded just such unexpected results, and that position was that the home-nine had everything to win by victory and little to lose by defeat, whereas the position of the opposing team was almost the reverse. At any rate, the effect was the same, and the result was a victory snatched from their opponents by the Clevelands in the very last inning of the game.[4]

Chicago had been "Chicagoed"—held scoreless—by the Cleveland Blues, 2–0. But the White Stockings did some "Chicagoing" of their own three days later when they beat

Cleveland, 3–0. On August 12 the White Stockings' record was 44–11–1, the day they lost on their home grounds for the first time all season. By then Chicago led the Providence Grays by 11½ games, and as the *Tribune* argued, "For Providence now to win the championship it would have to win every game from this time forth, and Chicago would have to lose half its games—a contingency, as everybody knows, too remote to be considered."

The *New York Clipper* pointed out that the White Stockings' lead would have been even greater if pitcher Fred Goldsmith had not been on the sick list for weeks. Even though Goldsmith's illness gave Larry Corcoran "double duty to attend to," on August 19 Corcoran managed to pitch the White Stockings' first-ever no-hitter. The *Chicago Times* covered the milestone in "Bootless Bean-Eaters: Boston's Batters Presented by Chicago's Silks with a Nice String of Nothings." The author of the ornately titled article wrote:

> The Chicagos administered a very lively trouncing to the Bostons on yesterday afternoon. They not only prevented them from making a run, but Corcoran proved so puzzling that they failed to make a single safe hit in the thirty times which they bestrode the plate. This is something that the little man had occasion to be proud of, as it is a pitching record which has not been equaled on these grounds this season, and the writer does not remember that it has been done before on Chicago grounds. The fielding of the home team was sharp and accurate, the four errors charged being excusable ones, due to the wet, slippery, loose-covered condition of the ball.[5]

The *Chicago Daily Tribune* wrote that the ball—and the grounds—were wet due to "some sharp showers which occurred in the third inning." Rain on September 1 postponed a game against the Troy Trojans until the following day, when the White Stockings played their first doubleheader. Larry Corcoran pitched both games, winning the morning match but losing the one in the afternoon. The White Stockings were still 11½ games in front of the Providence Grays, and Chicago clinched the National League championship on September 15 with a 5–2 victory over the Cincinnati Stars.

The *Tribune* knew who deserved much of the credit. In its game-day coverage, the newspaper declared that "the team has been handled with consummate ability by Capt. Anson, to whose remarkable executive force and genius for field management the success of the team is in no small degree attributable. He has at all times commanded the entire respect and good-will of his team, who without exception look up to him as always just in his acts toward them, and as almost infallible in judgment."[6]

Anson himself said that "the Chicago team of that season outclassed all of its competitors," despite the fact that the clubs it faced "were made up of first-class material in nearly every case." His judgment (and the White Stockings' considerable talent, of course) enabled the team to finish the season sitting comfortably atop the National League, 15 games in front of the Providence Grays and 20 ahead of the Cleveland Blues. Chicago's record of 67–17–2 gave the club an astonishing winning percentage of .798 and a record never since equaled.

Besides the 1880 league pennant, the White Stockings collectively took home a number of other laurels, such as the best team batting average (.279), as well as the most hits (876), runs (538), and runs batted in (378). George Gore led the league with his .360 batting average, while the trio of Cap Anson, Abner Dalrymple, and Tom Burns also topped the .300 mark. Dalrymple was also first in runs scored (91), and hits (126). Anson and Gore were not far behind him with their 120 and 116 hits. Pitcher Larry Corcoran, who compiled a win-loss record of 43–14, led the league in strikeouts with 268. He finished the year with an earned run average of 1.95 while Fred Goldsmith (21–3) ranked fourth in the league at 1.75.

The *Chicago Times* mentioned a few of these White Stockings honors and also discussed the significance of the "subtle factor of head-work" as it pertained to the team's success:

> It will be seen that the Chicagos, while they may have been—were, in fact,—excelled by some clubs in some points of play, nevertheless lead their opponents as an aggregate at every point. They were oftener at bat, made more base-hits, reached first base oftener, ran more bases, made more runs, had more fielding chances, and made fewer errors. Under these circumstances it is not surprising that they won the championship. One would think that, with such a marked superiority in every direction, they could not lose a game. Right here comes in the element of luck which plays such an interesting part in the game, together with the subtle factor of head-work, which is an important but unscorable element. It was nicely illustrated in the last regular game between Chicago and Buffalo. Kelly was on third when Anson knocked a safe drop fly to centre field. He was certain of his base, and, apparently, all Kelly had to do was to come in from third. He did come in, but in such a leisurely, careless way that the fielder was deceived into believing that he could catch him at the plate. The moment the ball left the fielder's hand, Kelly showed that he was wide awake and had gauged the chances very closely, for he made a quick run and fine slide, beating the ball by about two feet. The head-work shown was not in merely saving his run by a shave; but, in the fact that he drew the ball and gave Anson an opportunity to go to second, and, if the throw had been a wild one, he would have gone to third. As it was, a run resulted, whereas Anson would, otherwise, have died on third. This play of Kelly's is entirely beyond representation by figures. There is no means of crediting him with the base which he made it possible for Anson to get, and there would have been no way of charging him with an error had he run directly home and allowed the fielder to hold Anson on first. It is in this direction that Anson excels all other men in the league as a field-captain. He is quick to see and take advantage of a point, and it is safe to say that a dozen games have been won by the Chicagos this year by pure head-work.[7]

The 1880 White Stockings included, clockwise from top: Adrian "Cap" Anson, Fred Goldsmith, Ned Williamson, Tom Burns, Larry Corcoran, Tommy Beals, Joe Quest, and Frank Sylvester "Silver" Flint. In the center is George Gore and below him are Abner Dalrymple (left) and Mike Kelly (right). The team won the National League pennant with a record of 67-17-2 (Adrian C. Anson, *A Ball Player's Career*, 1900).

The *Times* added that "Chicago is the only club that has made money during the past season. One or two of the others have come out even, or nearly so; but the majority have fallen short several thousand dollars." Cincinnati was one of those teams that had "fallen short," which in turn led to more severe—and costly—problems for the baseball club. To secure much-needed revenue, it had leased its grounds to non-league clubs for Sunday games and had permitted the sale of liquor. At a special October meeting of the National League (undoubtedly called by an irate president William Hulbert), the delegates discussed whether they should amend the league constitution at the forthcoming annual meeting. All of the representatives except Cincinnati Stars owner W. H. Kennett pledged to support an amendment that would prohibit both the sale of liquor on league grounds and the playing of games, including amateur matches, on Sunday. Kennett's refusal to agree consequently cost the Cincinnati club its membership in the National League.

The *Cincinnati Enquirer* fumed that the Cincinnati Stars "were unceremoniously kicked out of the league" and that "Boss Hulbert engineered the job." National League delegates, however, obviously had different opinions about "Boss Hulbert." During the fifth annual meeting of the organization, held in New York that December, they adopted the following resolution:

> *Whereas*, Mr. W. A. Hulbert, of Chicago, Ill., has been president of this league since its organization, and has so performed the duties of such office as to reflect credit on the league and gain the hearty approval of all supporters of honest, manly, ball-playing; and,
>
> *Whereas*, We believe that to him more than to any other one man is due the credit of the practical reforms which have been accomplished during the past [five] years in the relations of clubs and players, the exhibition of the game of base-ball, and its elevation to the foremost rank among American field sports; therefore,
>
> *Resolved*, That we tender him our hearty thanks for his services, and express the hope that the league may have the benefit of his services as president for many years.[8]

Chicago's baseball fans probably cared more about Williams Hulbert's services as White Stocking president than they did his responsibilities as head of the National League. Could Hulbert keep the team together? Did the players want to remain in Chicago or would they look elsewhere? The *Chicago Daily Tribune* had reported in October that "it will be gratifying news to lovers of base-ball in this city to know that the team that won the pennant in 1880 will practically be the one that will play here next year. There was no need of any 'five-men reserve' in the case of the Chicagos, for all were apparently anxious to stay."[9]

More Cheers for Chicago (1881–1882)

Although the White Stockings team would basically stay the same for the new season, the club would see some changes on the field. During the National League's board of directors' meeting in New York, Hulbert and the other delegates revised some of the playing rules. For example, the pitcher would now have to stand fifty feet from home plate instead of forty-five feet. The batter would take first base after seven called balls (in December 1879 the number had been decreased from nine called balls to eight; the figure would vary during the 1880s until set at four in 1889). Also, the umpire's "good ball" warning to batters was eliminated. Since 1876 a rule had stipulated that before a batter was called out on three strikes, the umpire first had to warn him by calling out "good ball" if he did not swing at a well-pitched ball after the second strike. This had, in essence, given the batter an extra strike.[10]

Most of the White Stockings reported for duty by the last week of March, "hearty and sound in every respect," according to one report.[11] As the men worked out and prepared for Opening Day, newspapers published stories about the team and profiles of the various players.

"Ready for the Word. The Sporting Season Is on the 'Scratch,' and, at the Word 'Go,' Will Bound Away in the Race. The Big Chicago Base-Ball Team in Steady Daily Practice on White-Stocking Park. Its Members Show Up in Excellent Form—How Each Man Passed His Winter Vacation." *(Chicago) Times*, April 17, 1881, p. 11.

BASE-BALL.
THE WHITE STOCKINGS.

Now that the members of the Chicago team are all here and at work, it will not be uninteresting to the ball-loving public to know what their favorites have been doing during the past winter, and what their present condition is. In general, it may be said that they are men of exceptionally good habits, and that they have not run down, in bodily stamina, as many professional players do. Beyond a little soreness of muscle, in two or three cases, consequent upon their violent exercise after some months of rest, they feel as well as in the middle of the season.

To begin with Capt. Anson, he says he passed the winter playing the gentleman in Marshalltown, Iowa, though he occasionally renewed his muscle by shoveling snow and chopping firewood. He admits that he has studied up several new "wrinkles" in play, but refuses to give them away till he has won a few games with them. The first thing he did when he got back to the city was to take a few Turkish and vapor baths to get the "country" out of him.

[George] Gore spent the winter in Sac[c]arappa, Me., in the filial duty of caring for an invalid mother. On Sunday night last he received the sad intelligence of her death. He is in excellent physical trim.

[Silver] Flint passed a part of the winter in Chicago and a part in St. Louis, with his parents. He feels well and his hands are sound and hard, but he nevertheless rejoices in the fact that [Larry] Corcoran and [Fred] Goldsmith have been moved five feet farther away from him.[12] He has been in the gymnasium for a month.

[Mike] Kelly spent the early part of the winter in Paterson, N. J., and the other part in Cincinnati, where he practiced throwing and catching. He is longing for gentle spring, as, on the day following his arrival, most of his wardrobe was stolen, and he contracted a severe cold while going about in a duster.

Corcoran passed the winter in Brooklyn, with little opportunity to practice, on account of the weather. He is in good trim, however, and ready to take the chances with the other pitchers at fifty feet.

Goldsmith spent most of the winter in New Haven, coaching the Yale college nine. This, of course, gave him exercise. Moreover, he had free access to the gymnasium during the winter, and is in the very pink of condition. He promises to prove troublesome to the batters this season.

[Tom] Burns spent the winter in New Britain, Conn. and had no practice. He is as sound as a nut, however, and will be in good playing trim when the season opens.

[Abner] Dalrymple kept his muscle up during the winter by turning a brake on a Chicago, Burlington and Quincy train. He looks and feels in first-rate condition.

[Ned] Williamson made his home in Chicago and got callouses on his hands selling cigars and tobacco. He has been in the gymnasium for six weeks, and thinks he could hit for three bases if he had a chance.

[Joe] Quest also remained in Chicago and has been in gymnasium practice for a couple of months. He thinks he can still take care of second and a part of right.

[Andy] Piercy has been in New York a part of the time and in Chicago a part. Six weeks in the gymnasium have put him in trim. President [William] Hulbert feels sure that he will prove a valuable member of the team.

[Hugh] Nicol,[13] of Rockford, who is assisting in the practice, was with the Westerns, of Topeka, Kan., last season, and led the batting. He can play almost any position, including that of pitcher. He is a trained athlete, and professional gymnast, turning "cart-wheels," "twisters," and "flip-flaps" with ease. He is a stone and marble cutter by trade, and has kept his muscle hard during the winter at that business.

The diamond is still wet, notwithstanding the fact that large quantities of snow and i[ce] have been picked loose and carted away. A few more days of such weather as that of yesterday, however, will make it solid. The north end of the grounds are dry, and a diamond has been laid out there, where the game is practiced every day. Between the hours of practice, when they are together, there is no part of a circus which the members of the team do not go through, even to the calliope.[14]

◆ ◆ ◆

Joining Chicago in the National League for the 1881 season were teams from Boston, Buffalo, Cleveland, Providence, Troy, Worcester, and Detroit (taking Cincinnati's place). What with the White Stockings' tough schedule, Chicago's no-nonsense player-manager ensured that his men practiced diligently. As the *Chicago Daily Tribune* observed, "Capt. Anson is a firm believer in hard out-door work—batting, fielding, and base-running—as a preparation for effective play. Last year he put his team on the field in tiptop condition at the very outset, and he will do the same this year."

The Chicago players may have been in "tiptop condition," but they were not impressive on the ball field; they split their first six games with Cleveland and on May 18 were in fourth place, though only 2½ games behind Worcester.

At about this time, Mike Kelly was developing a reputation for "trickery," as the *Boston Herald* put it. The newspaper had a point, for on May 20 Boston lost to Chicago, 5–4, probably due to the right fielder's questionable behavior. In its game-day coverage, the *New York Clipper* wrote that Kelly was on second base when batter Cap Anson was called out on a close play at first base. "The umpire was giving his entire attention to the play at first, and Kelly, coming from second, seeing this, cut across the corner without touching third, and scored what proved to be the winning run. The claim was made by the Bostons that Kelly's run should not be counted; but the umpire did not see the play, and consequently allowed [t]he run."

Kelly also used his special tactics to prevent teams from scoring runs. For instance, he would conceal balls in the outfield grass, so if a long drive got by him, he could pick up one of his nearby hidden baseballs to rob the batter of an extra base or two. When an opposing player ran after a White Stocking fly ball, Kelly would occasionally try to confuse him by calling out the name of a different player to take the ball. Not surprisingly, the *Chicago Daily Tribune* did not see any "trickery" in Kelly's actions, instead opining that that no ballplayer "should be blamed for too much zeal in his endeavor to win."[15]

Kelly's teammates were no less zealous, and the White Stockings followed their May 20 victory with four more wins. On July 2, after three-game sweeps of the Providence Grays and Troy Trojans, Chicago led the second-place Buffalo Bisons by a healthy 4½ games. Center fielder George Gore, one of the league's speediest base runners—despite weighing 195 pounds and standing 5 feet, 11 inches—had particularly distinguished himself on June 25. As the *Chicago Daily Tribune* wrote, the 2,000 fans at the White Stockings' ballpark were treated to a 12–8 victory over Providence that was "full of action and at all times interesting.... Chicago won by virtue of superiority in every point of play, but notably so in base-running. Gore's performances in this respect were something phenomenal." He reached base in each of his five plate appearances, getting "three clean hits" and scoring five runs. He also "stole second base five times, and stole third base twice,—a record which as a whole has probably never been equalled in a League game."[16]

Chicago's schedule included a long road trip at the end of the season, so for the day of the club's last home game, August 25, it planned a grand celebration. The Chicago *Times* reported that "the management made some special preparations for the occasion. The club-house was dressed with flags, and many small flags ornamented the fences." The team, too, had some special preparations in mind for game day. That morning the players presented club president William Hulbert with a "massive" gold watch chain and locket "as a token of their respect and esteem." One side of the locket featured the initials "W. A. H." while "From the boys of '80 and '81" was inscribed on the other side. Inside the locket, the newspaper went on, "are little hinged ovals, capable of being folded and unfolded, for twelve portraits, which are yet to be put in. The occasion was as gratifying as it is unusual."

The festivities continued during the afternoon, which even included Hulbert's large black dog, Champion. As the game began, the crowd cheered as the two teams, with Champion, marched from the club house to home plate. The *Times* wrote that spectators received "engraved and perfumed score-cards," which "contained on the first page an engraved dog's head, with the legend: 'Champion: He feeds on visiting players.'"

Unfortunately, it was the Detroit Wolverines who did the feasting that day, as they chewed up the White Stockings, 7–5. That made little difference in the standings, however. Chicago still enjoyed a healthy lead over the other league teams, and with a record of 56 wins and 28 losses they once again ended the season in first place, 9 games in front of the Providence Grays and 10½ ahead of the Buffalo Bisons. The White Stockings also led the National League in hits (918), runs (550), runs batted in (400), and batting average (.295). Their earned run average of 2.43 was just slightly behind that of the Grays (2.40). Individual league honors were in the categories of hits (Cap Anson, 137); runs (George Gore, 86); runs batted in (Anson, 82); and wins (Larry Corcoran, 31). Anson's batting average of .399 was best in the league. Abner Dalrymple, Mike Kelly, and Silver Flint also hit over .300.[17]

The *New York Clipper* believed that Chicago owed its 1876, 1880, and 1881 championships to "superior play in the field in each of the departments of pitching, batting, and fielding." In addition, "each year competent club management was a prominent element of success—in 1876 under [Al] Spalding, and in 1880 and '81 under Anson." The *Chicago Daily Tribune* also singled out the club's administration, contending that the 1881 pennant "was a foregone conclusion from the first. The Chicago management had at the beginning of the year done a thing previously unheard of—had retained for a second season the identical team which won the championship in 1880, and the result justified the judgment which animated this action."

The White Stockings directors wisely kept the starting team members together for the 1882 season; in fact, the *Tribune* reported that in less than two weeks after Chicago secured its league victory, secretary Al Spalding had signed contracts from all of them. "Not one of these players hesitated an instant about signing, but all were only too glad to make sure of playing another year in Chicago. Not one asked for an increase of salary, but an increase was voluntarily allowed in one or two deserving instances."

The club could probably afford it. According to one report, most of the league teams at least broke even in 1881, "and some, notably the Detroit and Chicago clubs, have handsome balances in the treasury to begin on next year."[18]

That extra money would come in handy, as the National League would soon be competing with a new baseball league, the American Association. William Hulbert's strict administrative rules notwithstanding, the Cincinnati club had made it clear in 1880 that to attract spectators and turn a profit, it needed to sell alcohol at the park and play games on Sundays. Cincinnati and a few other teams also felt that the National League's set ticket price of fifty cents was too high, and they wanted the freedom to determine their own admission fees.

Baseball delegates formed the American Association in Cincinnati on November 2, 1881, and by the start of its inaugural season it would comprise teams from Baltimore, Cincinnati, Louisville, Philadelphia, Pittsburgh, and St. Louis. Although William Hulbert disagreed with the organization's philosophy, he appears to have enjoyed a spirited correspondence with its first president, Denny McKnight of the Pittsburgh Alleghenys. Hulbert even assured him that "speaking for myself, as a member of the Chicago Club and the League, I have not the slightest feeling antagonistic to the Am Ass^n."[19]

This sentiment may not have represented Hulbert's true feelings when it came to the new league and its advocacy for Sunday games, the sale of beer, and varied admission prices. On November 18 he emphatically wrote: "I tell you, M^r McKnight, many of the ideas upon which your Ass^n is based ... are each and all the rankest fallacies. Each and every 'departure' that I name, lowers the tone. You cannot afford that. You cannot afford to bid for the patronage of the degraded. If you are to be successful, you must secure recognition by the respectable. A Sunday playing club, that is at the same time accessory to beer hawking, is beyond doubt, a curse to any community."

Hulbert also informed McKnight that he was not a well man. He wrote that for "more than a month, I have been ailing. My doctors have let me out a few hours in the middle of pleasant days, but active attention to business is positively interdicted." A baseball man to the end, the 49-year-old Hulbert apparently disobeyed his doctor's orders for he continued to work on pressing business matters. "I am kept closely at home by illness," he told Walter S. Appleton of the New York Metropolitans in mid–January, "but I am up and about the house part of the day. I am a member of the [National League] schedule com^m, and I may as well employ my time drafting my plan for the schedule."[20]

Hulbert also spent his time following the White Stockings as they prepared for the 1882 season. He even intended to go to the ballpark on Saturday, April 8, to see them practice, but he was deterred by inclement weather. On Monday, as the *Chicago Daily Tribune* informed its readers, "he was feeling unusually well" but suffered a heart attack "and he died almost instantly." The cause of death was heart disease and dropsy.

Two days later, Chicago Ball Club stockholders, players, and friends of Hulbert gathered at the clubhouse at 108 Michigan Avenue. A special committee was appointed to draw up resolutions honoring the club president, and Al Spalding read aloud newspaper obituaries and telegrams of sympathy and condolence. The *Chicago Daily Tribune*, for example, declared that Hulbert's "great force of character, strong will, marked executive ability, unerring judgment of men and measures, and strict integrity and fairness were of incalculable value to the league, and he was rightly considered to be the brains and backbone of that organization." Prominent Chicago attorney W. I. Culver, a longtime friend of Hulbert, addressed the group, and Spalding published some of the remarks in a black-bordered obituary in his *Base Ball Guide and Official League Book*:

To those who were present at Mr. Hulbert's bedside during the weary nights of his long and fated illness, nothing was more suggestively prominent than the fact that he was dying as he lived—a sincere, earnest, energetic man. There was no mask for him to drop; he had worn none. Though impatient of suffering and of the restraint of his daily increasing weakness, he was bold and manly to the last; certain that his days were numbered, hopeless of cure, writhing at times in pain, he awaited the liberator death, with as much composure as he would have greeted a friend. He lived and died a man....

He was an originator, not an adopter of ideas. This is exemplified by the work he left behind, for it will be admitted without question that the league legislation was his creation, and its perfection of plan and detail, and the excellent results it has already accomplished, prove the foresight and comprehensiveness of mind of its originator.

In business and social relations, sincerity and candor attended his every act and word. He pretended nothing that he was not; he said nothing that he did not mean. No one ever doubted his word, or disbelieved his promise.

William Hulbert was interred in Chicago's Graceland Cemetery, with Cap Anson and Al Spalding serving as two of the pallbearers. The National League arranged to have placed near his gravestone a large baseball-shaped monument that, according to National League meeting minutes, had been "provided for by equal contributions of all the clubs that were members of the League at the time of his death." On the memorial stone was inscribed Hulbert's name, the words "National League," and the names of the 1882 league clubs: Boston, Buffalo, Chicago, Cleveland, Detroit, Providence, Troy, and Worcester.[21]

Hulbert's obituary appeared in Chicago newspapers as well as in publications across the country.

"The Last Run. Funeral of the Late W. A. Hulbert—Unusually Appropriate and Pleasing Floral Tributes." *(Chicago) Times*, April 14, 1882, p. 5.

FUNERAL OF W. A. HULBERT.

The funeral of the late W. A. Hulbert, president of the Chicago Base-Ball club and of the National league, took place yesterday morning at the family residence at No. 1,334 Fortieth street. The casket, which was covered with plain black velvet, was placed in the front parlor, and was fairly surrounded with beautiful floral pieces, the gifts of the associates of the deceased and his family friends. The most elaborate piece was a representation of a ballfield, nearly six feet square. The ground was of smilax. The bases and the pitcher's and catcher's stands were of white flowers. The running-paths were in blue flowers, and across the right field were the words, in floral inscription, "Our President." It was the tribute of the Chicago club. At the head of the casket a floral sphere about ten inches in diameter was supported by eight bats made of flowers. It represented the league of eight clubs, each bat bearing the name of a club, the Chicago bat being broken. It was the gift of the league. The Providence players presented a floral pillow, and there were numerous other floral tributes.

The entire Chicago club was present, and many of the friends of base ball in the city. Mayor [William G.] Thompson, of Detroit, and Josiah Jewett, of Buffalo, the presidents of the clubs of those cities, were also present.

The services were performed by the Rev. J. T. Burhoe, pastor of the Memorial Baptist church, and the Rev. E. F. Williams, pastor of the South Congregational church. After the reading of the scriptures by Mr. Burhoe, Mr. Williams delivered an address, in which he described the religious character of the deceased. Mr. Hulbert had been reticent about his inner sentiments, but those to whom he divulged them knew that he was a reader of the scriptures, and that before his demise he had expressed his willingness to die and his pious confidence in his future well-being. Mr. Williams paid a fine tribute to the strict integrity and uprightness of the deceased, and his desire that the organization over which he had presided should be characterized by purity, sobriety, and honesty. He commended these qualities to his friends and associates.

After prayer, a hymn was sung, and the remains were taken to Graceland for interment, the following being the pall-bearers:

J. B. Lyon, T. E. Courtney, A. C. Anson, A. G. Spalding, W. I. Culver, and C. T. Trego.

Upon Hulbert's death, league vice president Arthur H. Soden, the president of the Boston club, automatically assumed the presidency of the National League. The White Stockings' board underwent some changes as well; as reported in the *New York Clipper*, the Chicago Ball Club elected Al Spalding to take Hulbert's place as president and also appointed new officers:

> The recent death of the president of the club obliged the members to elect a successor, and on April 26, at a meeting of the stockholders, Mr. Spalding was unanimously elected president, and a better man for the position could not have been selected. Though his extensive business in Chicago and manufactory at Hastings, Mich., command his attention, he still finds time to attend to his club duties, and now, as its president, he will devote more of his efforts for its welfare and success than ever before, considerable as his services have been. The election of the new president was followed by the choice of the following well-known and influential citizens of Chicago as the club's new board of directors, viz., Messrs. John B. Lyon, Chas. T. Trego—members of the Chicago Board of Trade—John R. Walsh—President of the Chicago National Bank—and A. G. Mills, with President Spalding as a member *ex officio*. The new secretary is [Jonathan] H. Brown. The club is to be congratulated upon the high character of the gentlemen who have been chosen to govern it this season.[22]

The White Stockings opened the 1882 season on May 1, with each team member wearing a band of black crepe on his left sleeve in memory of William Hulbert. The wet and cold April had prevented much outdoor training and practice. Nevertheless, when the team surprisingly lost its first two games, the *Chicago Daily Tribune* offered some curt advice: "What the Chicagos need is a hard course of drill at home to work off the winter's laziness and looseness. In April, 1881, Capt. Anson had his men out an average of six hours a day playing against each other in a way that fitted them for the serious business ahead, and the good results of this policy were shown in the team's strong, steady play from the very beginning." This "strong, steady play," however, continued to elude the White Stockings, and on June 15 they were in fifth place in the National League with a record of 12-14. The *Tribune* predicted that "Chicago is virtually out of the race so far as first place is concerned."

Surprisingly, though, the team soon began chalking up increasing numbers of wins. Pitcher Larry Corcoran hit the team's first-ever grand slam home run on June 20 before two thousand spectators in a 13–3 victory over Worcester. Between June 26 and July 11 the White Stockings won nine games in a row, and on July 24 they pummeled the Cleveland Blues and pitcher Dave Rowe, 35-4. Seven Chicago players made four hits, six men scored four or more runs, and before the rout was over the covers were knocked off of two baseballs. The game had marked outfielder Rowe's first appearance for Cleveland as a pitcher, and the *New York Clipper* candidly dubbed him a "frightful failure, the score of clean hits, total bases and runs credited to the Chicagos being the largest ever made in a League championship game."[23]

The White Stockings' jubilance, unfortunately, was short-lived, perhaps due to

6. Successes and Struggles (1880–1884)

The 1882 Chicago White Stockings in a team engraving. Top row, from left: Ned Williamson, Mike Kelly, Silver Flint, and Fred Goldsmith. Middle row, from left: Joe Quest, Tom Burns, Cap Anson, Abner Dalrymple, George Gore. Bottom row, from left: Hugh Nicol, Larry Corcoran. The team finished first in the National League in 1882 (*Harper's Weekly*, October 14, 1882).

captain Anson's unnecessary tinkering with his players on the field. After Cap Anson moved several key men from their customary positions, both player errors and team losses began piling up and the team soon fell behind the Providence Grays. As the *Chicago Daily Tribune* groused, "A sorrier case of fall-down was never witnessed." Anson apparently saw the folly of his ways, for he returned the men to their normal positions, and on September 5, Chicago trounced the Troy Trojans, 10–0. "The original champion team of 1880 and 1881 was on the field," the *Tribune* rejoiced, "[Joe] Quest being restored to second, which he covered in very fine form, [Tom] Burns to short, where he seemed entirely at home, and [Mike] Kelly to right field, where he was all that could be asked."

By the middle of September, Chicago had passed Providence to seize first place, which the White Stockings managed to hold on to by winning 15 of their last 16 regular season games. The *New York Clipper* declared that the end of the season left "the Chicago Club once more in possession of the pennant, after the hardest struggle for it that any club has ever had in the League. It was a close and exciting race all the way through, not only for first place, but also for second, third and fourth positions" (which were occupied by the Providence, Boston, and Buffalo teams, respectively).

With its record of 55–29, Chicago walked off the field with not only the championship pennant but also other assorted honors, including best team batting average (.277), most hits (892), and most runs (604). George Gore scored the most runs with 99, followed by Abner Dalrymple with 96. Cap Anson ranked first in the league in runs batted in (83), though his batting average of .362 was second to Dan Brouthers of Buffalo (.368). George Gore and Mike Kelly also eclipsed the .300 mark. Pitcher Larry Corcoran led the league with a 1.95 earned run average.[24]

The baseball season had also been exciting—as well as lucrative—for the teams in the fledgling American Association. Enthusiastic spectators flocked to the ballparks of its six teams, and even Spalding's official *Base Ball Guide* allowed that the organization's first year was "attended by a degree of financial success unprecedented in the history of non–League professional clubs."

Cincinnati placed first in the Association, followed by Philadelphia and then Louisville. October 6 and 7 saw the two championship clubs in the country—the National League's Chicago White Stockings and the American Association's Cincinnati Red Stockings—face off in a two-game exhibition series in Cincinnati. The Red Stockings whitewashed their opponents, 4–0, in the first game, but Chicago came back and took the second, 2–0. The two clubs' previous commitments precluded a rubber match so, without a winner, the brief tournament was not a true World Series. But the contest was, as one modern baseball historian observes, "the first time two teams from different leagues played each other, and as such it takes its rightful place in baseball history."[25]

A Remodeled Ballpark but No Glory (1883–1884)

The 1883 season opened without the Troy and Worcester teams on the schedule. The clubs had played poorly for several years, and in 1882 they had finished seventh and eighth in the National League. With lackluster performances came sparse crowds and paltry gate receipts, and officials from the other teams voted to drop them from the league. Replacing the two were clubs from the much larger cities of Philadelphia and New York. "The reason given for kicking out Worcester and Troy," wrote the *New York Clipper*, "was that the patronage in either of these cities is not large enough to give the visiting clubs a share of gate-money sufficient to pay their expenses, and that, as New York and Philadelphia were anxious to be admitted, it was simply a question of business whether two non-paying cities should be continued in the copartnership [*sic*] when two paying cities could be secured to take their places."[26]

Chicago continued to be one of these "paying cities," and local newspapers bragged that Al Spalding easily retained the nucleus of his team for the upcoming season. (It did not hurt Spalding's recruiting efforts that in February 1883 the reserve rule was amended to allow each club to retain up to 11 of its members every season, an increase of six). Therefore, only a few White Stockings departed, including Joe Quest, who joined the Detroit Wolverines, and Hugh Nicol, who jumped to the American Association's St. Louis Browns. To refill his roster, Spalding signed Troy's Fred Pfeffer and acquired the amateur player Billy Sunday, who in later years would gain renown not as an athlete but as one of America's most celebrated evangelists.[27]

The new season would also usher in a renovated ballpark for the White Stockings. According to Cap Anson, even though the baseball grounds were "the most accessible of any in the country" and "within five minutes' walk from any part of the business district," the park was still quite small. Spalding solved the problem as well as capitalized on his team's burgeoning popularity by more than doubling the seating capacity. He added eighteen private boxes on top of the grandstand for the use of club officers, reporters, and, as the *Chicago Daily Tribune* noted, for "those who may wish to pay the extra charge for occupying them." A six-foot fence was erected to keep spectators off the field.

After extolling the amenities of the remodeled facility, the *Tribune* bragged that Chicago "now possesses the champion grounds." Other publications also covered the new ballpark, including the *New York Times*, the *New York Clipper*, *Sporting Life*, and *Harper's Weekly*.[28]

"The Chicago Base-Ball Grounds." *Harper's Weekly*, May 12, 1883, p. 299. [Note: This article originally appeared as one long passage, and a few paragraph breaks have been added for ease of readability.]

The grounds of the Chicago Ball Club, indisputably the finest in the world in respect of seating accommodations and conveniences, are located on what is known as the Lake Front property, the title to which is in the city of Chicago. The inclosure begins at Randolph Street on the north, and extends along the east line of Michigan Avenue southward to a point about midway between Washington and Madison streets. On the east are the tracks and switch yards of the Illinois Central Railroad Company, which has for several years past made a standing offer of $800,000 (not one-half its value) for the property; but as the city has been enjoined either

Billy Sunday was born near Ames, Iowa, in 1862. As a young man he competed in foot races and played on the baseball team in nearby Marshalltown, Cap Anson's hometown. Anson recalled in his autobiography that he happened to see Sunday run in a race "and it was the speed that he showed on that occasion that opened my eyes to his possibilities in the base-ball playing line." Anson signed him to the 1883 White Stockings as a substitute outfielder, and although he was a good fielder, he was not particularly strong at the plate (He played in 499 games during his career and batted .248.).

When Mike Kelly left Chicago for Boston in 1887, Billy Sunday took his place in the outfield. Sunday had begun attending church services in the mid-1880s, so when he was not playing baseball he was frequently addressing Sunday school classes and Young Men's Christian Associations. The Pittsburgh Alleghenys purchased his contract in 1888, and when *Sporting Life* mentioned his "brilliant work for the Pittsburgs" in its August 29, 1888, issue, it added that "Sunday is a Sunday school teacher and professing Christian, and yet he will deliberately steal—bases."

Sunday's last year as a professional ballplayer was 1890. The Philadelphia Phillies had signed him for the 1891 season, but he had taken a special YMCA course in Bible training, and he wanted to continue his studies. Right after Philadelphia granted his release, he started a job with the Chicago Y.M.C.A. He began holding revival meetings, and in 1903 was ordained as a minister in the Presbyterian Church. In the early twentieth century Sunday was the most famous evangelist in the United States, though by the 1920s his influence had declined, as had attendance at his revivals. Billy Sunday and his wife, Helen, had four children. He died in 1935 (Adrian C. Anson, *A Ball Player's Career*, 1900).

from selling the tract or from permitting its use for permanent buildings, the ball club has continued to enjoy the rare privilege of grounds situated within a two minutes' walk of State Street, the chief retail thoroughfare of Chicago.

Partly on account of the convenient location of the grounds, but more by reason of the exceptional management of the Chicago ball team, and its success in winning the National League championship for three successive seasons, beginning with 1881, the game of baseball is extremely popular in Chicago, and the average attendance at League championship games is considerably greater there than in any other city in the United States. During the season of 1882 the attendance at the forty-five League games played in Chicago was upward of 130,000, or an average of 3000 persons to a game.[29] With this fine patronage, made up in good part of the better classes of the community, the Chicago Club is amply able to maintain its costly team of players, and to equip its grounds and fixtures in a manner that by comparison with the usual style of base-ball appurtenances might be termed palatial.

At an outlay of $10,000 since the close of the playing season of 1882 the Chicago Club, under the direction of President SPALDING, has completely remodelled its seating arrangements. Every exposed surface is painted, so as to admit of thorough cleansing from dust, the item of paint alone amounting to $1800. The grand stand seats 2000 people, and the uncovered seats will accommodate 6000 more, so that with the standing room the total capacity is fully 10,000, and this without invading the playing-field. A fence six feet high encircles the field in front of all the seats, which are elevated so as to command the best view of the play. Overlooking the main entrance is a handsomely ornamented pagoda, built for a band stand, and to be occupied by the First Cavalry Band throughout the season.[30] Surmounting the grand stand is a row of eighteen private boxes, cozily draped with curtains to keep out wind and sun, and furnished with comfortable arm-chairs. By the use of the telephone and gong President SPALDING can conduct all the preliminary details of the game without leaving his private box.

Besides club officers and players, the services of forty-one persons are required at each game to attend to the grounds and seating arrangements, viz., seven ushers, six policemen, four ticket-sellers, four gate-keepers, three field-men, three cushion-renters, six refreshment boys, and eight musicians. Aside from players' salaries, ground rent, and including advertising, the cost per game on the Chicago grounds is $200; add to this the salaries of players, rent of grounds, travelling and hotel expenses, and $10,000 expended this year on improvements, and the total outlay for the season is $60,000, so that the Chicago Club must average $525 for each of the ninety-six League championship games to be played during 1883. But the patronage attracted by the famous champion team both at home and in other cities may be depended upon to make good this large sum, and possibly leave something besides for stockholders. The fact that so large an outlay can be safely made tells its own story of the popularity of base-ball.

◆ ◆ ◆

The White Stockings opened the 1883 season on the road with three wins against the Detroit Wolverines. Upon Chicago's return home, more than 5,000 excited fans braved a chilly May 5 afternoon to help the White Stockings inaugurate their remodeled park. "A great many of them must have been disappointed," the *Tribune* wrote, "not because the home club lost the game, but because of the wretched display they made against the Detroits—a club whom they had beaten three games straight."

The White Stockings lost the next two games as well, but by the end of the month their 15–6 record led the National League. On July 3 they rolled over the Buffalo Bisons,

31–7, pounding Buffalo's pitcher for 32 hits. Chicago was scheduled to play two games against the Cleveland Blues on the July 4 holiday, so members of the Ohio team had been in the stands and had witnessed the Buffalo carnage. According to the *Tribune*, "It is safe to say that no circus ever afforded [the Blues] greater enjoyment. Anson had a great run with the bat, going to the second bag four times. Each time he appeared [Jack] Glasscock, the shortstop of the Cleveland nine, would remark: 'Anson will now get two bases or kill an infielder.'"[31]

Glasscock may have been facetious, but Anson's ire was certainly on display on August 10 in Toledo, Ohio, where the White Stockings played an exhibition game against a local minor-league club. The Toledo Blue Stockings were in their first season as members of the Northwestern League, and scholar-athlete Moses Fleetwood "Fleet" Walker, an African American who had played baseball at both Oberlin College and the University of Michigan, was dazzling players and sports fans alike. Blacks had not yet played in the National League, however, and Anson had no intention of sharing the field with the young catcher.[32] The *Toledo Daily Blade* covered the game and reported on the shameful behavior of Anson (the "beefy bluffer") and the Chicago club:

> [Fleet] Walker, the colored catcher of the Toledo Base Ball Club, who, by the way, is a gentleman and a scholar, in the literal sense, was a source of contention between the home club and that swelled organization (literal, again) the Chicago Club. The National champions came to Toledo yesterday morning, and their arrival created quite a sensation at the Union depot, where it was first thought they were Haverly's Mast[o]dons or Callend[e]r's Consolidated, their sun burned faces leaving it a matter of doubt as to their being tainted with black blood.[33] They wore white tiles [*sic*] and blue uniforms, and under the command of the swelled baby (literal again) of Marshalltown, Capt. Anson, created a very considerable impression. Shortly after their arrival in the city the managing director of the Toledo Club was waited upon and informed that there was objection in the Chicago Club to Toledo's playing Walker, the colored catcher. It was not stated that Walker, being a "nigger," might contaminate the select organization of visitors, but that was the only inference to be drawn from the announcement. The New Yorks, Metropolitans, Columbus and St. Louis clubs, organizations outside of the N. W. League, had played with Walker against them and had experienced no unpleasant results save as his excellent play had militated against them, but the Chicago club was of more delicate fiber, more susceptible to deleterious [*sic*] influences and hence could not play, with a colored catcher against them.
>
> Walker has a very sore hand, and it had not been intended to play him in yesterday's game, and this was stated to the bearer of the announcement for the Chicagos. Not content with this, the visitors during their perambulations of the forenoon declared with the swagger for which they are noted, that they would play ball "with no d--d nigger," and when the Club arrived at the grounds Capt. Anson repeated this declaration to the Toledo management. What would have been gratifying to Toledoans would have been for the management to have ordered Capt. Anson and his crew off the grounds, without more ado, but this was not done. The management had put [Jack] McQuaid in to play, and as announced in the morning, had not intended to play Walker, but when Capt. Anson made his "break," the order was given, then and there, to play Walker and the beefy bluffer was informed that he could play his team or go, just as he blank pleased. Anson hauled in his horns somewhat and "consented" to play, remarking, "We'll play this here game, but won't play never no more with the nigger in." Walker was put in right field, and played a faultless game, despite his sore hand. Now for a brief comparison of men. The man whom the Chicago club played with under protest, and only to save their share of the gate money, is the superior intellectually of any man in the Chicago club. He differs from the "kicking" players in that he is a gentleman on or off the ball field, and entirely lacking in bummer instincts. As a ball player he is the equal of any of the visitors here yesterday. He has won the respect of all with whom he has been brought in contact since his engagement in Toledo, and it was just as well for the Chicago club yesterday that the crowd at League Park did not understand, during the game, the "break" that had been made. Walker is a law student of Ann Arbor University,

and stands well in his classes. As to the Chicago club, it is a fact not to be dis[p]uted that it contains a greater proportion of the "bum" element than any ball club in America, and it is likely to prove a very cold day when they again carry a substantial bundle of gate receipts out of Toledo.

The game was only a fair exhibition of ball playing. From the impression made by the Chicagos upon their arrival in the City, with their uniform suits of blue flannel and high white hats, it was expected by many that they would eclipse in point of appearance any club that has been seen at League Park this season. And they did. It is not putting it too strongly to say they were the most untidy looking lot of ballplayers that have ever graced the City with their presence. Their baggy white uniforms, dirty white stockings and varigarious [sic] assortment of caps gave them a slouchy, uncouth appearance which, with their brag[g]adocio manner, was in strange contrast with what most of the audience had expected to see.

The playing on both sides was characterized by heavy batting. The visitors hit [Sam] Moff[e]t quite freely, and the Toledos retaliated by batting [Fred] Goldsmith's pitching for 16 safe bases with a total of 20. During the first inning it was evident the Chicagos thought they had struck a picnic. But when the Toledos began rapping the ball about the diamond, and at the end of the second inning led them by four hits, they opened their eyes to the fact that unless they got down to business and that in pretty short order, the open air concert would be on the other side. For the remaining seven innings they accordingly did their best. The Toledos played a pretty game throughout. Their batting was unusually heavy, their base running was good and considering the number of men playing out of position, their fielding was excellent. It is safe to say had the home team been playing in their proper order the game would have been theirs. In the second, sixth and ninth innings the game was tied, and in the tenth the visitors won the victory by a single run, which was made on a series of bad plays for the Toledos. [Curt] Welch figured behind the bat yesterday, and did well. With practice he would soon become a valuable man in that position.[34]

A reporter for *Sporting Life* suggested that the Walker incident marked "the first time in base ball history that the color line had been drawn." The *Chicago Daily Tribune* did not mention the controversy in its sports pages. The newspaper devoted just two sentences to its account of the game, noting that it took the White Stockings ten innings to defeat the minor league team and that the "home nine felt proud of having succeeded in holding down the league champions." For their part, the Toledo manager and his men undoubtedly prided themselves for successfully defending their catcher against the tirade of "Baby" Anson (Anson's nickname, due to his childish outbursts, which the Toledo newspaper derisively used). The White Stockings' captain did not include the incident in his autobiography, though its pages are sprinkled with racist comments about Clarence Duval, an African American teenager whom the Chicago team engaged as a mascot for good luck in June 1888.

Some baseball writers maintain that Cap Anson, as an outspoken proponent of professional baseball's color line, single-handedly kept African American players out of professional baseball for decades. Others argue that he did not have this type of influential power; moreover, since his anti-integration beliefs mirrored those of many white players and officials of the time, it was not necessary for him to exert authority, even if he possessed it. While Anson was a superb player, his prickly disposition, combative personality, and boastful arrogance endeared him to few people. If baseball officials were undecided about breaking the color barrier, would they willingly go along with someone they heartily disliked? Chicago Cubs historian Ed Hartig believes that "Anson was so hated that if others were on the fence one-way-or-another, his views would have been enough to convince them to be contrary to Anson. That they weren't means that Anson's views were shared throughout the game."[35]

Chicago followed its win in Toledo with two more against the Buffalo Bisons. The White Stockings lost their next seven games, but the players managed an amazing comeback. On their way to 11 consecutive victories, they set a major league record on September 6 by scoring 18 runs in a single inning, hammering the Detroit Wolverines, 26–6. This win gave the White Stockings sole possession of first place in the National League. Boston, though, was right on their heels, and four losses to the Beaneaters shattered any Chicago hopes for a fourth straight pennant. Boston ended the season with a 63–35 record, four games in front of second-place Chicago.[36]

The White Stockings may not have walked off the field with a pennant, but they received other accolades. Due to the regulation that balls clearing Chicago's short outfield fences were counted as ground-rule doubles, the club easily led the league with 277 two-base hits (Boston was second with 68 fewer). Ned Williamson hit 49 doubles, the most among league players.

Cap Anson had long protested that such over-the-fence hits should be regarded as home runs. He finally got his wish with a rule change for the 1884 season. But the increase in runs did little to boost the team that year, nor the fans' low spirits. The White Stockings lost six of their first 10 games, and by mid–May Chicago was fifth among the National League's eight teams. The *Tribune* declared (rather presciently, as it turned out) on May 18 that there was "nothing to encourage the expectation that the Chicago Club will be better than fourth in the race, and will have hard work to get even that place."

Admittedly, poor weather had limited the ballplayers' outdoor practice, and catcher Silver Flint and shortstop Tom Burns spent appreciable time on the disabled list. Moreover, as the *Tribune* wrote, "Neither [Larry] Corcoran nor [Fred] Goldsmith have in the games thus far played shown the pitching form necessary to keep the club anywhere near the front."

By May 25 Chicago was in seventh place, and this time the newspaper pointed its finger at the players' lack of discipline, which apparently had been a reoccurring problem:

Members of the 1884 and 1885 Chicago White Stockings. Top row, from left: George Gore, Silver Flint, Cap Anson, Elmer "Sy" Sutcliffe, Mike Kelly, and Fred Pfeffer. Bottom row, from far left: Larry Corcoran, Ned Williamson, Abner Dalrymple, Tom Burns, John Clarkson, and Billy Sunday (Adrian C. Anson, *A Ball Player's Career*, 1900).

It is a club capable of the best and worst playing of any in the league, and it has with extraordinary persistency done its worst this year. Capt. Anson in April laid out a program very different from that which he has followed. He declared that he was not going to stand any foolishness this season—no late hours, no bumming, no indifferent play; that he would fine every man who fell short of strict obedience in this respect, and double the fine for each succeeding offense. Evidently he has not kept to his plan of action. President Spalding last week wrote him a very severe letter, ordering him to be more strict in discipline than ever before, and even to hire detectives, if necessary, to find out whether any of the players slipped out of the hotels after 11 o'clock and went on a carousal. Two of the players were fined $50 each for drunkenness while in Boston, and if half of the reports are true two or three more should have lost most of their salaries in fines long before this.[37]

Spalding's stern tactics may have worked. In late October a sportswriter pointed out that there had been a "marked improvement" in the players' "habits and behavior" during the last month of the season. The White Stockings won 21 of their last 25 games, but it was too little, too late; just as the *Tribune* had predicted in May, they ended the year disappointingly in fourth place. The 1884 post-season featured the first "championship of the United States," and the National League's Providence Grays defeated the American Association's New York Metropolitans in three straight games.

Despite the Chicago team's undistinguished 62–50 record, Mike Kelly won the batting championship with his .354 average. Furthermore, the White Stockings had taken advantage of the new home run rule and had clobbered 142 homers, with an astounding 131 hit in their own park (the team total the year before was 13). On May 30 Ned Williamson had become the first major league baseball player to hit three home runs in one game, and he topped the league that year with 27. The three leading 1884 home-run hitters behind him were all from Chicago: Fred Pfeffer (25), Abner Dalrymple (22), and Cap Anson (21). The White Stockings were also first in the league in runs batted in, with Anson (102), Pfeffer (101), Kelly (95), and Williamson (84) leading the way.[38]

Epilogue

The White Stockings would not have the opportunity to repeat their home run barrage, because in November the National League adopted a rule that allowed a batter just two bases if his ball cleared an outfield fence that was less than 210 feet from home plate. As it turned out, the rule would have had no effect on the team anyway, as the players were forced to abandon their cozy little park. Although the City of Chicago was in possession of the lake-front property, the United States owned the land and Chicago was merely its custodian and caretaker. In May 1884 the federal government had sued the City and the Chicago Ball Club, alleging that since the government held the property in trust for the public, Chicago did not have the authority to allow any party to use public land for private or commercial purposes. Federal Circuit Court Judge Henry Blodgett ordered that the City "absolutely desist and refrain from leasing the whole or any part of the public ground" and "absolutely desist and refrain from constructing on or occupying the whole or any part of the said public ground."

Judge Blodgett told the White Stockings that they had to leave their ballpark by November 1. Spalding decided to relocate to Chicago's heavily populated West Side, and he carefully selected a site that was both readily accessible to baseball fans and more spacious than the former grounds. The White Stockings president was confident that his ballpark would be as attractive as any in the National League. Moreover, after the team's winning performance during the last few weeks of the season, Spalding was just as confident that in 1885 the new park's flagpole would proudly be flying a league championship pennant.[39]

7

ON TOP OF THE LEAGUE
(1885–1886)

> It is indeed wonderful how this club holds its own against younger and equally ambitious rivals, as nearly all the players on this team are seasoned veterans and new young blood is only infused after careful consideration and long trial. In all other quarters the old material is rapidly deteriorating and being superseded by new men, but the Chicagos seem never to grow old or to weaken.
> —*Sporting Life*, October 14, 1885

A New Park and Another Pennant (1885)

The 1884 White Stockings owed much of their late-season success to pitcher John Clarkson. A sore arm had limited hurler Fred Goldsmith's effectiveness, and he was released in early August, which left Larry Corcoran to shoulder most of the pitching duties. Clarkson came on board later in the month, and although he lost his first game on August 27, he finished the season with a 10–3 record, which convinced one sportswriter that "there is very little doubt that if Clarkson had been available early in June Chicago would have won the championship of 1884."

Clarkson and his teammates each commanded excellent salaries—as much as $3,000 per year—and in 1884 the White Stockings' payroll was reportedly the highest in the National League. Club president Spalding needed thousands of fans to buy seats in his new ballpark so he could pay those salaries, and he announced that "no pains or expense will be spared to make these the finest base-ball and athletic grounds in America." He chose a city block bounded by Congress Street on the north, Harrison Street on the south, Loomis Street on the west, and Throop Street on the east. "Taken all in all," he said, "I think the selection the best that could have been made, for it is located near the centre of the West Side, which contains a larger population than the North and South Sides combined, and the transportation facilities are excellent."

Cap Anson looked forward to playing in the new park, telling a Chicago reporter that he hoped "some of these fellows who have been saying Anson can't bat will be there." Local newspapers, too, agreed with Spalding's choice of sites.[1]

"Sporting Notes. Description of the New West-Side Grounds of the Chicago Base-Ball Club." *(Chicago) Times*, March 1, 1885, p. 7.

7. On Top of the League (1885–1886)

BASE-BALL.
THE NEW GROUNDS.

The site of the new league ball grounds has been definitely fixed upon. The grounds will be located on the West side, extending from Throop to Loomis streets, and Congress to Harrison, being 660 × 400 feet in dimensions. The greater distance is in the course of the two latter streets, running east and west. The distance of the grounds from State street is not over one and a half miles, and they can be easily reached within ten minutes by a number of street-car lines. It is intended by the management of the Chicago club to make the grounds the most attractive and perfectly appointed in the country, and with that end in view it has already closed a number of contracts which tend to it. A long lease has been obtained, and about $25,000 will be expended for fitting up the grounds. The latter will be surrounded by a brick wall twelve feet in height.[2] At the west end of the grounds the grand and side stand will be erected in the form of a semicircle. The roof of the grand stand will be supported by trusses instead of posts, and private boxes will be placed along the entire roof front. Open seats to the number of about six thousand will be ranged on either side of the grand stand, and the latter will afford a seating capacity of twenty-five hundred.[3] The ticket offices, business office, and visiting players' dressing-rooms will be of brick, and situated just back of the grand stand, while the club-house and home players' rooms, also of brick, will be situated at the extreme east end of the field. The managers are likewise contemplating the erection of a number of club-houses on the grounds for cricket, lacrosse, bicycle, and other sports, and are accordingly consulting the wishes of such organizations before deciding upon a definite plan. There is a strong likelihood of building a fine cinder bicycle track around the edge of the wall, but that depends wholly upon the support the club shall receive from bicycle clubs. The extreme eastern end of the grounds will afford an excellent carriage court and entrances for vehicles will be put in at the northeastern and southeastern corners. There will be no Sunday playing on the grounds, and the sale of liquor or beer will not be tolerated, nor will open betting or pool-selling be allowed in any form.[4] The grounds will be excellently adapted for all kinds of outdoor sports and, except the lord's athletic grounds, of London, they will be the only grounds in the world enclosed by a brick wall. The selection of the grounds was not made until the club had carefully looked into and examined every tender of land made it.

◆ ◆ ◆

Spalding's West Side Park was oval-shaped, with both foul lines measuring 216 feet. In its illustrated article on the new baseball grounds, the *New York Clipper* noted that "on the roof is a row of private-boxes, lettered from A to L, and provided with chairs. A neatly-furnished toilet-room with a private entrance had been provided for the ladies.... Everything in the shape of wood-work is painted terra-cotta color." *Sporting Life* was similarly impressed with the grounds: "Beyond all question the Chicago base ball park will be the finest and best in the world. Its neat brick buildings, substantial wall, and well-kept lawns will place it far in advance of any other base ball grounds, and the cities of the East will undoubtedly pattern after Chicago's usual excellence as soon as they see how far they are surpassed."

Local bicycle enthusiasts heartily approved of the racing track that encircled the playing field, and riders formed the Chicago Bicycle Track Association to take advantage of the new facility and promote their sport. The *Chicago Daily Tribune* observed that "not only will the grounds be used for exhibitions of the National game, and for bicycling, but they are equally well adapted to cricket, lacrosse, lawn-tennis, running races, and athletic sports of every description."[5]

Upon the construction of the White Stockings' West Side Park in 1885, the *New York Clipper* published these sketches, along with a paragraph of commentary. "Chicago can now be congratulated on having a permanent ball-ground," the sportswriter wrote, "probably superior in many of its appointments to any other in this country, and President A. G. Spalding of the Chicago Club is deserving of commendation for the enterprise he has displayed in its completion" (*New York Clipper*, June 6, 1885).

The National League opened the 1885 season with teams from Boston, Buffalo, Chicago, Detroit, New York, Philadelphia, Providence, and also St. Louis (taking the place of Cleveland, which had left the league following its poor showing in 1884). The White Stockings' park was still under construction by the time clubs began spring training, so Chicago made plans to head south in early April to play exhibition games against teams from Louisville, Cincinnati, Nashville, Chattanooga, and Atlanta. The White Stockings would then spend two weeks practicing in New Orleans before opening the National League season in St. Louis. "Last year the club remained in Chicago," president Spalding told a local reporter, "and the backward spring prevented its doing any practice work at all. This season the boys will go south, where they will have every advantage in grounds and climate, and if there is any merit in early training we shall certainly have it."[6]

Spalding apparently also saw the merit of "late" training, for he announced that the players would be practicing in the evening as well as during the day. "Both President

Spalding and Capt. Anson intend bringing the team on to the field in such a way that they will work together like a machine," the Chicago *Times* declared, "and there need be no fear of a repetition of last season's disastrous opening."

The practice and discipline apparently paid off, for on April 2 the White Stockings defeated the Louisville Colonels of the American Association, 11–9. More pre-season victories followed, and the *Chicago Daily Tribune* soon predicted that the hometown team would win the league pennant. Cap Anson was similarly optimistic, and he told Spalding following spring training that "the White Stockings are in perfect trim.... Our trip South has done the boys a world of good. We have enjoyed excellent weather right along and every man in the club has been working industriously to harden his muscles and loosen his joints for our struggle with the St. Louis boys."[7]

Their rivalry began anew on April 30, when both teams played their first league game of the year. The Chicago ballplayers took the St. Louis field in new uniforms comprised of navy blue knit jerseys (collars and cuffs trimmed in white), navy blue pants, white caps, white belts, and, of course, white stockings. Despite a heavy rain that had rendered the grounds slippery and in poor condition, 7,000 fans flocked to the ballpark. "The greatest excitement prevailed," the Chicago *Times* recounted, "and the crowd yelled itself hoarse" during the thrilling battle between St. Louis pitcher Charlie Sweeney and the White Stockings' hurler Larry Corcoran. St. Louis managed to defeat the visitors, 3–2, but the White Stockings came back and won the last three games of the series, 9–5, 16–1, and 7–2.

President Spalding was on hand for the season's first three games, and when he returned to Chicago he remarked to a reporter how pleased he was with his men's performance on the field. "'I never saw the boys looking better,' said he, 'and if they don't come out a long way ahead in the race for the pennant, then my judgment as to what goes to make up a good base-ball nine is at fault.'" Spalding went on to say that he would be "well pleased" if the White Stockings won 16 games on their schedule before the first home game on June 6. "Our new grounds will be completed in ample time for the opening game," Spalding continued, "and I think I am safe in anticipating a great season for the game in Chicago."[8]

The ballplayers actually won 18 of 24 league games while on the road, which put them just one game behind the New York Giants in the National League standings. "The White Stockings are returning with a great record," raved the *Tribune*, "and the reception which the ball lovers of Chicago should tender them can not be too cordial."

The city's "ball lovers" apparently heeded the newspaper's suggestion, for more than 10,000 spectators inaugurated the new park on June 6, filling the grandstand, open seats, and chairs, as well as standing on the bicycle track that encircled the playing field. The *Tribune* wrote that "scattered throughout the grand stand were many of Chicago's most prominent citizens, nearly all being accompanied by their wives and daughters, there being in all fully 1,500 of the fairer sex upon the grounds."

The newspaper added that when captain Anson and his men walked onto the outfield, the "immense audience arose to its feet and gave them a welcome of which the club may well feel proud.... Every household and window commanding a view of the grounds was occupied by spectators, and at a rough estimate fully 2,000 people must have witnessed the game in this way. The east end of the grounds was filled with carriages, and quite a number of vehicles for want of room were compelled to stand outside on Congress, Throop, and Loomis streets." Center fielder George Gore "seemed to have his batting clothes on," and his two home runs, a triple, and a single helped Chicago soundly defeat St. Louis, 9–2. Chicago swept the remaining three games in the series, snatching first place in the National League away from New York on June 10.

The White Stockings continued their streak of victories for 10 more games, finally losing to Philadelphia on June 25, 2–0. With 32 wins and 7 losses (and a 14–1 record at home), Chicago still held only a slim 1½-game lead over the dogged New York Giants; furthermore, the team likely would have relinquished first place weeks earlier if not for John Clarkson. By June 25, not only had the pitcher won 22 games and lost just 5, but he also had helped fill in for Larry Corcoran, who had injured his arm in May. Spalding signed pitcher Jim McCormick from the Providence Grays in July and removed Corcoran from the White Stocking roster. The club president told a reporter that he had been "just about at my wit's end" trying to find a strong pitcher to assist Clarkson "when McCormick came to my relief. He is very popular with our boys, a good fellow, and a thoroughly good ball-player…. I believe, barring accident, that the Chicago's batteries will be as strong as any in the country."[9]

McCormick soon justified Spalding's faith in him. He pitched a one-hitter on July 31 as Chicago blanked Philadelphia, 9–0, and won his 14th straight game on September 4 with a 12–4 victory over Buffalo. John Clarkson continued to hold up his end of the pitching duties as well: on September 19 he won his 50th game of the season, a 10–3 victory over Boston.

The New York Giants, however, continued to nip at the White Stockings' heels. On September 28 Chicago led New York by just two games, and fans of both teams knew that the pennant rested upon the upcoming four-game series between the two teams. The next day more than 10,000 spectators packed West Side Park for the first game. As the *Chicago Daily Tribune* reported in its lengthy, illustrated, front-page coverage, "Every available foot of room was occupied, while hundreds witnessed the contest from adjoining house-tops."

Because fans even lined the playing field, New York insisted upon the "three-base rule"—that is, a player who hit a ball into the crowd would be awarded three bases. It was a stipulation that the Giants probably regretted, as the Chicago players hit six triples— Mike Kelly had three—while the Giants hit none. The White Stockings neatly won the game, 7–4. "To [Jim] McCormick and Kelly is due the greater share of the credit for the day's success," a sportswriter contended. "McCormick pitched a careful, steady, and at the same time brilliant game. He succeeded in making the New-Yorkers overanxious, as one by one they found themselves unable to hit him. They grew desperate, hit wildly, and, on the whole, ineffectually."

New York played better in the second game of the series, for as *Sporting Life* noted, "The question of superiority was undecided until the last man was out." Some 11,000 fans braved the rainy, cold weather to see pitcher John Clarkson and his teammates finally come out on top, 2–1. The Chicago *Daily Inter Ocean* bragged that by defeating the Giants, the White Stockings "have about made their title clear to the championship of the National League." Many New Yorkers had conceded defeat after the first game, and following the second, even the *New York Times* admitted in an editorial that the Giants' season was just about over:

> Yesterday's game of baseball probably disposes of the hopes of the New-York team for the championship. When the series of games of which two have now been played was begun, Chicago had three more victories and three less defeats than New-York, and each club had eight games to play, including

the four that they were to play with each other. The other four, it was not doubted, would be victories for both clubs. If New-York had won all four games with Chicago it would have been one game ahead. If it had won three the result would have been a tie. Chicago has now won two of the four games with New-York. Even if New-York wins the remaining two games, assuming that both clubs beat their other competitors, Chicago will still be one ahead, and will take the championship.[10]

An astute Chicago sportswriter made the observation that while the New Yorkers were adept at hitting, fielding, and base-running, "They do not possess the one great element of success so marked in the play of the home team—strategy. The White Stockings play the more brainy game, depending for victory as much upon their heads as upon their arms and legs." The "brainy" Chicagoans won again on October 1, 8–3, behind the pitching of Jim McCormick. The steamrolling White Stockings were now virtually assured of the National League pennant, and shortly before the start of the last game of the Chicago-New York series, the Giants formally presented their own pennant to their season-long rivals.[11]

"Courtesy to Chicago. New York's Players Present Spalding's Men with a Silken Emblem of Victory." *(Chicago) Daily Inter Ocean*, October 4, 1885, p. 3.

THE GIANT TEAMS.
NEW YORK PAYS TRIBUTE.
A WORTHY PRESENTATION.

One of the most disagreeable days on record for base ball playing was yesterday afternoon, and in spite of the cold, drizzly weather 10,000 people assembled at the ball park to witness the closing contest between the two great clubs. Before the game began Austin's [First Regiment] Band favored the crowd with funeral dirges and slow marches.[12] This sort of music was not pleasing to the crowd and the band soon found it out, and between innings they played jigs, to which the crowd danced. The first bell rang at 2:30 o'clock, and the band, headed by a drum major, went over to the club-house to escort the New Yorks upon the field. When they came up to the grand stand they were welcomed with a hearty cheer. At 2:45 the second bell rang and the New Yorks went to their bench. The drum major led his band out escorting the Chicagos, who came marching company front, with the little mascot, Willie Hahn, in the van.[13] As they neared the diamond, Captain [Monte] Ward, of the New Yorks, drew his men up in line at the home-plate, where the figures "1885" were clearly marked, and received the Chicagos, who formed a line facing the New Yorks. Captain Ward, taking a small but handsome

WHITE SILK FLAG

from an attendant, stepped in front of his men and said:

> Captain Anson, we came to Chicago hoping and expecting to win this last series of games. But you have beaten us fairly and by good ball-playing, and therefore we have no complaints to make. On the contrary, as a souvenir of the season's struggle and as an earnest [sic] of our friendly feeling, the New York Club presents to the Chicago Club this flag.

Thereupon he handed Captain Anson the flag, upon which were the words, "New York to Chicago, 1885," in gold letters. Captain Anson, taking the flag, said:

> Captain Ward, when after an earnest effort one competitor succeeds, and the other, in a spirit of fairness, kindly presents to the successful party so elegant a souvenir of victory as you have done and in so graceful a manner, it is a pleasant duty to acknowledge, as we do most sincerely, that we found in you gentlemen and ball players worthy to represent the National game. Our pleasure in any victory is tempered by regret that we should have won against such a generous foe. But the knowledge that we have won from giants leads us to hope that we shall meet again another year

when both of us shall do our best to please the public, and by so doing assure them that each club will do its best to win the championship of 1886.

The vast crowd cheered the two clubs to the echo, the mascot took the flag, and the band marched around the eighteen men playing "Auld Lang Syne," while the players all shook hands and the crowd went wild with enthusiasm.

◆ ◆ ◆

The enthusiasm was short-lived for the home crowd, as the Giants emerged victorious from the game, 12–8, with John Clarkson taking the loss. The White Stockings, though, clinched the pennant on October 6, following a Jim McCormick 9–4 win against the Philadelphia Phillies. The Chicagoans lost the remaining games of the series, their last three matches of the year, but they closed the regular season with a remarkable 87–25–1 record (a .777 winning percentage), two games in front of the New York Giants. In third place were the Philadelphia Phillies, who finished a whopping 30 games behind the White Stockings.

The *Chicago Daily News* reported in early October that the Chicago club grossed about $300,000 in 1885, giving the stockholders a more than 300 percent profit, since invested capital amounted to $50,000 and expenses and salaries about $40,000. (*Sporting Life*, on the other hand, argued in a follow-up article that if the club had earned that much, game attendance would have had to average "over 5,000 throughout the season, which is fully three times the actual average.") Whatever the exact figure was, the players also benefited from the successful season. They had signed temperance pledges in April before they left Chicago for spring training, and for keeping their word and for winning the league pennant, each man was promised $100.[14]

There were still, however, post-season games to play. In 1884 the leading teams of the National League and American Association had faced off in a series of games to determine the "United States Championship," and a similar series was planned between

After the White Stockings defeated the New York Giants and narrowly won the 1885 National League pennant, the New Yorkers presented their rivals with a congratulatory banner. Chicago's mascot, young Willie Hahn, is shown carrying the silk banner, on which is written "1885" and "New York to Chicago." Cap Anson wrote in his autobiography that Willie and his family lived near the team's West Side Park. "The first time that I ever saw him he came on the grounds arrayed in a miniature Chicago uniform," Anson remembered, "and so cunning was he that we at once adopted him as our 'mascot,' giving him the freedom of the grounds, and he was always on hand when the club was at home, being quite a feature, and one that pleased the lady patrons of the game immensely" (Adrian C. Anson, *A Ball Player's Career*, 1900).

the White Stockings and the association's St. Louis Browns. Unfortunately, it seemed that any sense of discipline the White Stockings had acquired during the long season had ended on October 6 with their league pennant win. After the three final losses to Philadelphia, Chicago's newspapers had pointedly criticized the players' apathy and lethargic performances on the field.

This "indifference and lack of interest in their work," as one reporter put it, apparently carried over to the national championship series. "The Chicagos played a very poor game both at bat and in the field," wrote the Chicago *Daily Inter Ocean* after the first match-up in Chicago on October 14, a 5–5 tie that was called on account of darkness after eight innings, "while the visitors played a creditable game at both points." The next day, with Chicago leading 5–4 in the sixth inning, the Browns forfeited the game after they walked off the field following a dispute with the umpire. The two teams split the next four games. Prior to Game Seven, the two managers agreed not to count the forfeited second match, which left the series even at two games each, and one tie. Only 1,200 spectators saw the deciding game on October 24, which Chicago lost by the score of 13–4.[15]

But that did not settle the championship. Chicago president Al Spalding, unwilling to accept the fact that his team lost, lashed out in the newspapers that Chicago had not agreed to disregard the second game and that the teams were now tied at 3–3. *Sporting Life* reported that "the Chicago Club is much chagrined at the defeats inflicted by St. Louis, a club they under-rated, and the loss of the 'world's championship,' a title which amounts to little, is yet irritating to the white-hosed lads." Spalding wanted the competitors to play one more game, but the teams disbanded at the end of October and the two clubs agreed to declare the contest a draw. That decision, *Sporting Life* concluded, "ends all further controversy on the subject."[16]

What did not end, though, was Spalding's frustration over his team's "miserable exhibition of ball-playing," as one sportswriter put it. Newspapers had reported that Cap Anson reprimanded center fielder George Gore for his laziness during Game One. Spalding had suspended the ballplayer without pay for the remaining games, with Billy Sunday taking Gore's place in the outfield. Spalding denied that Gore had been suspended, though the White Stockings president admitted that neither Gore nor his teammates had lived up to the club's high standards. "Unquestionably, our boys have played very poor ball during the entire series," Spalding said, "but their interest in play was gone."

Organized baseball certainly provided the players with few monetary incentives during the post-season. As *Sporting Life* pointed out, "The games amount to nothing financially, as they are recognized as exhibition games and but slimly patronized, especially as the interest in base ball games ends with the championship season." The White Stockings and the Browns had each contributed $500 towards prize money to be divided among the members of the winning team. Since the series ended in a tie, the $1,000 purse was split equally between the two ball clubs.[17]

Despite the loss of a championship title, the White Stockings' season had still been a memorable one. After the club had secured the National League pennant, the *New York Clipper* proclaimed "a great captain did it," for first baseman Cap Anson had led his team both figuratively as captain and literally with his 144 hits. He also had topped the National League with his runs batted in (108) and doubles (35). Outfielders Abner Dalrymple and Mike Kelly had headed the league in home runs with 11 and 9, respectively, and Kelly had led the league with 124 runs scored. The White Stockings certainly could not have won the league championship without John Clarkson. The National League had legalized overhand pitching at its November 1884 meeting, and Clarkson, in the words of Cap Anson, "was the possessor of a remarkable drop curve and fast overhand lifting speed, while his change of pace was most deceiving." In 623 innings, Clarkson won 53 contests, pitched 68 complete games, struck out 308 batters, and finished the season with a 1.85 earned run average.[18]

One More League Pennant (1886)

Assisted by a new league rule that allowed each club to retain up to 12 of its team members every season, White Stockings president Al Spalding lost little time in reserving his star players for 1886. By early November 1885, most had signed to play for Chicago, including center fielder George Gore, who evidently had gotten back in Spalding's good graces following his reported suspension during the post-season. Pitcher Jim McCormick was the only holdout, and he had told Spalding that he intended to retire from baseball and move back home to Paterson, New Jersey. In January the club president attended a National League meeting in New York, and he met with McCormick. "He came up to New York from his home in Paterson and signed willingly," Spalding told a reporter, "as I have all along anticipated he would." Spalding added that "with McCormick and [John] Clarkson I think we can hold our own with the best of the heavy batting nines that will enter the field this year."[19]

The National League teams included the New York Giants, the Philadelphia Phillies, the Boston Beaneaters, the St. Louis Maroons, and the Detroit Wolverines, all clubs whom the White Stocking had faced in 1885. The Providence Grays had drawn only small crowds at their games, resulting in little revenue, and were forced to drop out of the league. The Buffalo Bisons had also proven to be financially unsuccessful and were purchased by the Detroit franchise. To replace Providence and Buffalo, the league admitted the Kansas City Cowboys and the Washington Nationals.

Spalding knew that the forthcoming season would be a tough one, and to compete with the league's "heavy batting nines," as he called them, he signed pitcher John "Jocko" Flynn from Lawrence, Massachusetts, as well as Flynn's catcher on the Lawrence club, George Moolic. The *Chicago Daily Tribune* noted that all the team members were scheduled to meet in Chicago on March 13 and depart for Hot Springs, Arkansas, "where they will undergo a regular system of bathing and training until March 30." The men would then leave Hot Springs to play practice games with southern teams to prepare for the opening of the season on April 30.[20]

"Sporting Affairs. Departure of the Chicago Team To-day for Hot Springs—How the Men Look." *Chicago Daily Tribune*, March 13, 1886, p. 6. [Note: This article originally appeared as one long passage, and a few paragraph breaks have been added for ease of readability.]

For the last few days members of the Chicago League Club have been dropping in from their respective winter quarters, and when [Jim] McCormick and [Ned] Williamson arrive this morning from Philadelphia the entire team will be here to report at noon to President [Al] Spalding and receive their instructions for the coming training season in the South.[21] The first of the lads to get here was [Abner] Dalrymple. He came in ten days ago from his ranch in Nebraska, where he has been looking after about ninety head of stock bearing his brand of ownership. Dal[rymple] has raised a full beard, and, but for his muscular figure and springy step, might at first glance be mistaken for a theological student instead of the athlete and ball-player he is. Fred Pfeffer next arrived from Louisville looking as hale and handsome as when he last covered second for the Whites in the closing games with Philadelphia. Mike Kelly was the next to show up, and from all appearances his stay in New Orleans has resulted in putting him in splendid physical condition. "I never saw Kelly looking better," said President Spalding yesterday. This comment has been made by every man in the nine who has seen him. He speaks highly of the treatment he received in the Crescent City and says he never passed a pleasanter winter.

The next to come was John Clarkson and his bride. They came straight through from Boston after the wedding ceremony, and took rooms at the Matteson House, where they have since been quartered. John declares himself supremely happy as a married man and will take his wife with him upon his Southern trip with the club. He, too, is looking in first-class trim, and says he is not frightened in the least by the batting strength he will have to compete against this season. Billy Sunday came in from Marshalltown [Iowa] last Wednesday, and says he is ready to either play ball or run [Arlie] Latham another hundred yards.[22] He looks well, and is perhaps a trifle heavier than last seasson [sic]. On the same day [Jimmy] Ryan, [Jocko] Flynn, and [George] Moolic, the new members of the team, arrived from Lawrence, Mass., and reported to Capt. Anson. Ryan will be remembered at short and at centre field in the closing games with the Phillies last year. He made a very favorable impression at that time both as an in and out fielder and as a batter and baserunner, and Anson predicts a better showing for him this year than last, when he will have a far better opportunity to demonstrate his abilities as a player.

Flynn and Moolic will form the team's new battery. They have played together for several seasons, and both have excellent records with the New England leagues in which they worked. Flynn is the smallest man in the nine, being but a trifle taller and but little heavier than Larry Corcoran, who, by the way, has been signed by New York for the coming season. He is muscular and very active, however, and is thought very well of by both Anson and Spalding. Moolic in appearance is an ideal catcher for a crack team. He is about [Tom] Burns' h[e]ight, with a frame so sturdy and powerful that it would be odds against any pitcher knocking him out of his position behind the bat. He is quiet and gentlemanly in manner, and his record shows him to be a good ball-player.

Anson took all of the team who had arrived out to the park Thursday afternoon for a little practice, and the new battery acquitted itself to the entire satisfaction of the big Captain. Tom Burns arrived yesterday from his home in Connecticut, and declares himself in better trim than he has felt for two seasons. His right arm, which he injured [the] season before last and which troubled him greatly through all of last year's games, is now fully recovered, and the sturdy short-stop says that fewer balls will get past him this season than last. [George] Gore, [Silver] Flint, and Anson have remained in the city all winter taking life easy and resting up for the coming games. All carry considerable surplus flesh, but the month's training they will undergo will take this down and fit them for the work ahead. Williamson and McCormick, who will arrive this morning, have been East since the close of last season, the former in New York City and the latter at his home in Paterson, N. J. The big third-baseman is said to weigh 225 pounds, twenty-five of which he proposes to drop before meeting the "Cowboy" team at Kansas City.

Dating from today the members of the team will abstain altogether from beer, wine, whisky, or intoxicating drinks of any kind, and will continue to do so until the last ball in the coming championship series has been pitched. This evening all will leave for Hot Springs, Ark., and after a fortnight's stay there will depart for practice games at Nashville, Atlanta,

Savannah, Macon, and Memphis, with the Southern League teams at those points, reaching Kansas City to open the season there April [30].[23] The next appearance of the team in Chicago will be May 6, when they open the season here with the first of a series of three games with Detroit. The club uniform will be the same this year as last—viz.: navy blue with white stockings, white belts, and white caps. Both Anson and Spalding are highly pleased with the make-up of the team for the coming season and say that winning the pennant will be no harder for them this year than last, the increased strength of Detroit and St. Louis notwithstanding.[24]

◆ ◆ ◆

With prescient vision, Spalding predicted a "close and stubborn race" among the eight teams of the National League. His White Stockings got off to a fast start by sweeping the Kansas City Cowboys and taking two games out of three from the St. Louis Maroons. On May 6, two days after a bomb killed police officers and civilians during a labor rally in Chicago's Haymarket Square, 6,000 baseball fans converged on West Side Park for the White Stockings' home opener against Detroit. Austin's First Regiment Band celebrated the occasion by performing in front of the grandstand. The team itself was supposed to have marched through the city streets under the escort of 200 cadets, but as the *Chicago Daily Inter Ocean* noted, "In deference [to] the views of Mayor [Carter] Harrison, who disapproved of such a parade in view of the excited state of things, this programme was abandoned."

Perhaps it was just as well, as the weather was not particularly conducive to a parade. The Chicago *Times* believed that the spectators "would have enjoyed an interesting game had not the weather been so cold that enjoyment of anything but a red-hot stove was absolutely impossible. As it was, everybody stamped and pounded in a vain attempt to keep warm." The shivering spectators, though, got to cheer during their foot stamping when the White Stockings hoisted the 1885 National League pennant to the top of the West Side Park flag pole during the pre-game ceremonies. As the *Chicago Herald* reported, "The nine marched to the tall flagstaff at the southeast corner of the grounds, and with a lusty pull at the halyards sent the championship flag of 1885 swiftly to the top. The pennant is a large streamer of dark blue, with red edges dotted with white stars." Sportswriter Harry Palmer noted in *Sporting Life* that "the pennant is a handsome one, having a huge white ball in its centre inscribed 'Champions of the United States, 1885.'"

Chicago beat Detroit, 5–1, and ended up taking two games in the three-game series. Notwithstanding the victories, Anson and Spalding did not relax, as they knew that Detroit had strengthened its team during the off-season and was a formidable opponent. By the middle of June, in fact, the Wolverines were in first place, two games in front of Chicago. But the season was far from over, and even the *New York Times* admitted after the Giants went down, 3–2, at the hands of Chicago that the White Stockings "never lose heart, and they play a good game from the time the umpire orders the men on the field until the last man is retired in the ninth inning."

One of their notable victories was a 6–1 win over Kansas City on June 14, in which rookie Jocko Flynn struck out 13 batters. As the *Tribune* related, "Capt. Anson had seen fit to play the new battery—Flynn and [George] Moolic—and a prettier battery game will probably not be witnessed again in Chicago this season. Flynn seemed to have perfect command over the ball and the support he received was almost perfect."[25]

Anson's press coverage a week later was much different—and less admirable. The

7. On Top of the League (1885–1886)   153

White Stockings were playing the Wolverines in the rubber match of a three-game series at Detroit. Chicago ended up losing, 5–4, but "the most interesting incident" of the day, according to the Chicago *Times*, was umpire John Gaffney's "fining Anson $110. The first installment was $10 for 'back talk.' Anson permitted his zeal to overleap his customary discretion, and applied to Gaffney an epithet which is not heard in polite circles, whereupon an additional fine of $50 was imposed. The irate Anson gave vent to more indignation, and still another $50 was added."

The White Stockings soon had to face the Wolverines again, this time in Chicago from July 8 to 10. Detroit fans felt sure of victory; after all, the Wolverines had recently taken two games out of three from Chicago, in part due to the fine hitting and fielding of the well-known "Big Four" players Detroit had acquired from the Buffalo Bisons: Dan Brouthers, Hardy Richardson, Jack Rowe, and Deacon White. Four hundred Detroit fans traveled to Chicago for the series, and as the *Times* reported, "They had tin horns, rattles, and other ear-splitting and noise-spreading instruments, so they were in condition not only to prophecy victory, but celebrate it likewise." The Detroit revelers had no chance for celebration, however, for Chicago won all three games. As the *Chicago Herald* exulted on July 11:

> Detroit's big four
> And many more
> Came here with tin horns musical;
> Drums and a gong
> They brought along,
> And scores of things kazoosical.[26]

The White Stockings were now just 1½ games behind Detroit, and from July 14 to 23 they won 9 games in a row. Unfortunately, Detroit piled up the victories, too, and Chicago gained no ground in the standings. The White Stockings did, however, gain notoriety in the press, for newspapers reported that president Spalding had hired detectives to follow his players and report to him if any had broken the temperance pledges they had signed in March. Spalding was right to be suspicious. "A Bombshell in the Chicago Camp," blared the page-one headline in *Sporting Life*, followed by the subtitle, "Several Players Tripped Up."

As it turned out, more than just a few of them had "tripped up." The *Chicago Herald* disclosed on July 23 that "seven of the best players in the Chicago club, among them two of the new men, were yesterday fined $25 each by President [Al] Spalding for drinking. They were [Jim] McCormick, [Mike] Kelly, [Silver] Flint, [George] Gore, [Ned] Williamson, [Jocko] Flynn and [Jimmy] Ryan. That they were actually drunk was not charged, but it was reported that all of the seven had been drinking more or less for the past three weeks, especially when out of the city, and the fines were imposed merely as a warning."[27]

Kelly admitted to sportswriter Harry Palmer that "I have occasionally smothered my promise not to get full—*get full*, mind you—in a glass of the foaming or in a bracer with a little sugar. It did me good and I wanted it, and when I wanted it I got it. That's all there is to it." Spalding was reluctant to discuss the matter in public and merely told Palmer that "the boys have not been getting drunk or anything of that kind, but have forgotten themselves only so far as to take an occasional glass of beer or liquor in their rooms or at the bar, and their indiscreetness has resulted as you see. Reports have reached me which simply compelled me in the interests of the club, to take some action."

But some people thought Spalding was too hasty in taking action. The White Stockings had not lost a game since July 13, and a Chicago journalist ventured that "the fines would appear better timed" if they had been imposed after defeats rather than after victories. The timing, however, was of no concern to Spalding. He wanted the ballplayers to remember that from April 1 to November 1 they were under contract to the club, and he expected them to observe all training rules. Furthermore, as reported in the Chicago *Daily Inter Ocean*, "He did not propose to permit any lax habits to undo the playing qualities of his men, and, although they were playing well now, any irregularity would tell upon the team when they would be called upon to do their best." Spalding expected them to do their best; not surprisingly, when the disciplined players tried to get their fines rescinded, the club president refused to back down.[28]

To their credit, the disgruntled White Stockings did not let up in the pennant race, and the club managed to stay close behind first-place Detroit. Chicago swept Washington in early August, took two out of three games from St. Louis, and August 16–18 swept a three-game series from Kansas City. The second game of the Kansas City series, easily won by Chicago, 15–1, deserves special interest.

In the seventh inning, Cowboy Pete Conway hit a single and was heading for second on a passed ball when he heard Mike Kelly cry "foul!" (Kelly had started the game as catcher but hurt his hand in the fifth inning and had exchanged positions with first baseman Cap Anson.) Conway stopped at second and asked Kelly if the hit was a foul ball. Kelly said that it indeed was, and Conway turned and started walking back to first base. Pitcher Jim McCormick, who had the ball, threw it to second baseman Fred Pfeffer, who tagged Conway out. When Conway objected, Kelly innocently replied, "O, I thought you asked if that was a passed ball."

The Kansas City club members were livid. "We won't stand that," captain Dave Rowe shouted, running up to umpire Grayson "Gracie" Pierce. "You've no right to call that man out on such a play."

"What are you going to do about it?" Pierce asked Rowe. "I didn't tell him it was a foul."[29]

Mike Kelly had a reputation as an inveterate prankster as well as one of the league's top sluggers, and it was not surprising that sportswriters gleefully recounted his sly maneuver (a *Sporting Life* journalist chortled that Kelly's ploy was "characteristic of the great Sir Michael"). Others were not so charitable of either him or the club. John J. Rogers, for example, the secretary and treasurer of the Philadelphia Phillies, accused the White Stockings of winning games "by the use of questionable tactics and dishonest points of play."

One of Kelly's defenders was Eugene Field, a journalist for the *Chicago Daily News*. Although Field's literary reputation today rests largely on his children's poetry (such as "Little Boy Blue" and "Wynken, Blynken, and Nod"), during his career he was also well known for his humorous and satiric newspaper column, "Sharps and Flats." Field regularly commented and gossiped on a wide range of topics, including politics, culture, literature, sports, people, and assorted current events. As a baseball fan in the mid–1880s, he especially admired Mike Kelly.[30]

"Sharps and Flats." [By Eugene Field.] *Chicago Daily News*, August 26, 1886, morning edition, p. 2. [Note: Just the paragraphs about Mike Kelly are reprinted.]

Our valued exchange, the Detroit [Morning] Tribune, is sorely grieved because, as it alleges, "the Chicagos are always held up by base-ball enthusiasts as a model club. It is," explains the Tribune, "because they play with a view to 'getting there,' and many of their games are won by an audacity that sometimes carries them a little too far. To secure their end there is nothing they will not do, and [Mike] Kelly is chief among the originators of schemes." Then the Tribune narrates the story about how [Pete] Conway of the Kansas City club, having gone to second on a passed ball, asked Kelly if the ball was a foul tip, to which Kelly answered yes, and Conway was put out while walking back to first. For this trifling bit of shrewd humor on the part of Mr. Kelly the Chicago Base-Ball club is to be stigmatized as a set of schemers, eh?[31]

We will admit that Mr. Kelly is a humorist; we claim in his behalf that he has more brains than all the other members of the Chicago club combined. There is more pleasure to be derived from seeing him running the bases once around than is to be found in the entire nine innings of the average game of base ball. The average base-ball player goes about his business as a day laborer would go about sawing wood—he is an automaton, a mere thing moving in one, two, three motions; if he is at the bat, he strikes at the ball; if he is in the field, he goes through the conventional business. His theory of the game is to plod right along in the beaten path which dunderheads have trod from time immemorial—poor treadmill creature that he is! But Mr. Kelly believes it to be a part of the base-ball player's tactics to worry and to weary his opponents with all kinds of devices, and in the invention of these harassing devices we are free to say that Mr. Kelly is exceedingly felicitous and fertile.

Without such men as Mr. Kelly to redeem the game, base ball would soon sink to the level of an exhibition merely of brute force; there would be no prowess in the sport. It is when the intellectuals control and direct the muscles that athletic sports afford a special charm to an intelligent public.

We regard Mr. Kelly as a superb specimen of manhood—a gentleman in whom the intellectual and the physical are nicely balanced. We look upon him as the base-ball player of the future, and we commend him as an example to all ambitious beginners. That he is unappreciated by other base-ball players does not count for anything, because a large majority of the other base-ball players are simply abnormally developed chumps. With the public, however, Mr. Kelly is very popular; the public appreciates intelligence, shrewdness, and audacity. Still, Mr. Kelly is a rara avis, if not sui generis, and we are very sorry therefor[e]—we wish there were more of his kind.[32] He is alone in the Chicago club, and it were an insult to him to compare his coadjutors with him.

The public especially appreciated Kelly because his "intelligence, shrewdness, and audacity," to quote Eugene Field, helped the White Stockings win ball games. Shortly after his theatrics with Kansas City, *Sporting Life* declared that "Mike Kelly is only one-fourteenth of the Chicago Club, but he has made about one-sixth of the runs."

By August 19, the White Stockings had closed to just a half-game behind Detroit and were preparing to face the Wolverines in a crucial three-game series. After Chicago lost the first two, the *Chicago Herald* bemoaned that "Chicago is still struggling in second place." A sportswriter for the *Tribune* took a more pessimistic view when he sighed resignedly in a headline, "Farewell the Pennant."

Even with a few injured and sick team members, Chicago was not about to say "farewell" just yet. The White Stockings defeated Detroit on August 23 and followed that victory by sweeping Boston, Philadelphia, Washington, and New York. *Sporting Life* observed in its issue of September 8, the day the White Stockings took their 14th straight game, that "the Chicagos are pretty well bunged [sic] up; but still keep on winning just the same."[33]

By that time those victories had given them a three-game lead over the Wolverines. The rivalry between the two top teams was always intense, but probably never more so than on September 22 in Detroit. During the game, the Wolverines' fans protested some of umpire Phil Powers's calls and other decisions, and as the *Chicago Daily Tribune* noted, "They voiced their sentiments at the end of the fourth inning in a chorus of hisses and catcalls." Tempers only continued to flare, particularly when in the seventh inning, with Chicago leading Detroit, 6–3, Powers called the game on account of darkness. As the umpire walked back to the clubhouse, a spectator threw a cushion at him, which hit a policeman instead. "This was the signal for a rush," wrote the *Tribune*. "Between 300 and 400 men left their seats and started after him. Some one threw a stone which struck him in the back of the neck." Twelve policemen escorted Powers to the clubhouse, and from there he walked to his carriage to return to his hotel, though "the carriage was impeded in its course and was made the target for a fusillade of small stones and gravel, none of which, fortunately, did any damage."

The White Stockings were not as fortunate when they left the ballpark in their own carriages. As detailed in the Chicago *Times*:

> As the Chicago nine were driving along Brady street from Recreation park, this afternoon, a young scamp aged about 18 threw a stone into the second carriage, hitting one of the players. [Mike] Kelly immediately took after the fellow, but was hit by a man in the crowd, whom he therefore pursued, being joined by [Tom] Burns. The crowd closed in on them, and several umbrellas were brandished threateningly, Burns receiving one blow on the head, dislocating his thumb in striking his assailant. For a time a serious disturbance seemed imminent. The other players came up, and the crowd soon quieted down. Most of the crowd had no idea of the cause of the trouble, and denounced the throwing into the carriage as soon as it was known."

When the White Stockings' mascot, young Willie Hahn, heard about the attack on Kelly and Burns, he packed a small suitcase with a cap pistol and blow-gun and begged his father to buy him a train ticket for Detroit. As for Cap Anson, he shrugged off the incident, though he told a reporter that the Detroit ball club should employ a policeman armed "with a good, stout rawhide to lay over the shoulders of boys and men who begin such demonstrations as occurred today." As it turned out, the injury to Burns's thumb kept him out of Chicago's lineup for two weeks.[34]

Cap Anson believed that "at third base Burns was as good as the best of them." Anson was apparently not far off the mark, for after the mob attack in Detroit, the White Stockings, minus Burns, lost their next three games. The Wolverines were doing their part to overtake Chicago, and in early October they won six games in a row. The pennant race was tight through the rest of the season, and the league championship was not decided until the final games on October 9. "Throughout the day excitement in Chicago was intense," the *Chicago Herald* exclaimed, for if Detroit swept its two games with Philadelphia and Chicago lost its match against Boston, the Wolverines would secure the championship. But even though the Phillies were not in pennant contention, they were still strong competitors, and they dealt Detroit two humiliating losses in one day, 5–1 and 6–1. The White Stockings routed Boston, 12–3. From the *Herald*:

> All the morning crowds of men hung about the scores of tickers about the city, watching with absorbed interest the news that came over the wire.... When the news came in of Chicago's victory and Detroit's second defeat the cheering and applause were deafening.
>
> President Spalding's smile was as radiant as a sunrise in May. In the delirium of his joy he dashed off the following telegram to the boys:

CHICAGO, OCT. 9. A. C. ANSON, CAPTAIN CHICAGO BALL CLUB, BOSTON:—You have clinched the pennant in great style. Knew we could depend upon the old war horses in a pinch. You have won the League championship; now come home and win the world's championship. As a token of my appreciation of your work I herewith tender each man of the team a suit of clothes, awaiting their order, and the team collectively one-half the receipts in the coming series with St. Louis. Accept my hearty congratulations.

A. G. SPALDING.[35]

Spalding recalled the previous year's ill-fated world championship series with the American Association's St. Louis Browns, and he hoped that his generosity would motivate the Chicago players to take the 1886 games seriously. On September 25, Browns owner Chris Von der Ahe had written Spalding that "it now seems reasonably sure that the Chicago White Stockings and the St. Louis Brown Stockings will win the championship in their respective associations. I therefore take this opportunity of challenging your team on behalf of the Browns for a series of contests to be known as the 'world's championship series.'" Spalding had immediately accepted Von der Ahe's challenge, on the condition that the winning club "shall receive the total gross gate receipts, including the grand stand receipts." Spalding had also made stipulations concerning the playing rules and the selection of umpires, and he expected each team to pay its own traveling costs and other expenses. "In view of several misunderstandings that occurred in our series last season," he had told Von der Ahe, "I deem it wise to have all the conditions agreed upon and understood."

The Browns president did indeed understand, and the men agreed to play a best-of-seven series, with three games scheduled in Chicago (October 18–20) and three in St. Louis (October 21–23). If necessary, a seventh game would be played in a mutually agreed upon location.[36]

The temperature was only in the mid-fifties in Chicago on October 18, but nevertheless, every seat in the ballpark was filled for the first game between the National League and American Association champions. "Early in the contest," the Chicago *Times* reported, "the spectators found that it was warmer to stand up and yell than it was to sit still in silence, and in consequence the noise was something deafening." The home crowd was surely even more boisterous after John Clarkson pitched a magnificent 6–0 shutout. "We have heard a great deal about the prowess of these visitors at base-running," newspaper columnist Eugene Field wrote, "but we have not heard it demonstrated how base-running can avail a ball-player unless he is first able to get away from the home-plate."

Unfortunately for the White Stockings, the Browns were only too happy to show how it was done, as St. Louis mowed down Chicago in the second game, 12–0. "The visitors hit [Jim] McCormick with ease," a sportswriter observed, "and when they didn't knock the ball where a fielder couldn't get it some one of the Chicago men would make an error, so that between the two the Browns got around the bases pretty frequently." In the third game Clarkson once again pitched for Chicago, and the White Stockings managed an easy 11–4 win.[37]

With the White Stockings ahead, two games to one, the series moved to St. Louis. Cap Anson could rely on only Clarkson in the pitcher's box, as Jocko Flynn had a sore arm and McCormick complained of rheumatism in his feet (both men stayed home and did not even make the trip). The tired Clarkson made a valiant effort, but the Browns evened the series on October 21 with an 8–5 victory.

Shortly before the team left Chicago, Spalding had signed pitcher Mark Baldwin from the Northwestern League. The club president had told Anson that Baldwin would "come in handy if we g[e]t in a hole" in St. Louis. That hole appeared in Game Five, but Browns owner Chris Von der Ahe objected to Baldwin pitching as the new man had not played with the White Stockings during the regular season. Von der Ahe's protest was upheld by the series board of umpires, though merely with a yes / no flip of a coin. Anson needed to rest Clarkson, so the team captain had little choice but to start shortstop Ned Williamson as pitcher. Williamson pitched only into the second inning and was replaced by outfielder Jimmy Ryan. The Browns easily triumphed, 10–3, behind hurler Nat Hudson, who had started only 27 games throughout the regular season (as a comparison, John Clarkson had started 55).

Whispers of "hippodroming," or game fixing, had dogged both teams throughout the series, and the St. Louis victory did nothing to quell the rumors, unfounded though they probably were. "We have a higher opinion of the forbearance of the St. Louis public than we have had before," Eugene Field sarcastically wrote in his *Chicago Daily News* column. "We presume to say that if such a shameless farce had been attempted here in Chicago the conspirators and the co-conspirators would have been hooted off the field."[38]

Both teams were on the field October 23 for what turned out to be the final match of the series. Clarkson, throwing his fourth game in six days, masterfully carried a 3–0 lead into the eighth inning, but a St. Louis run, followed by left fielder Abner Dalrymple's misplay of Arlie Latham's deep fly ball, tied the score. The Browns's Curt Welch was on third base in the bottom of the tenth inning, when, according to the *Chicago Daily News*, third baseman Tom Burns "gave [catcher] Kelly a signal to catch Welch at third. Kelly played away from the plate for this purpose, but Clarkson put a ball over the plate which Kelly just touched with his fingers and bounded away to the grand stand, while Welch came in with the winning run."

With the victorious Browns receiving the total gate receipts of the series, this play has often been mythologized as "the $15,000 slide." No game-day accounts, however, indicate that Welch actually slid—*The Sporting News* reported that he "trotted home"—and the receipts from the six games amounted to $13,920.10, not $15,000. To confuse the situation even further, some contemporary articles make no mention of an attempted steal or pitchout, but note that Clarkson's throw was either a wild pitch or a passed ball.[39]

None of these details mattered to the disheartened (and unrewarded) White Stockings, who simply went back to their hotel after the game, had supper, and then boarded a train back to Chicago.[40]

"Departure of the Chicagos." *St. Louis Globe-Democrat*, October 24, 1886, p. 11.

The vanquished Chicago nine quietly and unostentatiously took their departure from the Union Depot last evening. There was an immense crowd of Saturday night travelers, but none of them knew that the windy city nine from Michigan Lake was about to make its retreat. There was no flag or proud banner to announce their presence, nor the sound of a fife or drum to tell where the breezy crew could be found. They refused an escort, preferring to straggle by ones and twos in the disguise of dudish attire into a Pullman, rather than attract humiliating attention from the busy throng. So quietly did they take passage that no one but the conductor knew who they were. There was no bluster in their midst, and they made a mournful-looking crowd, that reminded one more than anything else of a delegation of undertakers who had performed the last sad offices for a friend. The name of Chicago was not spoken, and the defeated ball-players who came from there looked sad at the thought of having to return. All the gush and sentiment usually displayed by them was suppressed, and they were silent. A Texan, who was escorting the Mexican Band to the State Fair at Dallas, discovered them and insisted on giving them a few lively beats of the drum, but St. Louis hospitality prevailed, and the crestfallen crowd was allowed to leave without any demonstration to emphasize their idea of fallen pride.

◆ ◆ ◆

As crestfallen as the White Stockings were, they could take pride in quite a few team and individual accomplishments. They had finished the regular season with a league-leading 90 wins, 34 losses, and 2 ties, for a winning percentage of .726, 2½ games in front of the second-place Detroit Wolverines. Although the Wolverines had totaled 1,260 hits to the White Stockings' 1,223, Chicago led the National League in runs (900), doubles (198), triples (87), runs batted in (673), bases on balls (460), and on-base percentage (.348). Chicago and Detroit had each hit 53 home runs; Detroit's team batting average was .280 while Chicago's was .279. Individual White Stocking honors were many. "Kelly leads them all," proclaimed the *Chicago Herald* at the end of October, while "Anson [is] second on the batting list." Mike Kelly had, indeed, led the league with a .388 batting average while Anson finished second at .371. Kelly was first in the league with 155 runs scored and an on-base percentage of .483, while Anson led with 147 runs batted in. The captain himself was proud of his men; Anson reminisced in his memoir that "the team that brought the pennant back to Chicago in the years 1885 and 1886 was, in my estimation, not only the strongest team that I ever had under my management but, taken all in all, one of the strongest teams that has ever been gotten together in the history of the [National] League."

That reliable workhorse, pitcher John Clarkson, won 36 games for Chicago (behind Charles "Lady" Baldwin of Detroit and Tim Keefe of New York, each with 42). John "Jocko" Flynn, who would pitch only one season, compiled a 23–6 mark with an earned run average of 2.24. Cap Anson recalled years later that he was a "good man in the twirling line." Flynn's last game as a Chicago pitcher was on October 5, for as Anson explained, "His arm gave out while he was with us, however, and besides that he got into fast company and, attempting to keep up the clip with his so-called friends, found the pace much too rapid for him and fell by the wayside." Still, though, Flynn holds a place in the record books for most wins by a one-year pitcher.[41]

Epilogue

On the day after the White Stockings lost the championship to the Browns, Chicago's *Daily Inter Ocean* published a poem that summed up the feelings of the city's discouraged baseball fans:

> Furl that Pennant, oh, 'tis weary!
> Round its staff it's drooping dreary,
> And the betting men feel sweary,
>   While all Chicago darkly frowns!
>
> Fold it gently and consign it
> To Mound City—we resign it![42]

> Spalding's champions now assign it
> To Von der A-he's howling Browns!

The White Stockings were bitter and disappointed following their defeat, for they had predicted an entirely different outcome. "I'll win the game or lose the use of my arm," John Clarkson had announced. And until the fateful eighth inning in Game Six, it had appeared that the pitcher's self-confidence was justified.

Abner Dalrymple, who had misjudged Arlie Latham's long fly ball in the eighth inning, was upset with himself, particularly as both his teammates and president Spalding blamed him for the loss. "Dal ought to have caught that ball," Spalding had said after the game, while a player remarked that "Ryan or Gore would have smothered it." Although various sportswriters chastised Dalrymple as well, Harry Palmer sensibly argued in *Sporting Life* that "Chicago had no business to permit the battle to become so close that its result would hinge upon the work of a single player in any particular game." Palmer added that some of the players had believed that their work was finished for the season "when they played the last game of the League championship series.... Had they entered the contest with the same ardor and determination that characterized the work of the Browns, the result might have been different."[43]

Besides being annoyed with Dalrymple, Spalding was also angry at Browns owner Chris Von der Ahe for objecting to Mark Baldwin pitching in Game Five. Spalding and Von de Ahe had summarily waved aside all rumors of game fixing, for both teams had played hard to win; Spalding simply believed that his men had not played hard enough. In St. Louis Spalding had told a reporter that "I've been so hot and mad over the way the club played ball or didn't play it," and he was still fuming after he returned home. The *Chicago Herald* observed that the defeat for the "championship of the world" was "humiliating" for him, and "it is an open secret that President Spalding hasn't had a good night's sleep since that memorable contest."[44]

The players' alcohol consumption was also an "open secret" and no doubt also kept him awake at night. "Beer Beats Them" was the headline, for example, of the *Daily Inter Ocean*'s article on the defeat of the White Stockings in Game Two. Sportswriter Henry Chadwick insisted that Chicago had lost that game because of Jim McCormick's "weak exhibition of pitching" due to his "over indulgence in drinking." Spalding discussed both McCormick and the club's temperance policy with a *Chicago Herald* reporter:

> "He drank about as much as all the rest of them put together," Mr. Spalding exclaimed, indignantly. "He lost all his effectiveness before the season was half over, and was a useless back number the latter part of the race. Then he said it was rheumatism [that] bothered him. Rheumatism! Bah! ... It was drink and nothing but drink. The influence of drinking men on the morals of the club is bad. Our policy is to use as much fresh blood as possible, and nothing in the world demoralizes a new player so quickly and so thoroughly as to see the older members taking their toddy right along. At any rate I won't have it and the newspapers can poke all the fun they want to at my 'temperance aggregation,' but I mean business and I'll stick to it to the end. I will not have a man in the club who will not sign a temperance pledge for the season—and keep it, too."[45]

Spalding's stubbornness—some might call it inflexibility—concerning his temperance policy naturally created resentment and outrage among the players, particularly when infractions cost them money. Less than a month after the Chicago team returned home from St. Louis, *Sporting Life* reported that Mike Kelly and Jim McCormick, the team's "famous battery," refused to sign their contracts. "They felt sorely hurt at the action of Manager Spalding in fining them $375 each," the publication asserted. Spalding quickly explained his actions in an interview with a Chicago sportswriter:

"As a matter of fact," President Spalding said to THE HERALD reporter, "when the men signed contracts for 1886 I told each one that there was a clause in the contract absolutely prohibiting them from drinking during the season. To each one I promised a certain sum if he would go through the season without drinking, and I also offered an additional sum in case they won the championship. I gave McCormick $2,000 for his salary and agreed to give him $350 if he let liquor alone, and $150 if we won the championship. Of course, when I settled up I did not give him the $350. He had been drinking all through the season and since July has been utterly useless. Kelly received an extra $200 for championship honors, but I did not give him the amount I promised in case he did not drink. Both he and McCormick were among the seven fined $25 each last August for drinking."[46]

Center fielder George Gore, one of the players fined, had wanted to leave the White Stockings for several years, but could not sign with another team because of baseball's reserve rule, which kept him bound to Chicago. (A reserved player could not sign with another club, nor could other clubs offer him a contract.) In November, however, the New York Giants purchased Gore's release, and he agreed to play for them.

Abner Dalrymple's teammates had continued to blame him for the loss of the deciding game in the championship series. He wanted a change, and after Spalding granted his release, he joined the American Association's Pittsburgh Alleghenys. "The releasing of Gore and Dalrymple thoroughly breaks up the best outfield that was ever seen on any grounds," declared the *Chicago Daily Tribune*. "Dalrymple at left, Gore at centre, and Kelly at right, were an unapproachable trio," the paper continued. "For five years they were the superiors of all rivals and won the admiration of the press and public throughout the country."

Kelly was still with the White Stockings by late November, as was the disgruntled Jim McCormick. The team's winning season had reportedly brought in some $62,000 for the club, and both Spalding and Cap Anson believed that Chicago would win again—with or without Kelly. "Who will be champions next year?" a *Chicago Herald* reporter asked Anson. "Chicago, of course," Anson immediately replied, adding that despite the loss of two key players and the possible loss of others, "We will put an invincible team in the field just the same."

The captain was well known for his annual predictions of White Stocking success, so his confident remarks probably came as no surprise. Privately, though, Anson might very well have held a different opinion. A *New York Times* reporter had observed that in Chicago "the impression ... is that the club which has won the League championship for three successive years will be composed largely of new and untried material next year." With his famed outfield in shambles, the baseball-savvy Anson likely had doubts about the "invincibility" of the 1887 White Stockings.[47]

8

FADING GLORY
(1887–1890)

> This season the champions were weakened considerably by the loss of the famous "Mike" Kelly, George Gore, Abner Dalrymple, and James McCormick.—*New York Times*, May 31, 1887

Chicago Loses Its $20,000 Battery (1887–1888)

With the departure of Abner Dalrymple and George Gore, White Stocking officials Al Spalding and Cap Anson were facing the new season with significant personnel changes in the team's lineup. The two men also knew that they might lose other key players as well, most notably the unhappy Mike Kelly. Their apprehensions proved justified, for in early 1887 Kelly announced that "I have determined not to play with the Chicagos any longer. President Spalding and Capt. Anson have not treated me properly, and for that reason I have made up my mind to sever my connection with the champions."

Since Kelly was a reserved player, he needed Spalding to approve his sale to another club (or else he would either have to stay with Chicago or not play professional baseball at all for the coming year). Spalding permitted Kelly to leave the White Stockings, telling a local sportswriter that "I did not care to interfere with him," even though "I had it in my power to keep him off the field for at least a year to come. Kelly was a good player, and I am sorry to lose his services, but I do not think the Chicagos will miss him much."

Spalding was shrewd enough to negotiate a substantial price for those services. He had suggested to Kelly that when the ballplayer was talking to reporters about wanting to play for another team, he "was at liberty to play the 'poor Base Ball slave' act to the limit," which would benefit both of them financially. The Boston Beaneaters' payment of $10,000 for Kelly's release from the White Stockings received widespread publicity as newspapers quickly began calling him "the $10,000 beauty." Kelly himself would receive $5,000 a year: the league's maximum salary of $2,000 plus $3,000 for rights to his picture. The *Chicago Herald* wrote that Boston Treasurer James B. Billings "conceived the idea of buying Kelly's release, and when he saw his efforts crowned with success at last his face beamed with a smile that would melt away the chilly sensations Captain Anson will experience when he learns that in the coming season he will have to pilot the Chicagos without the assistance of the able lieutenant he has had with him so long. As the genial Mike laid down the pen he said: 'Well, I am with you.'"

Just a few days after Kelly set his pen aside, a *New York Times* reporter asked him, "What do you think of the Chicagos' chances for the coming season?" He replied, "I don't think they will get there." The sportswriter for the *Chicago Herald* evidently shared the same opinion.[1]

"The Herald's Omnibus." *Chicago Herald*, February 17, 1887, p. 2.

With the loss of [Mike] Kelly the granite outfield of the Chicago base ball team is shattered. [Abner] Dalrymple, who for seven years guarded the left field for the White Stockings, has gone to Pittsburg; [George] Gore, the great center fielder, has been captured by New York, and now the telegraph brings the news of Kelly's removal to Boston. These three athletes made up one of the most invulnerable outfields ever seen on the ball field. The story that any one of these men ever won the championship for Chicago is bosh; but there is no denying the fact that all three contributed largely to the success of the club. As base runners their equals are not to be found in the league. As batsmen each was deservedly famous. Dalrymple headed the list in 1878, Gore was the king of batters in 1880, and Kelly clubbed his way to second place in the memorable struggle of last year.[2] As fielders all three ranked high, and as strategists they stood head and shoulders over all league players. Dalrymple was given his release because [Cap] Anson thought he had lost his grip on the stick. Gore was driven away by Anson's harsh treatment, and Kelly became so sick of the big captain's insolence that he at last resolved to quit the ball field forever rather than play under Spalding-Anson management again. The Chicago Club never won the championship by clean fielding. It captured the pennant by tremendous batting, daring base running and strategical [sic] work. With such men as Dalrymple, Gore, and Kelly no longer in the club—men who have raked many a chestnut out of the fire by some *coup de main*—the chances of Chicago winning the "rag" this season appear extremely attenuated.[3]

Just who Spalding will put in the outfield this year is not known. It is said that [Billy] Sunday, the Iowa sprinter and "bunt batter," will rattle around in Mike Kelly's shoes in right field. Sunday is as fleet as a deer, but he lacks the batting powers and all the other things that went to make Kelly the terror of all opposing pitchers. [Jimmy] Ryan, who will likely be placed in left field, is a colt. He started out last year by hitting the ball all over the field; but as the season advanced he tobogganed down the batting list at a furious rate. Fortunately, the schedule of games was played before the young man developed all the characteristics of the skyrocket. The gap in center field has not been filled, but it is probable that one of the howitzers from the formidable list of batteries will be planted in the garden.

It is possible, to be sure, that the new players will develop into giants, both in the field and at the bat, but this is hardly probable. There are too many of them.

◆ ◆ ◆

Chicagoans were dismayed that "the only Kelly"—an adulatory phrase that newspapers often used—was leaving the White Stockings. As the *New-York Tribune* editorialized, "He would appear to have done more than any other one man to develop and popularize the great American industry known as baseball." Fans still clung to pennant hopes, however, and *The Sporting News* reported in early March that people in Chicago were singing a baseball song that featured Kelly, written to the tune of "Climbing Up the Golden Stairs" (F. Heiser, 1884). The first verse and one of the choruses reveal the fans' despondency but also their sense of guarded optimism:

> Arrab [*sic*] Kelly's gone and left us,
>   Of his presence he's bereft us—
> Kelly of the diamond bold.
>   He's deserted us for Boston,
> Although Albert laid the cost on,
>   Ten thousand clear in Puritanic gold.
>
> CHORUS
>
> We may not have Mike Kelly,
>   Nor Mac, nor Dal, nor Gore,
> But we'll get there at the finish;
>   If—we don't get there before.[4]

Cap Anson hoped that "Mac" (Jim McCormick) would stay and help the team get to the finish, but if the pitcher wanted to leave he would not worry about it. "His case is just like Kelly's was," Anson told a reporter, "but he is reserved and he has either got to come here and play ball or somebody has got to buy his release, and they can't buy it for a song either, or he won't play ball this year." McCormick was determined not to play for Chicago, though, and he was conspicuously absent from spring training in Hot Springs, Arkansas. The Pittsburgh Alleghenys evidently offered enough money for him, as the pitcher joined the team in April.

With the ink barely dry on their signed temperance pledges, both old and new White Stockings got acquainted and set to work at Hot Springs. Sprinkled among the veteran players at the camp were pitcher Mark Baldwin (hired during the post-season the previous year), right fielder and catcher Dell Darling, left fielder Marty Sullivan, catcher Tom Daly, and pitcher Harry "Shadow" Pyle.[5]

The National League, like the White Stockings, also featured newcomers, and all the players would be taking the field under revised playing rules. The St. Louis Maroons had relocated in Indianapolis and became the Hoosiers, while the American Association's Pittsburgh Alleghenys had replaced the floundering Kansas City Cowboys. One of the new regulations for 1887 stipulated that a batter could no longer call for high or low balls; a "legally" delivered ball passed above the plate between his shoulders and knees.[6]

The league teams got to see how the rules played out when the baseball year opened at the end of April. Although Spalding had told a reporter that he predicted another "triumphant season" for the White Stockings, the first game did not particularly bode well for them. The *Chicago Daily Tribune* headlined its story of the team's 6–2 loss to the Alleghenys in Pittsburgh as "The Wrong Foot First: Chicago Makes a Bad Start in the League Ball Games." The White Stockings held its first home game on May 6, losing to Pittsburgh, 6–3. Chicago was "outbatted, outfielded and outplayed," according to the *Chicago Evening Journal*, and its fourth defeat in five games spurred two eastern dailies to reprint a passage from a Chicago newspaper:

> Never in Chicago's base ball history has the season opened so dismally and disastrously as to-day. The general feeling that the club management has sold out Chicago's chances for the league championship found expression in the most taunting remarks from the big crowd present. When Anson made a claim on the umpire such calls could be heard as "Sit down, you big duffer!" "You slave dealer!" "Sell some more men!" ... The only enthusiasm displayed was for the visiting club, [Abner] Dalrymple, in particular, receiving a hearty ovation. President Spalding was terribly mortified and industriously kept out of sight. The new talent gave a wretched exhibition and the only ball playing was that done by the old timers.

The "wretched exhibitions" continued, and the *Washington Post* reported that by May 18 Anson was "so disgusted" with the team he did not play in the game that day. Left fielder Marty Sullivan committed five errors in the 11–4 drubbing by the Washington Nationals, and center fielder Billy Sunday—who as a bench player in 1886 had played in only 28 games—"acted as if he wanted a net to stop the balls." The *Tribune* delivered similarly critical opinions: "The fielding of Sullivan and Sunday was simply outrageous and was in strong contrast to the work of the old outfield. There was no life or spirit in Chicago's play, and they went on the field as if defeat was a foregone conclusion."[7]

Chicago's old nemesis from 1886, the Detroit Wolverines, apparently played with a different mindset. By June 23 they led the National League with a 31-12 record (the White Stockings were 23-18-1 and in fourth place, seven games behind Detroit). The next day, though, was an exciting one for fans of Mike Kelly, as Boston faced the White Stockings in Chicago for the first time since Kelly was sold. Crowds cheered and applauded the Beaneaters at their hotel, and the *Washington Post* raved that the "$10,000 beauty" was "presented with more flowers to-day than a favorite prima donna on an opening night or a budding beauty at her first party."

The *New-York Tribune* editorialized about the grand festivities in Chicago:

> From all accounts the reception given by Chicago to "Mike" Kelly, the consummate flower of baseball who left her "immediate midst" to give tone and tonic to Boston's nine, was the most thrilling event that city has known since her colossal fire. The proud capital of the great Northwest caught him to her bosom with the impassioned love which a favorite son invariably inspires in the heart of his mother, and as she caught him she exclaimed with voice suffused with emotion: "Call for what you like, Mike." It made a superb picture for the instantaneous photograph. It was a scene never to be forgotten. Strong men bowed themselves and wept copiously; from ten thousand voices ascended the rapturous cry, "Kelly has come again"; business was practically suspended so as to enable everybody to weave garlands for the hero; leading saloons were compelled to engage extra bartenders; and the grand climax of enthusiasm was reached when, as Mike stepped into the chariot that was to bear him to the ball-grounds, the band struck up "Close Your Eyes, Lena." Lena doubtless closed her eyes. Like the rest of Chicago she must have been blinded by the excess of the light streaming of the ovation.

The White Stockings, including pitcher John Clarkson, seemed not to be intimidated or distracted by the attention given their former teammate. Down 5-1, Chicago scored eight runs in the sixth inning and six in the eighth, while the Beaneaters came back with two runs of their own in the eighth. Then "Boston made a good stand in the ninth," the *Washington Post* acknowledged, "rolling up six runs with two men out and [Joe] Hornung was on second when Kelly went to the bat the second time. Every one expected the game to be tied, but the $10,000 went out easily at first," with Chicago emerging victorious, 15–13.[8]

Clarkson followed this win with five more, finally losing on July 11 in the first of a three-game series against the Washington Nationals. The White Stockings split the remaining two games and were on their way to New York to play the Giants when they made a stop in New Jersey to play an exhibition game against the Newark Little Giants of the International League. Newark's battery featured two African Americans: pitcher George Stovey and catcher Moses Fleetwood "Fleet" Walker. Back in 1884, Cap Anson had objected to playing a game against the Toledo Blue Stockings because Walker was on the team. Now, three years later, the Chicago captain's racism was on public display again, for as *Sporting Life* remarked, "Anson wouldn't let Newark put in the colored battery." The minor-league team undoubtedly knew that the Chicago champions attracted paying customers, so rather than rebuff Anson for his demands—which Toledo had done—the ball club replaced Stovey and Walker with teammates Mickey Hughes and Bart Cantz. The Little Giants defeated Chicago pitcher Mark Baldwin and the White Stockings, 9–4. The *New York Herald* commented that it was "a very interesting game" and that "the home club hit Baldwin very hard, but the visitors were not so fortunate with Hughes."

On the same day as the Chicago-Newark game, the International League held a special meeting in which, as detailed in the *New York Clipper*, "The question of colored players was freely discussed." Some white players had threatened to leave the league, so the board directed the secretary "to approve of no more contracts with colored men." Sadly, racial discrimination would remain enforced throughout Organized Baseball for the next six decades.[9]

Following their loss to the Newark team, the White Stockings headed for New York City, where Clarkson beat the Giants on July 15. On August 1 the pitcher hit a home run and hurled a 13–0 shutout against Washington. Twelve thousand spectators filled the stands on August 13 to see Clarkson take on the Wolverines at West Side Park. He failed to pitch a shut-out, but the fans were not disappointed as he instead walloped two home runs in the 8–2 victory. Finley Peter Dunne, a notable *Chicago Daily News* sportswriter of this era who enlivened his baseball stories with colorful anecdotes, recorded his impressions:

> The Chicago audiences have been growing more and more enthusiastic as the champions advanced toward the leading position for the race. Saturday when [John] Clarkson made his second home run the crowd arose and advanced onto the diamond. Umbrellas wide open and silk hats sailed up into the air like bouquets, and from the bleaching-boards on the right and left the cushions were hurled out over the diamond and fell thick as hailstones. This performance has been repeated so frequently of late that the management have refused to rent the cushions to any except the reserved seats. Said Mr. [Jonathan] Brown [club secretary]: "The ladies, I guess, have been contented with clapping their hands and sending up little feminine yells when their favorite made a good hit, but there is no telling how soon they too will fall in with the habits of the men if this thing is not stopped."[10]

The White Stockings were then only one game behind Detroit, but they could not keep up the pace. By September 5 they were four games back, and when Clarkson and the White Stockings lost both games of a doubleheader against the Wolverines two days later, Chicago fans held little hope for a championship. As the *Tribune* observed, "By the loss of these games Chicago's chance of winning the pennant becomes so small as to hardly be worth talking about." The White Stockings finished the season in third place with a record of 71–50–6, 6½ games behind Detroit. Interestingly, Boston, with Mike "the only Kelly," had to settle for fifth place, 16½ games back.

Despite the disappointing season, Chicago was undoubtedly pleased to see that team captain Anson hit a solid .347 and that hurler John Clarkson took league honors with 38 wins, 523 innings pitched, and 56 complete games. Baseball historian Marshall D. Wright asserts in his history of nineteenth century baseball that Clarkson "singlehandedly pitched the team into third [place]; his 38 wins accounting for nearly 60 percent of the team's total."[11]

Chicago fans were no doubt dismayed when Clarkson announced in December that he wanted to play in Boston in 1888. He said that his family and friends lived in that area, and "I think it's about time that I should have something to say about where I shall play." When he was not pitching a baseball, Clarkson was employed alongside his father in their family jewelry and silver-plating business, and the ballplayer declared that if Spalding did not release him, "I will remain in Boston and work at my trade."

By the end of February, all of the major Chicago ballplayers except for Clarkson had signed their contracts. Boston was clearly interested in the pitcher; attendance at Boston games had risen dramatically since the arrival of Mike Kelly, and it was estimated that the club had taken in more than $60,000. The *New York Times* wrote that "in order to keep up the enthusiasm the managers sought to engage another player of national reputation." They offered $10,000 for Clarkson's release, which Spalding accepted.

As might be expected, the press immediately began referring to Kelly and Clarkson as the "$20,000 battery." The two took the field for the first time as Boston teammates on April 5, 1888, playing against some of the squad's "extra" members and a few local men. The club's marketing strategy appeared to have worked. As noted in the Chicago *Times* the next day, "It looked like rain before noontime, but 5,100 people gave up 50 cents a piece [*sic*] to stand in the rain, which commenced when three innings had been played.... Clarkson did not exert himself, but showed great speed." The Beaneaters won by the score of 7–2.[12]

Although Anson felt that the star pitcher could be temperamental and moody, especially when criticized, the White Stockings captain personally regretted seeing him leave Chicago. "The loss of Clarkson is a drawback," he admitted to a *Times* sportswriter. When the reporter asked him how he thought Chicago would do in the forthcoming run for the league pennant, Anson replied, "Oh, she's in the race. We've got a good team and will make a hard fight."

That fight began on April 20. "The Slugging Has Begun," the *Chicago Daily Tribune* exclaimed in its opening-day coverage of the White Stockings' away game against Indianapolis, a 5–4 Chicago win. The *Times* observed that "the Chicagos played a rattling good game of ball, and won by superior field play and opportune hitting." George Van Haltren, who had joined the White Stockings in June the previous year, "pitched good ball at critical points, and to that fact is largely due the success of the team."[13]

For the season's first home game, on May 1, spectators were surprised when the players took the field wearing light gray flannel uniforms—the word "Chicago" stitched in black across the shirt front—with black belts, black caps, and black stockings. The new uniforms were the idea of Cap Anson's wife, Virginia, and she had designed them and selected the colors. Newspapers soon informally began referring to the team as the "Black Stockings" or "Black Sox," though "White Stockings" would continue as the club name.[14]

Anson's men defeated Indianapolis, 8–4, and on May 14 they held a 14–3 record and sat atop the National League. The following day, they played Boston for the first time that season. Five thousand spectators were on hand in Chicago, for as the *New York Clipper* wrote, "The coming of Clarkson and Kelly was like unto the advent of a circus. It was a great popular event; it struck a responsive chord; our rural friends gave heed to the summons. They came on railroad train, in buggy and wagon."

The pre-game activities started ominously, however. As customary, the two teams arrived at the ballpark in horse-drawn carriages. The four horses pulling one of the carriages became startled by the cheers of the crowd and plunged into a platoon of marching policemen, severely injuring one of the men.

Spirits were further dampened when the players took the field on that rainy afternoon. "Base-ball is not a wet weather sport as a rule," the *Chicago Daily Tribune* opined, "but yesterday was an exception, and for once it ranked with fishing, duck hunting, snipe shooting, and such pastimes as people generally pursue in water-proof suits." Summed up the *Chicago Times*:

It was a cheerless sort of game anyhow. It was cheerless to the audience, which had to sit on the wet seats and absorb about half the rain in heaven. It was cheerless for the umpire, who has a bull-fiddle voice which the crowd caught onto early in the game. And oh! [M]y, but wasn't it cheerless for the Chicago ball club. The only people on the grounds who seemed to be enjoying themselves were [John] Clarkson and [Mike] Kelly. The unequaled Clarkson breathed on his enemies and they were as are the snow banks of last winter. The unrivaled Kelly smote the enemy's curves and they sailed away like robins seeking the summer. The two, with some assistance buried [George] Van Haltren and erected a mocking monument of twenty-one base hits above his remains.

The umpire finally—and mercifully—called the game after six innings, with the Beaneaters on top, 20–5. Clarkson did not pitch throughout the rest of the series, and Chicago won the remaining three games, maintaining its lead in the National League. The "Black Stockings" were still in first place on July 20, but then they lost six games in a row and soon dropped out of contention. They finished the 1888 season in second place, nine games behind the New York Giants. (Boston and the "$20,000 battery" were in fourth place, 15½ games back.) Cap Anson led the National League with his batting average of .344 and runs batted in (84), while Jimmy Ryan had a stellar year, ranking first in hits (182) and home runs (16).[15]

Even if they could not take the field in the post-season, the Chicago club members still had the opportunity to play more baseball. President Spalding had announced in March that he wanted to take two teams to Australia and a few other countries to promote baseball internationally (an enterprise that would also promote his own sporting goods firm). One team would include Chicago ballplayers while the second, called the "All-Americas," would comprise players from mainly other National League clubs. All of the athletes, Spalding said, needed to be "men of clean habits and attractive personality, men who would reflect credit upon the country and the game."[16] Soon after his announcement, Spalding discussed his plans with a Chicago *Times* reporter:

"I have been thinking about the matter in desultory fashion for a couple of years past. In February I sent Mr. Leigh S. Lynch to Australia with instructions to study the situation there, and to make necessary preliminary arrangements in case he thought the venture promised to prove successful. Mr. Lynch was for nine years manager of the Union Square theater, New York, and manager for Mrs. [Lillie] Langtry last year.[17] He is a man of much experience and good judgment. He reports in favor of the enterprise, and has engaged playing-grounds in all the large Australian cities.

"My intention is to take at least twenty of the best ballplayers along—enough to form two first-class teams. This will enable me to exhibit base-ball to the Antipodeans in its most perfect development of fielding, batting, base-running, pitching, and catching. We will sail from San Francisco in October or November. Our first stop will be at Honolulu, it having been arranged that the steamer will stay in port long enough to permit at least one game there. Then we will go direct to Australia and play games in Melbourne, Adelaide, Sydney, and other leading Australian cities. We will also play in Tasmania and New Zealand."

"What reason have you for thinking the trip will prove successful?"

"That is something that I will have to adventure in a measure. The expense, I believe, will be between $25,000 and $30,000. It will be my own individual undertaking, and whether I shall reap a profit or lose part of what it will cost me is a problem that will have to be solved by the event itself. But I am hopeful of the out, come [sic]. The Australians are more like the Americans than the English in their general characteristics, and as they are greatly devoted to out-of-door sports I think they will take kindly to base-ball. In fact, the game has a foothold there now, since I have filled Australian orders for base-ball goods. And besides, we shall be fully prepared to play cricket and foot-ball, as well as base-ball."

"How long will you remain away?"

"Something over four months, perhaps. Australia is distant between eight thousand and nine

Members of the New York theater community as well as the Chicago club members are shown in this photograph, which was taken in June 1888 when the baseball team was in New York to play the Giants. Top row, from left: Frank Lane (actor), Fred Pfeffer, Cap Anson, George Van Haltren. Directly in front of Anson is the Chicago club mascot, Clarence Duval, wearing a white drum major's hat and holding a baton. Bottom row, from left: Ariel Barney (theatrical manager), Jimmy Ryan, T. Henry French (theatrical manager and son of play publisher Samuel French), Ned Williamson, Charles "Duke" Farrell, Digby Bell (actor, wearing a white hat with a dark band), De Wolf Hopper (actor, wearing a dark hat), George Borchers, Tom Burns, and Tom Daly. The New York *Sun* of June 23, 1888, mentions Hopper and Bell of the McCaull Opera Company as being "sta[u]nch friends of the New York Giants" and notes that "the picture of the Chicago Club, taken on the Polo grounds, had these gentlemen as central figures."

In August the White Stockings played the Giants again in New York, and on the 14th both teams attended a special performance of the opera company at Wallack's Theatre. According to the next day's New York *Evening World*, "a scene of the wildest enthusiasm" followed Hopper's recitation of "Casey at the Bat." Hopper began to include Ernest Lawrence Thayer's classic poem into his stage repertoire, and during his career he would declaim "Casey" thousands of times (photograph by Joseph Hall of Brooklyn, New York; published in Adrian C. Anson, *A Ball Player's Career*, 1900).

thousand miles. The water trip will require about twenty-six days each way, and we will devote about two months to playing. However, we will arrive in time to take a good part in the league campaign of '89. I won't lose sight of that item while I am away."[18]

Spalding's World Tour (1888–1889)

To help promote what he called the "first world's tour of American Base Ball Players," Spalding invited a few sportswriters to accompany the group and chronicle the games and various other activities. The travelers (including family members, friends, and other guests) left Chicago for San Francisco via railway cars on October 20, 1888. "A crowd of people collected to see our departure," player Jimmy Ryan wrote in his diary that evening. After "the signal for starting" was given, "the train drew out of the Union station, amid the prolonged cheers of the multitude. The myriads of lights were fast receding in the distance but on we plunged into the dark hours of the night, taking our first step toward that far away goal."

As they made their way across the continent, the ballplayers stopped to play exhibition games in both large cities (St. Paul, Minneapolis, and Denver, for example) and much smaller ones (such as Cedar Rapids, Iowa, and Hastings, Nebraska). "The crowd waxed decidedly enthusiastic" during the game at St. Paul, Cap Anson said, but for that matter, according to Al Spalding, "Everywhere on this land journey the Base Ball Missionaries received splendid ovations."

On November 18 they boarded the steamship *Alameda* in San Francisco and set off for Honolulu, and from Hawaii sailed to New Zealand and Australia. After they played a ball game in Melbourne, the city's *Sportsman* newspaper observed that "the best evidence offered that Melbournites were pleased and interested in the exhibition lies in the fact that the crowd of nearly ten thousand people remained through not only nine but twelve innings of play, and then many of them staid [sic] to see a four inning game between the Chicago team and a nine composed mainly of our local cricket players, who made a very creditable show, considering the strength of the team they were playing against, and the fact that they were almost utter strangers to base ball."

The Americans also played games in Ceylon and at the base of Egypt's Great Pyramid of Giza. They climbed on top of the Sphinx to pose for a photograph, and took turns throwing baseballs at the Sphinx's right eye. (Tom Fogarty of the Philadelphia Phillies was "the only man who succeeded in giving the colossus a black eye," according to *Sporting Life*). They toured Italy, and in Naples had wanted to play two games in the Roman amphitheater of Pompeii, but "the offer was indignantly refused."[19]

Naples, Rome, and Florence were followed by a trip to Paris, where one of the Chicago players met with a freak accident. On March 8, 1889, the two teams were playing a game at the Parc Aristotique, along the River Seine near the Eiffel Tower. Shortstop Ned Williamson had taken first base on a walk, and when he tried to steal second, he tripped and fell, cutting his knee on the gravel that covered the ground. Williamson had been chronicling his experiences abroad for the *Cincinnati Enquirer*, and he wrote the newspaper after the injury that "I was advised to remain in Paris, but, stubborn as a mule, I refused, and left with the boys for London, crossing the channel. Oh, God! [W]hat a night I put in. Not only did my knee cause me excruciating pain, but I suffered greatly from sea sickness. In moving I tore one of the stitches from my knee. Immediately upon my arrival here I called in another physician and learned that the wound had not been thoroughly cleaned—result, here I am in bed in a city that I am more anxious to see than any I have yet visited."

While Williamson recuperated in a London bed, his anxious wife by his side, his teammates played baseball and toured England, Scotland, and Ireland. On March 28, 1889, the weary travelers (without Ned and Nettie Williamson), stepped on board the *Adriatic* and began their voyage home, reaching New York on April 6. "I am glad to get back," Spalding said, "for we have got the greatest country in the world. Australia is a nice place, so is England and the other countries we visited, but there is only room for one United States on this globe."[20]

The two teams continued to play ball as they made their way back to Chicago, taking the field together for the final game of their world tour on April 20 at West Side Park. *Sporting Life* correspondent Harry Palmer, who had accompanied the ballplayers on their nearly 32,000-mile trip spanning five continents and 13 foreign countries, recorded that the Chicago and All-America teams had played 53 games (of four innings or more) before over 200,000 people. Three games resulted in ties, and of the remaining 50, the All-Americas won 28 and Chicago 22. Spalding admitted a few months later that "we found very little interest in athletic sports in Italy and France," although "it was a great pleasure for our party to arrive in England, where we found an interest in out-door sports."[21]

As for the unlucky Ned Williamson, he and his wife had finally left England on April 10 aboard the steamship *Celtic*, arriving in New York nine days later. Although his wound had healed, he soon developed soreness or "rheumatic trouble" in both his legs, and in early June he sought relief in the soothing waters of Hot Springs, Arkansas, where the Chicago club held spring training. Williamson, "weak on his pins," did not return to the lineup until mid–August, but by then Chicago had faded out of pennant contention. The infield of Anson (first base), Fred Pfeffer (second base), Williamson (shortstop), and Tom Burns (third base) was known as "Chicago's stone wall," and Anson believed that Williamson's "absence hurt our chances very materially, as the old 'stone wall' infield was left in a crippled condition."[22]

Charlie Bastian from the

Following the 1888 season, Al Spalding embarked on what he called the "first world's tour of American Base Ball Players." To promote the sport of baseball internationally (and also his sporting goods firm), he took players and assorted guests on a trip spanning five continents and 13 foreign countries. The White Stockings and members from other teams played more than 50 games. *Sporting Life* chronicled the entire journey, and in a February 20, 1889, article about the travelers' visit to Egypt wrote that "after being photographed in front of the Sphinx the party proceeded to play a game of base ball in the shifting sand at the base of the pyramid of Cheops." Spalding, wearing a dark suit, is standing at the base of the Sphinx. Standing to his right is his mother, Harriet (Adrian C. Anson, *A Ball Player's Career*, 1900).

Phillies had replaced Williamson as shortstop, but he batted just .135 in 46 games. The crippled Chicago team closed the 1889 National League season in third place, 19 games behind the New York Giants. Boston pitcher John Clarkson claimed league honors in a number of categories, including complete games (68), innings pitched (620), wins (49), and earned run average (2.73), though in the tight pennant race he, Mike Kelly, and their fellow Beaneaters finished one game behind New York.[23]

The Players' League (1889–1890)

Spalding's Base Ball Guide observed about Boston and its famous "$20,000 battery" that "well managed and harmonious teams," not star players, win ball games. "Harmonious teams" would certainly not be a hallmark of the 1890 season. Ballplayers resented what they felt were the heavy-handed polices of owners, which left players, as *Sporting Life* put it, "bound hand and foot at the mercy of their clubs." The reserve rule, for instance, prohibited players "reserved" by team owners from joining other clubs. The 1883 Tripartite Agreement—also called the National Agreement—was a sort of "gentlemen's agreement" among the National League, the American Association, and the Northwestern League. It reinforced baseball's reserve clause, stipulating that club owners of each organization would not attempt to sign contracted players or negotiate with them.

Player salaries were generally between $1,000 and $2,000, but as Boston's purchase of Mike Kelly had shown, club owners ignored salary caps when they saw fit. On the other hand, they provided no money—and little sympathy—to sick or injured ballplayers. *Chicago Daily News* columnist Eugene Field wrote that when Ned Williamson injured his knee during Spalding's world tour, "Mr. Spalding deducted $800 from Williamson's salary on account of that protracted illness, and $500 more for Mrs. Williamson's expenses on the trip around the world!"[24]

John Montgomery "Monte" Ward, the popular shortstop of the New York Giants, had captained the All-America team during the trip abroad. An outspoken, articulate defender of the rights of ballplayers (and a law school graduate of Columbia College), Ward had helped organize a union in 1885, the National Brotherhood of Professional Base Ball Players. Two years later he published a widely circulated article in *Lippincott's Monthly Magazine* attacking the reserve clause, "Is the Base-Ball Player a Chattel?"

While Ward, the president of the Brotherhood, was out of the country playing ball, National League magnates met in New York and quietly passed a salary classification plan, which placed each ballplayer in one of five compensation categories, ranging from Class A ($2,500 a year) to Class E ($1,500). A player would be assigned to a particular classification grade—and awarded the appropriate salary—after being evaluated not just on his baseball skills, but also on "exemplary conduct, both on and off the field."

Newspapers across the United States published details of the plan. After Tim Keefe, the star pitcher of the New York Giants and secretary-treasurer of the Brotherhood, read the news in Boston, he told a *Sporting Life* reporter that the league's action was "in direct violation of our contract clause, which states that a player when reserved shall not receive less than he received the previous season." Keefe declared that the National League had acted unfairly as the touring Brotherhood members were not home to help fight the classification rule, adding, "Won't Ward and the others be mad?"[25]

Ward sarcastically derided the salary plan as a "wondrous scheme" when he and the other ballplayers read about it in American newspapers while they toured Italy. Upon the travelers' return to the United States, the members of the Brotherhood secretly met to determine a course of action. They felt that baseball needed to be run as a partnership between the owners and the players, not as an enterprise in which the players had no rights at all and were "cowed into submission."

By fall 1889, rumors that the ballplayers proposed to "branch out on their own hook and become something more than skilled hirelings" were circulating in the press and in baseball circles. Cap Anson heard the reports, and he said later that "I used what influence I possessed in trying to dissuade such of my players as was possible from taking what I then regarded as a foolish step." But the Brotherhood, which by then included most of the National League's stars, was not deterred and in November announced the formation of the Players' National League (more popularly known as the Players' League). "There was a time," the Brotherhood said in a public statement, "when the [National] League stood for integrity and fair dealing; to-day it stands for dollars and cents. Once it looked to the elevation of the game and an honest exhibition of the sport; to-day its eyes are upon the turnstile.... Players have been bought, sold and exchanged as though they were sheep instead of American citizens."

Players joining the new league were offered contracts that did not include a reserve clause and were promised that they and the financial backers would share revenues. "We believe that it is possible," the Brotherhood members continued, "to conduct our National game upon lines which will not infringe upon individual and natural rights. We ask to be judged solely by our own work, and ... we look forward with confidence to the support of the public and the future of the National game."[26]

The players would need the support of the public since they intended to launch clubs in cities that already boasted professional baseball teams (Boston, Brooklyn, Chicago, Cleveland, New York, Philadelphia, and Pittsburgh, as well as an eighth club in Buffalo). Cap Anson managed to retain pitcher Bill Hutchinson and third baseman Tom Burns, but he lost some of his best players to the newly organized Chicago Pirates, so named because of their black flag and dark uniforms. Fortunately, the minor leagues were thriving, and president Spalding reported that "I am receiving letters from every direction containing applications for positions under Anson." Chicago rookies had occasionally been referred to as "colts," and with new, young faces on board, many sportswriters adopted that nickname for Spalding and Anson's team. In an article titled "Well Pleased with the Colts," the *Chicago Daily Tribune* reprinted a letter from Anson to Spalding in which the captain gave his opinion of Chicago's National League players:

> I tell you I am much pleased with our team so far, and by the time the championship season is opened and we strike Chicago I am sure we will surprise and please our friends, and will also convince the brotherhood that they do not possess all the skillful players in the country.
> John Ward saw our game yesterday, and if he expresses his honest conviction I know he must have been surprised at the skill shown by some of our new men.... Just at present I do not think we want to sign any more players, and unless I am much mistaken our old players will be little missed.[27]

The Colts got off to a good start in 1890, winning six of their first nine games, and on May 1 were first in the National League. Although only 125 people attended a May 5 game with Cincinnati, the *Chicago Daily Tribune* reflected that "the turnstile wheels would have spun round with greater frequency no doubt had ... the cold north wind been out of town." With the score tied at 2–2 after nine innings and daylight disappearing and the temperature decreasing, the umpire called the game. "No one," added the *Tribune*, "offered any objection to quitting."

Low attendance, however, did plague professional baseball during the 1890 season, which included the eight teams of the National League, the nine in the American Association, and the eight in the Players' League. Since the clubs often played games on the same days in the same cities, turnstile counts naturally suffered, as did the profits. The financially struggling American Association "float[ed] along with the tide," coping as best it could. National and Players' League officials issued free passes to fill seats, and when talking to the press they inflated attendance figures to try to sway public opinion and boost fan interest.

The members of the National League soon realized that it was unlikely the fiscal situation would improve by the end of the year, so they counted on their capital to wait out the new teams' anxious and worried financial backers. "The salaries of the National League players," Spalding said in a May interview, "will come from the treasuries of the clubs and the Players' League salaries must come from the receipts after the expenses have been paid.... How long can this sort of thing continue? As long as the National League clubs can supply sufficient money and pay salaries, and as long as the Brotherhood leaders can keep the rank and file of their players satisfied with glittering promises instead of cash."[28]

The drawn-out fight between the rival factions was an open, nasty, no-holds-barred battle. As they scrambled to sign the best players, officials in both the National League and Players' League encouraged contract breaking, often through bribery. Sportswriters took sides, distorted facts, and confused readers in defamatory articles. Eventually the public grew weary of the "bickering among the clubs," as Players' League secretary Frank Brunell referred to the hostilities, and ballpark attendance—as well as profits—continued to fall.[29]

The National League's Brooklyn Bridegrooms finished the season 6½ games in front of Cap Anson's second-place Colts, while in the American Association the Louisville Colonels clinched the top spot. Leagues had held series of post-season championship games since 1884, though in 1890 the Players' League was not allowed to participate. To raise money, the Chicago Pirates and the National League's Cincinnati Reds played four exhibition games in mid–October. Crowds were small, however, and the Chicago-Cincinnati series was judged a failure.

Attendance at the championship National League-American Association games was meager as well. Both *Sporting Life* and *Sporting News* believed that the Boston Reds, the winner in the Players' League, should have been allowed to compete with Brooklyn and Louisville in the final showdown, which ended in a draw. "The old contests between the champions of the National League and the champions of the American Association meant something and solved a question which interested all base ball enthusiasts," bluntly asserted *Sporting Life*. "As things now are, the world's series represents but little and is such in name only, for the Players' League is as strong as the National League."[30]

The Players' League started crumbling when its financial backers decided it was too risky to continue supporting a venture that was obviously not going to turn a profit. "Money was lost so rapidly that the backers cried halt," the *New York Times* reported. Chicago Colts president Al Spalding was then head of a National League "war committee," which had been formed to challenge the Brotherhood and the rebel league. Years later he reminisced about the end of the long and costly fight:

It was with very great satisfaction, therefore, that in the fall of 1890, at the close of that season, I received a delegation from the management of the Players' League, bearing a flag of truce. I was not President of the National League, but, as chairman of its "War Committee," I was fully authorized to treat with those who came asking for terms. Of course, I was conversant with existing conditions in both organizations. I knew that they were on their last legs, and I was equally aware that we had troubles of our own. We had been playing two games all through—Base Ball and bluff. At this stage I put up the strongest play at the latter game I had ever presented. I informed the bearers of the truce that "unconditional surrender" was the only possible solution of the vexed problem. To my surprise, the terms were greedily accepted. I had supposed that they would at least ask for *something*.[31]

Epilogue

Shortly after Spalding met with the Brotherhood men, the Players' League clubs of New York, Brooklyn, and Pittsburgh merged with their National League counterparts in those cities. Spalding bought the Pirates for $18,565, plus $6,435 to settle unpaid player salaries, for a total of $25,000. "The Players' League is deader than the proverbial doornail," Spalding smugly decreed. "It is now undergoing the embalming process, and when this has been done it will be respectfully buried."

Brotherhood leader and champion of players' rights Monte Ward regretfully agreed with him. "Base-ball is a business, not simply a sport," he acknowledged. "It is no longer just a nice summer snap, but a business in which capital is invested." Both leagues had lost quite a bit of their capital during the baseball war of 1890. The *Chicago Daily Tribune* put the figures at $231,000 for the National League ($35,000 just for the Colts), and $125,000 for the Players' League ($16,000 for the Chicago Pirates). Assorted costs "to run the Players' League," according to the *Tribune*, totaled $45,000, "of which nearly $18,000 went for umpires and $10,000 to lawyers." The new league's investors had also spent $215,000 building and equipping the various club grounds, including $25,000 for the Pirates' ballpark at the corner of 35th Street and Wentworth Avenue.

As for Cap Anson, he declared after the baseball war that the "the hatchet must be buried" among the ballplayers. If he thought he could easily get back all his old men and that the former Players' League members would let bygones be bygones, it would not take long for him to be jolted back to reality. It had been a long, tension-filled season for everybody, but a particularly difficult and demanding one for the players.

And Anson would soon find out just how long their memories were.[32]

9

DARK DAYS AND GRIM YEARS (1891–1902)

> Bad luck frequently follows a change of long used distinctive color. The Chicago Club, for instance, has had more bad than good luck ever since it changed from the historic white stockings to black stockings.
> —*Sporting Life*, March 12, 1892

A Contested Pennant Race (1891)

Al Spalding's purchase of the Chicago Pirates following the baseball war of 1890 included the team's spacious Brotherhood Park. This ballpark, which would soon be called South Side Park, seemed ideal for him and the Colts. It could seat between 10,000 and 11,000 people, with room for 5,000 more; in addition, street car and railroad lines provided spectators with convenient transportation to the grounds. The ballpark land was owned by the estate of former Chicago mayor John "Long John" Wentworth (1815–1888), and the rent was only $1,500 a year, one-fifth the rent of the West Side Park. Spalding knew, however, that baseball fans on the West Side would object if he moved from the Congress Street grounds. South Side residents, on the other hand, would complain if he did not use the desirable, well-equipped facilities on 35th Street. The *Tribune* wrote that "letters protesting against the closing of either grounds came in numbers and couched in language which could not be mistaken." The Chicago club decided that the best way to solve the problem would be to schedule all Monday, Wednesday, and Friday games at the West Side Park and ones on Tuesday, Thursday, and Saturday at the grounds on the South Side (National League rules prohibited Sunday games).[1]

With the demise of the Players' League and some of the leading ball clubs consolidated, Anson thought that it would be easy for Chicago to build a team for the 1891 season. "But such was not the case," he recalled years later. He managed to secure some of his old players, but many were "scattered far and wide among the other League clubs, while others retired from the arena altogether. As a result it was a constant hustle on my part to secure new players." While the baseball clubs were "hustling" to secure the best men possible, Anson sought young players rather than established stars. He still, though, felt his team could compete well with the others, and as he told a sportswriter at the time, "You can rest assured it will be a strong one."[2]

In January Spalding returned from a grueling four-day National League conference in New York "worn out in mind and body." He had been neglecting his personal business interests due to his baseball duties, and he was still recovering from the stress of the previous year's clash with the Players' League. In March the Chicago executive announced his plans to retire as club president, though as a leading stockholder, he would still maintain ties to the club.

Cap Anson, he said, would continue to manage the Colts. To handle the club's administrative duties and business affairs, Spalding recommended James A. "Jim" Hart, who had assisted him with the players' world tour and who had experience managing baseball teams. Spalding was pleased when the Board of Directors elected Hart president and wrote to National League president Nicholas Young that "I bespeak for my successor the same courtesies that you have always extended to me, and I feel sure you will find in him a man thoroughly competent and well qualified by long experience to assist in league legislation."[3]

Anson, however, did not think much of Hart's knowledge of business ("no special qualifications") or of baseball ("an accredited failure") and was hurt that Spalding had not selected him as successor. Perhaps sensing his lieutenant's feelings, Spalding wrote Anson a long conciliatory letter to assure him that Hart was merely a figurehead in the Colts' organization under his, Spalding's, control. Anson, though, was not easily mollified. His friendship with Spalding would eventually sour, and the relationship between Anson and Hart, which had never been particularly cordial, would remain strained.

With no promotion, Anson had to be content with simply managing the players rather than the whole club's operations. He had first considered his young team with its new members to be "an experimental one," but on September 1 the Colts were in first place with a comfortable four-game lead over the Boston Beaneaters. The 39-year-old Anson had been with the Chicago team since 1876, and both sportswriters and players had fallen into the habit of poking fun at him and calling him such names as "the old man," "grandpa," "Pop Anson," or "Uncle Anse." Anson decided to have some fun of his own, and on September 4 he took the field in a game against Boston wearing a white wig and a white false beard that reached almost to his waist. "The grand old man of baseball was hurling defiance into the teeth of age by aping its appearance," wrote an amused local sportswriter. The 3,500 spectators laughed and applauded "Uncle Adrian," who kept the wig and whiskers on during the entire game. When he came to bat for the first time, he told umpire Tom Lynch that if the ball so much as brushed his beard, he would claim that he was hit by a pitch and insist on taking first base. "It might have been a fine point for Lynch to decide," the reporter continued, "but during the afternoon nothing disturbed the whiskers but Uncle's caresses and the nipping lake breeze."[4]

Chicago won the game, 5–3, extending its edge over Boston by seven games, and on September 15 the lead was 6½ games, with a mere 16 matches left in the Colts' season. "It is all over," *The Sporting News* proclaimed. "Let the town bells ring out the gladsome tidings and let the Windy City Cranks commence their great rejoicing for the pennant race is over." Unfortunately, though, the bell ringing was a bit premature. The Colts won just six of those final 16 games, while Boston, incredibly, lost only one of its remaining 20 games. At season's end Boston took the league pennant with a record of 87–51–2, while Chicago, at 82–53–2, finished 3½ games behind, in second place.

Various sportswriters wondered if eastern teams had deliberately lost to Boston to keep the pennant in the East. The New York Giants, for instance, did not use several of their star players during a five-game series with Boston in late September, and the

Beaneaters won all five games. Brooklyn lost four games in a row to Boston, while the Philadelphia Phillies lost five games out of six.

The New York *Evening Telegram* admitted that the Giants "put in about as weak a team as could be constructed at Boston." The *Boston Evening Record* made a similar comment, though it believed "the insinuation that New York is purposely surrendering the games or 'throwing' them is hardly worthy of consideration." Both newspapers mentioned that during the season Cap Anson had stirred up considerable resentment among the National League teams. "Anson, the brainiest and most tireless Captain in the country, is not at all popular," the *Record* observed, "partly from the reason that his team is composed of players, whose salaries are considerably less than those paid to the members of any of the other clubs, and partly because he has repeatedly made the boast that he would win the pennant with this raw material. He has made this boast in all of the cities, and it has not been relished East or West." After such public displays of grating arrogance, most teams were probably delighted that Boston won the pennant rather than Anson and Chicago.[5]

Few ballplayers could generate both cheers and jeers the way Cap Anson could. *Sporting Life* reverently called him "the greatest batsman the game ever produced.... As a field captain Anson has few equals and no superior." After Boston won the disputed pennant, the New York *Sun* editorialized that "Anson is one of the most genuine player[s] upon the field. No man can lick an awkward squad into the shape demanded by the League standard or keep his nine pegging away steadily from one end of a season to the other in comparison with him."

The members of Anson's nine might disagree, however, as he was a renowned taskmaster who expected them to work out both mornings and afternoons during spring training, even if they were stiff and sore from practice games and exercising. As one Chicago player bluntly stated, "Training under him was a nightmare." At Hot Springs, Anson would usually arrange games between the new players and the seasoned veterans. During one spring training trip he announced that he would play on the newcomers' team, "and we will make those old-timers hustle."

Anson also made the umpires hustle, as he constantly "kicked" (that is, argued) with officials about their calls during games. In fact, his tirades were occasionally featured more prominently in Chicago newspapers' game-day accounts than the actual plays of the games. One such article, titled "Anson and the Umpire," highlighted Anson's "kicks, protests, and wrangles" and noted it was fortunate that umpire Wallace Fessenden "is not a raving lunatic tonight."[6]

Perhaps Anson's abrasiveness had figured in Chicago's pennant loss. His contempt for the Players' League was well known, and some sportswriters conjectured that the Giants, which included members of the New York Brotherhood team, had decided to get even with him by losing games to Boston. "It is well known," the *Chicago Daily Tribune* claimed, "that the New York club was one of the sta[u]nchest in the Players' League and that its members have no love for Anson. The Brotherhood is dead, but its ghost is holding high revel in the National League at this moment."

Sporting Life dismissed this theory as "absurd," and many persons in baseball circles resented the attacks against the Giants and the other eastern clubs. In addition, it was pointed out that the Colts had struggled during the last couple of weeks of the season, and that perhaps what had hurt them more in the baseball pennant race were the games they had lost rather than the contests that their opponents had won.[7]

President Jim Hart still insisted that an investigative committee look into the matter, declaring in an interview that "were I under indictment for murder with the circumstantial evidence against me as strong as it appears to be against the New-York Club, I should expect to be hanged." As for Anson, he had at first believed there had been no dishonest playing, but later charged that "anybody that knows anything about the game knows that these games in Boston are not worthy the name." He had reason to be upset, as he was under suspicion himself. The American Association's Boston Reds had finished their own league season in first place. Newspapers had hinted that Anson and the eastern clubs had allowed the Beaneaters to win so that Boston's National League pennant victory would offset any prestige and glory accorded the Reds. Anson angrily denied the stories as "idiotic and unworthy of entertaining."

The Giants' Executive Committee met with the New York players on October 8 to examine the allegations. Five days later the committee issued a report that completely exonerated the men from all blame, prompting a swift editorial response from the *New York Times*:

> The investigation into the charges of bad faith brought, in the interest of the Chicago baseball team, against the New-York baseball team seems completely to have exploded those charges. There is no denying that New-York played a very weak game for the last week, and, indeed, for the last month of the season, but there appears to be no ground for saying that the team was purposely weakened in order that Boston might win. It is hard to see what the managers of the New-York team had to gain by the victory of Boston, and sentimental considerations have no weight at all with the professionals of baseball, either among players or managers. The Chicago team has never been remarkable for taking defeat gracefully, either in a single game, in a series, or in a season; but it appears at a particular disadvantage in trying to explain its defeat by Boston by imputing bad faith to New-York.[8]

For the rest of his life, Cap Anson remained convinced of New York's and the other eastern teams' "bad faith," and even charged in his memoir that the Colts "would have landed the pennant" if not for "the jealousy of the old players in the East." Anson finished the season with a league-leading 120 runs batted in, and "the old man" proved that he was not yet ready to retire by playing in all but one of the Colts' 137 games. Chicago pitcher Bill Hutchinson paced the National League by winning a staggering 44 games.

The National League's Boston club declined to play the American Association's Boston Reds in what would have been a lucrative championship series. The financially strapped Association officially disbanded in December 1891, with the National League absorbing teams from Baltimore, Louisville, St. Louis, and Washington. The Association's ticket price had been twenty-five cents, as opposed to the National League's fifty-cent charge. During the off-season, the league passed a rule stipulating that "the general admission fee to all championship games shall be 50 cents, but each club shall designate a part of its grounds, and provide seats thereon, the admission fee to which shall be 25 cents." In addition, for the first time the league allowed clubs the option of scheduling Sunday games, unless prohibited by city laws.[9]

From the South Side Park to the West Side Grounds (1892–1894)

There would be no Sunday games for the Colts, however, at either of their parks. As *Sporting Life* eloquently put it, the owners of the South Side Park were "as puritanical as a Quaker Sunday with a sprinkling of ash cloth and a thee and thou prayer." Also, Chicago president Hart decided to vacate the team's grounds on the city's West Side.[10]

"West-Side Park Abandoned. The 'Colts' Will Play All Their Games at the South-Side Grounds." *Chicago Times*, March 19, 1892, p. 7.

President James Hart of the Chicago club stated yesterday that the "colts" would play all their games on the South-side grounds this season. This fact was announced in THE TIMES a month ago, but there was a possibility that the West-side cranks would succeed in having a number of games played on the West-side grounds. Last year, when the games were equally divided between the West and South side parks there was a great deal of confusion. Despite the notices which were printed daily the patrons would "get their dates mixed" and go to one park when the club was playing at the other. The attendance was better at the South-side games, and this in a great measure brought about the abandonment of the Congress street grounds. The facilities for reaching the park were not as good as those on the South side, and the improvements were far below the standard. The club could not accommodate the 25-cent crowd on account of the size of the grounds and rather than build new double-decked stands, and then only have the use of them for a year, when the lease expires, it was decided to play all the games at the South-side grounds.

◆ ◆ ◆

With the addition of the American Association's four clubs, the National League now comprised 12 teams. League officials decided to split the 1892 season into two halves and expand the playing schedule from 140 games to 154, with each team playing every other club 14 times. The winners of the two half-season contests would then compete in a series of October championship games, in effect giving each team two chances to win the championship pennant.

Cap Anson expected to be a contender in that pennant race, but he would have to play without his famous "stone wall" infield. Third baseman Tom Burns signed a contract in May to manage and captain the Pittsburgh team. Shortstop Ned Williamson had retired from baseball in early 1891 and purchased a saloon in Chicago with former White Stocking Jimmy Wood. Second baseman Fred Pfeffer had played for the Chicago Pirates and the Players' League in 1890 and rejoined Anson for the 1891 season. He still, however, remained loyal to the Brotherhood. In September of that year, during a breakfast conversation while the Colts were in Cleveland, Pfeffer had become furious when Anson remarked, "If I had had my way about it every leader in the Brotherhood movement would have been barred forever from the national game" and immediately left the table without a word, his breakfast untouched. *Sporting Life* reported that "under no circumstances" would he play for Anson in 1892, and the second baseman was traded to his hometown team, the Louisville Colonels, in return for infielder Jim Canavan.[11]

Anson's veteran players included pitcher Bill Hutchinson and outfielder Jimmy Ryan. Anson had hoped to secure catcher Duke Farrell and outfielders George Van Haltren and Hugh Duffy, who had played with him in 1889, but other teams had already signed them. With the demise of the American Association, the National League's teams boasted an abundance of talent, though Anson, not surprisingly, claimed that his team outshone all others.

Sportswriters had their doubts, however. Frank H. Brunell of *The Sporting News* wrote in his column that "Anson talks about having a better team than that of 1891. He needs one. There's new and swifter blood in the League teams of this season.... The town isn't stuck on his outfit, and he needs a championship to get back into popularity. Anson is respected, but so is Christopher Columbus." Brunell added that the Chicago captain "has hopes of the pennant. You know Anson. He always has, and he'll bet you, too."[12]

Betting on the Colts was not a good idea in 1892. Although they won their first two games, they dropped the next nine. After they lost four games in a row in early July, the *Chicago Daily Tribune* speculated that there probably was not "an organization in existence worse than the Chicagos." They completed the season with a record of 70–76–1, in seventh place in the National League, with a winning percentage below .500 for the first time since 1877. Anson undoubtedly wished he had Fred Pfeffer back, as Jim Canavan hit only .166. The team's batting average had continued to fall since 1889: .276 in 1889, .260 in 1890, .253 in 1891, and .235 in 1892. Anson himself hit only .272, his worst performance at the plate since he joined the team in 1876. One bright spot was Bill Hutchinson, who pitched a league-leading 67 complete games. He and Cy Young of Cleveland finished first in the National League with 36 wins.

Despite his pre-season blustering, Anson had known early on that his team would not bring home any championship honors, especially without Van Haltren and Duffy. "I felt that I did not have a chance on earth from the beginning," he admitted, "and when things began to go wrong and I looked around in vain for reinforcements I got a bit discouraged and let things take their course for a time." President Hart had been able to acquire several additional players, and that helped the team improve somewhat; during the second half of the season the Colts won 39 games and lost 37 (as opposed to their record of 31–39–1 in the first half).[13]

Modest performance on the field undoubtedly accounted for empty seats in the ballpark, which certainly did not help the Colts' finances. Their year-long attendance of 109,067 placed them eleventh in the league, behind only Baltimore. Hart had remarked in early October that the Colts would not be playing any exhibition games after the regular season ended. "We have lost enough money now. I wouldn't care if the season closed to-morrow. It has been a bad year all around."[14]

Hart did have, however, a few money-making ideas, starting with a reorganization of the Chicago Ball Club. He and two associates, Charles M. Sherman, an attorney, and Thomas Barrett, a member of the Chicago Board of Trade, formed a stock company and purchased the National League franchise from its principal stockholders, Al Spalding and bankers John R. Walsh and Charles T. Trego. The latter three men remained owners of the old corporation, the assets of which consisted of spring training grounds in Hot Springs, Arkansas, and land on Polk Street on the West Side of Chicago, between Lincoln (later Wolcott) and Wood Streets. Hart obtained a ten-year lease on the Polk Street property for a new ballpark. He still planned to use the South Side Park, as its lease was held by his new company, called the Chicago League Ball Club.

The *New York Times* explained that with the purchase of the grounds in Hot Springs and the property on Polk Street, the original club had become, "from a financial standpoint, more of a land than an amusement company. It was therefore concluded to separate the two branches and allow the old corporation to look after the land end of the business, while the new corporation will do nothing but hunt the pennant.... Mr. Hart expresses himself firmly in the conviction that the new movement means Sunday games, especially in this city during the World's Fair."[15]

Millions of tourists were expected to throng Chicago's streets and lakefront when the "World's Columbian Exposition" opened in May 1893 on the city's South Side, and the club president was hoping that many of them would want to spend their afternoons—and money—watching the Colts play ball. The South Side Park is "central and convenient for World's Fair visitors," Hart told a reporter, "and we expect to draw large crowds."

Despite the opposition of many religious leaders and other defenders of "blue laws," the fair would remain open on most Sundays. "From a business point of view," Hart added, he favored Sunday games, though lease restrictions continued to prohibit the Colts from playing at the South Side Park on that day. Hart sold the old park on the West Side in August 1892 so the ball club could build a new facility on the grounds at Polk and Lincoln Streets. "We have labored to construct a park which shall be almost without a fault," Hart said upon its completion, "and I am confident that we have succeeded.... It is probable that we will play there next year, as the West Side is the best part of the city for ball games."

Chicago held its 1893 home opener at the South Side Park on Saturday, May 13, in a game against Cincinnati. The two teams moved to the West Side the next day. A lengthy illustrated article on the new grounds, where the Chicago team would play on Sundays, was featured in *The Sporting News* shortly before the park's inaugural game.[16]

"Chicago's New Park. It Is Located on the West Side and Is a Hummer. Something About the New Buildings and New Grounds." *The Sporting News*, April 22, 1893, p. 2. [Note: A diagram accompanying this article shows that the new park's boundaries were Polk Street (north), Taylor Street (south), Wood Street (east), and Lincoln Street (west). Home plate was near the corner of Polk Street and Lincoln Street.][17]

All the world of base ball is now notified that on May 14 the new West Side Base Ball Park at Chicago will throw open its doors to the public. It will be a red letter day indeed in Chicago base ball circles. It will not only mark the opening of a new park, but it will be memorable by reason of the fact that the first game ever played by National League Clubs in Chicago on a Sunday will then be played. On this notable occasion indeed the Chicago and Cincinnati Clubs will meet in a regular championship game. And in fact all the Sunday games to be played in Chicago during the World's Fair year will be played in this park. There is a clause in the lease held by the Chicago Club in the South Side grounds which prohibits the playing of Sunday games there. So all the Sunday games will be played in the West Side Grounds which have been specially fitted up to care for the big crowds which are expected to attend the Sunday games in Chicago this World's Fair year.

The grounds are roomy and the grand stand and open seats are massive and royal in their proportions. We present to-day cuts of the grand stand, the diamond and field, showing the grand stand and open seats and the building to be used for a ticket office and directors' room, together with portraits of President [Jim] Hart and Manager [Cap] Anson. The buildings were planned by Mr. John Addison, who made a record as the architect of the great Brotherhood Grounds in South Chicago and the contracting work was carried on by Contractor Charles Carpenter.

The base ball grounds proper are four hundred and seventy-five feet square, exclusive of the carriage yard. The grand stand contains three thousand folding opera chairs, five hundred arm chairs and fifty-six private boxes. In the covered pavillions [sic] there are four thousand five hundred seats and in the open seats there is room for eight thousand persons. Some idea of the immense amount of seating room may be gained when it is stated that eight hundred thousand feet of lumber were used in building the grand stand and open seats. The top floor

9. Dark Days and Grim Years (1891–1902)

According to the article that accompanied this illustration of the West Side Grounds, "almost one million feet of lumber" was used in the construction of the "magnificent" ballpark. "The new grand stand and grounds will be when finished one of the finest in the country" (*Chicago Evening Post*, April 16, 1893).

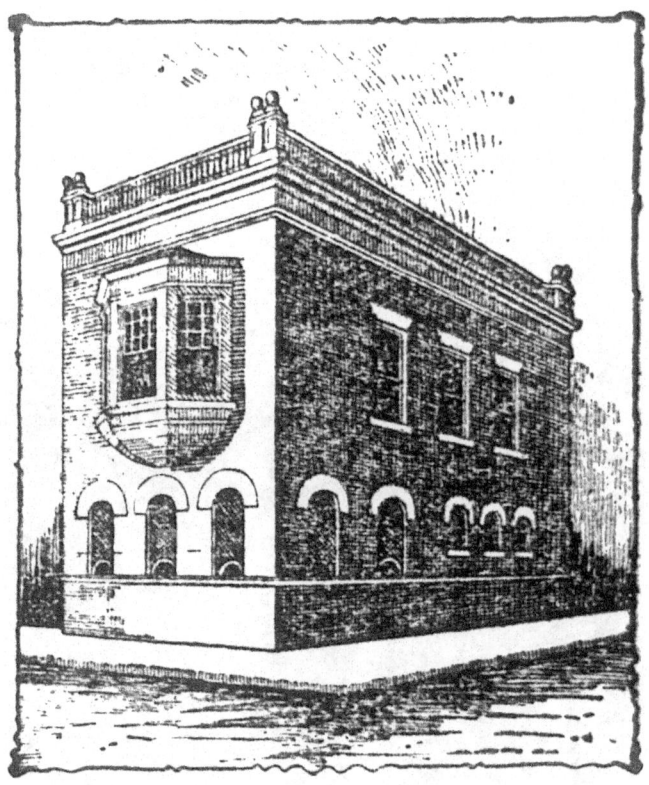

of the brick building at which we present a cut is to be used by the ticket sellers and for two toilet rooms. On the ground floor the directors' room and the ladies' retiring room is located. The diamond stands out ninety feet from the grand stand. The right and left field fences are five hundred and forty feet from the home plate, or one hundred and fifty feet further out than were the fences on the old West Side grounds.[18] The distance to the extreme center field corner is five hundred and sixty feet. There are dressing rooms for both the home and visiting clubs, each fitted with hot and cold water pipes, shower baths, closets and all that sort of thing.

As already stated these grounds will be the scene of the Sunday games played by the league Chicago year—the first ever attempted in Chicago—and, unless the calculations of President Hart and others interested in the game are greatly at fault

The clubhouse of the West Side Grounds was "supplied with lockers, with shower baths, with hot and cold water for the use of the players and with other conveniences that are considered necessary" (*Chicago Evening Post*, April 16, 1893).

will hold crowds of people such as were never seen at ball games there. The present calculations is for a seating capacity of 13,000, but this can be increased if it is seen that the crowd cannot be accommodated. Mr. Hart says that no more will be admitted to games than can be supplied with seats. "Experience has shown," said he, "crowds are much more unruly if not seated, and inasmuch as we expect to have the best of decorum at our Sunday games we will not tempt the disorderly element by letting them in without having a place for them to sit."

The grand stand, which is to be one of the largest in the country, is already assuming shape, but no work has yet been done on the "bleachers." A portion of these will be constructed between now and May 13 and the remainder later. They may eventually skirt the entire outfield. The work has progressed so rapidly during the recent pleasant weather that there is no longer any doubt about everything being in readiness for the first scheduled game, and President Hart, who spends much of his time at the new park, wears a broad smile of satisfaction. Almost the entire field will be "new," teams having been at work for two weeks hauling dirt and filling in so as to give an elevated surface that will dry rapidly after rains. The club calculates that it cannot afford to lose any games scheduled for Sunday because of inclement weather.

The worst defect about the grounds is a short right field. As a result right field hitters will have a rather easy task in putting the ball over the fence—but no more so than they had on the grounds at Congress and Loomis streets. The grand stand faces southeast, the main entrance being at the corner of Lincoln and Polk streets, but there will also be gates at which tickets will be sold to the "bleachers," with plenty of spaces for ingress and egress. The only public buildings of consequence in the vicinity are the county hospital and surrounding medical institutions, which are located one square to the north. The Ogden avenue, Harrison,

A postcard shows Chicago's West Side Grounds, facing Polk Street (the third base side of the ballpark). The buildings in the background were part of the old Cook County Hospital property (author's collection, courtesy of Tom Sheridan).

Van Buren, Taylor and 12th street car lines will afford transportation to the grounds this year. Next year the Metropolitan "L" will carry passengers near the gates.

The Chicago Club which is to occupy these grounds will this year be in charge of President James A. Hart and Captain-Manager A. C. Anson. Both are well and favorably known in base ball circles. Mr. Hart, before his election to the presidency of the Chicago Club managed several of the best teams in the country. Anson has been a member of the Chicago Club since 1876. His team this year will include: [Malachi] Kittridge, [Pop] Schriver and [Bill] Lange, catchers; [Bill] Hutchinson, [Gus] McGinnis, [Willie] McGill and [Hal] Mauck, pitchers; Anson, first base; [George] Decker and [Wallace] Taylor, second base; [Jiggs] Parrott, third base; [Jimmy] Ryan, short stop; [Bill] Dahlen, [Bob] Ca[ru]thers and [Sam] Dungan in the outfield.[19]

◆ ◆ ◆

Despite the Colts losing to Cincinnati, 13–12, on May 14, the *Chicago Evening Post* reported that everyone "went home well satisfied with the afternoon's entertainment if not thoroughly gratified with the result of the sport." President Hart said that he was especially pleased that the club could provide a baseball game on Sunday, as that was the one day of the week on which "people can get away from their work and it is only natural they should desire to see a ball game." Wrote the *Post* in its coverage of the momentous occasion:

> Sunday base ball in Chicago is a big success. That was demonstrated beyond all controversy by the great crowd that turned out to see the game between Chicago and Cincinnati at the West Side ball park. The event was an important one in base ball history and served to show clearly that Chicago is one of the best Sunday towns, if not the best, in the entire league. It was the first Sunday game the people of this city have had, and the hearty manner in which the people responded shows their appreciation. Base ball is an innocent open air amusement which appeals essentially to the working classes—to those who are compelled to labor in the employ of others for their livelihood and for whom Sunday is a day of recreative rest. In the great and beautifully constructed grand stand and pavilions of the new West Side park yesterday were gathered, by actual count, 13,233 spectators who enjoyed the game from the first inning to the last, notwithstanding the fact that it might have been played more artistically than it was.
> It was the first game, too, to be played in the new park, and in spite of that fact and the confusion that should have arisen in the seating of the people the vast crowd was as orderly as the congregation of a church, and not one unpleasant incident disturbed the serenity of the affair. The character of the vast concourse of citizens was above the average. A well-known court judge who was present looked around surprised and said: "This crowd is a revelation to me. I had no idea that this is what Sunday base ball is like. I have never before seen such a vast assemblage so completely free from every objectionable feature. These people are highly respectable, every one of them. Sunday ball is what Chicago has needed these many years, and I am amazed that we have not had it before. I must congratulate Chicago and the Chicago ball club, the first for being given this splendid out-of-door entertainment and the second for giving it."

The National League once again comprised 12 clubs, though the teams would play only 132 games with no split season and no double championship. The pitcher, who previously had stood within a chalked pitcher's box, now threw from a 12-inch by 4-inch rubber plate or slab. Ballplayers had discussed for several years the idea of moving the pitcher back "for the purpose of obtaining better batting," and the pitching distance to home plate was increased from 50 feet to 60 feet, 6 inches.[20]

Although the batting averages of numerous league players soon markedly increased, the new pitching rule did not materially help the Colts. Anson had remarked early in the

> WEST SIDE BALL PARK—Corner Polk and Lincoln-sts.
>
> # BASEBALL TODAY
>
> ## Cincinnati vs. Chicago.
>
> ADMISSION, 25c, 50c, 75c, $1. GAME CALLED AT 3:30 O'CLOCK
> SEATS FOR 13,000 SPECTATORS.
>
> Take Ogden-av. Car on Madison-st. Cable Train, Twelfth-st., Harrison-st., Van Buren-st., or Taylor-st. Cars.
> All games on week days are played at South Side Park, 35th-st. and Wentworth-av.

A newspaper advertisement publicizes the newly built West Side Grounds' first baseball game (*Chicago Daily Tribune*, May 14, 1893).

season that because of his many young players, "We have had to experiment a good deal, and will continue to do so." He added that he had confidence in his men and just wanted them to "be given a fair chance to show what they can do." By June 1 the Colts had had that "fair chance," but they had compiled just a 10–17 record and were in eleventh place in the National League. Later that month, Hart leased the South Side Park to the promoters of the World's Fair college baseball tournament, a series of games that would begin on June 26. He consequently moved all of the Colts' games to the West Side Grounds for the rest of the season.[21]

It was another losing season, too, what with Chicago's record of 56–71–1. But despite their ninth-place finish in the National League, 29 games behind Boston, the Colts' attendance was more than twice that of the previous year. *Sporting Life* found the high gate count, "considering the poor position" of the team, "hard to account for," though Hart attributed the large crowds to the team's relocation to the West Side Grounds, the park's 25-cent seats, and the public's interest in the club's new, young players.

The Colts did not return to the South Side Park. "We abandoned it as a ball park for league games," Hart later said. "We tried games at both the parks to see which would draw the best; and eventually decided that the west side ball park was best located for our games." Hart added that since the Chicago Ball Club owned the property on the West Side, "We preferred to play on what we might consider our own grounds."[22]

But they needed more than just enthusiastic fans in an attractive ballpark to win a pennant. "Never in the history of baseball has a Chicago team been so low in the race at this season of the year," the *Chicago Daily Tribune* had ranted in August. The angry and frustrated sportswriter may have been exaggerating, but the Colts' 1893 winning percentage of .441 tied the team's worst record set in 1877.

Perhaps the players needed a slight change in their uniforms. *Sporting Life* had occasionally commented that the club had never won the league championship after it adopted black stockings in 1888 (though "we have no desire to encourage superstition"). Chicago went back to the traditional white stockings in 1894.[23]

"Base Ball. Chicago Gleanings. A Wise Step Taken by the Club Management. The Club Returns to the Use of the Famous White Stockings." *Sporting Life*, April 21, 1894, p. 6.

Chicago, Ill., April 16.—When Captain Anson marches his Colts upon League fields hereafter they will be garbed in gray, and their shanks will be covered with white stockings. The Chicago ball players will return to the suits they wore when they won fame and pennants in the League.

BACK TO THE OLD SOX.

In discussing this matter the other day, Captain Anson looked wise and declared: "Yes, sir! This is our lucky year. We wore white when we were at the height of our prosperity, and had no business ever to discard it. This season we will stick to white hosiery at home and abroad. Now, Jim" [Hart], said he, turning to the gentleman who manages the business end of the club, "I want you to order the suits as soon as you can. We will wear all white at home. Abroad, of course, we have to wear gray uniforms, but will have white stockings, and the lettering across the breast will also be in white.

"How long since the Chicagos discarded white stockings?" "I don't believe I can say, but it has been several years. Why did we do it? Just because everybody else got to wearing them.[24] But it was a mistake. We ought to have stuck to them, as we made a name for them. I believe every club should have its colors, just as colleges do. The colors of the Chicago Club should be white and gray. There is not a prettier suit in the world than gray with white trimmings."

The new colors notwithstanding, most sportswriters continued to refer to the Chicago team as the Colts, although White Stockings was occasionally used. Cap Anson's hopes for a "lucky year," as he told *Sporting Life*, were dashed early on, for just a few days after the start of the 1894 season, the *Chicago Daily Tribune* observed that the players seemed to be "weak" and "hopelessly outclassed." The paper's sportswriter remarked that although they were "a nice, well-behaved, and praiseworthy body of young men that would do credit to any city," they simply could not play baseball. Anson, furthermore, did not seem to know what the problem was, but "the truth ... can be told him in a few words. His team plays ball with its hands and feet solely. Championship teams always use their heads. The Chicago club, individually and collectively, has none. There is one brainy man in the team, and he—Jimmy Ryan—is buried in the outfield. The infield is a joke pure and simple.... When Fred Pfeffer and Tom Burns left the Chicago club Anson's glory departed. Until he finds men with heads to take their places he will be near the foot of the championship ladder."[25]

By the first of August the hapless Colts were languishing near the bottom of that ladder, though they soon had more pressing, even perilous, concerns. On August 5, Chicago was leading the Reds, 8–1, in the seventh inning of a game at the West Side Grounds. Shortly before 5:00, right after Anson had struck out, a carelessly tossed match or cigar stub ignited some rubbish (or perhaps a small tool shed) beneath the west row of bleachers along Lincoln Street. The blaze, in turn, set fire to the wooden pine seats. Panicked spectators ran to escape the quickly spreading flames, but were trapped by strands of barbed wire that had been strung in front of the grandstand and bleachers to keep rowdy fans from running onto the field. The *Tribune* furnished particularly graphic details:

> The crowd was between the growing fire and the high, strong, barbed fence. Men began to clamber up these wires like rats in a cage and drop over into the field below. The first few got through easily enough. Others tried to slip between the wires and hung there, entangled fast in the barbs. Men and boys fought and clawed at each other to get a chance at the rasping barrier. The first ones through dropped on the ground half stunned; before they could get up heaps of others were piled upon them in crazy confusion. Men came popping out through the wires, their faces and hands torns [sic] and bloody, their clothes in rags, wild with fright. The crazed crowd behind pushed and pounded upon those near the barrier, driving them into the cruel barbs. Some of the men had sense enough to look after the few women in the bleachers—not over half a dozen. These were held back out of the mêlée.

The fire grew larger "as if it traveled on trains of powder," and president Hart ordered the fence behind the grandstand torn down. The ballplayers, led by Walt Wilmot, Jimmy Ryan, and George Decker, used their bats to beat down the barbed wire barricade, providing a gap that enabled hundreds to escape. "It seemed as if the entire field was covered with bleeding men," continued the *Tribune*, "some of them half stripped of their clothing. At least 500 people must have been more or less seriously hurt during the stampede."

Firemen eventually brought the fire under control, but not before it had caused some $15,000 damage to the grandstand and bleachers. The structures were fenced off so the game could be played the next day, and president Hart immediately made plans to repair the park.

The mood was a bit more lighthearted a few weeks later when the Colts were in Washington, D.C., to play the Nationals. Over the years, a desk clerk at the Arlington Hotel in Virginia had argued with Anson as to whether a player could catch a baseball thrown from the top of the Washington Monument. The clerk insisted that the force of the ball traveling 500 feet would break the bones in a man's hands, while Anson maintained that a good player could easily hold on to the ball. On August 24, Chicago catcher William "Pop" Schriver proved Anson correct when he caught a baseball tossed out of a north window of the monument by his teammate, pitcher Clark Griffith.[26]

Unfortunately, that catch was probably the high point of the Colts' whole year, for even Anson believed that his men had no chance to win the National League championship. On the last day of the 1894 season, the Chicago players found themselves in possession of the abysmal record of 57–75–5, in eighth place among the 12 teams, and 34 games behind the first-place Baltimore Orioles. Anson especially bemoaned Chicago's lack of pitching, for the team's earned run average was just 5.72. In a "review of the work of old Anson's team," *Sporting Life* declared that "this year, as in 1893, Anson's Colts had an off year.... From the outset the team was crippled by the poor work of its pitchers."

In the off-season, the club suffered another blow when fan-favorite Mike Kelly unexpectedly died of pneumonia on November 8 at the age of 36. He had traveled from his home in Paterson, New Jersey, to Boston to appear on stage with a local theatrical company. He had caught a cold on the boat from New York, and his health steadily declined after chilly weather and a storm hit the Boston area. The *Chicago Daily Tribune* reported that his former manager, Cap Anson, "seemed almost broken-hearted over Kelly's death." Anson was undoubtedly thinking of the state of his club when he declared that "I would willingly have had him on the Chicago team at any time."[27]

From Colts to Orphans to Cubs (1895–1902)

Although the Colts managed to compile winning seasons the next two years (72–58–3 in 1895 and 71–57–4 in 1896), they were not serious pennant contenders. One dedicated follower of the team was full-time traveling salesman and part-time writer L. Frank Baum, who lived with his family just a few blocks from the West Side Grounds. *The Wonderful Wizard of Oz* would earn Baum literary acclaim in 1900, but not many people recognized his name in 1896 when he contributed "Two Pictures" to the *Chicago Times-Herald*:

I.

With one tremendous, deaf'ning roar
    Ten thousand throats proclaim
Chicago has the biggest score,
    And Anson's won a game!

Ten thousand hats are toss'd in air,
    Their owners all aflame
With rapture, for they're well aware
    That "Uncle's" won a game!

Throughout the city flies the news
    That tells the city's fame,
While pandemonium ensues—
    For Anson's won a game!

All business worries are forgot,
    E'en politics seem tame;
Who cares for Cuba's woes a jot
    Since Anson's won a game?

II.

But hark! what means this muttered growl,
    This darksome look, this lowering scowl?
The "rooter's" ceased his joyous howl
    And hangs his head in shame.

And o'er the city falls a gloom
Unequaled save in gruesome tomb;
The reason is, we've met our doom
    And Anson's lost a game![28]

By this time, Chicago's fans had clearly grown weary of the old captain. Always stubborn and inflexible, he had refused to adjust to the nuances of the ever-changing sport and was "ten years behind the times," as one of his fellow managers said. "It isn't a very difficult task to see why Uncle Anson's Colts don't win more games," contended *Sporting Life*. "They aren't playing up-to-date base ball by several long shots. When, with two men on bases, a batter goes to the plate and tries to knock the ball out of the lot, instead of sacrificing, it's a good chance that not enough runs will be scored to beat a pudding. The Colts aren't the best fielders in the world. That is, they aren't sure fielders."

THE OPENING OF THE BASEBALL SEASON.

This cartoon, published on the day the 1896 baseball season opened, reflects fans' dissatisfaction with longtime Chicago team manager Cap Anson, who had not brought home a National League pennant since 1886. Note the derisive "Uncle Anse" on his sash (*Chicago Daily Tribune*, April 16, 1896).

Anson always liked to sign powerfully built ballplayers who could hit like him, even though they were usually slower than light, wiry men. He dismissed the importance of fielding, probably because he, himself, was a better offensive player than a defensive one. "I don't care if [players] can't field a little bit," he admitted. "In my experience I have found that a man can be taught to almost stop cannon balls, but it is a very difficult task to teach them to line 'em out."

It was also difficult for Anson to be tactful. His exacting demands as a manager, as well as his abrupt—often abrasive—manner won him few admirers among his men. For example, near the end of the 1896 season, with the Chicago Colts in fifth place in the league standings, he deliberately went "on record" with a newspaper reporter so he could publicly berate the players for their lack of discipline and for not showing up for practice games. "I can fine them for such conduct and cut off their salaries," he fumed, "and I may decide to do it. I see no reason why these men should be paid when they do no work nor even report for duty."[29]

Cap Anson was 45 years old in the spring of 1897, and his age and diminishing abilities were particularly noticeable on May 20, when Chicago lost to Washington, 16–14. The slow-footed Anson had inserted himself in the lineup as catcher rather than at his customary position at first base, and according to the *Washington Post*,

> At least three of the runs made by the Senators were due directly to the elderly gentleman's erratic passage of the ball to second and third base when the Senators moved along on steals.... The most

partisan of the Chicago fans cut loose with their throttles, and one reverberating bar[i]tone ensconced immediately behind the backstop, bawled:

"Papa, your trousers are bagging in the knees. You're a comedian as a catcher." ... Anson was cut to the quick by the shafts of persiflage and billingsgate hurled at him, and the Chicago papers of to-day demand the old gentleman's retirement from the game.

Chicago club president Jim Hart diplomatically said afterwards that "Anson realizes that there are stronger first basemen and catchers than himself. Our patrons didn't fancy his fielding as a first baseman, and they set up a howl. But he figured that he ought to be in the game for his hitting, and so he went behind the bat. Now they are up in arms against his catching."

Anson hit a respectable .285 in 1897, but he had averaged .331 in 1896, .335 in 1895, and .388 in 1894. He also scored only 67 runs in 1897, down from 72 in 1896 and 87 in 1895. He and his Colts ended the season in ninth place among the National League's 12 teams, 34 games behind league-leading Boston. Despite his team's poor record, he firmly announced that he had no plans to retire and that he intended to put on his baseball uniform again in 1898.[30]

Jim Hart, however, had his own ideas about Anson's future. The two men had disliked each other well before Spalding selected Hart over Anson in 1891 to head the Chicago ball club, and they were "not even distant friends," according to *Sporting Life*. Anson believed that Hart interfered with his management of the Colts; Hart purportedly had rescinded fines that Anson imposed on his men, which led to players treating Anson disrespectfully and ignoring his orders. For his part, Hart blamed Anson for the continual poor showing of the Chicago ball club. Anson had been manager of the team since 1879, and although he had brought home five National League championships, the last one was more than a decade ago and prospects for future pennants seemed rather slim.

Sharing Hart's dislike of Anson was John R. Walsh, a well-known Chicago banker and the principal stockholder of the baseball club. With the 1897 season over, a Boston sportswriter provided "a pretty fair idea of the Chicago situation" as he related how Hart and Walsh had tried to remove Anson as manager of the Chicago team:

> For several years Mr. Walsh has advised the release of Anson, but Anson's old friend, Spalding, came to the front and pleaded that he had not the heart to let Anson go. Jim Hart has fully agreed with Mr. Walsh, and during the last year or two the banker has obtained stock enough to control the club. A. G. Spalding was under heavy obligations to the Chicago banker when he started business in the Windy City about 20 years ago, and has grown tired of continually pleading for his old friend until the time has come when Hart as president can act without compromising himself with A. G. Spalding.[31]

That time came at the National League officials' annual fall meeting in November. Hart had asked Tom Burns—manager of the minor league Springfield Ponies in Massachusetts and Anson's former third baseman—to attend the conference. When the two men got together, the club president asked him if he would be interested in managing the Colts. "That would suit me all right if Anson has quit," Burns replied, "but I would not take the place for all the money in Chicago, though, if I thought I was to be the cause of Anson going." Hart assured him that Anson's 10-year contract would not be renewed after it expired in January.

Anson also attended the league meeting, and as he wandered around the lobby of his hotel, he wondered if he would have a job the following year. He soon realized what Hart and the club had in store for him, and remarked to a friend, "Well, it looks as if they were going to let the old man go, doesn't it?"

For a canny baseball man, Anson seemed remarkably obtuse about his impending dismissal. Fans for months had heard rumors that Anson would be leaving the Colts, so they were not at all surprised when they opened their newspapers on February 1, 1898, and read the news. "Adrian Constantine Anson is no longer at the head of the Colts," began the *Chicago Daily Tribune*. "With the expiration of his contract last night Anson's connection with the Chicago club ceased. He has not said a word, but has waited for the club to act while they waited for him to move."

Anson may not have said anything, but Hart released a public statement explaining that "it is the desire of the club to do exactly that which the public desires and the opinion of the majority of the stockholders is that the patrons of baseball in Chicago desire a change of management of the team; and because of that belief the directors have decided to not renew the contract with Mr. Anson which has just terminated."[32]

Even though many questioned whether Anson was the right man to lead the Colts, they still acknowledged his remarkable achievements. In an article titled "Greatest of All," for example,

Adrian Anson joined the Chicago White Stockings in 1876 and captained the team from 1879 to 1897. In his career with Chicago, he batted over .300 every year except 1891, 1892, and 1897. Upon his retirement in early 1898, *Sporting Life* listed his accomplishments in a February 12 article and declared that "as a consistent batsman no one ever equalled [*sic*] Anson." Some of his records have since been broken, of course—and his modern-day reputation is tainted by his racism—but according to the statistical resource Retrosheet, among the Chicago franchise's ballplayers he is the all-time leader in hits (3,012), runs (1,722), runs batted in (1,880), and doubles (529). He ranks second in games played (2,277), at-bats (9,104), and batting average (.331), behind, respectively, Ernie Banks (2,528), Banks (9,421), and Riggs Stephenson (.336).

Note Anson's black stockings in the photograph. His wife, Virginia, designed new light gray flannel uniforms for the team in 1888, with black belts, black caps, and black stockings. The players went back to their traditional white stockings in 1894.

After Cap Anson left the Chicago ball club, he briefly managed the New York Giants in the summer of 1898. After losing money in several business ventures, he toured the country on the vaudeville circuit and regaled audiences with baseball stories. In 1900 he published his memoirs, *A Ball Player's Career*. Anson died in Chicago on April 14, 1922, three days before his 70th birthday. His monument in the city's Oak Woods Cemetery features two crossed baseball bats laid on a wreath, beneath which is carved: "He Played the Game." Anson was enshrined in the National Baseball Hall of Fame at the hall's opening in 1939 (Adrian C. Anson, *A Ball Player's Career*, 1900).

Sporting Life singled out Anson's "handiness" with the bat, asserting that "he is probably the most consistent sticker in the history of base ball." Anson had joined the Chicago baseball team in 1876, and in only three years had he batted less than .300. He was also the first major league player credited with 3,000 hits.[33]

The Sporting News reminded its readers that new Colts manager Tom Burns had learned the fine points of baseball under the tutelage of his former mentor. Burns would certainly use some of "the Anson tricks," the paper said, "but of course he has ideas of his own regarding a team." One of these ideas centered on the team name. The men had often been referred to as "Colts" or "Anson's Colts," and Burns announced in March 1898 that he was looking for a new nickname.

Several hundred readers took the *Chicago Daily Tribune* up on the paper's invitation to send in some possibilities. Many fans preferred that the team simply be called the Chicagos. The word "Chicago" was supposedly derived from an Indian word meaning onion or wild onion; therefore, a few people suggested the Onions or Wild Onions. Other names included the Metropolitans, Napoleons, Burnsons, Hercules, and Phoenix. Former White Stocking Billy Sunday ("now engaged in evangelistic work," the *Tribune* noted), said that he wanted The Millionaires or The Brokers, as wealthy Chicago "always leads in works of charity and deeds of philanthropy," and because the Chicago ballplayers "are thrifty and provident."

Anson was often called "Pop Anson" during his later years as manager of the Colts. The *Tribune* related that it had received "at least a score of suggestions" similar to the one contributed by Frank L. Delbolf of Chicago: "I would suggest the name Orphans or Chicago Orphans for Burns' nine, since they have lost their pa-pa." Burns may or may not have liked the name, but reporters certainly did, and the nickname Orphans quickly became a fixture in newspapers' sports pages.[34]

With a new team name came a new uniform, though without the famous white stockings. "The Chicago club uniform has been neglected, and should be touched up," president Hart said. "The white stockings are unsightly after a couple of games. The men come up looking dirty, and some in various colored suits." Hart instead selected white uniforms with maroon stockings that the ballplayers wore for their first home game of the 1898 season, attended by 7,800 cheering spectators.[35]

The Orphans' 16–2 victory against the Louisville Colonels on April 29 was played less than a week after the United States declared war on Spain, following the sinking of the USS *Maine* in Cuba's Havana Harbor. War anxiety may have caused baseball interest to slump in some parts of the country, but Chicago's fans held high hopes for Tom Burns and his Orphans. One sportswriter emphasized that since the team was a "demoralized club, utterly lacking in the prime essentials, fire and ginger," it needed a quick start, which would help the players maintain a winning momentum. They won five of their first six games and wound up the 1898 season with a respectable record of 85-65-2. Moreover, the team's fourth-place finish in the National League standings was a huge improvement over the previous season.

In spite of this success, player grumbling and complaints had contributed to club dissension and squabbling, and it was unfortunate that Burns had not picked up at least a few tips on discipline from his former manager. Burns was "good-natured," as *Sporting Life* put it, and although he had wanted Jimmy Ryan to be the captain of the Orphans, he had let the players make the decision, and they selected shortstop Bill Dahlen. Dahlen had proven to be a "kicking, fault-finding captain," who had complained about the umpiring after every defeat and infected the team with his surliness. "To the mind," continued *Sporting Life*, "of a close observer of the work of the team all season the fault is right with the captain."

Dahlen was traded to the Baltimore Orioles in January 1899 for shortstop Gene DeMontreville. "The exchange was made in the interests of discipline and will strengthen the team in other ways as well," said Burns. "If I did not think so I should not have suggested it."[36]

Despite the removal of Dahlen and addition of DeMontreville, the baseball squad was not particularly strengthened. "The team is weak in more ways than one," *Sporting Life* argued, "even the sanguine and optimistic Burns can't deny it." Some of the men could not play due to sickness or injuries, others were hitting poorly, and the club lacked pitchers. Furthermore, players continued to rebel against managerial authority. For instance, many wanted Bill Lange as captain for the 1899 season, even though Jimmy Ryan was the logical choice, given his performance on the field, sound knowledge of the game, and seniority (he had joined the team in 1885). After Burns appointed Ryan to the position, a team delegation told Burns that they would not play under the new captain. One Chicago sportswriter insisted that Burns should have called the team's bluff and "put his foot down there and kept it down." Instead, Burns "bowed to the will of the team and asked Ryan to resign." Later in the season Burns compromised and appointed Bill Everitt as captain.

It was obvious that Burns had no control over his men, who ignored his directives and dismissed his authority. In August a Chicago newspaper announced that he "has been charged with 'failure as a disciplinarian,' because of the low estate to which the team has been reduced." The paper added that "the various troubles in the team, to be concise, consist of petty jealousies between players, real sickness, serious injuries and injuries magnified by lazy players, drunkenness on the part of a few, and last, but not least, a lack of courage, coupled with that self-satisfaction which comes only to ball players." It went on to say that "manager Burns, so his players say, is 'a good fellow,' which means that he has allowed them to do as they pleased, and has not taken their money away from them in fines.... The team is composed of strong, brilliant men, but, having put the machine together, Manager Burns cannot make it run."[37]

The machine continued to sputter in the succeeding weeks, and by mid–October the club had firmly settled in eighth place in the National League and "was in more disorganized condition than it ever was under Anson," according to a local sportswriter. Following the team's dismal 75-73-4 season, Hart released Burns—though some reports claimed that the manager had resigned—and the club president hired Tom Loftus to replace him. Loftus had played and managed in both the major and minor leagues and was well known for his skills in handling difficult ballplayers. "He is fearless," the *Chicago Daily Tribune* contended, "and not at all inclined to be easy-going when it comes to indulging the men in things which they should not have; so that, if the matter of discipline should again have an important bearing on the success of the Chicago team, it is reasonably safe to believe his engagement would greatly strengthen the team in one particular at least."[38]

Loftus wasted no time in getting to work, but even after signing a few more ballplayers, he was not particularly optimistic about the club's strength, an opinion shared by both sportswriters and fans alike. In addition, Loftus had to contend with the "indifferent attitude" of "malcontents" on the squad. "From all accounts the Chicago team is still a band of anarchists," *Sporting Life* reported during spring training, "and Manager Loftus is having the same trouble that beset ... other Chicago club managers."

The Orphans lost four of its first five games, and they ended the 1900 season with a disappointing 65–75–6 record. Early in the year the National League, considered "top-heavy and unmanageable," had voted to drop its four weakest clubs: Baltimore, Cleveland, Louisville, and Washington. Chicago had to settle for fifth place among the remaining eight teams, a distant 19 games back of first-place Brooklyn.[39]

The National League would soon be facing its biggest challenge since the formation of the Players' League. One of the prominent minor leagues during the 1890s had been the Western League, comprised of eight clubs from the Midwest. Western League president Byron Bancroft "Ban" Johnson wanted to expand his circuit and locate new teams in other areas, including cities in National League territory. Towards this goal, he shrewdly renamed his league the "American League" to remove the "hampering sectional basis" of the organization and "to place it in position to become nationally known."

Among the team executives he courted was Charles Comiskey, who joined the league and moved his St. Paul Saints to the South Side of Chicago. The baseball team would boast a new name as well as a new home field, as Comiskey, in a nod to the city's storied baseball history, rechristened his men the White Stockings, which sportswriters quickly shortened to White Sox. Other minor league club owners supported Johnson's endeavor, and in 1901 the new major league included eight teams, three of which were based in the National League's abandoned cities of Baltimore, Cleveland, and Washington.[40]

The American League included many familiar faces, as dozens of National League players left their teams to take advantage of the junior circuit's more lucrative salary offers. The Orphans were particularly "hard hit," one sportswriter noted, and "there appears to be no doubt that the American League agents have been after the Chicago players." Pitcher Clark Griffith was one of the first to transfer his allegiance from the city's West Side to the South Side, where he signed on as Comiskey's player-manager. Accounts of men switching leagues filled the sports pages, and as the *Washington Post* reported, "The fact that the best, or at any rate the high-priced players, are jumping around and leaving the old for the new order of things indicates that big things are going to take place in baseball this spring."

But no big things would be taking place on Chicago's National League team. Soon so many players had deserted the Orphans that sportswriters began calling the remaining club members the "Remnants." The imperturbable Jim Hart, when asked about the mass exodus, shrugged off the entire matter. "If some of our men are stolen it will be a blessing to the team—an unmixed blessing," he said. "Yes, sir—even if the men taken are all good." He coolly added that since there were numerous players on the Chicago squad, "Should the American [League] take some of them off our hands we shall not kick much. No, we will simply act as if the men were dead, and fill their places the best way we can."[41]

Unfortunately for Chicago, 15 other major league teams were all in competition for the same leading ballplayers. Tom Loftus and his "Remnants" spent much of the 1901 season bogged down at the bottom of the National League. In mid–July one local sportswriter sighed that "Loftus has made a grand effort to get the team into winning condition, but it seems useless. The American league's raid left him little to work with. He has kept the men keyed up almost to their limit, but defeat, accidents, and sickness have taken the courage out of them, and they seem to have contracted the losing spirit."

That spirit lingered into October, undoubtedly contributing to the team's 53–86–1 season record, its lowest winning percentage since the club was formed (.381). The players' morale certainly was not helped by the ascendancy of Comiskey's White Sox, who finished first in the American League. Tom Loftus, realizing that prospects did not look particularly bright for 1902, left the Orphans for the American League's Washington Senators. Although his successor, the highly regarded Frank Selee, won five pennants during twelve years as manager of the Boston Beaneaters, sportswriters were not at all hopeful about his chances in Chicago. The *Chicago Daily Tribune*, for example, maintained that "Selee assumes a Herculean task in attempting to build up a winning team from the mediocre remnants of the Remnants." The *Washington Post* was even more dismissive of the woeful leftover players:

> The Chicago National League club gains a good manager in Frank Selee, who was Boston's manager for so many years, but it is doubtful if Selee will do any more with the misfit crowd that masqueraded under the guise of the Chicago team last season than Tom Loftus did. Loftus had no more than five real ball players at Chicago last season, and the American League has secured three of these—[Topsy] Hartsel, [Danny] Green, and [Tom] Hughes. Selee is counted an excellent judge of young ball players, and if owner Hart will loosen the purse-strings a little, Selee says he will be able to add some first-class material to Hart's forlorn hope. Selee is the third manager of the Chicago team since the Anson dynasty. Tom Burns followed the Grand Old Man. Next came Loftus, and now an attempt will be made to convert Selee into a Moses.[42]

The *Post's* sportswriter may have overstated his Biblical allusion, but he was right on target when he emphasized Selee's keen ability to assess young players. One of the first men the new manager acquired was Joe Tinker, "a Kansas City youngster of much promise," according to one reporter. Because Selee intended to organize "a team of younger men who … will give their best services to the club at all times," he released Chicago's fiery team captain, Jack Doyle, fearing "the effects of his unruly temper upon the youngsters."

With a new managerial regime, it seemed fitting that the team should have a new name. The *Tribune* argued for a "revival of the old pseudonym of 'Colts' to designate the Chicago National league club. There are not enough of last year's Remnants left to make that a fitting name, they have long since outgrown the orphanage which followed Anson's retirement, and the present team is more generally composed of colts than any which ever carried that name in Anson's day."[43]

A *Chicago Daily News* sports reporter had something else in mind. Fred A. Hayner felt that "Orphans" was too long to put in headlines; moreover, he preferred a name that

SELEE PLACES HIS MEN

Manager of the Cubs Is In Doubt Only on Two Positions.

TEAM WORK HIS CHIEF AIM

Leader of West Side Club Thinks He Has Secured a Bunch of Fast Youngsters.

Frank Selee will devote his strongest efforts on the team work of the new Cubs this year. He made this announcement today when he returned from Hot Springs.

Chicago's National League baseball team acquired a new name when the *Chicago Daily News* used the word "Cubs" in its issue of March 27, 1902: "Frank Selee will devote his strongest efforts on the team work of the new Cubs this year" (author's collection).

would reflect Selee's rebuilding plan and the manager's emphasis on youth. In the opening sentence of an unsigned article in the March 27, 1902, *Daily News*, Hayner observed that "Frank Selee will devote his strongest efforts on the team work of the new Cubs this year."

Former *Daily News* city editor James Gilruth recalled years later that the name change was a result of a discussion with him, Hayner, *Daily News* assistant sports editor Charles Sensabaugh, and baseball reporter George C. Rice. Gilruth said that Hayner had objected to Orphans, so "we tried one name and another, then one of us, I don't recall who, came up with the name Cubs, and Cubs it was and Cubs it is even today."[44]

POSTSCRIPT: RETURN TO GREATNESS (1902–1908)

> With the crowd of youths the National League Club went on with their schedule, but the papers began calling the "kid" players "cubs." ... For awhile they were "cubs" in fact at the base ball business, but as time passed they grew into real champions.
> —*Sporting Life*, June 8, 1907

The name "Cubs" did not immediately catch on with baseball fans. Imaginative sportswriters often coined team names, and during the early 1900s the Chicago National League team was called the Colts, Orphans, Remnants, Cubs, Chicagos, Nationals, Sprouts, Seedlings, Recruits, Hartites, Microbes, Seleeites, Selee's Colts, and the Tribe of Selee. Reporters would occasionally even use two different names in the same newspaper article, if only as a literary device to avoid repetition. But by and large, according to one journalist, from 1902 through 1904 the players were "generally known as Selee's Colts although use of the word Cubs was gaining in popularity."[1]

Frank Selee continued to sign promising young players throughout the 1902 season. In August he acquired infielder Johnny Evers of Troy, New York, who would join fellow infielders Frank Chance and Joe Tinker at the West Side Grounds. On September 14, shortstop Tinker, second baseman Evers, and first baseman Chance made their first 6-4-3 double play. The trio completed another successful double play during the next game, inspiring the *Chicago Daily Tribune* to report that Evers "played second base without an error, accepting seven chances, and in addition secured a clean hit to center. The youngster is remarkably fast in relaying double plays."

Although the three ballplayers never did lead the league in double plays, the phrase "Tinker to Evers to Chance" achieved baseball immortality—as did the three men—when newspaper columnist and pundit Franklin P. Adams contributed the poem "That Double Play Again" to the New York *Evening Mail*:

> These are the saddest of possible words:
>   "Tinker to Evers to Chance."
> Trio of bear cubs, and fleeter than birds,
>   Tinker and Evers and Chance.
> Ruthlessly pricking our gonfalon bubble,
> Making a Giant hit into a double—
> Words that are heavy with nothing but trouble:
>   "Tinker to Evers to Chance."[2]

The Cubs' 1902 record of 68–69–6 (and a fifth-place finish in the National League) may not have resulted in a winning year for Selee, but it was an improvement over the previous season. Furthermore, the manager seemed to have laid the groundwork for future success. Chicago rose to third place in 1903, and to increase his team's chances in the 1904 pennant race, Selee acquired pitcher Mordecai Brown. "Brown is considered a coming twirler ... [with] the qualities of a winner," *Sporting Life* said about the three-fingered pitcher, who had lost the forefinger of his right hand in a childhood farming accident. Brown's earned run average of 1.86 helped the Cubs finish the 1904 National League season in second place, 13 games behind the New York Giants.

Frank Selee had to leave the club midway through the 1905 season due to illness, and Frank Chance assumed his managerial duties. The *Chicago Daily Tribune* praised Selee's baseball acumen and his "unerring instinct in selecting young talent," and declared that he "produced a team this season which, if it had not been deprived of his guidance before the middle of the race, would have been the strongest contender against the Giants, it is believed. Even without his fighting spirit, his experience, and calm encouragement the team is still in the race with every prospect of bettering its present position before the finish under the guidance of Capt. Chance, who will continue as acting manager."[3]

The Cubs' "present position" was then a solid fourth place in the National League. Frank Chance was clearly the right man to lead the Cubs, for by season's end they had climbed to third place, once again 13 games behind the Giants. President and controlling partner Jim Hart retired shortly thereafter, having sold his share of the club to Cincinnati newspaperman Charles W. Murphy. Chance would remain as manager, Murphy announced, for "he is not only a great all around player but undoubtedly a manager of tact, ability, and rare skill.... While I hope our club will be profitable, the greatest delight life now holds for me would be the winning of the national league championship."[4]

That was uppermost in Chance's mind, too. After an astounding record of 116–36–3—and a .763 winning percentage not equaled to this day—the Cubs clinched the 1906 National League pennant, 20 games in front of the New York Giants. A championship series between the National League and the American League had begun in 1903, and odds were on the Cubs to defeat easily Charles Comiskey's White Sox. But as baseball historian Lee Allen succinctly observed, in a short series "victory goes to the team with the hot hand," and the South Siders pulled off a stunning upset through superior pitching and timely batting. "We played our hardest to win," Chance said afterwards, "but in this series we did not show we were the best club. But we are just the same. Next year you will see the Cubs come back again for another battle, for I think we will again win the pennant."[5]

Player-manager Chance, also known as the Cubs' "peerless leader," followed through on his prediction by leading his team to another National League flag. The Cubs could not match their previous number of wins, but their 107–45–3 record bested the second-place Pittsburgh Pirates by 17 games. After the first game in the 1907 World Series was declared a tie on account of darkness, the Cubs efficiently dispensed with the American League's Detroit Tigers four games in a row to claim the championship.

By this time "Cubs" was generally accepted as the name of Chicago's National League team, and it regularly appeared on scorecards in 1907. Furthermore, bear cubs were emblazoned on the 14-karat gold medals that the World Series champions received in honor of their achievement.[6]

The Cub bear motif was continued in 1908, as the uniform jersey featured a standing bear cub holding a baseball bat, encircled by a round C. The Cubs hoisted the 1907 National League pennant on the ballpark's flag pole on April 22, the day of the team's

1908 home opener, and as part of the festivities, the park was decorated with bear cubs. In its game-day coverage, the *Tribune* related that "the Cub pennant for 1907 displays a white baseball on a blue [back]-ground and a restful white bear armed with a bat."[7]

Frank Chance and the Cubs needed their bats in 1908; sportswriters predicted a close race in the National League, and the Cubs clashed all season with both New York and Pittsburgh for bragging rights. It was "Crazy '08," as one baseball historian put it, for the pennant race was not settled until the very end of the season, with a dramatic winner-take-all Chicago victory against the team's arch-rivals, the New York Giants.

In the post-season, the Cubs once again defeated the Detroit Tigers in five games for Chicago's second consecutive World Series title. In his wrap-up of the series, renowned sportswriter Irving E. "Sy" Sanborn—who earlier that fall had helped organize the Base Ball Writers' Association of America—recalled the team's storied history. He wrote that when Chicago pitcher Orval Overall shut out the Tigers, 2–0, in the fifth and last game of the World Series, "He drove the final nail into the greatest honors that ever fell to one baseball club—two straight world's champi-

The Chicago Cubs players received 14-karat gold medals after they won the 1907 World Series. The *Chicago Daily Tribune* wrote that the medal's "center represents in rose gold the 'world,' on which is mounted in relief the profile of a bear cub holding a large diamond in his teeth, which are to be of aluminium [*sic*]. A ruby represents the cub's eye. The figures '1907' will be raised slightly. Circling this field is a band of Roman gold bearing the inscription 'World's Champions.' On the reverse side is a place for engraving each player's name" (*Chicago Daily Tribune*, November 24, 1907).

On October 14, 1908, the Chicago Cubs won their second consecutive World Series title. As this cartoon published the following day illustrates, fans also celebrated the team's third consecutive National League pennant victory (*Chicago Daily Tribune*, October 15, 1908).

onship pennants flaunting on top of three straight league championship emblems. There have been other clubs which wore the title of three times champions, but Chicago has worn it twice, once when Cap Anson's old White Stockings were at their best in the middle of the '80s and once again when Cap Chance developed and led an even greater team in the young years of the twentieth century."

Like Anson, the Cubs' captain adhered to a strict "play to win" philosophy. "Chance was one of the greatest leaders I ever saw," his old teammate Johnny Evers remembered years later. "He was a wonderful man to lead a charge on the baseball field, to drive and bully the men and get the last ounce of energy out of them."[8]

This passion and single-mindedness characterized the most successful of Chicago's club leaders—from Jimmy Wood to William Hulbert to Al Spalding to Cap Anson to Frank Selee and then to Frank Chance. Managers sporting white stockings led numerous

Opposite: The Cubs raised their blue 1907 National League championship pennant on April 22, 1908, the team's first home game of the season. The day's festivities included a 7-3 victory over the Cincinnati Reds (*Chicago Daily Tribune*, April 22, 1908).

charges on baseball fields, building championship teams that brought pride to nineteenth-century Chicago. Years later, after the club adoption of a name that had first inconspicuously appeared in a 1902 newspaper article, Frank Chance squeezed "the last ounce of energy" from his men and helped the Chicago Cubs create a dynasty of their own.[9]

Appendix: Year-End Standings of the Chicago Team, 1871–1908

These season-end league standings are from Retrosheet (http://www.retrosheet.org), a baseball resource that contains game logs and statistics for every major league game since 1871, the year the National Association of Professional Base Ball Players was founded. The information used here was obtained free of charge from and is copyrighted by Retrosheet. Interested parties may contact Retrosheet at www.retrosheet.org.

G = Games Played
GB = Games Behind
L = Losses
PCT = Winning Percentage [W / (W + L)]
T = Ties
W = Wins

Year	Finish	G	W	L	T	PCT	GB
1871	3rd	28	19	9	0	.679	2.0
1874	5th	59	28	31	0	.475	18.5
1875	6th	69	30	37	2	.448	35.0
1876	1st	66	52	14	0	.788	—
1877	5th	60	26	33	1	.441	15.5
1878	4th	61	30	30	1	.500	11.0
1879	4th	83	46	33	4	.582	10.5
1880	1st	86	67	17	2	.798	—
1881	1st	84	56	28	0	.667	—
1882	1st	84	55	29	0	.655	—
1883	2nd	98	59	39	0	.602	4.0
1884	4th	113	62	50	1	.554	22.0
1885	1st	113	87	25	1	.777	—
1886	1st	126	90	34	2	.726	—
1887	3rd	127	71	50	6	.587	6.5
1888	2nd	136	77	58	1	.570	9.0
1889	3rd	136	67	65	4	.508	19.0

Appendix

Year	Finish	G	W	L	T	PCT	GB
1890	2nd	139	83	53	3	.610	6.5
1891	2nd	137	82	53	2	.607	3.5
1892	7th	147	70	76	1	.479	30.0
1893	9th	128	56	71	1	.441	29.0
1894	8th	137	57	75	5	.432	34.0
1895	4th	133	72	58	3	.554	15.0
1896	5th	132	71	57	4	.555	18.5
1897	9th	138	59	73	6	.447	34.0
1898	4th	152	85	65	2	.567	17.5
1899	8th	152	75	73	4	.507	26.0
1900	5th	146	65	75	6	.464	19.0
1901	6th	140	53	86	1	.381	37.0
1902	5th	143	68	69	6	.496	34.0
1903	3rd	139	82	56	1	.594	8.0
1904	2nd	156	93	60	3	.608	13.0
1905	3rd	155	92	61	2	.601	13.0
1906	1st	155	116	36	3	.763	—
1907	1st	155	107	45	3	.704	—
1908	1st	158	99	55	4	.643	—

CHAPTER NOTES

The following abbreviations are used throughout the notes: *CDT (Chicago Daily Tribune); CT (Chicago Tribune); NYC (New York Clipper); NYT (New York Times); SL (Sporting Life); TSN (The Sporting News); WP (Washington Post)*

Preface

1. "Begged to differ" quotation is from "Letters to the Editor," Chicago Cubs *Vine Line*, June 2004, 7. Wrigley Field is included in Philip J. Lowry, *Green Cathedrals: The Ultimate Celebration of Major League and Negro League Ballparks* (New York: Walker, 2006), 54–58. Weeghman Park is in "Cubs vs. Pittsburgh," *CDT*, April 23, 1916, sec. 8, 2. Cubs Park is in "Amusements," *CDT*, June 30, 1919, 21. Wrigley Field is in "Cubs Name Miss Donahue as Secretary; Re-Elect Veeck," *NYT*, December 4, 1926, 21. Charles Weeghman resigned as Cubs president in December 1918, and William Wrigley, Jr., became the club majority stockholder. See "Fred Mitchell Cubs' Magnate," *Washington Herald*, December 8, 1918, 10; "Wrigley Returns from Cubs Camp Strong for Team," *CDT*, April 7, 1919, 19. Cubs always playing at Wrigley Field is in Patrick M. O'Connell, "Cubs Ruled at Long Gone West Side Grounds," *CT*, October 6, 2017, sec. 1, 11.

2. Chicago Base Ball Association reorganization is in "Bats Are Trumps," *(Chicago) Inter Ocean*, July 31, 1876, 8. Paul Hines letter is in "Sport of the Period," *Chicago Times*, November 4, 1877, 10. Billy Sunday is in [Finley Peter Dunne], "Giants Beaten," *Chicago Daily News*, August 8, 1887, evening issue, 1.

3. "Too soft" quotation is from "Sporting," *CDT*, May 17, 1877, 5. "Breathed on his" and "as no nine" quotations are from "Ah There, Captain Anson!" *Chicago Times*, May 16, 1888, 3. Tin horn award is in Peter Morris, "Pecatonica Base Ball Club," in *Base Ball Pioneers, 1850–1870: The Clubs and Players Who Spread the Sport Nationwide*, ed. Peter Morris and others (Jefferson, NC: McFarland, 2012), 236; Peter Morris and David Nemec, "Burroughs, Henry F. 'Henry,'" in *The Rank and File of 19th Century Major League Baseball: Biographies of 1,084 Players, Owners, Managers and Umpires*, by David Nemec (Jefferson, NC: McFarland, 2012), 222 (includes "the name Pecatonica" quotation).

4. Club stock ownership is in the postscript, note 4. "There are too many" quotation is from Ed Hartig, email message to author, December 10, 2017. Uniforms and black stockings are in chapter 8, note 14; chapter 9, note 23. Baseball tournament is in chapter 9, note 21. Kelly was usually called "Mike" in contemporary newspaper articles. See Peter Morris, *A Game of Inches: The Stories Behind the Innovations That Shaped Baseball*, rev. and exp. one-vol. ed. (Chicago: Ivan R. Dee, 2010), 11.

5. For a fine discussion of nineteenth-century standards of spelling, grammar, punctuation, and capitalization, see Peter Morris, "Note on Sources and Usage," in *Base Ball Founders: The Clubs, Players and Cities of the Northeast That Established the Game*, ed. Peter Morris and others (Jefferson, NC: McFarland, 2013), 5–6. The essay also appears in Morris's *Base Ball Pioneers*, 7–8.

Prologue

1. *Cincinnati Daily Gazette* quotations are from "Base Ball," *CT*, October 12, 1870, 4. *Tribune* quotation is from "The National Game," *CT*, October 12, 1870, 2. The Midwest was generally referred to as the Northwest or West in newspapers of the day.

2. "Chicago wasn't such" quotation is from James Wood to Frank G. Menke, "Baseball of Bygone Days," *El Paso (Texas) Herald*, August 17, 1916, home edition, 9.

3. The high-scoring game was on May 13 against the Bluff City Club of Memphis, Tennessee. See "Sporting Matters," *CT*, May 14, 1870, 4. "Proven themselves" quotation is from "Base-Ball," *Chicago Republican*, July 25, 1870, 4. "Infants" and succeeding *Tribune* quotations are from "Sporting Matters," *CT*, June 4, 1870, 4.

Chapter 1

1. Game-day account is in "Base Ball," *CT*, July 22, 1868, 4. Ballpark on State Street is in "Base Ball," *CT*, July 15, 1868, 4; "Sporting," *CT*, July 19, 1868, 4. See also Peter Morris, *But Didn't We Have Fun? An Informal History of Baseball's Pioneer Era, 1843–1870* (Chicago: Ivan R. Dee, 2008), 9–10: "Club names during the era were generally rendered with the nickname preceding the city name; e.g., the Eckford Base Ball Club of Brooklyn, or, for simplicity, the Eckfords of Brooklyn. Only as the era was ending did the order begin to be reversed."

2. Buckeyes game is in "Base Ball Match at Cincin-

nati," *NYT*, June 6, 1868, 5. Excelsiors game and "crack" ball club are in "Base Ball," *CT*, July 29, 1867, 4. For statistics on the Excelsior Club's seasons see Marshall D. Wright, *The National Association of Base Ball Players, 1857–1870* (Jefferson, NC: McFarland, 2000), 157, 210. See also "Sporting Gossip," *CT*, January 26, 1868, 4.

3. "Mediocre Playing" is the subtitle of "Base Ball," *CT*, July 22, 1868, 4. "Many persons" quotation is from "Base Ball," *Chicago Times*, July 22, 1868, 6 (this passage is usually cited incorrectly as appearing in the July 22 *Chicago Tribune*). "Muffing" refers to poor ball playing. See Paul Dickson, *The Dickson Baseball Dictionary*, 3rd ed. (New York: Norton, 2009), 561–62. See also "Base Ball as a Confidence Game," *CT*, July 28, 1867, 2: The Nationals "are professional athletes, while the Excelsiors are but amateurs."

4. "The Age of Base Ball," *CT*, July 22, 1866, 2; July 23, 1866, 2. See also "Sporters in for the War," *NYC*, June 22, 1861, 74 (notes that "many of the most active participants in sporting matters have enlisted"); "Old Time Base Ball," *Chicago Herald*, July 11, 1886, 5; Stephen Freedman, "The Baseball Fad in Chicago, 1865–1870: An Exploration of the Role of Sport in the Nineteenth-Century City," *Journal of Sport History* 5 (Summer 1978): 42–64. The Excelsiors are mentioned in "Base Ball," *Chicago Daily Press and Tribune*, August 26, 1858, 1. Peter Morris provides an excellent in-depth history of the Excelsior Club in his two-part essay: Peter Morris, "Excelsiors of Chicago, Prewar" and "Excelsiors of Chicago, Postwar," in *Base Ball Pioneers, 1850–1870: The Clubs and Players Who Spread the Sport Nationwide*, ed. Peter Morris and others (Jefferson, NC: McFarland, 2012), 206–10, 210–21. The Excelsior Club's prowess is also detailed in Mark Rucker and John Freyer, *19th Century Baseball in Chicago* (Charleston, SC: Arcadia, 2003), 14. See also Alfred H. Spink, *The National Game*, 2nd ed. (1911; repr., Carbondale: Southern Illinois University Press, 2000), 63; Federal Writers' Project (Illinois), Work Project Administration, *Baseball in Old Chicago* (Chicago: A. C. McClurg, 1939), 1–4. Three excellent histories of early baseball are George B. Kirsch, *Baseball in Blue and Gray: The National Pastime During the Civil War* (Princeton: Princeton University Press, 2003); Morris, *But Didn't We Have Fun?*; William J. Ryczek, *Baseball's First Inning: A History of the National Pastime Through the Civil War* (Jefferson, NC: McFarland, 2009).

5. Chicago's population is in "City Census," *CT*, November 12, 1868, 1; Susan B. Carter and others, *Historical Statistics of the United States*, millennial ed., vol. 1, *Population* (New York: Cambridge University Press), 1–110. Thirty-two clubs are noted in "Base Ball Convention," *CT*, December 10, 1866, 4. The Atlantic, Columbia, Excelsior, and Olympic teams are mentioned in Bessie Louise Pierce, *A History of Chicago*, vol. 2, *From Town to City, 1848–1871* (New York: Alfred A. Knopf, 1940), 470. In 1919, John Kelley compiled a list of "early day matches," and for the year 1860 he listed games between the Niagaras, Athletic Juniors, Atlantics, and the Excelsiors. See John Kelley, "White Stockings and Cincy Renew Feud from 1870," *CDT*, October 19, 1919, sec. 2, 4. Newspapers also covered black baseball teams, such as Chicago's Blue Stockings in "The Sporting World," *CT*, August 24, 1870, 4; "Base Ball," *CT*, September 17, 1870, 4.

6. "Raring to go" quotation is from Morris, "Excelsiors of Chicago, Postwar," 210. "Excelsior boys" quotation is from "Sporting," *CT*, September 20, 1868, 1. See also "Sporting Gossip," *CT*, September 27, 1868, 1. Fundraising quotation is from "Sporting," *CT*, July 24, 1868, 4. See also "The Excelsiors," *CT*, July 28, 1868, 3: A member of the Excelsior club "made several attempts to collect funds, but met with no success."

7. "Base Ball," *New-York Tribune*, April 3, 1869, 2 (article reprinted as "Base Ball," *CT*, April 7, 1869, 2). For statistics on the Excelsiors' 1868 season, see Wright, *The National Association of Base Ball Players*, 210.

8. The Cincinnati Red Stockings are examined in many books on early baseball history, including David Ball, "Cincinnati Base Ball Club ('Red Stockings')," in Morris, *Base Ball Pioneers*, 146–60; Harry Ellard, *Base Ball in Cincinnati: A History* (1907; repr., Jefferson, NC: McFarland, 2004); Stephen D. Guschov, *The Red Stockings of Cincinnati: Base Ball's First All-Professional Team and Its Historic 1869 and 1870 Seasons* (Jefferson, NC: McFarland, 1998); Tom Melville, *Early Baseball and the Rise of the National League* (Jefferson, NC: McFarland, 2001), 36–46; Morris, *But Didn't We Have Fun?*, 184–201; William J. Ryczek, *When Johnny Came Sliding Home: The Post-Civil War Baseball Boom, 1865–1870* (Jefferson, NC: McFarland, 1998), 168–93. See also David Nemec, *The Great Encyclopedia of Nineteenth Century Major League Baseball*, 2nd ed. (Tuscaloosa: University of Alabama Press, 2006). For statistics on the Red Stockings' seasons, see Wright, *The National Association of Base Ball Players*, 193, 238–43. "It is generally known" quotation is from "Sporting," *CT*, August 1, 1869, 4.

9. Cincinnati's and Chicago's rivalry is summarized in Ryczek, *When Johnny Came Sliding Home*, 200–202; Glenn Stout and Richard A. Johnson, *The Cubs: The Complete Story of Chicago Cubs Baseball* (Boston: Houghton Mifflin, 2007), 3–5. Comparisons between the cities are also in Robert G. Spinney, *City of Big Shoulders: A History of Chicago* (DeKalb: Northern Illinois University Press, 2000), 73–74; James R. Grossman, Ann Durkin Keating, and Janice L. Reiff, eds., *The Encyclopedia of Chicago* (Chicago: University of Chicago Press, 2004), 233, 341. "This was too much" quotation is from "Chit-Chat," *Western Monthly* 4 (November 1870): 326 (article abridged as "Base Ball as a Business" *(New York) Sun*, November 9, 1870, 3). See also "Base-Ball as a Pastime and as a Business," *Spirit of the Times*, November 26, 1870, 235; Richard Hershberger, "Chicago's Role in Early Professional Baseball," *Baseball Research Journal* 40 (Spring 2011): 9–11. "A meeting of all" quotation is from "Sporting," *CT*, September 28, 1869, 1. See also "Base Ball," *CT*, September 30, 1869, 1.

10. "Some of the most" quotation is from "Base Ball," *CT*, October 12, 1869, 1. The organization of the Chicago Base Ball Club is in "Base Ball," *CT*, October 13, 1869, 4; John Kelley, "White Stockings and Cincy Renew Feud from 1870," *CDT*, October 19, 1919, sec. 2, 4. Baseball's "professional" system is discussed in "Base Ball," *New-York Tribune*, April 3, 1869, 2 (article reprinted as "Base Ball," *CT*, April 7, 1869, 2). See also "Base Ball," *Brooklyn (NY) Daily Eagle*, January 24, 1871, 8; "The Coming Base-Ball Season," *NYT*, April 7, 1870, 5; *Baseball in Old Chicago*, 6–7. Gage's position as Chicago's treasurer is noted in "The City Deposit Question," *CT*, October 10, 1869, 2; "The City Treasurer," *CT*, December 8, 1869, 2. For a discussion of the committee members, see Larry

Names, *Bury My Heart at Wrigley Field: The History of the Chicago Cubs* (Neshkoro: Angel Press of Wisconsin, 1996), 45–51. Committee members are also listed in A. T. Andreas, *History of Chicago: From the Earliest Period to the Present Time*, vol. 2, *From 1857 Until the Fire of 1871* (Chicago: A. T. Andreas Co., 1885), 615. For information on Tom Foley see David Nemec, "Foley, Thomas J. 'Tom,'" in *The Rank and File of 19th Century Major League Baseball: Biographies of 1,084 Players, Owners, Managers and Umpires*, by David Nemec (Jefferson, NC: McFarland, 2012), 233. As Nemec points out, another Tom Foley of this era was a baseball player.

11. Fifteen professional teams for the 1870 season are listed in Wright, *The National Association of Base Ball Players*, 308; Gary Gillette and Pete Palmer, eds., *The ESPN Baseball Encyclopedia*, 4th ed. (New York: Sterling Publishing, 2007), 264. Concerning Chicago's need for immediate action, see "Base Ball," *CT*, October 12, 1869, 1: "Chicago's intentions ... have already been noticed in the Eastern papers, and the movement has no time to lose." The club's advertisements in the two publications are mentioned in "Sporting," *CT*, October 24, 1869, 2. See also items in the *Spirit of the Times*: October 9, 1869, 119; October 16, 1869, 135; and October 30, 1869, 171.

12. "Garden City" is a reference to Chicago; the city's motto, "Urbs in Horto" (City in a Garden), was adopted in 1837. See Ellen Eslinger, "Gardening," in Grossman, *The Encyclopedia of Chicago*, 325. A Chicago baseball team in the late 1860s and early 1870s was the Garden City Club. Due to Cincinnati's pig slaughterhouses and meat packing plants, the city's unofficial nickname was Porkopolis (the Red Stockings were sometimes called the Porkopolitans). See Jonathan Fraser Light, *The Cultural Encyclopedia of Baseball*, 2nd ed. (Jefferson, NC: McFarland, 2005), 191.

13. A picked nine is a baseball team whose players were selected or "picked" to play a game. See Dickson, *The Dickson Baseball Dictionary*, 634: "Picked nines were typically the best players from the teams in a single city, who played picked nines from other cities. The professional era of the 1870s essentially ended the practice of picked nines." See also "Athletic vs. Picked Nine," *NYC*, May 13, 1871, 45; "Sporting Matters," *Chicago Republican*, June 2, 1870, 4: "The 'picked up' nine was not a picked up, but a *picked* nine—all good amateur players."

14. "To secure talent" quotation is from "The Ball and Bat," *(New York) Sun*, November 25, 1869, 1 (article reprinted, with commentary, as "Sporting News," *CT*, December 1, 1869, 4). Some well-known teams played in the New York and Philadelphia areas, including the Brooklyn Eckfords, Philadelphia Athletics, Brooklyn Atlantics, and the New York Mutuals. Stock sales are in "Chit-Chat," *Western Monthly* 4 (November 1870): 327; "Sporting," *CT*, November 25, 1869, 4. See also "The Base Ball Market," *(New York) Sun*, December 2, 1869, 2, for the "latest quotations" of players' annual salaries, based on the competitive market: "Catchers, $2,000; Pitchers, $2,000; First base, $1,500; Second base (good general players), $2,500; Third base (great demand and few in market), $3,000; Short stop (good general players), $2,000; Fielders, $1,500." The article was reprinted as "The Base-Ball Market," *(Philadelphia) Evening Telegraph*, December 10, 1869, 1. The salaries were reprinted in "Sporting Matters," *CT*, December 9, 1869, 4.

15. "Special meeting" and "good progress" quotations are from "Sporting," *CT*, November 26, 1869, 4. "Bungling inefficiency" and "the thing has fizzled" quotations are from "Sporting Matters," *CT*, January 16, 1870, 4.

16. "When the club" and "thus far" quotations are from "Base Ball," *NYC*, January 15, 1870, 323. Although the *Clipper* wrote that Chicago had signed just Wood and Ned Cuthbert, it mentioned in December 1869 that Chicago had signed Fred Treacey of the Eckfords. See "Base Ball," *NYC*, December 4, 1869, 274. A club's business manager usually handled finances and the scheduling of games. See Peter Morris, *A Game of Inches: The Stories Behind the Innovations That Shaped Baseball*, rev. and exp. one-vol. ed. (Chicago: Ivan R. Dee, 2010), 206.

17. New officers and "the players will" quotation are in "Sporting," *CT*, January 18, 1870, 4: The club was "duly organized by the election of D[avid] A. Gage as President; W. F. Wentworth, Vice President; W. F. Tucker, Treasurer; W. Low, Recording Secretary; J. W. Bute, Corresponding Secretary; and J. H. McVicker, Philip Wadsworth, Gilbert Dutcher, Albert Crosby, and Thomas Foley, as the Board of Trustees." See also Names, *Bury My Heart at Wrigley Field*, 56.

18. Wood's signing with the team and his salary are in "The Ball and Bat," *(New York) Sun*, November 25, 1869, 1. "Is a fine looking" quotation is from "Sporting Matters," *CT*, March 13, 1870, 3. Eckfords' seasons are in Wright, *The National Association of Base Ball Players*, 67, 76. Wood signing the players is in "Sporting Matters," *CT*, January 23, 1870, 4. Team salaries are in "Chit-Chat," *Western Monthly* 4 (November 1870): 327 (mentions Wood receiving $2,000). An excellent biography of Wood is in William J. Ryczek and Peter Morris, "Eckford Base Ball Club," in *Base Ball Founders: The Clubs, Players and Cities of the Northeast That Established the Game*, ed. Peter Morris and others (Jefferson, NC: McFarland, 2013), 184–85.

19. Tom Foley's trip is in "Sporting Matters," *CT*, March 11, 1870, 3. Foley is referred to as the club's business manager in "Sporting Matters," *CT*, May 19, 1870, 4 (see also note 16). During a meeting of the Chicago Base Ball Club on January 17, 1870, Foley was elected a member of the organization's board of trustees. See "Sporting," *CT*, January 18, 1870, 4. "Not long since" quotation is from "Sporting Matters," *CT*, March 13, 1870, 3.

20. "As a nine" quotation is from "Base Ball," *NYC*, March 19, 1870, 394. "Probably has no equal" and "the responsibility" quotations are from "Sporting Matters," *CT*, March 13, 1870, 3.

21. "A total failure" quotation is from "Sporting Matters," *CT*, January 16, 1870, 4. An examination of the 1870 box scores shows that the players' positions and the roster changed throughout the season. See also *Baseball in Old Chicago*, 13. Quotations about ballplayers are from "Sporting Matters," *CT*, March 13, 1870, 3. The ballplayers profiled include James Wood, William C. Fisher, Michael McAtee, Charles Hodes, Marshall King, James White, William Flynn, Edgar Cuthbert, Frederick Treacey, and Levi Meyerle. Fisher and White were not with Chicago when the team began playing in late March 1870. By that time the club had added William "Bill" Craver and Edward "Ed" Pinkham. See "Base Ball," *CT*, March 27, 1870, 3; "Sporting Matters," *CT*, March 30, 1870, 4. See also Ryczek, *When Johnny Came Sliding Home*, 203–205. Chicago's players are also profiled in

Paul Batesel, *Players and Teams of the National Association, 1871–1875* (Jefferson, NC: McFarland, 2012).

22. "The boys had a bout" quotation is from "Sporting Matters," *CT*, March 30, 1870, 4. "A new professional nine" quotation is from "City Intelligence," *(Philadelphia) Evening Telegraph*, April 11, 1870, 8. "It is a strong team" quotation is from "The Coming Base-Ball Season," *NYT*, April 7, 1870, 5. Garden City game reported in "Sporting Matters," *CT*, April 24, 1870, 3. The Chicago professionals beat an amateur team, 75–12, in a practice game on April 22. See "Sporting Matters," *CT*, April 23, 1870, 4. See also "Sporting Matters," *CT*, April 10, 1870, 3: "The first base ball playing of the season took place yesterday afternoon ... between the Chicago Club and the Aetnas, of this city. Numerous other afternoons have been devoted to practice, but this was the only occasion when the play might be said to reach the dignity of a game of base ball."

23. All three Chicago names are in "Sporting Matters," *CT*, April 24, 1870, 3. See also note 1. Southern tours are discussed in Morris, *A Game of Inches*, 560–61: "Early clubs were ... aware that a trip through the South would be a wonderful way to prepare for the season."

24. "Sporting Matters," *CT*, April 30, 1870, 4. A match game was one played between two teams "that resulted from a formal challenge." See Dickson, *The Dickson Baseball Dictionary*, 536.

25. Game against the Empires is in "Sporting Matters," *CT*, May 1, 1870, 2. Team names are in John Snyder, *Cubs Journal: Year by Year and Day by Day with the Chicago Cubs Since 1876* (Cincinnati: Clerisy Press, 2008), 16–17.

26. This anecdote is repeated in "The League Champions," *SL*, October 28, 1885, 4.

27. Levi Meyerle's name was misspelled as "Myerle" in the original *CT* article. It has been silently corrected throughout the rest of this reprinting.

28. Fred Treacey's name was misspelled as "Treacy" in the original *CT* article. It has been silently corrected throughout the rest of this reprinting.

29. For the location of Ogden Park, see *Baseball in Old Chicago*, 10–11; "Sporting Matters," *CT*, May 18, 1870, 4 ("at the foot of Ontario street, on the lake shore"); "From the Tribune's Columns," *CDT*, December 14, 1924, 8; *Edwards' Annual Director [sic] to the Inhabitants, Institutions, [...] in the City of Chicago, for 1869–70* (St. Louis: Edwards & Co., 1869), 677 ("Ontario, cor. Seneca"). The game was on July 31, 1869. "It was very evident" quotation is from "Sporting," *CT*, August 1, 1869, 4. For a White Stockings game played at Ogden Park, see "Sporting Matters," *CT*, May 21, 1870, 4. A circa 1863 map of Chicago that "shows how the Chicago River divides the city into three divisions" is in Richard F. Bales, *The Great Chicago Fire and the Myth of Mrs. O'Leary's Cow* (Jefferson, NC: McFarland, 2002), 10.

30. *Baseball in Old Chicago*, 11–13 (quotations are on p. 12); "Sporting Matters," *CT*, May 27, 1870, 4 (mentions ease of getting to Dexter Park). See also Stout and Johnson, *The Cubs*, 5, 81; Randy Roberts and Carson Cunningham, eds., *Before the Curse: The Chicago Cubs' Glory Years, 1870–1945* (Urbana: University of Illinois Press, 2012), 14; Michael Benson, *Ballparks of North America: A Comprehensive Historical Reference to Baseball Grounds, Yards and Stadiums, 1845 to Present* (Jefferson, NC: McFarland, 1989), 79–80. The improvements to Dexter Park were discussed at a Chicago Base Ball Club stockholders' meeting on March 21, 1870. See "Sporting Matters," *CT*, March 22, 1870, 4.

31. The date in the article is June 15; the game was actually played on June 16.

32. The "practice game" is in "Sporting Matters," *CT*, June 4, 1870, 4. June 16 victory is in "The National Game," *CT*, June 17, 1870, 4. See also "Sporting Matters," *CT*, May 27, 1870, 4. Three articles that list games played at both Ogden Park and Dexter Park are "The National Game," *CT*, August 5, 1870, 4; "The Sporting World," *CT*, October 6, 1870, 4; "The Sporting World," *CT*, October 9, 1870, 3. Additional plans to improve Dexter Park with "seating accommodations for the multitude" are in "The National Game," *CT*, July 17, 1870, 4: "With these additions, ... it is believed that the White Stocking ground will be greatly superior to any in America, both as a ball field, and as furnishing unlimited accommodations for spectators."

33. Two *Tribune* quotations are from "Sporting Matters," *CT*, May 19, 1870, 4. "Fault of the Chicago" quotation is from "The National Game," *NYT*, November 27, 1870, 6. For information on Bill Craver's dismissal, see "The Sporting World," *CT*, August 21, 1870, 3; "The National Game," *CT*, August 22, 1870, 4; "The Sporting World," *CT*, December 3, 1870, 4; Peter Morris, David Ball, and David Nemec, "Craver, William H./'Bill,'" in *Major League Baseball Profiles, 1871–1900*, vol. 2, comp. and ed. David Nemec (Lincoln: University of Nebraska Press, 2011), 277–78. See also Ryczek, *When Johnny Came Sliding Home*, 206, 226.

34. References to the White Stockings' "lack of discipline" are in "Sporting Matters," *CT*, June 4, 1870, 4; "The National Game," *CT*, June 18, 1870, 4. A reference to the team's "careless playing" is in "Base Ball," *CT*, June 17, 1870, 2. "In the field" quotation is from "Base-Ball," *New-York Tribune*, July 5, 1870, 8. New York *Star* quotation is from "Sporting Matters," *Chicago Republican*, July 9, 1870, 4. "Wretched" and "the Mutuals waited" quotations are from "The National Game," *CT*, July 7, 1870, 4. The *Chicago Republican* wrote about the Mutuals game that "another such a cleaning out, and we shall begin to think that the White Stockings are, indeed, but a paper nine, and that their strength lies in the puffing they have received from Chicago journals." See "Sporting Matters," *Chicago Republican*, July 7, 1870, 4. On the other hand, the *NYT* wrote of the team that "this new-comer into the field of base-ball contests has already a brilliant record, and an ample field for future achievements." See "The White Stockings," *NYT*, July 6, 1870, 3.

35. Quotation about Bluff City Club is from "Sporting Matters," *CT*, May 14, 1870, 4. The *Chicago Republican* quotes the *Daily Memphis (TN) Avalanche*'s write-up of the Bluff City game: "The Chicago Club played splendidly, beating the Bluff City Club badly; but this result was expected by all persons who knew anything of the respective clubs. The Chicago boys are professional players, while the Bluff City boys merely engage in the game for amusement. Nevertheless, our boys played well, and gave promise of good play in the future." See "Sporting Matters," *Chicago Republican*, May 17, 1870, 4. Quotations about Forest City game are from "Sporting Matters," *CT*, June 4, 1870, 4. See note 16 for duties of a club's business manager.

36. For the season record of the White Stockings, see Wright, *The National Association of Base Ball Players*, 292–94. "Excellent health" quotation is from "The National Game," *CT*, July 21, 1870, 4. July 23 game is in "Out-Door Sports," *CT*, July 25, 1870, 4. Summary of July 23 game is in Richard Bogovich and Mark Pestana, "The First 'Chicago' Game," in *Inventing Baseball: The 100 Greatest Games of the 19th Century*, ed. Bill Felber (Phoenix: Society for American Baseball Research, 2013), 74–76. The history of the verb "Chicago," which signifies a team that was held scoreless in a game, is in Dickson, *The Dickson Baseball Dictionary*, 181–82. The term was used in sports articles in the nineteenth century and even in the early twentieth century. For example, see "Model 'Chicago' Games," *NYC*, September 2, 1876, 181; "Orphans Get Chicagoed," *CDT*, May 19, 1901, 17. See also John H. Gruber, "Unusual Baseball Games," *WP*, December 11, 1916, 4: "Occasionally even now we hear of a team being 'Chicagoed.'" Al Spalding even included National League "'Chicago' Games" in his annual baseball guides. For example, see *Spalding's Base Ball Guide and Official League Book for 1886* (1886; repr., St. Louis: Horton Pub. Co., 1987), 45. "It may be proper" quotation is from "The National Game," *New York Herald*, July 27, 1870, 5.

37. According to *The Sporting News*, "There were exactly five shutouts prior to 1870." On May 13, 1870, the Brooklyn Atlantics defeated the Resolutes of Elizabeth, New Jersey, 19–0. On June 15, 1870, the Cincinnati Red Stockings beat New York's Morrisania Unions, 14–0. See John H. Gruber, "Rules of the Game and Their History: Scoring of Runs," *TSN*, November 4, 1915, 4; Wright, *The National Association of Base Ball Players*, 297, 291.

38. Information on shutouts and pitching is in Light, *The Cultural Encyclopedia of Baseball*, 68–69, 724, 850–52; Morris, *A Game of Inches*, 17–21, 71–75, 136–37, 275–76; *Baseball in Old Chicago*, 15. The White Stockings' use of rubber baseballs is in "The National Game," *NYT*, November 27, 1870, 6. See also Ryczek, *When Johnny Came Sliding Home*, 146–48; Morris, *A Game of Inches*, 271–76. "Who would have thought it?" quotation is from "The National Game," *CT*, July 24, 1870, 4 (article reprinted as "Mutuals vs. White Stockings," *New York Herald*, July 27, 1870, 5). Baseball scores are in "The National Game," *CT*, July 27, 1870, 4; "The National Game," *CT*, August 2, 1870, 4 (include praise of players' batting and the "repeated drubbings" quotation); Wright, *The National Association of Base Ball Players*, 293.

39. "The mixture of merchant" quotation is from *Baseball in Old Chicago*, 20. Reorganization of the club and executive committee are in "The White Stockings," *CT*, August 11, 1870, 4; "The National Game," *CT*, September 12, 1870, 4; "Base Ball," *CT*, September 13, 1870, 4. Gassette's occupation is mentioned in "The Office of the Circuit Clerk," *CT*, June 22, 1869, 4; untitled editorial, *CT*, February 16, 1870, 2.

40. "Utter disregard of the rules" quotation is from "The Sporting World," *CT*, August 21, 1870, 3. Craver's dismissal is documented in note 33. Marshall King as catcher is in "The Sporting World," *CT*, August 25, 1870, 4. Ed Duffy as new player is in "The National Game," *CT*, August 27, 1870, 4; Ryczek, *When Johnny Came Sliding Home*, 226–27. See also "Out-Door Sports," *NYT*, September 28, 1870, 8. Baseball scores are in "The National Game," *CT*, August 31, 1870, 4; "The Sporting World," *CT*, September 6, 1870, 2 (includes "perfect harmony" quotation); Wright, *The National Association of Base Ball Players*, 240–42, 291, 293, 297–98. See note 34 for sportswriters' earlier criticisms of the White Stockings.

41. The White Stockings' schedule is in Wright, *The National Association of Base Ball Players*, 292–93. "Will take the field" quotation is from "The Sporting World," *CT*, September 6, 1870, 2. "The mission of the" quotation is from "White Above the Red," *CT*, September 8, 1870, 4. The White Stockings' goal of beating Cincinnati is also in "Base Ball," *CT*, May 15, 1870, 3; "The 'Red' and the 'White,'" *NYT*, October 16, 1870, 8; "The National Game," *NYT*, November 27, 1870, 6; untitled editorial, *CT*, November 28, 1870, 2. The derogatory $18,000 adjective is also in "A Victory for the $18,000 Nine," *New-York Tribune*, June 21, 1870, 5; "The National Game," *CT*, July 7, 1870, 4; "The National Game," *New York Herald*, July 7, 1870, 10; "Chicago on Its Nine," *Brooklyn (NY) Daily Eagle*, July 11, 1870, 3; "Base Ball," *CT*, September 13, 1870, 4; Ryczek, *When Johnny Came Sliding Home*, 200.

42. Grand celebration, George Wright absence, and request for rematch are from "The National Game," *CT*, September 9, 1870, 4. George Wright absence also in "Base-Ball," *NYT*, September 8, 1870, 1; "Sporting," *Chicago Times*, October 13, 1870, 8. "There arose a prolonged" and "Porkopolis" quotations are from "The National Game," *CT*, September 10, 1870, 4. See note 12 for meaning of "Porkopolis." Umpire's calls are in "White Above the Red," *CT*, September 8, 1870, 4; "The 'Red' and the 'White,'" *NYT*, October 16, 1870, 8. "The recent superb" quotation is from "Base Ball," *CT*, September 13, 1870, 4.

43. White Stockings leaving for New York is in "Sporting," *CT*, September 21, 1870, 4. The Mutuals beating the White Stockings twice is in "Base Ball," *CT*, September 22, 1870, 4. The Mutuals beating the Atlantics and the Athletics, the Chicagoans predicting a close game, and "that spectral" quotation are from "Sporting," *CT*, September 28, 1870, 4. The White Stockings' schedule is in Wright, *The National Association of Base Ball Players*, 292–93. "Was decidedly the best" quotation is from "Base-Ball," *NYT*, September 27, 1870, 1.

44. During the Franco-Prussian War, German forces decisively defeated Napoleon III and the French Army at Sedan, France, on September 1, 1870.

45. The White Stockings' schedule is in Wright, *The National Association of Base Ball Players*, 292–93. *Cincinnati Daily Gazette* quotation is from "Base Ball," *CT*, October 12, 1870, 4. "People who have been" quotation, people from other states, and excursion train are in "The National Game," *CT*, October 12, 1870, 2. Railway lines and "no lack of facilities" quotation are from "The Sporting World," *CT*, October 13, 1870, 4.

46. Umpire Bob Ferguson is in "Base Ball," *CT*, October 12, 1870, 4. Use of local umpires is in Morris, *A Game of Inches*, 252. George Wright and *Chicago Tribune* quotations are from "The Sporting World," *CT*, October 13, 1870, 4. "The pestilential air" quotation is from "Base Ball," *Cincinnati Daily Gazette*, October 14, 1870, 3 (the sportswriter's comments also appeared in: *CT*, October 15, 1870, 4; *Chicago Times*, October 15, 1870, 5; *NYT*, October 17, 1870, 5; *(Philadelphia) Evening Telegraph*, October 17, 1870, 1; *Saturday Evening Post*, November 5,

1870, 3). See also "Story of an Old Game," *CDT*, December 17, 1899, 18; John Kelley, "White Stockings and Cincy Renew Feud from 1870," *CDT*, October 19, 1919, sec. 2, 4.

47. According to the *Oxford English Dictionary*, "spraed" is the past tense of the obsolete use of the verb "spray," meaning "to spring, take rise."

48. See note 44 for use of Sedan.

49. After the White Stockings beat the Red Stockings, the *Cincinnati Commercial* wrote that the Chicagoans were "the champions of the country." See "Sporting," *Chicago Times*, October 15, 1870, 5. "Are in a demoralized" quotation is from "Base Ball," *Cincinnati Daily Gazette*, October 17, 1870, 1. Attendance declining is in Ryczek, *When Johnny Came Sliding Home*, 237–38; John Thorn, *Baseball in the Garden of Eden: The Secret History of the Early Game* (New York: Simon & Schuster, 2011), 147. "We have arrived" quotation is from "Base Ball," *Cincinnati Daily Gazette*, November 23, 1870, 1 (the board's letter is reprinted in "The 'Red Stockings,'" *NYT*, November 26, 1870, 6). See also "New Professional Nines," *NYT*, November 26, 1870, 2.

50. The Mutuals beating the Brooklyn Atlantics for the championship is in "Base-Ball," *NYT*, September 23, 1870, 3. The White Stockings first defeating the Mutuals is in "Out-Door Sports," *NYT*, September 28, 1870, 8. For rules concerning the championship, see "Who Are the Champions for 1870?," *NYC*, November 12, 1870, 250; "Base-Ball," *NYT*, March 13, 1871, 12; Wright, *The National Association of Base Ball Players*, 284–87; Ryczek, *When Johnny Came Sliding Home*, 214–17. "Games were scheduled" quotation is from *Baseball in Old Chicago*, 18.

51. Mutuals arriving in Chicago and rain storm are in "The Sporting World," *CT*, October 31, 1870, 4. "Double incentive" quotation is from "Sporting," *Chicago Times*, November 1, 1870, 5. Weather and grounds are in "Base Ball," *CT*, November 1, 1870, 4; "Base-Ball," *Chicago Times*, November 2, 1870, 2. *New York Times* quotations are from "Base-Ball," *NYT*, November 2, 1870, 1. In the early years of baseball, an umpire had a great deal of discretion in calling balls and strikes. See Morris, *A Game of Inches*, 17–20. Chicago-New York game is also in "The Sporting World," *CT*, November 2, 1870, 3; "Base Ball," *NYC*, November 12, 1870, 250; Bob Tiemann, "The Birth of the NA," in Felber, *Inventing Baseball*, 77–78. Chicago's record is in Wright, *The National Association of Base Ball Players*, 292–93; Harvey Frommer, *Old-Time Baseball: America's Pastime in the Gilded Age* (Lanham, MD: Taylor Trade Publishing, 2006), 186–87; "1870 National Association," Baseball-Reference.com, accessed January 15, 2018, https://www.baseball-reference.com/bullpen/1870_National_Association. The Mutuals refused to play a November 4 game against the White Stockings. See "The Sporting World," *CT*, November 4, 1870, 4.

52. The Mutuals' and the White Stockings' claims to the championship are in "The Sporting World," *CT*, November 3, 1870, 4; "Sporting," *Chicago Times*, November 3, 1870, 4; "The Sporting World," *CT*, November 12, 1870, 4; "Who Are the Champions for 1870?," *NYC*, November 12, 1870, 250 (includes "Who are the" quotation). Other teams' claims are in "Base Ball," *NYC*, November 5, 1870, 242; "Base-Ball," *NYT*, February 21, 1871, 8 (includes "it would puzzle" quotation); "Base-Ball," *NYT*, March 13, 1871, 12; Wright, *The National Association of Base Ball Players*, 286–87; Ryczek, *When Johnny Came Sliding Home*, 230–31. See also *Baseball in Old Chicago*, 18: "The mythical national title was principally a matter of opinion, based upon such comparisons as could be made from the games played." For an explanation of a "picked nine," see note 13.

53. Wood's six "as told to" Menke syndicated articles appeared in newspapers around the country. The main title of all of the articles, as published in the home edition of the *El Paso (Texas) Herald*, is "Baseball of Bygone Days." The six articles appeared in the newspaper from August 14–19, 1916.

54. See "Billiards," *(Chicago) Daily Inter Ocean*, November 16, 1885, 5: "He has been a member of the City Council, and for several seasons he was the manager of the famous Chicago White Stocking base ball team. Base ball for him has now almost lost its charms, and outside of billiards he has a fondness for horses." This article notes that Foley "was born in Cashel, Ireland, Aug. 16, 1842, and came to America with his parents in 1848, settling down among the farmers on Staten Island. In 1854 they removed to Chicago, and here young Tom began his battle with the world, earning his first dollar in the West in the billiard-room of the old Tremont House." See also J. G. Davis, "Tom Foley, Father of American Billiards," *CDT*, November 12, 1911, sec. 3, 4.

55. The Union Club stopped the tied game in the sixth inning following a disagreement with the umpire. The umpire then announced to the crowd, "I decide this game in favor of the Cincinnatis, because the Unions of Lansingburg refuse to continue it." See "Base Ball," *NYT*, August 27, 1869, 1.

56. Fisher did not stay with the White Stockings and was not with the team when it began playing in late March 1870. See note 21.

57. The White Stockings played more than two dozen games in June and July. They also lost to the Rockford, Illinois, Forest Citys on August 26 by the score of 14–7. See Wright, *The National Association of Base Ball Players*, 292–93; "The National Game," *CT*, August 27, 1870, 4.

58. The Red Stockings lost six games in 1870. See Wright, *The National Association of Base Ball Players*, 291–92.

59. According to the *Oxford English Dictionary*, the verb "job" means "to rebuke, reprove, or reprimand in a long and tedious harangue." The *Chicago Tribune* reported that "not far short of" 18,000 persons attended the game while the *Chicago Times* wrote that it was about 15,000. See "The Sporting World," *CT*, October 14, 1870, 4; "Sporting," *Chicago Times*, October 14, 1870, 4.

60. Potter Palmer was the club's first president. Philip Sheridan was a vice president.

61. Change players (such as a change catcher or change pitcher) are substitute or relief players. See Dickson, *The Dickson Baseball Dictionary*, 175.

62. Al Spink also writes about the White Stockings in his *One Thousand Sport Stories* (Chicago: Martin Co., 1921), 1: 80–83.

63. The captain of the Red Stockings was Harry Wright, George's older brother.

64. According to the *Oxford English Dictionary*, "to give one a back-cap" is a slang expression meaning "to disclose or state something to one's detriment; to run down."

Chapter 2

1. The club's debt is in "The Sporting World," *CT*, January 17, 1871, 4. "The stockholders have" quotation is from "The Sporting World," *CT*, November 13, 1870, 3. "The White Stocking nine" quotation is from "Sporting," *Chicago Republican*, January 20, 1871, 4. Tom Foley's recruitment of players is in "Our National Game," *Chicago Republican*, January 12, 1871, 5. Departing players are in "The Sporting World," *CT*, November 26, 1870, 4; "The Sporting World," *CT*, December 25, 1870, 4. Charlie Hodes rejoining the team is in "The Sporting World," *CT*, March 5, 1871, 3. New players are in "Base Ball," *CT*, January 18, 1871, 4. Red Stockings disbanding is in chapter 1, note 49. Baseball player Tom Foley is in chapter 1, note 10. Ned Cuthbert is in "Sporting Matters," *CT*, January 13, 1871, 4; "Base Ball," *CT*, February 19, 1871, 3; "The National Game," *CT*, March 30, 1871, 3. See also Larry Names, *Bury My Heart at Wrigley Field: The History of the Chicago Cubs* (Neshkoro: Angel Press of Wisconsin, 1996), 78–79.

2. National Association of Base Ball Players information is in "Base Ball Convention," *New York Herald*, March 14, 1858, 2; "Ball Play," *NYC*, March 20, 1858, 379; Marshall D. Wright, *The National Association of Base Ball Players, 1857–1870* (Jefferson, NC: McFarland, 2000), 15–16, 284–88; Gary Gillette and Pete Palmer, eds., *The ESPN Baseball Encyclopedia*, 4th ed. (New York: Sterling Publishing, 2007), 264. Disputes and conflicts are in William J. Ryczek, *When Johnny Came Sliding Home: The Post-Civil War Baseball Boom, 1865–1870* (Jefferson, NC: McFarland, 1998), 243–51. The editorial is "Base-Ball," *NYT*, July 3, 1870, 4. See also "The Ethics of Base Ball," *CT*, June 11, 1871, 2.

3. Baseball concerns are in Wright, *The National Association of Base Ball Players*, 284–85, 328–29; Peter Morris, *A Game of Inches: The Stories Behind the Innovations That Shaped Baseball*, rev. and exp. one-vol. ed. (Chicago: Ivan R. Dee, 2010), 534; Warren N. Wilbert, *Opening Pitch: Professional Baseball's Inaugural Season, 1871* (Lanham, MD: Scarecrow Press, 2008), xi–xii; Gillette and Palmer, *The ESPN Baseball Encyclopedia*, 264; Federal Writers' Project (Illinois), Work Project Administration, *Baseball in Old Chicago* (Chicago: A. C. McClurg, 1939), 21–22. "Attractive as is" quotation is from "The Sporting World," *CT*, December 11, 1870, 3. Baseball as a business is in Albert G. Spalding, *America's National Game: Historic Facts Concerning the Beginning, Evolution, Development and Popularity of Base Ball* (1911; repr., Lincoln: University of Nebraska Press, 1992), 159–60.

4. The founding of the National Association of Professional Base Ball Players is in "National Association of Professional Base-Ball Players," *NYT*, March 18, 1871, 8; William J. Ryczek, *Blackguards and Red Stockings: A History of Baseball's National Association, 1871–1875* (Wallingford, CT: Colebrook Press, 1999), 11–14; John Thorn, *Baseball in the Garden of Eden: The Secret History of the Early Game* (New York: Simon & Schuster, 2011), 148–49; David Nemec, *The Great Encyclopedia of Nineteenth Century Major League Baseball*, 2nd ed. (Tuscaloosa: University of Alabama Press, 2006), 9–10; David Pietrusza, *Major Leagues: The Formation, Sometimes Absorption, and Mostly Inevitable Demise of 18 Professional Baseball Organizations, 1871 to Present* (Jefferson, NC: McFarland, 2006), 5–9. Proceedings' quotations are from *Proceedings of Convention of the National Association of Professional Base Ball Players, Held in New York City, March 17, 1871* (Washington, D.C.: Beresford, 1871), 6, 7. Winning three out of five games equaled a series win. Participation of amateur clubs is in Tom Melville, *Early Baseball and the Rise of the National League* (Jefferson, NC: McFarland, 2001), 49. Southern tour quotations are from "The Sporting World," *CT*, March 7, 1871, 4. The White Stockings leaving for New Orleans is in "The National Game," *CT*, March 16, 1871, 4; "Sporting," *Chicago Times*, March 19, 1871, 10; "Base-Ball," *Chicago Republican*, March 17, 1871, 4: "The White Stocking party ... left the city last evening on the 9 o'clock train, Illinois Central road, for Cairo, where they take a steamer for New Orleans."

5. Dexter Park's inadequacies are in "Base Ball," *CT*, January 21, 1871, 4; "The Sporting World," *CT*, February 12, 1871, 3 (includes "in view of these facts" quotation); *Baseball in Old Chicago*, 12–13, 22–23; Names, *Bury My Heart at Wrigley Field*, 80; Steven A. Riess, *Touching Base: Professional Baseball and American Culture in the Progressive Era*, rev. ed. (Urbana: University of Illinois Press, 1999), 100. A horse car was a horse-drawn street car that ran on tracks. Leasing part of Lake Park to the White Stockings is in "Common Council," *CT*, February 21, 1871, 3; "The Sporting World," *CT*, March 5, 1871, 3; "Common Council," *CT*, March 7, 1871, 4; "Sporting," *Chicago Times*, March 7, 1871, 5; "Sporting Matters," *CT*, March 11, 1871, 4; "Base Ball," *NYC*, March 18, 1871, 394. The park's length of 375 feet and its names are in Philip J. Lowry, *Green Cathedrals: The Ultimate Celebration of Major League and Negro League Ballparks* (New York: Walker, 2006), 47. Lowry adds: "Left Field (E) Illinois Central RR tracks, then Lake Michigan; Third Base (N) Randolph St; First Base (W) Michigan Ave; Right Field (S) Madison St." He also notes that "although Washington is closer to what was then the boundary than Madison, Washington was then inside the park, so Madison is a better descriptor of the boundary than is Washington." The park now being part of Millennium Park is in Timothy J. Gilfoyle, in association with the Chicago History Museum, *Millennium Park: Creating a Chicago Landmark* (Chicago: University of Chicago Press, 2006), 12–14. The grounds are also discussed in "Base-Ball," *Chicago Times*, April 9, 1871, 11; "Base-Ball," *Chicago Times*, April 26, 1871, 8; "Base Ball Notes," *Chicago Republican*, April 26, 1871, 4; "The Sporting World," *CT*, May 5, 1871, 4 (mentions that the grounds "will have seating capacity for about 7,500 people; ... their cost will not be far from $5,000").

6. "The Sporting World," *CT*, March 8, 1871, 4.

7. "In good health" quotation is from "Base Ball," *CT*, March 22, 1871, 3. Work was scheduled to begin on the new park right after the players left Chicago. See "The National Game," *CT*, March 16, 1871, 4. Practice games are in "Base Ball," *CT*, March 23, 1871, 4; "Base Ball," *CT*, March 25, 1871, 4 (includes "are getting down" and "it is as first" quotations). March 26 game coverage is in "Base Ball," *CT*, March 27, 1871, 1. March 31 game coverage is in "The Sporting World," *CT*, April 1, 1871, 4 (includes "hankering" and "sorely" quotations). Zettlein is also in "Sporting," *Chicago Republican*, January 25, 1871, 4.

8. The White Stockings leaving New Orleans for Memphis and St. Louis is in "Base Ball," *CT*, April 16,

1871, 3; "The Sporting World," *CT*, April 20, 1871, 4. Team's record of victories and "may seem to show" quotation are in "The National Game," *CT*, April 24, 1871, 4. This article states that the White Stockings scored 479 runs during their southern tour in 1870. The correct total is 485. See "Sporting Matters, *CT*, May 19, 1870, 4; Wright, *The National Association of Base Ball Players*, 292. Characteristics of baseballs are in "New Rules of the Game," *CT*, November 16, 1870, 4; Ryczek, *When Johnny Came Sliding Home*, 146–48; Morris, *A Game of Inches*, 271–76. "Feeling and looking" quotation is from "Sporting," *Chicago Times*, April 25, 1871, 5.

9. The original phrase was "northeast to southwest," but home plate was actually in the northwest corner of the ball field.

10. Part of this article was reprinted in "Base Ball," *NYC*, May 13, 1871, 45. For an explanation of a "picked nine," see chapter 1, note 13. See also "The Sporting World," *CT*, April 18, 1871, 3: "It was announced about a week ago that the management of the Chicago Club had determined to divide the second floor of the grand stand into commodious seats and offer the same for sale for the season. The plan was drawn for the stand and it was found that there would be 497 first-rate seats that it would be feasible to sell immediately." There were two Tom Foleys with the Chicago club. One was a ballplayer and the other was a team official. See chapter 1, note 10.

11. Quotations are from "Sporting," *Chicago Times*, April 30, 1871, 10; "The Sporting World," *CT*, April 30, 1871, 2. See also "Base-Ball," *Chicago Republican*, May 1, 1871, 4; "Sporting," *Chicago Times*, April 28, 1871, 5: "As the occasion will be the opening of the grounds, it is proposed to give it as much *eclat* as possible. A band of music will be in attendance; a congratulatory speech will be made by a South-side alderman who is an ardent admirer of the national game, and an address of thanks, it is said, will be delivered by a gentleman of journalistic descent in behalf of the Chicago club to the mayor and common council. It is also rumored that there will be some champagne loafing around."

12. Teams playing in 1871 and the start of the new season are in Thorn, *Baseball in the Garden of Eden*, 149–50; Ryczek, *Blackguards and Red Stockings*, 1–3, 24, 39–41; Marshall D. Wright, *Nineteenth Century Baseball: Year-by-Year Statistics for the Major League Teams, 1871 Through 1900* (Jefferson, NC: McFarland, 1996), 6–7; http://www.retrosheet.org/.

13. May 8 game is described in "Games and Pastimes," *CT*, May 9, 1871, 4; "Our National Game," *Chicago Republican*, May 9, 1871, 4; "Forest City vs. Chicago," *NYC*, May 20, 1871, 53; Richard A. Puff, "Ezra Ballou Sutton," in *Nineteenth Century Stars*, ed. Robert L. Tiemann and Mark Rucker (Phoenix: Society for American Baseball Research, 2012), 253. The White Stockings' record is in http://www.retrosheet.org/. *Tribune* coverage of May 19 game is in "Games and Pastimes," *CT*, May 20, 1871, 4. *Chicago Republican* coverage and Jimmy Wood's discomfiture are in "Base-Ball," *Chicago Republican*, May 20, 1871, 1. Jimmy Wood quotation and verification of Lotta Crabtree's name are from *Baseball in Old Chicago*, 23–24. Paddy Quinn, the catcher for the White Stockings in 1875, called this game "the most remarkable game I have seen in forty years." See "Quinn Talks of Old Times," *CDT*, September 21, 1906, 10.

14. Record by May 27 and eastern tour are in "Games and Pastimes," *CT*, May 27, 1871, 4. Eastern tour is also in "Sporting Notes," *Chicago Republican*, May 27, 1871, 4. Win against the Eckfords is in "The National Game," *CT*, May 30, 1871, 1. Win against the Red Stockings is in "Games and Pastimes," *CT*, June 3, 1871, 4. Game against the Mutuals and "badly whipped" quotation are from "Base-Ball," *NYT*, June 6, 1871, 8. Haymakers' score is in "Base-Ball," *NYT*, May 26, 1871, 2. Philadelphia Athletics' victory is in "Games and Pastimes," *CT*, June 9, 1871, 4. On June 12, Chicago beat the Baltimore Pastimes, 38–17. See "Games and Pastimes," *CT*, June 13, 1871, 4. Olympics' victory and "were led to ask" quotation are in "Games and Pastimes," *CT*, June 14, 1871, 4.

15. White Stockings-Mutuals game postponed and Chicago record are in "Games and Pastimes," *CT*, June 16, 1871, 4. Game logs are in http://www.retrosheet.org/. "The steadiness with" quotation is from "Sporting," *Chicago Republican*, June 17, 1871, 4. "The players feel sore" and Tom Foley quotations are from "Games and Pastimes," *CT*, June 18, 1871, 3 (includes National Association records). Listing of "championship games played" is in "Boston vs. Rockfords," *CT*, August 18, 1871, 4. June 30 defeat is in "Games and Pastimes," *CT*, July 1, 1871, 4. August 10 loss is in "Base Ball," *CT*, August 11, 1871, 4. August 16 win is in "Games and Pastimes," *CT*, August 17, 1871, 4. September 29 victory is in "Games and Pastimes," *CT*, September 30, 1871, 4. A "standing of clubs contesting for the championship" is in "Games and Pastimes," *CT*, October 1, 1871, 2. Eastern tour and game with Athletics are from "Games and Pastimes," *CT*, October 6, 1871, 4.

16. Chicago Fire is in Richard F. Bales, *The Great Chicago Fire and the Myth of Mrs. O'Leary's Cow* (Jefferson, NC: McFarland, 2002), 16 (includes "a desiccated husk" quotation), 20, 41; "Everything," *CT*, October 14, 1871, 2 (includes "up to Sunday" quotation). According to the *Tribune* article, the only members of the White Stockings who did not lose their property were Tom Foley, Ed Atwater, and Jimmy Wood, "who all lived outside the limits of the fire." Canceling player contracts is in "Washington News," *NYT*, October 16, 1871, 8. "For the sufferers" quotation is from "Aid for Chicago," *NYC*, October 14, 1871, 219. "At quite a discount" quotation is from "Players on the Market," *NYC*, October 14, 1871, 219. Benefit baseball games are mentioned in "Aid from Abroad," *CT*, October 19, 1871, 2; "Local News in Brief," *NYT*, October 21, 1871, 10; "The Mutual-Athletic Benefit Games," *NYC*, October 28, 1871, 234; Wilbert, *Opening Pitch*, 50; David Quentin Voigt, *American Baseball*, vol. 1, *From Gentleman's Sport to the Commissioner System* (University Park: Pennsylvania State University Press, 1983), 39–40.

17. The October 12 game with the Haymakers is in "Base Ball," *CT*, October 4, 1871, 4. October 21 game against the Haymakers is in "Base Ball," *CT*, October 23, 1871, 1. "Much less feeling" and "the misfortunes" quotations are from "Base Ball," *CT*, October 23, 1871, 1. October 23 loss is in "Base-Ball," *NYT*, October 25, 1871, 8. The White Stockings traveling east is also in "Everything," *CT*, October 14, 1871, 2. "Not two of the nine" quotation is from "Base Ball," *CT*, November 3, 1871, 1. See also "The Champion Athletics," *New York Herald*, October 31, 1871, 3; Wilbert, *Opening Pitch*, 48–49; "Sporting Gossip," *Chicago Evening Journal*, October 25,

1871, 4: "The Chicago boys lost all their uniforms in the fire, and it is stated that Messrs. Peck & Snyder, of New York, refused to make new clothes unless they were paid for in advance."

18. Few opportunities for practice and October 30 game are in "Base Ball," *CT*, November 3, 1871, 1 (includes "and a large portion" quotation); "The Champion Athletics," *New York Herald*, October 31, 1871, 3; Bob Tiemann, "The First Pennant Race," in *Inventing Baseball: The 100 Greatest Games of the 19th Century*, ed. Bill Felber (Phoenix: Society for American Baseball Research, 2013), 81–83. The season's end is in Wilbert, *Opening Pitch*, 49–54 (mentions exhibition games on pp. 52–53); Thorn, *Baseball in the Garden of Eden*, 152–53; Wright, *Nineteenth Century Baseball*, 7–8; Ryczek, *Blackguards and Red Stockings*, 54–67 (mentions November 2 Haymakers game and National Association on p. 64); Paul Batesel, *Players and Teams of the National Association, 1871-1875* (Jefferson, NC: McFarland, 2012), 158–59; Preston D. Orem, *Baseball (1845-1881): From the Newspaper Accounts* (Altadena, CA: Preston D. Orem, 1961), 138–41 (exhibition games and rainy weather are on p. 140); Nemec, *The Great Encyclopedia of Nineteenth Century Major League Baseball*, 15, 18 ("official standings" are on pp. 19–30). November 2 game is in "Games and Pastimes," *CT*, November 8, 1871, 6. Philadelphia Athletics declared champions is in "The Athletic Ten for '71," *NYC*, November 18, 1871, 1; "Telegraphic Brevities," *NYT*, November 19, 1871, 1. Game logs and statistics are in http://www.retrosheet.org/; http://www.baseball-reference.com/.

19. New York Mutuals exhibition game is in "Games and Pastimes," *CT*, November 5, 1871, 4 (includes New York *World* quotation and White Stockings joining other teams); "Base Ball," *CT*, November 3, 1871, 4 (mentions White Stockings joining other teams, including Haymakers); Wilbert, *Opening Pitch*, 50. White Stockings joining Haymakers is in "Games and Pastimes," *CT*, November 10, 1871, 6; "Base Ball Notes," *CT*, November 11, 1871, 6; "Base Ball," *CT*, November 24, 1871, 6; "Base Ball," *CT*, December 4, 1871, 4.

20. Stockholders' meeting is in "Games and Pastimes," *CT*, November 13, 1871, 6. The club surrendering its stock is in "Games and Pastimes," *CT*, November 26, 1871, 2. See also "City Affairs in Brief," *CT*, March 2, 1872, 2: "The Committee was instructed to divide *pro rata* among the players of the Club what money remained of last year's earnings." An amateur club and the "no lack of interest" in it are in "Miscellaneous City Items," *CT*, January 12, 1872, 2. See also "Miscellaneous City Items," *CT*, March 20, 1872, 5; "Games and Pastimes," *CT*, March 29, 1872, 5.

Chapter 3

1. "Base-Ball Matters," *Spirit of the Times*, April 27, 1872, 165. See also "Base-Ball Notes," *NYT*, February 25, 1872, 6: "The Chicago fire has, for this season, banished the game from Illinois." Quotation about the Aetna Ball Club is from "Miscellaneous City Items," *CT*, January 12, 1872, 2. See also "Miscellaneous City News," *CT*, March 20, 1872, 5; "Games and Pastimes," *CT*, April 28, 1872, 3, "The National Game," *CT*, May 7, 1872, 2. The Aetna and Phoenix clubs are in "Games and Pastimes," *CT*, May 12, 1872, 10; "Games and Pastimes," *CT*, May 17, 1872, 6; "Games and Pastimes," *CT*, May 25, 1872, 6. The Active Base Ball Club is in "Games and Pastimes," *CT*, July 18, 1872, 6; "Base Ball," *CT*, July 20, 1872, 2; "Games and Pastimes," *CT*, July 25, 1872, 6 (includes quotation about new uniform).

2. The new baseball organization (originally called the Phoenix Base Ball Association) is in "Base Ball," *CT*, April 8, 1872, 6 (mentions Jimmy Wood wanting to play in Chicago); "Base-Ball," *NYT*, April 14, 1872, 1; "The National Game," *CT*, April 14, 1872, 8 (includes reference to the group changing its name to the Chicago Base Ball Association). The new grounds, the need for $4,000 and "had assurances" quotation are in "Games and Pastimes," *CT*, April 25, 1872, 6. In this article, which includes a list of the association's officers, the secretary's last name is spelled "Thacher." The correct spelling is "Thatcher." A reference to the "powerful professional team which Chicago would like to have this year" is in "Games and Pastimes," *CT*, April 28, 1872, 3. Information about the association earning money to obtain players for a team is in "The National Game," *CT*, January 14, 1873, 4. The new grounds and Jimmy Wood are also in "The Sporting World," *CT*, January 28, 1872, 2. See also Larry Names, *Bury My Heart at Wrigley Field: The History of the Chicago Cubs* (Neshkoro: Angel Press of Wisconsin, 1996), 91–93.

3. Particulars of May 6 meeting are in "The National Game," *CT*, May 7, 1872, 2. "The 'home plate' will" quotation, dimensions of the new ballpark, and use of the grounds by the Chicago Athletic Club are from "The National Game," *CT*, May 5, 1872, 2. "As in the case" quotation is from "Games and Pastimes," *CT*, May 12, 1872, 10. The athletic club and dressing room are in "Games and Pastimes," *CT*, May 19, 1872, 10. May 29 game between Baltimore and Cleveland is in "Inauguration of the New Chicago Base Ball Park," *CT*, May 30, 1872, 6.

4. The location of the park is in Philip J. Lowry, *Green Cathedrals: The Ultimate Celebration of Major League and Negro League Ballparks* (New York: Walker, 2006), 48. Lowry notes that when the park was built, stands were constructed on the west side of the field along Clark Street. Clark Street now ends on Cermak Road, so a present-day western boundary would be Federal Street. See "23rd Street Park," Seamheads.com, accessed January 19, 2018, http://www.seamheads.com/ballparks/ballpark.php?parkID=CHI02; Paul Batesel, *Players and Teams of the National Association, 1871-1875* (Jefferson, NC: McFarland, 2012), 157–58. "A side-track" quotation is from "Local Miscellany," *CDT*, April 5, 1874, 4. "The public has" quotation is from "Games and Pastimes," *Chicago Tribune*, May 26, 1872, 10.

5. Two Baltimore and Cleveland games are in "Inauguration of the New Chicago Base Ball Park," *CT*, May 30, 1872, 6; "Games and Pastimes," *CT*, May 31, 1872, 5. Ballpark's names are in "Turf and Field," *CDT*, July 13, 1873, 3; Lowry, *Green Cathedrals*, 47. Lowry notes that the park was also known as both the State Street Grounds and the 23rd Street Park. Aetnas-Evanston University game is in "Games and Pastimes," *CT*, June 1, 1872, 6. Fauntleroy quotation is from "Base-Ball," *Chicago Times*, June 8, 1873, 4; "The Sporting World," *CDT*, June 8, 1873, 3. Fauntleroy's position as the association's treasurer is verified in "Base-Ball," *Chicago Times*, July 17, 1873, 2; "Base Ball," *CDT*, July 17, 1873, 8. June 13 article is "Out Door Sports," *CT*, June 13, 1872, 5

(includes "to take time" and "it may transpire" quotations). Several players signed for Chicago for the 1872 season instead joined the Troy Haymakers, and on June 9 the *Tribune* published an article describing the Troy team's problems and its "sackcloth of defeat." See "The Chicago Club for 1872," *NYC*, October 21, 1871, 226; http://www.retrosheet.org/ (includes names of players); "Games and Pastimes," *CT*, June 9, 1872, 10. See chapter 1, note 3, for a discussion of "muffing."

6. July 1 meeting is in "Base Ball," *CT*, July 2, 1872, 6. "The financial difficulties" quotation is from "Base Ball," *CDT*, November 25, 1872, 8. Salary demands of Cincinnati Red Stockings are in "Base Ball," *Cincinnati Daily Gazette*, November 23, 1870, 1; John Thorn, *Baseball in the Garden of Eden: The Secret History of the Early Game* (New York: Simon & Schuster, 2011), 147–48. Heavy salary obligations and Forest Citys club are in United States. Congress. House. Committee on the Judiciary. *Organized Baseball: Report of the Subcommittee on Study of Monopoly Power of the Committee on the Judiciary Pursuant to H. Res. 95, 82d Cong., 1st sess., Authorizing the Committee on the Judiciary to Conduct Studies and Investigations Relating to Matters Within Its Jurisdiction* (Washington: U.S. Government Printing Office, 1952), 18; Harold Seymour, *Baseball: The Early Years* (New York: Oxford University Press, 1989), 75. July 28 untitled editorial is in *CT*, July 28, 1872, 4. See also editorial "The New Chicago," *CT*, July 28, 1872, 4; "Real Estate," *CT*, September 1, 1872, 3.

7. Game logs are in http://www.retrosheet.org/. Coverage of Chicago Base Ball Association's attempts to attract eastern clubs to Chicago and to secure players for 1874 is in "Base-Ball," *CDT*, June 1, 1873, 3; "The Ball Field," *CDT*, June 2, 1873, 3; "The Sporting World," *CDT*, June 3, 1873, 3; "The Sporting World," *CDT*, June 8, 1873, 3. Reorganization of association is in "Base Ball," *CDT*, July 17, 1873, 8; "The Sporting World," *CDT*, July 19, 1873, 8; "Base Ball," *CDT*, July 20, 1873, 3. *Chicago Times* quotations are from "Base-Ball," *Chicago Times*, July 21, 1873, 8. Weather and attendance figure of 6,000 are in "Sporting Matters," *CDT*, August 17, 1873, 3. August 16 game being first professional game in Chicago and "the attendance was very" quotation are from "Base Ball," *CDT*, August 18, 1873, 5. Norman Gassette's 1872 resignation is in "Games and Pastimes," *CT*, June 7, 1872, 6. Gassette's authority with association is in "Base Ball," *CT*, July 2, 1872, 6. Gassette promising to make a success of the club is in "The World of Sport," *Chicago Times*, July 19, 1873, 4. Gassette's announcement of new White Stocking team is in "Sporting Matters," *CDT*, August 16, 1873, 8.

8. Player transaction information is in Batesel, *Players and Teams of the National Association*, 9, 159; http://www.baseball-reference.com/; http://www.retrosheet.org/. "The members of both" quotation is from "Out-Door Amusements," *Chicago Times*, August 16, 1873, 3. Gate receipts and the money clubs made by renting their grounds are in Seymour, *Baseball: The Early Years*, 68; Names, *Bury My Heart at Wrigley Field*, 92–93; David Pietrusza, *Major Leagues: The Formation, Sometimes Absorption, and Mostly Inevitable Demise of 18 Professional Baseball Organizations, 1871 to Present* (Jefferson, NC: McFarland, 2006), 10. See also chapter 6, note 14. Two games between Boston and Philadelphia are in "Sporting Matters," *CDT*, August 17, 1873, 3; "Sporting," *CDT*, August 20, 1873, 5. Teams traveling to Chicago are in "Base Ball," *CDT*, August 31, 1873, 16 (article observes that the Philadelphia and Boston games "were remunerative enough to warrant the belief that an investment in similar ones will be a comparatively safe investment"); "Ba[s]e Ball," *CDT*, September 7, 1873, 3; "Base Ball," *CDT*, October 5, 1873, 1; "Base Ball," *CDT*, October 12, 1873, 3.

9. The end of the 1873 season is in "Base-Ball," *NYT*, October 26, 1873, 3. Game logs and statistics are in http://www.retrosheet.org/; http://www.baseball-reference.com/. The *Tribune*'s observations on the 1874 season are in "Sporting," *CDT*, November 10, 1873, 3.

10. March 7 article is "Base-Ball Notes," *NYT*, March 7, 1874, 3. New York *World* article quoted in "Local Miscellany," *CDT*, March 18, 1874, 3. March 19 article is "News Items," *Los Angeles Daily Herald*, March 19, 1874, 1. Park's seating capacity is in "Local Miscellany," *CDT*, April 5, 1874, 4. See also Lowry, *Green Cathedrals*, 47–48.

11. Jimmy Wood's condition and "every pleasant day," "composed of," and "the professionals" quotations are from "Sporting Gossip," *CDT*, April 19, 1874, 4 (this article notes that "while the club is out of town the grounds will be put in condition, and everything will be in readiness" for the May 13 game against the Athletics). Wood's accident is in "Base Ball," *(Chicago) Inter Ocean*, July 11, 1874, 9; "Sporting News," *CDT*, July 11, 1874, 7. "In a fair way" quotation is from "Local Miscellany," *CDT*, April 5, 1874, 4.

12. April 18 game and team leaving for St. Louis are in "Sporting Gossip," *CDT*, April 19, 1874, 4. Team practicing in St. Louis is in "Base Ball," *CDT*, April 28, 1874, 5. For White Stockings victories in St. Louis see *CDT* from April 24–May 3, 1874; "Base-Ball Notes," *NYT*, April 29, 1874, 5. *New York Herald* quotation, "the batting of the Reds" quotation, and White Stockings leaving St. Louis on good terms with local players are in "The Sporting World," *CDT*, May 3, 1874, 16 (this article notes that the Chicago grounds "are now in fine condition, so far as the sod is concerned, but the fencing and seating arrangements are not yet to the entire satisfaction of the management"). Pearls nickname is in David Nemec, *The Great Encyclopedia of Nineteenth Century Major League Baseball*, 2nd ed. (Tuscaloosa: University of Alabama Press, 2006), 67. To avoid confusion with the Chicago team, they are hereafter in this chapter referred to as the Pearls. For White Stockings victories in Chicago, see *CDT* from May 7–10, 1874. "All the practice necessary" quotation is from "Base Ball," *CDT*, April 26, 1874, 16.

13. "It was a most" quotation is from "Sporting Gossip," *CDT*, May 14, 1874, 8. "There is plenty" quotation is from "Sporting Gossip," *CDT*, May 24, 1874, 13. "The miserable play" quotation is from "Sporting News," *CDT*, June 18, 1874, 7. "Suspicion being openly" quotation and Waterloo reference are in "Sporting News," *CDT*, June 19, 1874, 8. The *Tribune* noted incorrectly that the score of the White Stockings-Mutuals game was 37–1. The *New York Times* included the right score and asserted that the match was "without exception the worst game two professional clubs have ever played in this vicinity" ("Base-Ball," *NYT*, June 19, 1874, 8). An untitled article in the *Tribune* declared that "the distress in Chicago over this news has no parallel since the Great Fire" (*CDT*, June 19, 1874, 4). Game logs are in http://www.retrosheet.org/. See also "The National Game," *New York Herald*,

June 19, 1874, 3; William J. Ryczek, *Blackguards and Red Stockings: A History of Baseball's National Association, 1871–1875* (Wallingford, CT: Colebrook Press, 1999), 153–54.

14. Pinkham's resignation, poor play of team members, changes in positions, and John Peters are in "Sporting Matters," *CDT*, May 23, 1874, 12. "Wander[ing] listlessly" quotation is from "Sporting Matters," *CDT*, June 25, 1874, 12. The White Stockings' record, game logs, and players' names are in http://www.baseball-reference.com/; http://www.retrosheet.org/. "The White Stockings have" quotation is from "Sporting Gossip," *CDT*, May 24, 1874, 13. Fergy Malone's hands and Dan Collins's pitching are in "Sporting News," *CDT*, June 19, 1874, 8. Malone's hands are also in "Sporting News," *CDT*, June 30, 1874, 5. The acquisition of Collins is in "Sporting News," *CDT*, June 9, 1874, 8. "Nearly all of" quotation is from "Base-Ball," *NYT*, June 19, 1874, 8. The team returning home on July 3 and "a party of much" quotation are in "Sporting Matters," *CDT*, July 4, 1874, 12. Player salaries are listed in "The Coming Base-Ball Season," *NYT*, February 19, 1874, 5; "Rational Pastimes," *Forest and Stream*, February 26, 1874, 35.

15. "The large attendance" quotation is from "The Fourth," *CDT*, July 5, 1874, 7. White Stockings' loss and win are in "Sporting News," *CDT*, July 7, 1874, 8; "Sporting News," *CDT*, July 9, 1874, 5. "If one might judge" quotation is from "Base Ball," *(Chicago) Inter Ocean*, July 11, 1874, 9. "An exceedingly commonplace" quotation is from "Base-Ball," *CDT*, July 12, 1874, 16. "This will be sad news" quotation is from "Sporting News," *CDT*, July 11, 1874, 7. Wood's signing with the White Stockings is in "Base Ball," *NYC*, January 15, 1870, 323; T. Z. Cowles, "Ye Sporting Ed of 1868 Harks Back 50 Years," *CDT*, May 26, 1918, sec. 2, 1.

16. Wood's benefit game is described in "Sporting Matters," *CDT*, July 30, 1874, 8. See also "Sporting News," *CDT*, July 26, 1874, 16; "Sporting Matters," *CDT*, July 28, 1874, 8.

17. Game logs are in http://www.retrosheet.org/. The departure and return of the Red Stockings and Athletics are in "The Traveling Base-Ball Clubs," *NYT*, July 15, 1874, 8; "Base Ball," *CDT*, September 10, 1874, 8; "The Returned Ball-Players," *NYT*, September 12, 1874, 4. Regarding Europeans' views of baseball, the London *Daily Telegraph* wrote on July 21 that "comparatively few of the youth of Great Britain will desert cricket, with its dignity, manliness, and system, for a rushing, helter-skelter game such as we are given to understand base-ball is" (as quoted in "The Base-Ball Tourists," *NYT*, August 3, 1874, 5). See also "Our Athletic Cousins," *NYT*, August 20, 1874, 3; Albert G. Spalding, *America's National Game: Historic Facts Concerning the Beginning, Evolution, Development and Popularity of Base Ball* (1911; repr., Lincoln: University of Nebraska Press, 1992), 175–86; Adrian C. Anson, *A Ball Player's Career, Being the Personal Experiences and Reminiscences of Adrian C. Anson* (1900; repr., Mattituck, NY: Amereon House, n.d.), 69–77; "The Tour of England in 1874," in *Spalding's Base Ball Guide and Official League Book for 1890* (1890; repr., St. Louis: Horton Pub. Co., 1989), 124–26; Ryczek, *Blackguards and Red Stockings*, 158–71; Thorn, *Baseball in the Garden of Eden*, 153–54; Nemec, *The Great Encyclopedia of Nineteenth Century Major League Baseball*, 70; Pietrusza, *Major Leagues*, 15–17.

18. Quotations are from "Base Ball," *CDT*, August 6, 1874, 8. See also Ryczek, *Blackguards and Red Stockings*, 167–68; Preston D. Orem, *Baseball (1845–1881): From the Newspaper Accounts* (Altadena, CA: Preston D. Orem, 1961), 194–96.

19. Affidavit is in "Sporting News," *CDT*, September 4, 1874, 8. Stockholders' meeting and "for the loose manner" quotation are in "Base-Ball," *NYT*, September 9, 1874, 5. Radcliff's reinstatement is in "Sporting News," *CDT*, March 7, 1875, 5; "Baseball," *NYC*, March 13, 1875, 397. Radcliff joining the Centennials is in Ryczek, *Blackguards and Red Stockings*, 169; "Philadelphia vs. Centennial," *NYC*, May 1, 1875, 35. Game logs and team rosters are in http://www.retrosheet.org/; http://www.baseball-reference.com/. See also "Sporting News," *CDT*, September 2, 1874, 8; "Base-Ball," *NYT*, September 4, 1874, 5; "Base Ball," *CDT*, September 9, 1874, 8; Orem, *Baseball (1845–1881)*, 198–99; David Nemec and David Ball, "Radcliff, John Young (aka Radcliffe)/'John,'" in *Major League Baseball Profiles, 1871–1900*, vol. 2, comp. and ed. David Nemec (Lincoln: University of Nebraska Press, 2011), 269–70. "The Chicagos made" quotation is from "Base-Ball," *CDT*, November 1, 1874, 16.

20. Problems and weaknesses of the National Association are in "Sporting," *CDT*, October 24, 1875, 12; "Base Ball," *CDT*, November 21, 1875, 12; Spalding, *America's National Game*, 189–93, 199–201; Pietrusza, *Major Leagues*, 17–22; Marshall D. Wright, *Nineteenth Century Baseball: Year-by-Year Statistics for the Major League Teams, 1871 Through 1900* (Jefferson, NC: McFarland, 1996), 31–32, 39–40; Tom Melville, *Early Baseball and the Rise of the National League* (Jefferson, NC: McFarland, 2001), 47–69; Thorn, *Baseball in the Garden of Eden*, 159–64; Andrew J. Schiff, *"The Father of Baseball": A Biography of Henry Chadwick* (Jefferson, NC: McFarland, 2008), 137–38; Thomas Gilbert, *Superstars and Monopoly Wars: Nineteenth-Century Major-League Baseball* (New York: Franklin Watts, 1995), 8–16; Daniel E. Ginsburg, *The Fix Is In: A History of Baseball Gambling and Game Fixing Scandals* (Jefferson, NC: McFarland, 2004), 15–36. Mills's comments are from A. G. Mills, "Reminiscences," in *Spalding's Official Base Ball Record, 1915*, ed. John B. Foster (New York: American Sports Publishing Co., 1915), 47. The banquet was in honor of the New York Giants and Chicago White Sox, who had recently returned from their world tour. Mills was elected president of the National League in December 1882, succeeding Arthur H. Soden, the interim president following William Hulbert's death in April. See "Base-Ball," *CDT*, December 8, 1882, 3.

21. Wealthy teams are in Lee Allen, *The National League Story: The Official History*, rev. ed. (New York: Hill and Wang, 1965), 4. Davy Force case is in "Sporting Matters," *CDT*, December 6, 1874, 2; "Rational Pastimes," *Forest and Stream*, March 4, 1875, 59 (notes that William Hulbert was present at the Philadelphia convention); "Sporting News," *CDT*, March 7, 1875, 5 (mentions William Hulbert); "Baseball," *NYC*, March 13, 1875, 395; "Sporting News," *CDT*, March 14, 1875, 8; "Base Ball," *CDT*, March 19, 1875, 7; "Harry Wright," *NYC*, March 20, 1875, 403; "Sporting News," *CDT*, March 21, 1875, 7 (observes that the Force case "has awakened an indignation among the most prominent of the professional nines"); "Sporting News," *CDT*, March 28, 1875, 12 (includes the report of the 1874 Judiciary Committee and

"imperfect" contract quotations); Ryczek, *Blackguards and Red Stockings*, 187–90 (includes an excellent analysis of the facts).

22. Hulbert's experience in Philadelphia is in "In Memoriam: William A. Hulbert, Esq., Founder and President of the National League," in *Spalding's Base Ball Guide and Official League Book for 1883* (1883; repr., St. Louis: Horton Pub. Co., 1988), 6; Nemec, *The Great Encyclopedia of Nineteenth Century Major League Baseball*, 85–86. Eastern bias of the National Association is in "Sporting News," *CDT*, March 21, 1875, 7; "Base Ball," *CDT*, November 21, 1875, 12; Glenn Stout and Richard A. Johnson, *The Cubs: The Complete Story of Chicago Cubs Baseball* (Boston: Houghton Mifflin, 2007), 7; Allen, *The National League Story*, 4.

23. Information on William Hulbert is in Robert Knight Barney and Frank Dallier, "'I'd Rather Be a Lamp Post in Chicago, Than a Millionaire in Any Other City': William A. Hulbert, Civic Pride, and the Birth of the National League," *NINE: A Journal of Baseball History and Social Policy Perspectives* 2 (Fall 1993): 40–42 (includes mention of Hulbert's 1870 purchase of stock); Tom Melville, "A League of His Own: William Hulbert and the Founding of the National League," *Chicago History* 29 (Fall 2000): 44–57; Bob Carroll, "For the Hall of Fame: Twelve Good Men," *National Pastime* 4 (Winter 1985): 20; John M. Rosenburg, *They Gave Us Baseball: The 12 Extraordinary Men Who Shaped the Major Leagues* (Harrisburg, PA: Stackpole Books, 1989), 15–22; William E. Akin, "William A. Hulbert," in *Nineteenth Century Stars*, ed. Robert L. Tiemann and Mark Rucker (Phoenix: Society for American Baseball Research, 2012), 135; David Ball and David Nemec, "Hulbert, William Ambrose/'Will' 'William,'" in *Major League Baseball Profiles, 1871–1900*, vol. 2, 35–36; Michael Haupert, "William Hulbert," SABR Baseball Biography Project, Society for American Baseball Research, accessed January 22, 2018, http://sabr.org/bioproj/person/d1d420b3. Hulbert's "lamp-post" quotation is from Spalding, *America's National Game*, 207–208 (according to an undated letter from Jim Hulbert to Chicago Cubs historian Art Ahrens, sent to the author by Ahrens, "My great grand uncle really said: 'I'd rather be a lamppost in Chicago than a streetcar in any other city'"). Hulbert's official positions in the White Stockings are in "Base Ball," *CT*, July 23, 1872, 2; "The Chicago Club," *NYC*, December 12, 1874, 290 (mentions correspondence, contracts, and Hulbert as "efficient secretary"); "Bats Are Trumps," *(Chicago) Inter Ocean*, July 31, 1876, 8; "William A. Hulbert, President of the Chicago Base-Ball Club and of the National League," *CDT*, April 11, 1882, 6; Melville, *Early Baseball and the Rise of the National League*, 77.

24. Game logs are in http://www.retrosheet.org/. "The St. Louis men" quotation is from "Sporting News," *CDT*, September 8, 1875, 5. On May 11, the White Stockings' win over the St. Louis Reds featured the sport's first 1–0 game. See "Chicago vs. St. Louis Reds," *NYC*, May 22, 1875, 58. The Philadelphia Pearls beat Chicago, 4–0, on July 28 in professional baseball's first no-hitter. See "Sporting News," *CDT*, July 29, 1875, 5; "Philadelphia vs. Chicago," *NYC*, August 7, 1875, 147; Casey Tibbitts, "The First Professional No-Hitter," in *Inventing Baseball: The 100 Greatest Games of the 19th Century*, ed. Bill Felber (Phoenix: Society for American Baseball Research, 2013), 95–96.

25. "The most brilliant contest" quotation is from "Whitewash," *CDT*, June 20, 1875, 14. "For the first time" quotation is from "The Championship Record," *NYC*, June 26, 1875, 98. The June 19 game, a mention of the May 11 game, pitchers' mastery of the curve ball, and baseball's low scores are in David Arcidiacono, "The 'Model' Game," in Felber, *Inventing Baseball*, 93: "For years baseball games had been dominated by offense. From 1871–74 the average number of runs in a National Association game was 19. Double-digit scores were common. The 1875 season was different. That year the league batting average plunged nearly 20 points from the previous season and total runs per game were down to 12." Game logs and team standings are in http://www.retrosheet.org/. Boston's record from 1871 to 1875 included seven tie games.

26. According to the July 3 minutes, Spalding initially wrote the association "offering his services as 'Manager'" of the team. Hulbert "was instructed to visit Boston, and confirm the best arrangement possible with Mr Spalding, and also to engage such players for the season of 1876" as both men saw fit. See Minutes of July 3, 1875, meeting of directors of the Chicago Base Ball Association, record book of the Board of Directors of the Chicago Base Ball Association, Chicago Cubs Records, box 4, volume 4, Chicago History Museum. See also Names, *Bury My Heart at Wrigley Field*, 111–12.

27. Hulbert acquiring Boston and Philadelphia players is also in Spalding, *America's National Game*, 201–203 (keeping it a secret is on p. 203); Peter Levine, *A. G. Spalding and the Rise of Baseball: The Promise of American Sport* (New York: Oxford University Press, 1985), 21–23; Neil W. MacDonald, *The League That Lasted: 1876 and the Founding of the National League of Professional Base Ball Clubs* (Jefferson, NC: McFarland, 2004), 12–20; Names, *Bury My Heart at Wrigley Field*, 108–17; Ryczek, *Blackguards and Red Stockings*, 216–18; Schiff, *"The Father of Baseball,"* 139–43; Pietrusza, *Major Leagues*, 25–27. Spalding's administrative positions with the White Stockings and the Chicago Base Ball Association are also mentioned in "Sporting News," *CDT*, November 28, 1875, 13. Sutton remaining with the Athletics is in Seymour, *Baseball: The Early Years*, 78. The *Tribune*'s coverage of the player signings is in "Base-Ball," *CDT*, July 20, 1875, 5; "Base Ball," *CDT*, July 24, 1875, 2 (includes "to say that" quotation). For references to the "Big Four," see Anson, *A Ball Player's Career*, 94, 95. Jimmy Wood, former captain of the White Stockings, reminisces about Anson in "Chats with the Ball Men," *TSN*, May 7, 1887, 5.

28. Deacon White's quotations are from "Sporting Notes," *Boston Daily Globe*, July 27, 1875, 8. References to "seceders" are in "The Seceding Players—How They Came to Secede," *Boston Daily Globe*, July 28, 1875, 8; "The Boston Seceders," *NYC*, July 31, 1875, 139; "The Professional Arena," *Forest and Stream*, August 5, 1875, 409. The *Forest and Stream* quotation is from "Rational Pastimes," *Forest and Stream*, July 29, 1875, 393. The untitled *New York Clipper* editorial is in *NYC*, August 7, 1875, 146. The *Clipper* declared that "Boston is very indignant at Chicago, and threatens to train up a new nine that shall make it warmer for Chicago than the big fire made it."

29. Biographical material on Spalding is in "A. G. Spalding, Pitcher and Manager," *NYC*, November 22,

1879, 277; Levine, *A. G. Spalding and the Rise of Baseball*; Arthur Bartlett, *Baseball and Mr. Spalding: The History and Romance of Baseball* (New York: Farrar, Straus and Young, 1951); William E. McMahon, "Albert Goodwill Spalding," in *Baseball's First Stars*, ed. Frederick Ivor-Campbell and others (Cleveland: Society for American Baseball Research, 1996), 154–55; David Ball and David Nemec, "Spalding, Albert Goodwill/'Al,'" in *Major League Baseball Profiles, 1871–1900*, vol. 2, 64–66; Bill McMahon, "Al Spalding," SABR Baseball Biography Project, Society for American Baseball Research, accessed January 19, 2018, http://sabr.org/bioproj/person/b99355e0; Spalding, *America's National Game*, 107–109, 116–18; 141–43; 511–14. Spalding's salary is in minutes of July 16, 1875, meeting of directors of the Chicago Base Ball Association, Chicago History Museum (see note 26); Names, *Bury My Heart at Wrigley Field*, 114.

30. Coverage of June 24 ball game is in "Base-Ball," *CDT*, June 25, 1875, 2. "There has been just" quotation is from "Base-Ball," *CDT*, June 26, 1875, 5. "There seems no good" quotation and Higham overthrowing second base are from "Sporting News," *CDT*, June 27, 1875, 14. "The recent revelations" quotation is from "The Turf," *CDT*, June 27, 1875, 14. Meeting of directors and decisions about Higham are in "Sporting News," *CDT*, June 29, 1875, 5. See also "Sporting," *CDT*, November 10, 1873, 3: "It is no longer a question whether honesty is the best policy in base-ball. It has been shown time and again that people will turn out to see a game between clubs that are known to be 'square,' and that, on the other hand, they will not go to see clubs play against whom there is a suspicion of dishonest playing." Game attendance and revenue are discussed in "Base Ball," *CDT*, November 21, 1875, 12.

31. Higham played in a July 3 game; see "Sporting," *CDT*, July 4, 1875, 13. "Gotten rid of" quotation is from "Sporting," *CDT*, November 7, 1875, 12. See also "Sporting News," *CDT*, November 11, 1875, 7. "The existing National" quotation is from "Rational Pastimes," *Forest and Stream*, February 17, 1876, 27. Rumors and "Western clique" quotation are from "Sporting News," *CDT*, October 3, 1875, 9 (periodicals at this time often referred to the Midwest as the West or Northwest); Melville, *Early Baseball and the Rise of the National League*, 76. Meacham's job as sportswriter is in "Obituary," *CDT*, October 3, 1878, 8. Hulbert's and Meacham's friendship is in O[liver] P. Caylor, "Men We Have Known," *SL*, February 10, 1886, 2; Names, *Bury My Heart at Wrigley Field*, 119–22; MacDonald, *The League That Lasted*, 4, 12, 15, 21–22; Schiff, *"The Father of Baseball,"* 139; Thorn, *Baseball in the Garden of Eden*, 160; Seymour, *Baseball: The Early Years*, 78, 89. Hulbert's obituary is "William A. Hulbert, President of the Chicago Base-Ball Club and of the National League," *CDT*, April 11, 1882, 6.

32. Additions in brackets are from Thorn, *Baseball in the Garden of Eden*, 160.

33. Baseball historian Tom Melville refers to the October 24, 1875, *Tribune* article as "something of a manifesto of the coming National League." See Melville, *Early Baseball and the Rise of the National League*, 78. Disbanded teams are in "The Professionals," *CDT*, June 20, 1875, 14; "The Championship Record," *NYC*, July 17, 1875, 123; Nemec, *The Great Encyclopedia of Nineteenth Century Major League Baseball*, 86. Game logs and player statistics are in http://www.retrosheet.org/. *Tribune* quotations are from "Sporting," *CDT*, October 31, 1875, 14. (The *Tribune*'s statistics are inaccurate. According to Retrosheet, base hits include: Barnes, 143 in 78 games; McVey, 138 in 82 games; and White, 136 in 80 games.) See also "Base Ball," *CDT*, November 21, 1875, 12; "The Base-Ball Championship," *NYT*, December 2, 1875, 8.

Chapter 4

1. Spalding quotations are from Albert G. Spalding, *America's National Game: Historic Facts Concerning the Beginning, Evolution, Development and Popularity of Base Ball* (1911; repr., Lincoln: University of Nebraska Press, 1992), 201, 213, 200. "Education and gentlemanly" quotation is from "The Baseball Tourists," *NYC*, July 25, 1874, 133. Baseball as a business is in "Games and Pastimes," *CDT*, February 13, 1876, 12; Spalding, *America's National Game*, 209; Robert Knight Barney and Frank Dallier, "'I'd Rather Be a Lamp Post in Chicago, Than a Millionaire in Any Other City': William A. Hulbert, Civic Pride, and the Birth of the National League," *NINE: A Journal of Baseball History and Social Policy Perspectives* 2 (Fall 1993): 45–47; Peter Levine, *A. G. Spalding and the Rise of Baseball: The Promise of American Sport* (New York: Oxford University Press, 1985), 21–27; Neil W. MacDonald, *The League That Lasted: 1876 and the Founding of the National League of Professional Base Ball Clubs* (Jefferson, NC: McFarland, 2004), 21–25. See also "The Boston Club in 1876," *NYC*, August 7, 1875, 147: "Hitherto Boston has somewhat 'monopolized things,' and it had come to be monotonous to hear of the Boston victories."

2. Ticket prices are in "Base-Ball," *NYT*, August 11, 1872, 8; "A Model Game of Base-Ball," *NYT*, May 28, 1871, 8; Tom Melville, *Early Baseball and the Rise of the National League* (Jefferson, NC: McFarland, 2001), 88–89 (a discussion of "Chicago's financial benefit to visiting clubs" is on p. 75). See also Richard Hershberger, "Chicago's Role in Early Professional Baseball," *Baseball Research Journal* 40 (Spring 2011): 11. June 8, 1875, game is in "Sporting News," *CDT*, June 9, 1875, 5 (attendance at this game was 5,509 according to http://www.retrosheet.org/).

3. Attendance at White Stockings games, "some financial figures," and division of gate receipts are in "Base Ball," *CDT*, November 21, 1875, 12. The clubs whose statistics the *Tribune* analyzed for 1874 and 1875 were the Philadelphia White Stockings, the Philadelphia Athletics, the New York Mutuals, the Hartford Dark Blues, the Boston Red Stockings, the Brooklyn Atlantics, the New Haven Elm Citys (1875), and the Baltimore Canaries (1874). The *Tribune* noted that St. Louis and Cincinnati were not included in the analysis because the newspaper wanted to compare Chicago with just eastern teams. The paper also stressed that the games with St. Louis and Cincinnati had been profitable ones. "It pays out there" quotation is from "Base-Ball Matters," *Spirit of the Times*, September 13, 1873, 115. See also "Base Ball," *CDT*, February 28, 1875, 10: "Chicago paid the highest prices for ball-tossers last year, and, notwithstanding the rent of their grounds costs them $2,400 a year, they came out at the end of last season with more in their treasury than all of the other professional clubs put together."

4. Meeting in Louisville, Kentucky, and "thorough and animated" quotation are from A. G. Spalding, "In

the Field Papers: Base-Ball," *Cosmopolitan: A Monthly Illustrated Magazine*, October 1889, 607. Meeting also in *Constitution and Playing Rules of the National League of Professional Base Ball Clubs: Official, 1876* (1876; repr., St. Louis: Horton Pub. Co., 1988), 23–24; *Spalding's Base Ball Guide and Official League Book for 1886* (1886; repr., St. Louis: Horton Pub. Co., 1987), 8–9 (mentions Meacham); Spalding, *America's National Game*, 209–10; Preston D. Orem, *Baseball (1845–1881): From the Newspaper Accounts* (Altadena, CA: Preston D. Orem, 1961), 243–44 (mentions Meacham). Hulbert's and Fowle's letter is from "Sporting Notes," *CDT*, February 7, 1876, 7. It also appeared in "The Proceedings at the Grand Central," *NYC*, February 12, 1876, 362. 12 m (meridiem) stands for noon.

5. "A forceful, magnetic" quotation is from Federal Writers' Project (Illinois), Work Project Administration, *Baseball in Old Chicago* (Chicago: A. C. McClurg, 1939), 29. Delegates at the New York meeting are in "The Proceedings at the Grand Central," *NYC*, February 12, 1876, 362; "Games and Pastimes," *CDT*, February 13, 1876, 12; Spalding, "In the Field Papers," 607 (includes "they entered into it" quotation). Constitution of the National League is in *Constitution and Playing Rules*, 6–24 ("except by unanimous" quotation is on p. 7 and "the emblem" quotation is on p. 20). Details about the New York meeting and the new league are also in "The Diamond Squared," *CDT*, February 4, 1876, 5; "Base-Ball," *NYT*, February 7, 1876, 2; "Sporting Notes," *CDT*, February 7, 1876, 7; "Baseball," *NYC*, February 12, 1876, 362; "Base-Ball," *NYT*, February 13, 1876, 2; *Spalding's Base Ball Guide and Official League Book for 1886*, 8–10; Harold Seymour, *Baseball: The Early Years* (New York: Oxford University Press, 1989), 78–85; David Quentin Voigt, *American Baseball*, vol. 1, *From Gentleman's Sport to the Commissioner System* (University Park: Pennsylvania State University Press, 1983), 63–66; John Thorn, *Baseball in the Garden of Eden: The Secret History of the Early Game* (New York: Simon & Schuster, 2011), 160–64; MacDonald, *The League That Lasted*, 52–58; Francis C. Richter, *Richter's History and Records of Base Ball: The American Nation's Chief Sport* (1914; repr., Jefferson, NC: McFarland, 2005), 49–54; Patrick Mallory, "The Game They All Played: Chicago Baseball, 1876–1906" (PhD diss., Loyola University Chicago, 2013), 36–43; Michael Haupert, "William Hulbert and the Birth of the National League," *Baseball Research Journal* 44 (Spring 2015): 83–92; "National League Plans Golden Jubilee Season," *WP*, February 2, 1925, 13 (article includes quotations from minutes of the league's first meeting).

6. "Effect of the formation" quotation is from "Games and Pastimes," *CDT*, February 13, 1876, 12. Hulbert working diligently is in most biographical works (see chapter 3, note 23). An article illustrating the decline of the National Association is "Games and Pastimes," *CDT*, March 5, 1876, 12. The presidency of the National League is in "The Proceedings at the Grand Central," *NYC*, February 12, 1876, 362; MacDonald, *The League That Lasted*, 56–57, 218; Seymour, *Baseball: The Early Years*, 84. A study of Bulkeley is David Krell, "Morgan Bulkeley: Founding Father or Figurehead?," *Base Ball: A Journal of the Early Game* 9 (2016): 45–52. A reference to the Chicago team and its "break up" of the Red Stockings is in "Rational Pastimes," *Forest and Stream*, July 29, 1875, 393. The *World*'s "the nine will contain" quotation is from "Sporting News," *CDT*, November 28, 1875, 13. "The Chicago Club is, individually" quotation is from "Out-Door Sports," *NYT*, January 30, 1876, 2. "Do their best" quotation is from "The Boston Club in 1876," *NYC*, August 7, 1875, 147.

7. Eight charter members of the National League are in *Constitution and Playing Rules*, 6–7; "Base-Ball," *NYT*, February 13, 1876, 2; "The Base-Ball League, *NYT*, March 23, 1876, 8. Players coming to Chicago and working out are in "Sports and Pastimes," *Chicago Post and Mail*, March 4, 1876, 4; "Games and Pastimes," *CDT*, March 5, 1876, 12. Information on the Chicago Athenaeum is in A. T. Andreas, *History of Chicago: From the Earliest Period to the Present Time*, vol. 3, *From the Fire of 1871 Until 1885* (Chicago: A. T. Andreas Co., 1886), 416–17. "A padded partition" quotation is from "Turf and Table," *Chicago Post and Mail*, March 18, 1876, 4. "Have now worked off" quotation is from "Sporting," *CDT*, March 19, 1876, 9.

8. "Handsomely embroidered" quotation is from "Sporting News," *CDT*, April 18, 1875, 15. Articles on new uniforms and caps include "Sports and Pastimes," *Chicago Post and Mail*, March 11, 1876, 4; "Games and Pastimes," *CDT*, March 12, 1876, 16 (includes "a collection of heads" quotation); "Sporting," *CDT*, March 19, 1876, 9; "The New Chicago Nine in the Field," *NYC*, April 29, 1876, 34 (notes that each man's cap "gives the spectator an impression that he is looking at a song-and-dance artist or a jockey. This, however, soon disappears as the ease in distinguishing the players by simply referring to the score-sheet becomes apparent"). The colors of the men's caps are in "Base-Ball," *CDT*, March 26, 1876, 5 (includes "it is fair to say" quotation); "Sporting News," *CDT*, April 21, 1876, 8; "Pastimes," *CDT*, April 23, 1876, 3; "Pastimes," *CDT*, April 22, 1877, 7.

9. Articles on the clubhouse include "Base-Ball," *CDT*, March 26, 1876, 5 (includes "the new move" quotation); "Pastimes," *CDT*, April 2, 1876, 5 (includes the "fine mansion" quotation); "Pastimes," *CDT*, April 9, 1876, 10 (mentions that the last three players to report for spring training arrived in Chicago "last week"); "The Club House," *Chicago Evening Journal*, May 11, 1876, 4 (mentions the various rooms in the clubhouse and that it opened on May 10); William Leonard, "When the 'Friendly Confines' Were at 23d and Dearborn," *CT Magazine*, April 4, 1976, 43. The ballpark needing attention is in "Sporting News," *CDT*, April 21, 1876, 8. A reporter writes in an interview with Al Spalding that "the grand stand will be raised and enlarged, and other improvements for the comfort of the spectators will soon be commenced.... There has been some talk of providing for carriages, and to do so a low fence will be run across one end, in the same manner as they do on the English cricket grounds." See "Sporting News," *CDT*, November 28, 1875, 13 (includes "you are perfectly" and "the Chicago nine consist" quotations). See also "Pastimes," *CDT*, October 1, 1876, 7: "For convenience of access and other merits the [23rd Street Grounds] has no equal in the city."

10. "Unkind weather" quotation is from "Pastimes," *CDT*, April 2, 1876, 5.

11. Tom Miller and George Bradley were catcher and pitcher respectively on the 1875 St. Louis Brown Stockings. Nat Hicks and Bobby Mathews were catcher and pitcher on the 1875 and 1876 New York Mutuals. John

Clapp and Dick McBride were catcher and pitcher on the Philadelphia Athletics from 1873 to 1875. See http://www.retrosheet.org/.

12. "Baseball," *NYC*, April 8, 1876, 13. This section of the article originally appeared as one long passage, and a few paragraph breaks have been added for ease of readability.

13. Anson's contract is in "Games and Pastimes," *CDT*, March 5, 1876, 12; Adrian C. Anson, *A Ball Player's Career, Being the Personal Experiences and Reminiscences of Adrian C. Anson* (1900; repr., Mattituck, NY: Amereon House, n.d.), 93–94; "Anson's Early Ball-Playing Days," *CDT*, May 3, 1897, 4. The wet grounds are in "Base-Ball," *CDT*, March 26, 1876, 5; "Pastimes," *CDT*, April 2, 1876, 5; "Pastimes," *CDT*, April 16, 1876, 6. April 20 game and "the grounds were found" quotation are from "Sporting News," *CDT*, April 21, 1876, 8. Coverage of April 22 game with Franklin club and quotations are from "Pastimes," *CDT*, April 23, 1876, 3.

14. Wood receiving an artificial leg is in "Base-Ball," *CDT*, April 4, 1875, 5. Wood as manager in 1875 is in "Sporting News," *CDT*, May 20, 1875, 5; "Sporting News," *CDT*, June 18, 1875, 2; Robert L. Tiemann, "James Leon Wood," in *Baseball's First Stars*, ed. Frederick Ivor-Campbell and others (Cleveland: Society for American Baseball Research, 1996), 174. "It is predicted" quotation is from "Pastimes," *CDT*, April 9, 1876, 10. Players taking advantage of Wood is in "Sporting: Pen and Ink Sketch of Capt. Jimmy Wood," *Chicago Republican*, January 27, 1871, 4. Warning rule is in *Constitution and Playing Rules*, 32; "Base-Ball," *NYT*, February 7, 1876, 2; "The Proceedings at the Grand Central," *NYC*, February 12, 1876, 362; "Games and Pastimes," *CDT*, February 13, 1876, 12; David Nemec, *The Great Encyclopedia of Nineteenth Century Major League Baseball*, 2nd ed. (Tuscaloosa: University of Alabama Press, 2006), 109. "The veteran Jimmy Wood" quotation is from "Pastimes," *CDT*, April 23, 1876, 3.

15. Home team providing game balls is in *Constitution and Playing Rules*, 25. "Be able to properly" quotation is from "Games and Pastimes," *CDT*, February 13, 1876, 12. Large amount of rubber is in John H. Gruber, "Unusual Baseball Games," *WP*, December 11, 1916, 4. "Hitting was an easy" quotation is from Peter Morris, *A Game of Inches: The Stories Behind the Innovations That Shaped Baseball*, rev. and exp. one-vol. ed. (Chicago: Ivan R. Dee, 2010), 28 ("insides" of the baseball is on pp. 275–76; high and low pitches and pitching distances are on pp. 20–21, 26–27, 72–75). Lively ball and dead ball are in Spalding, *America's National Game*, 223–25. "Not contain more" quotation is from *Constitution and Playing Rules*, 25 (see also pp. 4, 29, 32). Rubber content of a "dead" baseball are in display advertisements, *NYC*, April 22, 1876, 29; "Baseball," *NYC*, December 23, 1876, 307. Rubber strips inside baseballs are in Robert H. Schaefer, "The Legend of the Lively Ball," *Base Ball: A Journal of the Early Game* 3 (Fall 2009): 89. Teams using non-regulation baseballs are in "Sporting News," *CDT*, May 11, 1876, 8; William J. Ryczek, *When Johnny Came Sliding Home: The Post-Civil War Baseball Boom, 1865–1870* (Jefferson, NC: McFarland, 1998), 148. Pitchers completing 40 or more games and the use of the dead ball (with a "solid rubber center") are in Arthur R. Ahrens, "The Chicago National League Champions of 1876," *Baseball Research Journal* 11 (1982): 85–86. Complete games are also in http://www.baseball-reference.com/ and http://www.retrosheet.org/ (Al Spalding pitched 53 complete games and won 47 in 1876). See also John H. Gruber, "Development of the Playing Rules," *Sporting Life*, November 20, 1915, 2. Publication of the 1876 playing rules is in "Sporting News," *CDT*, February 27, 1876, 9; "Sporting," *CDT*, March 19, 1876, 9.

16. Balls, strikes, and umpires are in Morris, *A Game of Inches*, 17–22, 56–58; Ahrens, "The Chicago National League Champions of 1876," 85; *Constitution and Playing Rules*, 30–34; David L. Fleitz, *Cap Anson: The Grand Old Man of Baseball* (Jefferson, NC: McFarland, 2005), 20; Nemec, *The Great Encyclopedia of Nineteenth Century Major League Baseball*, 11–12, 109 (includes "to make a batter" quotation); Bill James, *The New Bill James Historical Baseball Abstract* (New York: Free Press, 2001), 9. High scores are in Warren Goldstein, *Playing for Keeps: A History of Early Baseball*, 20th anniversary ed. (Ithaca: Cornell University Press, 2009), 13–14. Ross Barnes is in Tim Murnan[e], "Then and Now," *Sporting Life*, March 24, 1886, 5; Frank V. Phelps, "Roscoe Conkling Barnes (Ross)," in *Nineteenth Century Stars*, ed. Robert L. Tiemann and Mark Rucker (Phoenix: Society for American Baseball Research, 2012), 19–20; Glenn Dickey, *The History of National League Baseball Since 1876* (New York: Stein and Day, 1979), 8; http://www.retrosheet.org/; http://www.baseball-reference.com/. See also chapter 6, note 10.

17. The White Stockings leaving for Louisville is in "Pastimes," *CDT*, April 23, 1876, 3. The western teams included Chicago, Cincinnati, St. Louis, and Louisville. "The first of the Centennial" quotation is from "The Louisvilles," *CDT*, April 16, 1876, 6. Alexander Graham Bell is in Charlotte Gray, *Reluctant Genius: Alexander Graham Bell and the Passion for Invention* (New York: Arcade Publishing, 2006), 121–22, 130–39. The first shutout of the season is verified in http://www.retrosheet.org/.

18. "First tally," "deeply chagrined," and "wait till Thursday" quotations are from "Sporting News," *CDT*, April 26, 1876, 1, 2. The White Stockings' 10–0 victory is in "Sporting News," *CDT*, April 28, 1876, 5. The two Cincinnati losses are in "Pastimes," *CDT*, April 30, 1876, 8; "Sporting News," *CDT*, May 3, 1876, 5 (includes "made the finest hit" quotation). First home run is in John Snyder, *Cubs Journal: Year by Year and Day by Day with the Chicago Cubs Since 1876* (Cincinnati: Clerisy Press, 2008), 13. "Was less worthy" quotation is from "News Items," *Chicago Evening Journal*, May 3, 1876, 1. "The White Stockings" quotation is from an untitled article on p. 1 of this issue of the *Evening Journal*.

19. Cal McVey's sick child and May 5 game are in "Sporting News," *CDT*, May 6, 1876, 2. McVey's absence is also in "Sporting News," *CDT*, May 3, 1876, 5. McVey married his wife, Abbey, in 1874. See Don Doxsie, *Iowa Baseball Greats: Sixteen Major Leaguers Who Were in the Game for Life* (Jefferson, NC: McFarland, 2015), 14. The quotations from the St. Louis newspapers are from "Pastimes," *CDT*, May 7, 1876, 7.

20. Chicago defeating St. Louis, 3–2, is in "Sporting News," *CDT*, May 9, 1876, 7. "Bringing with them" and "there will undoubtedly be" quotations are from "Sporting," *CDT*, May 10, 1876, 7. "Putty ball" and "simply gave" quotations are from "Sporting News," *CDT*, May 6, 1876, 2. Louis H. Mahn of Jamaica Plain is in Schaefer, "The

Legend of the Lively Ball," 90. Advertisements for Mahn's baseballs are in *NYC*, April 22, 1876, 29; *NYC*, May 20, 1876, 61. Double cover baseball is in Paul Dickson, *The Dickson Baseball Dictionary*, 3rd ed. (New York: Norton, 2009), 266. "It looks as if" quotation is from "Sporting News," *CDT*, May 11, 1876, 8.

21. "Anson at third" quotation is from "Whitewashed," *Chicago Evening Journal*, May 11, 1876, 4. "Spalding's pitching" quotation is from "Chicago vs. Cincinnati," *NYC*, May 20, 1876, 61. "The notable feature" quotation, in reference to an April 20 game, is from "The New Chicago Nine in the Field," *NYC*, April 29, 1876, 34. Chicago's second win against Cincinnati is in "Sporting News," *CDT*, May 12, 1876, 8. Chicago's two wins against Louisville are in "Pastimes," *CDT*, May 14, 1876, 7; "Chicago vs. Louisville," *NYC*, May 27, 1876, 69. "Goose-egged Chicago" quotation is from "Pastimes," *CDT*, May 7, 1876, 7. Chicago's loss to St. Louis and 8,000 in attendance are in "Four to One," *CDT*, May 20, 1876, 5. Standings of teams are in http://www.retrosheet.org/. Eastern trip and "nerve, work, running," "with an excellent record," and "this week will tell" quotations are from "Pastimes," *CDT*, May 21, 1876, 1.

22. Western teams traveling to the East and the excellent records of Chicago and Hartford are in "West vs. East," *NYC*, May 27, 1876, 67. *New York Clipper* quotations are from "The Professional Campaign," *NYC*, May 20, 1876, 59. Standings of teams are in http://www.retrosheet.org/. "The four Western" quotation is from an untitled editorial, *CDT*, May 28, 1876. 4.

23. Adrian Anson quotations are from Anson, *A Ball Player's Career*, 94–95, 96. Anson's book was ghostwritten by Chicago writer Richard Cary. See "Baseball Gossip," *St. Louis Post-Dispatch*, April 24, 1900, 6. The Boston team is now known as the Atlanta Braves. It and today's Chicago Cubs are the only two National League franchises that have operated continuously since 1876. "Boston had prepared" quotation is from Orem, *Baseball (1845–1881)*, 253–54. *Tribune* quotations about Boston game are from "Pastimes," *CDT*, May 31, 1876, 8. Chicago's third game against the Mutuals and the Whites returning home are in "Pastimes," *CDT*, June 18, 1876, 7; "Sporting," *CDT*, June 20, 1876, 5. Games won and lost and standings of teams are in http://www.retrosheet.org/.

24. "Judging of the new" quotation is from "Chicago vs. Mutual," *NYC*, June 24, 1876, 99. Historical facts for 1876 are in Arthur M. Schlesinger Jr., *The Almanac of American History* (New York: G. P. Putnam's Sons, 1983), 331–33. "Was ushered in" quotation is from "Chicago," *CDT*, July 5, 1876, 2.

25. "Pitched with a degree" quotation is from "Baseball," *NYC*, January 9, 1875, 322. "It is rather curious" quotation is from "Sporting," *CDT*, July 7, 1876, 8. The White Stockings' 9–3 victory is in "Pastimes," *CDT*, July 9, 1876, 7. July games are in "Pastimes," *CDT*, July 23, 1876, 7; "Base-Ball," *CDT*, July 26, 1876, 5; "Base-Ball," *CDT*, July 28, 1876, 5. See also Snyder, *Cubs Journal*, 14–15. Games won and lost and standings of teams are in http://www.retrosheet.org/.

26. "This may be" quotation is from "Next Year's Engagements," *CDT*, July 30, 1876, 3. Names of board members and "the affairs of the old" quotation are from "Field and Turf," *CDT*, March 18, 1877, 7. See also Orem, *Baseball (1845–1881)*, 258–59; Larry Names, *Bury My Heart at Wrigley Field: The History of the Chicago Cubs* (Neshkoro: Angel Press of Wisconsin, 1996), 139–42.

27. "To ascertain what" quotation is from "Gambols on the Green," *Chicago Times*, August 2, 1876, 2. Orem quotations are from Orem, *Baseball (1845–1881)*, 259. "Contains within" quotation is from "Field and Turf," *CDT*, March 18, 1877, 7. See also "Base Ball," *Chicago Evening Journal*, August 2, 1876, 4; "Sports and Pastimes," *Brooklyn (NY) Daily Eagle*, August 15, 1876, 3; Names, *Bury My Heart at Wrigley Field*, 140–42. September 17 *Tribune* quotations are from "Pastimes," *CDT*, September 17, 1876, 7. Road trip game logs are in http://www.retrosheet.org/.

28. Games won and lost, standings of teams, and player statistics are in http://www.retrosheet.org/. See also http://www.baseball-almanac.com/; Marshall D. Wright, *Nineteenth Century Baseball: Year-by-Year Statistics for the Major League Teams, 1871 Through 1900* (Jefferson, NC: McFarland, 1996), 39–44; "Pastimes," *CDT*, October 29, 1876, 6. "To give Chicago" quotation is from Nemec, *The Great Encyclopedia of Nineteenth Century Major League Baseball*, 114. "At last Chicago" quotation is from "Base Ball," *Chicago Evening Journal*, September 28, 1876, 2. "For a number" quotation is from "The Deciding Game," *Chicago Evening Journal*, September 27, 1876, 4. See also "Greeting the Champions," *CDT*, September 22, 1876, 2; "Pastimes," *CDT*, September 27, 1876, 5; "Pastimes," *CDT*, September 28, 1876, 5; "The League Championship," *NYC*, October 7, 1876, 219. Chicago in 1876 drew the highest attendance among the league teams with 65,441 spectators at the 23rd Street Grounds (Boston was second with 51,000). See Robert L. Tiemann, "Major League Attendance," in *Total Baseball: The Official Encyclopedia of Major League Baseball*, 7th ed., ed. John Thorn and others (Kingston, NY: Total Sports Publishing, 2001), 74.

29. The club's road schedule and "They take with them" quotation are from "The Champions Take Another Game," *Chicago Evening Journal*, September 28, 1876, 4. Chicago's playing in Minnesota and Milwaukee is in "Pastimes," *CDT*, October 15, 1876, 7. Mention of Deacon White, the club's return to Chicago, and *Tribune* quotations are from "The Last Game of the Season," *CDT*, October 22, 1876, 6. See also "The Campaign of 1876," *NYC*, October 28, 1876, 245.

Chapter 5

1. White Stockings returning to Chicago and Spalding's business are in "Sporting Matters," *CDT*, October 24, 1876, 5. "To open a large" quotation is from "Spalding's Opinion of the League," *CDT*, February 13, 1876, 12. The March opening of Spalding's business is in "Sports and Pastimes," *Chicago Post and Mail*, February 19, 1876, 4; "Sports and Pastimes," *Chicago Post and Mail*, March 4, 1876, 4; "Games and Pastimes," *CDT*, March 5, 1876, 12; "City Items," *Chicago Post and Mail*, March 8, 1876, 4; "Sports and Pastimes," *Chicago Post and Mail*, March 11, 1876, 4; "Games and Pastimes," *CDT*, March 12, 1876, 16; Peter Levine, *A. G. Spalding and the Rise of Baseball: The Promise of American Sport* (New York: Oxford University Press, 1985), 71–73. Advertisements for Spalding's store are in the *Chicago Post and Mail*, March 8, 1876, 1; *NYC*, April 8, 1876, 13; *CDT*, April 30, 1876, 1 (the *Clipper* spells "baseball" as one word in "Western Baseball Emporium" while the *Tribune* spells it as two

words). A description of Spalding's store is in "Pastime Notes," *CDT*, April 15, 1877, 7. See also "A. G. Spalding, Pitcher and Manager," *NYC*, November 22, 1879, 277; "Sporting Goods," *CDT*, January 1, 1883, 19.

2. *Clipper* advertisement is in "Sporting," *NYC*, April 8, 1876, 13 ("announce to the" quotation is from "Baseball Notes" on p. 10). "With great pleasure" quotation is from "Pastimes," *CDT*, September 17, 1876, 7. Bradley joining the White Stockings and "superseded" quotation is from "Pastimes," *CDT*, October 22, 1876, 6. Bradley's ERA is in http://www.retrosheet.org/. "New school of pitchers" quotation is from "Baseball," *NYC*, November 4, 1876, 253 (article mentioned in "Pastimes," *CDT*, November 5, 1876, 10). "The fact seems to be" quotation is from Arthur Bartlett, *Baseball and Mr. Spalding: The History and Romance of Baseball* (New York: Farrar, Straus and Young, 1951), 107. See also Levine, *A. G. Spalding*, 28–29 (mentions Spalding and Hulbert), 81 (mentions Louis Mahn).

3. Articles on the National League convention were published in *CDT*, December 7–10, 1876 (see especially "Pastimes," *CDT*, December 10, 1876, 7 [mentions Mahn ball and that Hulbert was "unanimously elected President"]). See also "The Base-Ball League," *NYT*, December 9, 1876, 1; "Rational Pastimes," *Forest and Stream*, December 14, 1876, 301; "Baseball," *NYC*, December 23, 1876, 307 (mentions Meacham). Reporter Lewis Meacham's baseball contributions are in "Obituary," *CDT*, October 3, 1878, 8; "Lewis Meacham," *CDT*, October 4, 1878, 3; "Lewis Meacham's Death," *NYC*, October 12, 1878, 227; "William A. Hulbert, President of the Chicago Base-Ball Club and of the National League," *CDT*, April 11, 1882, 6. New York Mutuals and Philadelphia Athletics are in convention articles and in "Pastimes," *CDT*, September 17, 1876, 7 (Athletics); "Pastimes," *CDT*, September 24, 1876, 3 (Mutuals); "Pastimes," *CDT*, October 22, 1876, 6; "Pastimes," *CDT*, December 3, 1876, 7 (both teams). Baseball rule about teams "forfeiting membership" in the National League "by failing or refusing to keep its engagements in regard to games with other clubs" is in *Constitution and Playing Rules of the National League of Professional Base Ball Clubs: Official, 1876* (1876; repr., St. Louis: Horton Pub. Co., 1988), 12. Spalding quotations are from A. G. Spalding, "In the Field Papers: Base-Ball," *Cosmopolitan: A Monthly Illustrated Magazine*, October 1889, 608. Baseball used in 1877 is in convention articles and in Robert H. Schaefer, "The Legend of the Lively Ball," *Base Ball: A Journal of the Early Game* 3, no. 2 (Fall 2009): 90–91; *Constitution and Playing Rules of the National League of Professional Base Ball Clubs: Official, 1877* (1877; repr., St. Louis: Horton Pub. Co., 1988), 23. This booklet also contains accounts of the 1876 Cleveland convention (pp. 41–47).

4. Finley under contract is in "Base-Ball," *CDT*, April 8, 1877, 7. "The most prominent" and "the attendance" quotations are from "Pastimes," *CDT*, April 22, 1877, 7.

5. Game logs are in http://www.retrosheet.org/. "It is getting to be" and "this will at the same" quotations are from "Sporting Matters," *CDT*, May 18, 1877, 7. Meeting called to consider league schedule is in "Pastimes," *CDT*, April 22, 1877, 7. "Too soft" and "had overdone the matter" quotations and the calling of Indianapolis meeting are from "Sporting," *CDT*, May 17, 1877, 5. "The only other" quotation is from "Field and Turf," *CDT*, April 29, 1877, 7. May 10 game and lively ball is in "Sporting," *CDT*, May 11, 1877, 5. Hartford club playing in Brooklyn is in "Pastimes," *CDT*, March 4, 1877, 7. According to David Nemec, the Hartfords of Brooklyn were "a team that officially represented Hartford [Connecticut] but was listed by most newspapers as Brooklyn in the daily standings because it played its home games at Brooklyn's Union Grounds" to attract larger crowds. See David Nemec, *The Great Encyclopedia of Nineteenth Century Major League Baseball*, 2nd ed. (Tuscaloosa: University of Alabama Press, 2006), 128. The new baseball is also in "The Ball Brigands," *Chicago Times*, May 17, 1877, 2; "Meeting of the National Association," *Chicago Times*, May 18, 1877, 5; "The Championship Campaign," *NYC*, May 26, 1877, 66; "The League Ball," *NYC*, June 16, 1877, 91.

6. "I tell you" quotation is from "Sporting," *CDT*, May 19, 1877, 2 (mentions Barnes going home to Rockford and Harry Smith taking his place). Barnes's illness is also in "The Field and Turf," *CDT*, May 20, 1877, 7; "The Field and Turf," *CDT*, June 10, 1877, 7; "Base-Ball," *CDT*, July 22, 1877, 7; "All at It," *CDT*, August 8, 1877, 5. Barnes suffering from ague is in Robert H. Schaefer, "The Lost Art of Fair-Foul Hitting," *National Pastime* 20 (2000): 6. Barnes returned to the Chicago lineup on August 28. See "Base-Ball," *CDT*, August 29, 1877, 2. "The great hitters" quotation is from "Sporting News," *CDT*, June 1, 1877, 5. "Loose fielding" and "it excited" quotations are from "The Field and Turf," *CDT*, June 3, 1877, 7. Game logs are in http://www.retrosheet.org/. June 19 game-day quotations are from "Sporting," *CDT*, June 20, 1877, 5. An example of another sarcastic comment is in "Base-Ball," *CDT*, May 29, 1877, 5: "The 'Great Chicagos,' as they have been called, were to-day beaten by. . ."

7. Game logs are in http://www.retrosheet.org/. "The ill-luck" quotation is from "Miserable Muffers," *Chicago Times*, May 31, 1877, 6 (mentions McVey's hands that "were so badly battered by Bradley's swift pitching"). Barnes's illness hurting team and "had no such" quotation are from "Masterly Muffers," *Chicago Times*, June 20, 1877, 6. Injuries to players are in "Field and Turf," *CDT*, June 6, 1877, 2 (mentions "too many errors" in the game); "Uphill Work," *CDT*, July 17, 1877, 5. McVey not being able to hold Bradley's fast pitches is in "The Championship Campaign," *NYC*, May 26, 1877, 66; "Base-Ball," *Chicago Times*, May 27, 1877, 4. Bradley's pitching is in "A Rattled King-Pin," *Chicago Times*, May 25, 1877, 5; "A Bit of Fun," *Chicago Times*, June 3, 1877, 4. Errors are in "Base-Ball," *CDT*, May 13, 1877, 7 (mentions Bradley's lack of support); "The Field and Turf," *CDT*, June 3, 1877, 7; "Field and Turf," *CDT*, June 12, 1877, 5; "Base-Ball," *CDT*, June 16, 1877, 7; "Sporting," *CDT*, June 20, 1877, 5; "Business with the Bat," *Chicago Times*, June 29, 1877, 3. May 12 game, 22 errors, and "a great deal" quotation are in "Boston vs. Chicago," *NYC*, May 19, 1877, 59. See also game-day coverage in "Base-Ball Games," *NYT*, May 13, 1877, 7. "When the Chicago Club" quotation is from "Baseball," *NYC*, June 30, 1877, 109 (the lengthy quotation originally appeared as one long passage, and a paragraph break has been added for ease of readability). The "Chicago experiment" article the *Clipper* mentions is probably "The League Club Teams for 1877," *NYC*, April 7, 1877, 10: "The Chicagos will ascertain whether Bradley or Spalding can pitch best for McVey's catching." A change catcher is a relief or substitute catcher. See Paul Dickson, *The Dickson Baseball Dictionary*, 3rd ed. (New York: Norton, 2009), 175.

8. "Particularly unfortunate" quotation and Hallinan's injury are in "Out-Door Sports," *CDT*, June 22, 1877, 2 (Chicago lost to the Hartfords, 6–0). "Had been in the" quotation is from "Base-Ball," *CDT*, June 23, 1877, 2. Hallinan and Jones playing in the St. Louis game are in "Athletic Sports," *CDT*, June 27, 1877, 5. "Seemed to put" quotation is from "The Day of Retribution," *Chicago Times*, June 27, 1877, 3. See also "Business with the Bat," *Chicago Times*, June 29, 1877, 3: "Hallinan and Jones brace up the bruised and crushed-down weaklings very materially. They give them confidence as well as strength."

9. Cincinnati disbanding is in "Sporting News," *CDT*, June 19, 1877, 5. Jones playing in a second game is in "Field and Turf," *CDT*, June 29, 1877, 2. Jones and reorganized Cincinnati club are in "Base-Ball," *CDT*, July 1, 1877, 7; Jim Sumner, "Charles Wesley Jones," in *Nineteenth Century Stars*, ed. Robert L. Tiemann and Mark Rucker (Phoenix: Society for American Baseball Research, 2012), 140. Game logs are in http://www.retrosheet.org/. "The White Stockings introduced" quotation is from "Mr. Bunker's Boys," *Chicago Times*, July 17, 1877, 6. Hulbert's letter is in "Sport of the Period," *Chicago Times*, November 4, 1877, 10.

10. The *Chicago Daily Tribune* noted on the same day that the *Chicago Times* reprinted Hines's letter that Hines "now causes the letter to be printed, though what he expects to prove by it does not so clearly appear" ("Sporting," *CDT*, November 4, 1877, 7). Batting averages and game logs are in http://www.retrosheet.org/. "Fielding honors" quotation is from "Bat and Whip," *CDT*, August 3, 1877, 5. Ross Barnes's August game is in "Base-Ball," *CDT*, August 29, 1877, 2; "Chicago vs. Buffalo," *NYC*, September 8, 1877, 187 (includes box score). "The Barnes of 1876" quotation is from "Nearly a Walk-Over," *NYC*, September 15, 1877, 197 (mentions Chicago's lack of a "first-class catcher"). "A year of disaster" quotation is from Adrian C. Anson, *A Ball Player's Career, Being the Personal Experiences and Reminiscences of Adrian C. Anson* (1900; repr., Mattituck, NY: Amereon House, n.d.), 97. "It is useless" quotation is from an untitled editorial, *CDT*, October 7, 1877, 4. "A dismal and" quotation is from "Sporting," *CDT*, October 28, 1877, 7 (subtitle of article is "Some Reasons Why the Chicago Club Could Not Retain the Championship"). The lack of a competent catcher is also mentioned in "Base-Ball," *NYT*, September 5, 1877, 8. "For integrity of character" quotation is from "Baseball," *NYC*, November 17, 1877, 266. On December 4, 1877, the National League directors voted to forfeit Cincinnati's league membership due to non-payment of dues (see "Sporting," *CDT*, December 9, 1877, 7; "Baseball," *NYC*, December 15, 1877, 298). Most modern baseball works, however, include the Cincinnati club in 1877 league standings.

11. Mrs. Spalding sewing names on uniforms is in Harriet I. Spalding, *Reminiscences of Harriet I. Spalding* (East Orange, NJ: Spalding, 1910), 97. Spalding's retirement is in "Land and Winter Sports," *CDT*, August 19, 1877, 7; "Al Spalding," *CDT*, December 23, 1877. 3; "Next Year's Champions," *Chicago Times*, November 13, 1877, 3; Levine, *A. G. Spalding and the Rise of Baseball*, 28–29. See also Bartlett, *Baseball and Mr. Spalding*, 118–19: Spalding "told his son, Keith, years afterward: 'I knew that I was slipping before anybody else did, and that it was time for me to retire. When a batter hit a ball in my direction, I noticed that I had to move around to locate it, instead of just sticking out my hand and catching it.'" Barnes signing with the Tecumsehs is in "Sporting," *CDT*, December 9, 1877, 7. Player statistics are in http://www.retrosheet.org/. Fair-foul rule is in "Pastimes," *CDT*, December 10, 1876, 7; "Baseball," *NYC*, December 23, 1876, 307. See also Robert H. Schaefer, "The Lost Art of Fair-Foul Hitting," *National Pastime* 20 (2000): 3–7; Frank V. Phelps, "Roscoe Conkling Barnes (Ross)," in Tiemann and Rucker, *Nineteenth Century Stars*, 19–20. Before 1877, a ball hit into fair territory was counted as a fair ball, even if it rolled foul before it passed first or third base.

12. Bradley signing with the New Bedfords is in "Sporting," *CDT*, March 10, 1878, 7. McVey and White joining Cincinnati are in "Pastimes," *CDT*, August 10, 1877, 5 (McVey); "Sporting," *CDT*, November 18, 1877, 7 (White). Paul Hines playing for Providence is in "Sporting," *CDT*, February 10, 1878, 7; "Sporting News," *CDT*, July 3, 1878, 8. "Dropped down" quotation is from "Sporting," *CDT*, October 28, 1877, 7. Player records in http://www.retrosheet.org/ indicate that Hines's 1877 fielding average at second base was .788. Wood umpiring games is in "Pastimes," *CDT*, April 23, 1876, 3; "Sporting," *CDT*, April 21, 1878, 7. Wood's baseball tournament is in "The Field and Turf," *CDT*, September 9, 1877, 7; "Games and Pastimes," *CDT*, September 16, 1877, 7. William J. Ryczek and Peter Morris write in their excellent biographical sketch of Wood that he led a "busy and productive" life. After he left the White Stockings, he "embarked on a series of new ventures that included running a saloon in Chicago, supervising orange orchards in Florida and running minor-league ball clubs in the South.... By 1927 he was living in New Orleans when he decided to travel to San Francisco for cataract surgery. There were complications and one of the pioneer era's greatest players and captains died there on November 30, 1927, one day shy of his 85th birthday." See William J. Ryczek and Peter Morris, "Eckford Base Ball Club," in *Base Ball Founders: The Clubs, Players and Cities of the Northeast That Established the Game*, ed. Peter Morris and others (Jefferson, NC: McFarland, 2013), 184–85. In late 1884 the *New York Clipper* observed that Wood "has returned to Chicago after an absence of several years in Florida" (see "Baseball," *NYC*, November 8, 1884, 540). His running a liquor store in Chicago is in Tim Murnan[e], "Then and Now," *Sporting Life*, March 24, 1886, 5. A mention of Wood working at a Memphis ballpark is in "Base-Ball Notes," *CDT*, March 27, 1890, 6. The article states that "the veteran is still engaged in the laundry business in Memphis." In early 1891 Wood and retired Chicago ballplayer Ned Williamson purchased a saloon in Chicago (see Joe Murphy, "Chicago Gleanings," *SL*, March 7, 1891, 5). See also "Jimmie Wood," *TSN*, September 19, 1891, 1; chapter 4, note 14.

13. Concerns about the 1878 team are in "The Field and Turf," *CDT*, September 9, 1877, 7; "Nip and Tuck," *Chicago Times*, September 9, 1877, 3; "Games and Pastimes," *CDT*, October 21, 1877, 7. White Stockings making a profit in 1876 is in "The Financial Outlook," *CDT*, August 13, 1876, 3; Preston D. Orem, *Baseball (1845–1881): From the Newspaper Accounts* (Altadena, CA: Preston D. Orem, 1961), 264–65; Harold Seymour, *Baseball: The Early Years* (New York: Oxford University Press, 1989), 86. Clubs losing money in 1877 is in "Base Ball," *Chicago Times*, September 30, 1877, 9; "Sporting," *CDT*, October 28, 1877, 7; "The Coming Season," *NYC*,

January 26, 1878, 349; "Sporting," *CDT*, January 27, 1878, 7; Seymour, *Baseball*, 86.

14. New ballpark is in "Next Year's Champions," *Chicago Times*, November 13, 1877, 3; "Sporting Events," *CDT*, November 13, 1877, 5; "The Council," *CDT*, November 27, 1877, 5; "The Ordinance Originators," *Chicago Times*, November 27, 1877, 3; "The Lake-Front Ballpark," *CDT*, March 18, 1878, 8; Philip J. Lowry, *Green Cathedrals: The Ultimate Celebration of Major League and Negro League Ballparks* (New York: Walker, 2006), 48. A map showing the ballpark located south of Randolph Street and north of Madison Street (Washington Street between them) is in Joseph D. Kearney and Thomas W. Merrill, "Private Rights in Public Lands: The Chicago Lakefront, Montgomery Ward, and the Public Dedication Doctrine," *Northwestern University Law Review* 105, no. 4 (2011): 1457. "Very desirable ball-field" quotation is from "The White Stockings for 1878," *NYC*, November 24, 1877, 274. The park was north of the Interstate Industrial Exposition Building, Chicago's first convention center (now the site of the Art Institute). See also "Base-Ball and Other Sports," *NYT*, January 28, 1884, 8: "The Chicago Base-ball Club has the best grounds in the country. Its diamond is on the lake front, and but a few minutes' walk from the business portion of the city. The patrons do not have to travel to the suburbs to witness a game of base-ball, as is the case in almost every other large city. In consequence the games are largely attended."

15. According to Lowry's *Green Cathedrals*, p. 48, the foul lines were actually the "shortest ever" in the major leagues: "186 to left in 1883 and only 180 in 1884, 196 to right."

16. In 1871 the grandstand was in the northwest corner of the park. See "The Sporting World," *CT*, March 8, 1871, 4. The new grandstand's location in the southwest corner of the park, "the field lying to the northeast," is corroborated in "Base-Ball," *Chicago Times*, March 24, 1878, 2. See also Timothy J. Gilfoyle, in association with the Chicago History Museum, *Millennium Park: Creating a Chicago Landmark* (Chicago: University of Chicago Press, 2006), 14.

17. "The old grounds" quotation is from "A Field for Fun," *Chicago Times*, November 14, 1877, 2. Park's seating is in "Suburban Gossip," *Chicago Times*, March 24, 1878, 5. Dressing rooms, the ticket office, and "the field has been" quotation are in "Sporting," *CDT*, April 7, 1878, 7. Chicago Fire rubble is in Gilfoyle, *Millennium Park*, 12; Dennis H. Cremin, "Waterfront," in *The Encyclopedia of Chicago*, ed. James R. Grossman, Ann Durkin Keating, and Janice L. Reiff (Chicago: University of Chicago Press, 2004), 865; Kearney and Merrill, "Private Rights in Public Lands," 1431. See also Lowry, *Green Cathedrals*, 48: "Infield was bumpy and uneven, littered with stones, boulders, ashes, glass, and broken bottles."

18. Foul lines are in Lowry, *Green Cathedrals*, 48. Ground-rule double is in "Sporting," *CDT*, March 24, 1878, 7; "Chicago vs. Detroit," *NYC*, June 7, 1884, 181; John Snyder, *Cubs Journal: Year by Year and Day by Day with the Chicago Cubs Since 1876* (Cincinnati: Clerisy Press, 2008), 19. Balls over the left- and right-field fences counting as doubles occasionally appear in game accounts. For example, see "Sporting," *CDT*, May 22, 1878, 5; "Sporting," *CDT*, July 7, 1878, 7; "The Chicagos Defeated," *CDT*, July 20, 1879, 6; "Chicago vs. Cleveland," *CDT*, May 23, 1880, 12; "'One And,'" *Chicago Times*, September 3, 1880, 4; "Base-Ball," *CDT*, May 15, 1881, 8; "Base-Ball," *CDT*, May 6, 1883, 11; "Chicago vs. Detroit," *NYC*, May 12, 1883, 114. See also chapter 6, note 37.

19. For financial costs, see note 13. St. Louis, Hartford, and Louisville are in "Baseball," *NYC*, December 15, 1877, 298; "Sporting," *CDT*, December 9, 1877, 7; Nemec, *The Great Encyclopedia of Nineteenth Century Major League Baseball*, 128–33. Louisville is also in "Disgraced," *CDT*, October 31, 1877, 5; "Sporting," *CDT*, March 10, 1878, 7. National League clubs of 1878 and "if the Boston nine" quotation are in "Baseball," *NYC*, March 23, 1878, 413. Game logs and team standings are in http://www.retrosheet.org/.

20. April 20 game is in "The Fun Has Begun," *Chicago Times*, April 21, 1878, 9. Game logs are in http://www.retrosheet.org/. "It will easily" quotation is from "Sporting Events," *CDT*, September 28, 1878, 5.

21. Newspaper quotations about Bob Ferguson are from "Next Year's Champions," *Chicago Times*, November 13, 1877, 3; "Sporting Events," *CDT*, November 13, 1877, 5. Batting average is in http://www.retrosheet.org/. Ferguson's temper and demeanor are in "Base-Ball," *NYC*, February 15, 1873, 364; "The Players of 1873," *NYC*, March 14, 1874, 397; Anson, *A Ball Player's Career*, 100–101. Spalding quotation is from Albert G. Spalding, *America's National Game: Historic Facts Concerning the Beginning, Evolution, Development and Popularity of Base Ball* (1911; repr., Lincoln: University of Nebraska Press, 1992), 195–96. Ferguson and Hulbert are in "The Springfield Club," *NYC*, December 7, 1878, 290; "Baseball," *NYC*, April 12, 1879, 19. The White Stockings not signing Ferguson is in "Sporting," *CDT*, September 15, 1878, 7; "Base-Ball," *CDT*, November 3, 1878, 12.

22. Anson as player-captain is in "Base-Ball," *CDT*, October 13, 1878, 7. Anson's "Cap" nickname is in "Chicago Still on Top: 'Cap' Anson's Aggregation Steadily Holds Its Lead," *CDT*, May 17, 1891, 4; Ed Hartig, "Illustrious … Inclement … Infamous," Chicago Cubs *Vine Line*, April 2002, 46; Glenn Stout and Richard A. Johnson, *The Cubs: The Complete Story of Chicago Cubs Baseball* (Boston: Houghton Mifflin, 2007), 10. "The Chicagos of 1879" is from "Sporting," *CDT*, September 15, 1878, 7. Team rosters, statistics, and league standings are in http://www.retrosheet.org/. Indianapolis and Milwaukee clubs are in "Base-Ball," *CDT*, October 27, 1878, 12; "Sporting," *CDT*, December 5, 1878, 5. George Gore of New Bedford is in "Sporting," *CDT*, September 29, 1878, 7. Gore had asked Al Spalding for a salary of $2,500 but settled on $1,900. See Arch Ward, "Talking It Over," *CDT*, January 25, 1933, 19. Game on April afternoon is in "Base-Ball," *CDT*, April 20, 1879, 7 (includes "like a shot" quotation); "Speaking of Sport," *Chicago Times*, April 20, 1879, 7.

23. Teams are listed in "Base-Ball," *CDT*, March 9, 1879, 12. Game logs are in http://www.retrosheet.org/. Dubuque game is in "Base-Ball," *CDT*, August 5, 1879, 5. This article reports that Flint "had two joints of his fingers dislocated." Others note that he injured his thumb ("Cincinnati vs. Chicago," *CDT*, August 10, 1879, 7). "Billious fever" quotation is from "Baseball Notes," *NYC*, August 16, 1879, 163 (also mentions Flint's finger). "The Whites not only" quotation is from "Anson's Liver," *CDT*, August 17, 1879, 7. Other articles on Anson's sickness include "Providence Defeats Troy," *CDT*, August 14,

1879, 5 (mentions Flint's thumb); "Sporting Events," *CDT*, August 20, 1879, 5; "Capt. Anson," *CDT*, September 14, 1879, 7; "Sporting News," *CDT*, September 29, 1879, 8.

24. Articles that mention Anson's inability to play include "Sporting Events," *CDT*, August 8, 1879, 5; "Sporting Events," *CDT*, August 21, 1879, 5; "Capt. Anson," *CDT*, August 24, 1879, 7. Anson did take the field in an August 14 game. See "Sporting Events," *CDT*, August 15, 1879, 5. Remsen is in "Base-Ball," *CDT*, August 13, 1879, 5. Game logs, team standings, and player statistics are in http://www.retrosheet.org/. "It looks now" quotation is from "Sporting Events," *CDT*, August 20, 1879, 5. Anson going home to Marshalltown, Iowa, is in "Capt. Anson," *CDT*, August 31, 1879, 7; "Baseball Notes," *NYC*, September 13, 1879, 197. Silver Flint as new captain is in "Baseball Notes," *NYC*, September 6, 1879, 189. "Accidents and misfortunes" and "simply an addition" quotations are from "Base-Ball," *CDT*, September 28, 1879, 7. See also "The Season's Work," *CDT*, September 14, 1879, 7, which mentions Flint as the new captain and that "the misfortune of losing Anson … was like taking a leg from a race-horse." The article also observes that "Larkin had incapacitated himself for play by injudicious conduct." "Though the Chicago" quotation is from "Field Facts," *Chicago Times*, October 5, 1879, 4 (this article notes that the team "dropped from first to third place"). "Facile princeps" indicates that Anson was easily the best.

25. The White Stockings earning a profit in 1878 and having the largest attendance among league teams is in "Base-Ball," *CDT*, October 27, 1878, 12. See also "The Base Ball Season," *WP*, November 12, 1878, 3. Chicago making a profit in 1879 and having the largest attendance is in "Notes of the Game," *CDT*, October 5, 1879, 7; "Field Facts," *Chicago Times*, October 5, 1879, 4. See also Levine, *A. G. Spalding*, 36. Furthermore, Cubs historian Ed Hartig observes that "Spalding was not out to lose money! If he was [losing money], he would have bailed" (Ed Hartig, email message to author, February 27, 2015). Attendance figures are in Robert L. Tiemann, "Major League Attendance," in *Total Baseball: The Official Encyclopedia of Major League Baseball*, 7th ed., ed. John Thorn and others (Kingston, NY: Total Sports Publishing, 2001), 74. See also "Chicago Cubs Attendance Data," Baseball Almanac, accessed November 18, 2017, http://www.baseball-almanac.com/teams/cubsatte.shtml. Finances of league clubs are in "Notes of the Game," *CDT*, September 28, 1879, 7; "Sporting Events," *CDT*, September 30, 1879, 5; "The League Meeting," *NYC*, October 11, 1879, 229. Spalding baseball is in "Sporting," *CDT*, December 6, 1878, 5; "Baseball Notes," *NYC*, March 1, 1879, 386; "Notes of the Game," *CDT*, December 7, 1879, 16; "Later Baseball Notes," *NYC*, December 13, 1879, 298.

26. "Looking as hearty" quotation is from "Local Happenings," *CDT*, September 28, 1879, 7. White Stockings' California trip is in "Sporting News," *CDT*, September 11, 1879, 5; "The California Trip," *CDT*, September 28, 1879, 7; "Notes of the Game," *CDT*, October 5, 1879, 7; "Sporting News," *CDT*, October 27, 1879, 5; *CDT*, November 21–25, 1879; "The Cincinnati-Chicago-California Fiasco," *NYC*, December 27, 1879, 317. "On the field" quotation is from "Sporting," *CDT*, November 12, 1879, 6. Optimism for 1880 is in "The Season's Work," *CDT*, September 14, 1879, 7. "So far as the home" quotation is from "Base-Ball," *Chicago Times*, October 12, 1879, 2. "Supremely happy" quotation is from "Notes of the Game," *CDT*, December 14, 1879, 12.

Chapter 6

1. Heavy rain and baseball practice is in "Slight Sport," *Chicago Times*, April 4, 1880, 9. Exhibition games are in "Coming Games," *Chicago Times*, April 11, 1880, 2. "The Chicago team kept" quotation is from "Base Ball," *Chicago Evening Journal*, April 15, 1880, 4. "Review of" and "in the Chicago team" quotations are from "Base Ball," *Chicago Evening Journal*, April 22, 1880, 2.

2. Descriptions of Kelly are in "M. J. Kelly," *NYC*, February 26, 1887, 793; "'King' Kelly Dies of Pneumonia," *NYT*, November 9, 1894, 1; "'King' Kelly Is Dead," *WP*, November 9, 1894, 1; "None Equals 'King Kelly,'" *WP*, November 13, 1904, Sporting sec., 2; "Hub Happenings," *SL*, November 17, 1894, 2; "Popular Idols," *NYC*, December 12, 1896, 655; "Talk of 'King Kel,'" *CDT*, January 15, 1898, 7; "Stars of the Old Days," *WP*, December 24, 1905, Sporting sec., 2; "Mike Kelly Had It on Present Day Crop of Ball Players," *WP*, July 21, 1907, Sporting sec., 4; Marty Appel, *Slide, Kelly, Slide: The Wild Life and Times of Mike "King" Kelly, Baseball's First Superstar* (Lanham, MD: Scarecrow Press, 1999); Michael J. Kelly, *"Play Ball": Stories of the Diamond Field and Other Historical Writings about the 19th Century Hall of Famer*, McFarland Historical Baseball Library, 9 (1888; repr., Jefferson, NC: McFarland, 2006). "Was a good fielder" quotation is from Adrian C. Anson, *A Ball Player's Career, Being the Personal Experiences and Reminiscences of Adrian C. Anson* (1900; repr., Mattituck, NY: Amereon House, n.d.), 115–16.

3. Team roster and game logs are in http://www.retrosheet.org/. Reserved players on a team could not sign with other clubs, nor could clubs offer contracts to these players. Reserve rule is in "Baseball Notes," *NYC*, October 18, 1879, 237; "Baseball Notes," *NYC*, October 25, 1879, 243; "Sporting," *CDT*, January 18, 1880, 8; "The Five-Men Rule," *NYC*, October 23, 1880, 245; Albert G. Spalding, *America's National Game: Historic Facts Concerning the Beginning, Evolution, Development and Popularity of Base Ball* (1911; repr., Lincoln: University of Nebraska Press, 1992), 229; Anson, *A Ball Player's Career*, 104 (also mentions Anson alternating pitchers). Cap Anson's health is in "Pure Fun," *Chicago Times*, March 14, 1880, 12. Anson alternated pitchers during a May 20 game. See "Sporting Events," *CDT*, May 21, 1880, 9: "With commendable prudence Capt. Anson laid off Corcoran and put in Goldsmith to pitch, the change being in the highest degree successful." New players for 1880 team are in "Sporting News," *CDT*, October 2, 1879, 5; "Sporting Events," *CDT*, October 4, 1879, 5 (also mentions Anson's "reappearance after [his] illness"); "Base-Ball," *CDT*, October 17, 1879, 5; "Notes of the Game," *CDT*, October 19, 1879, 7. "One of the most" quotation is from "Reviewing the Season," *NYC*, November 29, 1879, 285. "He has wonderful" quotation is from "Larry Corcoran, Pitcher," *NYC*, September 13, 1879, 197. "With a corking hit" quotation is from "Base-Ball," *CDT*, May 2, 1880, 7.

4. Game logs are in http://www.retrosheet.org/. "It has proved itself" quotation is from "Base-Ball," *CDT*, May 23, 1880, 12. "The one special attraction" quotation is from "The League Championship," *NYC*, July 17, 1880, 130.

5. See chapter 1, note 36, for discussion of verb "Chicago." Game logs are in http://www.retrosheet.org/ (Corcoran's profile on the website notes that he was 5 feet, 3 inches tall and weighed 127 pounds). Chicago-Cleveland games are in "Base-Ball," *CDT*, July 11, 1880, 6; "'Chicagoed,'" *Chicago Times*, July 11, 1880, 4; "Sporting Events," *CDT*, July 14, 1880, 8. "For Providence now" quotation is from "Base-Ball," *CDT*, August 15, 1880, 12. "Double duty to attend to" quotation is from "The League Championship," *NYC*, July 31, 1880, 146 (see also "Baseball Notes" in same issue, p. 149). "The Chicagos administered" quotation is from "Bootless Bean-Eaters," *Chicago Times*, August 20, 1880, 3. Larry Corcoran also pitched no-hitters on September 20, 1882 (against Worcester), and June 27, 1884 (against Providence). See "Chicago vs. Worcester," *NYC*, September 30, 1882, 450; "Base-Ball," *CDT*, June 28, 1884, 6.

6. "Some sharp showers" quotation is from "Sporting Events," *CDT*, August 20, 1880. Rain and doubleheader are in "'One And,'" *Chicago Times*, September 3, 1880, 4; "Sporting Events," *CDT*, September 3, 1880, 8. The *Times* noted that the doubleheader was necessary as Troy had to play Boston on September 4. Game logs are in http://www.retrosheet.org/. "The team has been handled" quotation is from "Sporting Events," *CDT*, September 16, 1880, 5.

7. "The Chicago team" quotation is from Anson, *A Ball Player's Career*, 104. Games won and lost, standings of teams, and player statistics are in http://www.retrosheet.org/. See also http://www.baseball-almanac.com/. "It will be seen" quotation is from "How They Won," *Chicago Times*, October 3, 1880, 4. Articles on the White Stockings winning the championship include "Around Town," *Chicago Evening Journal*, October 1, 1880, 4; "After the Ball," *Chicago Times*, October 1, 1880, 7; "The News," *Chicago Times*, October 1, 1880, 1; "Sporting Events," *CDT*, October 1, 1880, 8; "The League Championship," *NYC*, October 2, 1880, 218.

8. "Chicago is the only club" is from "How They Won," *Chicago Times*, October 3, 1880, 4. Chicago being the only club to turn a profit is also in Anson, *A Ball Player's Career*, 105. Cincinnati playing Sunday games and selling liquor is in "League Legislation," *CDT*, August 15, 1880, 12. National League's special meeting is in "Sporting Events," *CDT*, October 5, 1880, 3; "Sporting Events," *CDT*, October 7, 1880, 5; "After-Season Sport," *Chicago Times*, October 10, 1880, 15 (includes Cincinnati's financial problems and the "were unceremoniously kicked" quotation from the *Cincinnati Enquirer*); "The Rochester Meeting," *NYC*, October 16, 1880, 238. "Whereas, Mr. W. A. Hulbert" quotation is from "Base-Ball," *Chicago Times*, December 11, 1880, 7, and reprinted in *Spalding's Base Ball Guide and Official League Book for 1881* (1881; repr., St. Louis: Horton Pub. Co., 1988), 91–92 (the Cincinnati club forfeiting its membership is on p. 87 and Hulbert's "five" years of service is on p. 91). Morgan Bulkeley, not Hulbert, was the league's first president). For other details of the National League's annual meeting, see "The Base-Ball Players," *NYT*, December 9, 1880, 2; "Sporting Matters," *CDT*, December 9, 1880, 5; "Base-Ball," *CDT*, December 12, 1880, 13; "The League Convention," *NYC*, December 18, 1880, 309.

9. "It will be gratifying" quotation is from "Base-Ball," *CDT*, October 10, 1880, 7.

10. National League annual meeting and rules are in "The Base-Ball League," *Chicago Times*, December 10, 1880, 4; "The Base-Ball Players," *NYT*, December 10, 1880, 3; "Sporting Events," *CDT*, December 10, 1880, 6; *Spalding's Base Ball Guide and Official League Book for 1881*, 63, 71, 87–92. The 1879 rule change concerning called balls is in "Sporting," *CDT*, December 5, 1879, 6; "The Base Ball League," *WP*, December 6, 1879, 1. According to baseball historian Peter Morris, "The number of balls and strikes allowed changed frequently [during the 1880s] as rule makers sought the ideal balance between hitters and pitchers.... In 1889, three strikes and four balls were finally settled upon as the parameters for an at bat." See Peter Morris, *A Game of Inches: The Stories Behind the Innovations That Shaped Baseball*, rev. and exp. one-vol. ed. (Chicago: Ivan R. Dee, 2010), 19. See also "Baseball Rules Changed," *NYT*, November 15, 1887, 2; "To Improve the Batting," *NYT*, November 21, 1888, 2; chapter 4, note 16. Umpire's 1876 warning rule is in chapter 4, note 14.

11. "Hearty and sound" quotation is from "Base-Ball," *CDT*, March 27, 1881, 20. Four players arrived late. See "Base-Ball," *CDT*, April 3, 1881, 17.

12. Flint was a catcher, and beginning in 1881, pitchers stood fifty feet from home plate rather than forty-five feet.

13. Hugh Nicol's name was misspelled as "Nichols" in the original *Times* article.

14. Clubs often rented out their ballparks during the off-season or when their teams were playing away games. See "Amusements," *Chicago Republican*, April 29, 1871, 4; R. S. Dingess, "The Lake-Front Circus-Ground," *CDT*, February 14, 1880, 11; Steven A. Riess, *Touching Base: Professional Baseball and American Culture in the Progressive Era*, rev. ed. (Urbana: University of Illinois Press, 1999), 123: "Clubs rented their fields to promoters of other sporting events ... and to popular amusements like vaudeville and the circus." See also chapter 3, note 8.

15. Teams in National League are in "Base-Ball," *CDT*, January 2, 1881, 6; http://www.retrosheet.org/ (includes game logs). "Capt. Anson is a firm" quotation is from "Base-Ball," *CDT*, March 27, 1881, 20. Detroit taking Cincinnati's place is in "The League Convention," *NYC*, December 18, 1880, 309. *Boston Herald*'s "trickery," calling out players' names, and "should be blamed" quotation are from "Boston Foolishness," *CDT*, June 19, 1881, 10. "The umpire was giving" quotation is from "Chicago vs. Boston," *NYC*, May 28, 1881, 154. Hiding baseballs in the grass is from "Mark Baldwin Tells Things about Anse," *Brooklyn (NY) Daily Eagle*, July 16, 1916, Sporting sec., 5. See also "The Base Ball Conundrum," *(New York) Sun*, February 20, 1887, 7; "Baseball Chat," *Rock Island (IL) Argus*, November 23, 1904, 7.

16. Game logs and Gore's height and weight are in http://www.retrosheet.org/. Gore's speed is in "Baseball Notes," *NYC*, November 8, 1879, 261; "Gore Was Star Outfielder," *Chicago Eagle*, April 30, 1921, 2. "Full of action" quotation is from "Chicago vs. Providence," *CDT*, June 26, 1881, 16. See also "Base-Ball," *(Chicago) Times*, June 26, 1881, 12; "Chicago vs. Providence," *NYC*, July 2, 1881, 231; Jerry Grillo, "George Gore's Theft Spree," in *Inventing Baseball: The 100 Greatest Games of the 19th Century*, ed. Bill Felber (Phoenix: Society for American Baseball Research, 2013), 127–29. Gore reached base on three singles, a walk, and an error. Philadelphia Phillies

player Billy Hamilton stole seven bases in 1894. See "Two Games Are Lost," *WP*, September 1, 1894, 6.

17. Game logs, games won and lost, standings of teams, and player statistics are in http://www.retrosheet.org/. "The management made some" quotation and others from the *Times* are from "The Last Lost," *(Chicago) Times*, August 26, 1881, 4. In its game-day coverage, the *Tribune* wrote that the 12 persons who would be represented in the locket were the 12 "donors" of the nearly $200 for the gold watch chain: Cap Anson, Tom Burns, Larry Corcoran, Abner Dalrymple, Silver Flint, Fred Goldsmith, George Gore, Mike Kelly, Hugh Nicol, Joe Quest, Ned Williamson, and W. H. Finley, Hulbert's private secretary. See "Sporting Events," *CDT*, August 26, 1881, 6 (includes mention of a "big black dog"). Finley as Hulbert's secretary is in W. A. Hulbert "per Finley" to F[red] E. Goldsmith, 6 January 1882, Chicago Cubs Records, box 3, Chicago History Museum. Finley is also mentioned in "Gossip of the Game," *CDT*, May 21, 1882, 10. Hulbert's dog is in "Sporting Events," *CDT*, May 19, 1881, 8; "Sporting Events," *CDT*, May 21, 1881, 6; "Base-Ball," *CDT*, June 12, 1881, 16; "Base Ball," *(Chicago) Daily Inter Ocean*, August 26, 1881, 5. Articles on the White Stockings' championship include "Ball Bosses," *(Chicago) Times*, October 1, 1881, 7; "Sporting Events," *CDT*, October 1, 1881, 7.

18. "Superior play in the field" quotation is from "Baseball," *NYC*, October 8, 1881, 465. "Was a foregone conclusion" quotation is from "Sporting News," *CDT*, October 2, 1881, 10. "Not one of these players" quotation is from "Sporting Events," *CDT*, October 9, 1881, 10. See also "The League Meeting," *NYC*, October 8, 1881, 463. "And some, notably" quotation is from "Ball Bosses," *(Chicago) Times*, October 1, 1881, 7.

19. Cincinnati wanting to set its own rules is in "League Legislation," *CDT*, August 15, 1880, 12; "Base-Ball," *CDT*, October 31, 1880, 11. Ticket prices are in "Sporting," *CDT*, December 5, 1879, 6; "The League Rules," *NYC*, April 22, 1882, 75; "The Base-Ball Field," *NYT*, November 28, 1882, 2. The American Association is in "Sporting Events," *CDT*, November 2, 1881, 7 (mentions that "the price of admission to games will probably be put down to 25 cents"); "Sporting Events," *CDT*, November 3, 1881, 3; "Baseball," *NYC*, November 12, 1881, 556; "The American Association," *NYC*, March 18, 1882, 855. McKnight as Allegheny director is in David Ball and David Nemec, "McKnight, Harmar Denny/'Denny,'" in *Major League Baseball Profiles, 1871–1900*, vol. 2, comp. and ed. David Nemec (Lincoln: University of Nebraska Press, 2011), 172. "Speaking for myself" quotation is from W. A. Hulbert to H. D. McKnight, 29 November 1881, Chicago Cubs Records, box 3, Chicago History Museum.

20. "I tell you" and "more than a month" quotations are from W. A. Hulbert to H. D McKnight, 18 November 1881, Chicago Cubs Records, box 3, Chicago History Museum. "I am kept closely" quotation is from W. A. Hulbert to W. S. Appleton, 18 January 1882, Chicago Cubs Records, box 3, Chicago History Museum. Appleton, who helped organize the New York club, is in "Sporting Events," *CDT*, November 6, 1881, 7; "Chicago in Third Place," *CDT*, October 5, 1889, 6; Francis C. Richter, *Richter's History and Records of Base Ball: The American Nation's Chief Sport* (1914; repr., Jefferson, NC: McFarland, 2005), 401.

21. Hulbert's illness, death, and funeral are in "Obituary Notes," *NYT*, April 11, 1882, 5; "William A. Hulbert, President of the Chicago Base-Ball Club and of the National League," *CDT*, April 11, 1882, 6 (includes "he was feeling" and "great force of character" quotations); "The Last Run," *(Chicago) Times*, April 14, 1882, 5; "Death of the President of the League," *NYC*, April 15, 1882, 55; "The Funeral of President Hulbert," *NYC*, April 22, 1882, 73. Meeting of the Chicago Ball Club is in "Obituary," *CDT*, April 13, 1882, 8. Resolutions and tributes are in "Tender Tributes," *(Chicago) Times*, April 13, 1882, 7. "To those who were present" quotation, "provided for by equal" quotation, monument, and reprinted tributes and resolutions (including resolutions passed by the National League), are in *Spalding's Base Ball Guide and Official League Book for 1883* (1883; repr., St. Louis: Horton Pub. Co., 1988), 5–11, 97–99. The league meeting took place on December 6, 1882. Hulbert's monument is also in Robert Knight Barney and Frank Dallier, "'I'd Rather Be a Lamp Post in Chicago, Than a Millionaire in Any Other City': William A. Hulbert, Civic Pride, and the Birth of the National League," *NINE: A Journal of Baseball History and Social Policy Perspectives* 2 (Fall 1993): 53–54. See also "Base-Ball," *CDT*, December 7, 1882, 5; "The League Convention," *NYC*, December 16, 1882, 629.

22. Soden assuming presidency is in "Mr. Soden of the Bostons," *NYC*, April 22, 1882, 75: "Secretary [Nicholas] Young says: 'Mr. Soden is the right man as Mr. Hulbert's successor. He is a clear-headed and very able presiding officer, and of unquestioned integrity of character." See also "Base-Ball," *CDT*, September 23, 1882, 12. "The recent death" quotation is from "The Chicago Club," *NYC*, May 6, 1882, 107. New Chicago officers are also in Peter Levine, *A. G. Spalding and the Rise of Baseball: The Promise of American Sport* (New York: Oxford University Press, 1985), 29. After Hulbert's death, Spalding and White Stockings board member John R. Walsh were club majority stockholders. See "Sporting Gossip," *(Cincinnati) Sun*, November 22, 1885, 4; "Anson's Affairs," *Sporting Life*, January 4, 1902, 2; "Walsh Sells His Stock," *CDT*, May 21, 1902, 18. Abraham G. Mills was elected National League president in December 1882. See "Base-Ball," *CDT*, December 8, 1882, 3.

23. Game logs are in http://www.retrosheet.org/. Players wearing black crepe is in "Death of the President of the League," *NYC*, April 15, 1882, 55; "Sporting," *(Chicago) Times*, April 16, 1882, 13; "The Run Record," *(Chicago) Times*, May 2, 1882, 5. The wet April and "what the Chicagos need" quotation are from "Base-Ball," *CDT*, May 7, 1882, 7. "Chicago is virtually out" quotation is from "Base-Ball," *CDT*, June 18, 1882, 16. Chicago's first grand slam is in "Base-Ball Games," *CDT*, June 21, 1882, 8; "Home Influences," *(Chicago) Times*, June 21, 1882, 3; "Chicago vs. Worcester," *NYC*, July 1, 1882, 237; John Snyder, *Cubs Journal: Year by Year and Day by Day with the Chicago Cubs Since 1876* (Cincinnati: Clerisy Press, 2008), 32. "Frightful failure" quotation is from "The League Championship Games," *NYC*, July 29, 1882, 298. See also "Base-Ball Games," *CDT*, July 25, 1882, 7; "Dear Defeat," *(Chicago) Times*, July 25, 1882, 5.

24. Changes in players' positions and poor playing are in "Base-Ball Games," *CDT*, August 8, 1882, 3; "Base Ball," *CDT*, August 13, 1882, 7; "Base-Ball," *CDT*, August 23, 1882, 8; "Base-Ball Games, *CDT*, August 24, 1882, 8; "Base-Ball," *CDT*, September 3, 1882, 16 (includes "a sor-

rier case of fall-down" quotation). "The original champion team" quotation is from "Base-Ball Games," *CDT*, September 6, 1882, 7. "The Chicago Club once more" quotation is from "The League Championship," *NYC*, October 7, 1882, 466. See also "Base-Ball," *CDT*, October 1, 1882, 9; "The Championship," *(Chicago) Times*, October 1, 1882, "Supplement" sec., 8; "The Base-Ball Championships," *NYT*, October 2, 1882, 5; "The Chicago Base-Ball Club," *Harper's Weekly*, October 14, 1882, 646–47. Game logs, games won and lost, standings of teams, and player statistics are in http://www.retrosheet.org/.

25. Rivalry of two leagues is in "The League," *NYC*, September 30, 1882, 451. "Attended by a degree" quotation is from *Spalding's Base Ball Guide and Official League Book for 1883*, 31. The American Association's financial success is also in "The Base-Ball Champions," *NYT*, October 9, 1882, 5. The American Association's history is in David Nemec, *The Beer and Whisky League: The Illustrated History of the American Association—Baseball's Renegade Major League*, special rev. and expanded ed. (Guilford, CT: Lyons Press, 2004); David Pietrusza, *Major Leagues: The Formation, Sometimes Absorption, and Mostly Inevitable Demise of 18 Professional Baseball Organizations, 1871 to Present* (Jefferson, NC: McFarland, 2006), 61–79. Chicago and Cincinnati games are in "Base-Ball Games," *CDT*, October 7, 1882, 7; "Chicago 2, Cincinnati 0," *CDT*, October 8, 1882, 9; "Cincinnati vs. Chicago," *NYC*, October 14, 1882, 483; David Nemec, *The Great Encyclopedia of Nineteenth Century Major League Baseball*, 2nd ed. (Tuscaloosa: University of Alabama Press, 2006), 225; Edward Achorn, *The Summer of Beer and Whiskey: How Brewers, Barkeeps, Rowdies, Immigrants, and a Wild Pennant Fight Made Baseball America's Game* (New York: PublicAffairs, 2013), 36–37. "The first time" quotation is from Peter Golenbock, *Wrigleyville: A Magical History Tour of the Chicago Cubs* (New York: St. Martin's Press, 1996), 42. See also Jim Farmer, "The First Meeting of Champions," in *Inventing Baseball*, 147–48.

26. Game logs and team standings are in http://www.retrosheet.org/. "The reason given" quotation is from "The Late League Meeting," *NYC*, September 30, 1882, 448. See also "The League," *NYC*, September 30, 1882, 451; "National Base-Ball League," *NYT*, December 8, 1882, 2; "The League Convention," *NYC*, December 16, 1882, 629.

27. Chicago as a successful baseball city is in an editorial, *CDT*, September 29, 1882, 4; "Base-Ball and Other Sports," *NYT*, January 28, 1884, 8. The 1883 players are in "The Chicago Team of 1883," *CDT*, October 1, 1882, 9; "The Chicagos Re-engaged," *(Chicago) Times*, October 1, 1882, "Supplement" sec., 8; "Base-Ball," *CDT*, October 8, 1882, 9; "The Base-Ball Champions," *NYT*, October 9, 1882, 5. Reserve rule is in *Spalding's Base Ball Guide and Official League Book for 1883*, 59–60; "Base-Ball," *CDT*, February 18, 1883, 3; "Baseball," *NYC*, February 24, 1883, 790. Joe Quest is in "Base-Ball," *CDT*, March 25, 1883, 13. Hugh Nicol and Fred Pfeffer are in "The Coming Base-Ball Season," *NYT*, February 5, 1883, 8. Billy Sunday is in "Sporting," *CDT*, May 23, 1883, 6; "Notes and Comments," *SL*, August 29, 1888, 2. Game logs and team rosters are in http://www.retrosheet.org/.

28. "The most accessible" quotation is from Anson, *A Ball Player's Career*, 106. *Tribune* quotations are from "Base Ball," *CDT*, April 22, 1883, 7. New park is in "Base-ball," *NYC*, November 25, 1882, 583 (mentions fence and spectators); "The Chicago Base-Ball Park," *NYT*, April 22, 1883, 2; "Notes," *SL*, April 29, 1883, 4.

29. Chicago game attendance was 82,000 in 1881 and 125,452 in 1882, according to Robert L. Tiemann, "Major League Attendance," in *Total Baseball: The Official Encyclopedia of Major League Baseball*, 7th ed., ed. John Thorn and others (Kingston, NY: Total Sports Publishing, 2001), 74. The National League team with the second highest attendance was Detroit, with 53,720 in 1881 and 75,000 in 1882.

30. The band is briefly discussed in chapter 7, note 12.

31. Game logs and team standings are in http://www.retrosheet.org/. "A great many of them" quotation is from "Base-Ball," *CDT*, May 6, 1883, 11. "It is safe to say" quotation is from "Base-Ball," *CDT*, July 4, 1883, 7.

32. The Northwestern League was a minor-league baseball league with teams in the Northwest. See "Base-Ball," *CDT*, October 28, 1882, 8. Biographical information on Walker is in David W. Zang, *Fleet Walker's Divided Heart: The Life of Baseball's First Black Major Leaguer* (Lincoln: University of Nebraska Press, 1995); David Nemec and Peter Morris, "Walker, Moses Fleetwood/'Moses' 'Mose' 'Fleet,'" in *Major League Baseball Profiles, 1871–1900*, vol. 2, 347–48; Jerry Malloy, "Moses Fleetwood Walker," in *Nineteenth Century Stars*, ed. Robert L. Tiemann and Mark Rucker (Phoenix: Society for American Baseball Research, 2012), 272–73; John R. Husman, "Fleet Walker," SABR Baseball Biography Project, Society for American Baseball Research, accessed February 2, 2018, http://sabr.org/bioproj/person/9fc5f867. Anson and Walker is in John R. Husman, "Cap Anson vs. Fleet Walker," in *Inventing Baseball*, 149–51. Walker's prowess is mentioned in "On the Fly," *SL*, July 22, 1883, 7; "Manager McKee," *NYC*, July 21, 1883, 287; "Baseball," *NYC*, January 27, 1883, 728; Al Howell, "Al Howell's Toledo Tips," *SL*, August 30, 1913, 17, 19. The 1883 Toledo Blue Stockings are discussed in John R. Husman, *Baseball in Toledo* (Charleston, SC: Arcadia, 2003), 11.

33. Two nineteenth-century minstrel troupes were Haverly's United Mastodon Minstrels and Callender's Consolidated Colored Minstrels.

34. "Ball and Bat" (one of the subtitles is "Baby Anson and the Color Line"), *Toledo Daily Blade*, August 11, 1883, 3.

35. "The first time" quotation is from "The Browns' Strike," *SL*, September 21, 1887, 4. "Home nine felt proud" quotation is from "Base-Ball," *CDT*, August 11, 1883, 2. Before the start of the 1883 season, the Peoria, Illinois, baseball club unsuccessfully tried to ban African Americans (and Fleet Walker in particular) from the Northwestern League. See "Baseball," *NYC*, March 24, 1883, 7. For information on Cap Anson and segregation, see David L. Fleitz, *Cap Anson: The Grand Old Man of Baseball* (Jefferson, NC: McFarland, 2005), 111–14, 118–19, 152–54, 164–66, 186–87, 294–95; Achorn, *The Summer of Beer and Whiskey*, 151–67; Howard W. Rosenberg, *Cap Anson 4: Bigger Than Babe Ruth: Captain Anson of Chicago* ([Arlington, VA]: Tile Books, 2006), 423–46 ("Baby Anson" is on pp. 73–76 and nickname is also in Joe Murphy, "Baby Anson Slept," *TSN*, September 12, 1891, 1, and "News and Comment," *SL*, March 17, 1900, 7); Steve Andrews, "Making It Home: Cap Anson, Fleet

Walker, and the Romance of the National Pastime," in *Northsiders: Essays on the History and Culture of the Chicago Cubs*, ed. Gerald C. Wood and Andrew Hazucha (Jefferson, NC: McFarland, 2008), 69–85; Sol White, *Sol White's History of Colored Base Ball, with Other Documents on the Early Black Game, 1886-1936*, comp. Jerry Malloy (Lincoln: University of Nebraska Press, 1995), 76–77 (states that Anson had the power to keep black players out of baseball); Robert Peterson, *Only the Ball Was White* (Englewood Cliffs, NJ: Prentice-Hall, 1970), 29–30 (mentions that many baseball players shared Anson's views). Clarence Duval is in Anson, *A Ball Player's Career*, 148–50, 232; "Got a New Mascot," *CDT*, June 8, 1888, 7; "Our Ball Players," *Chicago Times*, June 8, 1888, 6 (mentions Duval's age as 14); "Nineteen to Two," *Chicago Times*, June 9, 1888, 3; "Midget Mascots," *Hot Springs (SD) Weekly Star*, July 22, 1892, 6; "Gossip of the Meeting," *Brooklyn (NY) Daily Eagle*, March 4, 1898, 4 (quotes the *St. Louis Globe-Democrat* as noting that the White Stockings regarded a mascot "as an omen of good luck" and that Anson firmly believed "in the ability of a mascot to down a hoodoo"); Larry G. Bowman, "Baseball Mascots in the Nineteenth Century," *National Pastime* 19 (1999): 107–110. "Anson was so hated" quotation is from Ed Hartig, email message to author, July 25, 2017. See also "The Color Line," *SL*, April 11, 1891, 6: "Probably in no other business in America is the color line so finely drawn as in base ball. An African who attempts to put on a uniform and go in among a lot of white players is taking his life in his hands."

36. Game logs and team standings are in http://www.retrosheet.org/. September 6 game, with major league record of 18 runs in the seventh inning, is in "Chicago Leads," *CDT*, September 7, 1883, 6; Arthur R. Ahrens, "Baseball's Biggest Inning," *Baseball Research Journal* 6 (1977) 59–62.

37. Statistics are in http://www.retrosheet.org/. New home run rule is in "Base-Ball," *CDT*, April 13, 1884, 11; "The National Game," *CDT*, May 30, 1884, 5; "Chicago vs. Detroit," *NYC*, June 7, 1884, 181. Balls over fences counting as home runs occasionally appear in game accounts. For example, see "Base-Ball," *CDT*, June 4, 1884, 7; "Base-Ball," *CDT*, July 1, 1884, 6; "New-York Wins at Last," *NYT*, October 4, 1885, 7. See also chapter 5, note 18. "Nothing to encourage" quotation is from "Sporting Events," *CDT*, May 18, 1884, 10. Poor weather, Flint, Burns, and "Neither [Larry] Corcoran" quotation are in "Sporting News," *CDT*, May 11, 1884, 11. Weather is also in "Base-Ball," *CDT*, April 20, 1884, 13. "It is a club" quotation is from "Sporting News," *CDT*, May 25, 1884, 14. Chicago's poor play is also mentioned in "New-York Defeats Chicago," *NYT*, July 9, 1884, 2; "Base-Ball," *CDT*, August 8, 1884, 7; "Base-Ball," *CDT*, August 13, 1884, 8. Anson's training regimen is in "Base-Ball," *CDT*, April 2, 1884, 3; "Base-Ball," *CDT*, April 6, 1884, 11.

38. "Marked improvement" quotation is from "Base-Ball," *CDT*, October 26, 1884, 8. Game logs, standings of teams, and player statistics are in http://www.retrosheet.org/. Buffalo was behind Chicago in home runs, with 39. May 30 home run is in "The National Game," *CDT*, May 31, 1884, 6. Chicago's home run record would stand until the 1927 New York Yankees hit 158. Chicago's home runs are in Snyder, *Cubs Journal*, 40; David Vincent, *Home Run: The Definitive History of Baseball's Ultimate Weapon* (Washington, DC: Potomac Books), 8–9, 66.

"Championship of the United States" quotation is from "The Baseball Field," *NYT*, October 24, 1884, 2. See also "Baseball," *NYC*, November 1, 1884, 523 (mentions "the United States championship").

39. New rule is in "Base-Ball," *CDT*, November 21, 1884, 2; "Sporting," *(Chicago) Times*, May 1, 1885, 5; "Sporting Affairs," *CDT*, May 9, 1885, 3. Lawsuit is in "The Lake Front," *CDT*, May 27, 1884, 8; "The Base-Ball Club," *CDT*, May 28, 1884, 8; "The Lake-Front," *CDT*, June 25, 1884, 11 (includes November 1 deadline); "The Lake-Front Sale," *CDT*, June 29, 1884, 4; untitled article, *NYC*, July 5, 1884, 245. "Absolutely desist" quotation is from "The Lake-Front," *CDT*, July 18, 1884, 8. An excellent summation of the legal situation is in Joseph D. Kearney and Thomas W. Merrill, "Private Rights in Public Lands: The Chicago Lakefront, Montgomery Ward, and the Public Dedication Doctrine," *Northwestern University Law Review* 105, no. 4 (2011): 1457–62. See also Lois Wille, *Forever Open, Clear, and Free: The Struggle for Chicago's Lakefront*, 2nd ed. (Chicago: University of Chicago Press, 1991). The new ballpark is in "Sporting Matters," *CDT*, February 24, 1885, 2; "Sporting," *CDT*, February 25, 1885, 6; "The Base-Ball Park," *(Chicago) Times*, March 1, 1885, 13. Spalding's confidence about the 1885 pennant is in "Base-Ball Notes," *(Chicago) Times*, March 11, 1885, 8; "Sporting," *CDT*, March 11, 1885, 6.

Chapter 7

1. Game logs and player statistics are in http://www.retrosheet.org/. Goldsmith is in "Sporting News," *CDT*, June 22, 1884, 11; "Base-Ball," *CDT*, July 9, 1884, 8; "Base-Ball," *CDT*, August 8, 1884, 7 (mentions that Corcoran was willing to pitch more games and that Goldsmith played for the American Association's Baltimore Orioles after he left Chicago). Clarkson joining team in August is in "Providence vs. Chicago," *NYC*, September 6, 1884, 393. "There is very little" quotation is from "Base-Ball," *CDT*, October 12, 1884, 15. High payroll is in "The Money in Baseball," *WP*, November 2, 1884, 6. "No pains or expense" and "taken all in all" quotations are from "Sporting," *CDT*, February 25, 1885, 6. "Some of these" quotation is from "Base-Ball," *CDT*, March 1, 1885, 3. A map of the park, showing the street boundaries, is in "The Chicago Club's Grounds," *NYC*, June 6, 1885, 179. See also "The Chicago Club," *NYC*, March 7, 1885, 813.

2. Spalding spent almost $30,000 on his new ballpark, with the brick wall costing $10,000. See "Completion of the Chicago Club's New Grounds," *CDT*, May 31, 1885, 17; "In the Baseball Field," *WP*, February 8, 1886, 2.

3. The park's seating capacity was 10,300, according to Philip J. Lowry, *Green Cathedrals: The Ultimate Celebration of Major League and Negro League Ballparks* (New York: Walker, 2006), 49.

4. Pool-selling was a form of wagering on the games. See David Pietrusza, *Major Leagues: The Formation, Sometimes Absorption, and Mostly Inevitable Demise of 18 Professional Baseball Organizations, 1871 to Present* (Jefferson, NC: McFarland, 2006), 33: "Pools" were not bets between two persons but instead "involved a third party who held the cash, and were formed in 'pool rooms' usually near the local park.... Prior to a game (actually days in advance), an auction was held, with bidding on the right to bet on favorite clubs. Then bids were made on the opposing nine. If the odds were not

favorable, bets could be withdrawn. The pool seller kept records of these transactions, paid the winners, tried to maintain a reputation for honesty and received a percentage of each bet."

5. Details of the ballpark are in Lowry, *Green Cathedrals*, 49 (notes foul lines); "The Chicago Club's Grounds," *NYC*, June 6, 1885, 179 (includes "on the roof" quotation); "The Chicago Club," *SL*, April 22, 1885, 4 (includes "beyond all question" quotation); "Completion of the Chicago Club's New Grounds," *CDT*, May 31, 1885, 17 (includes "not only will" quotation). Inaugural race meeting of the Chicago Bicycle Track Association is in "The Wheel," *CDT*, May 24, 1885, 11. Bicycle track is also in "Sporting News," *CDT*, April 17, 1885, 2; "The Wheel," *CDT*, May 3, 1885, 14.

6. National League season is in "Sporting Affairs," *CDT*, March 8, 1885, 14; "Base-Ball," *CDT*, April 26, 1885, 10. St. Louis and Cleveland clubs are in "Base-Ball," *CDT*, January 6, 1885, 5; "Base-Ball," *CDT*, January 11, 1885, 10; "Baseball," *NYC*, January 17, 1885, 700. In 1884 St. Louis was in the Union Association, a baseball league that lasted just one year. See "A New Association," *NYT*, September 13, 1883, 2; Francis C. Richter, "Two Big Wars Interrupted the Progress of the National Game," *SL*, March 14, 1908, 6; Pietrusza, *Major Leagues*, 80–98. Chicago in the South is in "Base-Ball Notes," *(Chicago) Times*, March 11, 1885, 8; "Sporting," *CDT*, March 11, 1885, 6 (includes "last year the club" quotation); "In General," *(Chicago) Times*, March 15, 1885, 3; "Base-Ball," *CDT*, March 29, 1885, 14. The "backward spring" is a reference to the cold and rainy weather. See, for example, "Base-Ball," *CDT*, April 20, 1884, 13.

7. "Both President Spalding" quotation is from "In General," *(Chicago) Times*, March 15, 1885, 3. Chicago beating Louisville is in "Opening of the Ball Season," *CDT*, April 3, 1885, 5. The Louisville team, the Colonels, is in http://www.retrosheet.org/. Pennant prediction is in "Base-Ball," *CDT*, April 26, 1885, 10. Cap Anson quotation and St. Louis game are in "Sporting News," *CDT*, April 30, 1885, 3.

8. Game logs are in http://www.retrosheet.org/. New uniforms are in "Sporting Affairs," *CDT*, March 15, 1885, 11. "The greatest excitement" is from "Sporting," *(Chicago) Times*, May 1, 1885, 5. See also "Sporting News," *CDT*, May 1, 1885, 3. "I never saw" quotation is from "Sporting News," *CDT*, May 5, 1885, 5.

9. Game logs and team standings are in http://www.retrosheet.org/. "The White Stockings are returning" quotation is from "The World of Sport," *CDT*, June 6, 1885, 6. "Scattered throughout," "immense audience," and "seemed to have" quotations are from "Sporting Affairs," *CDT*, June 7, 1885, 14. See also "Sporting," *(Chicago) Times*, June 7, 1885, 6 (notes that Gore hit two singles, not one). Corcoran injuring his arm and release from Chicago are in "Corcoran Signs with New York," *CDT*, July 19, 1885, 10; "Will Corcoran Play with the New Yorks?," *CDT*, July 21, 1885, 2; "Corcoran's Side of the Story," *CDT*, August 5, 1885, 6. Spalding signing McCormick and "just about at my" quotation are from "The Last Game at Home—McCormick to Pitch for the White Stockings," *CDT*, July 11, 1885, 3. Some sportswriters believed that Spalding was hesitant to obtain a pitcher earlier in the season because he had already spent thousands of dollars on the new ballpark. Spalding denied these reports. See "Notes and Comments," *SL*, July 15, 1885, 5; Remlap (the pen name of *SL* correspondent Harry Palmer, who spelled "Palmer" backwards), "From Chicago," *SL*, July 29, 1885, 4. See also "Sporting Affairs," *CDT*, June 22, 1885, 3; "Corcoran vs. the Chicago Club," *NYC*, August 1, 1885, 307; "Sporting Affairs," *CDT*, August 4, 1885, 3; "They Talk," *SL*, August 5, 1885, 1.

10. Game logs are in http://www.retrosheet.org/. McCormick's one-hitter is in "Sporting," *CDT*, August 1, 1885, 2; "Philadelphia vs. Chicago," *NYC*, August 8, 1885, 324. September 4 game is in "Sporting Affairs," *CDT*, September 5, 1885, 2. Clarkson's victory against Boston is in "Sporting Affairs," *CDT*, September 20, 1885, 10. "Every available foot" and "To [Jim] McCormick" quotations are from "We Win," *CDT*, September 30, 1885, 1. Three-base rule is in "Chicago Victorious," *WP*, September 30, 1885, 3; Games Played Sept. 29," *SL*, October 7, 1885, 4. "The question of" quotation is from "Games Played Sept. 30," *SL*, October 7, 1885, 4. "Have about made" quotation is from "Gotham Grieves," *(Chicago) Daily Inter Ocean*, October 1, 1885, 2. See also "New York Again Beaten," *CDT*, October 1, 1885, 3. New Yorkers conceding defeat is in "Didn't Affect the Result," *CDT*, September 30, 1885, 2. "Yesterday's game" quotation is from an untitled editorial, *NYT*, October 1, 1885, 4.

11. "They do not possess" quotation is from "We Win," *CDT*, September 30, 1885, 1. October 1 game is in "Will Fly the Flag," *(Chicago) Daily Inter Ocean*, October 2, 1885, 2; "A Bitter Dose," *CDT*, October 2, 1885, 3. Game logs are in http://www.retrosheet.org/.

12. Austin's First Regiment Band was a Chicago militia band, led and directed by Fred Austin. See "A New Band for Chicago," *Chicago Herald*, February 22, 1887, 2; Sandy R. Mazzola, "Bands, Early and Golden Age," in *The Encyclopedia of Chicago*, ed. James R. Grossman, Ann Durkin Keating, and Janice L. Reiff (Chicago: University of Chicago Press, 2004), 60.

13. Willie Hahn, a young Chicago boy, was the team's mascot. See "The Biggest Man in the Lot," *Chicago Herald*, October 4, 1885, 5 (notes Willie's age as six); "The Mascot Is on Hand," *CDT*, June 19, 1886, 1 (notes Willie's age as five); "Notes and Comments," *SL*, February 17, 1886, 5; "The National Game," *(New York) Sun*, April 18, 1887, 3; Adrian C. Anson, *A Ball Player's Career, Being the Personal Experiences and Reminiscences of Adrian C. Anson* (1900; repr., Mattituck, NY: Amereon House, n.d.), 134–35.

14. Game logs and team standings are in http://www.retrosheet.org/. October 3 game is in "Sporting Affairs," *CDT*, October 4, 1885, 11. Chicago winning the pennant is in "A Crowning Victory," *(Chicago) Daily Inter Ocean*, October 7, 1885, 3; "The Pennant Is Ours," *CDT*, October 7, 1885, 6; "The National League," *SL*, October 14, 1885, 4. *Chicago Daily News* report is in "Base Ball in Chicago," *WP*, October 7, 1885, 2 (mentions $100 bonuses). "Over 5,000 throughout" quotation is from "Moonshine," *SL*, October 21, 1885, 1. Temperance pledges are in "Base-Ball Notes," *CDT*, May 27, 1885, [3].

15. "United States championship" quotation is from "Baseball," *NYC*, November 1, 1884, 523. See also "The Baseball Field," *NYT*, October 24, 1884, 2; "American Association vs. National League," *NYC*, October 4, 1884, 464. Championship planned for 1885 is in "Gotham Grieves," *(Chicago) Daily Inter Ocean*, October 1, 1885, 2. Criticism of players is in "Sporting Affairs," *CDT*, October 11, 1885, 11 (includes "indifference and lack"

quotation); "Saturday's Games," *(Chicago) Daily Inter Ocean*, October 11, 1885, 5. "The Chicagos played" quotation is from "Sporting Events," *(Chicago) Daily Inter Ocean*, October 15, 1885, 5 (includes phrase "championship of the world"). Forfeiture of second game is in "Ended in a Row," *CDT*, October 16, 1885, 2. The decision not to count the second game is in "Chicago Badly Beaten by the St. Louis Browns," *CDT*, October 25, 1885, 11. The third, fourth, fifth, and sixth games were played on: October 16, won by St. Louis, 7–4; October 17, won by St. Louis, 3–2; October 22 and 23, each won by Chicago, 9–2. Game-day coverage is in Chicago's newspapers. See also Anson, *A Ball Player's Career*, 136; *Spalding's Base Ball Guide and Official League Book for 1886* (1886; repr., St. Louis: Horton Pub. Co., 1987), 66–67 (information is under the heading "The United States Championship"); Alfred H. Spink, *The National Game*, 2nd ed. (1911; repr., Carbondale: Southern Illinois University Press, 2000), 312–13.

16. Spalding's complaint is in "Sporting Affairs," *CDT*, October 26, 1885, 2. "The Chicago Club is much" quotation and teams disbanded are from "Exhibition Games," *SL*, November 4, 1885, 2. Series declared a draw and "ends all further" quotation are from "Chicago vs. St. Louis," *SL*, November 25, 1885, 4. See also Remlap (see note 9), "From Chicago," *SL*, November 11, 1885, 3; "Chicago vs. St. Louis," *NYC*, November 14, 1885, 555; Paul E. Doutrich, "Champions, Tantrums and Bad Umps: The 1885 'World Series,'" *Baseball Research Journal* 46, no. 2 (Fall 2017): 10–16.

17. "Miserable exhibition" quotation is from "Sporting Events," *CDT*, October 17, 1885, 2. Poor play of team is in "Other Sports," *(Chicago) Daily Inter Ocean*, October 24, 1885, 3; "Base Ball," *(Chicago) Daily Inter Ocean*, October 25, 1885, 5. Gore's suspension is in "Sporting Events," *(Chicago) Daily Inter Ocean*, October 16, 1885, 2; Remlap (see note 9), "From Chicago," *SL*, October 21, 1885, 1 (includes $500 contribution); "President Spalding on the New York Conference Committee and Other Matters," *CDT*, October 22, 1885, 7 (includes Spalding's denial about suspension); "Chicago News," *SL*, October 28, 1885, 4 (includes denial about suspension, statement about Gore's poor play, and "the games amount" quotation); "Sporting Affairs," *CDT*, October 29, 1885, 6. "Unquestionably, our boys" quotation is from "Sporting Affairs," *CDT*, October 26, 1885, 2 (includes $500 contribution). Spalding admitted that players made "fielding errors" during the season in "This Week's Joint Committee Meeting," *CDT*, October 14, 1885, 3. Each team receiving $500 is in "Chicago vs. St. Louis," *SL*, November 25, 1885, 4; *Spalding's Base Ball Guide and Official League Book for 1886*, 67.

18. "A great captain" quotation is from "A Great Captain Did It," *NYC*, October 10, 1885, 478. Games won and lost, standings of teams, and player statistics are in http://www.retrosheet.org/. See also "Bat and Sphere," *CDT*, October 13, 1885, 9. "Was the possessor" quotation is from Anson, *A Ball Player's Career*, 130. In the 1880s, pitchers were allowed to change their throwing techniques. See Bill Felber and Gary Gillette, "The Changing Game," in *Total Baseball: The Official Encyclopedia of Major League Baseball*, 7th ed., ed. John Thorn and others (Kingston, NY: Total Sports Publishing, 2001), 87: "The underhand delivery requirement gradually was modified to allow what in effect was a sidearm pitch in 1883, and a full overhand delivery the following year." See also "National Base-Ball League," *NYT*, December 8, 1882, 2; "Baseball," *NYC*, December 15, 1883, 649; "Baseball Rules Changed," *NYT*, November 21, 1884, 2. Biographical sketches of the players are in "The Champions," *SL*, October 14, 1885, 4.

19. New league rule is in "The Baseball Convention," *NYT*, October 18, 1885, 2 (the previous rule allowed 11 players); "Base Ball," *SL*, October 21, 1885, 1. Chicago's reserved players are in "Reserved by the League Clubs," *CDT*, October 26, 1885, 2. Spalding signing players is in "Base-Ball—How the Chicago Players Were Signed Yesterday," *CDT*, October 27, 1885, 2; "Base Ball," *SL*, November 11, 1885, 1; Remlap (see note 9), "From Chicago," *SL*, November 11, 1885, 3. McCormick wanting to retire is in Remlap, "From Chicago," *SL*, November 4, 1885, 1. "He came up to" quotation is from "Base Ball," *CDT*, January 24, 1886, 12. See also "Baseball," *NYC*, January 30, 1886, 730.

20. National League teams for 1886 are in "The League Schedule," *NYT*, March 5, 1886, 2; http://www.retrosheet.org/. Providence club is in "Baseball Magnates," *NYT*, November 19, 1885, 2; "The Providence Baseball Club," *NYT*, December 1, 1885, 2; "Straight Tips," *SL*, April 28, 1886, 1. Buffalo club is in "Buffalo's Club Sold," *NYT*, September 18, 1885, 3. Washington club is in "Baseball Plans," *NYT*, December 21, 1885, 5; "Washington in the League," *NYT*, January 17, 1886, 7. Kansas City club is in "The League Admits Kansas City," *NYT*, February 10, 1886, 5. Flynn and Moolic joining club is in Remlap (see note 9), "From Chicago," *SL*, November 18, 1885, 4; "Base-Ball—A New Catcher Signed," *CDT*, November 28, 1885, 3; "The Eastern New England League," *SL*, December 16, 1885, 4. "Where they will" quotation is from "Sporting Affairs," *CDT*, February 27, 1886, 2. Hot Springs is also mentioned in "Sporting Affairs," *CDT*, February 14, 1886, 2; "The Sporting Review," *CDT*, March 20, 1886, 9; "Sporting," *(Chicago) Times*, March 21, 1886, 16.

21. A speech that Spalding gave to the team members is in Remlap (see note 9), "'Remlaps'' Letter," *SL*, March 24, 1886, 5.

22. On November 8, 1885, Billy Sunday beat Walter Arlington "Arlie" Latham from the American Association's St. Louis Browns in a 100-yard race. See "Latham Beaten by Sunday," *NYT*, November 9, 1885, 1.

23. The date in the article is April 29; the season actually started on April 30. The Southern League was a minor-league baseball league in the South. See untitled article, *NYC*, January 24, 1885, 716; untitled article, *NYC*, February 28, 1885, 795.

24. Detroit improved its team by adding four members from the purchased Buffalo Bisons club. St. Louis also added some players, which particularly strengthened its infield. See "Detroit to Have the 'Big Four,'" *NYT*, November 20, 1885, 8; "Sporting Affairs," *CDT*, February 27, 1886, 2.

25. "Close and stubborn" quotation is from "Sporting Affairs," *CDT*, February 27, 1886, 2. Game logs are in http://www.retrosheet.org/. On May 4, 1886, demonstrators gathered at Chicago's Haymarket Square (near the corner of Randolph and Des Plaines Streets) in support of striking workers. As policemen tried to disperse the demonstrators, a bomb was thrown, killing officers and civilians. Austin's band and "the nine marched" quotation

are from "One More for Chicago," *Chicago Herald*, May 7, 1886, 3. "In deference" quotation is from "Detroit Drubbed," *(Chicago) Daily Inter Ocean*, May 7, 1886, 7. "Would have enjoyed" quotation is from "Sporting," *(Chicago) Times*, May 7, 1886, 8. "See also "The Chicagos at Home," *CDT*, May 7, 1886, 5. "The pennant is a handsome one" quotation is from Remlap (see note 9), "Remlap's Letter," *SL*, May 26, 1886, 1 (also mentions Fred Austin). Detroit strengthening its team is in "Sporting Affairs," *CDT*, March 13, 1886, 6. "Never lose heart" quotation is from "Chicago Men Win Again," *NYT*, June 9, 1886, 3. "Capt. Anson had seen" quotation is from "Chicago Is a Winner," *CDT*, June 15, 1886, 10.

26. Game logs are in http://www.retrosheet.org/. "The most interesting incident" quotation is from "Sporting," *(Chicago) Times*, June 23, 1886, 5. See also "Chicago Again Downed," *CDT*, June 23, 1886, 10. The "Big Four" players are in "Detroit to Have the 'Big Four,'" *NYT*, November 20, 1885, 8. "They had tin horns" quotation is from "A Bluff Called," *(Chicago) Times*, July 9, 1886, 2. "Detroit's big four" quotation is from "Detroit Waxed Again," *Chicago Herald*, July 11, 1886, 3. See also the editorial "Chicago Nerve," *Chicago Herald*, July 11, 1886, 4.

27. Game logs and team standings are in http://www.retrosheet.org/. Detectives and "A Bombshell" quotation are from Remlap (see note 9), "Late News," *SL*, July 28, 1886, 1. Temperance pledges are in "Notes and Comments," *SL*, March 24, 1886, 3; Remlap, "'Remlap's' Letter," *SL*, March 24, 1886, 5. "Seven of the best" quotation is from "Fined $25 All Around," *Chicago Herald*, July 23, 1886, 3 (the two new men were Flynn and Ryan). Spalding wrote in his autobiography that the accused men set their own fines. Since the detective agency's report cost $175.00, "one of the guilty" said, "There's just seven of us. Suppose we stand $25 apiece?" See Albert G. Spalding, *America's National Game: Historic Facts Concerning the Beginning, Evolution, Development and Popularity of Base Ball* (1911; repr., Lincoln: University of Nebraska Press, 1992), 525. See also "Punished Champions," *CDT*, July 23, 1886, 3.

28. Kelly's and Spalding's comments to Harry Palmer are from Remlap (see note 9), "A New Scheme," *SL*, August 4, 1886, 1. Spalding's reluctance and "the fines would appear" quotation are from "Paying the Piper," *(Chicago) Times*, July 23, 1886, 3. Men under contract and "he did not propose" quotation are from "Enforcing the Rules," *(Chicago) Daily Inter Ocean*, July 23, 1886, 2. Attempts to rescind fines is in "Notes and Comments," *SL*, August 25, 1886, 5. See also "Sporting News," *CDT*, May 5, 1885, 5; "Base-Ball Notes," *CDT*, May 27, 1885, [3]; D., M. C., "The League Champions," *SL*, May 27, 1885, 6; "Base Ball in Chicago," *WP*, October 7, 1885, 2; "Sporting Affairs," *CDT*, February 14, 1886, 2 (mentions players' "total-abstinence agreement"); "Sporting Affairs," *CDT*, March 13, 1886, 6; "Our Sporting Letter," *Salt Lake Herald*, August 8, 1886, 10.

29. Game logs and team standings are in http://www.retrosheet.org/. August 17 game is in "Chicagos, 15; Kansas Citys, 1," *Chicago Herald*, August 18, 1886, 3; "Visitors in the Diamond," *CDT*, August 18, 1886, 3. Game-day quotations are from both articles.

30. Game logs are in http://www.retrosheet.org/. "Characteristic" quotation is from "Characteristic of the Great Sir Michael," *SL*, September 1, 1886, 6. Rogers's accusation is in "A Furious Attack upon the Chicago Club by the Philadelphias' Secretary," *CDT*, September 22, 1886, 2. Eugene Field is in William H. Taft, "Eugene Field," in *American Newspaper Journalists, 1873–1900*, ed. Perry J. Ashley, vol. 23, *Dictionary of Literary Biography* (Detroit: Gale Research Co., 1983), 110–17; Lewis O. Saum, *Eugene Field and His Age* (Lincoln: University of Nebraska Press, 2001). Field's baseball interest is in Saum, pp. 130–62.

31. This news item originally appeared in "The World of Sport," *Detroit Morning Tribune*, August 22, 1886, 3. After the journalist summarized the Kelly-Conway altercation, he concluded: "This is a typical Chicago trick. They do not care what they do, so they win."

32. *Rara avis* is Latin for rare bird. *Sui generis* is also Latin, meaning of his or her own kind. The phrase indicates that Kelly was unique and in a class by himself.

33. "Mike Kelly is only" quotation is from "General Sporting Notes," *Chicago Herald*, August 22, 1886, 2. Game logs and team standings are in http://www.retrosheet.org/. *Herald* and *Tribune* quotations about the Chicago team are from "Detroit to the Front," *Chicago Herald*, August 22, 1886, 2; "Farewell the Pennant," *CDT*, August 22, 1886, 11. The health of players is in "Diamond Dust," *CDT*, August 4, 1886, 3; "How They Stand," *CDT*, August 8, 1886, 10; "Chicago Gaining," *(Chicago) Times*, August 25, 1886, 2; "Chicago Leads," *(Chicago) Times*, August 27, 1886, 5; "New York vs. Chicago," *NYC*, October 9, 1886, 474; "To Go at Them Again," *Chicago Herald*, December 4, 1886, 2; "In the Enemy's Camp," *CDT*, April 7, 1887, 2. "The Chicagos are pretty" quotation is from "Notes and Comments," *SL*, September 8, 1886, 5.

34. *Chicago Daily Tribune* and Cap Anson quotations on September 22 game are from "Mob Work in Detroit," *CDT*, September 23, 1886, 1. "As the Chicago nine" quotation is from "Just Like Clockwork," *(Chicago) Times*, September 23, 1886, 6. Recreation Park was the name of the Detroit Wolverines' ballpark. Willie Hahn is in "Sports and Pastimes," *Fort Worth (Texas) Daily Gazette*, October 11, 1886, 3. Burns out of the lineup is in box scores in Chicago's newspapers of the time. Burns returned to the lineup on October 8. See "Chicago Calcimined," *(Chicago) Daily Inter Ocean*, October 9, 1886, 4; "A League of but Two Games," *CDT*, October 9, 1886, 6. See also "Detroit vs. Chicago," *NYC*, October 2, 1886, 457.

35. "At third base" quotation is from Anson, *A Ball Player's Career*, 129. Game logs and team standings are in http://www.retrosheet.org/. "Throughout the day" and "all the morning" quotations are from "Brass Bands in Order," *Chicago Herald*, October 10, 1886, 2. See also "Chicagos Grandly Win," *CDT*, October 10, 1886, 10; "Why It Was Chicago Won," *CDT*, October 14, 1886, 3. The St. Louis Browns winning the American Association championship is in "The Browns Win the Association Championship," *CDT*, October 11, 1886, 3.

36. Spalding's motivation is in "A Big Stake," *St. Louis Post-Dispatch*, October 23, 1886, 8. "It now seems" quotation is from Joe Pritchard, "Base Ball News," *SL*, September 29, 1886, 1. See also "A Challenge from the Browns," *CDT*, September 26, 1886, 10. Spalding accepting Von der Ahe's challenge is in "A Meeting Between the Champions Nearly Certain," *SL*, October 6, 1886, 1. The best-of-seven series is in "Still Our Pennant," *(Chicago) Times*, October 10, 1886, 5. See also display advertisement, *CDT*, October 17, 1886, 7.

37. Early in the contest" quotation is from "Amusing Themselves," *(Chicago) Times*, October 19, 1886, 6. "We have heard" quotation is from [Eugene Field], "Sharps and Flats," *Chicago Daily News*, October 19, 1886, morning edition, 2. "The visitors hit" quotation is from "Browns Take Revenge," *CDT*, October 20, 1886, 2. Chicago's victory in the third game is in "Carruthers Hit Hard," *CDT*, October 21, 1886, 2.

38. Poor condition of pitchers is in "To Go at Them Again," *Chicago Herald*, December 4, 1886, 2; "Louisville Notes on Tuesday's Game," *CDT*, April 14, 1887, 2. Flynn's sore arm, Mark Baldwin, coin toss, and game fixing (hippodroming) are in "A Big Stake," *St. Louis Post-Dispatch*, October 23, 1886, 8 (during a discussion of Baldwin's eligibility, one of the four umpires on the series board of umpires could not be found, so the others "undertook to dispose of the matter by tossing a coin"). Baldwin's signing is also in "Gossip of the Game," *CDT*, October 21, 1886, 2. McCormick's rheumatism is in "Home Again," *St. Louis Post-Dispatch*, October 21, 1886, 8 (mentions hippodroming). Flynn and McCormick staying home and "come in handy" quotation are from "We Gave 'Em the Goose," *TSN*, October 30, 1886, 2 (mentions hippodroming). Game Four is in "Beaten by Missourians," *CDT*, October 22, 1886, 2 (mentions hippodroming). The Northwestern League was a minor-league baseball league with teams in the Northwest. See "Base-Ball," *CDT*, October 28, 1882, 8. Game Five is in "The Browns Win a Third," *CDT*, October 23, 1886, 6; "St. Louis Soars," *(Chicago) Daily Inter Ocean*, October 23, 1886, 4. Hudson's record is in http://www.retrosheet.org/. Hippodroming is also in "Return of the Champions," *Chicago Herald*, October 12, 1886, 2; O[liver] P. Caylor, "Base Ball," *SL*, October 27, 1886, 4; "A Reception on 'Change," *TSN*, October 30, 1886, 3. The definition of "hippodrome" is in Paul Dickson, *The Dickson Baseball Dictionary*, 3rd ed. (New York: Norton, 2009), 412: "A fraudulent baseball game in which the winner is determined beforehand; a rigged contest." "We have a higher" quotation is from [Eugene Field], "Sharps and Flats," *Chicago Daily News*, October 23, 1886, morning edition, 4.

39. Dalrymple's misplay and "gave [catcher] Kelly" quotation are from "The Cost of an Error," *Chicago Daily News*, October 25, 1886, morning edition, 4. Essays on "the $15,000 slide" are in G. W. Axelson, *"Commy": The Life Story of Charles A. Comiskey* (Chicago: Reilly & Lee Co., 1919), 77–92; Jerry Lansche, *Glory Fades Away: The Nineteenth-Century World Series Rediscovered* (Dallas: Taylor Publishing Co., 1991), 71–93; Marshall D. Wright, *Nineteenth Century Baseball: Year-by-Year Statistics for the Major League Teams, 1871 Through 1900* (Jefferson, NC: McFarland, 1996), 145–46; Bob Tiemann, "Curt Welch's Winning Slide," in *Inventing Baseball: The 100 Greatest Games of the 19th Century*, ed. Bill Felber (Phoenix: Society for American Baseball Research, 2013), 184–86. "Trotted home" quotation is from "The Game," *TSN*, October 30, 1886, 3. Gate receipts are in "The Receipts," *TSN*, October 30, 1886, 3 (the Browns "received half or $6,960. This divided among twelve players gave each member of the team $580. The remaining $6,960 went to Von der Ahe who out of it had to pay the salaries of the umpires and his other expenses"); "St. Louis vs. Chicago," *NYC*, November 6, 1886, 537 (total listed is $13,920.20, though the six daily figures are the same as in *TSN*). Wild pitch is in "Sporting," *St. Louis Globe-Democrat*, October 24, 1886, 11; "Chicago vs. St. Louis," *NYC*, October 30, 1886, 521; "The Game," *TSN*, October 30, 1886, 3. The write-ups in the following game-day accounts report that Welch scored on a passed ball, though the box scores indicate that Clarkson threw a wild pitch: "Beaten by the Browns," *(Chicago) Times*, October 24, 1886, 6; "Browns the Champions," *CDT*, October 24, 1886, 10; "Chicago Conquered," *(Chicago) Daily Inter Ocean*, October 24, 1886, 4; "St. Louis' Day of Bliss," *Chicago Herald*, October 24, 1886, 2.

40. Silver Flint, George Gore, Mike Kelly, and Ned Williamson stayed in St. Louis for a few days after the final game. See "The Game," *TSN*, October 30, 1886, 3 (mentions that the team had supper and took the train home).

41. Games won and lost, standings of teams, and player statistics are in http://www.retrosheet.org/. "Kelly Leads Them All" headline is in *Chicago Herald*, October 31, 1886, 2. John Clarkson won 36 games and lost 17. His ERA was 2.41. See also Shawn O'Hare, "John Clarkson, the 34 Million Dollar Man," in *Northsiders: Essays on the History and Culture of the Chicago Cubs*, ed. Gerald C. Wood and Andrew Hazucha (Jefferson, NC: McFarland, 2008), 159–64. "The team that brought" quotation is from Anson, *A Ball Player's Career*, 128 ("good man" and "his arm gave out" quotations are from p. 131). Flynn's last game is in "One for the New Yorks," *Chicago Herald*, October 6, 1886, 2. See also "Base Ball Notes," *(Washington, DC) Evening Star*, March 12, 1887, 2. Flynn's accomplishments are in David Nemec, *The Great Encyclopedia of Nineteenth Century Major League Baseball*, 2nd ed. (Tuscaloosa: University of Alabama Press, 2006), 375. Flynn played one game in right field for Chicago on May 23, 1887, and he played with the Western Association's Omaha team in 1888. See "On the Diamond," *CDT*, May 24, 1887, 3; "Omaha's Team," *SL*, January 18, 1888, 2.

42. St. Louis's nickname was Mound City, due to the city's many Native American earthwork mounds.

43. "Furl that pennant" quotation is from "Chicago Conquered," *(Chicago) Daily Inter Ocean*, October 24, 1886, 4. "I'll win the game" quotation and Dalrymple being upset are from "The Cost of an Error," *Chicago Daily News*, October 25, 1886, morning edition, 4 (mentions that Game Seven, if necessary, would have been played in Cincinnati on October 27). Dalrymple blamed for loss is in "The Game," *TSN*, October 30, 1886, 3 (includes quotations by Spalding and player); "Mad Players," *SL*, November 10, 1886, 1. "Chicago had no business" quotation is from Remlap (see note 9), "From Chicago," *SL*, November 3, 1886, 2. See also Anson, *A Ball Player's Career*, 137: "We were beaten, and fairly beaten, but had some of the players taken as good care of themselves prior to these games as they were in the habit of doing when the League season was in full swim, I am inclined to believe that there might have been a different tale to tell."

44. Spalding's anger, playing hard to win, and game fixing (hippodroming) are in "A Big Stake," *St. Louis Post-Dispatch*, October 23, 1886, 8. Spalding was "very wrathy at the kick made over Baldwin." See "Browns the Champions," *CDT*, October 24, 1886, 10. Teams playing hard to win are also in "Home Again," *St. Louis Post-Dispatch*, October 21, 1886, 8; "Chicago Conquered," *(Chicago) Daily Inter Ocean*, October 24, 1886, 4; O[liver] P. Caylor, "Base Ball," *SL*, October 27, 1886, 4; "A

Reception on 'Change," *TSN*, October 30, 1886, 3. "I've been so hot" quotation is from "A Big Stake," *St. Louis Post-Dispatch*, October 23, 1886, 8. Spalding still angry after returning home is in "The News in Chicago," *TSN*, October 30, 1886, 3. "Championship of the world" quotation is from "To Go at Them Again," *Chicago Herald*, December 4, 1886, 2.

45. "Beer Beats Them" headline is from the *(Chicago) Daily Inter Ocean*, October 20, 1886, 2. "Weak exhibition" quotation is from Henry Chadwick, "The Diamond Campaign," *Omaha (NE) Daily Bee*, November 7, 1886, 4. "He drank about" quotation is from "Must Sign the Pledge," *Chicago Herald*, January 16, 1887, 6. Spalding accusing McCormick of drinking is also in "Kelly Leads Them All," *Chicago Herald*, October 31, 1886, 2; "In the Arena of Sports," *CDT*, April 16, 1887, 2 (includes mention of McCormick's "bumming" and alleged rheumatism). McCormick's drinking is also in "Notes and Comments," *SL*, March 16, 1887, 3; "Louisville Notes on Tuesday's Game," *CDT*, April 14, 1887, 2. After he left baseball, he ran a saloon in Paterson, New Jersey. See "Notes and Comments," *SL*, September 26, 1888, 2.

46. Famous battery" and "they felt sorely" quotations are from "Is This True?," *SL*, November 10, 1886, 1 (reprinted in "Sprays of Sport," *(Chicago) Daily Inter Ocean*, November 10, 1886, 3). "As a matter of fact" quotation is from "Reviving Base Ball," *Chicago Herald*, November 14, 1886, 2 (interview with Spalding reprinted in "The White Stockings," *TSN*, November 25, 1886, 4, which also mentions the White Stockings blaming Dalrymple). The text of the temperance clause is in "Only Temperance Men," *CDT*, December 2, 1886, 2. See also "Sporting," *CDT*, December 1, 1886, 2; "What Made the Boys Mad," *NYT*, December 2, 1886, 5.

47. "Gore leaving Chicago is in "Gore Goes to New York," *Chicago Herald*, November 25, 1886, 2; "Gore to Play Here," *NYT*, November 25, 1886, 5. Dalrymple leaving Chicago is in "Base-Ball," *CDT*, November 27, 1886, 2 (includes "the releasing of Gore" quotation); "Dalrymple Leaves the Chicagos," *NYT*, November 27, 1886, 3. Chicago team earning $62,000 is in "Base Ball Notes," *(Washington, DC) Evening Star*, March 12, 1887, 2. Spalding and Anson predicting a winning season is in "The Kingdom of Sports," *CDT*, February 16, 1887, 2; "Gossip about Sports," *Chicago Herald*, February 20, 1887, 3. "Who will be" quotation is from "On the New Players," *Chicago Herald*, November 28, 1886, 2. Anson annually predicting success is in F[rank] H. Brunell, "Brunell Talks," *TSN*, March 19, 1892, 2; "Adrian C.'s Annual," *CDT*, December 26, 1892, 12; "Chicago's New Ball Players," *CDT*, December 17, 1899, 18. "The impression" quotation is from "The Chicago Ball Players," *NYT*, October 30, 1886, 3. See also David Ball with David Nemec, "The Dismantling of the National League's First Dynasty: Phase 1," *Base Ball: A Journal of the Early Game* 8 (Fall 2014): 104–25.

Chapter 8

1. "I have determined" quotation is from "Tired of Chicago," *NYT*, January 3, 1887, 8. The reserve system could force a contracted player "to either play at a reduced salary or play with no League club the coming year." See "Baseball Notes," *NYC*, October 18, 1879, 237. Sale of Kelly, "I did not care" quotation, and "conceived the idea" quotation are from "Mike Goes to Boston," *Chicago Herald*, February 15, 1887, 1. Spalding hoped that Kelly would stay in Chicago. See "Reviving Base Ball," *Chicago Herald*, November 14, 1886, 2; "Only Temperance Men," *CDT*, December 2, 1886, 2. "Was at liberty" quotation and salary are from Albert G. Spalding, *America's National Game: Historic Facts Concerning the Beginning, Evolution, Development and Popularity of Base Ball* (1911; repr., Lincoln: University of Nebraska Press, 1992), 517, 516. See also "Boston Secures Kelly," *CDT*, February 15, 1887, 3 (mentions picture); "The Kingdom of Sports," *CDT*, February 16, 1887, 2; "Kelly Will Eat Shortcake," *CDT*, February 21, 1887, 3. "$10,000 beauty" is in "Some of the Freshest Squibs," *Chicago Herald*, March 20, 1887, 2; "Yale Beats Boston," *SL*, May 4, 1887, 8; "Boston's $10,000 Beauty," *WP*, June 25, 1887, 2; "Ball Players Go West," *NYT*, October 26, 1887, 3. "What do you think" quotation is from "Kelly as a Prophet," *NYT*, February 21, 1887, 8. See also "Will the Chicagos Win?," *Chicago Herald*, April 3, 1887, 2; David Ball with David Nemec, "The Dismantling of the National League's First Dynasty: Phase 1," *Base Ball: A Journal of the Early Game* 8 (Fall 2014): 112–20.

2. Paul Hines of the Providence Grays actually led the National League in 1878 with his .358 batting average. Dalrymple was second with .354. In 1886, Kelly was first (.388) and Anson was second (.371).

3. A "coup de main" is a sudden surprise attack. "Rag" is slang for the pennant, and this article marks the first known use of the word. See Paul Dickson, *The Dickson Baseball Dictionary*, 3rd ed. (New York: Norton, 2009), 685.

4. "The only Kelly" is used, for example, in "Mike Goes to Boston: The Only Kelly Leaves Chicago," *Chicago Herald*, February 15, 1887, 1. "He would appear" quotation is from "Boston's Latest Achievement," *New-York Tribune*, February 17, 1887, 4 (after quote is "That's why he is the 'only' Kelly"). Chicago baseball song is in "Base Ball," *TSN*, March 5, 1887, 5.

5. "His case is just" quotation is from "In the Arena of Sports," *CDT*, April 16, 1887, 2. McCormick signing with Pittsburgh is in "In the Field of Sports," *CDT*, April 21, 1887, 5; "McCormick Signs with Pittsburg," *CDT*, April 30, 1887, 3. See also untitled article, *NYC*, April 9, 1887, 58. Players at spring training and temperance pledges are in "The White Stockings Ready to Leave for the Hot Springs," *CDT*, March 2, 1887, 7; "Spalding's New Nine," *Chicago Herald*, March 2, 1887, 3 (includes mention of McCormick's absence).

6. St. Louis team moving to Indianapolis, Kansas City leaving the National League, and Pittsburgh admitted to the league are in "Indianapolis Chosen," *NYT*, March 9, 1887, 8; "Kansas City Ousted," *Chicago Herald*, March 9, 1887, 1; "Pittsburg Comes In," *CDT*, November 18, 1886, 3. Composition of the National League is in http://www.retrosheet.org/; "When They Will Play," *NYT*, March 10, 1887, 8. Rules are in *Spalding's Base Ball Guide and Official League Book for 1887* (1887; repr., St. Louis: Horton Pub. Co., 1988), 127–32 (a "legally" delivered pitch is on p. 130); "The Baseball Rules," *NYT*, November 17, 1886, 5 (mentions that "five balls and four strikes will be allowed instead of six balls and three strikes, as heretofore"). Al Spalding and Cap Anson approved of the new rules. See "Almost Another Game," *Chicago Herald*, November 20, 1886, 2; "In the Arena of Sports," *CDT*, April 16, 1887, 2.

7. Game logs and player statistics are in http://www.retrosheet.org/. "Triumphant season" quotation is from an untitled article, *Chicago Daily News*, May 2, 1887, evening issue, 2. The Wrong Foot First" quotation is from *CDT*, May 1, 1887, 11. "Outbatted, outfielded" quotation is from "Sports and Sportsmen," *Chicago Evening Journal*, May 7, 1887, 12. "Never in Chicago's base ball" quotation is from "Boston Beaten," *Brooklyn (NY) Daily Eagle*, May 7, 1887, 1; "Chips from the Diamond," *(New York) Sun*, May 7, 1887, 3. "So disgusted" and "acted as if" quotations are from "Three Times and Out," *WP*, May 19, 1887, 2. "The fielding of Sullivan" quotation is from "Pitcher Geiss No Good," *CDT*, May 19, 1887, 3.

8. Game logs and team standings are in http://www.retrosheet.org/. "10,000 beauty," "presented with more," and "Boston made" quotations are from "Boston's $10,000 Beauty?," *WP*, June 25, 1887, 2. See also "Ah There, Mike, Old Boy?," *CDT*, June 25, 1887, 3. "From all accounts" quotation is from "Chicago's Ovation to Kelly," *New-York Tribune*, June 27, 1887, 4.

9. Game logs are in http://www.retrosheet.org/. The minor-league International League completed its first season in 1886 with teams from New York State and Canada. See "The International League," *NYT*, March 18, 1886, 1; "Baseball," *NYC*, January 8, 1887, 681. Newark's "favorite battery of Stovey and Walker" is mentioned in "The Newarks and the Giants," *NYT*, April 27, 1887, 2. "Anson wouldn't let" quotation is from "Notes and Comments," *SL*, August 3, 1887, 5. *New York Herald* quotations are from "Newark Defeats Chicago," *New York Herald*, July 15, 1887, 9. *NYC* quotations are from an untitled article, *NYC*, July 23, 1887, 296. See also "Chicago Plays a Game in Newark," *CDT*, July 15, 1887, 3; "Base Ball Notes," *SL*, June 1, 1887, 10 (mentions that an International League team had signed "a colored second baseman" and asks, "How far will this mania for engaging colored players go?"); Peter Mancuso, "The Color Line Is Drawn," in *Inventing Baseball: The 100 Greatest Games of the 19th Century*, ed. Bill Felber (Phoenix: Society for American Baseball Research, 2013), 189–91.

10. Game logs are in http://www.retrosheet.org/. August 1 game is in "Downing the Nationals," *CDT*, August 2, 1887, 3. August 13 game is in "It was Clarkson's Day," *CDT*, August 14, 1887, 6; "Chicago vs. Detroit," *NYC*, August 20, 1887, 362. "The Chicago audiences" quotation is from [Finley Peter Dunne], "Chicago Again," *Chicago Daily News*, August 15, 1887, evening issue, 1. See also Margaret A. Blanchard, "Finley Peter Dunne," in *American Newspaper Journalists, 1873–1900*, ed. Perry J. Ashley, vol. 23, *Dictionary of Literary Biography* (Detroit: Gale Research Co., 1983), 95–110; Elmer Ellis, *Mr. Dooley's America: A Life of Finley Peter Dunne* (New York: Alfred A. Knopf, 1941), 16–30; Charles Fanning, *Finley Peter Dunne & Mr. Dooley: The Chicago Years* (Lexington: University Press of Kentucky, 1978), 5–9. The definition of "bleaching boards" is in Dickson, *The Dickson Baseball Dictionary*, 115: "The planks laid lengthwise as spectator seats at baseball games. The term evolved into *bleachers*, but also coexisted with it."

11. Game logs, team standings, and player statistics are in http://www.retrosheet.org/. "By the loss" quotation is from "The Pennant Detroit's," *CDT*, September 8, 1887, 3. Anson's response to Boston's fifth-place finish was "'one swallow does not make a summer,' however, nor one ball player a whole team." See Adrian C. Anson, *A Ball Player's Career, Being the Personal Experiences and Reminiscences of Adrian C. Anson* (1900; repr., Mattituck, NY: Amereon House, n.d.), 138. "He singlehandedly pitched" quotation is from Marshall D. Wright, *Nineteenth Century Baseball: Year-by-Year Statistics for the Major League Teams, 1871 Through 1900* (Jefferson, NC: McFarland, 1996), 153. Bases on balls counted as hits in 1887, and Anson's 60 walks pushed his batting average to .421, best in the National League. Most baseball references disregard this one-year rule, leaving his batting average at .347. Detroit defeated the American Association's St. Louis Browns in the championship series.

12. "I think it's about" and "I will remain" quotations are from "Late News," *SL*, December 14, 1887, 1 (a similar quotation is in "Clarkson Dead Set Against Chicago," *CDT*, December 10, 1887, 2). Clarkson and family business is in "The Champions," *SL*, October 14, 1885, 4; "Notes and Comments," *SL*, November 2, 1887, 2; "Another $10,000 Beauty," *NYT*, April 4, 1888, 2 (includes Boston club's earnings, "in order to keep up" quotation, and Clarkson signing with Boston); "Clarkson, $10,000 Pitcher, Is Dead," *CDT*, February 5, 1909, 10. See also Mugwump [the pen name of *SL* correspondent Billy Sullivan], "Hub Happenings," *SL*, January 18, 1888, 2; "How Clarkson Talks," *(Chicago) Times*, April 9, 1888, 2; "Chicago's Backers," *SL*, November 20, 1889, 5. Ballplayers signing contracts is in "Players Who Have Signed," *WP*, February 26, 1888, 2. "$20,000 battery" is in "Base Ball on Many Fields," *(New York) Sun*, April 6, 1888, 3; "Notes and Comments," *Sporting Life*, April 11, 1888, 6; "Great Pitchers," *(Washington, DC) Evening Star*, April 26, 1888, 4. "Extra" and "it looked like rain" quotations are from "Clarkson as a 'Bean-Eater,'" *(Chicago) Times*, April 6, 1888, 3.

13. Anson's views on Clarkson are in Alfred H. Spink, *The National Game*, 2nd ed. (1911; repr., Carbondale: Southern Illinois University Press, 2000), 126; Anson, *A Ball Player's Career*, 130, 139–40. "The loss of Clarkson" quotation is from "An Interview with Anson," *(Chicago) Times*, April 6, 1888, 3. See also "John Clarkson Talks," *(New York) Evening World*, April 5, 1888, extra 1 p.m. edition, 1. "The slugging has begun" quotation is from "The Slugging Has Begun," *CDT*, April 21, 1888, 7. "The Chicagos played" quotation is from "Van's 'South Paw,'" *Chicago Times*, April 21, 1888, 1. See also "The Chicagos at Indianapolis," *Chicago Times*, April 20, 1888, 3. George Van Haltren joining the White Stockings is in "Can Give Curry Points," *CDT*, June 28, 1887, 3. For a pre-season summary of the 1888 White Stockings, see "The Chicagos of 1888," *(Chicago) Times*, March 24, 1888, 5.

14. The new uniforms are in "Their First Home Game," *CDT*, May 2, 1888, 3; "Victory Number Seven," *Chicago Times*, May 2, 1888, 3; Harry Palmer, "Chicago Gossip," *SL*, May 9, 1888, 8; Harry Palmer, "Baseball in Australia," *Outing: An Illustrated Monthly Magazine of Recreation*, November 1888, 166. Sportswriters' references to Chicago club as "Black Stockings" or "Black Sox" are in "The Game Went to the Bostons," *CDT*, July 10, 1888, 6; "The Black Sox Again Shut Out," *CDT*, September 20, 1888, 3; "A Defeat for All-America," *SL*, November 28, 1888, 4; "No Game at Washington," *CDT*, May 21, 1889, 3; "Chicago Again Wins from Pittsburg," *WP*, May 1, 1890, 6. The White Stockings name during 1888–1889 is in "Some Lively Batting," *CDT*, June 23, 1888, 7; Joe Pritchard, "St. Louis Siftings," *SL*, June 12,

1889, 6; http://www.baseball-almanac.com/; http://www.baseball-reference.com/; http://www.retrosheet.org/.

15. Game logs and team standings are in http://www.retrosheet.org/. "The coming of Clarkson" quotation is from "A Circus in Chicago," *NYC*, May 26, 1888, 173. Carriage accident, game attendance, and "it was a cheerless" quotation are from "Ah There, Captain Anson!," *Chicago Times*, May 16, 1888, 3. "Base-ball is not" quotation is from "An Uninteresting Game," *CDT*, May 16, 1888, 3. See also "Chicago vs. Boston," *NYC*, May 26, 1888, 174 (mentions Boston's 21 hits). New York defeated the American Association's St. Louis Browns in the championship series.

16. The promotion of Spalding's store is in Harry Palmer, "To Australia," *SL*, March 28, 1888, 1. Two teams and "men of clean habits" quotation are from Spalding, *America's National Game*, 252–53. Spalding had been a young pitcher on the Boston Red Stockings team that had sailed to England in 1874 to promote the sport of baseball. See "Base-Ball," *NYT*, August 17, 1874, 5. See also chapter 3, note 17.

17. Lillie (also Lily) Langtry (1853–1929) was a British actress.

18. "I have been thinking" quotation is from "Sports of the Spring," *(Chicago) Times*, March 25, 1888, "Supplement" sec., 20. See also "Base-Ball in Australia," *CDT*, March 25, 1888, 2; "A Trip to Australia," *NYC*, March 31, 1888, 45; "Chicago Ball-Tossers in Australia," *CDT*, August 26, 1888, 17; Harry Palmer, "Baseball in Australia," *Outing: An Illustrated Monthly Magazine of Recreation*, November 1888, 157–66.

19. "First world's tour" and "everywhere on this land" quotations are from Spalding, *America's National Game*, 251, 253; see also pp. 252–59. "A crowd of people" quotation from Ryan's diary is from Tom Shieber, "To Australia ... and Beyond," *Memories and Dreams* (official magazine of the Baseball Hall of Fame), Spring 2014, 45. "The crowd waxed" quotation is from Anson, *A Ball Player's Career*, 146. "The best evidence" quotation is from *Spalding's Base Ball Guide and Official League Book for 1890* (1890; repr., St. Louis: Horton Pub. Co., 1989), 123. "The only man" quotation is from "Base Ball," *SL*, February 20, 1889, 4. "The offer was" quotation is from "No Base Ball in the Coliseum," *SL*, February 20, 1889, 4.

20. Trip to Paris and game is in Harry Clay Palmer and others, *Athletic Sports in America, England and Australia* (Philadelphia: Hubbard Brothers, 1889), 391–402; 440–41; "The Spalding Tourists," *NYC*, March 16, 1889, 11; "The Spalding Tourists," *NYC*, March 23, 1889, 27; "Base Ball," *SL*, April 17, 1889, 6. Williamson and *Cincinnati Enquirer* is in "Notes and Comments," *SL*, April 3, 1889, 4. "I was advised" quotation is from "Williamson's Injury," *SL*, April 3, 1889, 1. Nettie Williamson is in Waller Wallace, "Off for Australia: Old Friends Meet Again," *SL*, December 5, 1888, 4. See also Anson, *A Ball Player's Career*, 256–57 (Williamson); 260–72 (team touring England, Scotland, and Ireland). Williamson staying in London and travelers leaving for home are in "Now Bound for America," *CDT*, March 29, 1889, 6; "End of the Trip—Off for Home," *SL*, April 3, 1889, 2. Ship arriving in New York is in "They're Home," *(New York) Evening World*, April 6, 1889, extra 2 o'clock edition, 1; "On Their Native Heath," *CDT*, April 7, 1889, 10. "I am glad" quotation is from [George] Stackhouse, "Home Again," *SL*, April 10, 1889, 1. See also articles in *NYC*, April 13, 1889, 79–80 (Anson mentions Williamson on p. 80, "whom we were obliged to leave abroad").

21. Ball playing in U.S. is in Anson, *A Ball Player's Career*, 275–85. Players returning to Chicago is in "Return of the Players," *CDT*, April 20, 1889, 3. April 20 game is in "Last Game of the Tour," *CDT*, April 21, 1889, 10. Travel distance of nearly 32,000 miles is in "Nineteen Men Signed," *WP*, April 7, 1889, 7. Palmer's records are in Palmer, *Athletic Sports in America, England and Australia*, 708–711; Harry Palmer, "Net Playing Results," *SL*, May 1, 1889, 2. Modern-day historians provide slightly different statistics. See Mark Lamster, *Spalding's World Tour: The Epic Adventure That Took Baseball Around the Globe—And Made it America's Game* (New York: Public Affairs, 2006), 250, 287–92 (57 games: All-America, 29 wins; Chicago, 23 wins; 4 ties; 1 unofficial game); Thomas W. Zeiler, *Ambassadors in Pinstripes: The Spalding World Baseball Tour and the Birth of the American Empire* (Lanham, MD: Rowman and Littlefield, 2006), 157, 178 (54 games: All-America, 30 wins; Chicago, 20 wins; 4 ties). The teams had also played a few exhibition games and cricket matches. "We found very" quotation is from A. G. Spalding, "In the Field Papers: Base-Ball," *Cosmopolitan: A Monthly Illustrated Magazine*, October 1889, 610.

22. Williamson is in "Ed Williamson Coming Home," *CDT*, April 10, 1889, 5; "Notes and Comments," *SL*, April 17, 1889, 4; "Short Stops," *NYT*, April 20, 1889, 3; "Williamson's Injuries," *CDT*, April 26, 1889, 7 (includes "rheumatic trouble" quotation); Joe Pritchard, "St. Louis Siftings," *SL*, June 12, 1889, 6 (left for Hot Springs on June 4); Harry Palmer, "Chicago Gleanings," *SL*, July 10, 1889, 1 (returned from Hot Springs on July 2); "Baseball," *NYC*, July 20, 1889, 310 (practiced with team on July 9); "Williamson Won a Game," *CDT*, August 16, 1889, 6 (includes "weak on his pins" quotation); "Stray Sparks from the Diamond," *NYC*, March 1, 1890, 843; Anson, *A Ball Player's Career*, 128 (includes "Chicago's stone wall" quotation), 256, 286 (includes "absence hurt" quotation). Anson makes a similar comment in an untitled article, *SL*, September 11, 1889, 4. Chicago's famous "stone wall infield" is also in "Pfeffer Is Released by Chicago," *CDT*, July 1, 1897, 4; "The Old Chicago Infield," *WP*, March 15, 1897, 8; "Tom Burns Dies," *CDT*, March 20, 1902, 6.

23. Bastian is in "Chicago's Old and New Players," *CDT*, April 26, 1889, 7; "Chicago Beaten Again," *NYT*, May 25, 1889, 2. Game logs, team standings, and player statistics are in http://www.retrosheet.org/. Clarkson's achievements are even more astounding when compared to those of the players in second place behind him: complete games (46, Harry Staley of Pittsburgh); innings pitched (420, Harry Staley); and wins (28, Charlie Buffinton of Philadelphia). New York defeated the American Association's Brooklyn Bridegrooms in the championship series. See also "Sketch of Carlson" in *Spalding's Base Ball Guide and Official League Book for 1890*, 48.

24. "Well managed" quotation is from *Spalding's Base Ball Guide and Official League Book for 1889* (1889; repr., St. Louis: Horton Pub. Co., 1988), 21. "Bound hand and foot" quotation is from "The Facts of the Situation," *SL*, December 18, 1889, 4. The reserve clause and Tripartite Agreement/National Agreement are in *Spalding's Base Ball Guide and Official League Book for 1883* (1883; repr.,

St. Louis: Horton Pub. Co., 1988), 58–60; "Baseball," *NYC*, March 17, 1883, 839; *Spalding's Base Ball Guide and Official League Book for 1886* (1886; repr., St. Louis: Horton Pub. Co., 1987), 22–27; John Montgomery Ward, "Is the Base-Ball Player a Chattel?," *Lippincott's Monthly Magazine*, August 1887, 310–14 (sick players are on p. 314). Salaries are in "The Baseball Convention," *NYT*, October 18, 1885, 2; "Base Ball," *SL*, October 21, 1885, 1. Owners ignoring salary caps is in Peter Morris, *A Game of Inches: The Stories Behind the Innovations That Shaped Baseball*, rev. and exp. one-vol. ed. (Chicago: Ivan R. Dee, 2010), 478. See also David Quentin Voigt, *Baseball: An Illustrated History* (University Park: Pennsylvania State University Press, 1994), 67: "Average players, especially those on the less profitable teams, typically earned less than $2,000 a year—considerably more than a factory worker and somewhat more than a state university professor, but less than a civil engineer. Outstanding players earned as much as $3,000 to $5,000, putting them in a class with mechanical engineers and Harvard professors." "Mr. Spalding deducted" quotation is from "Stray Sparks from the Diamond," *NYC*, March 1, 1890, 843. Spalding's treatment of Williamson is also in Joe Pritchard, "St. Louis Siftings," *SL*, June 12, 1889, 6; "Baseball," *NYC*, March 10, 1894, 10.

25. John "Monte" Ward is in "John M. Ward, New York's Short Stop," *NYC*, August 25, 1888, 381; Spalding, *America's National Game*, 253, 270–71 (mentions the National Brotherhood); David Stevens, *Baseball's Radical for All Seasons: A Biography of John Montgomery Ward* (Lanham, MD: Scarecrow Press, 1998); Bryan Di Salvatore, *A Clever Base-Ballist: The Life and Times of John Montgomery Ward* (New York: Pantheon Books, 1999). Ward's articles on the reserve clause include "The Reserve-Rule and Contract-Breakers," *NYC*, February 14, 1885, 763; "Is the Base-Ball Player a Chattel?," *Lippincott's Monthly Magazine*, August 1887, 310–19. Ward also wrote the book *Base-Ball: How to Become a Player, with the Origin, History, and Explanation of the Game* (Philadelphia: Athletic Pub. Co., 1888). Formation of the Brotherhood is in O[liver] P. Caylor, "Words of Sense," *SL*, February 24, 1886, 2; Layman (the pseudonym of James Blackhurst), "A Big Surprise," *SL*, August 4, 1886, 1; "Better Baseball Rules," *NYT*, November 15, 1886, 8; "The Players," *SL*, November 17, 1886, 1; Players' National League, *The Players' National League Base Ball Guide for 1890* (1890; repr., [St. Louis]: Horton Pub. Co., 1989), 7. Salary classification plan is in "Bombshell in Baseball," *NYT*, November 23, 1888, 2; "Ball-Players' Pay," *Chicago Times*, November 23, 1888, 3; "A Sensation!" *SL*, November 28, 1888, 1 (includes "exemplary conduct" quotation); "Talking Fight," *SL*, November 28, 1888, 1 (includes Tim Keefe quotations); R. M. Larner, "Late News," *SL*, November 28, 1888, 1.

26. Players in Italy is in John M. Ward, "Ward's Notes in Naples," *CDT*, March 17, 1889, 25 (includes "wondrous scheme" quotation); untitled article, *SL*, March 6, 1889, 4 (mentions that "as was to be expected, none of the players are in love with" the salary plan); "Rumors of Trouble in the League," *CDT*, May 7, 1889, 3 (includes players secretly meeting, which is also in "Trouble Feared," *SL*, May 8, 1889, 1). "Cowed into submission" quotation is from Ward, "Is the Base-Ball Player a Chattel?," 313. Rumors are in "The Ball Players' Revolt," *NYT*, September 23, 1889, 2; "The Baseball Brotherhood," *WP*, September 24, 1889, 4 (includes "branch out" quotation). "I used what influence" quotation is from Anson, *A Ball Player's Career*, 289. Formation of Players' National League is in "In Hostile Array," *SL*, November 13, 1889, 1 (includes "there was a time" and "we believe" quotations); "Players and Backers Meet," *SL*, November 13, 1889, 1–2; "Baseball," *NYC*, November 9, 1889, 588; "Baseball," *NYC*, November 16, 1889, 603; "The Ball Players Meet," *NYT*, December 17, 1889, 3; *Spalding's Base Ball Guide and Official League Book for 1890*, 14–17. Ward gave a lengthy interview on "the causes which led to the present revolt" in "Ward's Warnings," *SL*, January 22, 1890, 5.

27. New baseball teams are in "In Hostile Array," *SL*, November 13, 1889, 1. Pirates name is in "Players' League News Notes," *SL*, May 3, 1890, 8; "On the Road with the Players," *SL*, June 28, 1890, 4. Black flag is in "From League Headquarters," *SL*, April 19, 1890, 8. "I am receiving" quotation is from "Anxious to Play Under Anson," *CDT*, December 27, 1889, 6. Player profiles are in "They Play with Anson," *CDT*, April 20, 1890, 28. "I tell you" quotation is from "Well Pleased with the Colts," *CDT*, March 2, 1890, 3 (includes mention of Burns, Hutchinson, and Anson as the club's "old players"). Composition of the National League and names of players are in http://www.retrosheet.org/ (in Retrosheet the Chicago team is called the Colts for the first time in the 1890 league standings). Prior to 1890, Chicago club rookies had also been called "colts." See "Chips from the Diamond," *(New York) Sun*, May 7, 1887, 3; "On the Way to Hot Springs," *CDT*, March 4, 1888, 11; "Notes from the Hot Springs," *SL*, March 21, 1888, 5. See also "The Colts Are Laid Up," *CDT*, March 10, 1888, 6; "The Sporting World," *Chicago Times*, October 9, 1888, 3; "Anson's Men Defeated," *CDT*, October 23, 1888, 6; Harry Palmer, "Chicago Gleanings: The Colts Running at a Steadier Pace," *SL*, July 10, 1889, 1; "The Browns Defeated by the Colts," *SL*, April 19, 1890, 6.

28. Game logs and team standings are in http://www.retrosheet.org/. "The turnstile wheels" quotation is from "A Tie Game with Cincinnati," *CDT*, May 6, 1890, 6. See also "Chicago vs. Cincinnati," *NYC*, May 10, 1890, 138. Conflicting schedules is in "The Schedules Compared," *CDT*, March 24, 1890, 6; "Base Ball," *SL*, October 11, 1890, 4. "Float[ed] along" quotation is from "Base Ball," *SL*, November 1, 1890, 3. Financial condition of American Association is also in "Peace or War?," *SL*, August 2, 1890, 4 (mentions that the Association "cuts no figure in the fight"); "Base Ball," *SL*, October 18, 1890, 5. Free passes are in T[im] H. Murnane, "Murnane's Missive," *SL*, July 19, 1890, 7; "The Pass System," *SL*, July 19, 1890, 4; Henry Chadwick, "Chadwick's Chat," *SL*, August 16, 1890, 9. Padded attendance figures are in "Figures Will Lie," *SL*, August 9, 1890, 1; "Base Ball," *SL*, August 16, 1890, 10; Pickwick, "Wheeling Wirings," *SL*, September 27, 1890, 1. Attendance figures are in Robert L. Tiemann, "Major League Attendance," in *Total Baseball: The Official Encyclopedia of Major League Baseball*, 7th ed., ed. John Thorn and others (Kingston, NY: Total Sports Publishing, 2001), 74. The National League waiting out the Players' League is in "Two Clubs Dropped," *NYT*, March 23, 1890, 5; "The Base-Ball War," *Chicago Eagle*, May 31, 1890, 5 (includes "the salaries of the National" quotation).

29. Contract breaking is in "Players' League Means

Business," *CDT*, January 10, 1890, 6; "Managers of the Ball Field," *WP*, February 16, 1890, 14; "On Dangerous Ground," *SL*, August 16, 1890, 4 (mentions "disgust" of fans). Bribery is in "Baseball," *NYC*, March 1, 1890, 843; "From League Headquarters," *SL*, April 19, 1890, 8; "A Washington Plea," *SL*, October 4, 1890, 1. Sportswriters taking sides is in J. H. McDonough, "The Centre of the War," *SL*, June 7, 1890, 5; Henry Chadwick, "Chadwick's Chat," *SL*, June 28, 1890, 9; F. C. Anderson, "Base Ball," *SL*, September 20, 1890, 9. Public weariness is in "Compromise Talk," *SL*, October 4, 1890, 1; "Rogers' Review," *SL*, October 11, 1890, 2 (notes that the public was "disgusted"); Joe Murphy, "Brunell Bows Low," *TSN*, October 25, 1890, 1 (includes "bickering among" quotation).

30. Game logs and team standings are in http://www.retrosheet.org/. The 1884 championship series is in Peter Mancuso, "The First 'World Series': Metropolitans (AA) vs. Providence Grays (NL)," in *Inventing Baseball*, 172–74; chapter 6, note 38; chapter 7, note 15. The 1890 exhibition series is in "News Notes and Comments," *SL*, October 11, 1890, 4; "The Pirates Disband," *CDT*, October 21, 1890, 6 (mentions that the series was a failure); "Stray Sparks from the Diamond," *NYC*, October 25, 1890, 521. The championship is in "The World's Series," *TSN*, October 25, 1890, 2 (mentions that the Players' League team was not allowed to play); "Lines from Louisville," *SL*, November 1, 1890, 5 (includes attendance and "the old contests" quotation); *Spalding's Base Ball Guide and Official League Book for 1891* (1891; repr., St. Louis: Horton Pub. Co., 1989), 99–100. After Brooklyn and Louisville each won three of seven games, with one contest ending in a tie, the series was declared a draw "on account of the disagreeable state of the weather for ball playing." See "Louisville Wins Again," *NYT*, October 29, 1890, 8. The first modern World Series was held in 1903. See Frederick Ivor-Campbell and David Pietrusza, "Postseason Play," in *Total Baseball*, 265–66.

31. Backers and loss of money is in "The Great Baseball War," *NYT*, October 6, 1890, 2; "Another Baseball Row," *NYT*, October 19, 1890, 10 (includes "money was lost" quotation); "News Notes and Comments," *SL*, October 25, 1890, 3; "Late News by Wire," *SL*, November 8, 1890, 1; "Sale of a Baseball Club," *NYT*, November 14, 1890, 3; "Baseball Next Season," *WP*, November 17, 1890, 6; Ella Black, "The Big Wreck," *SL*, November 22, 1890, 7; *Spalding's Base Ball Guide and Official League Book for 1891*, 15–16. "It was with" quotation is from Spalding, *America's National Game*, 288.

32. Merging of clubs is in "End of the Baseball War," *NYT*, November 13, 1890, 3. Spalding buying the Pirates is in "Spalding Is the Victor," *CDT*, November 14, 1890, 6; "Spalding Owns Both," *CDT*, December 30, 1890, 5; Joe Murphy, "The Olive Branch," *TSN*, January 3, 1891, 1; "Baseball," *NYC*, January 10, 1891, 697 (includes purchase costs of $18,565 and $6,435). Figures of $18,564.33 and $5995.18 are in "Base Ball," *SL*, January 3, 1891, 3. The Players' League's Boston and Philadelphia teams wound up in the American Association in 1891. See "Three Clubs Sell Out," *WP*, January 17, 1891, 1. "The Players' League is deader" quotation is from "Spalding's Review," *SL*, November 29, 1890, 3. A similar quotation is in "Return of President Spalding," *CDT*, November 22, 1890, 6. Ward saying that the Players' League is defunct is in an untitled article, *NYC*, November 29, 1890, 602. "Base-ball is a business" quotation is from "Training in Base-Ball," *CDT*, March 20, 1887, 28. Baseball attendance is in "Facts in Figures," *SL*, August 2, 1890, 5. Baseball losses are in "Here Are the Figures," *CDT*, November 22, 1890, 6; David Quentin Voigt, *American Baseball*, vol. 1, *From Gentleman's Sport to the Commissioner System* (University Park: Pennsylvania State University Press, 1983), 167–68; F[rank] H. Brunell, "Base Ball," *SL*, November 29, 1890, 9. Comiskey Park would later be built near the site of the Pirates' ballpark. "The hatchet must" quotation is from "Will Have No Cliques," *CDT*, January 23, 1891, 7. See also Palmer, *Athletic Sports in America, England and Australia*, 120–29; Charles C. Alexander, *Turbulent Seasons: Baseball in 1890–1891* (Dallas: Southern Methodist University Press, 2011); Scott D. Peterson, *Reporting Baseball's Sensational Season of 1890: The Brotherhood War and the Rise of Modern Sports Journalism* (Jefferson, NC: McFarland, 2015); Robert B. Ross, *The Great Baseball Revolt: The Rise and Fall of the 1890 Players League* (Lincoln: University of Nebraska Press, 2016); David Pietrusza, *Major Leagues: The Formation, Sometimes Absorption, and Mostly Inevitable Demise of 18 Professional Baseball Organizations, 1871 to Present* (Jefferson, NC: McFarland, 2006), 99–126.

Chapter 9

1. Grounds are in "Brotherhood Ball Park," *CDT*, January 19, 1890, 7 (mentions railroad and cable car lines); "Players' Grounds," *SL*, January 22, 1890, 5 (mentions "Long John" Wentworth and rent of $1,500); "Base Ball," *SL*, February 12, 1890, 5; "Grounds of the Players' League," *CDT*, February 19, 1890, 6; "White Stocking News," *SL*, May 3, 1890, 8 (mentions the number of ballpark seats and "the State street cable road"); "Return of President Spalding," *CDT*, November 22, 1890, 6; F[rank] H. Brunell, "Base Ball," *SL*, November 29, 1890, 9; "Games at Both Parks," *CDT*, March 23, 1891, 10 (includes "letters protesting" quotation and schedule of games); "News, Gossip and Comment," *SL*, May 2, 1891, 2 (mentions South Side Park and schedules of games at both parks); "Chicago Still on Top," *CDT*, May 17, 1891, 4 (mentions the excellent "transportation facilities" at the South Side grounds); "News, Gossip and Comment," *SL*, May 23, 1891, 2; "Base Ball," *TSN*, January 9, 1892, 3; "Short but Sweet," *SL*, January 9, 1892, 11; "To Play Baseball," *CDT*, April 4, 1892, 10 (mentions ballparks' rents of $1,500 and $7,500). No Sunday baseball is in *Spalding's Base Ball Guide and Official League Book for 1891* (1891; repr., St. Louis: Horton Pub. Co., 1989), 38; F[rank] H. Brunell, "Base Ball," *SL*, November 29, 1890, 9.

2. "But such was not" quotation is from Adrian C. Anson, *A Ball Player's Career, Being the Personal Experiences and Reminiscences of Adrian C. Anson* (1900; repr., Mattituck, NY: Amereon House, n.d.), 294. Team rosters are in http://www.retrosheet.org/. High demand for players is in Joe Pritchard, "St. Louis Sayings," *SL*, January 3, 1891, 5. Anson's young players are in "What Chicago's Triumph Means," *SL*, August 29, 1891, 8. "You can rest assured" quotation is from Joe Murphy, "Base Ball," *SL*, January 10, 1891, 10.

3. "Worn out in mind" quotation is from Joe Murphy, "Chicago Gleanings," *SL*, January 24, 1891, 6. New York trip is also in "Baseball," *NYC*, January 24, 1891, 729. Retirement is in "Base Ball," *SL*, March 28, 1891, 3 (mentions

Players' League, Anson, and Hart); "Hart Is President Now," *CDT*, April 15, 1891, 5 (mentions stress of previous year and neglect of personal interests and includes "I bespeak for" quotation); Joe Murphy, "Al Spalding Resigns," *TSN*, April 18, 1891, 1. Spalding as major stockholder is in "Chicago's Wail," *SL*, October 10, 1891, 2. Spalding describes meeting Anson in O[liver] P. Caylor, "Stories About 'Old Anse,'" *Indianapolis Journal*, July 5, 1891, 9. Jim Hart is in Anson, *A Ball Player's Career*, 307–308; "Rough on Jim Hart," *SL*, November 28, 1888, 1; J. A., "Louisville Laconics," *SL*, December 5, 1888, 4; "Notes and Comments," *SL*, May 1, 1889, 4.

4. Anson's disenchantment with Spalding is in Anson, *A Ball Player's Career*, 304–14, and his relationship with Hart is on pp. 306–309 (Hart quotations are on p. 307, and "experimental one" quotation is on p. 295). Anson writes of both men in "Anson Replies to Hart," *CDT*, January 7, 1900, 17. Game logs are in http://www.retrosheet.org/. "Old man" and similar names are in "Should Let Up on the Old Man," *CDT*, July 24, 1888, 3; "Old Anse Talks Back," *CDT*, August 19, 1888, 14; Joe Murphy, "Chicago Gleanings," *SL*, April 25, 1891, 7; J. F. Donnolly, "Brooklyn Budget," *SL*, June 6, 1891, 5; "Chicago Defeated Again," *NYT*, June 14, 1891, 3 (mentions that spectators jeered Anson after Chicago lost); "Pop Anson Beats Wilcox," *Forest and Stream*, December 10, 1891, 419. September 4 game is in "National League," *WP*, September 5, 1891, 6; "Uncle Adrian Wears Whiskers," *CDT*, September 5, 1891, 6 (includes "the grand," "Uncle Adrian," and "it might" quotations); Joe Murphy, "Baby Anson Slept," *TSN*, September 12, 1891, 1.

5. Game logs and team standings are in http://www.retrosheet.org/. "It is all over" quotation is from Joe Murphy, "The Worlds [sic] Honors," *TSN*, September 19, 1891, 1. The definition of "crank" is in Paul Dickson, *The Dickson Baseball Dictionary*, 3rd ed. (New York: Norton, 2009), 223: "A baseball fan in the late 19th century." The *Telegram*'s "put in about" quotation is from "Is the East Against Anson?," *CDT*, September 30, 1891, 6, and "As to Thrown Games," *TSN*, October 3, 1891, 1. The *Record*'s "the insinuation" and "Anson, the brainiest" quotations are from "Plot Against Chicago," *CDT*, October 1, 1891, 6. See also "Late News by Wire," *SL*, October 3, 1891, 1: "It would be particularly humiliating to the high-priced Boston and New York teams to have the Chicago Club—generally admitted to be the cheapest organization in the League—to win the pennant."

6. "The greatest batsman" quotation is from "Adrian C. Anson," *SL*, June 13, 1891, 1. Anson is also praised in "A. C. Anson," *NYC*, November 10, 1888, 561. "Anson is one" quotation is from "Baseball," *(New York) Sun*, October 4, 1891, 6. Anson's training regimen is in "On the Way to Hot Springs," *CDT*, March 4, 1888, 11 (includes "and we will make" quotation); "Meeting on the Diamond," *CDT*, March 14, 1888, 3; "The Colts Are Laid Up," *CDT*, March 10, 1888, 6 (includes players practicing mornings and afternoons); John J. Evers and Hugh S. Fullerton, *Touching Second* (1910; repr., Jefferson, NC: McFarland, 2005), 204 (includes "training under him" quotation); Anson, *A Ball Player's Career*, 293. "Kicks" quotation is from "Anson and the Umpire," *CDT*, June 16, 1889, 12. See also "Baby Anson Objected," *WP*, September 3, 1890, 6.

7. "It is well known" quotation is from "Bowed Down with Sorrow," *CDT*, October 2, 1891, 6. "Absurd" quotation is from "Opening the Door," *SL*, October 10, 1891, 1. Resentment of attacks is in E. M. Guenther, "Excited Chicago," *SL*, October 3, 1891, 10 (mentions "a universal hatred toward Captain Anson"); "They Were All 'Indignant,'" *CDT*, October 9, 1891, 6; "No Dishonesty," *SL*, October 10, 1891, 2; Gotham, "The Giants Feel Aggrieved," *TSN*, October 17, 1891, 1. Colts losing games is in "Straight and Incorruptible," *SL*, October 10, 1891, 1.

8. "Were I under" quotation is from "President Hart Is Angry," *NYT*, October 4, 1891, 7. A nearly identical quotation is in "No Dishonesty," *SL*, October 10, 1891, 2 (includes Anson's "anybody that knows" and "idiotic and unworthy" quotations). Investigation is in "They Will Investigate," *(New York) Sun*, October 6, 1891, 4; "They Were All 'Indignant,'" *CDT*, October 9, 1891, 6 (mentions October 8 meeting). Anson's initial reaction about alleged crookedness is in "Brave Anson," *SL*, October 3, 1891, 1. The Giants offsetting the Reds' prestige is in "Plot Against Chicago," *CDT*, October 1, 1891, 6; "Late News by Wire," *SL*, October 3, 1891, 1; "Baseball Comment," *WP*, October 4, 1891, 6. New York exonerated is in "They Play Honest Ball," *NYT*, October 14, 1891, 8. "The investigation into" quotation is from an untitled editorial, *NYT*, October 14, 1891, 4. Comments from newspapers around the country about the matter are in "The Soiled Pennant," *CDT*, October 4, 1891, 13. See also Joe Murphy, "A Grand Hippodrome," *TSN*, October 3, 1891, 1; "New York's Treachery," *TSN*, October 10, 1891, 3; Charles C. Alexander, "Was the 1891 National League Pennant Thrown?," *Base Ball: A Journal of the Early Game* 2 (Fall 2008): 5–17.

9. Anson, *A Ball Player's Career*, 295. Game logs and player statistics are in http://www.retrosheet.org/. No championship series is in "Baseball," *NYC*, October 3, 1891, 509 (notes that American Association teams were offered "very liberal inducements" to play exhibition games after the season); "The Fall Season," *SL*, October 3, 1891, 1; "World's Pennant," *SL*, October 17, 1891, 1. Financially strapped American Association is in "Baseball," *NYC*, October 10, 1891, 525. American Association collapsing and "the general admission fee" quotation are in "Baseball," *NYC*, December 26, 1891, 703. See also [Francis C. Richter], "The Revolution!" *SL*, December 19, 1891, 1–2. Option of Sunday games is in "Fixing the Details," *CDT*, December 18, 1891, 7. See also "Uncle Anse Preferred," *CDT*, November 13, 1891, 7: "In regard to [President Jim Hart's] plans for seats he said that at the South Side grounds skeleton seats would be erected in deep center field where there was plenty of room. He thought that except on Saturdays and on holidays the eastern side of the present bleachers might be used for 25 cent seats."

10. "As puritanical" quotation is from Campbell, "St. Louis Siftings," *SL*, February 20, 1892, 3. No Sunday games are also in "Sunday Chicago League Games," *CDT*, April 26, 1892, 7. Leaving the West Side Park is also in "Active for Sports," *CDT*, March 20, 1892, 11; "To Play Baseball," *CDT*, April 4, 1892, 10. Plans for the South Side Park are in "Will Lose Good Men," *CDT*, December 22, 1891, 7.

11. Spalding formally named the league the National League and American Association of Professional Base Ball Clubs. See [Francis C. Richter], "Base Ball," *SL*, December 26, 1891, 4. Split season and schedule is in "Baseball," *NYC*, March 12, 1892, 9. For schedule see also

Elmer E. Bates, "Forest City Findings," *SL*, January 23, 1892, 4; Ronald G. Liebman, "Schedule Changes since 1876," *Baseball Research Journal* 2 (1973) 58–61; Charles C. Alexander, "Split Season: The National League in 1892," *Base Ball: A Journal of the Early Game* 7 (Fall 2013): 5–27. Anson intending to play in the championship is in "No Dishonesty," *SL*, October 10, 1891, 2. Tom Burns is in "Tom Burns Closes with Pittsburg," *CDT*, May 22, 1892, 7; "Pittsburg Pencillings," *SL*, August 6, 1892, 4. Williamson is in Joe Murphy, "Chicago Gleanings," *SL*, March 7, 1891, 5. "If I had had" quotation is from "Bowed Down with Sorrow," *CDT*, October 2, 1891, 6. Pfeffer unwilling to play for Anson is in [Francis C. Richter], "Base Ball," *SL*, January 2, 1892, 9; "Chicago Gleanings," *SL*, February 6, 1892, 11 (includes "under no circumstances" quotation). Pfeffer trade is in "Where His Houses Are," *WP*, January 18, 1892, 1; "Chicago Gleanings," *SL*, March 5, 1892, 9; "Anson's New Baseman," *CDT*, April 5, 1892, 7.

12. Chicago's team for 1892 is in http://www.retrosheet.org/ (includes game logs and team standings); "Will Lose Good Men," *CDT*, December 22, 1891, 7 (mentions three players Anson wanted and includes newspaper's doubts about the strength of the Colts); [Francis C. Richter], "Base Ball," *SL*, December 26, 1891, 4; "The New Ball League," *NYT*, January 3, 1892, 8; "Ready for Pasture," *CDT*, January 31, 1892, 6. Anson boasting of team is in "No Dishonesty," *SL*, October 10, 1891, 2; "Anson Not Saying Much," *TSN*, March 19, 1892, 1. "Anson talks about" quotation is from F[rank] H. Brunell, "Brunell Talks," *TSN*, March 19, 1892, 2. Chicago's dislike for Anson is also in "Late News by Wire," *SL*, June 4, 1892, 1.

13. Game logs, team standings, and player statistics are in http://www.retrosheet.org/. "An organization in" quotation is from "Washington Shuts Anson Out," *CDT*, July 8, 1892, 7. Anson's discouragement is in "The Chicagos in a Losing Rut," *CDT*, June 27, 1892, 10 (includes loss of Duffy and Van Haltren); "Adrian C.'s Annual," *CDT*, December 26, 1892, 12 (includes "I felt that I did" quotation). Addition of new players is in "Baseball Economy," *CDT*, July 4, 1892, 12; "To be Strengthened at Last," *CDT*, July 6, 1892, 7; "Editorial Views, News, Comment," *SL*, August 27, 1892, 2.

14. Attendance figures are in Robert L. Tiemann, "Major League Attendance," in *Total Baseball: The Official Encyclopedia of Major League Baseball*, 7th ed., ed. John Thorn and others (Kingston, NY: Total Sports Publishing, 2001), 75; "Chicago Cubs Attendance Data," Baseball Almanac, accessed November 18, 2017, http://www.baseball-almanac.com/teams/cubsatte.shtml (notes that the National League attendance average for 1892 was 151,882; on the other hand, Chicago's season attendance in 1888 was 228,906). "We have lost enough" quotation is from "Baseball Brevities," *NYT*, October 6, 1892, 3.

15. The capital stock was $100,000. Reorganization of Chicago Ball Club is in "Chicago Club Sold," *CDT*, December 18, 1892, 6; "New Owners for a Ball Club," *NYT*, December 18, 1892, 3 (includes "from a financial" quotation); "Chicago's Changes," *SL*, December 24, 1892, 1; "Diamond Field Gossip," *NYC*, December 24, 1892, 677; "Hart Tells the Story," *TSN*, December 24, 1892, 2; "Time's Changes," *SL*, January 11, 1913, 15; Anson, *A Ball Player's Career*, 309 (mentions new name of club). New name of club is also in "Hart Writes of Anson," *CDT*, December 31, 1899, 18; "Anson Replies to Hart," *CDT*, January 7, 1900, 17. Occupations of Walsh and Trego are in John J. Flinn, *Chicago, the Marvelous City of the West: A History, an Encyclopedia, and a Guide*, 2nd ed. (Chicago: National Book and Picture Co., 1893), 143, 150. When William Hulbert died in 1882, Walsh and Trego were elected officers of the ball club. See "The Chicago Club," *NYC*, May 6, 1882, 107. Grounds on Polk Street are also in "Sunday Chicago League Games," *CDT*, April 26, 1892, 7.

16. The World's Fair and the Chicago club are in F[rank] H. Brunell, "Base Ball," *SL*, November 29, 1890, 9; "Chicago Plans," *SL*, October 15, 1892, 1 (includes "central and convenient" and "from a business" quotations); "Base Ball," *SL*, November 26, 1892, 3; "Chicago's Changes," *SL*, December 24, 1892, 1. World's Fair being open on Sundays is in Rachel E. Bohlmann, "Sunday Closings," in *The Encyclopedia of Chicago*, ed. James R. Grossman, Ann Durkin Keating, and Janice L. Reiff (Chicago: University of Chicago Press, 2004), 805; David F. Burg, *Chicago's White City of 1893* (Lexington: University Press of Kentucky, 1976), 89–91. Sale of old West Side Park is in "Will Play Sundays Next Year," *CDT*, August 21, 1892, 4; "Old Landmark Gone," *(Chicago) Daily Inter Ocean*, August 28, 1892, 10 (the bricks, benches, boards, and other material were purchased for the construction of a hotel at Vernon Park Place and Fayette Court, "in the immediate vicinity" of the ballpark). "We have labored" quotation is from "Chicago Gleanings," *SL*, April 22, 1893, 3 (includes a detailed description of the new park and mentions that the Chicago Maroons of the Western Association had played on the grounds in 1888). West Side Grounds is also in "Chicago Gleanings," *SL*, February 11, 1893, 4; Philip J. Lowry, *Green Cathedrals: The Ultimate Celebration of Major League and Negro League Ballparks* (New York: Walker, 2006), 49. Sunday baseball is in Art Ahrens, "Challenging Sunday Baseball in Old Chicago," *Base Ball: A Journal of the Early Game* 9 (2016): 130–44; Charlie Bevis, *Sunday Baseball: The Major Leagues' Struggle to Play Baseball on the Lord's Day, 1876–1934* (Jefferson, NC: McFarland, 2003). Game logs are in http://www.retrosheet.org/. Home games against Cincinnati at the South Side Park are in "Do Not Feel Frisky," *Chicago Evening Post*, May 11, 1893, 3. The game on May 11 was rained out. See "Has Confidence Yet," *CDT*, May 12, 1893, 7.

17. This article originally appeared as several long paragraphs (the first paragraph ending after the words "'place for them to sit'" and the second paragraph ending after "passengers near the gates"). A few additional paragraph breaks have been added for ease of readability. Excellent drawings and maps of the new grounds are in Marc Okkonen, *Baseball Memories, 1900–1909* (New York: Sterling, 1992), 43.

18. The *Chicago Evening Post* wrote that the distant outfield fences "will in a large measure cut down the number of home runs, which were such a conspicuous feature of the game at the old grounds." See "New Base Ball Park," *Chicago Evening Post*, April 16, 1893, 7.

19. According to "Late Official News," *SL*, May 13, 1893, 1, Chicago "released" both Caruthers and Taylor.

20. Score is in "Chicago Sad Sunday Defeat," *CDT*, May 15, 1893, 12. *Post* quotations, including Hart's remarks, are from "'Twas a Big Success," *Chicago Evening*

Post, May 15, 1893, five o'clock edition, 8. The lengthy quotation originally appeared as one long passage, and a paragraph break has been added for ease of readability. See also "The Chicago's First," *TSN*, May 20, 1893, 1. Composition of the National League, no split season, and 132 games are in [Francis C. Richter], "The Big League," *SL*, October 8, 1892, 2; "Dates of Baseball," *CDT*, March 9, 1893, 7; "The New Rules Adopted," *NYT*, March 9, 1893, 3; "Puts Him Back Five Feet," *WP*, March 8, 1893, 6. The pitcher's box, pitching rubber, and pitching distance are in "The Rule Changes," *SL*, April 22, 1893, 2; Peter Morris, *A Game of Inches: The Stories Behind the Innovations That Shaped Baseball*, rev. and exp. one-vol. ed. (Chicago: Ivan R. Dee, 2010), 26–27, 75, 389–91: "The intention of the rule makers was to move the pitcher back about five feet. But the five-and-a-half-foot pitcher's box had required the pitcher to keep his *front* foot fifty feet from home plate while the new rubber effectively determined the location of the pitcher's *rear* foot. This created the historic distance of sixty feet, six inches, but it also changed what that figure represented, with the result that the change was much less than ten feet" (p. 27). The pitching distance has remained at that measurement. "For the purpose" quotation is from "Diamond Field Gossip," *NYC*, November 26, 1892, 608 (William "Buck" Ewing of the New York Giants noted that with a longer pitching distance, batters would "have a better chance to g[au]ge the ball and more time to prepare to meet it"). See also "All Ready to Play Ball," *WP*, March 12, 1893, 6 ("more batting is desired").

21. Game logs and team standings are in http://www.retrosheet.org/. Increased batting averages are in "Wonderful Batting Averages," *Chicago Evening Post*, May 19, 1893, 3. "We have had" and "be given a fair" quotations are in "Has Confidence Yet," *CDT*, May 12, 1893, 7; "Baseball Brevities," *NYT*, May 17, 1893, 3. Hart leasing the grounds for the tournament is in Truax, "Chicago Gleanings," *SL*, June 24, 1893, 13. Baseball tournament is also in "College Teams are Scheduled," *CDT*, June 22, 1893, 5; "Games to Commence," *CDT*, June 25, 1893, 5. Articles and game-day accounts verify that beginning on June 18, the Colts played all their home games at the West Side Grounds. For example, see "Base Ball Notes," *CDT*, June 19, 1893, 12; "Anson Opens at Home Tomorrow," *CDT*, June 25, 1893, 5; "Cincinnati Plays Here Today," *CDT*, August 10, 1893, 8; "Won by a Scratch," *WP*, September 23, 1893, 6.

22. Game logs and team standings are in http://www.retrosheet.org/. Attendance is in "Chicago Gleanings," *SL*, September 30, 1893, 10 (includes quotations and Hart's rationale); Tiemann, "Major League Attendance," 75 (109,067 in 1892 and 223,500 in 1893); "Chicago Cubs Attendance Data," Baseball Almanac, accessed August 11, 2017, http://www.baseball-almanac.com/teams/cubs atte.shtml; "Editorial Views, News, Comment," *SL*, December 30, 1893, 2. The other league teams were also financially successful. See "Chicago Earned a Profit, *CDT*, October 1, 1893, 4; "Base Ball," *SL*, October 7, 1893, 3; "Base Ball in Chicago," *SL*, October 28, 1893, 4. "We abandoned it" quotation is from Joseph Burke, "Chicago National League Ball Club Played at 35th & Wentworth Ave." (Chicago, 1950), typescript, p. 3, Chicago History Museum.

23. "Never in the" quotation is from "Their Memory Dear," *CDT*, August 21, 1893, 12. Team statistics are in http://www.retrosheet.org/. Comments about black stockings and the pennant are in untitled article, *SL*, June 12, 1889, 4 (includes "we have no desire" quotation); "News, Gossip and Comment," *SL*, October 17, 1891, 2; "Editorial Views, News, Comment," *SL*, March 12, 1892, 2. The team's black stockings are also mentioned in "Games Played Tuesday, October 1," *SL*, October 9, 1889, 2; F[rancis] C. R[ichter], "Philadelphia Pointers," *SL*, September 6, 1890, 4; "Chicago Gleanings," *SL*, April 1, 1893, 1. See also "Whims of Players," *SL*, April 26, 1890, 11.

24. See "Chicago Gossip," *SL*, May 9, 1888, 8: "Mrs. Captain Anson designed [the uniform] and selected the colors, and too much credit cannot be given that lady for the excellent taste she has displayed."

25. In http://www.retrosheet.org/, the Chicago team is called the Colts from 1890–1897. "Colts" and "White Stockings" occasionally appeared in the same article. See "Chicago Colts Collapsed," *WP*, May 20, 1894, 15; "Baltimore Beats the Colts," *CDT*, June 25, 1894, 8; "Giants Play a Snappy Game," *NYT*, June 29, 1894, 3; "Chicago Gleanings," *SL*, September 15, 1894, 9. "Weak" and subsequent quotations are from "Chicagos Are Weak," *CDT*, April 23, 1894, 11.

26. Game logs and team standings are in http://www.retrosheet.org/. Details about the fire are in "Flames Stop a Ball Game," *NYT*, August 6, 1894, 1; "Flames Stop a Game," *WP*, August 6, 1894, 6; "Panic at a Fire," *CDT*, August 6, 1894, 1 (includes quotations); "Two Theories as to Fire's Origin," *CDT*, August 6, 1894, 2; "Again the Flames," *SL*, August 11, 1894, 2; "Chicago Gleanings," *SL*, September 15, 1894, 9 (mentions that "carpenters have completed their work on the stands"). Washington Monument anecdote is in "Schriver's Great Feat," *WP*, August 26, 1894, 3; "Schriver's Feat," *SL*, September 1, 1894, 1; "Schriver Censured," *SL*, September 15, 1894, 1.

27. Game logs and team standings are in http://www.retrosheet.org/. Anson's comments about his team are in "League Gossip; General Comment," *SL*, August 11, 1894, 2. "Review of" and "this year" quotations are from "Chicago Gleanings," *SL*, October 20, 1894, 4. Mike Kelly is in "'King' Kelly Dies of Pneumonia," *NYT*, November 9, 1894, 1; "Mike Kelly Is Out," *CDT*, November 9, 1894, 11 (includes quotations); "Kelly's Last Trip," *SL*, November 17, 1894, 5. Kelly played for Boston in 1892 and New York in 1893. After he left the Giants in 1893, Kelly played with minor league teams in Allentown, Pennsylvania, and Yonkers, New York. Kelly "could never keep money," according to the *Sporting Life* obituary, and performed in variety shows to earn extra cash. He would often recite the baseball poem "Casey at the Bat." See "Editorial Views, News, Comment," *SL*, April 1, 1893, 2.

28. Game logs and team standings are in http://www.retrosheet.org/. Baum as traveling salesman, part-time writer, Colts fan, and *Oz* author are in Katharine M. Rogers, *L. Frank Baum: Creator of Oz* (New York: St. Martin's Press, 2002), 47, 54–55, 66, 85–88, 261n40. "Two Pictures" is from the *Chicago Times-Herald*, May 17, 1896, 19. "Cuba's woes" in the poem refers to the island's fight for independence in its war against Spain.

29. "Ten years behind" quotation is from "Magnates Discuss Anson," *CDT*, November 10, 1897, 4. "It isn't a very" quotation is from "Brooklyn Budget," *SL*, June 19, 1897, 10. Baseball manager Gus Schmelz said of Anson in 1897 that it was possible "the game has grown beyond

him." See "Schmelz's Tribute," *SL*, November 13, 1897, 3. Anson preferring big players is in "Chicago Gleanings," *SL*, April 14, 1894, 4; "Big or Little?," *SL*, November 13, 1897, 3. Anson was six feet, two inches tall and weighed 218 pounds. See *Spalding's Base Ball Guide and Official League Book for 1887* (1887; repr., St. Louis: Horton Pub. Co., 1988), 10. "I don't care" quotation is from "Diamond Field Gossip," *NYC*, January 9, 1892, 735. Anson's weaknesses as a fielder are in "Anson and Comiskey," *SL*, November 6, 1897, 6; "Played 3,000 Games," *CDT*, February 1, 1898, 4. "On record" and "I can fine them" quotations are from "Your Uncle Still Has Some Hopes," *CDT*, September 26, 1896, 7.

30. "At least three" and "Anson realizes" quotations are from "The Taunts Tire Him," *WP*, May 22, 1897, 8. See also the game-day coverage in "Five Runs at Finish," *WP*, May 21, 1897, 8. On May 4, the day of the team's home opener, the Chicago club celebrated Anson's career with "Anson Day." Anson unsuccessfully tried to steal second base, which prompted the *Chicago Daily Tribune* to refer to him as an "agile hippopotamus." See "Uncle Anson Has a Day," *CDT*, May 5, 1897, 4. Game logs, player statistics, and team standings are in http://www.retrosheet.org/. Anson having no plans to retire is in "Anson's Dinner," *SL*, October 16, 1897, 10; W[illiam] A. Phelon Jr., "Chicago Gleanings," *SL*, October 16, 1897, 10.

31. Anson's and Hart's relationship is in Anson, *A Ball Player's Career*, 306–309. "Not even distant" quotation and Hart rescinding fines are in W[illia]m F. H. Koelsch, "New York Nuggets," *SL*, March 19, 1898, 6. Hart blaming Anson and the Boston sportswriter's quotations are in Tim Murnane, "Anson's Future," *SL*, November 20, 1897, 9. See also "Tales of a Feud," *SL*, October 23, 1897, 5 (mentions that Hart had wanted to "dispense with the services" of Anson after Hart's first year with Chicago and that Hart had supposedly prevented Anson from releasing player Jim Connor in April 1897); "Magnates Discuss Anson," *CDT*, November 10, 1897, 4 (mentions the "strained relations" between Anson and Hart); "Anson May Get in Games," *CDT*, July 15, 1901, 2 (mentions that "Walsh [is] said to be unfriendly" to Anson); "Sporting Gossip," *(Cincinnati) Sun*, November 22, 1885, 4: "Walsh is president of the Western News company. When Spalding, on a capital of $700, opened a sporting goods emporium in Chicago, Walsh bought 10,000 baseballs from him for the News company. This placed Albert squarely on his feet. Walsh first advanced the money to organize and equip the Chicago team, giving Spalding a share of stock conditional upon profits. As the profits have been immense Spalding has made a small fortune." Walsh's career is in Joel A. Tarr, "J. R. Walsh of Chicago: A Case Study in Banking and Politics, 1881–1905," *Business History Review* 40, no. 4 (Winter 1966), 451–66. Anson's Chicago team won pennants in 1880, 1881, 1882, 1885, and 1886.

32. Burns and league meeting are in "Anson Likely to Go," *CDT*, November 11, 1897, 4 (includes "well, it looks" quotation); Tim Murnane, "Anson's Future," *SL*, November 20, 1897, 9 (includes "that would suit me" quotation). Rumors of Anson leaving are in "'Pop' Anson, After Thirty Years, Is to Retire," *SL*, May 29, 1897, 1; "Discuss Anson's Work," *CDT*, July 18, 1897, 28; "Capt. Anson May Retire," *NYT*, October 3, 1897, 6; Colt, "Passing of Anson," *TSN*, January 29, 1898, 1. Anson's dismissal is in "Anson's Last Day," *CDT*, January 31, 1898, 4 (mentions his contract expiring at midnight); "Played 3,000 Games," *CDT*, February 1, 1898, 4 (includes "Adrian Constantine Anson is no longer" quotation); "Good-by to Anson," *CDT*, February 2, 1898, 4 (includes "it is the desire" quotation); "Pop Anson Goes Down," *WP*, February 2, 1898, 8; W[illiam] A. Phelon Jr., "Chicago Gleanings," *SL*, February 5, 1898, 6; W[illiam] A. Phelon Jr., "Chicago Gleanings," *SL*, February 12, 1898, 5.

33. *Sporting Life* article is "Greatest of All," *SL*, February 12, 1898, 7 (notes that "he has been credited with 3034 base hits"). Anson's statistics are also in "Cap Anson," Retrosheet, accessed February 25, 2018, http://www.retrosheet.org/boxesetc/A/Pansoc101.htm. Some baseball statisticians question whether Anson made 3,000 hits. See David L. Fleitz, *Cap Anson: The Grand Old Man of Baseball* (Jefferson, NC: McFarland, 2005), 310. An excellent profile of Anson is David Ball, David Nemec, and Peter Morris, "Anson, Adrian Constantine/'Cap' 'Anse' 'Uncle' 'Pop' 'Baby,'" in *Major League Baseball Profiles, 1871–1900*, vol. 2, comp. and ed. David Nemec (Lincoln: University of Nebraska Press, 2011), 3–5.

34. "The Anson tricks" and "but of course" quotations are from John E. Calvin, "Anson Is Out," *TSN*, February 5, 1898, 1. Tom Burns taking charge of team is in "Burns Anson's Successor," *WP*, February 10, 1898, 8; "Tom Burns Is Here," *CDT*, February 24, 1898, 5; "Burns Is in Charge," *CDT*, March 5, 1898, 7. Burns wanting a new team name is in "Team at Waycross," *CDT*, March 15, 1898, 5; "News and Comment," *SL*, March 26, 1898, 5. Suggestions for new names are in "Suggest New Names," *CDT*, March 16, 1898, 4; "Pitchers in Form," *CDT*, March 19, 1898, 7; "Offer New Names," *CDT*, March 21, 1898, 9 (includes quotations); "News and Comment," *SL*, April 2, 1898, 5 (mentions Orphans); W[illiam] F. H. Koelsch, "Gotham's Grief," *SL*, October 21, 1899, 4. See note 32 for mention of "Pop Anson." Early-season articles that mention the name Orphans include Elmer E. Bates, "Cleveland Chatter," *SL*, May 21, 1898, 9; "Anson at the Game," *CDT*, May 22, 1898, 7; "Chicago, 20; Baltimore, 4," *NYT*, May 26, 1898, 10; "Orphans' Double Loss," *WP*, May 31, 1898, 8; J[ohn] E. Calvin, "Are Erratic," *TSN*, June 18, 1898, 1.

35. New uniforms are in "White Stockings Go," *CDT*, February 16, 1898, 4 (includes "the Chicago club" quotation and mentions that the old home uniform was white and the road uniform was "rebel gray and white"); "News and Comment," *SL*, February 26, 1898, 2; "Open with Victory," *CDT*, April 16, 1898, 7 (mentions the road "maroon and gray suits"); "News and Comment," *SL*, April 23, 1898, 5 (mentions Chicago's road "maroon suits"); "Season Well Begun," *CDT*, April 30, 1898, 7 (mentions the attendance and the home team "robed in white with maroon stockings"); "Burns Is the Captain," *CDT*, April 14, 1899, 4; "News and Comment," *SL*, April 22, 1899, 3 (mentions that the "Y" on the players' caps "is the emblem of the Windy City" and signifies "the 'city among the rivers'").

36. Slumping attendance is in "Pat No Pessimist," *SL*, October 15, 1898, 1. "Demoralized club" quotation is from W[illiam] A. Phelon Jr., "Chicago Gleanings," *SL*, February 5, 1898, 6. Game logs and team standings are in http://www.retrosheet.org/. Captaincy of team is in "The Chicago Captaincy," *SL*, April 2, 1898, 6. "Good-natured," "kicking," and "to the mind" quotations are

from "Burns' Orphans," *SL*, September 3, 1898, 8. Dahlen and his "kicking" are also in "Baseball," *NYC*, November 26, 1898, 663. Dahlen trade is in "Hart Favors Changes," *CDT*, November 29, 1898, 4; W[illiam] A. Phelon Jr., "Chicago Gleanings," *SL*, December 10, 1898, 6; "Burns Discusses the Trade," *CDT*, January 24, 1899, 4; "Dahlen Now an Oriole," *CDT*, January 26, 1899, 4; "In Interest of Discipline," *CDT*, January 26, 1899, 4 (includes "the exchange was made" quotation); "Demont Traded for Dahlen," *SL*, January 28, 1899, 3. Dahlen went to Brooklyn in February. See John B. Foster, "Foster's Fancies," *SL*, February 18, 1899, 5.

37. "The team is weak" quotation is from W[illiam] A. Phelon Jr., "Chicago Gleanings," *SL*, June 17, 1899, 7. Poor evaluation of team is also in "Baseball Outlook in the National League Cities," *CDT*, April 14, 1899, 4. Team captain is in W[illiam] A. Phelon Jr., "Phelon's Pennings," *SL*, March 18, 1899, 8; "Six Players Holding Out," *CDT*, March 26, 1899, sec. 4, 1; "Talk of Chicago's Team," *CDT*, August 28, 1899, 4 (includes "put his foot," "bowed to the will," "has been charged," and "manager Burns, so his" quotations); "Ever[i]tt Captain of the Orphans," *WP*, April 18, 1899, 8; "News and Comment," *SL*, April 22, 1899, 3 (mentions that Burns compromised). See also "Hart Hits Hard," *SL*, June 17, 1899, 7.

38. Settled in eighth place is in "Chicago Lands in Eighth Place," *CDT*, October 14, 1899, 6. Game logs and team standings are in http://www.retrosheet.org/ (Brooklyn ended the season in first place). "Was in more" quotation is from "Ball-Players' Records," *CDT*, October 15, 1899, 20. Burns's release and Loftus's hiring are in "Loftus to Be Manager," *CDT*, November 12, 1899, 20 (includes "he is fearless" quotation); "Loftus Has a Talk with Hart," *CDT*, November 17, 1899, 4; T[im] H. Murnane, "Say Burns Expected to Return," *CDT*, November 30, 1899, 7 (mentions that "Tom Burns must have been surprised when he learned that Chicago had accepted his resignation and signed Tom Loftus to manage the Chicago club"); "Burns' Belief," *SL*, December 9, 1899, 1; W[illiam] A. Phelon Jr., "Chicago Gleanings," *SL*, December 9, 1899, 5 (mentions that "not till Burns, down in Springfield, read the next morning's papers, did he know that he had 'resigned'"); Jacob C. Morse, "Hub Happenings," *SL*, December 16, 1899, 6. See also David Nemec, "Loftus, Thomas Joseph/'Tom,'" in *Major League Baseball Profiles, 1871–1900*, vol. 2, 131–32.

39. Loftus's efforts and various opinions of 1900 team are in "Loftus Will Come Saturday," *CDT*, December 7, 1899, 7; "Deals for New Players," *CDT*, December 12, 1899, 4; "Chicago's New Ball Players," *CDT*, December 17, 1899, 18; [William] A. Phelon Jr., "Chicago Gleanings," *SL*, March 31, 1900, 7 (mentions that the "fans are critical and dubious" about the team's chances for success); "Orphans Are in Poor Condition," *CDT*, April 1, 1900, 17; "The Same Old Gang," *SL*, April 7, 1900, 6 (includes "indifferent attitude" and "from all accounts" quotations); "Chicago's Grief," *SL*, April 14, 1900, 2 (mentions that "the Chicago Club of 1900 is not a pennant winner"); "News and Comment," *SL*, April 14, 1900, 5 (includes "malcontents" quotation and the statement that "Manager Tom Loftus does not seem very sanguine about the Orphans"); "Comparison of League Teams," *CDT*, April 15, 1900, 17. Game logs and team standings are in http://www.retrosheet.org/. Changes in National League are in Henry Chadwick, ed., *Spalding's Official Base Ball Guide [for 1901]*, 20th century ed. (New York: American Sports Pub. Co., 1901), 10 (includes "top-heavy and unmanageable" quotation); "Baseball Men Here," *NYT*, March 7, 1900, 9; "Agree on Eight Club Circuit," *CDT*, March 9, 1900, 4; "Baseball," *NYC*, March 17, 1900, 61; "The World of Base Ball," *SL*, March 17, 1900, 2.

40. Western League teams in the Midwest are in "The West Alive," *SL*, November 4, 1893, 1; "Made Up at Last," *SL*, November 25, 1893, 1 (mentions the election of Ban Johnson as league president). The Western League changing its name to the American League is in "American League," *SL*, October 21, 1899, 6 (includes "hampering" quotation). Articles on the new American League include "New League's Status," *WP*, November 10, 1899, 8; "More League Trouble," *WP*, March 5, 1900, 8; "Start a Second League," *CDT*, March 13, 1900, 6; "Eight in New League," *WP*, March 13, 1900, 8; "Baseball," *NYC*, March 17, 1900, 61; "New Baseball Faces," *CDT*, April 8, 1900, 18; "Magnates' Quick Work," *CDT*, April 13, 1900, 4; "American League Opening Today," *CDT*, April 21, 1900, 6 (also mentions Charles Comiskey and the White Stockings at their "new park at Thirty-ninth street and Wentworth avenue"). Charles Comiskey and the new league are in "St. Paul Safe," *SL*, November 25, 1899, 2; "A Triple Invasion," *SL*, December 2, 1899, 5; "Milwaukee Mems," *SL*, December 16, 1899, 3; F[rancis] C. R[ichter], "St. Paul Siftings," *SL*, December 23, 1899, 8; "Comiskey's Chaps," *SL*, April 14, 1900, 4; "Credit Due to Padden," *CDT*, September 16, 1900, 20; G. W. Axelson, *"Commy": The Life Story of Charles A. Comiskey* (Chicago: Reilly & Lee Co., 1919), 131–44. American League becoming a major league is in Francis C. Richter, "American League," *SL*, February 2, 1901, 4; "Baseball," *NYC*, February 9, 1901, 1113. White Sox name is in "Orphans Find Batting Eyes," *CDT*, April 12, 1901, 6. The 1901 American League teams are in http://www.retrosheet.org/. See also Lee Allen, *The American League Story*, rev. ed. (New York: Hill and Wang, 1965); Warren N. Wilbert, *The Arrival of the American League: Ban Johnson and the 1901 Challenge to National League Monopoly* (Jefferson, NC: McFarland, 2007).

41. "Hard hit" and "there appears" quotations are from W[illiam] A. Phelon Jr., "Chicago Gleanings," *SL*, March 16, 1901, 11. Griffith signed is in "Star Players for Comiskey," *CDT*, March 2, 1901, 6; "Clark Griffith Is Here," *CDT*, March 23, 1901, 6. Griffith would later become owner of the Washington Senators. "The fact" quotation is from "Managers Are Uneasy," *WP*, March 15, 1901, 8. "Remnants" is in "Six Orphans Make Trip," *CDT*, April 1, 1901, 8; "News and Comment," *SL*, April 27, 1901, 3; W[illiam] A. Phelon Jr., "Chicago Gleanings," *SL*, April 27, 1901, 12; "Remnants and the White Sox," *CDT*, July 24, 1901, 6 (mentions players leaving the Orphans). "If some of our men" quotation is from W[illiam] A. Phelon Jr., "Chicago Gleanings," *SL*, March 9, 1901, 4. Team composition is in http://www.retrosheet.org/.

42. Clubs competing for players is in "Old League Is Losing Prestige," *CDT*, October 6, 1901, 17 (mentions that "what was left [on the Chicago team] after the American league was through was mediocre material, and it was too late in the season to get other men"). "Loftus has made" quotation is from "Orphans in Other Clubs," *CDT*, July 14, 1901, 19. Game logs and team standings are in http://www.retrosheet.org/. See also "Sports

Review for Year 1901," *CDT*, December 31, 1901, 7. Loftus leaving the Orphans is in "Loftus Leaves the Remnants," *CDT*, October 26, 1901, 8. Loftus becoming manager of the Washington Senators is in "Split with Johnson," *WP*, October 30, 1901, 8; "Loftus Succeeds Manning," *WP*, November 2, 1901, 8. Frank Selee and pennants is in "Final Summons to Frank Selee," *CDT*, July 6, 1909, 16. "Selee assumes" quotation is from "Frank Selee Is the Man," *CDT*, October 27, 1901, 20. "The Chicago National League club" quotation is from "Baseball Notes," *WP*, October 29, 1901, 8.

43. "A Kansas City youngster" quotation is from "New Men for Remnants," *CDT*, December 22, 1901, 19. "A team of younger" and "the effects of" quotations are from "Selee Releases Captain Doyle," *CDT*, February 26, 1902, 6. Doyle's temper is in W[illia]m F. [H.] Koelsch, "Base Ball," *SL*, June 15, 1895, 10. See also "Doyle Done Over," *SL*, March 8, 1902, 7; "Lowe to Captain Remnants," *CDT*, April 3, 1902, 6 (mentions Bobby Lowe as new team captain). "Revival of the old" quotation is from "Baseball Season Begins Today," *CDT*, April 17, 1902, 6. Need for a new club name is also in "Selee Names Chicago's Team," *CDT*, February 9, 1902, 17.

44. Selee's young players are in W[illiam] A. Phelon Jr., "Chicago Gleanings," *SL*, March 15, 1902, 11; "To Weed the Remnants," *CDT*, April 13, 1902, 10; "Colts Off for Cincinnati," *CDT*, April 17, 1902, 6; W[illiam] A. Phelon Jr., "Chicago Gleanings," *SL*, April 19, 1902, 8. Fred A. Hayner is in Don Hayner, "His Family's Connection to the Cubs? Naming the Team," *Chicago Sun-Times*, October 26, 2016, 6. "Frank Selee will devote" quotation is from "Selee Places His Men," *Chicago Daily News*, March 27, 1902, 4 (one of the article's subtitles refers to Selee's "Bunch of Fast Youngsters"). James Gilruth and "we tried one name" quotation is in Donald Yabush, "Editor Recalls Days of Glory: Sandburg 'Pest,'" *CT*, October 12, 1972, sec. 4A, 3. See also Woodruff, Harvey T., "In the Wake of the News," *CDT*, October 2, 1932, sec. 2, 6; Dickson, *The Dickson Baseball Dictionary*, 229.

Postscript

1. "Colts" are in "Rain Balks the Colts," *CDT*, June 1, 1902, 9; "Jim Hart's Scheme," *SL*, December 27, 1902, 8. "Orphans" are in "News and Gossip," *SL*, April 26, 1902, 7; "One Orphan Got to Third," *WP*, April 27, 1902, 8. "Remnants" are in "Remnants Have Revenge," *CDT*, April 6, 1902, 9; "Nearly Closed the Gap," *WP*, May 27, 1902, 9. "Cubs" are in "Baseball Notes," *WP*, October 5, 1902, 8; W[illiam] A. Phelon Jr., "Chicago Gleanings," *SL*, March 14, 1903, 2. "Microbes" are in "Giants Losers in the First Game," *(New York) Evening World*, July 4, 1903, sporting edition, 1; "Microbes Lose Second Place to Giants," *Chicago Evening American*, September 26, 1903, sporting extra edition, 1. "Selee's Colts" are in "Fans Welcome Selee's Colts," *CDT*, April 22, 1902, 13; W[illia]m F. H. Koelsch, "New York Nuggets," *SL*, June 20, 1903, 5; "Giants 4 to the Chicagos 3," *(New York) Evening World*, August 3, 1904, evening edition, 1. Both "Colts" and "Cubs" are in W[illiam] A. Phelon Jr., "Chicago Gleanings," *SL*, May 3, 1902, 12; "Colts Defeat the Reds," *CDT*, June 22, 1902, 9; "Colts Leave for Coast," *CDT*, March 8, 1903, 9. Team names are in W[illiam] A. Phelon Jr., "Chicago Gleanings," *SL*, January 4, 1902, 5 (mentions the Nationals, Hartites, Remnants, Orphans, and the Tribe of Selee); "Pittsburg Easy for Selee's Men," *CDT*, June 27, 1904, 8 (mentions the Tribe of Selee); "Baseball Notes," *WP*, April 21, 1902, 8 (mentions Sprouts, Seedlings, Cubs, Remnants, Orphans, Recruits, Colts, Seleeites, and Chicagos). In 1899 the Chicago club held spring training in New Mexico, so the team was occasionally called the "Rough Riders." See "Start Play This Week," *CDT*, April 3, 1899, 6; W[illiam] A. Phelon Jr., "Cheerless Chicago," *SL*, September 2, 1899, 8. "Generally known as" quotation is from Woodruff, Harvey T., "In the Wake of the News," *CDT*, October 2, 1932, sec. 2, 6. See also John Snyder, *Cubs Journal: Year by Year and Day by Day with the Chicago Cubs Since 1876* (Cincinnati: Clerisy Press, 2008), 16–17.

2. Evers signed to team is in "New Infielder for the Colts," *CDT*, August 30, 1902, 6. Chance signed is in "May Let Decker Go," *CDT*, March 9, 1898, 6. Tinker signed is in "New Men for Remnants," *CDT*, December 22, 1901, 19. The signing of another player, Jim St. Vrain, is in "National News," *SL*, June 28, 1902, 9. Frank Chance originally joined the Chicago team as catcher but Selee later moved him to first base. See "In Los Angeles," *SL*, January 1, 1898, 7; W[illiam] A. Phelon Jr., "Chicago Gleanings," *SL*, August 2, 1902, 5. Two double plays are in "Two Defeats for Colts," *CDT*, September 15, 1902, 6; "Lundgren Holds Reds at Bay," *CDT*, September 16, 1902, 6; "Notes of the Colts," *CDT*, September 16, 1902, 6 (includes "played second base" quotation). The poem "That Double Play Again" is from Franklin P. Adams, "Always in Good Humor," *(New York) Evening Mail*, July 12, 1910, 6. The three players were inducted into the Baseball Hall of Fame together in 1946. Despite the tone of Adams's poem, he was actually a Cubs fan. See Jack Bales, with Tim Wiles, "Franklin P. Adams's 'Trio of Bear Cubs,'" *NINE: A Journal of Baseball History and Culture* 19, no. 2 (Spring 2011): 114–40.

3. Game logs, team standings, and player statistics are in http://www.retrosheet.org/. "Brown is considered" quotation is from "Post-Meeting Deals," *SL*, December 19, 1903, 7. Brown's farming accident is in "3 Finger Brown, Cubs' Former Pitcher, Dies," *CDT*, February 15, 1948, sec. 2, 1. Selee's illness is in "National League News," *SL*, July 22, 1905, 10 (mentions Chance); "Selee Is Forced to Quit the Game," *CDT*, July 29, 1905, 4 (includes "unerring instinct" and "produced a team" quotations); W[illiam] A. Phelon Jr., "Chicago Gleanings," *SL*, August 12, 1905, 5; "Breezy Baseball Babble," *WP*, August 12, 1906, Sporting sec., 2 (mentions Chance). Frank Chance as leader is also in John J. Evers and Hugh S. Fullerton, *Touching Second* (1910; repr., Jefferson, NC: McFarland, 2005), 30, 51–52.

4. Game logs, team standings, and player statistics are in http://www.retrosheet.org/. Hart and Murphy are in "Murphy Takes Up Hart's Burden," *CDT*, July 16, 1905, sec. 2, 1; "Murphy's Promotion," *SL*, July 22, 1905, 8; "Hart to Retire Oct. 15," *CDT*, July 29, 1905, 4; "Chicago Gleanings," *SL*, August 12, 1905, 5; "Local Baseball Deal Ratified," *CDT*, November 2, 1905, 10 (includes "he is not only" quotation); "Chicago's Change," *SL*, November 11, 1905, 7; "The New Magnate," *SL*, November 11, 1905, 7 (notes that Murphy bought the club with the financial backing of his friend Charles P. Taft. Taft was the half-brother of William Howard Taft, U.S. president from 1909–1913). Purchase price of club was $105,000. See "A Lucky Deal," *SL*, October 6, 1906, 11; "Murphy's Enter-

prise," *SL*, September 4, 1909, 15. Club ownership details at this time are unclear. Hart reportedly had purchased the club stock of John R. Walsh and Al Spalding in May 1902 (see "Walsh Sells His Stock," *CDT*, May 21, 1902, 18; "Mr. Hart's Confidence," *SL*, May 31, 1902, 4), but in 1913, *Sporting Life* wrote "it was Walsh's stock that Hart sold to C. W. Murphy for $105,000, including Hart's commission of $5000" (see "Time's Changes," *SL*, January 11, 1913, 15). See also "Facts and Fancy," *SL*, December 30, 1905, 4. Club stockholders in 1901 are in "Anson May Get in Games," *CDT*, July 15, 1901, 2.

5. Game logs and team standings are in http://www.retrosheet.org/. No World Series was played in 1904 as the two leagues could not reach a contractual agreement. Prediction of a Cubs win is in "Cubs Heavy Favorites," *WP*, October 9, 1906, 8; H[ugh] S. Fullerton, "Series Verifies Fullerton's Dope," *CDT*, October 15, 1906, 4. "Victory goes" quotation is from Lee Allen, *The World Series: The Story of Baseball's Annual Championship* (New York: G. P. Putnam's Sons, 1969), 61 (no World Series in 1904 is on pages 52–53). "We played our hardest" quotation is from "'Fairly Won,' Says Chance," *CDT*, October 15, 1906, 3. See also Francis C. Richter, "Result of Battle of the Major Giants," *SL*, October 20, 1906, 5; "Ovation for Winners," *SL*, October 20, 1906, 7; Bernard A. Weisberger, *When Chicago Ruled Baseball: The Cubs–White Sox World Series of 1906* (New York: William Morrow), 2006; Bruce A. Rubenstein, *Chicago in the World Series, 1903–2005: The Cubs and White Sox in Championship Play* (Jefferson, NC: McFarland, 2006), 3–17.

6. "Peerless Leader" is in L[ee] G. Allen, "Public Opinion," *SL*, September 14, 1907, 6; H[ugh] E. K[eough], "In the Wake of the News," *CDT*, December 5, 1907, 8. Game logs and team standings are in http://www.retrosheet.org/. The 1907 World Series is in Allen, *The World Series*, 61–63; Rubenstein, *Chicago in the World Series*, 18–29. Name on 1907 scorecards is in Arthur R. Ahrens, "How the Cubs Got Their Name," *Chicago History* 5, no. 1 (Spring 1976), 43; "1907 World Series," Baseball Almanac, accessed December 9, 2017, http://www.baseball-almanac.com/ws/yr1907ws.shtml. See also "Chicago 'Cubs,'" *SL*, June 8, 1907, 17; W[illiam] A. Phelon [Jr.], "Chicago Chat," *SL*, March 13, 1909, 15. Gold medals are in "Design for Cubs' World's Medals," *CDT*, November 24, 1907, sec., 3, 4. *Spalding's Official Base Ball Guide* mentions the "first division cubs" and "Cubs" in its 1903 edition, and "Cubs" would regularly be used beginning in the 1907 volume. See Henry Chadwick, ed., *Spalding's Official Base Ball Guide*, [1903] (New York: American Sports Pub. Co., 1903), 173, 203; Henry Chadwick, ed., *Spalding's Official Base Ball Guide, 1907* (New York: American Sports Pub. Co., 1907), 57, 131, 139, 141, 145, 149, 153.

7. The 1908 Cubs uniform is in Marc Okkonen, *Baseball Uniforms of the 20th Century: The Official Major League Baseball Guide* (New York: Sterling, 1993), 105. In 1913 the word "CUBS" replaced the jersey emblem of the bear with the baseball bat. The park decorated with bear cubs is in "Pennant to Fly," *SL*, April 11, 1908, 1. "The Cub pennant" quotation is in Charles Dryden, "Cubs Take Game by Clever Work," *CDT*, April 23, 1908, 8. A picture of the pennant is in "National League Pennant to Be Unfurled by Cubs This Afternoon," *CDT*, April 22, 1908, 13.

8. Game logs and team standings are in http://www.retrosheet.org/. Close race is in "National League Teams Are Ready for the 1908 Campaign, Which Is Expected to Be a Close Race," *WP*, January 19, 1908, Sporting sec., 3. "Crazy '08" is from Cait Murphy, *Crazy '08: How a Cast of Cranks, Rogues, Boneheads, and Magnates Created the Greatest Year in Baseball History* (New York: Smithsonian/Collins, 2007). See also G. H. Fleming, *The Unforgettable Season* (New York: Holt, Rinehart and Winston, 1981); David W. Anderson, *More Than Merkle: A History of the Best and Most Exciting Baseball Season in Human History* (Lincoln: University of Nebraska Press, 2000); George R. Matthews, *When the Cubs Won It All: The 1908 Championship Season* (Jefferson, NC: McFarland, 2009). New York as rivals is in I[rving] E. Sanborn, "Training Jaunts Start This Week," *CDT*, February 23, 1908, Sporting sec., 2. Sanborn and baseball organization is in "Scorers' Association," *SL*, October 24, 1908, 13. "He drove the final" quotation is from I[rving] E. Sanborn, "Cubs Supreme in Baseball World," *CDT*, October 15, 1908, 1. "Chance was one" quotation is from C. P. Stack, "A Day with John Evers," *Baseball Magazine*, February 1915, 74. See also Ren Mulford, Jr., "A Frank Chance Story," *SL*, October 26, 1907, 2, which mentions "Captain Chance" and his "ability to get the best out of the men" on his team.

9. As all Cubs fans know, the dynasty would not last. The Cubs finished second in the National League in 1909, and although they took the league pennant in 1910, they fell to the Philadelphia Athletics in the World Series. The Cubs clinched the National League pennant in 1918, 1929, 1932, 1935, 1938, and 1945, but would not claim another World Series title until 2016, 100 years after they moved to Weeghman Park, later called Wrigley Field.

Bibliography

Books

Allen, Lee. *The National League Story: The Official History*. Rev. ed. New York: Hill and Wang, 1965.

Anson, Adrian C. *A Ball Player's Career, Being the Personal Experiences and Reminiscences of Adrian C. Anson*. 1900. Reprint, Mattituck, NY: Amereon House, n.d.

Bartlett, Arthur. *Baseball and Mr. Spalding: The History and Romance of Baseball*. New York: Farrar, Straus and Young, 1951.

Batesel, Paul. *Players and Teams of the National Association, 1871–1875*. Jefferson, NC: McFarland, 2012.

Dickson, Paul. *The Dickson Baseball Dictionary*. 3rd ed. New York: Norton, 2009.

Evers, John J., and Hugh S. Fullerton. *Touching Second*. 1910. Reprint, Jefferson, NC: McFarland, 2005.

Federal Writers' Project (Illinois), Work Project Administration. *Baseball in Old Chicago*. Chicago: A. C. McClurg, 1939.

Felber, Bill, ed. *Inventing Baseball: The 100 Greatest Games of the 19th Century*. Phoenix: Society for American Baseball Research, 2013.

Fleitz, David L. *Cap Anson: The Grand Old Man of Baseball*. Jefferson, NC: McFarland, 2005.

Gillette, Gary, and Pete Palmer, eds. *The ESPN Baseball Encyclopedia*. 4th ed. New York: Sterling Publishing, 2007.

Gold, Eddie, and Art Ahrens. *The Golden Era Cubs, 1876–1940*. Chicago: Bonus Books, 1985.

Goldstein, Warren. *Playing for Keeps: A History of Early Baseball*. 20th anniversary ed. Ithaca: Cornell University Press, 2009.

Golenbock, Peter. *Wrigleyville: A Magical History Tour of the Chicago Cubs*. New York: St. Martin's Press, 1996.

Ivor-Campbell, Frederick, and others, eds. *Baseball's First Stars*. Cleveland: Society for American Baseball Research, 1996.

James, Bill. *The New Bill James Historical Baseball Abstract*. New York: Free Press, 2001.

Levine, Peter. *A. G. Spalding and the Rise of Baseball: The Promise of American Sport*. New York: Oxford University Press, 1985.

Light, Jonathan Fraser. *The Cultural Encyclopedia of Baseball*. 2nd ed. Jefferson, NC: McFarland, 2005.

Lowry, Philip J. *Green Cathedrals: The Ultimate Celebration of Major League and Negro League Ballparks*. New York: Walker, 2006.

MacDonald, Neil W. *The League That Lasted: 1876 and the Founding of the National League of Professional Base Ball Clubs*. Jefferson, NC: McFarland, 2004.

Melville, Tom. *Early Baseball and the Rise of the National League*. Jefferson, NC: McFarland, 2001.

Morris, Peter. *But Didn't We Have Fun? An Informal History of Baseball's Pioneer Era, 1843–1870*. Chicago: Ivan R. Dee, 2008.

_____. *A Game of Inches: The Stories Behind the Innovations That Shaped Baseball*. Rev. and exp. one-vol. ed. Chicago: Ivan R. Dee, 2010.

_____, and others, eds. *Base Ball Founders: The Clubs, Players and Cities of the Northeast That Established the Game*. Jefferson, NC: McFarland, 2013.

_____, and others, eds. *Base Ball Pioneers, 1850–1870: The Clubs and Players Who Spread the Sport Nationwide*. Jefferson, NC: McFarland, 2012.

Names, Larry. *Bury My Heart at Wrigley Field: The History of the Chicago Cubs*. Neshkoro: Angel Press of Wisconsin, 1996.

Nemec, David. *The Great Encyclopedia of Nineteenth Century Major League Baseball*. 2nd ed. Tuscaloosa: University of Alabama Press, 2006.

_____. *The Rank and File of 19th Century Major League Baseball: Biographies of 1,084 Players, Owners, Managers and Umpires*. Jefferson, NC: McFarland, 2012.

_____, comp. and ed. *Major League Baseball Profiles, 1871–1900*. 2 vols. Lincoln: University of Nebraska Press, 2011. Vol. 1, *The Ballplayers Who Built the Game*. Vol. 2, *The Hall of Famers and Memorable Personalities Who Shaped the Game*.

Orem, Preston D. *Baseball (1845–1881): From the Newspaper Accounts.* Altadena, CA: Preston D. Orem, 1961.

Pietrusza, David. *Major Leagues: The Formation, Sometimes Absorption, and Mostly Inevitable Demise of 18 Professional Baseball Organizations, 1871 to Present.* Jefferson, NC: McFarland, 2006.

Richter, Francis C. *Richter's History and Records of Base Ball: The American Nation's Chief Sport.* 1914. Reprint, Jefferson, NC: McFarland, 2005.

Riess, Steven A. *Touching Base: Professional Baseball and American Culture in the Progressive Era.* Rev. ed. Urbana: University of Illinois Press, 1999.

Roberts, Randy, and Carson Cunningham, eds. *Before the Curse: The Chicago Cubs' Glory Years, 1870–1945.* Urbana: University of Illinois Press, 2012.

Rosenberg, Howard W. *Cap Anson.* 4 vols. [Arlington, VA]: Tile Books, 2003–2006.

Rucker, Mark, and John Freyer. *19th Century Baseball in Chicago.* Charleston, SC: Arcadia, 2003.

Ryczek, William J. *Blackguards and Red Stockings: A History of Baseball's National Association, 1871–1875.* Wallingford, CT: Colebrook Press, 1999.

_____. *When Johnny Came Sliding Home: The Post-Civil War Baseball Boom, 1865–1870.* Jefferson, NC: McFarland, 1998.

Schiff, Andrew J. *"The Father of Baseball": A Biography of Henry Chadwick.* Jefferson, NC: McFarland, 2008.

Seymour, Harold. *Baseball: The Early Years.* New York: Oxford University Press, 1989.

Snyder, John. *Cubs Journal: Year by Year and Day by Day with the Chicago Cubs Since 1876.* Cincinnati: Clerisy Press, 2008.

Spalding, Albert G. *America's National Game: Historic Facts Concerning the Beginning, Evolution, Development and Popularity of Base Ball.* 1911. Reprint, Lincoln: University of Nebraska Press, 1992.

Spalding's Base Ball Guide and Official League Book (assorted annual volumes).

Spink, Alfred H. *The National Game.* 2nd ed. 1911. Reprint, Carbondale: Southern Illinois University Press, 2000.

Stout, Glenn, and Richard A. Johnson. *The Cubs: The Complete Story of Chicago Cubs Baseball.* Boston: Houghton Mifflin, 2007.

Sullivan, Dean A., comp. and ed. *Early Innings: A Documentary History of Baseball, 1825–1908.* Lincoln: University of Nebraska Press, 1997.

Thorn, John. *Baseball in the Garden of Eden: The Secret History of the Early Game.* New York: Simon & Schuster, 2011.

_____, and others, eds. *Total Baseball: The Official Encyclopedia of Major League Baseball.* 7th ed. Kingston, NY: Total Sports Publishing, 2001.

Tiemann, Robert L., and Mark Rucker, eds. *Nineteenth Century Stars.* Phoenix: Society for American Baseball Research, 2012.

Voigt, David Quentin. *American Baseball.* Vol. 1, *From Gentleman's Sport to the Commissioner System.* University Park: Pennsylvania State University Press, 1983.

Wilbert, Warren N. *Opening Pitch: Professional Baseball's Inaugural Season, 1871.* Lanham, MD: Scarecrow Press, 2008.

Wood, Gerald C., and Andrew Hazucha. *Northsiders: Essays on the History and Culture of the Chicago Cubs.* Jefferson, NC: McFarland, 2008.

Wright, Marshall D. *The National Association of Base Ball Players, 1857–1870.* Jefferson, NC: McFarland, 2000.

_____. *Nineteenth Century Baseball: Year-by-Year Statistics for the Major League Teams, 1871 Through 1900.* Jefferson, NC: McFarland, 1996.

Newspapers and Sporting Periodicals

Chicago Evening Journal
Chicago Evening Post
Chicago Herald
(Chicago) Inter Ocean; (Chicago) Daily Inter Ocean
Chicago Post and Mail
Chicago Republican
Chicago Times; (Chicago) Times
Chicago Times-Herald
Chicago Tribune; Chicago Daily Tribune
New York Clipper
New York Times
Sporting Life
The Sporting News
Washington Post

Websites

http://www.baseball-almanac.com/
https://www.baseball-reference.com/
http://www.retrosheet.org/
http://www.sabr.org/

INDEX

*Numbers in **bold italics** indicate pages with illustrations*

Actives *see* Chicago Actives
Adams, Franklin P. 198
Addison, John 182
Addy, Bob 90–92, 96–97, *100*, 103
admission fees to games *see* ticket prices and sales
Aetnas *see* Chicago Aetnas
African Americans in baseball 137–38, 165–66, 206n5
alcohol: sold at games 125–26, 130, 143; use among players 40–41, 48, 75, 120, 122, 140, 148, 151, 153–54, 160–61, 164, 194
Algiers Atlantics *see* New Orleans Atlantics
Alleghenys *see* Pittsburgh Alleghenys
Allen, Lee 77, 199
Allison, Doug 35, 36, 56
American Association 134, 140, 145, 148–49, 157, 161, 164, 172, 180; and alcohol sold at games 130; disbanding 179; finances 174, 179; founding 130; and Sunday games 130; ticket prices 130, 179
American League 195–96, 199
Americus *see* Philadelphia Americus
Anderson, W.H. 14
Andrus, Fred 92, *100*
Anson, Adrian "Cap" 3, 41, 44, 69, 90–92, *93*, 96–97, *100*, 101–3, 106–7, 110, 113–15, 118–24, *125*, 127–29, 131–32, *133*, 134, *135*, 137, *139*, 140, 142, 145, 147, *148*, 149–52, 154, 156–59, 161, 165–68, *169*, 170–71, 176, 180–82, 185, 187–89, *190*, 191, *192*, 194, 196, 201; accusations of game fixing 179; and Al Spalding 140, 162–63, 173, 177, 191; and alternation of pitchers 123; *A Ball Player's Career* 102, *192*; boasting 138, 161, 178, 180–81; criticism 103, 113, 137–38, 162–66, 177–78, 189, *190*, 191; death *192*; decline and forced retirement 189–92; illness 119–21, 123; and Jim Hart 177, 191–92; nicknames 118, 138, 177, 189, *190*, 193; and player discipline 132, 140, 145, 149, 163, 178, 190–91; and Players' League 173–76, 178–80; praise of 101, 118–20, 124–25, 178, 192–93; racism 137–38, 165–66, *192*; records *192*; signing with White Stockings 78, 93; and umpires 153, 164, 178
Anson, Virginia 3, 167, *192*
Apollonio, Nicholas 80, 88
Appleton, Walter S. 130
Athletics *see* Philadelphia Athletics
Atlantics (Brooklyn) *see* Brooklyn Atlantics
Atlantics (New Orleans) *see* New Orleans Atlantics
attendance at games *see* Chicago Colts (1890–1897); Chicago White Stockings (1870–1889)
Atwater, Ed 36, 47, 50, 52, 212n16
Auburn (New York) Citizen 40, 45
Austin's First Regiment Band 147, 152
Australia 168, 170

bad luck *see* superstitions and bad luck
Baldwin, Charles "Lady" 159
Baldwin, Mark 157–58, 160, 164, 166
ballparks *see* Brotherhood Park; Dexter Park; Ogden Park; South Side Park; 23rd Street Grounds; West Side Grounds (1893–1915); West Side Park (1885–1891); White Stocking Grounds (1871); White Stocking Park (1878–1884)
balls and strikes, rules *see* rules and rule changes: balls and strikes
Baltimore American Association Team 130
Baltimore Canaries 61–62, 65, 68, 70–71
Baltimore Marylands 24
Baltimore Orioles 179, 181, 188, 194–95
Baltimore Pastimes 24
Barnes, Ross 64, 78–80, 85–86, 90–92, 95–98, *100*, 101–7, 110, 112–15
Barney, Ariel *169*
Barrett, Thomas 181
Bartlett, Arthur 109
Bartlett, Charles S. 78–79, 105
Base Ball Guide and Official League Book 130, 134, 172
Base Ball Writers' Association of America 200
baseball as a source of civic pride 11–13, 48, 136
Baseball in Old Chicago 25, 30, 38, 88
baseball parks *see* ballparks
baseballs: composition 94, 99–100, 109–12; "dead" ball 2, 50, 94, 99–100, 109–12; "lively" ball 29, 50, 94, 99–100, 109–12, 115; Spalding League Ball 108, 121; *see also* rules and rule changes
bases on balls counting as hits, rules *see* rules and rule changes: bases on balls counting as hits
Bastian, Charlie 171–72
batters, rules *see* rules and rule changes: batters
Battin, Joe 69
Baum, L. Frank 189
Beals, Tommy 122, *125*
Beaneaters *see* Boston Beaneaters
Bechtel, George 96–97
beer *see* alcohol
behavior of fans *see* fans' disruptive behavior
Bell, Alexander Graham 95
Bell, Digby *169*
bicycles 143, 145
Bielaski, Oscar 90–92, *100*, 103
Big Four (Boston) 79, 102, 115
Big Four (Detroit) 153
billiards, *14*, 39–40, 43, 45, 90

247

Index

Billings, James B. 162
Bisons *see* Buffalo Bisons
Black Stockings *see* Chicago Black Stockings
black stockings of Chicago team 167–68, 176, 187, **192**
blacks in baseball 137–38, 165–66, 206*n*5
Blodgett, Henry 140
Blue Stockings *see* Toledo Blue Stockings
Blues (Cleveland) *see* Cleveland Blues
Blues (Indianapolis) *see* Indianapolis Blues
Bluff Citys *see* Memphis Bluff Citys
Bond, Tommy 77, 104
Bonte, A.P.C. 36, 38
Booth, Amos 101
Borchers, George **169**
Boston Beaneaters/Boston National League team 2, 3, 83, 85–89, 101–3, 106–7, 110, 112, 114, 117–21, 123–24, 128, 131–33, 139, 144, 146, 150, 155–56, 162–63, 165–68, 172, 177–79, 191, 196
Boston Daily Advertiser 79–80
Boston Daily Globe 80
Boston Evening Record 178
Boston Harvards 24, 30
Boston Herald 128
Boston Lowells 24
Boston Red Stockings 52, 54–55, 58, 63–68, 70–71, 73–75, 77–80, 90–91, **121**
Boston Reds (American Association) 179
Boston Reds (Players' League) 173–74
Boston Trimountains 24
Bradley, George 92, 98, 101, 108–13, 115
Brainard, Asa 35, 36
Bridegrooms *see* Brooklyn Bridegrooms
Briggs House (Chicago) 13, 14, 36
Brooklyn Atlantics 24, 27, 30–33, 35–39, 42, 47, 64, 68, 72, 82–85
Brooklyn Bridegrooms 174, 178
Brooklyn Eckfords 16–18, 24, 30–2, 43, 54, 56, 58, 64–65
Brooklyn Hartfords *see* Hartfords of Brooklyn
Brooklyn Superbas 195
Brotherhood *see* National Brotherhood of Professional Base Ball Players
Brotherhood Park 175–76, 182; *see also* South Side Park
Brouthers, Dan 134, 153
Brown, Jonathan 132, 166
Brown, Mordecai 199
Brown Stockings *see* St. Louis Brown Stockings
Browns *see* St. Louis Browns
Brunell, Frank 174, 180–81
Buckeyes *see* Cincinnati Buckeyes
Budd, F.W. 14

Buffalo Bisons 83, 114, 119–20, 123, 125, 128–29, 131, 133–34, 136–38, 144, 146, 150, 153, 230*n*24
Buffalo Niagaras 23
Bulkeley, Morgan 88, 89
Burhoe, J.T. 131
Burns, Mark 29
Burns, Tom: as manager 191, 193–94, 196; as player 122–24, **125**, 127, **133, 139,** 151, 156, 158, **169,** 171, 173, 180, 187
Burnside Street 61–62

Cambridge Harvards 24, 30
Cammeyer, William H. 88
Canaries *see* Baltimore Canaries
Canavan, Jim 180–81
Cantz, Bart 166
Carbine, John 96–97
Carpenter, Charles 182
carriages 11, 19, 26, 49, 98, 143, 145, 156, 167, 182
Caruthers, Bob 185
"Casey at the Bat" **169**
Centennials *see* Philadelphia Centennials
Cermark Road 61
Ceylon 170
Chadwick, Henry 160
Champion (William Hulbert's dog) 129
championship wins, calculating 48, 58
championships of Chicago teams: (1870) 38–39; (1876) 106–7; (1880) 124–25; (1881) 129; (1882) 133–34; (1885) 147–48; (1886) 156–57; (1906) 199, **201**, 202; (1907) 199, **200, 201**, 202; (1908) 200, **201**, 202; *see also* Chicago Cubs (1902–); Chicago White Stockings (1870–1889)
Chance, Frank 198–202
Chapman, Jack 96–97
Chase, Charles E. 87
Chicago, Illinois: desire for first-rate baseball team 9–17, 40, 43; early baseball clubs 9, 11–13; lawsuit against the city and Chicago Ball Club 140; population 12; rivalry with Cincinnati 9–11, 13, 15–16, 30–31, 40, 45
Chicago Actives 60
Chicago Aetnas 60, 62
Chicago Athenaeum 89
Chicago Athletic Club 61
Chicago Ball Club 2, 104, 114, 116, 130–32, 135, 140, 142–43, 155, 157, 181, 185–86, 191; *see also* Chicago Base Ball Association; Chicago Base Ball Club
Chicago Base Ball Association 2, 60, 62–65, 74, 77–78, 80, **82**, 104–7; *see also* Chicago Ball Club; Chicago Base Ball Club
Chicago Base Ball Club 14–18, 27, 30, 58–60, **72**; *see also* Chicago Ball Club; Chicago Base Ball Association

Chicago Bicycle Track Association 143
Chicago Black Stockings 3, 167–68
Chicago Board of Trade 14, 77, 132, 181
Chicago Colts (1890–1897): black stockings 3, 176, 187, **192**; (1890) 172–75; club lost money 175, 181; (1891) 176–79; (1892) 179–81; (1893) 182–87; (1894) 187–89; (1895) 189; (1896) 189–90; (1897) 190–91; game attendance 181, 186; origin of team name 173; reorganization 181–82; *see also* Chicago Cubs (1902–); Chicago Orphans (1898–1901); Chicago White Stockings (1870–1889); team names
Chicago Cubs (1902–): cub bear motif 199, **200, 201**; (1902) 196–99; (1903) 199; (1904) 199; (1905) 199; (1906) 199; (1907) 199–200; (1908) 200–2; origin of team name 1, 196–97; ownership of club 2–3, 244*n*4; *see also* championships of Chicago teams; Chicago Colts (1890–1897); Chicago Orphans (1898–1901); Chicago White Stockings (1870–1889); team names; World Series
Chicago *Daily Inter Ocean* 146–47, 149, 152, 154, 159–60; *see also* Chicago *Inter Ocean*
Chicago Daily News 1, 2, 148, 154, 158, 166, 172, **196**, 197
Chicago Daily Tribune 2, 39, 42, 60, 64, 66, 68–71, 73–74, 77, 79, 81–82, 85–87, 89, 90, 93–95, 98–104, 106–21, 124–30, 132–33, 135–40, 143, 145–46, 150, 152, 155–56, 161, 164–67, 173–76, 178, 181, 186–89, 192–94, 196; 198–200; *see also* Chicago *Tribune*
Chicago Evening Journal 98, 101, 107, 122, 164
Chicago Evening Post **183**, 185
Chicago Excelsiors 11, **12**, 13
Chicago Fire 47, **53**, 55–59, 63, 116
Chicago Franklins 93–94
Chicago Garden City Club 18
Chicago Herald 152–53, 155–56, 159–63
Chicago History Museum 1, 78
Chicago *Inter Ocean* 2, 71–72, 76, 104–6; *see also* Chicago *Daily Inter Ocean*
Chicago League Ball Club 181
Chicago Orphans (1898–1901): (1898) 192–94; (1899) 194; (1900) 194–95; (1901) 195–96; origin of team name 193; *see also* Chicago Colts (1890–1897); Chicago Cubs (1902–); Chicago White Stockings (1870–1889); team names
Chicago Phoenixes 60
Chicago Pirates 173–76, 180; ballpark 175–76

Index

Chicago Post and Mail 89, **109**
Chicago Republican 9, 28, 47, 51, 54, 72
Chicago Times/Chicago Times 2, 11, 14, 33–34, 38, 51–52, 63, 65, 106, 112–14, 116, 118–21, 124–27, 129–31, 142, 145, 152–53, 156–57, 167–68, 180
Chicago Times-Herald 189
Chicago Tribune 9, 11–14, 16–21, 26–31, 33, 39; 43, 47–50, 52–55, 57–60, 62; *see also Chicago Daily Tribune*
Chicago White Sox 195–96, 199
Chicago White Stockings (1870–1889): black stockings 3, 167–68, **192**; championship 38–39; championship pennant description 39; (1870) 9–10, 17–46; (1871) 47–59; (1874) 63–76; (1875) 76–85; (1876) 88–109, 129; (1877) 106–17; (1878) 115–19; (1879) 118–21; (1880) 121–26, 129; (1881) 126–30; (1882) 129–34; (1883) 134–39; (1884) 139–41; (1885) 142–50; (1886) 150–61; (1887) 162–66; (1888) 166–68; (1889) 171–73; first grand-slam home run 132; first home run 98; first no-hitter 124; first run 98; first shutout 28, 95, 98; formation 13–17; game attendance 87, 121, 136, 220n28; gymnasium 89, 92, 110, 122, 127; lost money 45, 47, 55–59, 116–17; mismanagement 16, 30; origin of team name 18–20; pennant description 152; profit 105, 116, 121, 125, 129–30, 158, 161; reorganization 30, 58–59, 63, 104–6; stock purchasing 15–16, 45, 47, 59–61, 104–6; *see also* championships of Chicago teams; Chicago Colts (1890–1897); Chicago Cubs (1902–); Chicago Orphans (1898–1901); team names
"Chicagoed" 28, 30–31, 123–24
Chicago's early baseball clubs *see* early baseball clubs in Chicago
Cincinnati, Ohio: rivalry with Chicago, Illinois 9–11, 13, 15–16, 30–31, 40, 45
Cincinnati Buckeyes 11, **12**
Cincinnati Daily Gazette 9, 33, 36, 38
Cincinnati Enquirer 36, 126, 170
Cincinnati Red Stockings (National Association) 9–10, 13, 15–17, 23–24, 27, 29–42, 45, 47, 63–66, 81
Cincinnati Red Stockings/Reds (American Association) 130, 134
Cincinnati Red Stockings/Reds (National League) 83, 85, 87–90, 98–99, 101–2, 104, 107, 110, 113–15, 117–20, 173–74, 182, 185, 187, 201
Cincinnati Stars 123–26

circus 128
Civil War 12, 14
Clapp, John 92, 113
Clark Street 43, 61, **109**
Clarkson, John 2, **139**, 142, 146, 148–51, 157–60, 165–68, 172
Cleveland, Ohio 109
Cleveland Blues 83, 119–20, 123–24, 128, 131–32, 137, 144
Cleveland Forest Citys 23, 27–28, 52–55, 61–63, 90
"Climbing Up the Golden Stairs" 163–64
Collier's Rooms 48
Collins, Dan 70
Collins, Eddie 43
Colonels *see* Louisville Colonels
Colts *see* Chicago Colts (1890–1897)
Comiskey, Charles 195–96, 199
Cone, Fred 90–93, 98
Congress Street 142–43, 145, 176, 180, 184
contract breaking 41, 48, 75–76, 93
Conway, Pete 154–55
Corcoran, Larry 44, 122–24, **125**, 127, 129, 132, **133**, 134, **139**, 142, 145–46, 151
Corre, A.G. 36
Courtney, T.E. 132
Cowboys *see* Kansas City Cowboys
Cowles, T.Z. 14–15, 39–40, 42–44
Crabtree, Lotta 54
Craver, Bill 16, 18, **19**, 21–22, 27, 29–30, 32, 41, 43, 45–46, 74
Creighton, Jim 64
cricket 73, **109**, 143, 168, 170
Cuba 189, 193
Cubs *see* Chicago Cubs (1902–)
Cubs Park 1
Culver, W.I. 130, 132
Cummings, Candy 57, 74
curve ball throwing 77, 109, 111, 123, 150
Custer, General George 103
Cuthbert, Ned 16, 18, **19**, 22, 32, 35, 37, 43, 45, 47, 56, 65, 67, 69–71

Dahlen, Bill 185, 193–94
Dalrymple, Abner 44, 119–20, 122–24, **125**, 127, 129, **133**, 134, **139**, 140, 149–51, 158, 160–64
Daly, Tom 164, **169**
Dark Blues *see* Hartford Dark Blues
Darling, Dell 164
Davis, S.S. 36
Dearborn Street 61
Decker, George 185, 188
DeKoven, J. 105
Delbolf, Frank L. 193
Democratic Party 103
DeMontreville, Gene 194
Detroit Morning Tribune 154–55
Detroit Tigers 199–200
Detroit Wolverines 128–31, 134, 136, 139, 144, 150, 152–56, 159, 165–66
Devlin, Jim 65, 67, 69, 71, 96–98
Dexter, Edwin F. 61, 78–79, 104–5
Dexter Park 24, **25**, 26–27, 32–34, 37, 38–39, 45, 49, 52; clubhouse 26
discipline, players' lack of *see* players' lack of discipline and poor performances
doubles: rules *see* rules and rule changes: doubles
Doyle, Jack 196
Doyle, Larry 43
drinking *see* alcohol
Duffy, Ed 30, 32, 35, 38
Duffy, Hugh 180–81
Dungan, Sam 185
Dunne, Finley Peter 2, 166
Duval, Clarence 138, **169**

early baseball clubs in Chicago 9, 11–13
eastern teams and western teams *see* teams, eastern and western
eastern tours *see* tours (traveling to games)
Eckfords *see* Brooklyn Eckfords
Eclipse *see* Louisville Eclipse
Eggler, Dave 32
Egypt 170, **171**
El Paso (Texas) Herald 40
Empires *see* St. Louis Empires
England 73, 90–91, 170–71, 235n16
Erby, Fred 14
errors in baseball's early games 95
Everitt, Bill 194
Evers, Johnny 198, 201
Excelsiors (Chicago) *see* Chicago Excelsiors
Excelsiors (New Orleans) *see* New Orleans Excelsiors
exhibition games 39, 57–58, 68, 72–73, 84, 107–8, 118–19, 121–22, 134, 137, 144, 149, 165, 170, 174, 181; *see also* spring training and pre-season games; tours (traveling to games)
expenses, team *see* team expenses

fair-foul singles, rules *see* rules and rule changes: fair-foul singles
Fairbanks Club 110
fans' disruptive behavior 156, 166, 184
Farrell, Charles "Duke" **169**, 180
Farwell, Charles B. 14
Fauntleroy, T.S. 60, 62
female baseball fans *see* women baseball fans
Ferguson, Bob 33, 35–37, 118
Fessenden, Wallace 178
Field, Eugene 154–55, 157–58, 172
finances, team *see* stock purchasing; team expenses; team profits and losses
Finley, M.L. 110
Finley, W.H. 226n17

First Cavalry Band 136
Fisher, William Charles "Cherokee" 41
Fisler, Wes 16, 69
Flint, Frank Sylvester "Silver" 119–20, 122–23, *125*, 127, 129, *133*, *139*, 151, 153
Flynn, John "Jocko" 150–53, 157, 159
Flynn, William "Clipper" 18, *19*, 22, 32, 35–36, 43, 45, 47
Foley, Tom (baseball player) 47, 52, 207*n*10
Foley, Tom (club official) *14*, 16–17, 20, 28, 30, 39, 41, 43, 45–47, 52, 54; 212*n*16
football 168
Force, Davy 56, 64, 67, 69, 71, 75–76, 87
Forest and Stream 80–81
Forest Citys (Cleveland) *see* Cleveland Forest Citys
Forest Citys (Rockford) *see* Rockford Forest Citys
Forgarty, Tom 170
Fort Wayne Kekiongas 24, 33, 52
42nd Street 25
foul balls, rules *see* rules and rule changes: foul balls
Fowle, Charles E. 87–88
France 170–71
Franklins *see* Chicago Franklins
French, Samuel *169*
French, T. Henry *169*
Fulmer, Chick 96–97

Gaffney, John 153
Gage, David A. 14–15
Gage, George W. 77–79, 105
gambling and game fixing 27–28, 30, 40–41, 48, 70, 73–75, 81, 88, 92, 117, 143, 160; newspaper criticism 48, 81–82, 158
game admission fees *see* ticket prices and sales
game balls, rules *see* rules and rule changes: game balls
game scheduling 27, 38, 41–42, 48, 88–89
Garden City Club *see* Chicago Garden City Club
Gassette, Norman T. 30, 52, 54, 63–65, 105
Gedney, Count 69
Gerhardt, Joe 96–97
Giants *see* New York Giants
Gilruth, James 197
Glasscock, Jack 137
Glenn, John 65, 69, 81, 90–92, 96–98, *100*, 103, 110
Goldsmith, Fred 122–24, *125*, 127, *133*, 138–39, 142
Gore, George 44, 119–20, 122–24, *125*, 127–29, *133*, 134, *139*, 145, 149–51, 153, 160–64
Gould, Charlie 35–36
Grand Central Hotel (New York) 88
Grays (Louisville) *see* Louisville Grays

Grays (Providence) *see* Providence Grays
Green, Danny 196
Griffith, Clark 188, 195
Griswold, A.M. 36
Grove Citys *see* Kankakee Grove Citys

Hahn, Willie 147, *148*, 156
Haldeman, Walter N. 87
Hall, George 106
Hallinan, Jimmy 113–14
Halsted Street 25
Harper's Weekly *53*, *117*, *122*, *133*, 135
Harrison, Carter 152
Harrison Street 142–43, 184–85
Hart, Jim 3, 177, 179–88, 193–96, 199; and Adrian "Cap" Anson 177, 191–92; and Al Spalding 177, 181; and Sunday games 182, 184–85
Hart, Toby 20
Hartford Dark Blues 68, 70, 77, 83, 85, 88–89, 91, 101–4, 106
Hartfords of Brooklyn 110–12, 114, 117–18
Hartig, Ed 3, 138, 224*n*25
Hartsel, Topsy 196
Hastings, Scott 96–97
Hatfield, John 16, 32
Hawaii 168, 170
Hayes, Rutherford B. 103
Hayhurst, Hicks 64
Haymakers *see* Troy Haymakers
Haymarket Square 152
Hayner, Fred A. 196–97
Hazard, Nathaniel 87
Henderson, Alexander 36
Hicks, Nat 74, 92
Higham, Dick 81
Hines, Paul 2, 66–70, 90–92, 96–98, *100*, 103, 106, 110, 114–15
hippodroming *see* gambling and game fixing
Hodes, Charlie 18, *19*, 22, 39, 43, 47, 50, 56, 58
home plate: rules *see* rules and rule changes: home plate
home runs, rules *see* rules and rule changes: home runs
Honolulu, Hawaii 168
Hoosiers *see* Indianapolis Hoosiers
Hopper, De Wolf *169*
Hornung, Joe 165
horse cars *see* street cars
Hot Springs, Arkansas 150–51, 164, 171, 178, 181
Hough, Charles 105
Hough, Walter 105
Hudson, Nat 158
Hughes, Mickey 166
Hughes, Tom 196
Hulbert, William A. 2, 44, 74–78, 81, *82*, 85–90, 93, 102, 104–6, 111, 113–14, 116, 120, 125–27, 129–31, 201; and Al Spalding 78–81, 86, 109–10, 115, 118, *121*, 130–31; and

alcohol at games 125–26, 130; and American Association 130; criticism of eastern clubs 75–77, 87; death 82, 130–32; and gambling 74, 81; and National Baseball Hall of Fame *82*; and National League *82*, 87–90; praise of *82*, 126, 130–32; and Sunday games 130
Hutchinson, Bill 173, 179–81, 185

inclement weather 57, 89, 92, 122, 132, 139, 144, 146, 152, 167–68, 173–74, 184
Indianapolis Blues 118–19
Indianapolis Hoosiers 164, 167
International League 165–66
Ireland 73, 170, 173
Italy 170–71, 173

James, Bill 95
Jewett, Josiah 131
Johnson, Byron Bancroft "Ban" 195
Jones, Charley 100, 113
Joyce, John A. 64, 87

Kankakee Grove Citys 22–23, 46
Kansas City Cowboys 150, 152, 154–55, 164
Keefe, Tim 159, 172
Keerl, George 39
Kekiongas *see* Fort Wayne Kekiongas
Kelly, Mike "King" 2, 3, 44, 122–23, *125*, 127–29, *133*, 134, *135*, *139*, 140, 146, 149, 151, 153–56, 158–63; antics and tricks 122–23, 128, 154–55; and the Boston Beaneaters 162–68, 172; death 188–89; drinking 122–23; nickname of "the only Kelly" 163, 166; nickname of "the $10,000 beauty" 162, 165; sliding into bases 122
Kennett, W.H. 126
Keokuk Westerns 84–85
King, Marshall 18, *19*, 22, 30, 32, 35–37, 43–46, 58
Kittridge, Malachi 185

Lake Front Park (1871) *see* White Stocking Grounds (1871)
Lake Front Park (1878–1884) *see* White Stocking Park (1878–1884)
Lake Michigan 24, *53*, *117*
Lake Park (1871) *see* White Stocking Grounds (1871)
Lake Park (1878–1884) *see* White Stocking Park (1878–1884)
Lake Shore Park (1871) *see* White Stocking Grounds (1871)
Lane, Frank *169*
Lange, Bill 185, 194
Langtry, Lillie 168
Lansingburgh Unions 18, 40; *see also* Troy Haymakers
Larkin, Terry 119–20

Latham, Arlie 151, 158, 160
Lees *see* New Orleans Robert E. Lees
Leonard, Andy 35–36
Lincoln Street 181–82, 184, 188
Lippincott's Monthly Magazine 172
liquor *see* alcohol
Loftus, Tom 194–96
London, England 170
Lone Stars *see* New Orleans Lone Stars
Loomis Street 142–43, 145, 184
Los Angeles Daily Herald 66
losses of teams *see* team profits and losses
Louisville Colonels 145, 174, 179–80, 193
(Louisville) Courier-Journal 96, 98
Louisville Eclipse 130, 134
Louisville Grays 83, 85, 87–90, 95–98, 101, 104, 110, 117
Lowry, Philip J. 3
Lynch, Leigh S. 168
Lynch, Tom 177
Lyon, John B. 104, 132

Mack, Denny 74
Madison Street, 62, 135
Mahn, Louis H. 99–100, 108–9, 111–12
Malone, Fergy 64–67, 69–70, 73
Maroons *see* St. Louis Maroons
Marshalltown, Iowa 107, 119, 127, **135**, 137, 151
Martin, Phonney 32, 56–57
mascots 138, 147, **148**, 156, **169**
Mathews, Bobby 73–74, 92
Mauck, Hal 185
McAtee, Michael "Bub" 18, **19**, 22, 32, 35, 36–38, 43, 45, 58
McBride, Dick 16, 69, 92
McCaull Opera Company **169**
McCormick, Jim 146–48, 150–51, 153–54, 157, 160–62, 164
McGeary, Mike 56, 69
McGill, Willie 185
McGinnis, Gus 185
McKnight, Denny 130
McLean, Billy 74
McMullin, John 69
McQuaid, Jack 137
McVey, Cal 35–36, 78–80, 85–86, 90–92, 96–99, **100**, 101–4, 106–7, 110–13, 115
Meacham, Lewis 82, 85, 87, 90, 109
Medill, Joseph 14
Medill, Samuel J. 14, 43
Melbourne Sportsman 170
Memphis, Tennessee 22, 50
Memphis Bluff Citys 22–23, 28, 41, 46
Menke, Frank G. 39–40
Metropolitans *see* New York Metropolitans
Meyerle, Levi 18, **19**, 21–22, 32, 35–37, 43, 45, 47, 65, 67, 69, 70–71, 73
Michigan Avenue 49, 51, **53**, 116, 130, 135

Midgley, J.W. 14
Millennium Park 49
Miller, Joseph M. 36
Miller, Tom 92
Mills, Abraham G. 75, 132
Mills, Charlie 16, 32
Mills, Everett 32, 56
Milwaukee National League team 118–19
Milwaukee West End club 107
Moffet, Sam 138
Moolic, George 150–52
Morris, Peter 2, 94
Morrisania Unions 24
muffinism *see* players' lack of discipline and poor performances
Murphy, Charles W. 199
Murray, William M. 104–5
Mutuals *see* New York Mutuals

names of teams *see* team names
National Agreement 172
National Association of Base Ball Players 47; first shutout 28
National Association of Professional Base Ball Players (National Association) 48, 52, 54–55, 57–59, 68, 70, 73–77, 81, 85–86, 88–89, 95, 109, 203; and article on association's problems 82–85; first home run 53; first no-hitter 77; first 1–0 game 77
National Brotherhood of Professional Base Ball Players 172–75, 178, 180
National League: championship pennant description 88–89, 111; (1876) 88–109; (1877) 106–17; (1878) 115–19; (1879) 118–21; (1880) 121–26; (1881) 126–30; (1882) 129–34; (1883) 134–39; (1884) 139–41; (1885) 142–50; (1886) 150–61; (1887) 162–66; (1888) 167–68; (1889) 171–73; (1890) 172–75; (1891) 176–79; (1892) 179–81; (1893) 182–87; (1894) 187–89; (1895) 189; (1896) 189–90; (1897) 190–91; (1898) 192–94; (1899) 194; first championship of the United States 134, 140; first shutout 95, 98; founding 82, 87–89; (1900) 194–95; (1901) 195–96; (1902) 196–99; (1903) 199; (1904) 199; (1905) 199; (1906) 199; (1906) 199; (1907) 199–200; (1908) 200–2; ticket prices 130, 179–80, 186; *see also* Chicago Colts (1890–1897); Chicago Cubs (1902–); Chicago Orphans (1898–1901); Chicago White Stockings (1870–1889)
National League of Professional Base Ball Clubs *see* National League
Nationals *see* Washington Nationals
Nelson, Candy 16, 56
Nelson, John 32

Nemec, David 2, 106
New Bedfords 115, 119
New Haven Elm Citys 82–85
New Haven Yales 24
New Orleans, Louisiana 20–21, 41, 49–50, 144, 151
New Orleans Atlantics 20–22, 46
New Orleans Excelsiors 50
New Orleans Lone Stars 20–21, 23, 46, 49, 50
New Orleans Robert E. Lees 21, 23, 46
New Orleans Southerns 21, 23, 46
New York Clipper 15, 16–17, 39, 55–57, 76–77, 80, 86, 89, 92–93, 101, 103–4, 108–9, 113–16, 118, 123–24, 128–29, 132–33, 135, 143, **144**, 149, 166–67
New York *Evening Mail* 198
New York *Evening Telegram* 178
New York *Evening World* **169**
New York Giants 144–48, 150–52, 155, 159, 161, 163, 165–66, 168, **169**, 172, 177–79, **192**, 199–200
New York Herald 28, 47, 68, 166
New York Metropolitans 130, 137, 140
New York Mutuals 16, 24, 27–29, 31–33, 38–39, 52, 54, 57–58, 67–68, 70, 73–75, 83, 85, 88–89, 101, 103, 109
New York Sportsman 86
New York *Star* 27
New York *Sun* 11, 15, **169**, 178
New York Times 18, 27, 31–32, 38–39, 48, 54, 66, 68, 70, 89, 135, 146, 152, 161–63, 167, 174, 179, 181
New-York Tribune 13, 27, 163, 165
New York *World* 58, 66, 89
New Zealand 168, 170
Newark Little Giants 165–66
nicknames of teams *see* team names
Nicol, Hugh 127, **133**, 134
Noble, William P. 36, 38
Northwestern League 137, 158, 172

Oberlander, Johnnie 20
Ogden Park 24, 27
O'Leary, Patrick and Catherine 55
Olympics (Washington, D.C.) *see* Washington Olympics
Ontario Street 24
Orem, Preston D. 102, 106
Orioles *see* Baltimore Orioles
Orphans *see* Chicago Orphans (1898–1901)
O'Shaughnessy, Louis 36
Oswego Ontarios 24
Overall, Orval 200

Palmer, Harry 152–53, 160, 170–71
Palmer, Potter 14, 15, 40
Paris, France 170
Parrott, Jiggs 185
Paterson, New Jersey 127, 150–51, 188
Patterson, Dan 32

Index

Pearce, Dickie 64
Pearls *see* Philadelphia White Stockings
Peters, John 70, 78, 89–92, 96–97, **100**, 103, 106–7, 110
Pecatonica Blues 2
Pfeffer, Fred 43, 134, **139**, 140, 151, 154, **169**, 171, 180–81, 187
Philadelphia Americus 83
Philadelphia Athletics 11, 16, 18, 24, 30–32, 47, 52, 54–55, 57–58, 64–65, 67–70, 73–78, 83–85, 87–89, 101, 103, 106–7, 109, 130, 134
Philadelphia Centennials 74, 84–85
Philadelphia *Evening Telegraph* 18
Philadelphia Keystones 24
Philadelphia Olympics 65
Philadelphia Pearls *see* Philadelphia White Stockings
Philadelphia Phillies **135**, 144, 146, 148–51, 154–56, 170, 172, 178
Philadelphia White Stockings 63–66, 68–69, 73–74, 81, 83–84, 87, 91
Phoenixes *see* Chicago Phoenixes
picked nine 15, 23, 39, 52, 207n13
Pierce, Grayson "Gracie" 154
Piercy, Andy 127
Pinkham, Ed 18, **19**, 22, 32, 35, 45, 47, 56, 67, 70
Pirates (Chicago) *see* Chicago Pirates
Pirates (Pittsburgh) *see* Pittsburgh Pirates
pitchers, rules *see* rules and rule changes: pitchers
Pittsburgh Alleghenys 24, 130, **135**, 161, 164
Pittsburgh Pirates 180, 199–200
players' lack of discipline and poor performances 11–12, 23, 27–29, 54, 62, 69–71, 73–74, 112–15, 139–40, 149, 157, 159–60, 190, 193–96
Players' League 172–78, 180
Polk Street 181–82, **184**
poor playing *see* players' lack of discipline and poor performances
Powers, Phil 156
profits of teams *see* team profits and losses
Providence Grays 115, 118–20, 123–24, 128–29, 131, 133, 140, 144, 146, 150
Pullman, George M. 14
Pyle, Harry "Shadow" 164
Pyramid of Giza 170, **171**

Quest, Joe 119, 122–23, **125**, 127, **133**, 134

racism in baseball 137–38, 165–66, **192**
Radcliff, John 74
railroads 14, 25–26, 31, 33–34, 49–50, 52, **53**, 56–58, 61, 101, 116, 127, 135, 158, 169, 176

Randolph Street 49, **53**, 108, **109**, 110, 116, 135
Reach, Al 69, 88
Red Stockings (Boston) *see* Boston Red Stockings
Red Stockings (Cincinnati) *see* Cincinnati Red Stockings
Red Stockings (St. Louis) *see* St. Louis Red Stockings
Reds (Boston) *see* Boston Reds
Remsen, Jack 119–20
Renner, Matthew 14
Republican Party 103
reserved players, rules *see* rules and rule changes: reserved players
revolvers *see* contract breaking
Rice, George C. 197
Richards, J.M. 14
Richardson, Hardy 153
Robert E. Lees *see* New Orleans Robert E. Lees
Rochester Excelsiors 65
Rochester Flour Cities 24
Rockford Forest Citys 16, 24, 26–27, 30, 38–39, 41, 47, 52, 81, 91
Rogers, John J. 154
rowdiness *see* fans' disruptive behavior
Rowe, Dave 112, 132, 154
Rowe, Jack 153
rules and rule changes: balls and strikes 94–95, 126, 233n6; bases on balls counting as hits 234n11; batters 29, 94–95, 126, 164; doubles 117, 139–40; errors 95; fair-foul singles 95, 106, 115; foul balls 94, 115; game balls 94, 99, 109; home plate 94, 126, 185; home runs 117, 139–40; pitchers 29, 94, 126, 149–50, 164, 185; reserved players 123, 126, 134, 150, 161–62, 164, 172; Sunday games 88, 125–26, 130, 143, 176, 179–85; "three-base rule" 146, 148; walks 95, 126; *see also* baseballs
Ryan, Jimmy 151, 153, 158, 160, 163, 168, **169**, 180–81, 185, 187–88, 193–94

St. Louis Brown Stockings 77, 83, 85, 87–90, 98–99, 101, 106, 108, 110, 113–14, 117
St. Louis Browns 130, 134, 149, 157–60, 179
St. Louis Empires 18–20, 22, 46, 67
St. Louis *Globe-Democrat* 98, 158
St. Louis Maroons 144–46, 150, 152, 154, 164
St. Louis Red Stockings 67–68, 70
St. Louis Reds 82–85
St. Louis Unions 18–20, 22, 46
St. Paul Saints 195
Saints *see* St. Paul Saints
salaries of baseball players *see* team salaries
San Francisco, California **72**, 168–69

Sanborn, Irving E. "Sy" 200
scheduling of games *see* game scheduling
Schriver, William "Pop" 185, 188
Scotland 170
Selee, Frank 196–99, 201
Senators *see* Washington Senators
Sensabaugh, Charles 197
Sensenderfer, Count 16, 69
Shafer, George "Orator" 119
"Sharps and Flats" 154
Sheridan, Philip H. 14, 40, 43
Sherman, Charles M. 181
Shirley, Thomas 87
Simmons, Joe 47, 50
Smith, Harry 110, 112
Snyder, Charles "Pop" 96–97, 113
Soden, Arthur H. 132
Somerville, Ed 97
South Side Park 3, 176, 179–82, 186; game scheduling 176, 180; Sunday games 176, 179–80, 182; and World's Fair college baseball tournament 186; *see also* Brotherhood Park
Southern League 152
southern tours *see* tours (traveling to games)
Southerns *see* New Orleans Southerns
Spalding, Albert G. "Al": and Adrian "Cap" Anson 140, 162–63, 173, 177, 191; *America's National Game* **121**; baseball guide **121**, 130, 134, 172; and Jim Hart 177, 181; and National Baseball Hall of Fame **121**; opposition to players drinking alcohol 140, 153–54, 160–61; as player 16, 41, 46, 78, 81, 89–93, 95–99, **100**, 101–12, 115, 118, **121**, 129, 201; and player discipline 140, 149, 153–54, 160–61; and Players' League 173–75, 177; as president of club 132, 134–36, 140–46, 149–54, 156–58, 162–64, 166–67, 176–77, 244n4; retirement 115, **121**, 177; salary 78, 80–81; signing with White Stockings 78–81; sporting goods store 108, **109**, 115, **121**, 191, 241n31; trip to England in 1874 91, 235n16; and William Hulbert 78–81, 86, 88, 109–10, 115, 118, **121**, 130–32; world tour of 1888–1889 168–70, **171**, 172–73
Spalding, Harriet 115, **171**
Spalding, Walter 108, **109**, 115
Spalding League Ball 108, 121
Spalding's Base Ball Guide and Official League Book **121**, 130, 134, 172
Sphinx 170, **171**
Spink, Al 45
The Spirit of the Times 15, 60, 87
Sporting Life 135, 138, 142–43, 146, 148–49, 152–55, 160, 165, 170, **171**, 172, 174, 176, 178–80, 186–89, 191, **192**, 193–95, 198–99

The Sporting News 158, 163, 174, 177, 180, 182, 193
Sportsman 170
spring training and pre-season games 18–24; 41, 46, 48–50, 90, 144–45, 148, 150–51, 164, 171, 178, 181, 195; *see also* exhibition games; tours (traveling to games)
Springfield Ponies 191
Stars (Cincinnati) *see* Cincinnati Stars
Stars (Syracuse) *see* Syracuse Stars
Start, Joe 16
State Street 11, 61–62, 67, 136, 143
stone wall infield 171, 180
Stovey, George 165–66
street cars 25–26, 49, 61, 176, 184–85
strikes and balls, rules *see* rules and rule changes: balls and strikes
Sullivan, Marty 164–65
Sunday, Billy 2, 134, *135*, *139*, 149, 151, 163, 165, 193
Sunday games 88, 125–26, 130, 143, 176, 179–85
superstitions and bad luck 3, 112, 120, 176, 187
Sutcliffe, Elmer "Sy" *139*
Sutton, Ezra 53, 69, 78
Swandell, Marty 32
Sweasy, Charlie 35–36, 101
Sweeney, Charlie 145
Syracuse Central City 24
Syracuse Stars 119

Taft, Charles P. 243*n*4
Tanner, F.H. 14
Tanner, S.W. 14
Taylor, Wallace 185
Taylor Street 182, 185
team expenses 38, 40–41, 45, 47–48, 58–59, 63, 75, 83–84, 87, 117, 136, 148, 175; *see also* team profits and losses; team salaries
team names 19–20, 198, 205*ch*1*n*1; origin of Colts 173; origin of Cubs 1, 196–97; origin of Orphans 193; origin of White Stockings 18–20; other names: Black Stockings 167–68, *192*; Chicagos 198; Hartites 198; Microbes 198; Nationals 198; Recruits 198; Remnants 195–96, 198; Rough Riders 243*n*1; Seedlings 198; Seleeites 198; Selee's Colts 198; Sprouts 198; Tribe of Selee 198; *see also* Chicago Colts (1890–1897); Chicago Cubs (1902–); Chicago Orphans (1898–1901); Chicago White Stockings (1870–1889)
team profits and losses 12, 38, 45, 47, 55–59; 75, 83–84, 87, 105, 116–17, 121, 125, 129–30, 134, 136, 148, 161, 175, 181; *see also* team expenses; team salaries

team salaries 1, 15–17, 38, 41, 45, 47, 56, 58, 63, 70–71, 75, 78–80, 84, 91, 136, 142, 148, 161–62, 172, 174–75, 178, 195, 207*n*14, 223*n*22, 236*n*24; *see also* team expenses; team profits and losses
teams, eastern and western 29, 45–46, 75–77, 87–90, 101–2, 113, 120, 123, 178–79
Tecumseh Club 115
temperance *see* alcohol
"That Double Play Again" 198
Thatcher, J.M. 36, 52, 54, 58, 60–62
Thayer, Ernest Lawrence *169*
35th Street 175–76
Thompson, George W. 88
Thompson, William G. 131
"three-base rule" *see* rules and rule changes: "three-base rule"
Throop Street 142–43, 145
ticket prices and sales 32, 87, 130, 179–80, 186
Tigers *see* Detroit Tigers
Tilden, Samuel J. 103
Tinker, Joe 196, 198
Toledo Blue Stockings 137–38, 165–66
Toledo Daily Blade 137–38
Topeka Westerns 127
tours (traveling to games) 18–24; 31, 41, 46, 48–50, 67, 70–71, 101, 106, 144–45, 150–51; *see also* exhibition games; spring training and pre-season games
trains *see* railroads
Treacey, Fred 18, *19*, 22, 32, 35–36, 45, 56, 58, 65, 67, 69
Treadway, George 14
Trego, Charles T. 132, 181
Tripartite Agreement *see* National Agreement
Trojans *see* Troy Trojans
Troy Haymakers 18, 24, 41, 43, 52, 54–55, 57–58, 60–61, 64; *see also* Lansingburgh Unions
Troy Trojans 119, 123–24, 128, 131, 133–34
22nd Street 61, 78
23rd Street 61, 90
23rd Street Grounds 1, 61–63, 65–69, 71, 73, 77, 87, 90, 93, 115–16; clubhouse 90
"Two Pictures" 189

Uhlich House (Chicago) 60
umpires and umpiring 21, 31, 36, 38–39, 46, 74, 93–95, 97–98, 126, 128, 153–54, 156, 158, 177–78
uniforms of Chicago teams: (1870) 19–20; (1871) 52, 57–58; (1875) 89–90; (1876) 89–90, 93; (1877) 111; (1883) 138; (1885) 145; (1888) 167, *192*; (1894) 187; (1898) 193; (1908) 199–200
Union Association 229*n*6
Union Base-Ball Grounds *see* White Stocking Grounds (1871)
Union Stock Yards *25*

Unions (Lansingburgh) *see* Lansingburgh Unions
Unions (St. Louis) *see* St. Louis Unions
United States championship 148–49

Van Haltren, George 167–68, *169*, 180–81
Von der Ahe, Chris 157–58, 160

Wabash Avenue 90
Wadsworth, Philip 78–79
Waitt, Charlie 110
Walker, Moses Fleetwood "Fleet" 137–38, 165–66
walks, rules *see* rules and rule changes: walks
Wallack's Theatre *169*
Walsh, John R. 132, 181, 191, 244*n*4
Ward, John Montgomery "Monte" 147, 172, 175
Warren, L.B. 97
Washington Monument 188
Washington Nationals 24, 81, 83–85, 150, 154–55, 165–66, 179, 188, 190
Washington Olympics 24, 52–55, 58, 64–65
Washington Post 165, 190, 195–96
Washington Senators 190–91, 196
Washington Street 49, 89
Waterman, Fred 35–36
weather, inclement *see* inclement weather
Weeghman Park 1, 244*n*9
Welch, Curt 138, 158
Wentworth, John 176
Wentworth Avenue 175
West Side Grounds (1893–1915) 1, 3, 182, *183*, *184*, 185, *186*, 187–89, 198; clubhouse *183*; fire 187–88; Sunday games 182–85
West Side Park (1885–1891) 140–43, *144*, 145–46, 152, 166, 170, 176, 180, 182–84; bicycle track 143, 145; clubhouse 143, 147; game scheduling 176, 180; Sunday games 176, 179–80
Western Base Ball Emporium 108, *109*, 115, *121*
Western League 195
Western Monthly 13
western teams compared to eastern teams *see* teams, eastern and western
Westerns *see* Keokuk Westerns
whip pennant 32, 38–39, 67, 80, 107, 120
White, James "Deacon" 78–80, 85–86, 89, 90, 92, 96–98, *100*, 102–3, 107, 110, 113, 115, 153
White Sox *see* Chicago White Sox
White Stocking Grounds (1871) 45, 49–52, *53*, 55, 61
White Stocking Park (1878–1884) 116, *117*, 118, 134–36, 139–40; clubhouse 129–30
White Stockings (Chicago) *see*

Chicago White Stockings (1870–1889)
White Stockings (Philadelphia) see Philadelphia White Stockings
Wilkie, Franc B. 14
Will, George 1
Williams, E.F. 131
Williamson, Edward "Ned" 119–20, 122–23, *125*, 127, *133*, *139*, 140, 150–51, 153, 158, *169*, 180; injury during world tour 170–72; three home runs in one game 140
Williamson, Nettie 170–72
Wilmot, Walt 188
Wolcott Street 181
Wolters, Rynie 16, 32, 38–39
Wolverines see Detroit Wolverines
women baseball fans 11, *12*, 26, 34, 37, 49, 54, 69, 143, 145, *148*, 166, 183, 188
The Wonderful Wizard of Oz 189
Wood, Jimmy 9, 16–18, *19*, 21–23; 28, 32, 35–37, 39–43, 45, 53–56, 58, 60, 64–67, *72*, 73, 78, 115, 180, 201; 212n16; as first White Stocking, 17, 43, 71, *72*; infection and removal of leg 66, 68, 70–72, 93; as umpire 93–94, 115, 118
Wood Street 181–82
Worcester (Massachusetts) Daily Spy 79
Worcester National League team 123, 128, 131–32, 134
Work Projects Administration (Illinois) 25
World Series: (1907) 199, *200*, *201*, 202; (1908) 200, *201*, 202; see also Chicago Cubs (1902–)
world tour of 1888–1889 168–70, *171*, 172–73
World's Columbian Exposition/World's Fair of 1893 181–82; and baseball tournament 186
Wright, George 16, 31, 33, 35–36, 45, 107
Wright, Harry 35–36, 40, 64, 79–81, 88, 91
Wright, Marshall D. 166
Wrigley Field 1, 244n9

Young, Cy 181
Young, Nicholas "Nick" E. 56, 64–67, 70, 88, 110, 177

Zettlein, George 40, 43, 46–47, 50, 56, 58, 64–65, 67, 69–71

www.ingramcontent.com/pod-product-compliance
Lightning Source LLC
Chambersburg PA
CBHW081547300426
44116CB00015B/2792